T0311258

"A Great Many of Us Have Good Farms"

Agent Peter Ronan Reports on the Flathead Indian Reservation, Montana, 1877–1887

Peter Ronan
1839–1893

"A Great Many of Us Have Good Farms"

Agent Peter Ronan Reports on the Flathead Indian Reservation, Montana, 1877–1887

Peter Ronan

edited by Robert J. Bigart

published by
Salish Kootenai College Press
Pablo, Montana

distributed by
University of Nebraska Press
Lincoln, Nebraska

Cover illustrations. *Top:* Ronan family and residence. Photograph by F. Jay Haynes, Flathead Indian Agency, Jocko, Montana, 1884. Montana Historical Society Photograph Archives, Helena, negative H-1271. *Bottom left:* Chief Arlee. Peter Ronan, *Historical Sketch of the Flathead-Indians from the Year 1813 to 1890* (Helena, Mont.: Journal Publishing Co., 1890), page 78. *Bottom right:* Chief Michelle: Drawing by Gustavus Sohon, National Anthropological Archives, Smithsonian Institution, Washington, D.C. (negative number 08501400). *Back cover:* Flathead Indian Agent Peter Ronan. Montana Historical Society Photograph Archives, Helena, negative MMM900-004.

Frontpiece. Flathead Indian Agent Peter Ronan. Montana Historical Society Photograph Archives, Helena, negative MMM900-004.

Library of Congress Cataloging-in-Publication Data:
Ronan, Peter, 1839-1893.
    "A great many of us have good farms" : agent Peter Ronan reports on the Flathead Indian Reservation, Montana, 1877-1887 / Peter Ronan ; edited by Robert J. Bigart.
    p. cm.
    Includes bibliographical references and index.
    ISBN 978-1-934594-10-0
    l. Salish Indians--History--19th century--Sources. 2. Kootenai Indians--History--19th century--Sources. 3. Flathead Indian Reservation (Mont.)--History--19th century--Sources. I. Bigart, Robert, editor. II. Title.
E99.S2R69 2014
978.6'802--dc23

                                                            2013051323

Distributed by University of Nebraska Press, 1111 Lincoln Mall, Lincoln, NE 68588-0630, order 1-800-755-1105, www.nebraskapress.unl.edu.

Editor's Dedication

Thurman Trosper
and
Lucille Trosper Roullier Otter

Two tribal members who had positive impacts
on the reservation and the country.
They grew up on the reservation when succeeding
was not easy for tribal members.

Preface

The idea of publishing an edited version of Peter Ronan's reports from the Flathead Indian Reservation in western Montana first occurred to me in the middle 1970s when I was reading the letters in the old Natural Resources Reading Room at the National Archives in Washington, D.C. I had the good fortune of having the late Dr. John Ewers of the Smithsonian Institution sponsor my research in Flathead Reservation history as a Smithsonian Fellow.

It has been a long journey of research and detours over the years until two or three years ago when I was able to begin the project in earnest for the Salish Kootenai College Press. Many people and libraries over the years have made this publication possible. In addition to the exciting chance to work with Dr. Ewers, Richard Crawford, and many helpful staff people at the National Archives in the 1970s were invaluable. Dr. Joe McDonald, President Emeritus, and Gerald Slater, the late Academic Vice President, of Salish Kootenai College, encouraged and supported my research and writing.

The two most important people whose generous help made these volumes possible were Mary Frances Ronan, Reference Librarian, Natural Resources Division, National Archives, Washington, D.C.; and Bill Bennington, Salish Kootenai College. See the next page for more detail on the great assistance they gave. Penny McPherson of the National Archives went out of her way to make sure my xerox orders of Ronan materials did not get lost in the shuffle.

Several people have been willing to read and comment on portions of the manuscript including Tom Smith, Salish Pend d'Oreille Culture Committee, St. Ignatius, Montana; George Price, Native American Studies, University of Montana, Missoula; Steve Lozar, Confederated Salish and Kootenai Tribes; and Mike Dolson, Salish Kootenai College. A special thank you is due Richard Malouf of Twin Falls, Idaho, who read through the entire manuscript and made many helpful suggestions. He also helped revise the index to clear up some of the name references. Richard graciously listened to my occasional phone calls reporting on my progress with the project.

Martha Kohl of the Montana Historical Society and Geoff Wyatt of Wyatt Designs, Helena, shared some great ideas for the format and design of the Ronan volumes.

Thank you all for your encouragement and support!! However, I, of course, am responsible for the mistakes and weaknesses that remain in the publication.

A companion volume of Peter Ronan's letters from 1888-1893 accompanied by Biographical Sketches of the major tribal leaders has been published under the title: *Justice To Be Accorded To the Indians.*

I am especially thrilled to be able to make an important historical source on Flathead Reservation history easily available to tribal members and researchers in reservation and Montana history. No one has to travel to Washington, D.C., any more to read these documents.

Sincerely,
Bob Bigart
Salish Kootenai College
Pablo, Montana

Special Thanks

Very special thanks are due two people who played critical roles in making these volumes possible:

Mary Frances Ronan, Reference Librarian, Natural Resources Division, National Archives, Washington, D.C.

Ms. Ronan [no relation to Peter Ronan] gave above and beyond the call of duty in tracking down the references I had compiled in the 1970s to locate Ronan letters in Record Group 75 or Records of the Commissioner of Indian Affairs. During the 1970s I did not have funds enough to make xerox copies of all the Ronan letters that were of interest, so I took notes and file information from many of the letters. To publish the letters, however, I needed to work from xerox copies to increase the accuracy of the transcriptions. Mary Frances patiently and graciously made it possible for me to order copies without having to travel to Washington, D.C. Thank you again for your personal interest and assistance that made this publication possible.

Bill Bennington, Salish Kootenai College, Pablo, Montana.

Carefully proofing the transcription of 800 single space pages of manuscript typed from xeroxes of original letters required two people. Bill kindly donated several hundred hours over several years to listen to me drone on reading the letters while checking the typed version. He helped find many typos and transcription errors which greatly improved the accuracy of the finished publication. Thank you again for your interest and invaluable help with the Ronan letters project.

Table of Contents

Introduction

Flathead Indian Agent Peter Ronan was a man of his time. He accepted many of the prejudices and bigotry of the late nineteenth century, but was also able to treat the Salish, Pend d'Oreille, and Kootenai people with enough respect to work with them towards shared goals. When he was appointed agent in 1877, the tribal economy was still based on buffalo hunting and gathering wild foods. In 1877 the traditional tribal chiefs controlled the tribal police and enforced law and order on the reservation. When Ronan died in 1893, the reservation economy was largely based on ranching and farming. Even with this dramatic economic change, the tribes were still basically self-supporting. In 1893 the Flathead Indian Agent directed a police and court system that was funded with federal money. Ronan and tribal leaders worked hard to protect reservation resources from encroachment and to get justice from white courts and the federal government.

The Bitterroot Salish, Upper Pend d'Oreille, and Lower Kootenai Indians had lived for generations in the northern Rocky Mountains and northwestern Great Plains. Their economy was based on hunting buffalo and other wild game and gathering the roots, berries, and plants that grew in the region. After getting horses in the eighteenth century, the tribal economies prospered.

The 1780 smallpox epidemic and the expansion of enemy Plains tribes greatly reduced tribal population and territory. During the early nineteenth century, the Salish, Pend d'Oreille, and Kootenai allied themselves with the new tribe of white men against the Blackfeet, Sioux, and other Plains Indians.

White religious teachers brought news of new spiritual powers that could be combined with traditional Indian beliefs to strengthen the tribal fight against the much larger enemy tribes. The missionaries established St. Ignatius Mission and schools to teach the young people new crafts, mathematics, and English. Traders brought valuable metal tools, tobacco, and guns and ammunition.

The strange customs of the white men called for a peace treaty even with their allies. The 1855 Hellgate Treaty with the United States government called for the tribes to continue to share their hunting and gathering resources with white people, but strangely also talked about transferring most of the land to white settlers and leaving "reservations" for Indian people. In the second half of the nineteenth century, the white population in western Montana exploded and white people began to build fences to keep Indians and other people out, rather than sharing the land. This crisis threatened the economic and political independence of the tribes and formed the basis for the challenges facing tribal leaders between 1877 and 1893 as they tried to navigate the new landscape and protect the lives and interests of tribal people.

The Hellgate Treaty provided for a reservation in the Jocko and Lower Flathead Valleys and, provisionally, another reservation in the Bitterroot Valley. Ronan's letters document events on the Jocko or Flathead Indian Reservation as the tribes were coping with dramatic change. They present his viewpoint, but they also give us remarkable detail about life on the reservation between 1877 and 1893.

These two volumes of Agent Peter Ronan's reports on Flathead Indian Agency affairs lead us on a remarkable trip through reservation and western

Montana affairs during a critical time. Between the wise and capable tribal leadership and the efforts of Ronan, the tribes reached 1893 at peace with the white men and economically self-supporting. Many challenges faced the tribes in the years after 1893, but between 1877 and 1893 potential catastrophes were averted and a base was built from which tribal leaders could work to defend the tribes in the twentieth century. Some of these twentieth century battles were lost, but the tribes never stopped working to defend their lives, property, and values.

Editorial Notes

The Peter Ronan letters included in this collection were selected because they had something to say about Flathead Indian Reservation affairs. I used the subject indexes to the Commissioner of Indian Affairs correspondence at the National Archives. I probably missed some good letters which were indexed under topics that I did not expect to be of interest.

I did not include routine bureaucratic correspondence such as requests for stationery or submissions of business paperwork. I also did not include the letters, mostly now at the Montana Historical Society Archives, which discussed Ronan's patronage and campaign work in Montana politics. Possibly the most important limiting factor, though, was that not all of his correspondence to the Commissioner was preserved at the National Archives. At some point, most of his monthly reports, in particular, were discarded. I am sure that a number of those missing reports had valuable information about reservation history, but unfortunately they are no longer available.

Since the quantity of letters was so large, the editor divided the collection into two volumes. Each volume has footnotes and an index for that volume. The full introduction and map are included only in volume one. The biographical sketches of a few tribal leaders who needed extended treatment are included after the letters in volume two. References to other Ronan letters give the dates under which those letters can be located in this collection. Some of the cross references to biographical information in the annotations and other letters on the same subject can refer to the other volume in the collection. I hope the division into two volumes will not inconvenience too many readers

Ronan enclosed unidentified newspaper clippings in a number of his letters. Some which had new information are reproduced here with the letters. I have added the location citation for those articles which I could identify, but some are reproduced as "unidentified clippings."

Terms which are offensive to many twenty first century Americans, such as "squaw," "breed," "savage," etc., have not been changed. While they are rightly objectionable to contemporary ears, it is important to note the context where they are used. In almost all cases, Ronan did not use them in a negative way.

The editor has tried to transcribe the letters as accurately as possible, but the handwriting of some clerks involved very inconsistent capitalization. Many would occasionally make the first letter of a word half as tall as their capitals. I have tried to render the capitalization as accurately as possible given the limits of modern typography.

"Sic" was used sparingly, in hopes of making the letters easier to read. This meant that many misspelled, but phonetically pronounceable words, in the original documents are not followed by [sic]. Brackets and italics are used

Above: Flathead Indian Agent Peter Ronan. Montana Historical Society Photograph Archives, Helena, negative MMM900-004.
Below: Mary Ronan, wife of Peter Ronan. Archives and Special Collections, Mansfield Library, University of Montana, Missoula, negative 83-138.

to indicate comments or insertions by the editor. [* * * *] has been used in those few cases where I was unable to read the original text. Ellipses in some of the newspaper articles indicate omitted material, and in almost all cases the material was omitted in the original newspaper publication.

The text of the original letters and newspaper articles included in the collection is reproduced in Times Europa Roman font. The editor's annotations to the letters are in *Times Europa Italic Font* and Myriad Pro Light Condensed Font.

Transcribing Indian names in the letters proved especially challenging. Many of the names were hard to read accurately given the penmanship. Readers should be careful, because more than one person often had the same Christian name. The spelling of the Indian names varied greatly and one name could be spelled in a number of different ways over the years. The spelling of the names in the annotations usually follows the spelling in the document being discussed. For example Michel, Michelle, and Michael could easily be the same person.

I hope the conventions I have chosen will be obvious and easy for the reader to follow.

Peter Ronan (1839-1893): A Biographical Sketch

Flathead Indian Agent Peter Ronan and the Salish and Kootenai chiefs and headmen shared some goals and were able to cooperate to reach these common objectives. In areas where they disagreed, Ronan seems to have moved slowly and generally avoided confrontations with tribal members when possible. Apparently Ronan was able to treat Indian people with respect.

In 1883, Indian Inspector S. S. Benedict recorded the complaints of Chief Arlee and Duncan McDonald about the St. Ignatius Mission schools and the Flathead Agency and then went on to conclude: "Agent Ronan is quite popular with these Indians. They speak in high terms of his honesty, and fair treatment."[1] A short magazine article commenting on Ronan's reappointment in 1890 observed: "The Indians in his charge all like and respect him. . . He has no hobbies about the treatment of Indians and does not expect to make white men of them in a single generation." This article, probably written by journalist E. V. Smalley, summarized Ronan's low pressure approach: "He never tries to boss them except when necessary to preserve order and keep things moving in the right way."[2] In 1895, Inspector P. McCormick noted that Ronan had been more popular with the tribal members than his successor, Joseph Carter, because Ronan humored the Indians more than Carter did.[3]

Despite Ronan's ability to respect Indian people and work with tribal leaders in areas where their goals overlapped, he was very much a late nineteenth century American. He accepted the white American ideology of the superiority of "civilized" over "savage" life and saw his mission as helping the Salish and Kootenai people progress beyond their "uncivilized" and "savage" traditional lifestyles. Many tribal members supported the St. Ignatius Mission schools because they taught the students English literacy, mathematics, and useful economic and trade skills. Ronan agreed that these practical benefits of white education were good, but also saw education as an antidote to "the demoralizing influence of Indian home surroundings."[4] For Ronan and most nineteenth century Americans, white American society was civilized and good; tribal life and values were savage and bad. The white belief system was clearly expressed in Ronan's description of the importance of educating Indian children at a young age:

> The children, if taken into school at the age of two or three or four years and kept there, only occasionally visited by their parents, will when grown up know nothing of Indian ways and habits. They will, with ease, be thoroughly, though imperceptibly, formed to the ways of the whites in their habits, their thoughts, and their aspirations. They will not know, in fact be completely ignorant of the Indian language; will know only English. One generation will accomplish what the past system will require generations to effect. The affection of the child being gained at its youngest age, it is likely to grow up with a love for the whites instead of the hatred, or at least diffidence, as is the case to a great extent at present. The training of the children in later years in the various departments of an industrial-school education will be much facilitated, its latent talents discovered and better cultivated, never having tasted of the roaming, free and easy-going, lazy life of the older Indian and not having been spoiled by the indulgence of parent or near relatives, which is generally the case with all grown children. This love for a roaming, lazy life makes it at all times hard to get a boy or a girl of ordinary school age to resign himself or herself to the confinement of a boarding school.[5]

One expression of this prejudiced ideology can be seen in Ronan's attitude towards work. In 1890, he described those Kootenai Indians who followed a traditional lifestyle as "thriftless, lazy, and filthy" because they supported themselves through hunting, fishing, and odd labor around the white settlements. In contrast, acceptable or "real" work was raising grain and cattle on the reservation farms like white people. This viewpoint was blind to the amount of effort, skill, and ecological knowledge required to be a successful hunter, fisherman, and gatherer. Ronan supported the development of agriculture on the reservation because the "cultivation of the soil" represented "the adoption of the pursuits of advancing civilization." Many tribal members agreed with expanding agriculture and ranching on the reservation, but for a very different reason: They wanted to maintain the economic independence of the tribes. For Ronan, agriculture was good only if carried out in small family farms. He disapproved of the common field farmed by the Kootenai village at Elmo in the 1880s because it violated his nineteenth century sense of propriety.[6] By 1890, Ronan's influence had grown to the point that he used the government paid police force to suppress an "outbreak" of Indian dancing and gambling. Details are sketchy, but Ronan discharged some of the police for failing to enforce his orders.[7]

As agent, Ronan frequently argued in favor of tribal requests and interests in his correspondence with the Office of Indian Affairs. One example was the northern boundary of the reservation which nineteenth century surveys located several miles south of the line recognized by the Elmo Kootenai. Ronan requested that the Kootenai version of the boundary be recognized over the United States Geological Survey line. The Commissioner of Indian Affairs insisted on using the official survey.[8] Ronan's defense of tribal members might not have met twenty-first century standards, but one anti-Indian newspaper correspondent in 1889 accused him of being "not only an eager champion of the aborigines" but of being "activated by a prejudice against those of his own color."[9]

The two areas where Ronan and most tribal members had complimentary goals were (1) developing agriculture and ranching on the reservation to take up the economic slack caused by the loss of the buffalo and the decline of other wild game, root, and berry resources; and (2) keeping the peace on the reservation and not giving the U.S. Army or the Missoula County Sheriff excuses to intervene in reservation affairs.

Chief Arlee was a frequent critic of Flathead Agency operations and strenuously objected to tribal judges under the agent's control and trying Indians accused of crimes against other Indians in white Montana courts. In December 1885, however, when a fatal fight broke out between two Indians and the white trader and postmaster at the Arlee railroad station, Chief Arlee met Ronan at the scene and consented to sending the white men who did the shooting and a wounded Indian who survived the fracas to be tried by the courts in Missoula. The Missoula courts quickly released the wounded Indian, Big Jim, for lack of evidence and the two white men involved were judged to have acted in self-defense.[10] Chief Arlee, the headmen, and Ronan acted to keep the conflict from escalating into a full fledged confrontation with army troops and the Missoula sheriff.

A continuing aggravation for the chiefs and Ronan was the problem of uneven justice in late nineteenth century Montana. Cases of Indians accused of murdering white men were pursued vigorously by the white justice officials and the courts, but those involving Indian people murdered by whites were largely ignored. Four Indians convicted of murdering white men, mainly on Indian testimony, were hung in Missoula on December 20, 1890. The murderers of Chief Eneas' son in Demersville and Chief Michelle's relatives in eastern Montana about the same time were never caught or punished. Ronan wrote to Washington, D.C., frequently about the problem, but his calls for equal justice were not answered.[11]

One of the more important contributions Ronan made to the tribal economy on the reservation was to postpone the imposition of the General Allotment Act on the reservation for twenty years. The new policy provided for each tribal member to receive an individual allotment or portion of reservation land formerly held in common by the tribes. The policy was an attempt to forcibly convert Indian tribal hunter/gatherers to small independent farmers on the Euro-American model. Two principal impacts of the policy on the Flathead Indian Reservation were: (1) land claims on the reservation were to be standardized and made legally more secure, and (2) "surplus" lands left after allotments were made to tribal members were to be sold to white farmers at considerably less than their real value. The first part of the policy could have been positive for the development of ranching and agriculture on the reservation, but the second part was little more than coerced asset loss, or robbery.

In 1885, Ronan supported allotment on the reservation — or at least the first part of the policy — and thought he could convince the tribes to go along.[12] In 1887, however, when the Commissioner of Indian Affairs suggested that the new allotment act be applied to Flathead, Ronan demurred because of tribal complaints about boundary surveys that had worked against their interests and asked for "ample time to the Agent and his employes to induce the Indians to take allotments in sev[e]ralty, and to pursuade [sic] them to forget their prejudices against the word 'Survey.'"[13] Five years later, in 1892, Ronan again recommended that allotment not be forced on the Flathead Reservation tribes: "I do not believe it would be wise to negotiate with them for the cession of any surplus lands, or to attempt at present to have the lands surveyed and allotted."[14]

Ronan may have personally believed in the allotment policy, but his opposition to forcing allotment on the reservation delayed it for twenty years from about 1890 to 1910. Federal policy changes during the early twentieth century progressively weakened the trust protection of the allotments, but since the protection of the allotment patents expired after 25 years under the policy, an 1890 allotment would have resulted in even fewer restrictions on the sale of tribal member lands during the 1910s and 1920s. Since the reservation was not opened until 1910, it meant that the trust protection was set to expire during the 1930s, when government policy changed and continued the trust status indefinitely. Ironically, Ronan's avoidance of conflict with the tribes protected the tribes, despite his personal beliefs about the allotment policy.

Peter Ronan was born on June 1, 1839, at Antogomish, Nova Scotia, Canada.[15] He attended a village school in Nova Scotia before his family moved to Rhode Island when he was thirteen years old. At fourteen he was apprenticed at a print shop in Rhode Island. When he was seventeen he became foreman of the book and job printing office of M. B. Young, Providence, Rhode Island. Between 1854 and 1860, he worked as a compositor for a Dubuque, Iowa, newspaper. For two years following the Pike's Peak gold rush he prospected in the Rocky Mountains, and then he returned to Kansas to work as a partner in a Democratic newspaper. After being caught up in the political turmoil surrounding the Civil War, in 1863, Ronan headed to Alder Gulch or Virginia City in what became Montana. Ronan spent several years in mining before starting a series of newspapers in Virginia City and Helena with various partners, including Martin Maginnis, who was later to become his political patron. Ronan's newspaper was burned out by the Helena fires of 1872 and 1874 and he returned to mining. He was under sheriff of Lewis and Clark County when he was appointed as Flathead Indian Agent in 1877. His twin interests in mining and journalism continued as he speculated in various mining ventures during his years at the Jocko Agency and exhibited his journalistic skills in his voluminous correspondence as agent.

Since the Flathead Agency burned down in 1898, most of his correspondence as agent is no longer available. We do have his letters to the Commissioner of Indian Affairs which survived in the National Archives in Washington, D.C. His communications to other correspondents between 1877 and his death in 1893 would have filled in many details about Flathead Reservation affairs during that period, but only a few letters have survived in the collections of the Montana Historical Society Archives in Helena.

The *Rocky Mountain Gazette* published by Ronan and his partner in 1872 and 1873 carried several editorials about Indian policy in Montana, but there is no way to tell if these editorials represented Ronan's personal views. In October 1872, the *Gazette* endorsed the federal policy of cutting off supplies of guns and ammunition Indians used for hunting and using military force to confine Indian people to reservations, forcing them to farm, and treating all off-reservation Indians as hostiles. In December 1872 the newspaper approved of a congressional bill to transfer Indian affairs to the U.S. War Department. In August 1873, the paper argued for a reduction of the reservation for the Blackfeet, River Crow, and Gros Ventres Indians in northern Montana. None of these editorials were signed to indicate whose views they represented.[16]

Ronan had a reputation for honesty and in 1890 the *Northwest Illustrated Monthly Magazine* noted, "The Major has served a long time at the [Flathead] agency and is one of the few Indian agents who have made no money.[17] When Ronan died at the Jocko Agency on August 20, 1893, he left assets in Missoula County appraised at $5,402.88, mostly in cattle, real estate, and various mining claims.[18] But most of these assets had been purchased with borrowed money. The probate court allowed a $1,500 family allowance for the widow and her children. On June 8, 1896, the estate still had outstanding debts of $5,251.83. Most of the money was owed to Ronan's friends from his mining days. In 1896, $4,017.90 was owed to Henry Bratnober, who made a fortune from the Drum Lummon Mine at Marysville, near Helena, and was a hunting partner with Ronan in 1890.[19] Ronan's second large debt was $2,208.33, owed to William A. Clark, the famous Butte Copper King and Montana politician. In 1867 William and his brother, Joseph, ran a mail line between Missoula and Walla Walla, Washington, which traversed the Flathead Reservation.[20] When the Ronan estate was finally settled in 1907, interest had increased the debts to $7,211.83 with only $277.33 in cash available. The outstanding debts were settled for less than four cents on the dollar. Clearly Ronan had not grown personally rich from his position and his death left his family in straightened circumstances.

Peter Ronan was a nineteenth century white American who exhibited many of the cultural prejudices of his time. But he was also able to work with the Salish and Kootenai tribal community and leaders in keeping law and order on the reservation and growing the reservation ranching and agricultural economy. Sometimes he worked against the wishes of the tribes, but, in those areas where their goals intersected, Ronan proved a positive force for stability and protected the tribal community during a period of rapid cultural and economic change.

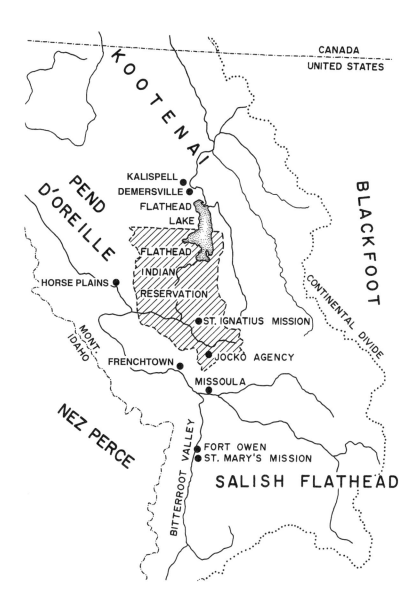

**Flathead Indian Reservation
Showing Tribal Territories
and Surrounding Towns**

1877

June 1, 1877
U.S. Office of Indian Affairs, "Letters Received by the Office of Indian Affairs, 1824-1880," National Archives Microfilm Publication M234, reel 507, frames 177-178.

Flathead Agency, M.T.
June 1st, 1877

To the
Hon. J. Q. Smith, Comr. Ind. Aff'rs
Washington, D.C.
  Sir:
  I have the honor to report that, in pursuance to instructions, I have this day assumed charge of this Agency, relieving C. S. Medary and receipting to him for all property pertaining to said Agency; that as soon as practicable, I will report as to the condition of the Indians etc, under my charge.

Very respectfully
Your obdt srvt
Peter Ronan
U.S. Ind. Agent.

June 23, 1877
Margaret Ronan, "Memoirs of a Frontiers Woman: Mary C. Ronan," unpublished masters thesis, State University of Montana, Missoula, 1932, pages 276-278. A foot-note has been omitted.[1]

By 1877 most of the Flathead Reservation Indians were at least nominally Catholic, and church festivals at St. Ignatius Mission had become major community events. The mission and its schools taught Western European Christian beliefs and values and also pressured tribal members to give up their tribal customs, values, and languages. The historical evidence is sketchy, but most tribal members probably disagreed with some of the church's goals and some, like Chief Arlee, were in frequent conflict with the priests.[2] Mary and Peter Ronan were devout Catholics and actively supported the work of St. Ignatius Mission on the reservation.

Rev. James O'Connor, Bishop of Omaha, was born in Ireland in 1823. Between 1876 and his death in 1890, he served as Vicar-apostolic of Nebraska and later Bishop of Omaha. His jurisdiction included Nebraska, Wyoming, Montana, and the Dakotas.[3] Father Lawrence Palladino, S.J., was born in Italy in 1837. He entered the Jesuits in 1855, served at St. Ignatius Mission between 1867 and 1873, and was stationed at Helena between 1874 and 1894. In 1894 he published the first edition of *Indian and White in the Northwest*, his history of the first half century of the Catholic Church in Montana. He was stationed at Missoula and other Pacific Northwest parishes during the twentieth century until his death in 1927.[4] Father Leopold Van Gorp, S.J., was Belgian. Between 1875 and 1890, he was Superior and then later temporal administrator at St. Ignatius Mission. He died in 1905 after a short second term as Superior at St. Ignatius Mission.[5] Father Joseph Bandini, S.J., was an Italian who had a long career as a missionary to the Indians. Bandini was stationed at St. Ignatius in the mid-1870s, where he was responsible, among other things, for visiting the outlying tribes. In the 1880s and 1890s, he became well know as a missionary to the Crow Indians.[6]

[Mary Ronan:] In the very midst of the furor and excitement of the Nez Perce trouble, the first of our long series of distinguished visitors arrived, Bishop [James] O'Connor of Omaha, whose diocese then extended into Montana. Accompanied by Father [Lawrence] Palladino from Helena and Father [Leopold] Van Gorp, superior at St. Ignatius Mission, the Bishop drove from Missoula and reached the Agency at noon on July [June] 22, 1877. The members of the party spent a few hours looking over the mills, workshops, office, storehouse, garden, and farm. They were our guests at dinner before they proceeded to St. Ignatius Mission. Mr. Ronan had dispatched Indian runners the length and breadth of the Reservation with the message that the "Chief of the Black Robes" had arrived and would say Mass and speak to the Indians at St. Ignatius Mission on Sunday morning, July [June] 23. Mr. Ronan went to the Mission with the Bishop and his party. This is his account of the occasion, preserved in the Old Scrap Book:

> The chiefs and head men of the three confederated tribes — Flatheads, Pend d'Oreilles and Kootenais — accompanied by their warriors, squaws, and papooses, came flocking in. At nine o'clock Sunday morning his Grace celebrated Mass in the commodious Mission Church, which was crowded to excess, and some hundred and fifty Indians and squaws received Holy Communion from his hands. The Bishop addressed the Indians in English, which was interpreted to them by father [Joseph] Bandini.
>
> "I am very happy, my dear friends, to be with you today. When a boy, with glowing enthusiasm, I read of your tribe. I remember your first deputation sent to St. Louis to ask that Catholic missionaries be sent among you to preach the Gospel of Christ and to spread the word of truth. I also remember of their departure and of their having been killed on the way. I have read of the other deputation which followed and heard of the readiness with which you embraced the faith. One of the principal objects of my long journey from the East was my hope of visiting this place, and I assure you, my dear friends, I am not disappointed. I am truly edified by your devotion to your religion and the duties it imposes. Your chief business at the Mission is to glorify God. Men of the world spend their lives in seeking gold. You are more wise in spending your time in adoring God. Your daily occupation is the wisest, the holiest, the most sublime. Having come far to see you my advice is this: Love one another, remain united in charity, have no hatreds, no quarrels among yourselves. God tells you this in the Gospel of the Mass today. We are all children of God. It would make your hearts sad to see your children hate each other. If you know and feel that your children should love each other, why should not all people love each other?
>
> "As Christians you are bound to love even those who are your enemies. It is hard, indeed, to love our enemies, but the

Great Spirit in Heaven commands us to love each other, and in order to be Christians and to be saved we must obey his commands. When our divine Lord came down from heaven to save us, He had His enemies. They reviled Him, they insulted Him, they nailed Him to the cross, and they put Him to death. Did He hate them? No. He prayed for them. He blessed them. He forgave them.

"To love our enemies requires courage. A coward can hate. It requires a brave man to forgive. The Indians are brave in the chase; they are brave in battle; they are brave against all danger. Show your courage and your bravery by forgiving your enemies. Misunderstandings will arise; quarrels will come up. You will find men who will behave badly to you; but you have the father here to advise you. For love of you the black-gowns left their homes and far-off country and came to dwell in your midst and to teach and advise you. You can rely with confidence on what they tell you. Come to the black-gowns for comfort, for solace, for advice. I will not ask you to love them, for I see you do love and revere them.

"I am very happy to tell you that your Catholic brethren in the East love you, and that the great heart of the American people and the Great Father in Washington love you and re-gret the wrongs you have had to suffer. The American people condemn the action of bad men. I am glad to inform you that you have a good Agent, Major Ronan, one of your own faith, loved and revered by his friends, and respected by all who know him, without regard to creed or country. — Goodbye; God bless you all, my children."

It interests me to note how the Bishop studiously avoided any direct ref-erence to the Nez Perce war and even more any reference what ever to the news that three days before Nez Perces had been seen in the Bitter Root Valley and that it was being whispered that the Selish would not remain true to the pledged words of their chiefs to protect the white settlers and to take no side with Chief Joseph. Indeed on the very day Bishop O'Connor was pleading for peace and brotherly love, the Nez Perces, in war array were warily skirting the entrenchments of Captain [Charles C.] Rawn.

July 2, 1877a
The Helena Independent *(daily), July 6, 1877, page 3, col. 3.*

Almost immediately after he took charge of Flathead Agency, Ronan faced a maelstrom spilling over from Idaho Territory. Nez Perce Chief Joseph had worked for years to avoid con-flict with the invading white settlers in Idaho while protecting his tribe's homeland. The Nez Perce had been friends with the white men since meeting the Lewis and Clark Expedition early in the nineteenth century. They joined the white trappers and the Flathead Reserva-tion tribes in fighting the Blackfeet and Sioux on the plains. But United States government policy was to force the Nez Perce onto a much reduced reservation which would remove many Nez Perce from their traditional home areas. Government bungling and white hostil-ity finally touched off a war. Since the Nez Perce were traditional friends and allies of the

Salish and Pend d'Oreille Indians, many Montana whites feared they would side with the Nez Perce. Ronan consulted with the western Montana chiefs and then reassured the U.S. Army, federal officials, and local white settlers of the peaceful intentions of the local tribes. Western Montana whites were hostile and suspicious, but the Bitterroot Salish sent Chief Adolph to Missoula to assure the settlers of the tribe's desire to avoid war.[7] When the Nez Perce did arrive in the Bitterroot Valley, the Salish refused to attack the Nez Perce but actively protected their white neighbors.

The tribal leaders Ronan talked to on the reservation probably sincerely wanted to avoid conflict with the United States Army, but likely also sympathized with the Nez Perce and felt the Nez Perce had been wronged. Andrew Garcia's Nez Perce wife, In-who-lise, told of an 1877 visit to the Nez Perce camp at Lolo by nineteen Pend d'Oreille warriors who encouraged the Nez Perce to avoid the white settlements and travel north to Canada through the remote parts of the Flathead Reservation.[8]

Benjamin F. Potts was Governor of Montana Territory between 1870 and 1883. An Ohioan and Civil War veteran, Potts worked hard to build the Republican Party in Montana with only limited success. During the Nez Perce War he tried to organize and arm a large militia force to fight the Nez Perce fleeing through the territory. The U.S. War Department declined to fund Potts' militia and most of it disbanded without encountering the Nez Perce.[9] Captain Charles C. Rawn commanded the U.S. Army troops that had just arrived in western Montana and were still engaged in building Fort Missoula. When Chief Joseph and the hostile Nez Perce fled Idaho by the Lolo Trail, Rawn gathered his troops and Bitterroot Salish and local white volunteers at a barricade at the western end of the trail where it comes into the Bitterroot Valley. Rawn tried to prevent the Nez Perce from entering the valley, but they found a way around his position without fighting. The barricade has since been known as "Fort Fizzle." Rawn and his troops later attacked the Nez Perce in the Battle of the Big Hole. Rawn enlisted in the army from Pennsylvania in 1861 and became a captain in 1863 and a major in 1884. He died in 1887.[10]

The Flatheads.
Letter from Agent Ronan to Governor Potts.
Missoula, July 2, 1877.

Governor B. F. Potts:

Dear Sir:— I came down from the Jocko reservation to-day to confer in regard to the threatened Indian difficulties. * * *

If it should happen that the hostiles come this way, (by way of the Spokane) and can form an alliance with the Coeur d'Alenes, Spokanes and Colville Indians, they can make a clean sweep, as the confederate tribes of this agency are almost entirely without arms. From assurances from the chiefs and head men of this reservation, I have no fears that they will join the hostiles, but I intend to be vigilant and watch their movements. A delegation of Indians and half breeds came to me yesterday and desired that I should send to you for arms and amunition. There are no arms at the reservation, and, after a conference with Capt. [Charles C.] Rawn, I was advised by him to ask you for about sixty stand of arms and two thousand rounds of amunition. The Indians are anxious to scout and form themselves into companies, and at the least warning to concentrate at the agency where arms and amunition can be furnished by me if necessity requires it.

By giving my request your earliest consideration, I remain,

Your obedient servant,
Peter Ronan,
U.S. Indian Agent.

July 2, 1877b

U.S. Office of Indian Affairs, "Letters Received by the Office of Indian Affairs, 1824-1880," National Archives Microfilm Publication M234, reel 507, frames 242-244.

In response to this letter, the Commissioner of Indian Affairs refused to authorize subsistence for Flathead Agency employees but offered to consider raising the salaries and reducing the number of employees if absolutely necessary.[11] This letter illustrated the continuing problem Ronan had in securing good employees at the agency.

Flathead Agency, M.T.
July 2d, 1877

Hon. J. Q. Smith
Commissioner Indian Affairs
Washington, D.C.

Sir:

With reference to instructions, contained in your letter of June 6th, to the late Agent, Chas. S. Medary, disallowing any expenditure for subsistence for Employés after July 1st 1877, I have the honor to state that I have put on a full complement of hands, as will be seen by the accompanying "Report of Changes in Employés," but they have only agreed to serve for one month *without subsistence*, and at the end of that time I will be without men to perform the work necessary to be done at the Agency. It is impossible to get skilled labor for the salaries allowed by Government, in a country where wages are so high and work so plenty as in Montana, unless subsistence is furnished. I can of course find men, occasionally, who are without means and are willing to work for a week and may be a month, long enough to enable them to get money sufficient to keep them for a time without work; but such labor is neither profitable nor reliable, and, though it will cripple very much the force so necessary to the economical management of the Agency, I respectfully ask that I may be allowed to dispense with the services of two hands and apply the sum appropriated for their salaries to the subsistence of the balance of the employés, so as to enable me to keep a few good hands at the Agency constantly.

Very respectfully
Your obdt servt
Peter Ronan
U.S. Ind Agent

July 11, 1877

U.S. Office of Indian Affairs, "Letters Received by the Office of Indian Affairs, 1824-1880," National Archives Microfilm Publication M234, reel 507, frames 268-280.

See the Biographical Sketches for information on Charlo, Michelle, Arlee, and Louison. Note Charlo's description of the Salish economy in 1877. The Salish had added planting and harvesting crops to the traditional cycle of hunting, fishing, and digging camas and other roots. The Salish were familiar enough with the economy of the whites to expect payment for time spent scouting and defending the white settlers.

According to Michel Revais, Andre, the second chief of the Pend d'Oreille in the 1870s, declined election as head chief in 1868 when Chief Alexander died. Michelle was elected head chief instead. During a buffalo hunting expedition in 1873, Andre carried with him "an American flag as an evidence of his friendship for the white man and the [U.S.] Government." In 1874 and 1875, embattled Flathead Agent Charles S. Medary tried to get the government to recognize Andre as Pend d'Oreille head chief in place of Chief Michelle. Andre lived at the St. Ignatius Mission with the bulk of the Pend d'Oreille tribe, while Michelle lived in the Jocko Valley near the agency. In August 13, 1877, Ronan reported Andre had organized a police force in the Mission Valley; in November 27, 1878, Ronan mentioned Andre led a buffalo hunting party that returned from the plains without hunting in order to avoid a war with the plains tribes; and, in an April 12, 1878, interview by Ronan, Andre refuted charges of cruelty to prisoners in the Mission jail.[12]

John Sheehan was a merchant who in 1877 worked for D. J. Welch and Thos. Williams in Missoula.[13] For biographical information on Baptist Marengo see the annotation to Ronan's August 27, 1877, letter. Father Jerome D'Aste, S.J., was an Italian mathematician and priest recruited by Father Pierre DeSmet in 1858. D'Aste worked at St. Mary's Mission between 1869 and 1891. When the Salish moved to the Flathead Reservation, he transferred to St. Ignatius Mission, where he served until his death in 1910. D'Aste became close to Chief Charlo.[14] Red Owl, a Nez Perce chief also known as Koolkool Snehee or Snene which is Salish for Red Owl, was in Looking Glass' camp in Idaho in July 1877 when it was attacked by soldiers under General O. O. Howard, but he was not killed there. He survived to take part in the Battle of the Bear's Paw. Duncan McDonald described him as "eloquent, sagacious . . . noted as an Apollo among belles of the tribe."[15] According to Mary Ronan, Eagle-of-the-Light and eleven lodges of his band of Nez Perce opposed the 1877 war with the whites. In order to keep out of the conflict, Eagle-of-the-Light and his people camped near the Flathead Agency in the Jocko Valley for the duration of the the crisis. Eagle-of-the-Light spoke during the 1879 conference between Ronan, Father J. M. Cataldo, S.J., and a group of Nez Perce refugees seeking to return to Montana. See Ronan's November 10, 1879, letter. In 1880, he pleaded with army and government officials to allow Chief Joseph and the surviving Nez Perce prisoners to settle on the Flathead Reservation.[16]

Flathead Agency, M.T.
July 11th, 1877

Hon. J. Q. Smith
Commissioner Ind. Affairs
Washington, D.C.

Sir:

I have the honor to transmit herewith copies of a letter received from Governor Potts requesting me to make a report to him of the feeling, etc., of the Indians under my charge as to the Nez Perce outbreak, and my report to him.

Very respectfully

Your obdt srvt
Peter Ronan
U.S. Ind. Agent

First Enclosure:

Territory of Montana
Executive Department
Helena, M. T., June 29th 1877

Sir:

In view of the anticipated Indian troubles in your locality, I request that you, with some of your most influential Fathers, seek the Flathead Indian Camp — Charlos' Camp — and have a talk with the Indians and Counsel peace and alliance with the Whites. In an interview such as suggested you can gain much valuable information about their intentions and the probable action of the other Indians. Let this meeting take place at an early day and report to me such information as you may be able to obtain.

Yours Truly
<signed> B. F. Potts

Peter Ronan, Esqr.
Agent Flathead Indians
Missoula, Montana
Second Enclosure:

Missoula, M. T.
July 10th 1877

Hon. B. F. Potts.
Govr. Montana
Helena, M. T.

Sir:

On the 5th day of July I received your letter of June 29th, requesting that I, with some of the most influential Fathers, seek the Flathead Camp — Charlos' band — and have a talk with the Indians, and to counsel peace, and alliance with the Whites; also, to gain whatever information I could and report to you.

On the day of the reception of your letter Capt. Rawn, in command of the Military Post near Missoula, arrived at the Agency for the purpose of gaining some knowledge of the Indians of this Reservation, and before proceeding to Charlos' camp, I concluded to hold a council with the Chiefs and head-men of the Confederated Tribes of my Agency, and for that purpose, in company with Captain C. C. Rawn and John Sheehan, taking with me an Interpreter we proceeded to the Mission.

On our way to the Mission we met Michelle, head chief of the Pen d'Oreilles, returning from a visit to his sister at the Lakes, who agreed to talk with me at the Agency on my return. On the morning of the 6th, André Second Chief of the Pen d'Oreilles, called into the Council representatives of the three confederated Tribes, viz: Flathead, Pen d'Oreill[e]s and Kootenais. Father Van Gorp and Father Bendini were also present. The Indians gave us unqualified assurance of their loyalty to the Whites, and stated that upon emergency they were ready to go to War with any tribe or confederation of tribes who might attempt to make war upon the settlers of Montana. Capt Rawn asked for Indian scouts to guard the passes, but the Indians were unwilling to go into service unless the Captain or myself could give them assurance of payment, a proposition neither of us would accede to, without instructions from our respective Departments, and we were both unwilling to make any promises that we could not fulfill to the letter.

The Indians, therefore, would not agree to act as scouts unless fully assured of payment but said, upon the reception of any news of danger, they would immediately dispatch messengers to the Military Post at Missoula, and to the Agency. After the conference we returned to the Agency where we met Arlee, Chief of the Flathead reservation Indians, who denounced, as false the intimation that he ever stated that any of his people had any intention of Joining the hostiles. He stated that they were peaceable and friendly to a man and would defend with their lives, if necessary, the Whites. Michelle, the Pen d'Oreille Chief, expressed himself in the same terms. Feeling fully satisfied of the peaceful intentions of the Reservation Indians, I proceeded to Charlos' Camp, up the Bitter Root Valley, in company with Captain Rawn and my official Interpreter, Baptiste Marengo, and on Sunday July 8th arrived at St. Mary's Mission, where we met Charlos, who with his family, was in attendance at Mass. Father D'Asti [Jerome D'Aste, S.J.], in charge of St. Mary's Mission, arranged preliminaries for our talk with the Chief.

Charlos greeted us in a frank and manly way and stated that his heart was glad to meet us, as bad stories had been put in circulation about himself and his people, and he hoped now he would have a chance to have the truth told of him to his White friends. In answer to my question "Where are your people?" he said: "This broad Country is our home — it is usual every year, after my people put in their crops, for them to go to the different Camas prairies, for the purpose of digging those roots for winter use, and while the squaws and Children perform that duty, the young men hunt and fish —

When the crops begin to ripen they return to their homes — They are on their ways home now, as I am informed by one of my young men, and twenty lodges are encamped near Missoula, the rest will soon follow." I then asked him how he felt in regard to the Whites, and he answered: "My father's name was Victor — he was the head Chief of this nation; he made the treaty with Governor Stephens [Issac I. Stevens], eighteen years ago; It was my father's boast that the blood of a Whiteman never reddened the hands of a single Indian of the Flathead tribe. My father died with that boast on his lips — I am my father's son, and will leave that same boast to my children."

In answer to my question "Will you join the Whites, with your warriors, and make war on the Nez Perces?" he stated "If danger threatens I will send runners to inform the settlers and the captain of the soldiers, and you, the Agent, I will do all in my power to defend the Whites and their homes, but I cannot send my young men out to make war on the Nez Perces. When my old enemy, the Blackfeet, came here to redden the Valley with my people's blood, the Nez Perces assisted us and, helped to drive them away. No, I cannot send my young men out to fight them, but I will help to protect the Whiteman's home."

I then asked him the news, and he said he was sorry to state that Red Owl, a Nez Perce Chief, and father of Louison, a Half-breed Flathead, who lives at my Agency was Killed by the Whites, on the head of the Clearwater River, together with fifteen lodges of his people. Red Owl was friendly to the Whites and asked the White people to designate a safe place for him to camp, with his people, which was done, and the Chief went into camp feeling that he was safe from the Whites. In the meantime a company of soldiers arrived in the vicinity of Red Owl's camp, where they captured one of Joseph's band, and they promised him his liberty on condition that he would guide them to Joseph's Camp. The Indian agreed to the proposition, but instead of taking them to Joseph's camp, he guided them to Red Owl's lodges, and the Whites fell upon this friendly band and Killed them all. This news, Charlos stated, he got from reliable sources and as Red Owl was known in Montana, he sent Messengers to different Indian camps to tell the truth concerning the death of Red Owl, and to say that the whites deplored the treachery and the snare that they were led into by Joseph's renegade.

On our way up the Bitter Root, we met Eagle-of-the-Light, formerly Chief of Joseph's band of non-treaty Nez Perces who was driving a band of loose horses, and we were informed that he was going up the Lo Lo Pass to bring back the Nez Perce camp, which left Missoula some three weeks ago with the intention of going over to the Nez Perce country, but who were met by a runner who informed them of the uprising of Joseph's band against the Whites and they went into camp and sent Word to their friends here of the trouble and asked advice. Eagle-of-the-Light advised peace and the return of the tribe to Missoula, there to camp in the vicinity of the Military post until peace was made, and for that purpose he was going out with fresh horses to assist them in; this was the Indian statement, and of course I give it as repeated.

There are a number of wild stories afloat in regard to Indian massacres lately perpetrated, but I cannot trace them to any reliable source and will refrain from making any mention of them. I feel perfectly confident, however, of the good faith of Charlos, the "original" Flathead Chief, and his band as well as all of the confederate tribes under my Jurisdiction but of course this will not prevent me from taking every precaution to guard against danger or surprise.

The only danger I apprehend at present is from the Indians of the Snake and Columbia rivers, as far north as Colville, who may possibly be influenced to Join the hostiles, in that case, if they come through this country it seems to me that the Chiefs, no matter what their influence may be in their tribes, will be unable wholly to restrain their young men, as there are restless and adventurous spirits among the Indians, as well as among the Whites who would be only too glad for an op[p]ortunity for plunder and rapine.

Very respectfully
Peter Ronan
U.S. Ind. Agt.

August 6, 1877

U.S. Office of Indian Affairs, "Letters Received by the Office of Indian Affairs, 1824-1880," National Archives Microfilm Publication M234, reel 507, frames 347-348.

> The patents mentioned below were an unresolved aftermath of James A. Garfield's 1872 visit to the Bitterroot Valley Salish. Garfield was an Ohio congressman who may have accepted the assignment to negotiate with the Salish to avoid having to campaign for President Ulysses S. Grant's reelection. His arrogance and impatience must have made the negotiations with Charlo and the Bitterroot Salish a mockery. Charlo refused to remove to the Jocko Reservation and was offended when the published report seemed to indicate he

had signed the agreement with Garfield. Garfield went on to become President in 1880 but was assassinated a few months after taking office.[17]

Federal law required that Salish farmers accept patents on 160 acres of land in order to remain in the Bitterroot Valley. The patents were issued by the General Land Office, but Charlo and the Salish declined delivery because acceptance would imply the dissolution of tribal relations and an obligation to pay taxes to Missoula County. The law also provided for white settlement and title to all of the Bitterroot Valley outside of the Salish allotments. The Salish saw this as a violation of the 1855 Hellgate Treaty which provided for Salish owner-ship of the Bitterroot if the valley was "better adapted to the wants of the Flathead tribe." See also Ronan letter of October 31, 1877b.

Flathead Agency, M.T.
August 6th, 1877

Hon. J. Q. Smith
Commissioner Ind. Affairs,
Washington, D.C.
    Sir:
    Among the miscellaneous papers turned over to me by the late Agent, upon my taking charge of this Agency, were 51 Land Patents for members of the Flathead, Kootenai and Pen d'Oreille Confederated tribes, bearing date March 13th 1876. Accompanying them was a letter, dated April 4th 1876, from the Hon. Commissioner, which ordered immediate action to be taken relative to the distribution of the same. As I am not aware what action, if any, was taken by the late Agent, I have the honor to request that instructions as to the dispo-sition of the patents be given me.

Respectfully,
Your obdt servt,
Peter Ronan
U.S. Ind. Agent.

August 13, 1877

U.S. Commissioner of Indian Affairs, Annual Report of the Commissioner of Indian Affairs *(Washington, D.C.: U.S. Government Printing Office, 1877), pages 530-533.*

Ronan often waxed philosophical in his annual reports showing the assumptions and prejudices that colored his views of tribal life. In this report he defined progress in terms of expansion of individual farms. Most tribal leaders supported expanding cattle herds and farms to make up for the declining plains buffalo herds, but many probably would have preferred cooperative agriculture over individual holdings. His prejudices against gambling reflect the views of his time and class, not the opinions of many tribal members. The priests also campaigned against gambling. In 1877 the Indian Police on the reservation were or-ganized and controlled by the traditional chiefs, not the agent. In the 1880s Ronan and the traditional chiefs fought over control of the Indian police and courts. His conclusion that the agency physician "has the full confidence of the Indians" and that there were no traditional healers on the reservation is questionable. For biographical information on Kootenai Chief Eneas see the Biographical Sketches. The report refers to moving the Flathead Agency from

the Jocko Valley to a more central location on the reservation, but cost considerations delayed moving the agency until well into the twentieth century.

Office of Flathead Agency,
Montana Territory, August 13, 1877.

Sir: In compliance with instructions contained in a letter from your office,
dated July 10, 1877, I have the honor of submitting this, my first annual report,
and in doing so, it gives me great pleasure to state that notwithstanding the
fears and predictions of the people generally of the Territory of Montana, the
Indians of this reservation have remained faithful and friendly to the whites,
although their relatives and allies, the Nez Percés, have been on the war-path
and marched in triumph through the Territory within a few miles of this agency, when they sent their runners and scouts to try to seduce the reservation
Indians to join their cause. But, thanks to the activity of the chiefs, to the religious and moral influence of the fathers in charge of Saint Ignatius and Saint
Mary's missions, and to the good sense of the Indians themselves, they not only
refrained from joining their ancient allies, the Nez Percés, but they gave them
warning that if an outrage was committed, either to the person or property
of any settler of the Bitter Root Valley, in their retreat before General [O. O.]
Howard's advancing troops, they would immediately make war upon them; and
to this worthy action of Charlos, the non-treaty Flathead chief, and the chiefs
and headmen of this reservation, do the white settlers of the Bitter Root Valley owe their preservation of life and property during those trying days. The
Indians belonging to this reservation are the confederated tribes of Flatheads,
Upper Pend d'Oreilles, and Kootenais.

The Flatheads,

as a tribe, are not surpassed by any Indians I know of in intelligence, civilization, and disposition of kindness and good-will toward the whites. Under
the Garfield agreement of August 27, 1872, a few families (not over twenty)
were induced to remove from the Bitter Root Valley and settle in close proximity to this agency, under the chieftainship of Arlee, second chief of the tribe,
who signed the agreement, and it was confidently expected that the balance
of the tribe would soon follow; but Charlos, the son of Victor, and hereditary
chief of the tribe, chose not to sign the agreement, and still resides in the Bitter Root Valley, where he cultivates the soil and refuses to leave the home of
his fathers. The whole Flathead tribe, consisting of nearly four hundred souls,
with the exception of the few families who removed to this agency, adhere to
Charlos and follow his fortunes, choosing rather to eke out a livelihood by their
own exertions in the neighborhood of their venerated chief than to accept the
bounty of the Government and leave their homes. The Flathead families who
reside at the agency are in comfortable circumstances, as the $5,000 annually
appropriated to the tribe, under the conditions of the Garfield agreement, is
paid wholly to them, and is generally expended in improvements, and in purchasing stock.

The Kootenais.

It is a pleasant duty for me to inform you of the advance of the Kootenais,
consisting of about 315 souls, settled on the Jocko reservation, a tribe hitherto
reported as a lazy, thriftless set. This year six families of that tribe have entered upon civilizing pursuits and have excellent crops of wheat, oats, potatoes,
onions, turnips, &c. The tribe also owns 100 head of horned stock and 300 head

of horses. These poor people, above all others on this reservation, need encouragement and assistance, as they are furnished with hardly any implements of labor worth speaking of. A few weeks ago Eneas, the Kootenai chief, who, by the way, is better respected and has more influence among his people than any other chief on the reservation, purchased for the use of his tribe a mowing and reaping machine and a set of blacksmith's tools, pledging in payment the money coming to him from Government for the next two quarters as chief of the tribe. Eneas is a good man, kind and generous, and spends all the money he receives from Government in relieving the wants of his poor and struggling people.

The Kootenais live near the Flathead Lake, nearly 100 miles from the agency, and have no means of hauling lumber from the agency mill, and therefore have no houses to live in. If means are given these people to continue their efforts and encourage their civilizing pursuits, under the chieftainship of Eneas, whom the whole tribe respect and venerate, a very short time will elapse before they become a happy and prosperous people, as their land is productive and their grazing facilities unsurpassed. I would therefore recommend that the case of the Kootenais be carefully considered and prompt action be taken in furnishing them with implements of labor.

The Pend d'Oreilles,

numbering about 847, reside near Saint Ignatius Mission, some twenty miles from the agency, where they are generally engaged in the cultivation of the soil as far as the limited facilities will allow. Michelle, their chief, although a good-meaning man, has lost caste among his people, and a great deal of dissatisfaction exists among the tribe. I went to some pains to obtain the bottom facts, so that I might in some way try to conciliate and bring about a better understanding. It seems that the tribe are dissatisfied because Michelle lives near the agency some 20 miles from his people, who are located near Saint Ignatius Mission, and when business is to be settled, and decisions to be made by the chief, the Indians must come a long distance to consult him; therefore, André, second chief, who lives with the tribe, takes the responsibility upon himself and decides a great many of their cases. Sometimes, when the adverse party is dissatisfied, an appeal to Michelle is taken, who generally reverses André's decisions, to the vexation of all concerned. The influence of the chiefs on this reservation consists mainly in oratory, and Michelle, being crippled and away from his tribe, has in a great measure lost control, a fact which he is well aware of himself, as he came to consult in regard to removing from the agency and going back among his people, with a view of regaining his lost influence. I held my decision in this case for further information and advice.

The Location of the Agency.

It seems to me that a great error was committed in locating this agency upon its present site, in an out-of-the-way corner of the reservation, if it was the intention to gather the Indians around the vicinity of the agency, where plenty of good agricultural land could be procured for the Indians to settle upon. The Jocko valley is very limited in agricultural land, being rocky, gravelly, and poor, but cannot be surpassed for grazing and timber; while further on toward the lakes, and more in the center of the reservation, where the Pend d'Oreilles reside, the agricultural land is excellent, and an unlimited number of farms [c]an be opened up with timber, meadow, pasturage, and water-power that cannot be excelled. Of course it would cost quite a sum of money to remove the agency more to the center of the reservation, but in the end it would be economy, as it would tend to bring the Indians together and harmonise existing quarrels, especially among the Pend d'Orielles, which may terminate in the severance of the tribe in case they may undertake to depose Michelle. Outside of these matters the best of

Good Feeling Prevails,

and no case of outrage or drunkenness has been reported to me since taking charge. The Indians seem to be contented and happy, and are pursuing their avocations with patience and good humor. The harvest is upon us, and all are engaged in gathering in their crops, which are very good this season, as a kind Providence has so far averted storms and drought, and an abundant yield is sure to bless their toil.

Gambling and Horse-Racing

in the vicinity of the agency, since I have taken charge, is entirely discountenanced, and with the aid of the chiefs and mission Indian police, I have succeeded in prohibiting it almost entirely, and if indulged in at all, is carried on in the most secret manner. On Saturday afternoons, when the young men wish to try the speed of their horses, they ask permission with a pledge that no betting will be indulged in.

Indian Police.

Under the supervision of André, second chief of the Pend d'Oreilles, a very efficient force of Indian police is organized, who have their headquarters at the mission, where a jail has been erected. Upon information being lodged with André that any outrage against whites, or infraction of Indian law has been committed, the culprit is arrested and punished by imprisonment or labor, according to the nature of the crime. This force of police is composed of the very best men of the tribes, who perform any duty required of them by their chief without any payment. Their service is also at the disposal of the agent, and to their activity and efficiency I owe in a great measure the healthy moral state of affairs at this agency; and I would suggest that some recognition of their organization be made, and that the agent be empowered to at least furnish them with arms and necessary clothing for each year, as a reward for their sterling service. I will here cite an instance: Upon the approach of Joseph's band of hostile Nez Percés, and while the people of this county were trembling for their safety, and fearful that the reservation Indians would join the hostiles, the mission-police placed themselves at the agent's service and received orders from their chiefs to immediately arrest and incarcerate in the Indian jail any disaffected reservation Indian who might attempt to join the hostiles. This prompt action had a salutary effect upon the malcontents, and we had no occasion to arrest any one.

The Sanitary Condition of the Indians

is excellent, and at this time but few cases of sickness are reported on the reservation. The medical service is in charge of an able and efficient physician, who has the full confidence of the Indians. Such thing as Indian "Medicine Men" have no existence, to my knowledge, on this reservation. I am in receipt of a fine supply of medical stores from the Department, which is one of the principal causes of the excellent health which prevails on the reservation.

The School

is under the supervision of the missionaries, and the boarding-school is taught by the Sisters of Charity, and owing to their untiring devotion the progress made by the children is highly gratifying. Besides the ordinary branches of education, the girls are taught sewing, knitting, to cut and make their own clothes, and house-keeping, cooking, &c. The boarding-school subsists through the salary granted to the teachers by Government treaty, alms, and labor of the Sisters of Charity. The day school for boys is not a success, as it is impossible to induce them to confine themselves to the school-house. An industrial school, where attendance can be compelled, is the only practicable institution for boys. Industry is the great civilizer, and it is only by leading the rising generation into habits of industry, as well as education, that they will be brought to the understanding of the advantage and elevation of labor and agricultural pursuits.

Very respectfully, your obedient servant,

Peter Ronan.
United States Indian Agent

The Commissioner of Indian Affairs.

August 20, 1877

U.S. Office of Indian Affairs, "Letters Received by the Office of Indian Affairs, 1824-1880," National Archives Microfilm Publication M234, reel 507, frames 378-388.

Despite the demonstrated fidelity of the Salish, Pend d'Oreille, and Kootenai tribes during the Nez Perce War, the federal government responded by including the friendly tribes in a military order banning sales of guns and ammunition. The western Montana tribes desperately needed access to ammunition for hunting and self-defense. Ronan lobbied to have the order modified and/or have the government feed the tribes. Ronan was able to get the order slightly modified and did get authority to purchase subsistence supplies, but it took time for the bureaucracy to respond, and, in the meantime, the tribes had to purchase ammunition at high prices from independent white traders in the buffalo country. Ronan must have had considerable difficulty explaining the fickle behavior of the government to the Indian people. See especially Ronan's August 21, 1877, letter to Montana Territory Delegate Martin Maginnis. *The Helena Daily Herald* editorialized that the Flathead "are peaceable, their crops are deficient, and they have to get meat, steal or starve. Give them the ammunition."[18] For Henry A Lambert, Flathead Agency farmer and clerk in 1877, see Ronan's September 7, 1889, letter and annotation.

Flathead Agency, M.T.
August 20th 1877

To the
Hon. Commissioner Indian Affairs
Washington, D.C.

Sir:

I have the honor to forward herewith special Estimate for Supplies which the exigency of the case demands immediate attention. In making my Estimate for subsistence and clothing for the Indians of this reservation I most respectfully submit the following facts:

Owing to the Order from your office, dated August 3d, 1877, the sale of arms and ammunition will be prohibited, and your suggestions obeyed to the letter, but in depriving the Indians of this Reservation of the means of procuring game particularly the Kootenais, who, with the exception of six families, have no other means of support, they will be reduced to hunger and desperation, and I fear the consequences.

The Pen d'Oreilles, a large tribe, consisting of over eight hundred, belonging to this reservation, although farming to some extent, depend chiefly on the Chase for a livelyhood. It is true that but a few of them went on a summer hunt this year, but all are preparing for their annual Winter hunt, and when the harvest is gathered, nothing but force will prevent them from going and I fear they will use force in procuring ammunition, unless their necessities are supplied.

The Flatheads are in better circumstances owing to the money paid to them according to the Garfield agreement; but their young men will not be restrained if the Pen d'Oreilles and Kootenais make up their minds to have food or War.

For over thirty years these Indians have procured their ammunition and guns without restraint, and during all that time their loyalty and friendship to the Whites has not been questioned; and now during the bloody war which is raging in our Territory these Indians stand foremost, with arms in their hands, in defence of the Whites, and to their address and intrepidity do the people of the county of Missoula owe (and are not ashamed to own it) their lives and property; and for this service, instead of praise and encouragement, they are to be prohibited from supporting their families, and will be compelled either to fight or famish unless my request is granted.

The necessity of the case makes me thus plainly state matters, and I trust my suggestions will be duly acted upon. Enclosed You will find a letter just received by me from one of the Missionaries of this reservation who is with the troops. He makes some suggestions which will bear me out in my view of the situation.

Very respectfully
Your obdt servt,
Peter Ronan
U.S. Ind Agent.

First Enclosure: "Special Estimate of Indian Supplies, &c., Required at the Flathead Agency, During 3 and 4th quarters 1877, and 1st and 2d Quarters 1878," August 20, 1877. Estimate for $5,232.00 for blankets, bacon, beans, beef, carrots, candles, coffee, denims, domestic, flour, fishhooks, matches, needles, potatoes, pork, prints, rice, sugar, salt, soda, soap, tea, tobacco, ticking, and thread. The purpose of the purchase would be "To subsist the Indians who are prevented from going on their annual hunts by the law forbidding the sale of arms and ammunition to them." Second Enclosure:

Deer Lodge
Aug. 15th/ 77

Peter Ronan U. S. I. A.

Dear Sir:

Under the present excitement which is all over the country on this side of the range more than at fever heat; it is exceedingly dangerous for any of our indians to pass any where through this country. Intentionally or unintentionally they are likely to be mistaken for hostiles and be destroyed. I am of opinion that it is their very best course to keep close to their Reservation and Missions, till this great excitement subsides. Should they have to suffer in consequence of giving up their hunting expeditions, for peace's sake, and for their own good; it seem to me that it would be adviseable for you to represent these matters to Washington and apply for such subsistence from the Government as should meet the wants of those hiding under the circumstances.

I am just in from the battle grounds on the Big Hole. It must have been a very bloody and desperate contest. The wounded, all told 39, are being brought into Deer Lodge. They will reach here by next friday.

My best regards to Molly also to Mr. & Mrs. Lambert.

Your obt Servant in X
L. Palladino S.J.

Third Enclosure:

Stevensville, Aug 18th 77

Major P. Ronan
Dear Major,

I am in receipt of a letter from Rev. Father Palladino. He tells me that all through the country on the other side of the range there is a terrible and fieverish excitement about the Indians in general and counsel me to exert myself to stop our Indians from going to buffalo. But in the starving condition in which our Indians are at present for the scarcity of the grain they put in, because they had no seed, and the visitation of the hail storm we had here in the valley, seems no possibility of stopping them from going to buffalo. So that either of the two things should be done, to obtain from the Government some support for next winter, or to direct the Indians authoritatively to go to buffalo by the Kootenais trail. I wished you could take this matter in your hand and see what can be done for the best of the country and Indians.

My best respects to your lady.

Yours Respectfully
J. d'aste, S.J.

This letter refers to the non-treaty Flatheads under Chief Charlos.

Peter Ronan
U.S. Ind. Agent

Endorsement on Peter Ronan's August 20, 1877, letter:

Interior Dept.
Ofc. Ind. Affairs,
Sept. 6, 1877.

Respectfully forwarded to the Hon. Secretary of the Interior, recommending that agent Ronan be authorized to advertise in the Helena "Independent," inviting proposals for furnishing such of the within supplies as are absolutely required, and to enter into contract therefore with the lowest responsible bidders, at a cost not to exceed $5,000.— providing that if the exigencies of the service require it, the agent may buy, in open market, pending execution of contracts, supplies not exceeding $1000. in amount.

J. Q. Smith
Commissioner

Second Endorsement on Peter Ronan letter:

Department of the Interior
Sept. 6, 1877

Respectfully returned to the Commissioner of Indian Affairs approved as recommended.

C. Schurz
Secretary.

August 21, 1877
Martin Maginnis Papers, MC 50, box 2, folder 25, Montana Historical Society Archives, Helena, Montana.

> Martin Maginnis was the Montana Territory Delegate to the U.S. House of Representatives for six terms. He was first elected in 1872 and served until 1885. A Civil War veteran, he worked variously in mining and journalism in Montana before being elected Territorial Delegate.[19] In the 1860s Maginnis had been Ronan's partner in the newspaper business in Helena. The Maginnises and Ronans were longtime friends and Martin was Ronan's political patron, who supported his appointment as Flathead Indian Agent and helped pressure the Indian Office to respond favorably to Ronan's requests.[20] This letter and Ronan's September 20, 1877, letter which was referred by Maginnis to the Commissioner of Indian Affairs on October 17, 1877, illustrate Ronan's efforts to reverse the ban on the sale of guns and ammunition to the Bitterroot Salish and Flathead Reservation tribes.

Missoula, Aug. 21, 1877.

Dear Major:

I came down here yesterday from the Agency with a hope of meeting you. It is almost imperative that you make a trip here in order to have convincing proofs of the great blunders which are being made at Washington — blunders which are more than likely to plunge this country into another Indian war and God knows we have had had [sic] enough of that business.

Among several of those incendiary orders which I have lately received, is one to prohibit the sale of amunition and arms to the Indians of this reservation. If such an order is carried into effect the Government must make provisions to support the Indians who depend upon the hunt for a livelyhood, *or hunger will compel them to fight for food.* For thirty years those Indians have had full license to purchase all the amunition as they needed and during all this time their loyalty to the whites has never been questioned. And now after having stood forward with arms in defence of their white neighbors and after having by their address and firmness saved the people of Missoula and the Bitterroot from death and devastation, they naturally feel that in depriving them of their means of living that a great wrong is committed, and if things are pressed, without providing for their wants war will be sure to follow. Do not leave Montana without making me a visit. Come to stay for a few days and post yourself, and I know you will be able to prevent in a measure, the crimes of a handful of Nez Percz outlaws from being visited upon the heads of the unfortunate Indians of this reservation.

Respectfully Yours
Peter Ronan

August 27, 1877
U.S. Office of Indian Affairs, "Letters Received by the Office of Indian Affairs, 1824-1880," National Archives Microfilm Publication M234, reel 507, frames 414-416.

> Baptiste Marengo was the son of a French trapper named Louis Raboin (nicknamed Maringouin) and an unidentified Indian woman. In March 1860 he married Harriet Boisvert, a mixed blood lady, and they lived in the Bitterroot Valley until moving to the Jocko Valley in 1873. He served as interpreter during Congressman James A. Garfield's negotiations with the

Bitterroot Salish in 1872.[21] In 1880, Nez Perce Chief Eagle-of-the-Light described Marengo as "a good interpreter."[22] According to a January 29, 1879, letter from Pend d'Oreille Chief Michelle to Big Canoe, Marengo died on New Years 1879.[23]

Flathead Agency, M.T.
August 27th, 1877

To the
Hon. Commissioner Ind. Affairs
Washington, D.C.

Sir:

In compliance with your letter of July 12th, 1877, requesting me to make a full investigation of the case of Baptiste Marengo relative to the annuity money alleged to be due him, I have the honor to report as follows:

The books of the office show that the payment of the annuity money claimed by the said Marengo has been duly made as follows: The 2d quarter, 1876 – to claimant – amt 58^{14}/100; the 3d quarter, 1876, to Agent Medary, amt 56^{82}/100; the 4th quarter, 1876, to Arlee, Chief of Flatheads, amt. with remarks in red ink "$56^{82}/100 due for 3d Quarter 76" amt 56^{82}/100; 1st and 2d Quarters, 1877, to Arlee, with remarks, "69.87 due Medary" – amt 119.05.

The Chief, Arlee, states that he received but $105.00 from the late Agent, to be paid to Marengo, which amount Marengo acknowledges to have received.

The amount of pay for 3d Quarter 1876, for which the order was given to Decker (and payment of same refused by the Agent) was paid to the late Agent, by himself, as shown by the entry upon the Ledger.

Though the books show to the contrary, Marengo claims that the sum of $185^{82}/100 the total amount (less the amount of $105.00 received from Arlee) of 5 quarters pay is still due him.

Very respectfully,
Your obdt servt,
Peter Ronan
U.S. Ind. Agent.

Action notation on letter is "Copy to 2nd Auditor for consideration with accs of Medary. Jany 6th/ 78."

October 1, 1877

U.S. Office of Indian Affairs, "Letters Received by the Office of Indian Affairs, 1824-1880," National Archives Microfilm Publication M234, reel 507, frames 465-472.

Flathead Agency, M.T.
October 1st 1877

To the Hon. Commissioner of Indian Affairs
Washington D. C.

Sir:

Enclosed please find copy of letter from Rev. Fr. D'Astie of St. Mary's Mission Bitter Root, and my reply thereto which explains itself.

In regard to the Flatheads who adhere to their homes in the Bitter Root, from all the information I can gain they are in very destitute circumstances, owing in part to a partial destruction of their crops by a hail storm, and to the fact that they were prevented in a great measure from harvesting what was not destroyed, by the excitement caused by the march of the Nez Percés through their country. Charlos the Chief of the Non-Treaty Flatheads, called all his men around him and warned the Nez Percés that if any outrage against the whites or a theft was committed by them in the Bitter Root valley that he would immediately fall upon them with his warriors. Joseph's band heeded Charlos' warning and not a single outrage was committed by the hostile Nez Percés upon the white citizens of that rich and thickly settled valley, and to Charlos and his Indians do the citizens owe their preservation. In view of this fact I write to you for permission to distribute some of the goods amongst those Indians, which has been so generously permitted me to purchase by special estimate.

Very respectfully
Your obedient Servant
Peter Ronan
U.S. Indian Agent

First Enclosure:

Stevensville, Sep. 20th 77

Major P. Ronan
    Dear Major
    Our Indians are starting for buffalo. Could you do something for them. They have scarcely any ammunition and feel very bad. Charlot and other leading men were saying to me. The whites, Captain Rawn and the Governor told us that they were very pleased with us, and now that the danger is passed they want us to starve and refuse us the only means of living we have now. How can we believe them to be sincere in their talks?
    Please to give my best respects to your lady.

Yours respectfully
J. d'aste S.J.

Second Enclosure:

Flathead Agency, M.T.
September 21st 1877

Father D'Aste:
    Reverend Sir:
    Yours of the 20th received, and in reply I would say, that inasmuch as the Flatheads of the Bitter Root still adhere to their homes in that Valley, and refuse to remove to the Jocko and come under the arrangements of the Garfield Agreement, that they are entirely outside of my Jurisdiction, and have no claims upon this Agency. I sincerely sympathize with the Flatheads of the Bitter Root and in view of the very exigency you state, made a requisition on the Government for permission to purchase food and clothing for the indigent Indians of this reservation to a limited extent which has been generously granted, but I am not advised yet if the Department will allow me to distribute the goods among Indians who refuse to come on the reservation.
    My construction of duty is to give to those who come to live on the reservation and I cannot depart from it without special instructions from the Department. I will ask for permission to aid your Indians to the Extent of the appropriation granted and if given permission will only too gladly avail myself of the opportunity to relieve their immediate wants. In regard to ammunition, orders are imperative against the sale to any Indians and however deplorable, must be obeyed.

I remain Yours, truly
Peter Ronan
U.S. Ind Agent

October 17, 1877

U.S. Office of Indian Affairs, "Letters Received by the Office of Indian Affairs, 1824-1880," National Archives Microfilm Publication M234, reel 508, frames 321-325.

> In September 1877, Civil War hero General William T. Sherman was at Fort Missoula on an inspection tour and met with Agent Ronan and an unnamed priest, presumably Father Leopold Van Gorp, S.J. Ronan pleaded for subsistence for the Flathead Reservation and Bitterroot Valley tribes or ammunition for a buffalo hunt. Sherman noted that "These Indians, the Flatheads, are friendly, but they must go for buffalo or starve. If they go for buffalo they may come in contact with white settlers who know not the difference between Nez Perces and Flatheads, and trouble may result."[24]

House of Representatives
Washington, D C., Oct. 17, 1877

To the Hon
The Commissioner of Indian Affairs
    Sir:
    I have the honor to enclose a letter from Maj Ronan Agent for the Flatheads. He was in doubt in regard to the construction of the President's order. In the opinion of Gen'l [William T.] Sherman, visiting Missoula, and those whom the question was submitted, the order permitted Mr. Ronan to allow powder and lead to be issued or sold to the Flatheads. They being our allies, and the ammunition necessary to their subsistence. From the enclosed it would seem that Mr Ronan is anxious to learn if the Department places the same construction upon the order.
    The Flatheads were a great aid in the protection of Western Montana during the recent Nez Perces invasion, they receive no subsistence, are largely dependent on the chase, Armed with breech loaders. The order will work great hardship upon them even with the most liberal construction. I request if it meets with your pleasure that Mr Ronan be advised of the sense of the Department in this matter.

Respectfully
Martin Maginnis

Enclosure:

Flathead Agency
Sept. 20, 1877

Major Maginnis
    Dear Friend:
    Everything is satisfactory in regard to "Employees" as I have received instructions to put the hands on again. I am also advised that funds have been placed to my credit. In regard to amunition, will you be kind enough to have me advised *at once*, whether the construction yourself and General Sherman put upon the order in regard to giving the Indians permission to purchase *powder lead and caps* is the correct one, as understood at the Department, as I am harrassed beyond measure by the Indians to give the storekeepers orders to sell loose amunition, since you told "Arllee" that it was your opinion and the opinion of Gen Sherman that they could make such purchases. The storekeepers refuse to sell loose powder, lead and caps unless I give my consent, and I hesitate to do so unless assured of its correctness, in view of the strenious [sic] orders from the Department. By promptly attending to this matter you will

confer a great favor upon me and relieve me from much trouble and annoyance.

Yours as ever,
Peter Ronan
U.S. Ind. Agent.

October 31, 1877a

U.S. Office of Indian Affairs, "Letters Received by the Office of Indian Affairs, 1824-1880," National Archives Microfilm Publication M234, reel 507, frames 557-558.

Flathead Agency, M.T.
October 31st, 1877

To the
Hon. Commissioner of Ind. Affairs
Washington, D.C.
Sir:
I have the honor to state that on account of the absence of the majority of the Indians of this reservation, on their annual Buffalo hunt, it will be impossible to take the census of said Indians until the Coming spring, when they will have returned to their homes. This census was ordered by office letter "A" of August 3d 1877 (Roberts).

Very respectfully,
Your obdt servt,
Peter Ronan
U.S. Ind. Agent.

October 31, 1877b

U.S. Office of Indian Affairs, "Letters Received by the Office of Indian Affairs, 1824-1880," National Archives Microfilm Publication M234, reel 507, frames 567-568.

Flathead Agency, M.T.
October 31st, 1877

To the
Hon. Commissioner of Ind. Affairs
Washington, D.C.
Sir:
By Office letter "L" dated August 23d, 1877, I was ordered to deliver to the Indians living in Bitter Root Valley certain land patents, with reference thereto I have the honor to state that when the letter, above referred to, reached me, the Bitter Root Indians had gone on their winter buffalo hunt, and that until their return it will be impossible to comply with said instructions.

Very respectfully,
Your obdt servt,
Peter Ronan
U.S. Ind. Agent.

December 10, 1877

U.S. Office of Indian Affairs, "Letters Received by the Office of Indian Affairs, 1824-1880," National Archives Microfilm Publication M234, reel 507, frames 612-616.

The Lower Pend d'Oreille Indians under Petah [identified as Victor in Ronan's letter of December 30, 1878], who lived along the Clark Fork and Pend d'Oreille Rivers, were not included in the 1855 Hellgate Treaty signed by the Upper Pend d'Oreille, Bitterroot Salish, and Lower Kootenai Indians. Victor was the son of Chief Loyola of the Lower Pend d'Oreille who died in 1846. In 1854 he moved to the Lower Flathead Valley with most of his tribe when the St. Ignatius Mission was relocated. He and his tribe soon returned to their traditional homes on the Pend d'Oreille River. In 1859 he accompanied Father Pierre DeSmet and a delegation of other chiefs to Fort Vancouver to assure U.S. Army General William Harney of their desire for peace with the whites. At the 1877 council at Spokane Bridge with Col. Frank Wheaton, he declared his intention of staying out of the Nez Perce War. After 1877 he continued to work for a reservation for his people on the Pend d'Oreille River. He worked for peaceful relations with the white settlers, but was considered irresolute and weak by the priests.[25] Simon was a subchief among the Lower Pend d'Oreille and brother of Victor, the head chief.[26]

Charles A. Lynch and his brother, Neptune Lynch, were among the earliest white settlers on Horse Plains. He was a farmer and rancher, carried the mail, and operated a store in Horse Plains.[27]

Since the Lower Pend d'Oreille were not parties to a treaty, conflicting claims to river bottom lands between the new white settlers and the Indians led to continuing friction during the late nineteenth century.[28] The Indian side of the story was not recorded in detail. See Ronan's January 2, 1878, report on his meeting with Simon at St. Ignatius Mission on December 26, 1877.

Flathead Agency, M.T.
December 10th, 1877

To the
Hon. Commissioner of Ind. Affairs
Washington, D.C.

Sir:

I have the honor to state that in pursuance of instructions (Communication "C") received by me from your office, bearing date October 10th, 1877, — copy of which I herewith transmit — I left the Agency on the 3d day of December, taking with me the Agency Interpreter and an employè, and proceeded on my Journey to Horse Plains, to enquire into and to institute measures to put a stop to outrages committed by Indians against settlers, as charged by Mr. Charles A. Lynch, and forwarded to the commanding officer of Fort Missoula. Having previously consulted with the chiefs of this reservation, I was informed that no Indians belonging to the Confederate Tribes of the Jocko reservation claimed homes on Horse Plains, or were guilty, in any way, of trespassing upon the Whites; but that the Lower Pen d'Oreilles, who have no reservation, or who are under no treaty stipulations were the guilty parties. I therefore sent out a runner to inform Petah, the head-chief of the Lower Pen d'Oreilles to meet me at Horse Plains, that we might enquire into the charges made against his people.

Below the mouth of the Jocko, I was compelled to leave my team and employ saddle horses and a pack animal, and having been ferried across the Pen d'Oreille river proceeded down the right bank of that stream to a point about twenty miles from Horse Plains, where we were met by a messenger who informed us that the Second chief of the Lower Pen d'Oreilles would meet me at that point, provided I would encamp and await him there. The weather was intensely cold but we found a deserted cabin where we made ourselves as comfortable as could be under the circumstances. During the night the second chief arrived, who called himself "Simon." I found him an intelligent, well-meaning Indian, who expressed himself as being a Christian and in favor of living on friendly terms with the Whites; he said also that friendship and good feeling towards the Whites was the general disposition of the tribe and its head-men; they had among them, he said, a few uncontrolable spirits — young men who would pick a quarrel and involve his people in trouble — but they were watched and punished on every occasion of offense. Horse Plains, he said, was a long distance from where his people made their home, but a few Indians of the band had taken up farms there among the Whites, and Complained that the Whites encroached upon their rights — the Whites claimed it was the fault of the Indians — he was not prepared to say then who was to blame or to make arrangements for the future conduct of his people — they were all out hunting and he would like to call them in and have a talk and a fair understanding before them all and explain to them the consequences should they perpetrate any more depredations against the settlers.

It was finally agreed between us that he would bring all the Indians of Horse Plains to St. Ignatius Mission, on Christmas; and, Mr. Lynch and another settler from Horse Plains having arrived at the camp, it was agreed that all should meet at the Mission on Christmas and make a settlement of the difficulties if possible. I informed the Chief that it was my intention, if any depredation was committed by his people, to have them arrested by the United States authorities, I also informed Mr. Lynch and his companion that the settlers would be dealt with in the same manner if it was conclusively shown to me that the Whites were the aggressors.

I then broke camp and returned to the Agency, having to swim our horses through the floating ice across the Pen d'Oreille river, the ferry boat being frozen in.

After the meeting on Christmas at St. Ignatius Mission, I will report to you the full proceedings, in the mean time the slightest danger of any trouble between the settlers, and the Indians need not be apprehended by the Department, as I am fully convinced of the sincerety of the motives of the Chief.

Very respectfully,
Your obedient Servt,
Peter Ronan
U.S. Ind. Agent.

December 24, 1877

U.S. Office of Indian Affairs, "Letters Received by the Office of Indian Affairs, 1824-1880," National Archives Microfilm Publication M234, reel 511, frames 478-480.

Flathead Agency, M.T.
December 24th, 1877

To the
Hon. Commissioner of Ind. Affairs
Washington, D.C.

Sir:

I have the honor to state that there are now in the neighborhood of one thousand Indians encamped close to this Agency, nearly all of whom belong to this reservation, who have returned from their buffalo hunt, and among whom the knowledge of the fact that I have contracted for certain goods, to be furnished to them, is widely spread. In view of this fact, and the promise that I made, that the poor and needy — the old and decriped [decrepit] of the tribes should receive sustenance, while the young men would be furnished employment in splitting rails, hauling logs, etc., for their own benefit, and the benefit of the nation, and be paid for their work out of the supplies, I hereby request that authority be given me to order the immediate delivery at this Agency of the goods contracted for with John D. Sheean and Co., of Missoula, M.T.

Very respectfully,
Your obedient Servant,
Peter Ronan
U.S. Ind. Agent.

1878

January 2, 1878

U.S. Office of Indian Affairs, "Letters Received by the Office of Indian Affairs, 1824-1880," National Archives Microfilm Publication M234, reel 511, frames 484-495.

> Charles Lynch and John Haas, two white settlers in Plains, made many charges against the local Indians, but Ronan's letter makes clear that the Indians also had problems with the conduct of the settlers. Unfortunately only a few of the Indian complaints made it into the written record. John Haas moved to Horse Plains in the fall of 1876 and took up farming.[1] See also Ronan's December 10, 1877, report on the conflict at Horse Plains.[2]

Flathead Agency, M.T.
January 2d, 1878

To the
Hon. Commissioner of Indian Affairs
Washington, D.C.

Sir:

Pursuant to arrangements made with "Simon," 2d Chief of the Lower Pend 'Oreilles or Kalispels, and brother of "Petah" head-chief of that tribe, information of which was given to you in my special report bearing date December 10th, 1877, I met that chief at St. Ignatius Mission, on the 26th day of December. All the Indians who make Horse Plains their home, when not hunting, consisting of some thirty warriors, accompanied "Simon," and several of the White settlers of that place, including Charles A. Lynch, the complainant, were also present.

Having called the parties together I stated, through my interpreter, that complaints had been forwarded to Washington against the Indians by the White settlers of Horse Plains, claiming that the Indians were committing depredations in throwing down their fences, Killing their hogs and cattle, ruining their crops by driving their herds to graze upon them, and other offences; and that I was directed to inquire into the matter, and to take prompt measures to protect the settlers against such outrages.

Simon replied that the general home of the Lower Pen d'Oreilles was far to the West of Horse Plains, on the Columbia river, but the Indians who I saw before me, deeming Horse Plains an Indian country, and better adapted to their wants as it was in the vicinity of game and fish, and also a good grazing country, made it their home. Of late years several White men settled among them — he did not dispute their right to do so — but there were wrongs Committed on both sides, and as the Whites made their statements he desired that the Indians should now make theirs.

From the various grievances stated by the Indians against the settlers from poisoning their dogs to altering stallions, I will cite one as it related directly to Mr. Charles A. Lynch, the complainant, and was not denied by him, and as showing that the Indians have also their grievances.

An old Indian rose in his turn and said, "One day I came up to this Mission and my heart did not feel easy — at last a raven or a crow or something else whispered in my ear 'go home to Horse Plains' — I went back and found Charla (meaning Mr. Lynch) had my horses caught up and was using them to thresh his grain. The horses looked bad and I felt bad. I demanded five dollars Charla said he would give me three — I did not like to take three — but when I thought it over I took three dollars because I always think it is better to take half a cup of coffee if I cannot get a full one."

From all the information I could gain I am led to believe that offences have been committed on both sides, but no serious trouble has yet occurred; but in an isolated place like Horse Plains, where the settlement consists of only six families, it is a matter of surprise to me that greater offences have not been committed by the Indians, when it is reflected that the Indians occupying the vast region extending from the Flathead reservation to the Columbia river are under no treaty stipulations, have no reservation and receive no aid from government. In his remarks Simon said: "Our people had a talk last summer with a man sent by the Great Father to Spokane bridge to meet us — there were six tribes present — we did not understand all he wanted of us, but our people thought he wanted to put us into Coralls instead of reservations. Tell the Great Father in Washington we like the country around Horse Plains and I think our people would like to have their reservation to take in that country — I do not say this for sure, but I think so." Here I would remark that I consider it a great misfortune, both for the Indians and the Whites, that a settlement was made upon Horse Plains as the place is situated some ninety miles west of Missoula, the nearest white settlement to the east, and to the West stretches that vast Indian country to the Columbia river only occupied by Indians.

There are no inducements for settlement west of Horse Plains, and to the East the Jocko Reservation precludes settlement, so that little valley is now, and to all appearances must remain, an isolated settlement of six or eight families in the heart of an Indian Country. Under those circumstances if I might be permitted to make a suggestion, it would redound to the interest both of the Whites and Indians that Horse Plains either be included in the Jocko reservation, or be set aside as a reservation for the Lower Pen d'Oreilles.

I finally settled all past difficulties between the settlers and the Indians, in a seemingly satisfactory manner to all concerned by suggesting that both parties were, in a measure to blame and it was desirable that the past should be forgotten, and that in future they live in peace to-gether. I stated to the Indians that if any depredations were reported to me in the future I would have the guilty party arrested and punished, and that the settlers would be treated in like manner. Simon said he would remain all Winter at Horse Plains and would arrest and punish any of his people who might do wrong, but in case they resisted his power he would call upon me to aid him.

The settlers feel perfectly assured that no trouble will occur while Simon remains on the Plains, but fear the worst when he returns to the lower country. Some inducement should be held out to Simon to remain at Horse Plains, as it would be a cheaper and better mode of providing against trouble than by stationing military there for the purpose of protecting six or eight settlers, who are disappointed and chagrined at the delay of the North Pacific Railroad company in building their road through the country as was supposed would be the result when the land was occupied by them, and thus afford an outlet and a market.

No doubt some of the Indians of Horse Plains are overbearing, disagreeable, mischievous, and tantalize the Whites by their petty thefts and depredating proclivities, but no serious difficulty has yet transpired.

I trust, as they do not belong on this reservation, that special instructions be given me if I am supposed to be accountable for their future behavior.

I have the honor to enclose complaints from one of the settlers, — who failed to attend the meeting, — preferring to put them in writing.

Very respectfully,
Your obdt servt,
Peter Ronan
U.S. Ind. Agent.

Enclosure. Periods have been added by the editor at the end of sentences:

Horse Plains Jan 2nd/ 78

Major P. Ronan, U.S. Indian Agent

Dear Sir I wish to state to you a few facts in regard to the non treaty Calespelle Indians that live on horse Plains. first as for thare cheifs Brother Simon who seems to have some little infleuance over them he is a well dispoesed Indian but as for thare chief I never saw chief Petall. All the Indians here tell me that Petall tells them that all of this country belongs to the Indians and that the whites have no right to it. they allso say that thare chief Petall would did not have any thing to do with the peace treaty held on the Spokanne by Col. [Frank] Wheaton last summer they camp around our houses some times in our yards and allways Keeping a large pack of starved dogs that so much worse than Wolfes. they never feed them so they have got to hunt thare living. consequently they ramsack our houses when ever thare is any show sometimes having holes in the doors Kill and eat our chickens our hogs and sometimes our calves.

when we ask them to do something with thare dogs they laugh at us and we cant Keep our dogs tied up we allways let them run loose and if you dont like our dogs you had better leave here as you have no right here any way. we some times threaten to Kill them and they say if we do the[y] wil Kill our horses or cattle and in one instance they missed a dog and claimed that white man had Killed it and shortly after wards that man found a fine mare worth $150 with Several large gashes in her apparently cut with an ax which caused her death in a few days and we supposed it to have been done by the Indians. since I have lived here they have done hundreds of simuilar tricks to numerous to mention. they at one time drove my wife out of my house with a butcher knife in his hand for asking them to stop smoking in the house and when she ran for assistance they consented that she might go in to the Kitchen and get her meal but that they would hold possession of the room they were in until they got ready to leave. when I came home one of them flourished a knife around me and told me that if I did not like the way the Indians done that I had better get up and leave as I had no right here any way. that this country belongs to the Indians.

they invariably with the exception of the sub chief and 2 or 3 more tell us that it is thare land and we have no right here. thare is a lady in this vally now that has just thrown her crutch awy which she has been carrying for six weeks. the caus of which was she got scared at a yung Buck Indian of 13 or 14 summers a chaceing her two little girls with a butcher knife in his hand in the abcence of any man being around at the time and in runing to thare assestance Strained her ankle. they at one time last summer came in a band after night howling and shouting and scared the parties from there house. the women and children runing over the prairie bear footed and cut the ferry boat loose on the same night. They throw down our fences in a carless Kind of maner make througher fares of our fields, Some times go into our fields and camp heard thare Stock on our crops. when we drive them out they drive them back. help them Selves to any thing they find in our fields that they want and upon being talked to on the

conduct only say to us that we own this land and you have no right here and if
you dont like the way we do you had better get up and leave. they seem to try
to agrivate us in every way immaginable calling us cowards Saying we would
not do to fight Squaws and all Such so that they Seem to want a fight and want
us to Start it. it is a Shure thing that the Indians cant run wild depending on
thare gun and dog for a living amongst white Settlers whare they claim that the
whites have no right with out it ending enventualy in blood Shed and such.

Yours Truely,
John Haas.

January 10, 1878
*U.S. Office of Indian Affairs, "Letters Received by the Office of Indian Affairs, 1824-
1880," National Archives Microfilm Publication M234, reel 511, frames 505-522.*

> The conflict between Watson and Blain, sheep herders, and Charlo's band of Salish on October 29, 1877, illustrated the type of incidents which challenged the Salish leaders as they worked to keep the peace with the white settlers while exercising their treaty guaranteed hunting rights. Diamond City was near the Continental Divide, northeast of Townsend, Montana. See Ronan's letter of September 14, 1878, for a description of Charlo's reaction to this claim. The claim dragged on for years and was apparently settled for $220.50 in 1893.[3]
>
> Adolphe, mentioned in Watson & Blain's letter quoted by Ronan, was recognized by the government as the third ranking chief of the Bitterroot Salish. He had a long record as a leader and warrior. In 1859, he accompanied Father DeSmet to Fort Vancouver to assure the U.S. Army of the peaceful intentions of the Salish. In 1872, he signed the agreement with Congressman James A. Garfield to move to the Jocko Valley, but later decided to remain in the Bitterroot Valley with Chief Charlo and the bulk of the Salish. In July 1877, during the Nez Perce War crisis, Charlo sent Adolphe to Missoula to assure the townspeople of the friendship and loyalty of the Bitterroot Salish. While camped near Missoula on this mission, some white people started shooting at Adolphe's camp. Instead of shooting back, which could have ignited a general war, he complained to the local military and the white aggressors backed off.[4] The identity of "Little Big Man" is unknown. General John Gibbon commanded the U.S. Army District of Montana in 1878. He was a veteran of the Civil War, the Sioux campaign of 1876, and the Nez Perce War of 1877.[5] In the summer of 1881 he visited the Flathead Agency with Delegate Martin Maginnis and other army officers. See letter from Martin Maginnis to Commissioner of Indian Affairs, December 14, 1881, enclosing Ronan letter of October 21, 1881, to Maginnis.

Flathead Agency
10th January 1878

To the
Hon. Commissioner of Indian Affairs
Washington, D.C.
    Sir:
    In answer to your letter of December 20th, 1877 ("C" Stephen) calling to
my attention a report from Col. C. C. Gilbert, Commanding Officer at Camp
Baker, Montana, received from the War department, in relation to the complaints of Ranchmen against roaming Indians, accompanied by a copy of letter

to him from Watson and Blain, and in order that the matter be fully understood by you, I herewith transmit copies of my correspondence in the matter:

Diamond City, Meagher County, Montana
Nov. 6th, 1877

Mr. Ronan,
Agent Flathead Indians
    Sir,
    We find it necessary to inform you that the Indians while passing on their way to the Buffalo Country, Oct. 29th allowed their dogs to attack our sheep and scatter them in every direction, Killing seven outright and severely injuring eight others, some of which will no doubt die from the effects. They also threw our fences down and passed through our field leaving the fences down and when spoken to regarding it they were very saucy and would give no satisfaction. This is the fourth time we sustained loss by their dogs; last fall they Killed twenty five sheep for us. I wrote to the Agent stating the case but received no reply; we also notified the Military, and our complaint was forwarded to Department Head quarters. As we are poor Men, trying to get a start in the world and have only a little flock of 400 heads we find it rather discouraging to see our property destroyed in such a manner. We have again notified the Commander at Camp Baker (Col. [C. C.] Gilbert) of our grievance, and as we have heard you are not the same person who had charge of these Indians last year, we thought we would inform you of the facts in the case with the hope that you will be so Kind as to reply and let us Know what means of redress we have (if any) and whether there is not some way to prevent a recurrence of the Same every time they (the Indians) pass. Our loss by their dogs is not less than forty sheep in the four raids they have made upon us, and we paid four dollars per head for them which is a dead loss of $160.00 without counting the loss of time in getting them up after such scattering and doctering [sic] the injured ones. Now we propose to recover damages if there is any law for so doing, and of that there can be little doubt. Please answer immediately and let us Know what you can do about it, and what shape we ought to proceed in the matter and you will greatly oblige.

Very respectfully Yours
Watson & Blain

    P.S. If this is not attended to by *either* the Military or Yourself, whichever has the right to attend to it, we will send our Complaint to the Secretary of the Interior and employ some one who can and will put the case through for us, for we will have satisfaction if it is to be had. Hoping you will take no offence at this (which is of course no personal matter) and that you will give it your earliest attention we are with respect.

Watson & Blain

Upon receipt of above I transmitted the following letter:

Flathead Agency, Montana Territory
November 14th, 1877

Messrs. Watson & Blaine:
    Gentlemen:
    Your letter of Nov. 6th, 1877, in regard to the Killing of your sheep by Indian dogs is at hand, and in reply I would say that you failed to state what Tribe or band of Indians committed the depredations. I have under my charge Flatheads, Pen d'Oreilles and Kootenais. Charlos band of Flatheads who live in the Bitter Root Valley, having failed to come under the treaty stipulations,

do not reside on this reservation, and claim, I believe, to be independent of the Reservation instructions. I believe it was Charlo's band of Indians who passed through your country. Make inquiries as to what band you have complaint against and write me. While it is not in my power to indemnify you, I will lay your case and complaint before the proper authorities in Washington.

Yours Respectfully
Peter Ronan
U.S. Indian Agent.

In answer to above the following reply was received:

Diamond City, Nov. 30th, 1877

Peter Ronan Esq.

Sir,

Yours of the 14th is at hand — have made inquiries regarding which Band of Indians committed the depredations and find that they claimed to be Charlo's Band. Two other Indians who seemed to cut considerable of a figure amongst them were recognized by the "Post Trader at Camp Baker" Adolphe and Little Big Man. But I enclose statement of Col. Gilbert in reply to our inquiry to whom I sent your letter. Please do all you can for us and you will greatly oblige.

Very Respectfully
Yours
Watson & Blain.

Accompanying above is the letter of Col. Gilbert, which shows conclusively that I was correct in my surmises as regarding the identity of the Band:

Camp Baker, Montana Territory
Nov. 28th, 1877

Messrs Watson & Blain
Benton Gulch, M. T.

Gentlemen:

I[n] reply to your letter of the 27th instant, I can only state that the Post Trader says he recognized Adolphe as one of the Indians in the Band of which you make complaint. Another Indian of importance among them was Little Big Man.

In my report to District Head Quarters this Band (30 Lodges) is called Charlo's Band, and very likely it was "Charlos" as the Agent surmises.

The Indians have their jokes and as I have no interpreter they can tell me what they please as to who their head men are and accordingly I place little confidence in what they say.

Enclosed I return the Agent's letter.

Very respectfully
C. C. Gilbert.
Lieut. Col. 7th, Infantry Commanding.

As the information in regard to the Indians of this reservation, and the Flatheads of the Bitter Root Valley, having received permission to purchase ammunition in limited quantities for hunting purposes was not received by me until the 26th day of November, And as Messrs Watson & Blain complain the depredations were committed on the 29th of October, and some two hundred Miles East of this Reservation, you will readily perceive that the claims cannot attach to any abuse of the privilege so Kindly granted, as Charlo's Band left the Bitter Root Valley over a month before he could claim the privilege of purchasing an ounce of powder for the hunting grounds in the Judieth basin. At

Helena the Indians called upon Governor [Benjamin F.] Potts and urged their necessity to procure ammunition, but I am informed they obtained none, and proceeded on their hunt unprovided with any, unless they obtained it through Gen. [John] Gibbon, or by some elicit means.

The Indians who properly belong to this Reservation have returned from their hunt with few exceptions and are now living in their homes. No case of depredation or insubordination has been reported against them.

Charlo's Band who are now out hunting and who, no doubt, in spring will return home through Messrs Blain & Watson's Ranch, live in the Bitter Root Valley where they claim their home, and refuse to remove to the Jocko Reservation, and receive no aid from the Government. Last Summer during Nez Percez invasion, Charlo and his band protected the white Settlers from outrage and bloodshed during the march of Joseph and his Warriors through the Bitter Root, and on that account his people, to a great extent neglected their crops, and a hail storm destroyed nearly all that was cultivated by the few. Having no other means Charlo was Compelled to take his people to the Buffalo Country. Before going they begged for ammunition, but could procure none, as orders did not arrive until a month after they left the Valley, giving them permission to purchase, and on the 26th of November I addressed the following to the traders at Stephens ville in the Bitter Root Valley:

Messrs Buck Bros. and J. Fay

Gentlemen:

You are hereby granted permission to sell to Charlo's Band of Flathead Indians Powder, Lead and Caps (but not metalic ammunition). Sell to no other Indians except Flatheads and limit your sales to such quantities as in your judgment is sufficient for the purpose of hunting game.

Your Obedient Servant
Peter Ronan
U.S. Indian Agent.

I now take the liberty to refer the Hon. Commissioner to his answer dated October 22nd, 1877, to my letter, urging a distribution of supplies among Charlo's people to prevent the necessity of their leaving their home in the Bitter Root.

Department of the Interior
Office of Indian Affairs
Washington, October 22d/77.

Peter Ronan
Indian Agent, Flathead Agency, via Missoula.

Sir:

Replying to your letter of the first instant, requesting permission to distribute a portion of the goods which you have purchased for the Indians on the Jocko Reservation among those who have refused to remove from the Bitter Root Valley to the said Reservation, I have to say that as those remaining in the Bitter Root Valley are non-treaty Indians, Authority cannot be granted for you to distribute among them goods that belong to those who are subject to treaty stipulations.

I very much regret the necessity for this refusal as I should like to reward these Indians for their fidelity to the Government and but for want of funds applicable to the purpose would grant your request.

Very Respectfully,
E. A. Hayt
Commissioner.

I call your attention to the foregoing letter, which I infer, gives me no authority to dictate to the Bitter Root Indians either as to their going or returning from their hunt, or any other matter, as they are called non-Treaty Indians. "Adolphe" spoken of by Col. Gilbert is the second Chief of the Bitter Root Flatheads, and his name will be found attached to the Garfield agreement. Little Big Man also referred to by Col. Gilbert is the 3d Chief of the Tribe. Charlo is the Son of the deceased Victor and is now the hereditary head chief of the Nation. His name appears on the Garfield agreement, but he claims never to have signed that document. Charlo is a good and just man, and if he was with his people at the time of the depredations complained of (which I doubt) I am very much surprised. You will please inform me if I am to take any further steps in this matter, or if it is expected by the Department, in view that these Indians do not belong to this Reservation, that I provide against further depredations by them, while returning, in Spring, from the Buffalo Country to the Bitter Root Valley.

Very Respectfully
Your Obedient Servant,
Peter Ronan
U.S. Ind. Agent.

January 15, 1878
U.S. Office of Indian Affairs, "Letters Received by the Office of Indian Affairs, 1824-1880," National Archives Microfilm Publication M234, reel 511, frames 500-504.

Flathead Agency, M.T.
January 15, 1878

To the
Hon. Commissioner of Indian Affairs
Washington, D.C.
Sir:

I have the honor to state that during the Nez Perce invasion in July last, I purchased on my own responsibility, and from my own private means, a quantity of goods for the Indians of this reservation, in order to satisfy and keep them on the reservation, to encourage them in their allegiance to the Government, and to induce them to resist the entreaties to join them, of their relatives, friends and al[l]ies in the hostile camp. In making the purchases above referred to, I took into consideration the fact that I had no recourse to the Department for reimbursement, but to insure the safety from an alliance with the hostiles, and to save Montana from the horrors of an Indian war from her own reservation Indians, which a spark would have ignited, among a few of the restless ones and whose actions would have involved the whole of the tribes and the nation, I expended from my private means the money necessary for the goods. I desire to present for your consideration the above facts, hoping that if in your judgment I am entitled to reimbursement for my expenditures as above stated authority will be given me to pay myself out of either of the funds which you may designate and state vouchers for same to accompany my next account.

In addition to the purchases before mentioned I made others during Christmas week — also out of my private means. The whole tribe of Kootenais, and destitute Indians from the other tribes, came to the Agency expecting to receive some of the goods for which contract has been made, but as the same had not yet been ordered to be received by me, I was compelled to purchase two hundred bushels of wheat, (which I ground into flour) and other supplies and issued the same, so as to prevent hunger and want. This also I did with the full knowledge that I had no recourse to the government for reimbursement for my outlay; but when I took into consideration the fact that I have had no authority from your office since my appointment in June last, to purchase and issue to them anything but the thousand dollars worth authorized by you, which was issued to them soon as purchased, and as there is indigence and want among some of them, particularly the Kootenais, I could not resist the promptings of humanity, and rather than see their sufferings continue I took my own means (which I can ill afford to loose) and purchased what was necessary to relieve them. Of course I do not present this as a claim on the Government, for I well know I have no right to look to it for payment of the expenses above incurred in the face of my instructions on this subject, unless your judgment will confirm my action. The long delay in the receipt of goods contracted for sometimes necessitates prompt and intelligent action, as Indians are like children, and cannot take into their brain the necessity of delay when a thing is promised.

Very respectfully,
Your Obedient Servant,
Peter Ronan
U.S. Indian Agent.

January 16, 1878

U.S. Office of Indian Affairs, "Letters Received by the Office of Indian Affairs, 1824-1880," National Archives Microfilm Publication M234, reel 511, frames 523-534.

The government's 1877 prohibition of gun and ammunition sales to the Bitterroot Salish and Flathead Reservation tribes continued to bedevil tribal efforts to support and defend themselves.

Flathead Agency, M.T.
January 16, 1878.

To the Hon. Commissioner of Indian Affairs:
Washington, D.C.
Sir:—
I have the honor to submit for your information and suggestions the following correspondence in regard to the sale of arms and amunition to the Flathead Nation:

Flathead Agency, M.T.
November 26, 1877.

John R. Brooke
Lieut Col. 3d Infantry.
Commanding Fort Missoula, M. T.
Sir:
On the 23d day of August, 1877, I had the honor of addressing a letter to Captain C. C. Rawn, then in Command of Post, in regard to the sale of Arms and Amunition to the Indians of the Flathead Nation under my charge. The letter having been transmitted through the several Head Quarters was returned to me with the following:

6th Endorsement
Head Quarters Dist. Montana.
Fort Shaw, M. T. Oct. 4th 1877.

Respectfully returned to Mr. Peter Ronan, U.S. Indian
Agent, Flathead Agency, M. T., through Commanding officer
Post near Missoula:

Authority is hereby granted to permit each warrior of the
Flathead tribe to supply himself with one rifle and not to exceed sixty rounds of amunition.

In the present unsettled condition of Indian Affairs in the
District, it is not deemed advisable to remove all restrictions
to the arms and amunition trade, and Agent Ronan is requested to take such steps as may be necessary to insure that the
limit authorized is not exceeded.

By order of Col. John Gibbon
Levi T. Burnett
1st Lieut and Agt 7th Infty.

In answer to above endorsement, I called attention of
Col. Gibbon, through Captain Rawn to the fact that his endorsement only gave permission to the Flatheads to procure
amunition, and that I desired the privilege extended to the
other tribes under my charge consisting of the Pen 'd Oerelles
and Kootenais, which communication was returned with following:

2d Endorsement.
Head Quarters Dist. Montana,
Fort Shaw M. T. Nov. 8, 1877.

Respectfully returned to Mr. Peter Ronan, Indian Agent
Flathead Nation, through commanding officer Post near Missoula.

The authority granted regarding arms and amunition to
be allowed the Flatheads is extended to all the confederated
tribes under charge of Agent Ronan.

John Gibbon
Col. 7th Infantry,
Commanding Dist.

Upon receipt of the above I repaired to Missoula to arrange for the In-
dians to purchase arms and amunition, under restrictions ordered by Col.
Gibbon, when I received the following communication from the Secretary of
War through the Indian Department:

War Department,
Washington City
Oct. 3d 1877.

Sir: —

I have the honor to acknowledge the receipt of your letter
of the 19th inst., transmitting a copy of one from commissioner of Indian Affairs, and its enclosures relating to supplying
arms and amunition to the Indians of the Flathead Agency
and subjoin here to the remarks of General Sherman on the
subject, viz:

"From personal observation I think the Flathead Indians behaved so well in the recent Nez Perce war, that we can
safely allow them to purchase of the traders powder, lead, and
caps, for muzzel loaders — good enough for hunting but not

metalic amunition, used only in war."

These views are concurred in by the Department.

Very respectfully
Your obedient servant
George W. McCrary
Secretary of War

To the Honorable
The Secretary of the Interior

With above I received the following instructions from the Hon. Commissioner of Indian Affairs:

Department of Interior
Office of Indian Affairs
Washington, Nov. 6, 1877.

Peter Ronan
U.S. Indian Agent
Missoula Montana

Sir: —

Referring to your letter of Sept. 30th last transmitted by Hon Martin Maginnis in relation to supplying amunition to the Indians of your agency, I have to state that the same was referred by the Department on the recommendation of this office to the Honorable Secretary of War on the 19th ult inst and herewith is a copy of his reply thereto granting permission to the Indians to purchase of the traders powder lead and caps for muzzel loaders only. The purchases should be made on your order and in such quantities as you may judge to be necessary.

Very respectfully
E. A. Hayt,
Commissioner.

Having submitted all the papers, I would respectfully ask through your Head Quarters, if I can go on under Col. Gibbons order, and allow the warriors of the Flathead Nation to purchase arms under the restrictions in his endorsement, or will I only obey the order granting loose amunition.

The Indians of this Reservation have never before been prohibited from a free purchase of amunition, and as a greater portion of the tribes support themselves and families by hunting, to be restricted from this purchase of Metalic cartridges and breach loading guns with which to hunt bear, buffalo and other large game, which cannot be procured very well with muzzel loaders, will cause a great deal of dissatisfaction, particularly as it is well known by the District Commander the peaceful and friendly disposition of the tribes.

Trusting you will give this matter your earliest attention

I am
very respectfully
Peter Ronan
U.S. Indian Agent
Flathead Nation

In reply to the foregoing, I received the following

Head Quarters
Fort Missoula, M. T.
January 8th 1878

To Mr. Peter Ronan
U.S. Indian Agent
Flathead Nation
        Sir:
        The following endorsement on your letter of 26th of No-
vember, asking information in regard to sale of Amunition
&c., to Indians of the Flathead Nation is furnished for your
information and guidance.

2d Endorsement
Head Quarters District of Montana
Fort Shaw, M. T. Jan. 1st 1878

        Respectfully returned to Lieut. Col. John R. Brooke, 3d
Infty, Commanding Fort Missoula, M. T., who will notify Mr.
Ronan that under instructions from the Department Commander, the District commander decides that the Authority
given by Endorsements October 4th and November 8th 1877,
from these Headquarters, will continue to govern the matter
of trade in Amunition to the Flathead Nation.

By order of
Col. John Gibbon
(sgd) Lieut J. Burnett
1st Lieut. and Adjt 7th Inf'ty
A.A.A.G.

I am very respectfully

Your obedient Servant
John R. Brooke
Lieut. Col. 3d Inf'ty
Commanding Post

        I would respectfully inform the Hon. Commissioner of Indian Affairs, that
previous to the receipt of authority to allow the Indians of this Nation to procure arms or amunition of any description, the various bands living on the
Reservation, through their head men, informed me that they were going to the
buffalo country to hunt with what arms and amunition they then possessed,
and they intended to trade and barter ponies and other property for buffalo
meat with Blackfeet and other tribes, they also said they would go to the Buffalo country and return, by a Northerly trail, which though a longer rout[e],
would avoid the necessity of passing through any white settlement. The Indians have returned and are now on the reservation. They Kept their word and
avoided the settlements, and I have heard of no complaint against them.
        Charlos band of Flatheads proceeded to the Buffalo country early last fall,
passing through the very heart of the settlements — Deer Lodge, Helena, and
Meagher county. As this band lives in the Bitter Root valley, and refuse to remove to the Jocko Reservation, they ask nor received no instructions from the
Agent in regard to their going away or return to their homes in the Bitter Root.
On account of the excellent conduct of Charlos and his Warriors during the Nez
Percz war, and the distruction of their crops by a hailstorm and the prevention
of attending to their agricultural pursuits by the excitement of the times last
summer, I was induced to make an effort to at least give them the privilege
of purchasing amunition. The order came too late and they proceeded on to
the Judieth Basin, making efforts in every settlement they passed through to
procure amunition, but I am unable to say whether they got supplies or not.

General Gibbon admired Charlo's conduct in the Indian war and as that chiefs rout to the hunting ground passed in the vicinity of Fort Shaw, it may be possible the General issued him a small quantity but I am not cognisant of the fact. This band will not return to the Bitter root until spring.

It is my intention, with your concurrence, not to allow the sale of a gun or metalic amunition to any Indian, (to whom permission is granted to purchase,) unless he is thoroughly vouched for by his chief, and personally known to me.

Trusting these views will meet your approbation, and that I may have your council and instructions in regard to the matter, I have fully submitted it to you.

Very respectfully
Your Obedient Servant
Peter Ronan
U.S. Indian Agent
Flathead Agency
Montana

February 4, 1878a
U.S. Office of Indian Affairs, "Letters Received by the Office of Indian Affairs, 1824-1880," National Archives Microfilm Publication M234, reel 511, frames 551-553.

> In this letter Ronan was referring to Duncan McDonald (1849-1937), son of Angus McDonald, Hudson's Bay Company trader, and his Nez Perce wife, Catherine. Duncan operated a store at Jocko Agency in the late 1870s and later had a hotel, general store, livery, blacksmith, stage line, and orchard at Ravalli, Montana. Duncan was in frequent conflict with various Flathead Indian Agents, wrote extensively on Indian affairs, and was a cultural broker between the tribes and the white settlers.[6]

Flathead Agency, M.T.
February 4th, 1878

To the Hon. Commissioner Indian Affairs
Washington, D.C.

Sir:

I have the honor to represent that when I took charge of this Agency I found a trader here who claimed to be an Indian and trading under that title without any license from the Department.

This person is a half-breed — with an Indian mother and Scotch father and is named Macdonald; He has always conducted himself in a gentlemanly manner and to my knowledge has violated no laws governing the trade with Indians, but, Sec. 2133 of "laws and Regulations relating to Trade with Indians" states that: "Any person other than an *Indian* who shall attempt to reside in an Indian country as *trader*, or to introduce goods, or to trade therein without such license, shall forfeit all merchandise offered for sale to the Indians or found in his possession, and shall moreover be liable to a penalty of five hundred dollars." and I request information as to whether it applies to the person mentioned or to any other Halfbreed trading on the Reservation without a license from the proper authority.

Very respectfully,
Your obdt servt,
Peter Ronan
U.S. Indian Agent.

February 4, 1878b
*U.S. Office of Indian Affairs, "Letters Received by the Office of Indian Affairs, 1824-
1880," National Archives Microfilm Publication M234, reel 511, frames 302-306.*

As this letter indicates, most of the agency employees who were officially providing services
to tribal members were actually doing clerical work at the agency or working on the agency
farm which provided subsistence to the government employees.

The only action notation on the letter is "File," indicating the Indian Office did not even
reply to the request despite the endorsement by Martin Maginnis, the Montana Territory
Delegate to Congress.

Flathead Agency, M.T.
February 4th, 1878

Hon. Martin Maginnis,
Washington, D.C.
Dear Sir:

It has always been the custom at this Agency to employ a Head Farmer and
place him in the office to discharge the duties thereof and to put the Assistant
Farmer in charge of the Agency farm and allow him to have the general supervision of the Indians who desire to learn the use of Agricultural implements
and practical farming; but under a recent circular from the Commissioner the
duties of the farmer have been made more numerous, so many in fact that to
discharge them all conscientiously it will require his entire time leaving me to
do all the office work performed by him. It is utterly impossible for me to do
this work and at the same time perform the other duties required of me, such
as travelling over the reservation to take the census of all the Indians; taking
the same journey to enable me to make a statement of the number of head
of all Kinds of domestic animals on the reservation; to visit the schools; to go
to Bitter Root Valley in the Spring to deliver Indian land patents; to have a
general supervision of all the various departments of the Agency and all the
other numerous duties pertaining to my office. The head-farmer is constantly
employed in the office and with the additional work given him to do, according
to the circular referred to, his time would be accupied [sic] night and day and
the consequence would be that neither branch of the service under his care
would receive the attention necessary. I have therefore to request that you
represent this state of affairs to the proper authorities and discover whether it
will not be possible to have authority given me to employ a clerk in addition to
the employés already allowed this Agency. As your visit here last Summer will
enable you to state from personal Knowledge the great necessity of a clerk at
this Agency no one can be better fitted to represent the same to the Hon. Commissioner of Indian Affairs.

Respectfully,
Peter Ronan
U.S. Ind. Agent.

Endorsement on above letter from Peter Ronan:
Respectfully forwarded approved. The situation of these Indians, being at four
different places viz the Bitter Root, the Jocko, the Mission & Flathead Lake,
Valleys some hundreds or more miles apart makes hard work for the Agent.

The present Agent is a thoroughly correct and conscientious man and desires to square all his actions with the rules of the Department.

Respectfully
Martin Maginnis

February 19, 1878
U.S. Office of Indian Affairs, "Letters Received by the Office of Indian Affairs, 1824-1880," National Archives Microfilm Publication M234, reel 511, frames 566-580.

T. J. or Telesphore Jacques DeMers was a leading merchant and businessman in western Montana in the late 1870s. He was based out of Frenchtown, Montana, and married to a Pend d'Oreille/French lady named Clara, the sister of Michel Revais, the blind interpreter at the Jocko Agency.[7]

Flathead Agency, M.T.
February 19th, 1878

To the
Hon. Commissioner Indian Affairs
Washington, D.C.
    Sir:
    In compliance with paragraph 9th, of "laws and regulations relating to trade with Indian tribes," I have the honor to transmit herewith a certified copy, under oath, of the original invoice of goods received by T. J. Demers at his trading post at this Agency. Also a statement of the retail prices of such goods as will be offered for sale by said trader, as they are quoted at Missoula and Frenchtown, M.T., the nearest points of trade to this Agency; also a copy of a list of prices, which will be posted in a conspicuous place in the store of said trader.
    In relation to the prices at which the goods, to be offered for sale by the trader, shall be sold, I have the honor to state that, in my opinion, the prices prevailing at Missoula and Frenchtown should govern those of the trader at this Agency, allowing a little advance for freight.
    With reference to the cash value of robes and furs I have to state that the trader informs me that he will not touch furs as they do not pay to ship to the East. No person at Missoula or Frenchtown can give me the prices of said articles of trade with the Indians; the merchants all refusing to trade for such articles on account of their great decrease in value in the East. Therefore I am unable to report the cash value of robes and furs as required by aforesaid paragraph.

Very respectfully,
Your obd't servt,
Peter Ronan
U.S. Indian Agent.

The invoices and price list Ronan referred to were not filed with the letter. Only the eleven page list of goods for sale at Jocko with prices charged in Missoula and Frenchtown has survived. A small sampling from the list follows: vermillion, $1.17/ lb.; narrow ribbon, 55¢/piece; colored silk, 4²/₅¢/skein; shot, 19¹/₈¢/lb.; ¹/₂# cans gunpowder, 45¢/ea.; candles, 22¢/lb.; candy, 33¢/lb.; traps no. 1, $4.20/doz.; traps no. 3, $14.04/doz.; matches, 99¢/caddy; sugar, $20.90/sack; nails, 11¢/lb.; salt, 11¢/lb.; tobacco, 62³/₄¢/lb.; S. K. flour, $5.50/100 lbs.; and coarse flour, $1.90/100 lbs.

February 21, 1878

U.S. Office of Indian Affairs, "Letters Received by the Office of Indian Affairs, 1824-1880," National Archives Microfilm Publication M234, reel 511, frames 581-582.

> This Ronan letter and many following ones emphasize that in the nineteenth century the tribes were not supported by the federal government. The agency provided only occasional gifts and employment for most tribal members. The old, sick, and indigent did get rations, but probably not enough to live on.

Flathead Agency, M.T.
February 21st, 1878

To the
Hon. Commissioner Indian Affairs
Washington, D.C.
Sir:

With reference to circular No. 6, dated January 23d, 1878, I have the honor to ask whether it applies to this Agency. There are no rations issued to the Indians under my charge, neither do they receive annuities but there is a "Beneficial Fund," $3000.00 per annum, which is applied to the purchase of necessary articles of clothing, food, etc., for sick and indigent Indians. As the same families are not at all times dependent upon the Agency it would be very difficult to certify to a list of Indians who are entitled to receive subsistence under the provisions of the "Beneficial Fund."

I ask that instructions be given me in the matter.

Very respectfully,
Your obdt servt,
Peter Ronan
U.S. Indian Agent.

March 19, 1878

U.S. Office of Indian Affairs, "Letters Received by the Office of Indian Affairs, 1824-1880," National Archives Microfilm Publication M234, reel 511, frames 591-602.

> The number of hogs and cattle recorded here suggest the reservation economy was diversifying during the 1870s to replace the declining plains buffalo herds. Most of the hogs were owned by mixed blood tribal members but many of the cattle were owned by fullbloods. Surprisingly the inventory found tribal members owned more cattle than horses.

Flathead Agency, M.T.
March 19th, 1878

To the
Hon. Commissioner Indian Affairs
Washington, D.C.
Sir:

I have the honor to transmit herewith a statement of the number of head of domestic animals on this reservation, with information in relation to same, as required by circular no. 1, dated January 8th, 1878.

Very respectfully
Your obedient servt.
Peter Ronan
U.S. Ind Agent.

Enclosure:

Statement of number of head of domestic animals on Flathead Reservation, Montana Territory. Submitted March 19th, 1878, by Peter Ronan, U.S. Indian Agent.

Owner	Hogs	Cattle	Horses	Total
Line 2: Location, distance and direction from Agency, etc.				

Arlee, Chief of Flatheads; Antoine, Son of above; Agut, daughter of above

	2	100	100	202

One Mile W. Arlee married Flathead; an undivided interest held by each owner in each animal.

Baptiste Bason		12	10	22

Two miles W. Halfbreed married Flathead.

Toma Aslan		4	3	7

Two and one half miles W. Married Flathead.

Antoine		2	6	8

3 miles W. Single.

Michel, Chief of Pen d'Oreills		26	19	45

3 miles W. Flathead married Pend d'Oreill.

Joseph Coture	16	50	19	85

3½ miles W. Frenchman married Flathead.

Joseph La Rose		16	4	20

3¾ miles W. Frenchman married Pend d'Oreill.

Peter Finley	8	50	28	86

4 miles W. Halfbreed married Flathead.

Bazile Finly and mother, Mary Finley	6	20	21	47

4½ miles W. Bazile, Half-breed not married. Each undivided int. in all.

Francois Nichola and mother, Sussette		1	11	12

5 miles NW. Halfbreed married Hfbreed.

Isadore Laderoote	14	25	22	61

6 miles NW. Halfbreed married Spokane.

Alex Porya	4	22	14	40

7 miles NW. Halfbreed married Flathead.

Isadore Finley		2	8	10

7¼ miles NW. Halfbreed married Spokan.

Alex. Morriseau	5	40	42	87

8 miles NW. Halfbreed married Hfbreed.

Alex. Dimoe			5	5

22 miles NW. Halfbreed married Flathead.

Alex. Sorrelle		25	10	35

23 miles NW. Halfbreed married Flathead.

Pierish Aslaw		6	8	14

24 miles NW. Halfbreed married Pend d'Oreille.

Louise Decker		30	3	33

1 mile E. Halfbreed Flathead wife of Agency Miller.

Joseph Touse			2	2

1 miles E. Halfbreed married Flathead.

Can-cau-su		8	11	19

1½ miles E. Flathead married Flathead.

Eneas Lorrette		5	4	9

1 mile E. Flathead married Pend d'Oreille.

Dominic Finley		5	12	17

1¼ mile NW. Halfbreed married Pend d'Oreille.

Louison		60	65	125

½ mile E. Nez Perce married Flathead.

Owner	Hogs	Cattle	Horses	Total
Line 2: Location, distance and direction from Agency, etc.				
La-Sa		3	5	8
½ mile W. Flathead married Flathead.				
Big Sam		27	50	77
¼ mile W. Flathead married Flathead.				
Baptiste Marengo		27	29	56
1 mile E. Halfbreed married Flathead.				
Duncan McDonald, Archibald McDonald, Angus McDonald, Joseph McDonald, Thomas McDonald		500	50	550
25 Miles NW. Halfbreed brothers — own undivided interest in band.				
Tin As			2	2
3 miles W. Unmarried Pend d'Oreille.				
Tenome Finley		4	20	24
5 miles W. Married Pend d'Oreille.				
Hardlots		6	12	18
8 miles NW. Unmarried Pend d'Oreille.				
Ambroise		12	3	15
1 mile W. Unmarried Flathead.				
Baptiste Eneas	15	14	16	45
15 miles NW. Halfbreed married Pend d'Oreille.				
Loui Com-Com		1	6	7
16 miles NW. Pend d'Oreill married Pend d'Oreille.				
Peter J. Matte	15		1	16
15 miles NW. Unmarried Halfbreed.				
Ske-ki-em			5	5
15½ miles NW. Pend d'Oreille married P. d'Oreill.				
Big Head		85	82	167
14 miles NW. Pend d'Oreille married P. d'Oreill.				
Antoine Rivais	25	100	25	150
20 miles NW. H.B. married P. d'Oreill.				
Michel Rivais, son of Antoine		6	12	18
20 miles NW. H.B. married P. d'Oreill.				
Roman Nose		16	32	48
20 miles NW. H.B. married P. d'Oreill.				
Qual-Qua-Pa or, Felicite		4	33	37
20 miles NW. Pend d'Oreille, wife of Roman Nose.				
Sa-tee (Leo)		8	26	34
26 miles NW. Pend d'Oreille, married Pend d'Oreill.				
Le-La			6	6
26 miles NW. Pend d'Oreille, married Pend d'Oreill.				
Paul			9	9
26 miles NW. Pend d'Oreille, married Pend d'Oreill.				
Alel — or, Cha Soos			10	10
28 miles NW. Pend d'Oreill married Pend d'Oreill.				
Isaac — or, Qua Quad.		5	12	17
22 miles NW. Pend d'Oreill married Pend d'Oreill.				
Joseph — or Tel-Sel-Pa		35	33	68
25 miles NW. Pend d'Oreill married Pend d'Oreill.				
Sopha, wife of Louie Pier		60	10	70
25 miles NW. Pend d'Oreill married Pend d'Oreill.				
Simon, or, Sin Ta		8	15	23
25 miles NW. Pend d'Oreill married Pend d'Oreill.				
Mac-Sim		6	12	18
25 miles NW. Pend d'Oreill married Spokane.				

Owner	Hogs	Cattle	Horses	Total
Line 2: Location, distance and direction from Agency, etc.				
Pier Paul			10	10
25 miles NW. Pend d'Oreill married Spokane.				
E-Shee-Tee			8	8
25 miles NW. Pend d'Oreill unmarried.				
David, or Ta Peet			8	8
25 miles NW. Pend d'Oreill married Pend d'Oreill.				
Alex Matte		55	35	90
¼ mile NW. Halfbreed married Flathead.				
Francois Cammile	7	15	14	36
17 miles NW. at Mission. Halfbreed married Spokane.				
James Burns	8	410	20	438
17 miles NW. at Mission. White-man married to Pend d'Oreill.				
Chabrain, Wife of James Burns		40	5	45
17 miles NW. at Mission. Pen d'Oreille woman.				
Isaac, or Kicking Horse			8	8
17 miles NW. at Mission. Pend d'Oreille married Pend d'Oreill.				
Pe-El-Ka		2	10	12
17 miles NW. at Mission. Pend d'Oreille married Pend d'Oreill.				
Loui Sack		61	52	113
17 miles NW. at Mission. Halfbreed married Pend d'Oreill.				
Hes-i-ca-ia			7	7
17 miles NW. at Mission. Pend d'Oreill married Pend d'Oreill.				
Lucy			4	4
17 miles NW. at Mission. Pend d'Oreill woman.				
Francois			5	5
17 miles NW. at Mission. Pend d'Oreill married Pend d'Oreill.				
Poless			12	12
17 miles NW. at Mission. Pend d'Oreill married Pend d'Oreill.				
Therese Mole			3	3
17 miles NW. at Mission. Pend d'Oreill woman.				
To-Ro-da			1	1
17 miles NW. at Mission. Pend d'Oreill woman.				
Eneas Pe-Ell		5	9	14
17 miles NW. at Mission. Pend d'Oreill married Pend d'Oreill woman.				
Joseph		2	2	4
17 miles NW. at Mission. Pend d'Oreill married Pend d'Oreill woman.				
John Che-Tast			7	7
17 miles NW. at Mission. Pend d'Oreill married Pend d'Oreill.				
Cammile		9	10	19
17 miles NW. at Mission. Pend d'Oreill married Pend d'Oreill.				
Michel Loui			5	5
17 miles NW. at Mission. Pend d'Oreill unmarried.				
Ge-Ey-Tim		20	10	30
17 miles NW. at Mission. Pend d'Oreill married P. D'O.				
Swallow-the-ax			6	6
17 miles NW. at Mission. Pend d'Oreill married P. D'O.				
Antelle, 2d Chief Pend'Oreills		1	17	18
17 miles NW. at Mission. Pend d'Oreill married P. D'O.				
El-Louise			6	6
17 miles NW. at Mission. Pend d'Oreill woman.				
En-Quan-Quan			4	4
17 miles NW. at Mission. Pend d'Oreill married P. d'O.				

Owner	Hogs	Cattle	Horses	Total
Line 2: Location, distance and direction from Agency, etc.				
Marie			4	4
17 miles NW. at Mission. Pend d'Oreill woman.				
Che-Tast-Partee			5	5
17 miles NW. at Mission. Pend d'Oreill married P. d'O.				
Mary Malay			1	1
17 miles NW. at Mission. Pend d'Oreill woman.				
To-Malse			7	7
17 miles NW. at Mission. Pend d'Oreill married P. d'O.				
Old-Pe-Ell		35	30	65
17 miles NW. at Mission. Pend d'Oreill married P. d'O.				
Pe-Ell's wife		10	2	12
17 miles NW. at Mission. Pend d'Oreill woman.				
Therese		5	4	9
17 miles NW. at Mission. Pend d'Oreill woman.				
Joseph, husband of Therese		7	7	14
17 miles NW. at Mission. Pend d'Oreill.				
Susanne, Wife of Spokane Bill		4	10	14
17 miles NW. at Mission. Pend d'Oreill woman.				
Young Joseph			9	9
17 miles NW. at Mission. Pend d'Oreill married P. d'O woman.				
Che-ha-pa			11	11
17 miles NW. at Mission. Pend d'Oreill unmarried.				
Joseph, Alexander's Son		8	26	34
17 miles NW. at Mission. Pend d'Oreill unmarried.				
Catherine			3	3
17 miles NW. at Mission. Pend d'Oreill woman.				
Che-Pa		8	1	9
17 miles NW. at Mission. Pend d'Oreill married P. d'O man.				
Loui & Wife Luset			4	4
17 miles NW. at Mission. Pend d'Oreill married P. d'O woman.				
Loui Pa Cile			3	3
17 miles NW. at Mission. Pend d'Oreill married P. d'O woman.				
Paul, and Mary, his wife			4	4
17 miles NW. Pend d'Oreills at Mission, undivided int. each.				
Small John		2	12	14
17 miles NW. at Mission. Pend d'Oreill married to P. d'O woman.				
Michel and Mary, his wife	1	66	30	97
17 miles NW. at Mission. Colvilles. Undivided int. in band.				
Joseph and wife, Christine			20	20
17 miles NW. at Mission. Pend d'Oreill's. Undivided int. in band.				
Martin and son, Clum Qual-Qual			21	21
17 miles NW. at Mission. Pend d'Oreill's married P. d'O women. Undivided int. in band.				
Joseph		55	80	135
17 miles NW. at Mission. Pend d'Oreill married P. d'O woman.				
Lucy, wife of Joseph			12	12
17 miles NW. at Mission. Pend d'Oreill.				
Charlie Anne and wife		42	25	67
17 miles NW. at Mission. Pend d'Oreill's undivided int. in band.				
Lawman and Partee, sons of Joseph		30	25	55
17 miles N.W. Pend d'Oreill's, both married ½ int. each in band.				
Widow Anne Tim Isaac			11	11
17 miles N.W. Pend d'Oreill's.				

Owner	Hogs	Cattle	Horses	Total
Line 2: Location, distance and direction from Agency, etc.				
Adolph		3	2	5
17 miles N.W. Pend d'Oreill married Pd'O woman.				
Pen-Mel-cha		8	10	18
17 miles N.W. Pend d'Oreill married Pd'O woman.				
Camele Lato		6	25	31
17 miles N.W. Whiteman married Pd'O woman.				
Sisters of Charity	3	14	5	22
17 miles N.W. White women.				
St. Ignatius Missionaries (Jesuites)	90	355	110	555
17 miles N.W. Whitemen.				
Philip Kin-nit			5	5
28 miles NW. at Crow Creek. Pend d'Oreill married P.d'O woman.				
Pem-mel-cha		8	10	18
17 miles NW. at Mission. Pend d'Oreill married P.d'O woman.				
Charlo-mole-man		22	21	43
30 miles NW. at Crow Creek. Pend d'Oreill married P.d'O woman.				
Pe-Ell		5	8	13
30 miles NW. at Crow Creek. Pend d'Oreill married P.d'O woman.				
Loui-Jos. hu-ka			7	7
30 miles NW. at Crow Creek. Pend d'Oreill married P.d'O woman.				
Se-la and Susan, his daughter			18	18
30 miles NW. at Crow Creek. Pend d'Oreills undivided int. in band.				
Pe-Ell. Sin-ka		6	5	11
30 miles NW. at Crow Creek. Pend d'Oreill married to P.d'O woman.				
David Polson		80	4	84
48 miles NW. at foot of Flathead Lake. Whiteman married Nez Perce woman.				
Michel Pablo	4	320	22	346
48 miles NW. at foot of Flathead Lake. Halfbreed married Hfbd. woman.				
Raphael Bisson	15	110	12	137
49 miles NW. at foot of Flathead Lake. Whiteman married to HB. woman.				
Joseph Ashlin	20	33	16	69
49 miles NW. at foot of Flathead Lake. Whiteman married Kootenai woman.				
Cammile Dupee	10	30	20	60
49 miles NW. at foot of Flathead Lake. Whiteman married HB. woman.				
Abraham Finley			7	7
49 miles NW. at foot of Flathead Lake. Halfbreed married HB. woman.				
Nels-qua-kui-pa		20	15	35
49 miles NW. at foot of Flathead Lake. Pend d'Oreill widow.				
James Dugan	5	355	20	380
70 miles NW. Little Bitter Root. Whiteman, u[n]married. Residing on Reservation with permission of Chiefs.				
Daniel Sullivan		275	5	280
70 miles NW. Little Bitter Root. Whiteman, u[n]married. Residing on Reservation with permission of Chiefs.				
Jim Grass		125	20	145
70 miles NW. Little Bitter Root. H.B. married Kootenai.				
Francois Pardo		60	20	80
38 miles NW. Head Mud Creek. Pend d'Oreill married Kootenai woman.				
Ma-quau-Sau Finley		6	12	18
40 miles NW. Head Mud Creek. H.B. married P. d'O. woman.				

Owner	Hogs	Cattle	Horses	Total
Line 2: Location, distance and direction from Agency, etc.				
Red river Finley		3	3	6
40 miles NW. Head Mud Creek. H.B. married H.B. woman.				
Pin-e-wa			15	15
40 miles NW. Head Mud Creek. Pend d'Oreille. married P. d'O. woman.				
Boneparte		6	25	31
24 miles NW. Hudson's Bay Post Creek. H.B. married Nez Perce woman.				
Louis Jim		51	18	69
24 miles NW. Hudson's Bay Post Creek. Colville Indian married Nez Perce woman.				
Em-pe-ka-ha			9	9
60 miles NW. Dayton Creek. Kootenai married Kootenai woman.				
Pe-tell			5	5
60 miles NW. Dayton Creek. Kootenai married Kootenai woman.				
George Kooenten			4	4
60 miles NW. Dayton Creek. Kootenai married Kootenai woman.				
Pe-ell-ball			6	6
60 miles NW. Dayton Creek. Kootenai married Kootenai woman.				
John Cha-chel-E-la		8	9	17
60 miles NW. Dayton Creek. Kootenai married Kootenai woman.				
Isald Cha-chelk		8		8
60 miles NW. Dayton Creek. Kootenai woman.				
André		3	7	10
60 miles NW. Dayton Creek. Kootenai Indian married Kootenai woman.				
Dug-an		4	4	8
60 miles NW. Dayton Creek. Kootenai Indian married Kootenai woman.				
Kas-mure			6	6
60 miles NW. Dayton Creek. Kootenai Indian married Kootenai woman.				
En-ne-will			4	4
60 miles NW. Dayton Creek. Kootenai Indian married Kootenai woman.				
Mary She-El-Ee			5	5
60 miles NW. Dayton Creek. Kootenai woman.				
Enas Paul, Kootenai Chief		50	38	88
60 miles NW. Dayton Creek. Kootenai married Kootenai woman.				
Louison		30	10	40
60 miles NW. Dayton Creek. Kootenai married Kootenai woman.				
Little Breech-clout			10	10
60 miles NW. Dayton Creek. Kootenai married Kootenai woman.				
Par-ciel, Little breech-clout's son		5	6	11
60 miles NW. Dayton Creek. Kootenai married Kootenai woman.				
Ole-Em		6	8	14
60 miles NW. Dayton Creek. Kootenai married Kootenai woman.				
Ka-ka-kish, or Harry		8	5	13
60 miles NW. Dayton Creek. Kootenai married Kootenai woman.				
To-mah, or broken arm		5	12	17
60 miles NW. Dayton Creek. Kootenai married Kootenai woman.				
Mal-tah		45	25	70
60 miles NW. Dayton Creek. Kootenai married Kootenai woman.				
Joe Finley		7	8	15
60 miles NW. Dayton Creek. Halfbreed married Kootenai woman.				
St. Paul		3	7	10
60 miles NW. Dayton Creek. Kootenai married Kootenai woman.				
Ka-cee-ell or Army blanket		9	7	16
60 miles NW. Dayton Creek. Kootenai married Kootenai woman.				

Owner	Hogs	Cattle	Horses	Total
Line 2: Location, distance and direction from Agency, etc.				
Baptist		10	3	13
60 miles NW. Dayton Creek. Kootenai married Kootenai woman.				
Ah-ka-sie		5	8	13
60 miles NW. Dayton Creek. Kootenai widow.				
Martin Ion-com			7	7
60 miles NW. Dayton Creek. Kootenai married Kootenai woman.				
Mathias			12	12
60 miles NW. Dayton Creek. Kootenai married Kootenai woman.				
Camile			5	5
60 miles NW. Dayton Creek. Kootenai married Kootenai woman.				
Pla-ce-wa			2	2
60 miles NW. Dayton Creek. Kootenai married Kootenai woman.				
Marcelleas			6	6
60 miles NW. Dayton Creek. Kootenai married Kootenai woman.				
Ma-till-Ann			7	7
60 miles NW. Dayton Creek. Kootenai widow.				
Little Parcile		5	5	10
60 miles NW. Dayton Creek. Kootenai married Kootenai woman.				
Paul			3	3
60 miles NW. Dayton Creek. Kootenai married Kootenai woman.				
Pier Kal-qual			6	6
60 miles NW. Dayton Creek. Kootenai married Kootenai woman.				
Alexander			5	5
60 miles NW. Dayton Creek. Kootenai unmarried boy.				
Mars-la			3	3
60 miles NW. Dayton Creek. Kootenai married Kootenai woman.				
Koo-la-mi-nee			11	11
60 miles NW. Dayton Creek. Kootenai married Kootenai woman.				
André or Kui-Mich			12	12
60 miles NW. Dayton Creek. Kootenai married Kootenai woman.				
Old Pe-Ell			1	1
60 miles NW. Dayton Creek. Kootenai married Kootenai woman.				
St. Pier			6	6
60 miles NW. Dayton Creek. Kootenai married Kootenai woman.				
Fetice-anne			2	2
60 miles NW. Dayton Creek. Kootenai married Kootenai woman.				
Pas-cal			1	1
60 miles NW. Dayton Creek. Kootenai married Kootenai woman.				
Dominic, or Big Head		3	16	19
60 miles NW. Dayton Creek. Kootenai married Kootenai woman.				
Eneas, Dominics' brother			7	7
60 miles NW. Dayton Creek. Kootenai married Kootenai woman.				
Little St. Pier			3	3
60 miles NW. Dayton Creek. Kootenai unmarried.				
Mal-Kee			4	4
60 miles NW. Dayton Creek. Kootenai married Kootenai woman.				
Young Paul Eneas			4	4
60 miles NW. Dayton Creek. Kootenai unmarried.				
Pe-Ell or Big-Bear			6	6
60 miles NW. Dayton Creek. Kootenai married Kootenai woman.				
Paul Euar or Fine-nose			12	12
60 miles NW. Dayton Creek. Kootenai married Kootenai woman.				

Owner	Hogs	Cattle	Horses	Total

Line 2: Location, distance and direction from Agency, etc.

Abraham or Kis-he-na 5 5
60 miles NW. Dayton Creek. Kootenai married Kootenai woman.
Kia-sa-mire 15 15
60 miles NW. Dayton Creek. Kootenai married Kootenai woman.
Enas Pa-las-sa-wa 8 8
60 miles NW. Dayton Creek. Kootenai married Kootenai woman.
Paul or "Friday" 1 1 2
60 miles NW. Dayton Creek. Kootenai married Kootenai woman.
Anes-tah 4 4
60 miles NW. Dayton Creek. Kootenai married Kootenai woman.
Little John 2 2
60 miles NW. Dayton Creek. Kootenai married Kootenai woman.
Andés 3 3 6
60 miles NW. Dayton Creek. Kootenai married Kootenai woman.
Pier Sui-a-pie 8 8
60 miles NW. Dayton Creek. Kootenai married Kootenai woman.
Flathead Indian Agency 9 6 15

I certify that the foregoing is a true statement.

Peter Ronan
U.S. Ind Agent

Flathead Agency, M.T.
March 19th, 1878

Remarks.

All of the domestic animals mentioned in the foregoing statement — with the exception of the Agency horses and cattle — live the entire year by feeding upon the Reservation lands.

The food furnished the Agency horses consists of hay and oats; about 80 tons of hay for horses and cattle, and 500 bushels of oats for horses — and they are fed hay for about 9 months during the year on account of the constant labor which they are obliged to perform. The hay and oats are paid for by the Government.

Peter Ronan
U.S. Ind. Agent.

Flathead Agency, M.T.
March 19th, 1878

	Hogs	Cattle	Horses
Indians & H.B.'s	175	3,323	2,286
Missionaries	93	369	115
Other Whites	5	755	45
Agency stock	—	9	6
Totals	273	4,456	2,452.

April 1, 1878

U.S. Office of Indian Affairs, "Letters Received by the Office of Indian Affairs, 1824-1880," National Archives Microfilm Publication M234, reel 511, frames 603-612.

Williams & Company was a general merchandise store operated in Missoula by Thomas Williams and Daniel J. Welch. Williams had previously operated stores in Virginia City and Cedar Creek. Between 1880 and 1886 he was Missoula County Treasurer.[8]

Flathead Agency, M.T.
April 1st, 1878

The
Hon. Commissioner of Indian Affairs
Washington, D.C.

Sir:

In reply to your communication "F. Montana. R. 45-78," I have the honor to transmit herewith the original invoices of goods purchased, handed me at the time I bought the articles referred to in my letter of January 15th, 1878.

As to the exigency which demanded the purchase of goods during the Nez Percé troubles I have to say, that some of the young warriors of the three tribes, viz: Flatheads, Kootenais and Pend d'Oreills, were assuming a war-like and restless attitude, which indicated that, unless something was done to conciliate them, trouble of the most serious nature might follow.

At the time of the advance of the Nez Percés quite a number of the Indians of this reservation were at the town of Missoula, and the citizens of that place waited upon me and implored me to take them (the Indians) back to the Agency. I went to the Indian camp and told them that they must return to the reservation; they said that if I insisted upon their doing so, they would, but that there was nothing at the Agency for them to live upon and that at Missoula they could saw wood and do light work which supplied them, at least, with food. I then promised them that as soon as I could get goods out from Missoula I would have plenty of provisions for them — This seemed to satisfy them for they thanked me and immediately struck their lodges and started home. This latter fact and the before-mentioned restless condition of the young warriors in the vicinity of the Agency impressed me with the belief that unless something was done immediately, I would be unable to prevent an alliance of a portion of the reservation Indians with the advancing Nez Percés; and feeling that the lives of the citizens of the county of Missoula depended upon my prompt action, I made the purchases mentioned on invoice dated July 26th, 1877. I had no funds to my credit nor had I authority to purchase on account, chargeable to the Department, therefore I bought the goods on my own responsibility and am compelled to pay for them out of my private funds unless the purchase is authorized by you. The exigency is certainly as great a one as could very well arise for action under Paragraph 2 of Instructions to Superintendents and Agents, dated July 1st, 1877.

At the date of the second purchase, Dec. 20th, 1877, there were no goods at the Agency and the Indians had collected in the vicinity of the Mission and Agency in great numbers to perform the religious duties at Christmas, and were very destitute. Daily, appeals were made to me for flour and tobacco, the Indians saying that they had heard I had received a large lot of goods and that they were starving, which their condition very plainly indicated. I purchased for them 200 bushels of Wheat and 100# of tobacco as is shown on invoice dated Dec. 20th, 1877.

I did not mention any of these goods on my property return as I did not Expect them to be allowed as purchases by the Department of the Interior.

Up to the present date I have not received authority to order the delivery of the goods authorized to be contracted for by the Hon. Secretary of the Interior September 8th, 1877, a contract for which was let, and duly approved by you, on the 30th day of October, 1877, to John D. Sheean & Co., and, although the time for their pressing delivery, — the winter months — are passed there are a large number of old, indigent and sick Indians, who must be supported by the Agent, or starve.

Very respectfully,
Your obdt. servt.
Peter Ronan
U.S. Indian Agent.

Enclosed is an invoice from Williams & Co., Missoula, M.T., for $1054.93, for sugar coffee, bacon, tobacco, prints, and denims, dated July 26, 1877, and a second invoice from the same company for $277.63 for wheat and tobacco, dated December 20, 1877.

April 12, 1878
The Weekly Missoulian, *April 12, 1878, page 3, col. 3-4.*

> This Ronan letter, published in a Missoula newspaper, gives valuable insights into problems melding traditional Pend d'Oreille punishments with the sensitivities and regulations of white American society. The use of jail and prisons was new to the Pend d'Oreille who had relied on social ostracism and floggings to discipline errant behavior. Andra, or Andre, worked closely with the missionaries and the agent, but the evidence suggests he was also supported by many tribal members. The priests and agent were particularly concerned about controlling marriage. There is no way to tell how the woman's testimony was affected by the presence of the chief of police and agent at the interview. By undermining the authority of the chiefs, the agent and missionaries weakened the traditional social structure and increased the law and order problems on the reservation during the 1880s and later.

The Indian Side of the Question.

The question of Indian cruelty assumed a tangible shape here some two weeks ago. An old Indian woman was circulating disparaging reports, and appealed to the citizens to interfere in behalf of humanity. In no spirit of officiousness, but as friends of the Agent, and well-wishers for a correct administration of affairs upon the reservation, two citizens of this place joined in a letter to the agent. Here is the letter, and the proceedings thereon:

Missoula, Montana, April 2, 1878.

Maj. Ronan:

Dear Sir — This old woman says her daughter has been in the Indian jail twenty-one days; that her wrists have been tied with cords until her hands are fearfully swollen. For the credit of the Agency, it seems a case requiring your investigation, and, if the case is as reported, you ought to stretch your authority to see that she has better treatment.

———

Gentlemen:

Your letter of April 2d reached me by messenger on the same date, and on the 3d I repaired to the Mission, taking with me the bearer of the letter and my official interpreter. I was much pleased that the opportunity arose, through your letter, to set the good people of Missoula and elsewhere right upon the matter referred to, as interested parties, as my investigation proves, have foully and wilfully misrepresented the conduct of Indian laws and discipline upon this reservation.

Andra, one of the head men and chief of Indian police, immediately upon my arrival, called his policemen together in council, and I told my interpreter to carefully interpret your letter, as I read it word for word, to them, and ask if it contained the truth.

Andra made the following reply to it:

"I am now sixty-eight years of age — I never committed a cruel act in my life. The daughter of this woman, who brought that letter to you, is in jail under sentence of 26 days; her time will expire on Sunday morning, when she will be let out, and her lawful husband will be here to take her to his lodge. Her husband is an older man than I am, a chief in our tribe; his name is 'Big Lance.' She deserted him, and ran off with a young Indian of the Spokane tribe. I heard of it, and sent out my police and overhauled them at Horse Plains, and brought them back. The Spokane Indian I will keep in jail for 30 days, and then send him back to his people, who will again punish him — perhaps not so much, but he will be punished. The woman, on next Sunday, I will give to her husband, who will be here to take her to his lodge. Is there anything wrong in this?"

Agent — "The letter says the woman's wrists are tied and lacerated."

Andra — "Your government built the jail; no separate rooms are made. I keep a guard about the jail nearly all the time. When we have a pair of adulterers in jail, we must keep them separate. When my gaurd [sic] goes away, they are tied to keep them apart, but never to hurt them."

Agent — "The letter says the woman is starved to a skeleton."

Andra — "The letter lies. Three times a day the prisoners are fed everything that my people and my family have to eat themselves; and three times a day they are taken out to walk in the air and sun — all day Sunday they are allowed out under a guard."

Agent — (to the woman) — "Have you seen your daughter, and are you satisfied with her treatment?"

Woman — "I have seen her, and she is sorry for what she has done; she is not badly treated."

Agent — "Why did you bring me such a letter?"

Woman — "A young Indian told me a lie at Missoula."

Agent — "Are you satisfied with what Andra says?"

Woman — "Yes, Andra told me to live and eat with his family until Sunday, when he will let my daughter go back to her husband's lodge, and I will stay and visit her, and try make it up between them."

Agent — "Then you are satisfied."

Woman — "Yes."

Agent — "It has been written to Missoula, and printed in the paper, that you whip prisoners in the dead hour of night."

Andra — "Indians are not cowards; if we had any whipping to do, we would do it in the day-time."

Agent — "Then you do not whip prisoners."

Andra — "For over a year that law is changed, and no one is whipped; nor has any one been whipped for any offense. I try to keep my Indians good. The most of them are good; but it takes force to keep some in the straight road."

Agent — "What crimes are punishable?"

Andra — "Every wrong that is done: stealing from each other, gambling, adultery, drunkenness, or anything else that is wrong. You white men have a law to send your people to jail for many months for giving whisky to Indians. Now, I can send any one of my young men to Missoula, and give him something to trade, and he will come back with all the whisky I want; but I do not let them trade for whisky; they go to jail if they do — it is our law. In Missoula, they can get drunk and get whisky. You have a law against it, why is it not enforced. Why do not the white people drive our bad Indians away from their town. They hide bad people when I send for them. White men would not like to have me hide their bad people here. You said it was printed in the paper that my prisoners were whipped in the dead of night. Who is my enemy that told such a lie?"

Agent — "It will do you no good to know."

May 1, 1878

U.S. Office of Indian Affairs, "Letters Received by the Office of Indian Affairs, 1824-1880," National Archives Microfilm Publication M234, reel 511, frames 633-639.

Federal prohibitions limiting the access of friendly Montana Indians to ammunition and guns still continued to cripple the ability of the western Montana tribes to defend and support themselves. See the July 5, 1878, letter below for further difficulties caused by restrictions on guns and ammunition.

Michelle Rivais, was half French and half Pend d'Oreille. A gifted linguist, he was Flathead Agency interpreter between 1877 and 1911. He could speak English, French, and a number of Indian languages. Totally blind, he was led around by his wife. He was the main source for the Salish ethnography of James A. Teit.[9] For biographical information about Henry A. Lambert, Flathead Agency farmer and clerk in 1878, see Ronan's letter of September 7, 1889, and annotation. Big Canoe was the Pend d'Oreille war chief in 1878. At the Hellgate Treaty negotiations in 1855, he asked why a treaty was needed when the Pend d'Oreille Indians were not at war with the whites. He asked the whites to stop trading with the Blackfeet for guns and ammunition: "Now I and you, you white man, both die with your own powder and ball. . . . Sometimes my people get mad when the Blackfeet kill us." He did not understand why the discussion of land and reservations was needed, but signed the document at the end. He died in 1880 at the reported age of 83 years.[10]

Flathead Agency, M.T.
May 1st, 1878

To the
Hon. Commissioner Indian Affairs
Washington, D.C.
Sir:

In compliance with the wishes of the three Head-chiefs of the Confederate tribes, I transmit herewith a letter dictated by them and interpreted by the Agency Interpreter, in which they ask that they may be allowed to purchase breech-loading guns and fixed ammunition. They have repeatedly asked me to apply to you for permission for them to purchase said guns and ammunition, since your refusal to permit the same; I told them that the Secretary of the Interior had refused, for the reasons given by him in letter of last fall, and they then requested of me to allow them to address the inclosed letter to you.

Very respectfully,
Your obedient servant
Peter Ronan
U.S. Indian Agent.

Enclosure:

Flathead Agency, M.T.
May 1st, 1878

E. A. Hayt,
Commissioner Indian Affairs,
Washington, D.C.

Honored Sir:

We cannot read words, but from those we hear spoken from our Agent, and others we feel that you have a good heart for the Indian and, whenever it is in your power, you will try to do him justice and smooth his rough road. For over thirty years we have had missionaries among us, who teach us the gospel and try to point out the trail which will lead to the whiteman's road. A great many of us have houses to live in — have good farms fenced in — have good crops now planted — have families growing up around us; and our laws forbid that we have more than one wife. We never have had war or trouble with your people, and during all our lives, until last summer, we could go to traders and buy guns and ammunition. While the Nez Percés were on the war path we did not care to buy ammunition or guns, as it might look bad to the whites as that tribe has always been our friends against the Blackfeet and Sioux. But when the war was over and our young men after laboring in the fields and gathering in their crops thought it hard when the Agent told them they could not buy ammunition with which to hunt. Our crops are now in and the buffalo are only a short distance from us, across a northern trail which leads through no white settlements, and our young men desire to hunt them and procure meat while the old people stay at home and look after the crops until they ripen when all return from the hunt and help to gather them; but our Agent tells us we cannot buy ammunition except powder, lead and caps. Powder, lead and caps are of no use to us as we have no muzzle-loading guns, nor could we buy them if we had the money as there are none to buy that we know of. We cannot throw away our good guns as they cost us very much — and we have forgotten the use of the bow and arrow. Our Agent tells us that it is your wish that we all should stay at home and work upon our farms — this is good advice — we are doing our best to bring our children up to work, but when the crops are planted and nothing to do, we feel that it would be a great wrong to force our children to stay at home when they so much love to hunt the buffalo and return at the time work commences, cheerful and happy and well supplied with meat and furs. The time is fast coming when we will be in our graves for we are three old men; we love our children and our people, and we hope you will not refuse us the only source of great pleasure we have in our lives; — the opportunity to have guns and ammunition with which we can kill game. The Great Spirit knows we do not want them for war — for when your people were few in our country we always treated them as friends. The chief of the Soldiers, — General Gibbon, who was among us and knew us, was willing that we should have metallic ammunition fit to hunt with, but our Agent says that a greater Chief gave orders that we should not have any. Now we will await anxiously to hear your words and hope our prayers will be granted.

Your friends,
Arlee, his X mark, Head-chief of Flatheads
Michel, his X mark, Head-chief of Pend d'Oreills
Eneas, his X mark, Head-chief of Kootenais

Interpreter: Michel, his X mark, Rivais
Witness foregoing marks:
H. A. Lambert
Big, his X mark, Canoe, Hunting-Chief.

July 1, 1878

Excerpted from "Affairs at Indian Agencies: Official Reports — Efforts of the Agents to Maintain Peace," The New-York Times, July 24, 1878, page 5, col. 2. The original monthly report has not survived in the National Archives. The text below which appeared in the newspaper report was rewritten from the original which would have been dated July 1, 1878.

The June report from the Indian Agency at Flathead, Montana, says the past month has been very propitious, the cloudy weather and copious showers rendering it unnecessary thus far for the Indians to irrigate the growing crops, which are looking heavy and well. As yet no grasshoppers have appeared in the Jocko Valley, but as they have made their appearance at the foot of Flathead Lake, Dayton Creek, and the Mission, they are daily expected at the agency. The agent reports the citizens of the country as being greatly excited and apprehensive of a general uprising of the Indians, owing to the troubles among the Bannocks, and wild rumors are published in the Territorial press to the effect that the Spokane and other tribes of the Columbia River and surrounding country are dissatisfied with negotiations now going on with them, and contemplate taking the war-path. The agent has been informed from the Town of Missoula that the Spokanes attacked the military post at Spokane Bridge. A trustworthy Indian, however, brought him word that all was quiet and peaceable thus far among the Indians and military in that locality. No fears are entertained by the agent that the Indians on his reservation will join the Spokanes if trouble should occur, although they are nearly related and intermarried. He feels confident of his ability to restrain and guide his people from mixing with the Columbia River Indian quarrel.

July 5, 1878

U.S. Office of Indian Affairs, "Letters Received by the Office of Indian Affairs, 1824-1880," National Archives Microfilm Publication M234, reel 511, frames 674-679.

This letter is hard to follow in places, but it is apparent that the tribal members were quick to defend their rights under the 1855 Hellgate Treaty. They also felt no obligation to work for a gratuity from the government after the government had crippled their efforts at self-support by banning ammunition and gun sales.

Flathead Agency, M.T.
July 5th, 1878

To the
Hon. Commissioner of Indian Affairs
Washington, D.C.
    Sir:

On the 20th of August, 1877, I made a special requisition for various supplies for the Indians of this reservation, to be issued to them as a recognition by the United States Government of their good conduct during the Nez Perces troubles of last Summer, and to enable them to subsist without the necessity of hunting which they claimed was rendered impossible by the order from your office dated October 3d, 1877, prohibiting the sale of arms and ammunition to them.

Upon receipt of your letter granting me authority to make a contract for the goods mentioned in my requisition, I informed the Indians (who were getting restive on account of not being allowed to procure ammunition and the prospect of starvation during the winter) that you have permitted the purchase of these goods to enable them to live without the necessity of hunting and as a reward for their good faith with the Government during the recent Indian troubles. This seemed to satisfy them and no more inquietude was apparant among them. But upon the arrival of the goods last month and the information being given them that issues of coffee, tea, tobacco and sugar would not be made unless work was done therefore, they stated that if these goods were furnished to enable them to live without hunting and were a part of the pay due them for the lands sold to the Government they did not consider it just that they should give their labor for what belonged to them by virtue of the country already transferred to the United States therefore; but that they did not consider it as a part of what is known as the "Beneficial object" fund but as a gratuity as a reward for not joining the Nez Perces last year, and a recompense for not being allowed to purchase arms and ammunition with which to hunt and that they desired that what they considered due them from the sale of their lands should be expended (as they told me a month previous and upon which I based my requisition then made) (for plows, harness and wagons.) In reply to this I told them that the object of the Hon. Commissioner in prohibiting the issues of Coffee, tobacco, tea and Sugar except in payment for labor, was intended for their interest and to teach them to become conversant with the modes of civilized life so that when the time came when no more goods would be given them, they would know how to work for themselves and become self supporting; that unless some of them were compelled to work now, they would be unable to keep themselves and families from starvation when the issues were stopped and necessity would render it imperative for them to do some thing for their own support. In answer they said that they were all able and knew how to till their farms and raise cattle, and what they wanted in addition to these goods — which they considered a present from the Great Father — was the agricultural implements already mentioned, to be purchased with the balance of the money due them for last year.

I would state that I think in view of their understanding of the matter and the impossibility to convince them of the facts, and also, the very unsettled condition of the neighboring Indians, it would be the better policy to issue them the goods received in addition to the blankets due on the contract, as the gratuity intended by myself and apparantly understood by the late Hon. Commissioner of Indian Affairs, J. Q. Smith, and to apply the balance of the "Beneficial Object," fund for 1878, to the purchase of the articles mentioned in my requisition of May 25th, 1878.

Finally, I have the honor to say that from my experience among the Indians of this reservation I do not think that it will be possible to compel them to work to obtain the coffee, tobacco, tea and sugar purchased for them and that from their utterances when told of the decision of the Hon. Commissioner, it will be the cause of trouble if enforced — In stating this I have only the desire to Express my opinion derived from my Experience among the Indians, not to pretend any superior judgement to the Honorable Commissioner.

Very respectfully,
Your obdt. serv't.
Peter Ronan
U.S. Indian Agent.

July 15, 1878
U.S. Office of Indian Affairs, "Letters Received by the Office of Indian Affairs, 1824-1880," National Archives Microfilm Publication M234, reel 511, frames 685-688.

Flathead Agency, M.T.
July 15th, 1878

To the
Hon. Commissioner of Indian Affairs
Washington, D.C.

Sir:

In reply to your letter "A" June 14th, 1878, calling my attention to Circular No. 6, Jany 23d '78, directing me to forward a list of the heads of families and individual Indians at this Agency entitled to receive supplies, I have the honor to say that on the 21st of February, 1878, I wrote you relative to said Circular and received in reply the following: (The date of the letter is March 23d, 1878, "A Montana R. 149 1878")

"Your letter of February 21st relative to Census Roll asked for by office Circular No. 6 has been received.

"In reply I have to say that while this roll is not needed from your Agency for the purposes mentioned in the above Circular, still it is desired to complete the records of this office.

"You are requested therefore to prepare and forward, as soon as practicable a list of all heads of families and individual Indians at your Agency, preparing the list as opportunity may be afforded, but without incurring additional expense for the same.

Respectfully
(Sgd) E. A. Hayt
Commissioner"

I[n] compliance with the foregoing letter of instructions I have taken the names of such Indians as presented themselves at the office to receive supplies but the number does not represent one-fifth of those entitled to receive supplies, and to fully comply with the requirements of Circular No. 6, it will be necessary for me to make a tour of the reservation. Expenses will be incurred on such a trip, and the above quoted letter forbids me to "incur any additional expense." It will be impossible for me to make a complete list of the heads of Families and individual Indians and certify to the same according to the certificate in above mentioned Circular unless every facility is allowed me for making a correct census. Therefore, I have the honor to request that authority be granted me to incur such expense as may be necessary to make a complete and correct return as contemplated in Circular No. 6, Jany 23d, 1878.

Very respectfully,
Your obdt. serv't.
Peter Ronan
U.S. Ind. Agent.

July 24, 1878

Extract from [Peter Ronan,] "Stories of Life : Some Scraps of Indian History in Montana's Early Days," The Anaconda Standard, *March 6, 1892, page 9, col. 1-3.*

Ronan refers below to a July 24, 1878, report to the Commissioner of Indian Affairs about the trials of Captain George, a Nez Perce man looking for his lost daughter. Unfortunately that report did not survive with Ronan's other letters in the Records of the Commissioner of Indian Affairs in the National Archives, Washington, D.C., so his 1892 version is included here. No further biographical information about Captain George or his family was located. The poignant experiences of Captain George and his daughter during the war between the Nez Perce and the United States government and its aftermath highlight the human cost of war.

White Bird was the chief who led the Nez Perce who escaped to Canada from the Battle of Bear's Paw in the fall of 1877. White Bird refused repeated American attempts to lure him back to the United States, but many individual Nez Perce refugees fled south during 1878 and 1879 attempting to return to their homes in Idaho. White Bird was murdered in Canada by another Nez Perce in 1892.[11] John Hill was half Delaware and half Nez Perce and lived in the Bitterroot as part of Chief Charlo's band. He had been wounded in the hand while serving in the Union Army in the American Civil War. In 1884, he was part of the Bitterroot Salish delegation to Washington, D.C., led by Chief Charlo that negotiated for Salish land rights in the Bitterroot Valley.[12]

While the Indian excitement was at its height in Missoula and throughout the west side of the state, one day [in 1878] two heavily armed strange Indians dismounted at the dwelling of Agent Ronan and entered. Mrs. Ronan, the nurse girl and children were alone in the house. The girl at once recognized the Indians as Nez Perces, and so informed the family, and the Indians announced that their camp was on the Jocko, and this led to the inference that White Bird's hostiles would soon surround the agency. After the warriors sat for some time in silence one of them produced some letters and said they were from General Miles. This brought considerable relief to the household. As the incident connected with the arrival of the Indians at the agency was rather of a romantic character, we will commence the narrative by first giving place to the letter from General Miles and the other correspondence which was handed to the agent.

Headquarters District of Montana,
Terry's Landing, Mont., June 21, 1878.

To the Commanding Officers of the District of Montana:

The bearer "Captain George" (so-called) is a Nez Perces, who came through with General Howard to get his daughter, who was in the hostile camp. He was very useful as an interpreter at the surrender of Chief Joseph and his band of warriors, and after the Nez Perces camp was secured. I sent

him to Sitting Bull's camp for his daughter, got as far as Carroll, or near there, where he was foully dealt with by miserable
white men — was shot in several places, as his unhealed
wounds will show, and his young girl used worse. I presume he
was left for dead, but succeeded in reaching the Crow camp.
His daughter was taken, I understand, to Benton, where she
remained at last accounts.

For his good service, and to repair, as far as possible the
wrong done, I send him with two government ponies to you,
and one other Nez Perces, hoping that he may yet recover his
child. Should he do so, please send him back to his home, or
make such disposition of them as you deem best. The ponies I
would like sent back, as they belong to my regiment.

If the white men who committed the crime are caught I
would suggest that you report to department headquarters, as
the department commander ordered the affair investigated. I
am, sir, very respectfully your obedient servant,

Nelson A. Miles,

Colonel Fifth Infantry, Brevt Major General
United States Army, Commanding.

————

Fort Ellis, Mont., July 5, 1878.

To Whom it May Concern:

The bearer of this "Captain George," a Nez Perces Indian, arrived here, and goes to Benton to find his daughter who
was stolen from him by some white men. Citizens along the
road between here and Benton are forbidden to harm Captain
George and his companion, and should give him every assistance in their power in recovering his child, as he has been
badly treated by the whites.

Jas. T. Brisbin,

Major Second Cavalry, Commanding.

It was on Friday, July 14, 1878, when Captain George presented himself
at the Flathead agency with the above quoted letters, also one from the commanding officer at Benton to Agent Ronan.

The poor Indian father related that a young warrior of Chief Joseph's hostile band carried off his daughter, who was 16 years of age, from his home
at the crossing of Camai, in Idaho, and she was with the Indians in all their
battles and retreat, followed by General Howard and his troops, including the
battle of Bighole, at the head of Bitter Root valley, where General [John] Gibbon was wounded, Captain [William] Logan, Lieutenant [William L.] English
and other brave officers and men of the Seventh regiment from Fort Missoula
were killed; and on for hundreds of miles, through the National park, across
the Missouria river, and away north until intercepted by General [Nelson A.]
Miles, who accomplished the surrender of Chief Joseph and his warriors. But
White Bird and 40 of his braves escaped from the surrender and pushed their
way on to the camp of Sitting Bull. The abductor of the daughter of Captain
George was one of the band that escaped and with him went the girl. As related
in the letter of General Miles, Captain George rescued his daughter from the
camp of Sitting Bull, only to be shot down like a dog by a white fiend near the

town of Carroll, a short distance from Benton, Mont., while making his way to Idaho. He was left for dead on the plains, while his daughter was again taken into captivity, this time, however, by a white brute. Captain George traveled more than 2,000 miles in search of his daughter, on horseback, before his arrival at the Flathead agency on that July morning in 1878.

Let the official report of Agent Ronan to the commissioner of Indian affairs at Washington, dated July 24, of that year, tell the end of Captain George's search for his daughter:

Learning from the Indians of this reservation that a young squaw answering the description of the daughter of Captain George, whom they rescued early in the spring from her white captors near Fort Benton, and whom they brought through with them over the Indian trail through the Caddot pass to this agency and sent home under Indian escort to Camai, by the Lo Lo pass, above Fort Missoula, to Idaho, I directed her father and companion to remain at the agency, as it was dangerous for them to travel through Missoula county, as they might be taken for members of the Nez Perces band of murderers who passed through the county only a week before, leaving death and destruction along their trail. I sent out runners to gather whatever information they could in regard to the fate of the girl, and started myself to Lo Lo pass to meet a camp of Indians that I learned were coming over that trail from Idaho, and were traveling towards Bitter Root valley.

On the trail I met an Indian in advance named John Nill [Hill], or "Ta-Netchet," which means Hand Shot-Off, and he assured me that eight days previous to our meeting he camped at the home of Captain George at the crossing of Camai, beyond the Bitter Root range of mountains, and that the girl in question was home with her mother, having been brought there by some Indians from the Flathead agency, who took her away from white men at Benton. I returned to the agency and related the news to Captain George, who was wild with delight, and stated that he knew the news was true, as "Ta-Netchet" was his friend and would not send a lie to him. From the agency I sent Captain George and his companion to Fort Missoula, with a trusted guard and a letter to Major [H. L.] Chipman, the commanding officer. That the brave, intrepid and devoted Indian father reached his home in safety and found his child after his perilous journey of more than 2,000 miles of search on horseback, I can vouch, as the following letter will show, and also a letter from himself, which it is not necessary to publish:

Fort Missoula, Mont., July 25, 1878.

Peter Ronan, Flathead Agent, Montana.

Sir: Captain George and companion, the Nez Perces Indians you sent here, were escorted to the Lo Lo pass, near Stevensville, Bitter Root valley, on the day succeeding their arrival here. They found a number of Indian friends at that place, with whom they will return to their homes at the crossing of the Camai in Idaho. Very respectfully yours,

H. L. Chipman,
Major Third Infantry, Commanding.

July 29, 1878

U.S. Office of Indian Affairs, "Letters Received by the Office of Indian Affairs, 1824-1880," National Archives Microfilm Publication M234, reel 511, frames 705-712. Note: The first part of Ronan's July 14, 1879, letter to Governor B. F. Potts is missing from the original of this letter in the National Archives. The missing text was found in "Indian Matters," The Helena Independent (daily), July 21, 1878, page 3, col. 3.

Murders committed by a small band of Nez Perce refugees returning to Idaho through Montana in 1878 severely tested the ability of Salish, Pend d'Oreille, and Kootenai leaders to maintain peace with the whites. According to newspaper reports, most white people could not distinguish a friendly Salish party from a group of hostile Nez Perce, but some may have used this as an excuse to vent their bigotry.[13] Duncan McDonald, a mixed blood trader on the reservation, was a voice of reason calling on white people to not take their vengeance out on friendly Indian hunters.[14] At this time McDonald was publishing an Indian account of "The Nez Perces: The History of Their Troubles and the Campaign of 1877," in the Deer Lodge newspaper, *The New North-West*, and even traveled to Canada to interview the Nez Perce refugees there.

Chief Moses was the nineteenth century leader of the Columbias, an interior Salish speaking tribe living on the middle Columbia river in Washington State. His efforts to stay in his homeland resulted in conflict with local whites who squatted on land used by the tribe. He and his people ended up on the Colville Reservation in Washington.[15]

Flathead Agency, M.T.
July 29, 1878

To the
Hon. Commissioner of Indian Affairs
Washington, D.C.
Sir:

I have the honor to make the following special report in regard to the recent Indian troubles in this portion of Montana which has caused and is still the cause of great excitement and most extravagant rumors among the settlers and in the Territorial press reports.

About the eight of July an Indian rumor reached me that a party of Nez Perczs had left White Bird's band in the British possessions and were making their way towards Idaho by Caddotts pass, and fearing that they might turn this way and come in by the Agency over the Jocko trail I sent out a runner to ascertain the facts. On the 11th of July the runner returned and gave me information that a band of Nez Percz Indians numbering about eighteen crossed the North Fork of Sun river and had taken a trail leading towards Missoula. Hardly had the runner delivered his message, when a messenger arrived from the town of Missoula with the news of the murder of two men on the Deerborn and also two men on Deep Creek, about one day's travel nearer this way on the trail the Indians in question had taken. The letter of the messenger from Missoula informed me that it was the general belief that the authors of the crimes were Indians from this reservation; but from the information I possessed I felt as[s]ured it was the party of Nez Perczs who crossed the Sun River, and I immediately sent a messenger to Fort Missoula with word of the rout[e] they had taken. Troops were at once sent out to intercept them, the Indians in the mean time having killed three more men on Rock Creek as they passed on towards Rosses Hole.

My next step was to visit Machell Head Chief of the Pend d'Orilles, and deeming it my duty made the following report to the Governor.

Flathead Agency, M.T.
July 14th, 1878.

B. F. Potts, Governor Montana Territory
Helena, M.T.

Sir —

I have to report the following council held with Michel, head chief of the Pen d'Oreilles, Sunday, July 14th, for your information, and any action you may suggest:

Having narrated to Chief Michel the particulars of the murders committed by a band of Nez Perces, who came from the North by the way of the north fork of Sun river, murdering as they came along two men at the Dearborn, in Lewis and Clark county; two men at Deep creek, Bear gulch, Deer Lodge county, and four or five miners at the head of Rock creek, in Missoula county; all of which murders were committed in the direct Nez Perces trail from the North to Idaho Territory, known as the Elk city trail. In reply the chief said:

"A few days ago a messenger came to me from Sitting Bull's camp with word from that chief, that if I valued the lives and welfare of my people to gather them together and leave the reservation — if I did not feel like joining him and making war upon the whites — that after he had done his work among the settlers myself and people could come back again and occupy our land without fear of obtrusion."

Agent — "What reply did you send back?"

Michel — "I told the runner to tell his chief that the Pen d'Oreilles were friends of the whites; that years ago, when I was young, the Pen d'Oreilles and the Sioux had met in battle and were enemies. We are now quietly settled down, supporting our families by raising stock and planting crops. Our homes we love. Our lands are beautiful. The crops are ripening, and we will soon be gathering them in. We are not well armed, and have nearly forgotten the modes of war; but a mouse, though small, if trodden upon will turn and bite. Tell your chief if he comes we will give him battle, and die by our homes. This is my answer."

Agent — "What do you think of the murders just committed?"

Michel — "I think that perhaps White Bird — the Nez Perces chief, whose voice is for war — has arranged with Sitting Bull and has sent out small murdering parties to come through Montana to the Lapwai reserve in Idaho, to murder as they go through this country and commit all sorts of crimes in Idaho, and incite the reservation Nez Perces to war, with a promise that Sitting Bull with his warriors will come and help them. This is only my opinion. Perhaps this band of marauders has broken away from White Bird without his consent."

Agent — "Do you not think it best, in order to be prepared, to send scouts on the two trails leading from the North through this reservation?"

Michel — "It is the only way to protect the country. Indians can scout on the trails north of here, and can give you and me information in time to head them off?"

Agent — "Will you send out scouts?"

Michel — "Yes; if they can have arms, ammunition, blankets and provisions, and some hope of reward."

Agent — "Providing I can get you these things will you be willing to have white men go with them?"

Michel — "Yes; provided you choose the white men and half-breeds, and that the scouts will be under your and my own control and report to you, when you can easily report to the soldiers when signs are seen. Three lodges of my people are camped on the trail leading in by the Jocko, I will send them word to look out for Nez Perces and bring in news of what route they take. These people are fishing at the lake and are not well armed; they cannot fight, but they can bring us news. If regular scouts go they should be armed, because they cannot otherwise protect themselves if they get into a fight, which they would be apt to do, as the Nez Perces do not feel friendly because we would not join their cause last summer."

Very respectfully,
Peter Ronan,
U.S. Indian Agent.

A wild rumor prevailed among the settlers that the Columbia river Indians under Chief Moses, had gone on the war-path and were marching this way. People were deserting their homes and coming into the towns for protection, and in order to allay the excitement I sent a runner to that country for news. There is no mail route across the country, and all the mail matter must be sent by special messenger, or be mailed around by San Francisco, which involves great delay. My messenger returned with the following letter, which had a tendency of allaying the excitement:

— Some two weeks ago, Major Ronan sent a runner over to the Cœur d'Alene Post, to get positive information in regard to the rumored "coming of Moses" in our direction. As there are some badly frightened people on the supposed route of this chieftain, we publish the copy, (kindly furnished us by Major Ronan,) for their information:

Camp Cœur d'Alene, July 14, 1878.
Peter Ronan, Esq., U.S. Indian Agent.

Sir: — Your letter of the 5th inst. was received at this post several days ago, but until to-day, the bearer of it has been away. In reply to it, I would state, that all the Indian tribes in our vicinity are peaceable and quiet. We hear of no actions of any of them that would indicate hostilities. To-day I received news that the hostiles, at present being pressed by General [O. O.] Howard, have turned to the eastward, instead of trying to come north of the Columbia river. I should say that there is nothing at present to indicate that the Columbia river Indians, nor those in our vicinity, intend to take the warpath. I shall be glad to hear from you at any time, if anything in your section should indicate the movement of hostile Indians in this direction.

Very Respectfully.

Wm. Mills,

Captain 25th Infantry, Commanding.

From the annexed letter it will be seen that my information to the Post Commander at Fort Missoula was correct, and that the Murdering band of Nez Perczs were overtaken and punished:

Fort Missoula, M.T.

July 25, 1878

Peter Ronan

Flathead Agency, M.T.

Sir:

Deeming it of interest to you I make the following extracts from a note (pencil) from Lieut. [Thomas S.] Wallace dated "Eight miles from Corvallis, July 25, 1878.

Fifteen miles from Clearwater, the Indians "not six hours ahead" the main body of citizens left, stating that their horses were too tired to go any further.

* * * * * *

I proceeded with 13 men of my own my guide and two citizens, volunteers. About 4 a.m. crossed N. fork Clearwater and struck the Indians moving on the middle Fork same river. After selecting a spot to place my horses and fall back upon in case of need I opened the ball [battle?] with a charge. The Indians numbered about 17 bucks and two squaws. They fought like devils but were surprised so we had a little advantage. The fight lasted two hours. Loss: Indians six killed. — three wounded that we know of. Ponies and mules 23 Killed — 31 captured which I have with me. Two horses were wounded — the g[u]ides and the one Sergt Webber rides — the latter slightly in the leg. These horses were wounded by the Indians returning to the attack about sun down. They then left us.

* * * * * *

"Captain George and companion — the Nez Perczs you sent here — were escorted to Stephensville, on the day succeeding their arrival here. They found a number of friends at that place.

Very respectfully yours

H. L. Chipman

Major 3d Infantry

Commanding Post.

The most intense excitement yet prevails and I am doing all in my power to keep the reservation Indians from leaving home. I have succeeded in gathering them all in with the exception of some three lodges that went to the Buffalo Country early in spring and who are now North of the American line. I expect them home in a few days by a Northern trail which will avoid all settlements, having sent them word of the troubles now existing. My supplies are very limited and I fear a scarcity of provisions before the new crops will be harvested.

> Very respectfully,
> Your obedient servant
> Peter Ronan
> U.S. Ind. Agent.

August 2, 1878
U.S. Office of Indian Affairs, "Letters Received by the Office of Indian Affairs, 1824-1880," National Archives Microfilm Publication M234, reel 511, frames 713-716.

> In 1878 Ronan had to rely on persuasion to influence the volunteer police force. The agent's ability to force unpopular actions in this situation would have been seriously limited. In the middle 1880s Ronan established a paid Indian police force under his control which resulted in considerable conflict with the traditional chiefs. The government policy of undermining the tribal social structure and the authority of the chiefs was counterproductive because it resulted in increased law and order problems on the reservation.

> Flathead Agency, M.T.
> August 2d, 1878

To the
Hon. Commissioner of Indian Affairs
Washington, D.C.

    Sir:

After having made several attempts to organize a police force at this Agency, in accordance with your instructions and without success, I have the honor to make the following report:

For a long time past there has been in existence among the Confederate tribes of this reserve, a police force composed of about twenty of the best Indians of the three tribes. They have been very successful in their efforts to maintain order and discipline among the Indians and have always been willing to obey any orders given by me to them to make arrests. Their services were especially useful during the Nez Perce trouble of last summer, as will be seen from my report for July, last year, and my report to Gov. Potts, — copy of which was transmitted to you July 11th, 1877 — During the excitement of the past month they have also been very diligent in Keeping the Indians on the reserve. The service which this force has rendered has never been compensated by the Government. Small presents of Coffee, tea and tobacco, and such other supplies as happened to be at the Agency, have been issued to them as to other Indians, but nothing more.

The reason for my failure to establish a force of police according to your instructions is this: The Indians say that "if we four Indians are made policemen we will be looked upon as pets of the Government and the others will be jealous of us; the old police force will say that we receive pay and clothing for doing what they have done all this time for nothing; that we are no better than they are and that they should be paid for what they have done. The result will be that we will stand alone among our people, and when you order us to make arrests the offender will resist and other Indians will help him, and we will get into trouble, may be Killed and war will follow. We will not be policemen; let everything stay as it is now." This is the only reply that I have received in my several attempts to obey your instructions, and I therefore report to you the facts, and would respectfully suggest that, to avoid dissension among these people, who are now getting on very pleasantly together, the arms, ammunition, clothing, rations etc., be given to the old force of something like twenty men, pro rata, which will cause them to continue in their efforts to keep order on the reserve. I am of the opinion that it will be impossible to organize a force of police in accordance with the rules and regulations established.

If there had been no police regulations among the Indians prior to your instructions, it would have been an easy matter to obey them to the letter, but, as before suggested, I would earnestly request that I be allowed to let the old force remain — of course, exercising, as I have always done, a strict vigilance over their actions.

Very respectfully,
Your obdt servt,
Peter Ronan
U.S. Ind. Agent.

August 12, 1878

U.S. Commissioner of Indian Affairs, Annual Report of the Commissioner of Indian Affairs *(Washington, D.C.: U.S. Government Printing Office, 1878), pages 87-89.*

> Ronan mentions Chief Eneas' use of personal funds to encourage farming among the Kootenai. The collapse of the buffalo herds and other game resources, undermined the ability of the Kootenai and other tribes to support themselves through traditional hunting and gathering.

Flathead Agency, Mont., August 12, 1878.

Sir: In compliance with instructions received from your office, under date of July 1, 1878, I have the honor to transmit herewith my second annual report.

General Topography.

On a small tributary of the Jocko River, and distant about two miles from that stream, at the head of the Jocko Valley, is situated the Flathead Agency. One mile to the rear of the agency buildings a chain of lofty mountains rise abruptly from the valley, forming no foot-hills, and towering grandly above the scene. The mountains are covered with a dense forest of fir, pine, and tamarack, which grows very large and furnishes excellent lumber. In the lofty range, and in close proximity to the agency, are several clear mountain lakes, abounding in speckled trout, and from one of those lakes a water-fall or cataract over 1,000 feet high, of great beauty and grandeur, falls into the valley, about 8 miles northwest of the agency, forming one of the tributaries of the Jocko River.

The valley is formed in a sort of triangular square, about 5 miles in breadth and 12 in length. Along the river and tributaries there is some very excellent farming-land, cultivated mostly by *Flatheads* and half-breeds, but a large portion of it is rocky and gravelly. Following down the Jocko to its confluence with the Pend d'Oreille River the valley closes, and for a few miles the Jocko rushes through a narrow gorge, but before joining its waters with the Pend d'Oreille the valley again opens into a rich and fertile plain, where a large number of Indian farms are located. Good log-houses and well-fenced farms with waving fields of grain give evidence of husbandry and thrift.

Leaving the Jocko Valley to the left and passing through a narrow cañon and over a low divide of hills, which form the north side of that valley, the road leads to Saint Ignatius Mission, some 17 miles from the agency, where the Indian school is located, and is taught by Sisters of Charity. A large church, convent, and dwelling-house for the missionaries are surrounded by some 70 log-houses, where principally *Pend d'Oreille* Indians dwell and cultivate the soil in the surrounding valley. The Mission Valley is a very broad and fertile plain, well watered by streams which flow from the ranges of mountains that rise on both sides of the valley, and from the mission to the Flathead Lake and around its borders there is farming-land sufficient for thousands of settlers. Along the plain from the mission to the foot of the Flathead Lake, a distance of some 30 miles, are scattered Indian farms and habitations.

Flathead Lake.

This beautiful sheet of water is some 28 miles in length and has an average width of 10 miles. Around the foot of the lake and amid the most delightful scenes that the mind can well picture is grouped another Indian settlement, where houses and crops give every evidence of thrift.

Crossing the lake by canoe or boat, and following a northeasterly direction to Dayton Creek, you will find the homes of the Kootenays, living mostly in lodges; but this spring they have commenced the erection of a few houses. The Kootenays live chiefly by hunting and fishing. A large prairie in the vicinity of their village furnishes them with camas and bitter-root, which they dig and dry in the spring for winter use. In brief, it is hardly possible in any country to surpass the natural resources of the Jocko Reservation as to agriculture, grazing, timber, and water-power. The fishing is excellent in all the rivers, lakes, and mountain streams, and the hunting is good in the surrounding country.

The Crops.

We are now in the midst of harvest, and although the grasshoppers made sad havoc among some of the Indian fields, particularly the oat crop, we will have a good yield of wheat, and among the thrifty class who remained away from the chase and gave attention to the cultivation of their farms there will be an abundance. Much attention was paid by the Indians to the cultivation of small vegetable gardens this season, with very good result.

Although the Indians have large bands of horses and cattle, they pay very little attention to the curing of hay, giving as a reason that there is no necessity to provide hay or shelter for stock, as the winters are too mild to require it. I very much fear, however, that an unusually cold winter may yet find them unprovided and occasion great loss. To guard against this to some extent I intend to see that all the straw from the crops is carefully stacked.

Building.

This year some good, substantial houses have been erected by the Indians, and lumber and shingles from the mill have been in great demand. The Indians cut and haul their own logs to the mill, and the agency miller saws them into lumber to suit their convenience. Several more houses would have been erected by the Kootenays but for the fact that the mill is some 60 miles distant from their village, and there are but three wagons in the tribe with which to do their hauling and farming. The chief of the Kootenays is doing all in his power to induce his people to follow the thrifty habits of the generality of the Flatheads and Pend d'Oreilles, and from his own private means has purchased for the use of his tribe a combined mowing and reaping machine, a set of carpenter tools, also, a set of blacksmith tools. I would again urge the necessity of encouraging these people by assisting them with agricultural implements, wagons, and harness, as well as the needy of the other two tribes.

Crime.

But very little crime of any description can be charged to the Indians of this reservation. The missionary work performed by the fathers of Saint Ignatius Mission has its salutary effect upon the Indians, keeping them in wholesome restraint, guarding their morals, and gradually leading them to the pursuit of happiness through sturdy toil, morality, and self-dependence. The tribal laws and the law of religion forbid polygamy and adultery among these people, and in my opinion it would be hard to find a community of the same number, even among christianized civilization, where as few of these crimes are in practice. Of course there are some uncontrollable characters of both sexes, who visit the neighboring towns, and through the demoralizing effects of whisky cause disgrace to themselves and scandal to the tribes.

At Home.

The Indians, with the exception of a very few, are now at home, and I am doing all in my power to keep them there. The chiefs are lending me all the aid they can to accomplish this, and doing all in their power to keep their people out of trouble.

The excitement of the past few months, caused by the Bannack war, and the murders committed by the Nez Percés in close proximity to this reservation, has given me a great deal of anxiety, fearing that the settlers or military might mistake these people for hostiles, and by attacking them plunge the tribes into war. But every precaution having been taken to gather the Indians home and to warn them of their danger, I feel that all danger is past. The chiefs fear that the hostiles may commit murder on the reservation or in some of the neighboring settlements, which may be attributed to their people and hastily acted upon by the whites and cause trouble.

The Boarding School,

under the charge of the Sisters of Charity, is in a flourishing condition, and is an excellent institution of learning for girls, and the pupils are making excellent progress in the common English branches. A large number of them can read and write the English language understandingly, and work in the first four rules of arithmetic. Singing and music are also taught, the Indian girls forming the choir in the Catholic church for Sunday service; also, house-keeping generally is taught, viz, washing of clothes, floors, &c., baking, cooking, ironing, sewing, and mending of clothes, quilting, knitting, laundry work, &c. As far as the education of the girls is concerned, the school is a success; but the education of boys cannot be successfully accomplished without the establishment of an industrial and agricultural boarding school, compelling attendance. I very much question the policy of day schools for Indian boys, as it has been tried at the mission for years with very indifferent success. The chiefs and headmen are very anxious to educate their boys, and I am constantly referred to the fifth article of the treaty and asked why it is not complied with, in regard to the establishment of an industrial school, and I can only echo — why?

The Sanitary Condition of the Indians

for the year has been very good until about the first of the present month, when the weather set in intensely hot, causing a great deal of sickness. The physician is in constant employment, and reports that few cases have proved fatal so far.

The Grist-Mill

has but one set of burrs, and is kept almost constantly employed in grinding Indian wheat. Last year the unprecedented amount of nine thousand bushels of wheat was made into flour, the product of Indian toil and thrift on the Jocko Reservation.

Very respectfully, your obedient servant,

Peter Ronan,
United States Indian Agent.

The Commissioner of Indian Affairs.

August 20, 1878a

U.S. Office of Indian Affairs, "Letters Received by the Office of Indian Affairs, 1824-1880," National Archives Microfilm Publication M234, reel 511, frames 723-730.

This letter illustrates the problems caused for Indian agents by unrealistic orders from Washington, D.C., to force an end to tribal buffalo hunts. The government made no provision to support those who still relied on the hunt for subsistence. Tribal members were also well aware of their treaty right to hunt off the reservation.

Flathead Agency, M.T.
August 20th, 1878

Hon. Commissioner of Indian Affairs
Washington, D.C.

Sir,

Referring to letter "C. Montana 1295–78" bearing date August 3d, 1878, I have to report as follows:

The Flathead Indians residing in the Bitter Root Valley, as will be seen from the following letter addressed to me from your Office under date of October 22d, 1877, are not considered by the Department as being under treaty restraint, and therefore hold little or no communication with this Agency and go to and return from the hunting ground without consulting my views:

Peter Ronan
Indian Agent
Flathead Agency.

Sir,

Referring to your letter of the 1st instant requesting permission to distribute a portion of the goods which you have purchased for the Indians on the Jocko reservation, among those who have refused to remove from the Bitter Root Valley to the said reservation, I have to say that as those remaining on the Bitter Root Valley are non-treaty Indians, authority cannot be granted for you to distribute among them goods that belong to those who are subject to treaty stipulations.

I very much regret the necessity for this refusal as I should like to reward these Indians for their fidelity to the Government, and but for want of funds applicable to the purpose would grant your request.

Very respectfully.
E. A. Hayt
Commissioner

The Bitter Root Flatheads having lost all their crop last year principally by neglect caused by their devotion to their white neighbours, whom they aided to protect from the murderous hands of Joseph's Band of Nez Percez, while marching through the Bitter Root valley, and having no other hope of Sustaining life during the Winter, Charlos and his people saught [sic] the hunting grounds of the Judith Basin, where they remained until this Summer. As their route lay though the thickly settled portions of Montana, Some ravages were committed by their dogs upon a Sheep herd, complaint of which was made to me, and which is now under investigation and will be reported upon at an early day. Charlos and his people will be compelled to go again to the hunting grounds this Fall or Starve, and as a matter of humanity I would suggest that they be not restrained from the chase unless some aid or assistance be furnished by the Government. It seems to me the most feasable plan to furnish them with a small escort from Fort Missoula to Camp Baker who will prevent all depredations in their route, and when returning home they could report at Camp Baker and an escort sent back with them to Fort Missoula, a small allowance of fixed amunition should also be allowed them as their necessities will compel them to hunt for subsistence.

In regard to the Indians of the Jocko Reservation, but few of them were out last year and as they went to the hunting ground and returned by a Northerly trail which avoids all settlements, no complaints ever reached me of any sort against them, — a few Flatheads and Pend 'Oreilles however, from the Reservation did go by way of Big Blackfoot and Fort Shaw, but they were in charge of a trusty Chief, and I have learned of no complaints against them. I use every persuasion and inducement in my power to prevent hunting parties from leaving the reservation; but in view of the fact that no beef or rations are issued to those Indians, and that allthough a large majority of them have adopted civilizing pursuits and are extensively engaged in the raising of grain and cattle, yet there are a great number of them who depend chiefly upon hunting for the support of their families; and if prevented from doing so must be supported by the Government, and as the Agent is powerless to issue rations where none are supplied, except from the beneficial fund of three thousand dollars a year which is not adequate to supply the wants of the aged, the infirm and the indigent. Besides, those Indians claim the right under existing treaty to a common hunting ground, where they have equal and uninterrupted rights of hunting, fishing and gathering fruits, grazing animals, curing meat and dressing robes, and refer to the sixth article of said treaty, concluded at the council ground on the Upper Missouri river, near the mouth of the Judith Basin (River) on the 17th of October 1855, which says "the aforesaid nations and Tribes of Indians parties to this treaty agree and consent to remain within their own respective countries, *except when going to or from, or whilst hunting upon the* ["]*common hunting ground*" or when visiting each other for purposes of trade or social intercourse," and claim if those rights are abrogated, they were never officially notified of it.

In view of the fact that I Know of nor cannot learn of any depredations committed by the Indians of the *Jocko Reservation* while going to or returning from their hunting ground, I do not feel justified in adopting "stringent measures to Keep the Indians upon the Reservation," unless so ordered, as year by year the number who seek the hunting grounds grow less, and will soon entirely cease. Last year not to exceed fifteen men of the Jocko reservation

Indians passed through the Settlements for hunting purposes, and they state to me that in their hunting excursions this Fall they will all go by the Northern trail before mentioned where no settlements lay in their route.

Very respectfully,
Your Obedient Servant
Peter Ronan
U.S. Indian Agent.

August 20, 1878b

U.S. Office of Indian Affairs, "Letters Received by the Office of Indian Affairs, 1824-1880," National Archives Microfilm Publication M234, reel 511, frames 731-740.

> Conflict over Salish claims to the Bitterroot Valley was to ebb and flow until 1889 when a dramatic drought finally crushed the efforts of the Salish to maintain an economically independent Indian community in the valley. The Salish refused to accept the patents because they believed the patents violated the 1855 Hellgate Treaty, but, since the patents had been issued, at least some land was safe from encroachment by white settlers.

Flathead Agency, M.T.
August 20th, 1878

Hon. Commissioner of Indian Affairs
Washington, D.C.
    Sir:
    Referring to letter "L." dated at Washington August 23d, 1877, which is in the following language: to wit:

> Peter Ronan
> U.S. Indian Agent
> Flathead Agency Montana
>   Sir,
>   In answer to your letter of the 6th instant asking for directions relative to 51 patents for certain Indians, you are instructed to proceed without unnecessary delay to carry out the instructions to which you referred, as given to your predecessor under date of April 4th, 1876, namely: to deliver the patents to the Indians and take their receipt properly witnessed therefor.

Very respectfully
J. Q. Smith
Commissioner

    Montana F310/77
    In regard to the foregoing I have the honor to make the following Special report: At the time of the receipt of instructions great turmoil and excitement prevailed in the Bitter Root Valley owing to the Nez Perces War, and the march of Joseph's Band through that country, and also to the fact that the Flatheads lost their crops, owing in part to neglect caused by assisting the Whites in guarding their homes, and to a hail storm which cut everything down before it that season, leaving them destitute, and compelling them to go to the Buffalo country to Sustain life by the chase, as they were refused any assistance by the Government, although I made an earnest appeal, in their behalf, at the time. Therefore I could not confer with them as they remained out all Winter, and

only during the present month was I informed that all the Bitter Root Flat-heads had returned to their homes, hence the delay in conferring with them according to instructions:

Having gathered the principal men of the tribe together, with their Chief Charlos, at the St. Mary's Mission, through my interpreter I stated the nature of my visit to the Indians. Charlos the Chief refused to accept his patent and, of course, all the Indians present followed his example. In explanation he said in Substance that the treaty agreed upon between his Father Victor, head Chief of the Flathead Nation, and other Indian Chiefs, and Governor Stephens on the part of the Government, on the 6th of July 1855, provided that the Bitter Root Valley above the LoLo Fork, should be set apart as a separate Reservation for the Flathead tribe. *I explained to him that the 11th article as it* reads in the Hell Gate treaty, gave the President of the United States the power to cause the Bitter Root Valley above the LoLo Fork to be surveyed and examined, and if in his judgment, it should be found better adapted to the wants of the Flathead Tribe, as a reservation for said Tribe it should be so set apart and reserved, and that the President on the 14th of November 1871, issued an order setting forth that the "Bitter Root Valley had been carefully surveyed and examined in accordance with said treaty, and ordered" that all Indians residing in said Bitter Root Valley be removed as soon as practicable to the Jocko reservation, and that a just compensation be made for improvements, made by them in the Bitter Root Valley. That in accordance with that Section an agreement was intered into by and between Gen. [James] Garfield on the part of the United S[t]ates and himself (Charlos) head Chief, Arlee, 2d Chief and Adolphe 3d Chief on the part of the Flathead tribe to remove to the Jocko reservation and to abandon the Bitter Root Valley — that the Government tried to carry out the Garfield Agreement in every particular, but that Charlos and Adolphe, after signing the agreement refused to remove with their People, and that Arlee, the 2d Chief was the only one who removed with his followers and was reaping the benefit of the Agreement. Charlos replied that he did not sign the Garfield Agreement, and if it appeared on the paper it was not his fault; and that the Stephens treaty gave to his Father the Valley of the Bitter Root for a Sepa-rate reservation from the Jocko; he Seemed to cling to the opinion that on the treaty ground it was then and there understood by the Flathead Tribe never to be disturbed unless specially agreed to by the Indians — that they were to be consulted and have a choice between the Jocko Reserve and the Bitter Root. In regard to the issue of the patents Charlos claims that that matter was never properly explained to him or his people, and when they gave their names for title they simply understood they were signing a petition to the President to allow them to retain the Bitter Root Valley as a separate reservation from the Jocko as agreed upon by the 11th article of the treaty. I found it in vain to try to explain the precise meaning and wording of this clause as he persisted that it was the Indian understanding that according to the Stephen's treaty they have a valid right and title to the Bitter Root Valley as a reservation. It was also inferred by him that if his People did accept the patents they would not Know where to find their land as a part of what he claimed to be his land has already been taken away from him by a white man who claimed his line ran through it; taxation and the breaking up of tribal relations is another objection; and also an utter lack of appreciation or confidence in the good intentions of the Government. He fully appreciates the Strength of the Government and the fact that he can be forced into measures, but he claims if it should come to that he will only ask the privilege to Seek another home in another Country of his own Choice rather than give up his title to the Bitter Root as a Reservation by accepting a patent for his farm or by removing to the Jocko.

I would state to the Hon. Commissioner, that the Affairs of the Flathead of the Bitter Root Valley are in a most deplorable and unsatisfactory Condition, and my motive in entering into so many details is to place the matter before you in as intelligent form as I can, so that Some action may be taken to settle the question definately, without resort to force.

The time is Surely approaching when the Bitter Root Land question will lead to serious difficulty as the valley is fast being settled by thrifty farmers. The Chief Charlos is a good and peaceable Indian and well respected by the Whites, but he clings to the Notion that his people have been wronged in regard to the Bitter Root question. The Jocko reservation, in my opinion, is a superior country to the Bitter Root Valley; but as matters now stand, Charlos will not consent to remove to it except by force, nor accept a Patent for his land in the Bitter Root, and give up tribal relations, and his people will cling to his fortunes and bide by the Consequences. It is clearly necessary, in my opinion, that some steps be taken to settle the question either by sending a commissioner with power and instructions to act or by inviting Charlos to a conference at Washington, where the intentions of the Government for the welfare of his people might be thoroughly impressed upon him. An imperfect apprehension of the terms of the Stephen's treaty, as understood by the Authorities of the United States, is the cause of all the trouble. It requires time and patience to impress the exact terms of an agreement upon the Indian mind, but when once stamped there, it is my experience, they are the last to break their obligations, but the foremost to insist upon all the terms of the bond, as by them understood.

Very respectfully,
Your obedient Servant
Peter Ronan
U.S. Indian Agent.

August 26, 1878
U.S. Office of Indian Affairs, "Letters Received by the Office of Indian Affairs, 1824-1880," National Archives Microfilm Publication M234, reel 511, frames 749-751.

Ronan made an effort to purchase supplies from tribal members to help develop the reservation economy. In this case he purchased 6,000 pounds of beef from Duncan McDonald, a tribal member trader. See also Ronan's October 14, 1878, letter to the Commissioner of Indian Affairs.

Flathead Agency, M.T.
August 26th, 1878

To the
Hon. Commissioner of Indian Affairs
Washington, D.C.
    Sir:
    I have the honor to forward herewith letter received from Cashier Missoula National Bank relative to a lost or stolen check on U.S. Asst. Treasurer at

New York drawn by me favor Duncan McDonald, in payment for 6000 lbs beef, amounting to $240.00. As there are no instructions on file in this office as to the issuing of duplicate drafts in such cases I have to request that I be informed as to the manner of procedure.

Very respectfully
Your obdt servt
Peter Ronan
U.S. Ind. Agent

Enclosed August 19, 1878, letter from the Missoula National Bank requesting a duplicate draft for the $240.

September 14, 1878

From Watson and Blain, Depredation Claim 1783, RG 75, National Archives, Washington, D.C.

> See above under date of January 10, 1878, for more detail about the conflict between the Salish dogs and Watson and Blain's sheep in central Montana. This letter from the depredation claim file describes Charlo's reaction to the charges.

(Copy)

Flathead Agency, M.T.
September 14, 1878.

To the Hon. Commissioner of Indian Affairs,
Washington, D.C.

Sir:

In reference to your letter "C" "Montana R42" dated Feb. 5th 1878, I herewith submit report of the proceedings had together with all papers.

Upon receipt of instructions, conveyed with above letter, I wrote as follows to Messers. Watson and Blain.

* * * * * *

In reply to my letter I received annexed application for indemnity, marked "B" and having ascertained by inquiry of reliable persons, that the prices fixed by the claimants upon the sheep killed by Indian dogs were not in excess of those ruling in this Territory; and I also obtained the knowledge to my satisfaction that Messrs. Watson and Blain are reliable and truthful men, and that the statements as set forth in their application for indemnity are truthful and just, to the best of my knowledge and belief. Whereupon I proceeded to the Bitter Root valley with my Interpreter, and stated the case to Charlos, head Chief of the Bitter Root Flatheads, and after fully explaining to him and his head men the whole case, then and there demanded satisfaction for the claimant. Charlos admitted that the Flathead dogs did attack a herd of sheep in the Country described by claimant, and that the military authorities at Camp Baker made complaint to him of the fact, and that he immediately took steps to prevent a recurrence of the same. He refused to make any satisfaction to claimants, giving as a reason that claimants or their agents, killed enough of their dogs to make up for the sheep.

This seems to be the Indian mode of satisfying a claim and Charlos considers the account squared.

Very respectfully,
Your obdt. servt.
Peter Ronan
U.S. Ind. Agt.

September 28, 1878

The Pilot *(Boston, Mass.), September 28, 1878, page 1, col. 1.*

Catholicity Among the Indians in Montana

The following extract from a letter received by a gentleman in Boston from Mr. Peter Ronan, an Indian Agent in Montana Territory, will be interesting to our readers:—

"I have the government of three Indian tribes, namely, the Flatheads, Pond d'Orrelles, and Kootenas. They have given me very little trouble so far, as they are on the highway to Christianity and civilization. Most of them live in houses, cultivate farms, raise stock, and are very devoted to their religion. Forty years ago, a portion of the tribes I have in charge, at their own instance, sent a delegation of their own people to St. Louis for Catholic missionaries, and in response to their request, Father [Pierre] De Smet came with them to this country, accompanied by a few Jesuit priests and lay brothers, and established the first mission in this region. To show how their religious teachings have taken root I will state that in July last, on St. Ignatius' Day, the Patron Saint of this reservation, I witnessed at our mission about five hundred Indians receive Holy Communion. Six Jesuit missionary priests conducted the services on the altar, and there were also five lay brothers. Among the latter were two who accompanied Father De Smet to the Rocky Mountains in 1841. One of the officiating priests was the Superior-General of the Order in the Rocky Mountains. . . . The country here is beautiful beyond my power of description, and the most bother I have is with tourists, pleasure-seekers, and army officers, who come here to enjoy themselves, visiting the beautiful lakes, water-falls, and trout streams."

Mr. Ronan, the writer of the above, is an old Boston printer, and his parents now live in the neighboring town of Malden. He was appointed Indian Agent of the Flatheads about two years ago, through the recommendation of the Jesuit Missionaries and the influence of his former business partner, Hon. Martin Maginnis, member of Congress for Montana Territory. He has given complete satisfaction to the government of the Indians under his charge, and if all of the Indian agents were like him, we would hear very little about Indian disturbances. He says:— "No doubt your reading of 'Indian rings' and thieving agents gives you the idea that it is hard for human nature to withstand the temptation of becoming a public robber, but make your mind easy on that score. I came into the office with clean hands, and with clean hands shall I go out. The conscientious scruples instilled into my mind in childhood by my good old parents, and the teaching of our grand old religion will prevent me, with God's help, from indulging in any such transactions."

Mr. Ronan, or Mayor [sic] Ronan, as he is now titled, has led an eventful life for the past fourteen years in the Rocky Mountains, and is thoroughly qualified for the responsible position he now holds. He has been journalist, miner, hunter, city marshal and farmer at different times, and in all positions has won the respect of every honest man.

October 14, 1878

U.S. Office of Indian Affairs, "Letters Received by the Office of Indian Affairs, 1824-1880," National Archives Microfilm Publication M234, reel 511, frames 775-776.

> In this letter, Ronan identified the traders near the agency at Jocko. Other traders operated elsewhere on the reservation.

Flathead Agency, M.T.
October 14th, 1878

To the
Hon. Commissioner of Indian Affairs
Washington, D.C.
Sir:
In compliance with Circular No. 24, Sept. 20th, 1878, I have the honor to state that the traders at this Agency are as follows: Telesphore Jacques Demers; White — Store a short distance from Agency buildings; Date of license July 29th, 1878. License granted by the Hon. Secretary of the Interior.

Duncan McDonald, Halfbreed — Store a short distance (about one-quarter of a mile) from the Agency buildings. No license. Authority granted is such as is given to one Indian to trade with another.

Very respectfully
Your obdt servt,
Peter Ronan
U.S. Ind. Agent.

November 1, 1878

The Weekly Missoulian, *November 1, 1878, page 2, col. 4.*

The original report of trouble between Mrs. McCabe and a party of unnamed Indians at her "station" thirteen miles west of Frenchtown appeared in *The Weekly Missoulian*.[16] Frenchtown was on the traditional Indian travel route between Montana and eastern Washington which became a major transportation corridor for the white settlers.

Mrs. Annie McCabe was a white Frenchtown resident who came to Montana in 1864. She was described as "a popular and successful teacher." In 1879, she married Archie McPhail and moved to the mining camp, New Chicago, near Drummond. They had three children.[17] No information was found about Camile, but Charloaine appeared later in Ronan's letters. In August 1885, he had a farm in Mission Valley and he served as a tribal judge in 1889.[18]

Commendably Prompt Action.

The people of this region can congratulate themselves that there is an agent at the head of affairs in this county, who is solicitous for the security and peace of the inhabitants of this section. It has transpired that the Indians who perpetrated the outrage at Mrs. McCabe's last week were Lower Calispels. They had been hunting in the vicinity for some time. They are of the insolent band which makes Horse Plains anything but a desirable place to live. We trust that matters will be so shaped that these vagabonds will be taught that they cannot remain in Missoula county unless they behave themselves and become subject to the agent and chiefs upon the reservation. It is as proper that that [sic] this should be so as that no foreign people should come into this country with an allegiance to some outside power. A private letter from Agent Ronan has this to say in regard to the matter:

"Having noticed in the last issue of your paper an account of the distardly [i.e., dastardly] outrage perpetrated by Indians upon Mrs. McCabe and her daughter at their ranch some thirteen miles below Frenchtown, and fearing that the crime might have been committed by Indians from this reservation, I proceeded to Chief Michell's house and made a statement to him of the facts.

The chief assured me that there are none of his people encamped in the vicinity of Missoula except two families, namely, that of "Camile" and "Charloaine," both of whom are considered among the very best Indians of the tribes, neither of whom, or any member of their families would be capable of committing any such an outrage. The lower Calispels, who live and roam from the Columbia river up to Horse Plains and to Frenchtown, and who are in no way under restraint of the chiefs or agent of this reservation, he think committed the crime, and he has agreed to do all in his power to ferret out the perpetrators and help to bring them to justice. If it should turn out that the Indians belong here, you may rest assured I will do all in my power to secure them to justice."

November 27, 1878
U.S. Office of Indian Affairs, "Letters Received by the Office of Indian Affairs, 1824-1880," National Archives Microfilm Publication M234, reel 511, frames 797-803.

By 1878 intertribal competition for the shrinking buffalo herds on the plains was becoming intense, and unsuccessful hunts were more frequent.

Flathead Agency, M.T.
November 27th, 1878

To the
Hon. Commissioner of Indian Affairs
Washington, D.C.
Sir:
I have to report that the band of Indians who left this reservation, in charge of André, the efficient chief of reservation police, for the purpose of securing a supply of meat for winter use, by hunting buffalo in the north, across the British line, are reported to me to be returning home without having secured any game, and report that upon arriving in the Buffalo Country, word was sent them by the Blackfeet and Assinaboines to return to their own country and not to attempt to kill buffalo on their range, unless they were prepared for war. André wisely concluded not to plunge his people into war for the sake of a few buffaloe, and turned back. I consider it a fortunate circumstance for the Indians that their hunting expedition was a failure as it deter[s] them from going out next season, and have a tendency to make them more devoted to the care of their stock and crops in the future; but unless I can relieve them there will be some suffering for the want of meat, and I would respectfully ask permission to purchase for them the beef and flour mentioned on the inclosed estimate for general distribution during the holidays.

A surplus of flour has been raised this year by the Indians of this reservation were it equally divided among them; but while the thrifty ones who remained at home will have flour and meat in abundance, the warriors and hunters will suffer unless relieved; besides, a distribution of flour and meat when the Indians are all gathered at the Mission on Christmas or New Years is as much looked for by the poorer Indians as the coming of the holidays, as, I am informed, it has been the uniform custom of my predecessors to make a distribution among them at that time.

Very respectfully,
Your obdt servt,
Peter Ronan
U.S. Indian Agent.

Enclosed is an "Estimate of Indian Supplies, &c." for $480 to cover the cost of 6000 lbs of beef at 4 cents a pound and 6000# of flour at 4 cents a pound.

December 10, 1878

U.S. Office of Indian Affairs, "Letters Received by the Office of Indian Affairs, 1824-1880," National Archives Microfilm Publication M234, reel 511, frames 812-814.

This is another example of local purchases by the Flathead Agency. Baptiste Eneas was Iroquois/Kootenai and lived at the foot of Flathead Lake. He farmed and operated a ferry across the Flathead River near the site of Polson.[19] See also Ronan letter of December 14, 1878.

Flathead Agency, M.T.
December 10th, 1878

To the
Hon. Commissioner of Indian Affairs
Washington, D.C.

Sir:

I have the honor to transmit herewith invoice of 1248 lbs. of white clay purchased by me this day for the purpose of white washing the out and insides of the Agency buildings.

The buildings are very much in need of a coat of white-wash as they have never received any since they were erected and this white-clay, a natural product of the reservation is much superior for the purpose and cheaper than the lime to be procured in this Territory. I respectfully request that you authorize the purchase.

Your obedient servant
Peter Ronan
U.S. Ind. Agent

Enclosed is an invoice for 6 sacks, 1248 lbs. white clay at 3 cents per lb. to Babtiste Eneas for $37.44.

December 14, 1878

U.S. Office of Indian Affairs, "Letters Received by the Office of Indian Affairs, 1824-1880," National Archives Microfilm Publication M234, reel 511, frames 815-817.

Flathead Agency, M.T.
December 14th, 1878

To the
Hon. Commissioner of Indian Affairs
Washington, D.C.

Sir:

With this letter I take the liberty of forwarding to you a small bag containing sample of wheat grown on this reservation at the foot of the Flathead Lake, by a full blood Indian named Baptiste Eneas. The land planted by the Indian produced sixty bushels of wheat to the acre, of which the sample forwarded is a specimen. No irrigation whatever was required as the mist from the Lake furnished the necessary moisture for the growth of produce of all Kinds.

I also transmit to you sample of a formation found in the bed of a lake now dried up, which, when mixed to consistency of starch with flour and water, makes a most brilliant white-wash, far superior to lime, as it will not rub off, and seems to stand the weather better. I have procured a supply of it and intend to whiten all the Agency buildings, which look gloomy and dingy at present. The white-washing of the buildings, I think, will have the effect of bringing the material into notice and give the Indians of the reservation a source of employment and revenue, by digging it out and furnishing to pur-chasers in the neighboring towns.

Very respectfully,
Your obdt. servt.
Peter Ronan
U.S. Ind. Agent

December 28, 1878
U.S. Office of Indian Affairs, "Letters Received by the Office of Indian Affairs, 1824-1880," National Archives Microfilm Publication M234, reel 515, frames 12-14.

In this letter and one dated February 5, 1879, Ronan pleaded to be able to employ Baptiste Matt, a good worker who in 1878 had a legal problem in the Bitterroot Valley resulting from a personal feud. Ronan's arguments did not sway the Indian Office clerks and Matt lost his job.[20] John Baptiste Matt was born in 1849 to a white blacksmith and a Blackfoot woman, Louis and Teresa Matt. The family was adopted into the Bitterroot Salish tribe and lived in Stevensville for many years. Matt married a mixed blood lady and they had eleven children. In 1889 he killed Benoit or Seven Pipes, but the court decided the killing was in self-defense. Between 1894 and 1896 he was an Indian policeman on the Flathead Reservation.[21] Judge Hiram Knowles, from Maine, was a judge on the Montana Territory Supreme Court in 1878. In 1890 he was appointed to the U.S. District Court. He also spent many years in private legal practice.[22]

Flathead Agency, M.T.
December 28th, 1878

To the
Hon. Commissioner of Indian Affairs
Washington, D.C.
Sir:
I have the honor to lay before you the following facts:
Baptiste Matte, the gunsmith at this Agency was indicted and tried before the United States Court at the last session at Missoula for trading liquor to Indians in the Bitter Root Valley some two years previous to his employment at this Agency and found guilty. The jury refused to bring in a verdict in the case unless the judge ([Hiram] Knowles) would allow them to fix the penalty; they fin[e]d him $100.00 and costs, and he was sentenced to one day in the Penitentiary. This is the lowest possible punishment under the law. The judge, jury and people of the county condemn the prosecution as a piece of petty revenge on the part of the prosecuting witness for some quarrel had between Baptiste Matte and said Witness.

Matte is a sober, industrious man and good mechanic. He is married to a Flathead woman and has a large family to whose support his salary is devoted. I may say I have no better workman at the Agency. Upon his conviction he immediately paid his fine and, placing a man to fulfil his duties here, proceeded to Deer Lodge and served out his sentence of one day's confinement in the Penitentiary. Since his return I have continued him in service as I feel that his prosecution was unwarranted. Judge Knowles himself stated to me that he was sure that the charge was only brought against him (Matte) to gratify the petty spite of the prosecuting witness, and, if necessary, I can procure a certificate to this effect from the Judge.

I request that my action be approved and that said Matte be continued in service.

Very respectfully,
Your obdt. servt.
Peter Ronan
U.S. Ind. Agent

December 30, 1878
U.S. Office of Indian Affairs, "Letters Received by the Office of Indian Affairs, 1824-1880," National Archives Microfilm Publication M234, reel 515, frames 15-28.

> In this report on Indian-white conflict in the Horse Plains area west of the reservation, Ronan was able to secure testimony and letters giving two sides of the story. Elize's account of working with the white man named John suggests mutually profitable cooperation until John sold his claim to James Laughlin and failed to inform Laughlin of Elize's interest in the ranch. Cultural differences, translation problems, and verbal agreements conspired to complicate relations between the parties and leave the agent a Gordian knot to unravel. Instead of trying to figure out who was right and wrong, Ronan punted and suggested the Missoula County courts sort out the conflict. No record has been found of how the case of Louie Cultis-toe and his mother Elize was resolved.
>
> James Laughlin came to Montana in 1864. In 1870, he was a butcher at Cedar Junction near Superior. In 1876 his place at Horse Plains was called "attractive and well-improved," and in 1884 he and his eldest son, Denver, were raising and selling vegetables in the Thompson Falls area.[23]

Flathead Agency, M.T.
December 30th, 1878

To the
Hon. Commissioner of Indian Affairs
Washington, D.C.
    Sir:
    I have the honor to communicate the following correspondence, and the result of my investigation, together with suggestions in connection with the affair:

Missoula City, Dec. 9th.
    Agent Ronan,
        Dear Sir:
        I have been informed by several parties that the Indians that roam between the Agency and Horse Plains, have broken open my house, and taken possession of my ranche at Horse Plains, and used and destroyed a lot of vegetables I had put away there, and other plunder that I had left there. I had made arrangements with Duncan McDonald to take the place, and a day or so ago I received a letter from him (Duncan) that he started down to the ranche and only got as far as the crossing of the Pend d'Oreille river, and the Indian known as Louis

Cultis-toe told him he would neither let Indian or whiteman go on the Ranche as it belonged to him. About a year ago his mother, old Mrs. Cultis-toe, wanted to build a house there to put her grub or Camas in and I gave her permission to build some distance from my house, and even gave her harness and tools to build with, and now he acts in this way. I hope you will look after this Indian or Indians, and if you cannot do anything I will take the matter in my own hands, and protect my rights and will find plenty friends to help me.

(sgd) James Laughlin.

The foregoing letter did not reach me for some ten days after it was written, owing to the fact that it remained in the coat pocket of the carrier, and in the mean time I received the following from the same party:

Missoula, Dec. 21st, 1878

Agent Ronan,

Dear Sir:

I wrote you a letter some time ago in regard to the Indians that had taken possession of my ranche at Horse Plains, not Knowing whether or not you received it I here write you a few lines as I just have been talking to Mr. Duncan McDonald, and also some others, and I understand the Indians have completely destroyed almost everything on the ranche. When I left Horse Plains I left my ranche in possession of Mr. Tranum, for I was so annoyed by the Indians that I could not stay there in peace, and as Mr. Tranum changed his mind and left there, as I was about to sell or trade the ranche to an Indian by the name of McSims, and in the mean time Louie Cultistoe went to him and told him I owed his mother some wheat, which is a falsehood for an excuse to steal and plunder. When Mr. Tranum went back this Louie Indian had keys and unlocked my door and divided up with other Indians my potatoes and other things, to get those Indians to help him hold my ranche — he is the meanest Indian in that tribe. I have been annoyed and lost more by him than any other Indian. He has camped in my pasture which was well fenced when I forbid him to, and many such instances I could name which others could tell you, I paid three hundred and fifty dollars for the ranche with but few improvements on it, and have worked on it for 6 years, and now for a lazy Indian to take it from me, it is more than I can tolerate, I send this by D. McDonald. If there is not something done I have friends enough to go with me, and I'll surely protect my rights, as I have plenty witnesses who have seen what him and his band have done.

(Sgd) James Laughlin

On Friday, December 27th I summoned those Horse Plains Indians to the Agency, although they live and have what they call their home at Horse Plains, outside of the reservation and claim "Petal" or "Victor," Chief of the Lower Kalispels as their Chief, who resides in Washington Territory; and after having had carefully interpreted to them the charges of James Laughlin as contained in the foregoing letter, Elize, Loui Cultis-toe's mother, made the following statement:

"A number of years ago a whiteman called John came to the Horse Plains, where I lived, and fenced in the land that I claimed — he did all the work — and when the fence was done he took me into the field, made a mark and said one-half is yours and one half is mine — he gave me my choice of the division — John plowed up a portion of the field, and had no seed to sow on his share. I had wheat enough to plant all the plowed land. John sowed the wheat and told me I could go off with my people whereever they went, and to come back at harvest time and help gather the crop, and it would be then taken to the mill and made into flour and after the flour was brought home I could get half. I went back at harvest time and John told me as there was not much wheat it would be better to keep it for seed and sow it all in the spring, when he would plow up a bigger piece of land and sow it all with our wheat and that I would have half the crop. When the second crop was raised John advised me to let the division of the wheat go until the next season, and said the third yield would give us both plenty. I agreed to it, and after the crop was in went out to pick and dry berries for winter. I came back to help to harvest and divide our produce but did not find John — he was gone — but there was a whiteman there with a family. This man was Laughlin. I asked him where John was, he told me John got a letter and was gone to see his mother. I asked if John left any word for me. Laughlin said no. I told Laughlin that half the growing crop was mine. He told me I lied. I went to a white neighbor named McMiller, who carried the mail last winter, and who lives at Horse Plains now, and who knows all about my trade with John, and I told him what Laughlin said. McMiller told me to keep quiet, not to take anything away, and if Laughlin did not give me anything to leave it to some good man and he thought Laughlin would do right with me. I never got my wheat. That is all I have to say."

Louie Cultis-toe, son of Elize, said:

"I was out hunting in the summer and when I came back, I found Laughlin had gone away from his place, and heard he moved away from Horse Plains. I found this old man Se-lah, and my mother camped near the house. The doors were open and I went in. There was nothing in the house except some potatoes in a cellar. As the house was open I thought the potatoes would be taken, and my people blamed for it, and I dug a hole away from the house and covered them up and they are there yet. I met Duncan McDonald at McSims and told him I took the potatoes and hid them, and who ever owned them could come to me and I would show him where they were. I had some talk with Duncan who claimed the ranche. I told him that half of it rightfully belonged to my mother, and that half of the crop which was growing when Laughlin came there was hers but she never got anything. Duncan said the ranche was his, and he wanted to send his father-in-law there to live, but the old man did not want to go; he also said he wanted his bother-in-law to go but he would not go. I then told Duncan he need not send anyone there, as I thought I had more right to it than anyone else if Laughlin left it. When I said I owned the house, Duncan said, 'all right; that is all I want to know.' I told Duncan in our talk that I thought I had a better right to it than anybody else, if Laughlin left it, because the first whiteman who lived there cheated my mother out of her wheat. Duncan said, 'how much wheat does your mother claim?' I said, 'you can figure; he owes her for half the crop for three years, and I think that is worth the whole of the field.' — But I will say no more — my mother is old and poor — if I do not protect her who will? I tell the truth; she tells the truth. I leave it to the whiteman to do her Justice. Any body who comes there to live with your knowledge will not be molested by me because I think you will tell the truth about it as we have told you. I am done."

Agent to Se-lah: — "Louis Tranum complains that you took his gun out of Laughlin's house."

Selah: — "I did, and have it safe for him. Tranum lives at Horse Plains, and as the house was open I thought the gun would be stolen. I took it and left it at a whiteman's house and told the whiteman to give it to Tranum."

Upon this evidence I wrote the following letter to Mr. Laughlin:

Flathead Agency, M.T.
December 28th, 1878.

Mr. James Laughlin,
Missoula,
Missoula Co., M.T.

Sir:

Your letter of Dec 9th, after a delay of some ten days came to hand and in the mean-time I received your letter of Dec 21st, and immediately took measures to investigate the charges preferred by you against Loui Cultis-toe, an Indian claiming his home at Horse Plains. The band of Indians who claim Horse Plains and of which Cultis-toe and his mother are members are a fragment of "Petals" or "Victors" tribe of Lower Kalispel Indians who have their head-quarters on the Pend d'Oreille river in Washington Territory and do not claim this Agent or any chief of this reservation as having jurisdiction over them. It is my opinion that as you pay taxes in Missoula County which is a regularly organized county of Montana, and a roaming Indian over whom the Agent can claim no control because he claims no allegiance to the chiefs of this reservation, is amenable to the laws of the Territory, and that you should regularly proceed against him according to the statutes; however, this is but my own opinion. I have laid your Complaint and also the statement of Cultis-toe and his mother before the Hon. Com. of Indian Affairs, and asked instructions as to whom this business properly belongs. In the mean time, if yourself or any agent you may designate will call upon me I will put you in possession of the ranche and see that you will not be molested by Indians until I am properly informed as to the modes of proceedure.

Yours respectfully,
(Sgd) Peter Ronan.
U.S. Ind. Agt.

In connection with all of the forgoing, I would respectfully call the attention of the Hon. Commissioner of Indian Affairs to Communication "C" dated Office Indian Affairs, Oct. 10th, 1877, and my reply thereto, dated at this office December 10th, 1877; also to my report in connection with the matter then brought before me, dated January 2d, 1877 [sic, 1878].

In reviewing the whole matter it will be seen that a few families of white settlers not over six in number have taken up ranches at Horse Plains, outside of the western boundaries of the Jocko Reservation; that a fragment of a band of Indians belonging to "Petals" or "Victors" tribe of Lower Kalispels, who have their home on the Pend d'Oreilles river, claim a right to some of the land occupied by the whites — that the conflicting claims engender bad feelings, which may result some time in the near future, in precipitating a fight which may result in an Indian war. The settlers look to me for protection against the Indians — while the Indians naturally resort to me with their complaints against the whites, and as the settlement is outside of the limits of the reserve and inside of the boundaries of an organized county, to the revenues of which the settlers contribute by the annual levy of tax; and, also, as the Indians are a fragment of a band claiming the Chieftainship of a chief who has his home in Washington Territory, I have expressed the opinion that their intricate disputes on questions of land and other annoying disputes properly belong in the Territorial courts; unless Horse Plains be declared a portion of this reservation, the settlers indemnified for their improvements, and this band either compelled to come under the Control of this Agency and acknowledge the authority of the proper chiefs of the reservation or move off to the home of their own chief in Washington Territory. All of which I respectfully submit with the hope that I may be fully and plainly instructed in the matter, so that I can take prompt and efficient action or give intelligent instructions to the disputants.

Very respectfully,
Your obedient servant,
Peter Ronan
U.S. Ind. Agent

A view of St. Ignatius Mission in 1878.
Jesuit Oregon Province Archives, Gonzaga University,
Spokane, Washington, negative 114.4.08c

1879

January 27, 1879
U.S. Office of Indian Affairs, "Letters Received by the Office of Indian Affairs, 1824-1880," National Archives Microfilm Publication M234, reel 514, frames 646-656. No date on endorsement, but received by Office of Indian Affairs on January 27, 1879.

> Ronan's description of Salish and Kootenai culture as "barboruous habits" show that even though he was able to work with tribal members, he still saw the world through the bigotry of nineteenth century white American values.

Respectfully referred to the Hon Com of Indian Affairs. I think some measures ought to be at once taken for the relief of the Flathead & other Confederated tribes of Indians.

Respectfully
Martin Maginnis
Delegate

Letter enclosed with above endorsement:

Flathead Agency, M.T.
December 5th, 1878

Hon. M. Maginnis,
Washington, D.C.
Dear Friend:

Inclosed you will find copy of a report I made to the Commissioner of Indian Affairs in regard to the Bitter Root land question. I concluded to make a copy and send it to you, as you will find in it as truthful and explicit a narrative of the affair as I could furnish, and as it may come before Congress for legislation I thought the inclosed would give you an intelligent view of the case. I do not understand the official etiquette of furnishing copies of reports from this office, but of course you will know how to use it.

I would also call your attention to the fact that the provisions of the treaty between the Flatheads, Kootenais and Pen d'Orielles, expire after January, 1879, and I trust you will do all in your power to secure to them another appropriation. If their appropriations are withdrawn and they are turned adrift the most unfortunate results are sure to follow.

The Indians of this reservation are only just beginning to realize and appreciate the benefit of their schools, shops and mills, and are fast turning their attention to stock raising and farming, and to withdraw the fostering care of the Government would be to plunge them back into their old and barboruous habits. I trust you will give this matter your earnest attention.

I may not be here long as Agent, but since coming among them I have taken a great interest in their welfare and I sincerely trust you will sharply look out for these Indians as they are surely deserving above all others in our Territory.

With regard to the removal of the Agency to the Mission, you can use your own judgement, but, to tell you the truth, I think the money it would cost would be better expended in buying them agricultural implements and let the Agency buildings rest where they are.

Very respectfully,
Peter Ronan
U.S. Ind. Agent

Enclosed is a copy of the August 20, 1878a, letter from Ronan to the Commissioner of Indian Affairs regarding the Bitter Root Valley allotments which was printed above. Action notations are "Note & file" and "See estimates — Flathead Agency."

February 5, 1879
U.S. Office of Indian Affairs, "Letters Received by the Office of Indian Affairs, 1824-1880," National Archives Microfilm Publication M234, reel 515, frames 69-73.

> The action notation on this letter is "Filed," which means no action was taken. See also Ronan's December 28, 1878, letter regarding Baptiste Matt's legal difficulties.

Flathead Agency, M.T.
February 5th, 1879

To the
Hon. Commissioner of Indian Affairs,
Washington, D.C.

Sir:

Referring to your letter "A Montana R 26 1879." I would state that in accordance with instructions therein contained, I have discharged from service at this Agency Baptiste Matt, and nominated another man to fill his position; and in connection therewith I take the liberty of making this statement in regard to the circumstances which led to the indictment and trial of Matt, in the hope that mercy tempered with Justice may be shown the man, and that I may again be empowered by you to give him employment; and in making the statement I have no other object in view than the well-being of every family connected with this Agency.

Baptiste Matt is of Canadian extraction, the son of a blacksmith and gunsmith brought to this country thirty years ago by the Hudson Bay Company. He worked with his father until of age when he married a Flathead woman and settled in the Bitter Root valley. The Bitter Root valley not being considered an Indian country, is thickly settled with whites, and ardent spirits are sold and vended there among the whites, there being several public houses in the valley. Some two years before the employment and removal of Matt and his family to this reservation (at that time being a man who occasionally drank) Matt had a bottle of liquor in his pocket, and meeting a neighbor, he proffered him a drink from the bottle, and in the mean time a man of Indian blood came up to whom Matt ignorantly passed the bottle, and who drank from it. Two years after the circumstance, when Matt became a temperate man, removed his family to this reservation and received employment here, from the wages of which he was making his family comfortable, the Bitter Root neighbor whom he treated from the bottle remembered the circumstance of a man of Indian blood having also drank from the same bottle, and having had a quarrel with Matt his conscience suddenly impelled him to go before the Grand Jury and prefer a charge of giving whisky to Indians, which resulted in the manner as narrated in my letter of December 28th, 1878.

It has been my policy, since assuming charge of this Agency, to employ no man known to be addicted to drinking, and to punish by the heavy hand of the law any person who might attempt to bring ardent spirits upon the reservation;

but in this transgression of Matt which occurred outside of an Indian country, and at a time long previous to his employment here, and before he knew the benefit of a temperate life; and also far as education is concerned being almost as ignorant as the Indians, having been born among them. I looked upon his case with leniency, and trust that the Honorable Commissioner, will appreciate my motives in asking to reinstate this man, in order to secure happiness and comfort for his large family of Flathead Indian children.

Very respectfully,
Your obedt. servt.
Peter Ronan
U.S. Ind. Agent

February 24, 1879
U.S. Office of Indian Affairs, "Letters Received by the Office of Indian Affairs, 1824-1880," National Archives Microfilm Publication M234, reel 515, frames 83-85.

Ronan purchased 1,000 pounds of oats from Espaniole Finley, a 19 year old tribal member farmer. In 1885 an Indian inspector reported that in 1884 he had 160 acres of land fenced and harvested 800 bushels of grain.[1] The 1888 Flathead Reservation census had Española Finley, age 28, living with his wife, Sophy, and two sons and a daughter between the ages of 6 and 1 year old.[2] No further information was found about Espaniole Finley.

Flathead Agency, M.T.
February 24th, 1879

To the
Hon. Commissioner of Indian Affairs,
Washington, D.C.
    Sir:
    I have the honor to forward herewith invoice of 1000 lbs. of oats purchased by me in open market without special authority. The supply of oats on hand being very small and the necessity for feeding for some time yet, is my reason for making the purchase. I respectfully ask that my action be approved.

Your obedient servant,
Peter Ronan
U.S. Ind. Agent

Enclosed is an invoice made out to Espaniole Finley for 1000 lbs. oats at @ 2 cents per pound, total $20.00.

March 3, 1879a
U.S. Office of Indian Affairs, "Letters Received by the Office of Indian Affairs, 1824-1880," National Archives Microfilm Publication M234, reel 515, frames 97-104.

The white legal system in 1879 considered the Bitterroot Salish "non-treaty" Indians as a consequence of the 1872 Garfield agreement. The Bitterroot Salish, however, understood that the provisions of the 1855 Hellgate Treaty entitled them to live in the Bitterroot Valley as a tribal community.

    Patrick "Pishena" Finley was the son of a French-Canadian father and a Chippewa Indian mother. He worked for many years as a trapper and hunter for the Hudson's Bay Company. In 1871, he had a farm in the Jocko Valley and lost his crop to hail. His entry in the Book of Deaths at Frenchtown says he was 90 years old when he died suddenly at Frenchtown.[3]

Flathead Agency,
March 3d, 1879

To the
Hon. Commissioner of Indian Affairs,
Washington, D.C.

Sir:

Referring to letter from your office ("C Montana No 345 '79") I would state that no band of Indians from this reservation are or have been away from here, to my knowledge, since last September, with exception of about twenty lodges of Pend d'Oreilles, under "Big Canoe," who left here last fall to hunt buffalo, with my permission, and the permission of the commanding officer of the District of Montana, who furnished them a proper military escort. And as evidence of the discipline I try to exercise over those bands even while under charge of a military escort, I herewith enclose copy of letter sent to Big Canoe by Chief Michel, at my suggestion, and Agent [John] Young's reply thereto. In accordance with instructions given in Office Circular of December 23d, 1878, I notified my Indians that "they must confine their movements wholly within the limits of their reservation and that under no pretext will they be permitted to cease the same without a special permit in writing from the agent approved by your Office," and in no case do I hear of those orders having been violated, except in cases of u[n]restrainable gamblers who seek the neighboring towns to indulge in whiskey-drinking and gaming, but who are immediately brought back to the reservation by Indian police, when the fact of their absence becomes known to me.

As to the "non-treaty" Bitter Root valley Flatheads, I have no intercourse with them as they hold no communication with the Jocko Reservation, and I would suggest that the Commanding officer at Fort Missoula is the proper person to put them under restraint in regard to leaving the Bitter Root valley for the purpose of hunting, as the Bitter Root valley is not considered an Indian Country and is located a long distance from this reservation and does not come under the jurisdiction of this Agency; and also, the Bitter Root Valley Indians are designated as "non treaty Indians" and so consider themselves.

Very respectfully,
Your obedient servant,
Peter Ronan
U.S. Ind. Agent

First Enclosure:

Flathead Agency
Jan. 29, 1879

Big Canoe

Friend I send you this letter to tell you the news from our Country.

Baptist Maringo died at New Years. Margarette Chem-Che-Na — the mother of Enyas Francois' wife died at the Mission. Thomas brother of Ee-Cheite, died at the Mission two days after Christmas. The son of old Sela, also died at the Mission about Christmas. Before Christmas I organized my policemen again, but one of the best of them died about New Years, Pe-Ell-Sa-kee which gives us great sorrow. The girl who was at school and who married Paul from Colville, died about Christmas. Old Patrick or Pishena Finley died at Frenchtown about New Years. Mary the wife of Michael from Colville died at the Mission since Christmas. "Chit-aste" Partee and and [sic] Old Andra, were both very sick but are now well. Tell our people not to be afraid about their cattle. We had some snow and cold weather but it is now warm and the snow is nearly all gone. The cattle did not suffer for grass. This all the news I have now. When you get this letter send one back to me and give me all the news about my people and anything else that you think I would like to hear.

Now Big Canoe and Enyas and Te-mal-tee Clom-Nah, I want you to see that you do not allow any of my people who are with you to steel [sic] any horses either from white men or from Indians, for if any stolen horses are brought here to this reservation we will arrest the thieves and send the horses back. See that none of my people commit depredations against any-one.

I remain your Chief
Michael his X mark
Chief Pend 'd Orelles

Second Enclosure:

Blackfeet Agency, M.T.
February 18, 1879

Peter Ronan, Esq.
U.S. Indian Agent
Flathead Agency, M.T.

Dear Sirs:

I am in receipt of your favor of the 1st inst. enclosing a letter for "Big Canoe."

I do not Know his present whereabouts, but will make inquiries of my Indians as they come in from the hunt, and endeavor to have him come here for his letter. Should he desire to send a reply, I will take pleasure in forwarding it to you.

Very Respectfully
John Young
U.S. Indian Agent.

March 3, 1879b

U.S. Office of Indian Affairs, "Letters Received by the Office of Indian Affairs, 1824-1880," National Archives Microfilm Publication M234, reel 515, frames 108-110.

This letter illustrates Ronan's attempt to cope with unrealistic orders from Washington, D.C. Ronan was not in a position to force tribal members to remain on the reservation and give up their treaty-guaranteed right to hunt buffalo.

Flathead Agency, M.T.
March 3d, 1879

To the
Hon. Commissioner of Indian Affairs,
Washington, D.C.

Sir:

In reference to office circular of December 23d, 1878, I would respectfully report to the Hon. Commissioner, that it has been the habit of a small portion of the Indians of this reservation every spring and fall to seek the buffalo country for the purpose of hunting. One route leads through a thickly settled portion of Montana, while the other route is by the head of the Flathead Lake, and leads to the buffaloe country without passing through any country inhabited by white settlers. Now, it will impose a great hardship, and to the Indian mind, a great wrong upon them, by prohibiting them from going out to hunt the buffalo, and I would respectfully ask that I be empowered to issue such band as may wish to go by the Northern route, under charge of an escort of Indian police of my own choice, a special permit in writing to do so.

The hunting parties are growing less every year as the Indians are brought to see the great benefits that accrue to those who remain at home and take care of their farms and stock, and but a short time will elapse until the habit will entirely cease. I desire permission therefore, to allow the Indians to leave the reservation, when, in my Judgement I deem it either necessary or Judicious, to issue a permit, with proper guard, and restrictions.

Very respectfully,
Your obedient servant,
Peter Ronan
U.S. Ind. Agent

March 10, 1879

U.S. Office of Indian Affairs, "Letters Received by the Office of Indian Affairs, 1824-1880," National Archives Microfilm Publication M234, reel 515, frames 115-118.

The fallout in human suffering from the war between the Nez Perce and the U.S. Army was still impacting lives in 1879. Families were broken up and Nez Perce refugees were learning about the suffering of Joseph and the prisoners in Oklahoma. See also Ronan's letters of June 18, 1879, and August 23, 1879.

Flathead Agency, M.T.
March 10th, 1879

To the
Hon. Commissioner of Indian Affairs,
Washington, D.C.

Sir:

I would respectfully report that two Nez Perce women of Joseph's tribe, came to this Agency last fall, in a most destitute condition, and claimed my charity and protection. I provided for their wants at the time and am still doing so, from my private means as I have no supplies here for issue to Indians, none having been received from last year's requisition — their wants, however, are few, but I deemed their case a sad one and of sufficient importance to lay the matter before you, with the hope that something may be done to either restore them to their children and relatives, or make provision for their care, as they seem to be well-behaved and good women, of comely and neat appearance, and, I would judge to be from twenty-two to twenty-five years of age. I submitted the following querries to them, which I give with their answers:

"What is your name?" "Mean Sher." "To what tribe do you belong?" "To Joseph's tribe of the Nez Perces." "Was you with Joseph when he was captured?" "Yes; I was with him and the tribe all through the war, and when the fight commenced in which he was captured, I was watching the horses." "How did you escape?" "When the fight was going on I was afraid to go to Joseph's camp, and I took a good horse and fled to the Sioux, where White Bird went." "How did you come to this reservation?" "Eight of us ran away from White Bird's camp to try to get home to our country. When I got here I heard my husband was in jail at Fort Missoula." "Where is your husband now?" "He got away from the soldiers and I heard he went to Lapawai." "Have you any children?" "Yes, I have three." "Where are they now?" "They are with Chief Joseph, if they have not died." "Do you wish to go and see your children and live with them at Joseph's home?" "I am afraid; I would rather live here if I can."

To the second Nez Perce woman:

"What is your name?" "Tartermer." "Are you a Nez Perce?" "Yes, and I was married to a Nez Perce warrior." "Where is your husband now?" "He was killed at the battle of the Big Hole." "Have you any children?" "I have no children." "Would you like to go and live with your chief Joseph in his new home or would you like to go to the reservation at Lapawai?" "I am afraid to go anywhere. I would like to live here with these people."

In connection with this matter I would state that the fears of the women are exagerated by the stories told by half-breeds of the disease and suffering of Joseph's people in the Indian Territory, and I suppose the peace and quiet they have enjoyed for the past few months gives them a preference to reside here, but those fears can be easily eradicated, I think, by a proper explanation, and I therefore submit this report with the hope that some provision may be made for these two unfortunate women.

Your obedient servant,
Peter Ronan
U.S. Ind. Agent

March 29, 1879
U.S. Office of Indian Affairs, "Letters Received by the Office of Indian Affairs, 1824-1880," National Archives Microfilm Publication M234, reel 515, frames 136-139.

Flathead Agency
March 29, 1879

To the
Hon. Commissioner of Indian Affairs,
Washington, D.C.

Sir:

I wish to call your attention to my letter of March 3d, 1879 and the request therein made in regard to modification of Office Circular of December 23d, 1878 as to the issue of passes to Indians leaving the Reservation. As yet I have received no reply in regard to the matter, and as an exigency arose on the 26th inst., wherein I deemed it necessary and prudent to issue a pass, as the matter could not be delayed for reference to your office:

The following letter states the case:

Flathead Agency,
March 26, 1879,

H. L. Chipman
Major 3d Infantry
Commanding Fort Missoula
Sir:
The Flathead Chief "Arlee" of this Reservation learning that the Bitter Root Indians are returning from their hunt and that their horses are poor and giving out, sends out to-day a

band of fresh horses to assist those people to return home with the spoils of the chase. The following named Indians will have charge of the band of fresh horses going to meet the Bitter Root Indians, to whom I have given a pass, and who will deliver this letter to you. I trust you will also furnish them with a letter, which will show who they are and the nature of their business traveling with a large band of horses:

"Louison" "Louie Tin-Sa" "Enyas Lorette" and wife.

Very respectfully
Your obedient servant,
Peter Ronan
U.S. Ind. Agent

I trust that my action in this matter will meet with your approbation as I deemed it beneficial to the service, and a case which would admit of no delay.

Your obedient servant,
Peter Ronan
U.S. Ind. Agent

April 17, 1879
U.S. Office of Indian Affairs, "Letters Received by the Office of Indian Affairs, 1824-1880," National Archives Microfilm Publication M234, reel 515, frames 153-158.

See Ronan's letters of December 10, 1877, and January 2, 1878, for more information about the Lower Kalispel Indians in the Horse Plains area. Frenchtown was located on a traditional travel route between western Montana and eastern Washington.

Flathead Agency, M.T.
April 17th, 1879

To the
Hon. Commissioner of Indian Affairs,
Washington, D.C.

Sir:

In reply to your letter of March 27th, 1879 "C. Montana. M. 580. '79" and enclosure, I would state that at the time the depredations therein mentioned, were committed, I repaired to Frenchtown, and having investigated the matter, found that the perpetrators did not belong to this reservation but belonged to a band of vagrants from the Spokane and Columbia river country who yearly infest this part of the Country, gambling, drinking, and carrousing around the white settlements.

The Chiefs of the Flathead Reservation refuse to have anything to do with them, claiming that they do not belong to their people and are desirous that they be kept away from the Reservation, as, the[y] claim, they lead their people into bad habits.

In my communications I have frequently alluded to those Indians — particularly to a band who make their home occasionally at Horse Plains, a tract of land adjoining the Reservation, and who claim to belong to "Petalts" tribe of Lower Pend d'Oreilles. These Horse Plains Indians are far removed from their Chief, who resides in Washington Territory, and as they do not acknowledge the chiefs of this reservation, nor the authority of the Agent here, they are always a source of annoyance to the settlers. "Petalts" band, as I understand it, are Lower Pend d'Oreilles, and are attached to the Colville Agency. Until those detached bands are concentrated and compelled to reside at their reservation or Agency, complaints from settlers will never cease, as they will continue to be an eternal source of trouble. As for the Indians of this reservation, I again repeat they are contented, peacefully inclined, and are now generally engaged in putting in their crops and fencing their fields. There are, of course, a few wild, and disolute young men on the reservation, who occasionally visit the settlements and get into trouble — but no serious trouble has occurred from any reservation Indian since I have taken charge here. The bands of hunters who occasionally leave the reservation for game are another source of annoyance, as they can always trade their furs in the settlements for whiskey. One of those bands who left the reservation last fall, is still out, but I learn are on their return home — the party consists of only a few lodges and were under military escort. In accordance with your instructions I informed the chiefs that they must restrain their people from leaving their reservation for hunting or any other purpose; they have signified their willingness to do all in their power to keep their people home.

Inclosed you will find a communication signed by Mr. T. J. Demers, acknowledging his error in regard to the identity of the Indians complained of in his communication to Hon. M. Maginnis.

Very respectfully,
Your obedient servant,
Peter Ronan
U.S. Ind. Agent

Enclosure:

Frenchtown, M.T.
April 17th, 1879

The
Hon. Commissioner of Indian Affairs,
Washington, D.C.

Sir:

After due investigation and proof in the matter, I wish to state that in my complaint against certain Indian depredations, and threats made by them, in a communication to Hon. M. Maginnis, delegate from Montana, date March 5th, 1879, I was mistaken in the identity of the Indians. When I wrote the communication I was under the impression that the Indians in question properly belonged to the Flathead Agency, but I have since learned to my satisfaction that they were a band of wandering vagrants from the different bands and tribes of the Columbia river country, who do not acknowledge any authority over them by the agent or chiefs of the Flathead Reservation. I make this statement in Justice to the general good conduct and behavior of the tribes who properly belong to the Flathead reservation.

Very respectfully,
T. J. DeMers.

May 6, 1879
U.S. Office of Indian Affairs, "Letters Received by the Office of Indian Affairs, 1824-1880," National Archives Microfilm Publication M234, reel 515, frames 167-170.

On May 22, 1879, the Commissioner of Indian Affairs approved granting the permits to hunt buffalo.[4]

Flathead Agency, M.T.
May 6th, 1879

To the
Hon. Commissioner of Indian Affairs,
Washington, D.C.

Sir,

The Chiefs of this Reservation, namely "Michel" Chief of Pend d'Oreilles; "Arlee" Chief of Flatheads; and "Ignace" Chief of Kootenais, formally called upon me recently to urgently request permission from your Office to allow some of their young men to go Buffalo hunting, about the tenth of June, after their crops are all planted. The Chiefs state that as one of the incentatives [sic] to labor, in the early Spring, such as ploughing, harrowing, fencing, planting and sowing, was a promise which they (the Chiefs) gave that a certain number of their people could go hunting, while others remained to take care of the herds and crops. They also state that if this promise is not complied with on their part, that it will be impossible to prevent scattering bands from slipping away from the reservation, without Authority, and who, while under no restraint from Chiefs, or Police, or Military Authority are liable to commit excesses. The Chiefs themselves, say that they, — or at least two of them, will accompany the hunters and hold themselves responsible in every way for the good conduct of their people. In view of the fact that the Chiefs are doing all in their power to gradually induce their people to labor, as they show the example by toiling in the fields themselves, I do not think it would be judicious to refuse permission for them to go, or cause them to break their promise to the hunters, as the hunt is planned for recreation, almost the same as that of a pleasure excursion of the Whites; and I think in no event will it be likely to prove disadvantageous to the Indian Service.

Very Respectfully,
Your Obedient Servant,
Peter Ronan
U.S. Indian Agent

May 7, 1879

U.S. Office of Indian Affairs, "Letters Received by the Office of Indian Affairs, 1824-1880," National Archives Microfilm Publication M234, reel 515, frames 161-166.

Ronan struggled with orders from D.C., to prevent tribal members from leaving the reservation and worked with the chiefs and the U.S. Army to avoid conflict between Indians and white settlers off the reservation. Some of the white complaints about Indian people from various tribes camped near Missoula and the efforts of the chiefs to get them to return to their reservations were described in *The Weekly Missoulian*.[5]

The legality of ordering the Pend d'Oreille lodges to return to the reservation may have been questionable, but the presence of the soldiers from Fort Missoula made it effective. Ronan mentioned that the Pend d'Oreille lodges supported themselves doing odd jobs and occasional work for white residents of Missoula. In 1942, the legal scholar, Felix Cohen, found that, despite decades of Office of Indian Affairs policy, there never was any statutory basis for trying to confine Indian people to reservations.[6]

Mary Sabine Walking Coyote or Wuh-Wah was the Pend d'Oreille wife of Samuel Walking Coyote and mother of Joseph Attahe (Latatie) or Blanket Hawk, the Pend d'Oreille Indians responsible for taming and driving a small herd of buffalo calves to the Flathead Reservation in the late 1870s. In 1879 she was the widow of a white man and sold over 200 head of cattle, depositing the money in a Missoula bank for her children's education. About 1879 she was shot in the shoulder by her then husband while he was drunk. The injury caused her continuing trouble until she was operated on in St. Patrick Hospital in Missoula in 1891. See Ronan's February 27, 1892, letter about the case.[7]

Flathead Agency, M.T.
May 7th, 1879

To the
Hon. Commissioner of Indian Affairs,
Washington, D.C.

Sir:

In reference to circular letter C. from your Office, under date of December 23d, 1879 [sic, 1878], and instructions therein contained in regards to restriction of Indians wholly to their reservation, I wish to make the following report with a view that my action may meet with your approbation.

For the past fifteen years some eight lodges of Pend d'Oreilles have made their home and encampment in the Town of Missoula, where they made a living by doing odd jobs for Whites, and if left to themselves and their own exertions, were a harmless and industrious community of Indians; but every year renegade Spokanes, Umatillas, Colville, Lower Pend d'Oreilles and other Indians from the Lower Country, came up and infested the Towns, and generally made encampments with said eight lodges, who properly belonged to this reservation. The drinking, gambling and carrousals of the lower Country Indians would be reported in the local press, and as a matter of course, all excesses were laid at the door of the Indians of this reservation. Last week I ordered the eight lodges to the reservation, and also ordered all foreign Indians to their homes, and was assisted in the enforcement of the order by the Commanding Officer at Fort Missoula, who sent an Officer and Men to tell the Indians to break up their encampment and move, which they did without any difficulty. I would suggest that the military Authorities at Spokane Bridge and other Posts in that country be instructed not to allow those lower country Indians to come up to this country without proper passes and escort.

The Flatheads of the Jocko and the Bitter Root Valley visit each other often, and their social intercourse has a tendency of inducing the latter to remove here; in fact one large family has already done so this Spring. To prevent an occasional visit of Flatheads to their relatives in the Bitter Root Valley, would cause most bitter feelings in both Sections, and I have allowed two or three parties of women and Children to go under instructions to return in from five to ten days. Those visits are purely business, and social intercourse of relatives and friends, and in no way detrimental to the Indian Service.

There are also well to-do Indian Farmers on the reservation, who wish, like all other people to dispose of their surplus crops and stock to the best advantage, and if prevented from going to the Towns to do so, and to make purchases, will be left to the mercy of the Traders. I cite an instance to-day: "Sabin" a full blooded Pend d'Oreille woman, the widow of a white man, who lived on the reservation, made a sale of over two hundred head of surplus cattle, most of the proceeds of which she intends placing in some safe institution for the benefit and education of her child. To-day, she proceeded to Missoula to receive her money at the Bank and properly attend to her business in person. It will therefore be seen by Your Honor that although I have my share of worthless and trifling Indians under my charge, over whom it is well to draw a tight curb, I have thrifty, ambitious, honest Indians, to whom some freedom should be allowed in their movements and business transaction, and with this explanation, I trust, I may be allowed some discretion in issuing passes where in my judgement it would be detrimental to the Indian Service to refuse, or cause a delay of over thirty days to have the same approved at your Office.

Very Respectfully,
Your Obedient Servant,
Peter Ronan
U.S. Indian Agent

May 20, 1879
U.S. Office of Indian Affairs, "Letters Received by the Office of Indian Affairs, 1824-1880," National Archives Microfilm Publication M234, reel 515, frames 171-173.

Flathead Agency, M.T.
May 20th, 1879

Respectfully forwarded to the Hon. Commissioner of Indian Affairs, calling his attention to my letter dated May 6th, 1879, relative to this matter.

Peter Ronan
U.S. Indian Agent

Enclosed extract copy of letter:

Headquarters Fort Missoula M. T.
April 18th, 1879

To the Actg. Asst. Adjt. General
Hdqrs. Dist. of Montana
Fort Shaw M.T.
(Extract)
Sir:
Chiefs Arlee (Flathead) and Aeneas (Kootenais) belonging to the Flathead Agency desire to visit the buffalo country east of the mountains as soon as they have finished putting in their crops. They wish to go in one party which will consist of about 20 or 30 lodges. In view of the fact that these Indians are well behaved, and friendly to the whites, and are at emnity with the Sioux, I deem it proper to ask that the permission to go on the hunt be given them.
* * * * *

Your obedient servant
(Signed): H. L. Chipman
Major 3d Inf. Com'dg Post

First endorsement on letter:

Headqrs. Dept. of Dakota
Saint Paul Minn. May 2d, 1879

Respectfully returned to the Commanding Officer Fort Missoula. It is for the Indian Agents, and not for the military authorities to give permission to these Indians to visit the buffalo Country. If such permission be given, a small escort of troops may, if desirable, be sent with these Indians.

By Command of
Brigadier General Terry
(Sgd) Geo. D. Ruggles
Asst Adjt. General

Added note:

Headqrs. Fort Missoula M. T.
May 15, 1879.

Official copy respectfully furnished Major Peter Ronan, Agent Flathead Nation, for his information.

H. L. Chipman
Major 3d Infantry.
Commd'g Post.

June 18, 1879

U.S. Office of Indian Affairs, "Letters Received by the Office of Indian Affairs, 1824-1880," National Archives Microfilm Publication M234, reel 515, frames 177-179.

See also Ronan's letters of March 10, 1879, and August 23, 1879, for similar cases.

Flathead Agency, M.T.
June 18, 1879

Hon. Commissioner Indian Affairs
Washington, D.C.
    Sir:
    Referring to office letter "M Idaho No. 1107, '79" bearing date of May 22d '79, referring to the proper steps to be taken in regard to two Nez Perce women, at this reservation, I would state that the women in question are now across the Flathead lake, on a distant portion of the reservation with a party of Pend d'Orielles, gathering camas, and owing to high water it would be difficult for me to communicate with them. I would also state that from previous conversations with said women, I am confident that they will not remove to the Indian Territory unless made prisoners of and enforced to, as a bitter prejudice has been inculcated into the Indian mind by half breeds and others against the Indian Territory, it being stated among other things that more than half of Joseph's people have died since the removal of his tribe to that country. However, soon, as I can hold communication with them I will report their decission and ask for instructions.

Very respectfully
Your obedient servt
Peter Ronan
U.S. Indian Agent

July 9, 1879

The New North-West *(Deer Lodge, Mont.), July 18, 1879, page 3, col. 2.*

Conflicting versions of the Lincoln Gulch incident were published in local newspapers.[8] Ronan related the Indian side of the story to white Montanans in a newspaper article,[9] and Duncan McDonald wrote a plea for justice for the Indian victim.[10] According to a report in the Deer Lodge newspaper, charges were brought against the white man accused of murdering the Indian, but the Indian witnesses failed to show up in court even after the local sheriff made a special trip to the reservation to convince them to appear. The case against the white man was dismissed.[11]

An Indian Row.

One White Man Killed and Another Wounded — An Indian Also Murdered.

Some miners from the Whippoorwill District were on a fishing excursion to the Big Blackfoot last week. A party of Flathead Indians came up and proposed trading horses. A trade was made and the Indians shortly after attempted to steal from the white men the horse which they had traded them. This was objected to by the whites, and the Indians drew their arms and fired on the whites, killing J. Eagleson and wounding a man named R. Evans. This is the story of the latter, now in Helena for treatment of his wounds. District Attorney Mayhew conversed with Evans and the latter emphatically denies that the Indians were furnished with whisky by his party. He says the trade was made, the Indians attempted to regain possession of the animal they had traded and a fight ensued. That an Indian killed his comrade and he in turn killed the Indian. He expressed a willingness to deliver himself up to the authorities should they so desired [sic].

Sheriff McAndrews is in receipt of the following letter from Agent Ronan giving the Indian version of the story. It will be seen the accounts are widely at variance:

Missoula, July 9, 1879.

Mr. James S. McAndrews,
Sheriff Deer Lodge County:

Dear Sir: To-day Michell, chief of Pend d'Oreilles, with a party of his head men came to the Agency and gave me the following version of a difficulty at or near Lincoln Gulch, in your county, which resulted in the death of an Indian and a white man:

It appears, according to the chief's information, that two white men came to an Indian encampment of three men and one woman. The white men had two bottles of whisky, and induced one of the Indians to go with them from the camp. The other two Indians and the squaw went out to a deer lick to watch for deer, and while there saw the Indian and two white men pass, and while yet in sight, heard the report of a gun and saw the Indian down and one of the white men clubbing him with his gun. The Indians started for their companion — the whitemen fled. On coming up, they found the Indian dead, shot through, his throat cut and his head beaten to a jelly. They followed the white men, one of whom they overtook and killed, the other escaped. The same night a party of white men fired into another Indian encampment. All of these matters have created excitement among the Indians and I started at once for Missoula, but nothing is known of the matter here. Will you be kind enough to send me at once full particulars, and if the case is in accordance with the Indian version. Also, if any steps have been taken in the matter. The mail is in and I know nothing save the Indian story.

Peter Ronan, U.S. Ind. Agt.,
Jocko Reservation.

July 24, 1879

U.S. Office of Indian Affairs, "Letters Received by the Office of Indian Affairs, 1824-1880," National Archives Microfilm Publication M234, reel 515, frames 202-204.

> Ronan was the intermediary in the long and tortured negotiations between the Nez Perce refugees in Tobacco Plains, British Columbia, and the Office of Indian Affairs in Washington, D.C. Finally on July 28, 1880, Ronan reported that the Nez Perce were coming south to the Flathead Reservation to surrender "subject to the clemency of the Government." See also Ronan's letters of October 6 and November 10, 1879, and July 28, 1880, for more information about this group of Nez Perce refugees.

Flathead Agency, M.T.
July 24th, 1879

The Hon. Commissioner of Indian Affairs
Washington, D.C.

Sir:

I have the honor to report that on this date Eneas, Chief of the Kootenais, came to the Agency and reported to me that ten lodges of Nez Perces, deserted from White Bird's band of hostiles are now encamped on Tobacco Plains about forty miles North of the border of this reservation and just over the British line. The Nez Perces sent a runner to Eneas' camp desiring that that chief would give the Nez Perces permission to cross the border and come on the reservation and live here in peace. Eneas deferred an answer untill I was consulted, and I therefore directed him to send a runner to the Nez Perce camp, and state to those Indians that in accordance with instructions from your office dated April 2d, 1879, in case they crossed the border and came upon this reservation, I would demand of them the surrender of their arms and horses, and receive them as prisoners, subject to the direction of the Government. That in case they refused to surrender, I would call upon the Indian Police of the reservation enforce the demand; and if refused aid from the Indians would call upon the military Power. Eneas promised to communicate this to the Nez Perces, and to let me know their decision, and also, to keep me informed as to their movements and destination in case they do not conclude to come upon this reservation.

Eneas also informed me that an encampment of eight Nez Perces, who were following those now encamped at Tobacco Plaines, from the north, were attacked by a war party supposed to have been Gros Ventres and massacred.

All of which I respectfully submit.
Your obedient servant,
Peter Ronan
U.S. Ind. Agent

August 8, 1879

Excerpt from The New North-West *(Deer Lodge, Mont.), August 8, 1879, page 2, col. 6-7. Written by Peter Ronan according to Margaret Ronan.[12] The portion of the article dealing with Seghers' visit to the Coeur d'Alene Mission has not been reproduced here.*

> Charles John Seghers was born in Belgium, came to the Pacific Northwest in 1863 and was appointed bishop in 1873. He was very active in support of the Indian missions and visited

western Montana in 1879 and 1882. After visiting St. Ignatius and the Flathead Reservation, Seghers and his party visited St. Mary's Mission in the Bitterroot Valley. Much of Segher's later work was in British Columbia and Alaska before he was assassinated in Alaska in 1886.[13] Dr. L. H. Choquette was born in Canada, trained at Victoria University, and came to western Montana in 1877. He was Flathead Agency physician between 1877 and 1882, and also maintained a private practice in Missoula. After he resigned his Flathead Reservation position, he continued his private practice in Missoula until 1885 when he returned to Canada.[14] Joseph Giorda, S.J., an Italian, was Superior-General of the Rocky Mountain Indian Missions during 1862-1866 and 1869-1877. In 1862, he expanded the missions which had been greatly reduced by his predecessor. He died at Sacred Heart Mission among the Coeur d'Alene Indians in 1882.[15]

Visit of Archbishop Seghers
to the Catholic Missions of the Rocky Mountains.

Route and Incidents of His Journeyings.
Special Correspondence New North-West.

. . . .

From the old [Coeur d'Alene] mission the Bishop and his escort of Jesuit missionaries and Indian chiefs proceeded Montanawards over the old Mullan road, and in this hurried sketch we will not stop nor attempt to describe the wild grandeur, the lofty scenes, the rushing torrents, the tortuous trail, but land His Grace across the Coeur d'Alenes and in his encampment at Schafer's ranch, six miles below Frenchtown, in Missoula county, Montana, on the evening of July 28th, [1879,] where mass was celebrated and sermon preached by His Grace. On the morning of the 29th he was met by a procession consisting of all the men, women and children of Frenchtown, headed by T. J. Demers, who was followed by some twenty wagons and buggies and a large cavalcade of horsemen. A band of music was also in attendance, the village blacksmith fired a salute from his anvils, a balloon ascension was made, shops were closed and a general holiday inaugurated. An address was delivered to the dwellers of Frenchtown by the Bishop, who promised to visit their village again on the second Sunday in August and administer confirmation.

After being hospitably entertained at the private residence of Mr. T. J. Demers, His Grace, accompanied by his missionary companions and Indian escort, proceeded fo[r] the Flathead Agency, driven in a fine carriage by Bonacina, of Frenchtown, who gracefully handled the ribbons, and at six o'clock the whole party were welcomed by Agent Ronan, wife and family, H. A. Lambert and family, Dr. Choquette and family and the agency employees. At the home of Major Ronan the Bishop and party were entertained and remained all night. In the morning His Grace celebrated mass in the mill, preached an edifying sermon and administered confirmation. After breakfast His Grace visited the Agency surroundings, with which he expressed great pleasure, and after partaking of luncheon with the Agent and family the whole party started for St. Ignatius Mission, a drive of seventeen miles. Two miles from St. Ignatius Mission the party was met by a cavalcade of some two hundred mounted Indians of the Flathead reservation, who ranged themselves in line and, as the carriages containing the Bishop, missionaries, Agent and others passed, fired a salute, and ranging themselves in a sort of wing or skirmish line on either side of the bishop's carriage, dashed off into a gallop, the drivers of the carriages whipped up their horses, and the whole cavalcade came over the hills to the Mission at a racing speed. They were halted by Father [Joseph] Giorda at the Indian burying ground, some five hundred yards from the beautiful Mission church, where a procession was formed, and beneath a silk and richly embroidered canopy, borne by four men, the Bishop walked followed by eight Jesuit missionaries with rich vestments, and a procession formed of at least eleven hundred Indian men, women and children. Just ahead of the Bishop two little dusky maidens walked backwards strewing flowers in his path. Arriving at the church benediction was given, the responses, *"Tantum Ergo"* and *"O Salutaris"* were delightfully rendered by the Indian girls of the choir, after which came the kissing of the ring by the eleven hundred Indians who knelt to receive the Bishop's blessing. His Grace remained at the Mission until Sunday for the purpose of assisting at the Feast of St. Ignatius, in the meantime blessing the church, consecrating the burying ground, visiting the Boys' Industrial School and the Girls' Boarding School, where he was edified and astonished at the wonderful progress of the children in all the branches of industry and education. The address of welcome written, read and presented to him by a full-blooded Indian girl on this occasion is one of the treasures of his visit.

On Sunday morning, at 9 o'clock, a procession was formed by the Mission School children and Indians, and as the Bishop passed to the front a salute was fired by forty Indian policemen ranged along the line, and all marched to the church, which is a large edifice 103 feet long and 43 feet wide, but it was incapable of holding the dense mass which filed in, there being by fair computation some fourteen hundred Indians present with a fair sprinkling of whites. High Pontifical Mass was celebrated, a sermon preached in English by His Grace, and translated by the Missionaries present into four different Indian tongues. Confirmation was then administered to one hundred and eighty Indian children and grown persons. After the service the procession was reformed and His Grace escorted to the residence. A public feast was then given to all the Indians present, and while regaling themselves upon the delicacies of the season they were addressed by their chiefs and head men, some of the speeches rendered in the grandest style of Indian oratory.

The next visit of the Bishop will be back again to the Flathead Agency, where he will lay the cornerstone of a new Indian church to be erected at that place, and then will continue his visit to Missoula, Deer Lodge and all the principal towns in Montana.

. . . .

August 12, 1879

U.S. Commissioner of Indian Affairs, Annual Report of the Commissioner of Indian Affairs *(Washington, D.C.: U.S. Government Printing Office, 1879), pages 94-95.*

In many of his annual reports Ronan displays his prejudice and bigotry. He makes clear his moral preference for farming over hunting and gathering, but shrinking game resources were also leading many tribal members to support expanding farms and herds. The 1855 Hellgate Treaty, ratified by Congress in 1859, provided for twenty years of payments to the tribes for ceded lands. The financial provisions of the treaty expired in 1879. There is good reason to question his conclusion that no traditional healers remained.

The *Dictionary of the Kalispel or Flat-head Indian Language* was printed at St. Ignatius Mission over a three year period and represented the culmination of thirty years of work by a succession of Jesuit missionaries to the Salish tribes. Much of the early work was done by Father Gregory Mengarini, S.J., in the 1840s. The entire dictionary was 1,148 pages long. The type was set by Indian student apprentice printers.[16]

Andrew Seltice (or Seltis) was chief of the Coeur d'Alene Indians in Idaho between 1865 and his death in 1902. He was strongly pro-Catholic and won great respect over the years for his efforts to help his people adjust to the loss of the buffalo and defend their interests against predatory white neighbors.[17]

Flathead Agency, Montana,
August 12, 1879.

Sir: The Flathead reservation, consisting of 1,433,600 acres of land, a large portion of which being well adapted to agricultural pursuits and grazing purposes, is dotted everywhere with Indian farms and habitations, where heavy crops of wheat, besides other grains and vegetables, are raised; and the past year shows a steady increase in the number of Indians thus engaged in civilized pursuits. The fact is beginning forcibly to dawn upon them that food and raiment must be obtained from mother earth, and slowly, but surely, they are advancing step by step in agricultural pursuits. But they need encouragement and assistance in the way of implements of labor, a supply of which should always be at the agent's command, so that when an Indian is induced to fence in a farm he can be assisted. Such a line of policy in a few years would put every head of a family upon a permanent home, and from past experience I find that the Indian who has once tasted the benefits of civilizing pursuits becomes anxious and ambitious to extend his operations, increase his herds, and surround his family with the comforts of life.

By reference to accompanying statistics it will be seen that an estimate of some 20,000 bushels of wheat, 4,000 bushels of oats, besides large quantities of potatoes, turnips, and other vegetables has been made of the product of the reservation during this season, which is a large increase over last year.

Education.

Tho [sic] establishment last year of a boarding and industrial school for boys and girls on this reservation was a most judicious step, but the fund for feeding and clothing the children is altogether too small, as the desire among parents for the education of their children is so general that the number far exceeds the amount appropriated to provide for them. The school is in a flourishing condition, and under the present management of the Sisters of Charity, who have competent teachers for boys in field, mills, and shops, as well as the school-room, the children are making rapid progress. A printing-office is also in operation at the mission where one of the boys receives instructions in the art of printing. A dictionary of the Kalispel or Flathead Indian language, compiled by the missionaries of the Society of Jesus, containing 640 pages, has just been completed at this office, and in order to show its character I copy the following preface from its pages:

The design of the present work is to afford assistance in the study of the language, mainly to those who have dedicated themselves to the teaching and regeneration of these Indian tribes.

The method of classifying the Indian words according to their etymology, or under the roots from which they originate, though fraught with no little difficulty to the unlearned, has, however, been pursued, and by many advised, as the only proper one in view of the highly educated character of the missionaries for whose perusal the work is intended.

That a better order, a better diction, and a better typographical dress could have been made use of, is freely acknowledged by the author, who labored under no inconsiderable difficulties to bring this edition, such as it is, to consummation, and he hopes that others, availing themselves of his labor, may correct the many blunders, and give it that finish of which the language is capable.

The author owes much to the manuscript dictionary of Rev. G. Mengarini, who, first of all the Jesuit missionaries, possessed himself of the genius of this language, and besides speaking it with the perfection of a native Indian, reduced it also to the rules of a grammar.

The abbreviations used in the dictionary seem plain enough without further explanation.

The Arabic numbers between parentheses refer to the different conjugations, which will be found in the appendix.

Saint Ignatius Mission, M. T., *July* 31, 1879.

Missionary Labors.

All of the Indians of this reservation are brought under the influence of religion and are practical Catholics. Polygamy is punished as a crime by tribal law, and the marriage rite, which in every case is performed by the missionaries, is respected and enforced. On Sunday, the 3d day of August, upon the occasion of a visit to St. Ignatius Mission by his grace Charles John Seghers, bishop coadjutor to the archbishop of Oregon (whose diocese extends over this reservation), some 1,400 Indians, men, women, and children, greeted him at the mission church, and knelt before him for his blessing. On that day the rite of confirmation was administered by the bishop to 108 Indian children. On Thursday, the 7th day of August, his grace laid the corner-stone of a new church at the agency, now in course of construction by the missionaries aided by Indians. Logs were delivered at the agency saw-mill by them, and they also assisted in the labor of sawing. Twenty-two thousand feet of lumber is now carefully piled upon the ground, to be used in construction of the church, the labor and expense of which will be borne by the missionaries. The influence of religion and education is the true source of the regeneration of these Indian tribes, and it should be the care of all connected with the Indian service, no matter in what capacity, to foster and encourage its advancement upon the reservation. The archbishop was accompanied here by several missionaries from the different Catholic Indian missions, and also a delegation of chiefs and headmen from the Nez Percés, Cœur d'Alénes, and Umatillas; among the latter was head-chief How-lish-wam-poo, who accompanied Chief Moses to Washington on his recent visit; and of the Cœur d'Alénes, head-chief Seltis. The visit of those chiefs to this reservation had a good effect, as in their council with the Indians all spoke of the great advantage of cultivating the land, adopting the white men's habits, and educating their children to industry and self-reliance.

Encouragement.

The arrival this month of the agricultural implements, wagons, iron, steel, &c., forwarded upon my requisition to your office, is a great source of encouragement to the Indians, particularly the Kootenais, who are very poor and ill-provided for in the way of implements of labor. The home of those people is some 80 miles from the agency, and owing to the great distance but little supervision can be given by the agent over their planting, fencing, and improvements, but their chief, Eneas, is an excellent man, and is using all his efforts to induce his people to cultivate the land. The Indians of this tribe are naturally a set of wandering and thriftless vagrants, and until the last two years did not attempt to cultivate the soil, living chiefly by hunting, fishing, and gathering berries and roots. But at present, under the good influence of their chief and other encouragements, several farms have been inclosed by them, and they promise to inclose more land this fall. The Flatheads and Pend d'Oreilles, more especially the former, are far in advance of the Kootenais in all the pursuits of labor, education, and self-reliance.

Expiration of the Treaty.

In view of the fact that the treaty existing between the government and the tribes of this reservation expires this year, before they have reached a point where government aid can be dispensed with, some new arrangement should be made and conclusion reached in regard to the removal or permanent settlement of the Bitter Root Flatheads, and all the vexatious questions in regard to them. Under Chief Charlos some 350 Flatheads still cling to their homes in the Bitter Root Valley, refusing to remove to this reservation. The rapid settling up of the valley by a white population has hedged those people in so closely that there is scarcely grazing room for their cattle and horses, and although in my opinion the Jocko Reservation far exceeds the Bitter Root Valley in all the advantages of agriculture, grazing, water and timber, for some cause those people refuse to take advantage of the inducements offered to remove here, and also refuse to accept the patents issued by the government for their lands.

The Sanitary

condition of the Indians has been good, and the resident physician has the confidence and respect of the Indians. "Medicine-men" are not now known to these tribes, and the doctor's prescriptions and advice are generally carefully followed by patients.

Very respectfully, your obedient servant,

Peter Ronan,
United States Indian Agent.

The Commissioner of Indian Affairs.

August 15, 1879

U.S. Office of Indian Affairs, "Letters Received by the Office of Indian Affairs, 1824-1880," National Archives Microfilm Publication M234, reel 515, frames 218-219.

Grain farming on the reservation was extensive enough by 1879 to require a new threshing machine.

Flathead Agency, M.T.
August 15th, 1879

The
Hon. Commissioner of Indian Affairs
Washington, D.C.

Sir:

In my estimate of annuity goods required for the Indians of this reservation for the year 1879-'80 I mentioned one threshing machine, and not having received information whether the same has been purchased I have the honor to request that I be informed relative thereto for the reason that the thresher at this agency is worn out beyond repair and, unless some arrangement can be made, the Indians will suffer a heavy loss in their very large crop of grain on account of their inability to thresh it. If the thresher has not been purchased for this place I would respectfully request authority to hire one to thresh the wheat for winter use.

Your obedt servt,
Peter Ronan
U.S. Ind. Agent.

August 23, 1879a

U.S. Office of Indian Affairs, "Letters Received by the Office of Indian Affairs, 1824-1880," National Archives Microfilm Publication M234, reel 515, frames 235-237.

For the resolution of the status of this particular Nez Perce refugee see Ronan's letter of September 1, 1879.

Flathead Indian Agency, Montana.
August 23d, 1879

The
Hon. Commissioner Indian Affairs
Washington, D.C.

Sir:

I have the honor to report that on this day "Arlee," chief of Flatheads, reported as follows:

On Arlee's recent hunting excursion a wounded Nez Perce came to his camp severely hurt by a charge of buckshot, who informed him (Arlee) that he was one of a party of five Nez Perces who deserted White Bird's camp across the British line, and attempted to return to their home in Idaho; that having got into Montana they were informed by Indians that if they returned to their country they would be killed or imprisoned by the whites, and thereupon concluded to turn back; and they also decided to make a raid upon settlers' horses and succeeded in running off a band, but were followed by the settlers who recovered the horses from them, shooting him with a charge of buckshot and leaving him as they supposed, dead; that after recovering strength enough he dragged himself to Arlee's camp and begged that chief's hospitality. His wounds were dressed and Arlee brought him to his home on the reservation where he now lives, and reported to me as above. I instructed Arlee to take care of him, and to be responsible for him until I reported the case to your office. The Indian in question is one of Joseph's band and begs to be allowed to live with the Indians of this reserve promising most faithfully to always remain on the reservation and to become a "good" Indian, and, at the request of the chief, I repeat his request to you, that he be allowed to remain here.

The wounded Nez Perce is now virtually a prisoner in charge of Arlee, and I desire instructions in regard to what disposition I will make of him.

Very respectfully,
Peter Ronan
U.S. Ind. Agent.

August 23, 1879b

U.S. Office of Indian Affairs, "Letters Received by the Office of Indian Affairs, 1824-1880," National Archives Microfilm Publication M234, reel 515, frames 238-241.

No further biographical information was located about Amos or his family. See also Ronan's letters of March 10 and June 18, 1879, for similar cases.

Flathead Indian Agency, Montana.
August 23d, 1879

To the
Hon. Commissioner Indian Affairs
Washington, D.C.

Sir:

I have the honor to report that one "Amos" a Nez Perce Indian, who was taken prisoner in the Lo Lo Pass by Captain [C. C.] Rawn's Command of the 7th Infantry, during the march of the Nez Perces through that pass, and who, after several months of imprisonment was discharged, it appearing upon investigation that he was not only innocent of being upon the war path, at the time of his arrest; but was using all his power and influence to prevent bloodshed, and was always a friend of the whites and opposed to the war which was then waged by Joseph, sought this reservation with a pass from the Agent at Lapwai, and informed me that during his incarceration at Fort Missoula, his wife and children were forced off with Joseph's hostile band, and at the surrender to Col. [Nelson] Miles, the wife became separated from the children, she escaping with White Bird, while the children were taken with Joseph. Not having heard from his wife and supposing her dead he married again, and is living with his second wife on Clearwater, near the Nez Perce Agency; but upon coming on a visit to this reservation he learned that his former wife was here, who is one of the women alluded to in my communications to your office under the respective dates of March 10th and June 18th, 1879. Amos claims that he is able to take care of his children, now supposed to be with Joseph, and earnestly desired me to communicate to you the particulars of the separation of his family, and asks as a matter of justice and generosity that his children be restored to him. They are described as follows:

A boy five years old; two girls, one seven the other eight years of age; the oldest girl being sickly at the time of separation, thinks perhaps she may be dead. The mother of the Children was called "Li-li-Cola," the father was known as "Amos."

Very respectfully,
Your obedient servant
Peter Ronan
U.S. Indian Agent.

August 26, 1879

U.S. Office of Indian Affairs, "Letters Received by the Office of Indian Affairs, 1824-1880," National Archives Microfilm Publication M234, reel 515, frames 248-250.

Little is known about the details of this program to apprentice Indian youth to agency mechanics, but see Ronan's letter of December 18, 1880, requesting that the program be ended on Flathead.

Flathead Indian Agency, Montana.
August 26th, 1879

The
Hon. Commissioner of Indian Affairs
Washington, D.C.

Sir:

I have the honor to forward herewith invoice of subsistence supplies purchased for use of apprentices — The purchase was rendered necessary in consequence of the non-arrival of subsistence supplies for which requisition was made February 28th, 1879. The prices are reasonable and the lowest obtainable and I would respectfully request that my action in this matter be approved.

Your obedt servt,
Peter Ronan
U.S. Ind. Agent.

Enclosed invoice from T. J. Demers, Frenchtown, M.T., dated August 26, 1879:

July 25, To 1 Pr. Pants Antoine Apprentice, $2.75.
July 28, To 1 Pr. Pants Tenass Apprentice, $2.50
July 28, To 550 lbs flour, $8.75.
July 31, To 60 lbs Bacon, $7.20.
August 2, To 1 Hat (By Gabriel) $3.50, 1 Shirt $2.50, Gabriel, $6.00.
August 4, To 1 Pr. Pants Michelle Apprentice, $3.75.
August 4, To 200 lbs flour, $5.00.
August 7, To 100 lbs flour, $2.50.
August 7, To 64 lbs Beef, 7 cents, $4.48.
August 11, To 100 lbs flour, $2.50.
August 15, To 1 Pr. Pants Lóni Apprentice, $3.50.
August 15, To 50 lbs flour, $1.25.
August 17, To 42 lbs Bacon, $5.45.
August 21, To 55 lbs Bacon, $6.87½.
August 21, To 100 lbs Beef, $7.00.
   Total $69.50½.

September 1, 1879

U.S. Office of Indian Affairs, "Letters Received by the Office of Indian Affairs, 1824-1880," National Archives Microfilm Publication M234, reel 515, frames 253-255.

See also Ronan's letter of August 23, 1879a, for more information about this case.

Flathead Indian Agency, Montana.
September 1st, 1879

The
Hon. Commissioner of Indian Affairs
Washington, D.C.

Sir:

Alluding to my communication to you of August 23rd, '79, in regard to a wounded Nez Perce from White Bird's camp, a prisoner under charge of Arlee, chief of Flatheads, I would respectfully report that said wounded Indian repaid Arlee for his nursing and attention to his wounds by watching an opportunity and making his escape, stealing from the Chief and his relatives a gun and two horses. The Flatheads are now in pursuit of him and if caught he will be summarely dealt with by them. I respectfully suggest that the orders in regard to hostile prisoners contained in your letter of April 21st, 1879, be so modified that I be empowered to deliver such prisoners over immediately to the nearest military post or to the civil authorities, to be fed and confined until further instructions can be received from your office, I make this suggestion to prevent future escapes, in case of making prisoners, as I have no suitable way of confining them.

Very respectfully,
Your obedt. servt,
Peter Ronan
U.S. Ind. Agent.

October 6, 1879

U.S. Office of Indian Affairs, "Letters Received by the Office of Indian Affairs, 1824-1880," National Archives Microfilm Publication M234, reel 515, frames 261-265.

See also Ronan's letters of July 24, 1879, and November 10, 1879, and July 28, 1880, for more information about this group of Nez Perce refugees.

Flathead Indian Agency, Montana.
October 6th, 1879

The
Hon. Commissioner of Indian Affairs
Washington, D.C.

Sir:

As heretofore communicated to you in my letter of July 24th, 1879, there are and have been encamped just across the border of the British line and within a few miles of the northwestern boundary of the Flathead reservation, some fifteen lodges of Nez Perces; a remnant of the band who escaped under the chieftainship of "White Bird," at the surrender of Joseph's band to Col. Miles. From the best information I can gain, the fifteen lodges in question left the encampment of White Bird in the North and under the direction of the brother of the celebrated "Looking Glass" (who fell during the Nez Perce campaigne) who acts as chief, and the brother of the equally celebrated "Eagle of the Light," who is second chief, have sought their present encampment with the hope that Government will make some arrangement by which they can cross the Border and settle down to peaceful pursuits. I also learn that the Indians of this encampment are among the best and the bravest of the unfortunate Nez Perces, who were drawn into the war by evil influences and evil counsel; that they are overwhelmed by their misfortunes and utterly subdued by their chastisement, but owing to the exaggerated reports of the unhealthy climate in which Joseph is located, and the stories told to them that the tribe of Joseph is fast disappearing from the face of the earth, by pestilence and death, they would rather face famine, or death by the whites, than consent to take their families to Joseph's reservation. They have also sent an intimation that they would like to hold a council with me, with a view of having their case laid before the Indian Office. They intimate by their messenger:

1st. If the Government is willing to give them a home at the head of the Flathead Lake, which is unoccupied by Whites or Indians, and is no part of the Flathead reserve, they would be willing to give up their arms, abandon the chase and settle down to peaceful pursuits, and never leave their homes without consent of the Government.

2d. With consent of the tribes of this reservation, they would accept a home on any part of the reserve, and bind themselves to obey all rules and restrictions that the Government, through the Agent here, might impose.

3d. That if either of those propositions would be concurred in, they would remove without delay and accept any assistance that might be offered to open farms and settle themselves down to pursuits of husbandry and would influence White Bird and the remaining Nez Perces in the North to join their community and accept the same terms.

Inasmuch as winter is fast approaching and those people are encamped in a bleak and sterile country where game and fish are scarce and hunger may drive them to acts of lawlessness, I have taken the liberty to make this statement and ask that I may have authority to treat with them in some way. If either of the above propositions, if offered by the Indians, as intimated, would not meet the views of the Government, could I offer them some place to live and means to support them through the winter or until the Commission arrives here which is expected to settle the affairs of the tribes under my charge whose treaty expires at the end of this year.

If authority is granted I will proceed to their camp or have them meet me half way, and obey any instructions in the matter which you may be pleased to give me.

Very respectfully,
Your obedt. servt.,
Peter Ronan
U.S. Ind. Agent.

October 8, 1879
U.S. Office of Indian Affairs, "Letters Received by the Office of Indian Affairs, 1824-1880," National Archives Microfilm Publication M234, reel 515, frames 258-260.

> The federal government purchasing system in 1879 was slow and cumbersome. Ronan's experiences show how it complicated running the agency. The bureaucratic problems must have considerably reduced the services and goods the agency supplied tribal members.

Flathead Indian Agency, Montana.
October 8, 1879

The
Hon. Commissioner of Indian Affairs
Washington, D.C.

Sir:

I would respectfully state that in accordance with my requisition for Shop material (made March 1878) a quantity of wagon-fellows and Spokes were sent to me but they are totally unfit for use, being intended for those immense "Murphy" wagons which were used on the plains in the early days of transportation and were drawn by sixteen to thirty yoke of cattle, and as the Indians' wagons are light two and four horse wagons it will be easily seen that I cannot make use of them in repairs. I will therefore be compelled to purchase such articles in open-market, or leave the Indians' wagons piled up in front of the shop, unrepaired.

In the same requisition I asked for one dozen blacksmith drills at a cost of 50 cts. a piece, instead of which, were sent me 12 enormous machine shop drills, for which I have no use, whereas the small drills are greatly needed. I, also, asked for one set each of hollow and round planes, Sizes from 1 to 2 inch, instead of which I received one-half dozen each of hollows and rounds, all of the *same size*. In place of one box of 10 x 14 inch glass, there was sent me the same quantity of *10 x 12* glass, which, even were not the greater portion of it broken, is of no use to me unless cut into 8 x 10 lights for windows of the Indians' houses.

Your Honor will plainly perceive that occasional open-market purchases of mill and shop supplies cannot be avoided, owing to accidents and other causes, and I trust that my action in such cases, which in the future as well as in the past, will always be made with a view to economy and the best interests of the service, may meet your approbation.

Your obedient servant,
Peter Ronan
U.S. Indian Agent.

October 30, 1879

The Council Fire *(Washington, D.C.), vol. 2, no. 12 (December 1879), page 192.*

> *The Council Fire* was a Quaker publication working to reform federal Indian policy and was part of the Friends of the Indian movement that promoted the allotment policy on reservations.

Flathead Indian Agency,
Montana, October 30, 1879.

A. B. Meacham,
Editor of the Council Fire.

Dear Sir: Inclosed find five-dollar draft, for which you will please forward *The Council Fire* to the following address: Peter Ronan, Agent Flatheads, H. A. Lambert, John Reed, John C. Dooley, Philip Hogan, Missoula, Co., Montana Territory.

Very respectfully, and with heartfelt wishes for the success of The Council Fire, I remain, yours truly

Peter Ronan,
United States Indian Agent.

November 4, 1879

U.S. Office of Indian Affairs, "Letters Received by the Office of Indian Affairs, 1824-1880," National Archives Microfilm Publication M234, reel 515, frames 276-280.

> It is hard to believe that in 1879 the "great majority" of the Indian people on the reservation had no Indian names. Pressures from the agency and the missionaries were undermining traditional Salish and Kootenai naming customs. The changes often make it difficult to determine just who is being referred to in historical documents.

Flathead Indian Agency, Montana.
November 4th, 1879

The
Hon. Commissioner of Indian Affairs
Washington, D.C.

Sir:

In reply to your communication "A" October 10th, 1879, returning vouchers 1, 2, & 3 to abstract "D" Property Return for 1st Quarter, 1879, and voucher 1 & 2 to same abstract & return for 2d Quarter, 1879. I have the honor to make the following statement and explanation:

The great majority of the Indians of this reservation have no Indian names and are only known by their Christian names given them in Baptism by the missionaries, and they seem to be decidedly opposed to adopting a surname — having a feeling that the name received when adopting their religion is sufficient to designate them. I will try to overcome this opposition but I fear that it is impossible. Hereafter I will insist upon the Indians who receive articles of Issue to give their Indian names borne before baptism if I cannot succeed in getting them to adopt a surname. With reference to the vouchers returned to me I would say that the Indians live in various parts of the reservation, very long distances from the agency and only come here from their homes and farms when they need some article, or to have repairs done at the Shops. For this reason I would respectfully request that I be allowed to return the vouchers signed as they are and have credit given me for the issues made and receipted for. There would be some expense attendant on a trip to the homes of the various Indians who have signed these vouchers, which I would not wish to incur unless ordered by the Hon. Commissioner. I will retain the vouchers until I receive information from you relative to my action in the premises.

Relative to issuance of subsistence supplies for a longer period than one week, I would state that the Indians are settled on various portions of the reservation ranging in distance from 20 to 80 miles from the Agency and that it would be imposing a hardship on them to compel them to come to the agency every week for what little articles they might need & for the small amount of goods allowed them under the appropriation of $3000 per year. These Indians are not allowed rations, but receive articles of subsistence, etc., to the amount of $3000.00 per annum for their indigent and sick and issues are made to such only and not to the healthy Indians who can work and are selfsustaining. I would respectfully call your attention to your letter of Aug. 6th, 1878 "A." Mont R565-'78 in reply to mine of July 15th, 1878. I would also suggest that to make weekly issues of goods to the poor and sick of the tribes would necessitate their camping at the agency during the entire year, which would encourage indolence in those who are poor, while on the other hand, if they, after receiving what they require return to their homes and then witness the success of those who apply themselves to husbandry, they will therefore receive encouragement to follow the example of the prosperous.

As to issuing such large quantities of seed oats, etc., to single families: The Indians who received seeds the last spring were generally those who had just started farming and were unprovided with such articles to sow the large area of ground broken by them.

Your obedient servant,
Peter Ronan
U.S. Ind. Agent.

November 5, 1879
U.S. Office of Indian Affairs, "Letters Received by the Office of Indian Affairs, 1824-1880," National Archives Microfilm Publication M234, reel 515, frames 281-284.

> This report on trade and credit on the reservation gives us a glimpse of the reservation economy in 1879. Ronan's letter indicates that by 1879 many tribal members had some involvement in the white cash economy. Credit provided a service to tribal members, but also restricted their shopping options. See also Ronan's report on traders on December 29, 1879.

Flathead Indian Agency, Montana.
November 5th, 1879

The
Hon. Commissioner of Indian Affairs
Washington, D.C.

Sir:

Referring to Circular No. 35 instructing me to notify all licensed traders on this reservation that in future when making purchase from or sales to Indians, money only must be used, I would respectfully call your attention to the following facts:

The Indians of this reservation are, to a great extent, agriculturalists and stock raisers, and the surplus of the thrifty ones is hauled or driven to the neighboring towns or to the traders store, and there disposed of at the ruling prices, sometimes for cash but generally in exchange for groceries and the necessary articles for family consumption. This season the grain crop has been so heavy that the market is glutted, and traders outside of the reservation in the neighboring towns of Missoula County, refuse cash for grain to white farmers, and refuse to purchase unless a portion of the price is taken in trade. You will perceive under these circumstances that the trader at the reservation cannot compete with merchants in surrounding towns if he is compelled to pay cash for his purchase from Indians, and would be compelled to close his store, and in such event the Indians will be obliged to do all their trading in the towns, on the same terms they would get here from the trader, if untransmuted by this order, and the demoralizing effect of such procedure can be seen at a glance. I would also state that as a general thing the reservation Indians are fully capable of protecting themselves in trade, and when prices do not suit them at the licensed trading post, (being well informed as to prices) they have an intelligent and and [sic] independent way (like white people) of hitching up their teams and carting their produce to where they can make the best terms. The trader here is aware of this fact and it is not to his interests to over-charge or under-pay an Indian in his barter. The use of tokens or tickets is not in vogue here; but the trader keeps a set of books and opens regular accounts with some of the surrounding Indian farmers and when the farmer harvests his crops, or has a steer or a horse to sell he settles his account just the same as the white farmers. Of course it is not to the traders interest to give promiscuous credit. In view of all these facts I would respectfully suggest that the inforcement of instructions in Cir. No. 35 would be of great injustice both to the Indians generally of this reservation and to the trader, and would ask that they be not enforced here.

Very respectfully,
Peter Ronan
U.S. Ind. Agent.

November 10, 1879

U.S. Office of Indian Affairs, "Letters Received by the Office of Indian Affairs, 1824-1880," National Archives Microfilm Publication M234, reel 515, frames 289-296.

See also Ronan's letters of July 24 and October 6, and July 28, 1880, for more information about this group of Nez Perce refugees.

Joseph M. Cataldo, S.J., was an Italian missionary who spent many years among the Nez Perce Indians. Between 1877 and 1893, he was the Superior-General in charge of all the Jesuit Rocky Mountain Indian Missions. A gifted linguist, he was said to have mastered twenty Indian and European languages.[18] For more information on Eagle-of-the-Light, Nez Perce chief, see Ronan's July 11, 1877, letter and annotation. A slightly different version of Eagle-of-the-Light's 1879 speech was published in Mary Ronan's memoirs.[19] The Nez Perce Chief Tuk-Alik-Shimi (or No Hunter or Hunter No More) had taken part in the July 1878 negotiations in Canada between the refugee Nez Perce, Col. James F. McLeod of the Northwest Mounted Police, and a representative of Gen. Nelson A. Miles of the United States Army. Duncan McDonald was an interpreter at this meeting. The United States Army representative tried to convince the Nez Perce to return to the United States, but failed. No Hunter or Tuk-Alik-Shimsi was a brother of Chief Looking Glass who was killed at the Battle of Bear's Paw in 1877.[20]

Flathead Indian Agency, Montana.
November 10th, 1879

The
Hon. Commissioner of Indian Affairs
Washington, D.C.

Sir:

In accordance with previous agreement with the Indians, upon the receipt of the following telegram from you, I made arrangements for a meeting with the Nez Perces, whose case I fully reported to you in my letter of October 6th, 1879:

Washington, October 23d, 1879.

To Agent Ronan,
Flathead Agency, Montana.

In reply to your letter of October Sixth you can say to the Nez Perces, if they choose to come upon your reservation and be fed they must do so as prisoners of war and trust to the clemency of the Government.

E. A. Hayt,
Commissioner.

The meeting was held at St. Ignatius Mission, Rev. J. M. Cataldo acting as Interpreter. The Nez Perces were represented by "Eagle of the Light," a former Chief of Joseph's band, but who took no part in the outbreak and who was living here before and since the war; "Red Mountain" another Nez Perce who lived here during the trouble and Tuk-Alik-Shimsi, the brother of the celebrated "Looking Glass." The latter fought with Joseph through all the war and was among the party who escaped at the surrender to Colonel Miles. To him I explained your telegram and its conditions. For his own part he was willing to accept, but would not speak for his people. They (his people) would probably think it was a trap to turn them over to the military who would carry them as prisoners to the Indian Territory, a calamity which they would rather face death than submit to. He would explain it to his people and come again in the Spring, when he could cross the mountains from the British Possessions, where the encampment is now situated, and let me know their decision. He then made a speech and asked if I would "take his words down for the eyes of the Chief in Washington.["]

Speech of Tuk-Alik-Shimsi, or Hunter No More — Tuk-Alik-Shimsi, is my name, I am the son of old Looking Glass, and brother of the chief and warrior of that name who fell in battle with the white Soldiers. My friend I heard and understand very well what you say; you speak indeed very well; you are truly an Agent-chief. Though I do not know you personally you have a good name among your people. Look at me my friend and look at my breathing, and you will see that my breath is not right, and therefore my friend have pity on my heart on account of its sorrow. As you speak well, so you have a right to expect that I should answer well, and I beg that the Great Chief in Washington shall hear my words through you. Would that that Great Chief and I would hear well and understand each other! You advise well that my children should have a home and grow in this world, and therefore, together, we send a letter to Washington, and now both of us are giving news about our people. — Peace and friendship are good and we should love them. I think that your proposal to give up this wandering life and have a home to live is very good; but give us a home here where our children can grow! My heart is seeking to find a place to stop for good. I did not wish any more to have a great many breaths, but if my people can live somewhere in this country my breath will be good and my heart will be whole again. You know that the soldiers and the Nez Perces had a war, and numbers were killed on both sides. It was not my fault that we had battles, and when I saw our people and the white people falling I was, as it were, deaf; my eyes became almost blind and I did not wish to see any more the whites or the Indians. When General Howard said "Now we are done fighting" and I hear the white soldiers and chiefs say "truly we are done," then and there I was very glad — so much so that my body had life again, my ears could hear and my eyes could see. I was glad for my heart said "Now we will only hear of peace and friendship." Then I thought: now I will meet whites as friends and have trouble no more — and those good words I have always kept in my heart. If anyone would try to give me a bad heart I would not take it. If my people would do anything with a bad heart I would not follow them; but if they try to good actions my heart will not only follow but try to lead them. You are our friend. I want a few more words to go to the great chief: My heart aches every moment of every day that the sun shines, for the needless death in battle of so many white soldiers and Indian warriors; and now I beg for peace and friendship for myself and those who follow me. We want a home here; your Indians are willing that we shall come upon their lands, or live somewhere here as neighbors. Oh! ask your chief to forgive the past and make our hearts live again; give us a home among our friends, where our children will grow up and follow the whiteman's road. I have spoken all.

At the conclusion of this speech, "Eagle of the Light" or "Te-peah-lena-caoph," arose and said to the Interpreter: "Do you perfectly understand our language? I do not wish my words here to be lost. Tuk-Alik-Shemsi has spoken for his followers, I wish to speak for all the Nez Perces, I heard all that you wrote to the Great Chief in Washington and understand, in turn, I want to be understood:

"I am very poor now! I lost all my children, all my brothers, all my women in the war, although I took no part in it. I was here before the war and stopped around here to see how it would end. Now I wish to speak as clear as the light of the morning; as in the morning the sun is clear after the darkness of the night, so shall my words be clear. I speak, as it were, from earth and from heaven; because both the Indians and the whites are made strong and weak from Him above. I know that all of my people who are in the Indian Territory (among who are some of my relatives) are very sad because a great many are dead and I hear the rest are fast dying. So here, from afar, great white chiefs who are in Washington! I beg of you to give my people all a home in the North. We are now as it were in the midday — there is the sun in the heavens very bright. It is by the law of that light that I ask from you to give me back my people. I am sorry now and sick at heart on account of my people now dead, and I think now that we should stop the dying of my children. You are a chief and I am a chief and we should agree in not having any more of our people die unnecessarily — that is why, I say again, give us back our people —"

Being told by the Agent that he was not there to discuss the affairs of Joseph or the people who were in the Indian Territory but simply to offer a home to the band of Nez Perces across the British line, providing they come in and give themselves up as prisoners and throw themselves upon the mercy of the Government, he replied: "I understand well — but my heart told me to speak for Joseph also, and I hope that the Great Chief in Washington will see and hear my words — I have done —"

Tuk-Alik-Shimsi informed me that some Nez Perces from the North, with renegade Spokanes and Palouses, made a raid last summer into Washington Territory, where they captured several horses and drove them to his camp, whereupon, Tuk-Alik-Shimsi demanded them from the thieves on the ground that his people would be accused by the whites of committing the depredation, and compelled them to give them up and has them now in charge and sent word that he had the horses and would give them up when called for by the owners. Among the persons whom Indian said he held stolen horses for he gave me the address of William Cassalman, Colfax, Washington Territory for whom he held nineteen head captured by him from the thieves.

Very respectfully,
Your obedient servant,
Peter Ronan
U.S. Ind. Agent.

December 9, 1879
From George Conford, Depredation Claim 1863, RG 75, National Archives, Washington, D.C.

According to the charges in this claim, Maxime and other unnamed Pend d'Oreilles took a moored ferry boat and other property of George Conford from the present day site of Superior, Montana, about February 28, 1878. The boat was allegedly moved down the Clark Fork River to the junction with the Flathead River and then about twenty miles up the Flathead River to approximately the present site of Perma. Maxime had been careful to get what he thought was permission from the owner, but he took the wrong boat. Ronan vouched for Maxime's character and honesty. As to the other missing property, Maxime's statement suggests it may have been stolen before he reached Superior. An affidavit by Neptune Lynch, an early white settler in Plains, claimed to have witnessed a group of Pend d'Oreille Indians moving a ferry boat loaded with boxes, block and pulleys, and chains. The Office of Indian Affairs file does not reconcile the conflicting testimony regarding the other property, but in 1881 the Commissioner of Indian Affairs awarded Conford the value of the boat, $400. No further biographical information about Conford was located. See also Ronan's letter of August 30, 1881, on this claim.[21]

Frank H. Woody, Conford's attorney, first came to western Montana in 1856 and held various positions in Missoula County government before being admitted to the bar in 1877. In the 1890s he was elected as a district judge.[22]

Flathead Agency, Montana.
December 9th, 1879

The Hon. Commissioner of Indian Affairs,
Washington, D.C.

Sir:

Having received from Frank H. Woody, attorney for claimant, annexed application for indemnity, marked "B" — and having ascertained by personal inquiry of reliable parties, that the prices fixed by the claimant upon the articles said to have been stolen by the Indians were not in excess of those ruling in this Territory at the time of the committal of the claimed depredation, and I also obtained the knowledge to my satisfaction, that the claimant, George Conford, is a reliable and good citizen of the county of Missoula, Territory of Montana, as are also the witnesses in the case, and that the statement as set forth in his application is truthful and just to the best of my knowledge and belief. Whereupon I called a council of the Indians of the reservation, taking care to bring in the suspected parties to the depredation, and after fully explaining to them through my official interpreter the whole case, there demanded satisfaction for the claimant. An Indian well known to me, and of good character, who is called by his tribe, the Pend d'Oreilles, "Maxime," stated that "while hunting down the Pend d'Oreille river he saw two boats which he supposed were lost by their owners and had drifted down the river; the one I took was tied but I supposed it was tied up by some one who did not want it to float down any further, and that it was abandoned by the owner. The boats were about five hundred yards apart. I wanted a boat for I knew I could make a living for my family if I could get it up to my house on the Pend d'Oreille river, by ferrying travelers across. I did not take the boat at that time, but came up to Frenchtown where T. J. Demers keeps a store and who is also the licensed trader at the Agency. I asked Demers if he thought it would be any harm to take the boat, he, Demers, replied that he knew a man who had lost two boats by the currents having carried them down, that he would ask him if I could take one. Demers spoke to the owner and he told me that it would cost more than a boat was worth to get it up the river; that he had two adrift and I was welcome to take one or both of his boats if I could find them. The man's name was Warren, who gave me this permission. I then went back with a party of Indians and worked a long time to get the boat up. It was tied but I thought it was tied by some one who saw it adrift. I did not think I was stealing the boat."

In reply to my question about the other articles in claimants list, the Indian said: "I found an unoccupied house not far from where the boat was, there was no one living there, the doors were open, the windows broken, with exception of a few panes of glass; a door and an old sleigh which was broken; a piece of wire-rope and a chain; this is all I took, and I saw nobody else take anything. I did not think I was stealing; I thought the boat was given to me, and I thought the owner of the house had abandoned the things I took. If a horse will pay him for those things, I will give him one — that is all I can do."

I interviewed Mr. Demers and Mr. Warren, alluded to by the Indian as having given him permission to take the boat. Both of these gentlemen verified the Indian's Statement as to getting Mr Warren's permission to take his boat but were of the opinion that he took Conford's (the claimant) boat, which was fastened and moored within a short distance of where it was built. The other articles mentioned in claimant's demand, outside of those confessed as having been taken by Maxime (the Indian in question) were not known of by any of the Indians. I herewith submit all papers bearing on the case.

Very respectfully,
Peter Ronan
U.S. Indian Agent.

December 29, 1879a

U.S. Office of Indian Affairs, "Letters Received by the Office of Indian Affairs, 1824-1880," National Archives Microfilm Publication M234, reel 517, frames 575-577.

Flathead Indian Agency, Montana.
December 29th, 1879

The
Hon. Commissioner of Indian Affairs
Washington, D.C.
Sir:

In reply to your letter of Dec. 12th "Montana R866 867. I2466. '79" in which you say that I did not make requisition in February last for a set of buggy harness, my purchase of the same in open market, will not be approved, I have the honor to state that the buggy harness at the Agency when I took charge had then been in service for a year or more but was in fair condition; that I have used the harness for more than two years; that at the time of making my requisition for the present fiscal year I considered the harness sufficiently strong to last for one year; and, not to incur an unnecessary expense, I delayed making requisition for a new set until I thought it absolutely required. That I was compelled to purchase the harness through the result of an accident, or, I should say, two accidents, which occurred as follows: The first was during a visit of the Hon. Martin Maginnis, Delegate from Montana. While he was here I had occasion to make a trip to Missoula and during my trip — (accompanied by Mr. Maginnis) — towards the Agency met a heavily loaded team on the road;

in attempting to turn out of the way the lines broke and the horses cramping the buggy upset the same breaking the harness. After having the harness repaired I was compelled to visit Missoula on official business and when some three miles from the Agency the "Kingbolt" of the buggy gave way and threw me out, and losing control of the horses I was forced to let them go, the result being the entire demolition of the harness. These accidents being unforeseen I did not include a set of buggy harness in my requisition of February last. I would respectfully request that in consideration of the foregoing facts you approve my action in making this purchase. In my requisition I aim to state such articles as will be necessary for use at the Agency for one year, but when accidents occur, I am, of course, compelled to repair them, if absolutely necessary, as in the case just stated.

Your obedient servant,
Peter Ronan
U.S. Ind. Agent.

December 29, 1879b
U.S. Office of Indian Affairs, "Letters Received by the Office of Indian Affairs, 1824-1880," National Archives Microfilm Publication M234, reel 517, frames 578-581.

> See also Ronan's letter of November 5, 1879, for more information about traders and business on the reservation.
>
> Antoine Rivais, or Revais, was part French, Pend d'Oreille, and Salish. His blind eldest son, Michel Revais, was the long time interpreter for the Flathead Agency. For some years Antoine farmed and operated a ferry on the Lower Flathead River in addition to the small store Ronan described. In the summer of 1882, Ernest Ingersoll saw the ferry: "It was a small scow suspended by two pulleys upon a wire-cable stretched high above the water, and operated by the force of the current against which it was set at an angle." Antoine's nearby ranch had "a score or so of log-houses and stables huddled together and surrounded by redskin teepees, corrals, and small stagings sustaining harness, etc., out of reach of dogs and coyotes," and "a long line of well-fenced fields and meadows." In Ronan's August 1, 1882, letter, he wrote that Revais wanted to sell the ferry because the rush of traffic connected to the construction of the Northern Pacific Railroad would be more than he could handle at 68 years of age. In 1885, an Indian inspector reported in 1884 Antoine had a 300 acre farm along the Pend d'Oreille or Lower Flathead River and harvested 200 bushels of grain.[23] Joseph Loyola was born at the Colville Mission and moved to the Flathead when he was young. He attended the St. Ignatius Mission school before becoming a merchant. In 1879 he subscribed to *The Weekly Missoulian* newspaper. He died on the reservation in 1885.[24]

Flathead Indian Agency, Montana.
December 29th, 1879

The
Hon. Commissioner of Indian Affairs
Washington, D.C.
    Sir:
    In reply to your circular of Dec 3d, 1879 in regard to the "names of all persons trading on this reservation," etc., I would state that there are now three trading Posts on this reservation; one kept by a half-breed by the name of

Antoine Rivais, who keeps a small quantity of articles for trade to the Indians, consisting of prints, shirting, sheeting, tobacco, matches, soap, etc., Said Rivais is a man of excellent character and deals, in his small way, with the Indians, in a perfectly honorable manner and does not use or bring upon the reservation spirituous liquors, or sell or buy any article forbidden by the laws of the trade. This post is situated at Rivais' farm, on the Pen d'Oreille river, some twenty miles from the Agency. A second small establishment with about the same quantity and list of articles is kept by an Indian by the name of Joseph Loyola, who can speak and read and write the English language, to a limited extent. This post is situated at St. Ignatius Mission, some seventeen miles from the Agency and no complaints of wrong-doings by the Indian proprietor, has come to my knowledge; the Indians claiming the privilege under the law to carry on the trade. The third is a regularly licensed store, kept by Telesphore Jacques Demers, within half a mile of the Agency. The proprietor is an honorable dealer and has the confidence of the Indians, and never to my knowledge, transgressed any of the rules and regulations governing trade, which are from time to time transmitted from your office for my guidance the Premises. I would state that no tokens or tickets have ever been used at either of the trading stores since I have taken charge here. All are cash transactions or trades of merchandise for articles the Indians may have to barter. As stated in my letter of November 5th, 1879, to which I again call your attention, traders (at least the licensed trader) have kept regular book accounts with Indians, and I see no reason why an Indian should be deprived of credit, at the post trader's store, when he can go to the neighboring towns and procure credit, where the merchants are only too glad to cultivate the Indian trade; as the Indians of this reservation are regarded as honest and punctual in their payments. If the trader is prohibited from crediting a trustworthy Indian, he will naturally seek the neighboring town for trade, and it is needless for me to state to your Honor the demoralizing effects such visits have upon the character of an Indian, where whiskey traffic and the lawlessness of the frontier town prevails.

Respectfully,
Your obedt servt,
Peter Ronan
U.S. Ind. Agent.

1880

March 1, 1880
U.S. Office of Indian Affairs, "Letters Received by the Office of Indian Affairs, 1824-1880," National Archives Microfilm Publication M234, reel 517, frames 645-646.

> In 1880, according to this letter, tribal members were fully exploiting the grazing and hay resources of the Jocko Valley.

Flathead Indian Agency, Montana.
March 1st, 1880

The
Hon. Commissioner of Indian Affairs
Washington, D.C.
    Sir:
    I see the statement in the Hon. Commissioner's report for 1879, that a contract has been given for the delivery in Spring at this Agency of 200 head of Stock cattle. As the small valley of the Jocko, where the Agency is located, has been stocked for several years with a large number of Indian ponies and cattle belonging to half-breeds who reside here and as the range is limited and pretty well eaten off, and, also, as there are no unoccupied meadowlands where hay can be cut, I would respectfully ask that I may be permitted to incur the expense of establishing a stock-ranche for the cattle in some unoccupied neighboring valley and to erect sheds and a branding corral, the whole cost of which not to exceed three hundred dollars. I would also ask authority to employ a competent herder, upon arrival of the cattle, to take charge of the band, at a salary of fifty dollars per month.

Very respectfully,
Peter Ronan
U.S. Ind. Agent.

March 26, 1880
The New North-West *(Deer Lodge, Mont.), March 26, 1880, page 3, col. 1.*

> In this letter Ronan repeats the official government position that the Bitterroot Salish were independent of the Flathead Reservation. According to the federal government, the Salish had severed their tribal relations by remaining in the Bitterroot Valley after the 1872 Garfield agreement. See Ronan's May 10, 1880, letter enclosing a copy of his May 5, 1880, report to General Thomas Ruger where Ronan spells out the Salish argument that they were promised a reservation in the Bitterroot in 1855 and so were in compliance with the terms of the 1855 treaty. The Salish would not agree that the whites had any moral or legal right to order them to give up their treaty guaranteed right to hunt off the reservation.
>
>   Col. George Gibson was a Civil War veteran who enlisted from Pennsylvania and died in 1888. He commanded Fort Missoula during the early 1880s.[1]

Roving Indians.

———

Some Erroneous Impressions Corrected by Agent Ronan.

We have urged the Department time and again to put an end to the present system of allowing reservation Indians to prowl through the country at will, but in vain. — *Husbandman.*

What can the Department do after the Ponca decision at Omaha last summer? You might as well urge the Agricultural Department to prohibit a New North-West canvassing agent from visiting Meagher county. There must [be] other law now if the Flathead Indians are to be kept on their reservation. These nomads are a nuisance to the settlements, but they cannot be restrained by action of Agent Ronan or the Indian Commissioner. — *New North-West.*

———

Editor New North-West —

Dear Sir: — Referring to the above, I desire to correct an erroneous impression which seems to prevail throughout the settlements of Montana, that the roving bands of Indians who cross from the West Side to the Eastern slope on hunting excursions are reservation Indians from the Jocko. This is not a fact. Those bands are generally composed of Bitter Root Flatheads and Spokanes from the lower country. The Indians of the Jocko reservation are all at home attending to their farms and herds; occasionally a few of them slip off to hunt with the Bitter Root Flatheads, but as a rule their own sense teaches them it is not to their interest to leave their farms and stock for the chase, and I am happy to add that every year diminishes the number of hunters from this reservation, and at present the number is so small and insignificant that if any are away I am not aware of it. It also seems to be the public impression that the Flathead Agent is responsible for the movements of the Bitter Root Indians, and in order to correct this error I enclose the following correspondence, which explains the matter:

> *Peter Ronan, U.S. Indian Agent, Flathead Agency:*
>
> Sir — Referring to your letter of the 1st inst., requesting permission to distribute a portion of the goods which you have purchased for the Indians on the Jocko reservation among those who have refused to move from Bitter Root valley to said reservation, I have to say that as those remaining in the Bitter Root valley are non-treaty Indians, authority cannot be granted for you to distribute among them goods that belong to those subject to treaty stipulations. I very much regret the necessity for this refusal, as I should like to reward these Indians for their fidelity to the government, and but for want of funds applicable to the purpose would grant your request.
>
> Very respectfully,
> (Signed) E. A. Hayt,
> Com. Indian Affairs.

Washington, Oct. 22, 1877.

———

Headquarters of the Army,
Adjutant General's Office,
Washington, June 4, 1879.

To the Commanding General, Department of Dakota,
through Headquarters Division of the Missouri:

Sir: Referring to your endorsement of the 21st ultimo, upon communication of the commanding officer, Fort Missoula, asking definite information as to jurisdiction of the military over "peaceable" Indians, "non-treaty," and those of the reservation, I have the honor to invite your attention to the following views of the General of the Army endorsed thereon, which are concurred in by the Secretary of War:

"The circular of December 28, 1878, is addressed to Indian agents, and is not obligatory on commanding officers of posts like Missoula; such passes, however, where given should be respected."

The Flathead Indians in the Bitter Root valley are domesticated Indians, and should be allowed to come and go as free as citizens subject to the laws of Montana. Troops should act to protect troops as against whites only when the local civil authorities are unable to keep the peace. When the civil power is sufficient, the military should abstain from any action.

I am, sir, very respectfully,

Your obedient servant,
(Signed) E. D. Townsend,
Adjutant General.

———

Headquarters,
Fort Missoula, M.T., Feb. 13, 1880.
Official copy respectfully furnished Peter Ronan, Esq.,
U.S. Indian Agent, Flathead Agency, M.T.

(Signed) Geo. Gibson,
Lieut.-Col. 3d Infantry,
Commanding Post.
Respectfully yours,
Peter Ronan, Agent.

Jocko Agency, M.T., March 20, 1880.

April 7, 1880

U.S. Office of Indian Affairs, "Letters Received by the Office of Indian Affairs, 1824-1880," National Archives Microfilm Publication M234, reel 517, frames 651-657.

Flathead Indian Agency, Montana.
April 7th, 1880

The
Hon. Commissioner of Indian Affairs
Washington, D.C.

Sir:

I have the honor to enclose herewith letter from the Superior of St. Ignatius Mission, located on this reservation, who has charge of the Indian School, and in connection therewith, would respectfully call your attention to the following correspondence held with your predecessor, last year in regard to the same matter:

Flathead Agency, M.T. March 5th, 1879
Hon. Commissioner Indian Affairs, Washington, D.C.

Sir:

I have the honor to request instructions relative to the disbursement of the "Fund for Schools" which is in the amount of $300.00 per annum, and is placed to my credit in quarterly installments of $75.00. The School at this Agency being under contract made in Washington, cannot, as I understand, come into the benefit of this fund, unless I am specially authorized by you to pay the same to them. This authority I ask for the reason that the schools are maintaining a number of scholars in excess of those provided for under the contract and that tools and agricultural implements are very necessary for their better advancement. I would respectfully request that permission be given me to purchase out of this fund such tools and implements as are necessary for the scholars at the Industrial and Agricultural School.

Your Obedient Servant
Peter Ronan,
U.S. Ind. Agent

To the above letter I received the following response and complied with its instructions:

Dept. of Interior, Office Indian Affairs,
Washington, March 28, 1879.

Peter Ronan, Ind. Agent,
Flathead Agency, Montana.
Sir:

Agreeably with the request contained in your letter dated the 5th instant, you have been authorized by the Hon. the Secretary of the Interior to expend a sum not to exceed $300 in purchasing in open-market Agricultural implements and tools, for use of the children attending the boarding School at your Agency. Payment for the purchases made under this authority to be from the funds named in your said letter.

Very respectfully
E. A. Hayt
Commissioner

Pugh

So there is now placed to my credit under the same restriction, I consider it, as explained in correspondence, a like amount ($300.00) of "School Fund," I respectfully request permission to purchase a reaping machine or other necessary implements of labor (to be paid for from said fund) for the use of the children attending the School, as I consider it necessary for the use and instruction of the Scholars.

Very respectfully,
Your obedt Servt,
Peter Ronan
U.S. Ind. Agent.

Enclosed letter:

St. Ignatius Mission March 30th, 1880

Major P. Ronan U.S. Ind. Agent
Dear Sir:

I would respectfully call your attention to the need we have of more farming implements for carrying on the Industrial School for the Indian boys of these Confederated tribes. Our greatest want for the present is a machine to

reap the grain. According to the terms of the contract, the government promises to furnish all necessary farming tools.

You have lately examined the School, & expressed your surprise at the
progress made by the children. You are aware that instead of limiting ourselves
to the number of children called for by the contract, viz. 40, we have had at no
time less than from 55 to 60. There is great anxiety on the part of the parents
to place their Children at school, but for lack of means we are unable to give
admittance to any more at present. I trust that you will use every exertion
to encourage us in the work which we have undertaken for the good of these
Indians.

Respectfully yours
L. Van Gorp, S.J.

May 10, 1880
*U.S. Office of Indian Affairs, "Letters Received by the Office of Indian Affairs, 1824-
1880," National Archives Microfilm Publication M234, reel 517, frames 669-675.*

> In this letter Ronan outlined why the Bitterroot Salish considered themselves in compliance
> with the 1855 Hellgate Treaty, despite the 1872 Garfield agreement which Charlo did not
> sign. Charlo believed a correct interpretation of the Hellgate Treaty entitled the Salish to a
> reservation in the Bitterroot Valley.

Flathead Indian Agency, Montana.
May 10th, 1880

The
Hon. Commissioner of Indian Affairs,
Washington, D.C.
    Sir:
    I have the honor to forward herewith copy of a report made to Gen. Ruger,
18th U.S. Infantry, Helena, Montana, in reply to a letter requesting a general
description of the Indians under my charge, their reservation and the country
adjacent thereto, and of the neighboring tribes.

Very respectfully,
Peter Ronan
U.S. Ind. Agent.

Enclosed letter:

Flathead Indian Agency, Montana.
May 5th, 1880

Col. [sic] [Thomas] Ruger,
18th Infantry, Commanding,
Helena, Montana
    Sir:
    I have the honor of acknowledging the receipt of yours of the 24th of April
in reply to your inquiries in regard to the number of Indians on this reservation
and other matters of information which you wished to obtain pertaining to the
tribes, I would state, that to my knowledge no census has ever been taken, but
by a careful estimate of numbers, I place them as follows:

Flatheads residing on reservation	100
Pen d'Oreilles residing on reservation	900
Kootenais residing on reservation	350
Bitter Root Flatheads (who do not live on reserve)	375

Under the chieftainship of Arlee, of Flatheads, Michel of the Pen d'Oreilles, and Eneas of the Kootenais, the confederated tribes of this reservation are rapidly advancing in the arts of civilization; having good bands of horses and cattle, a large number of well-fenced farms with dwellings and outbuildings. From their fields over twenty-thousand bushels of wheat, four thousand bushels of oats, besides large quantities of vegetables were raised last year, and the present season bids fair to exceed the last in the matter of crops as a large number have engaged in farming this Spring. A few more years of encouragement in the way of agricultural implements, and in keeping their Shops and Mills running, will make those people independent of Government aid, as their reservation is one of the finest agricultural and stock ranges in Montana. No rations are issued here, and very few of the Indians leave the Reservation for the chase, relying principally upon their farms for support.

The Flatheads occupying the Bitter Root valley having refused to remove to this reservation, under the Garfield Agreement are looked upon, I believe, (by the Department) as non-treaty Indians, as they share in no manner whatever in any of the benefits conferred upon the reservation Indians by the Government. I hold fifty-two patents issued by Government to the Bitter Root Flatheads several years ago, for farms; but upon calling a council of those Indians for the purpose of presenting the patents to those entitled to them, all refused to accept them, claiming that the Bitter Root valley from the crossing of the Lo Lo to the range at the head of the valley belonged to them as a reservation — and they claimed it all as their country, and desire no other title than that of "right and occupancy." In reply to my question to Charlos, the Chief, "why himself and his people asked the Government for separate titles to their lands and then refused to accept them when offered," he replied, in substance, as follows: "Myself nor my People ever asked for such titles. When we signed a paper which was carried around, and gave our names, we did so under the impression that we were asking the Great Father in Washington, to give us the Bitter Root Valley as a reservation."

This Chief also stated to me that notwithstanding his name appeared on the Garfield agreement, he never signed that document or authorized his signature to be placed there. I give you these lengthy details inasmuch as the War Department designates the Bitter Root Flatheads as "domesticated Indians, free to come and go as any other persons amenable to the laws of the Territory." But, to say the least of it, I fear their case will yet lead to complications unless settled definitely and satisfactorily both as to Indians and whites in the Bitter Root valley.

About Eighty or ninety miles west of Fort Missoula, on the Pen d'Oreille River, on the outside of the boundaries of this reservation at a place called Horse Plains, several stock-men have located ranches. A small band of Indians, not exceeding thirty men, women and children, also make their homes at the Plains, and claim a right to the land. As the country is not included in the reservation, the settlers, of course, will pay no attention to the Indians and their controversies are sometimes troublesome to me. The Indians in question are a detached band or fragment of a tribe of Lower Kalispels, who have their headquarters on the Pen d'Oreille river, in Washington Territory, and whose chief is called "Petal" or "Victor." As this Horse Plain band claims Petal as chief, I think, in the interest of settlers as well as Indians, they should live with their tribe in Washington Territory.

From the Lower Country, — Columbia river — we have visits every summer from roving bands of Indians, made up from all the different tribes; but, outside of whiskey drinking and its attendant vices, I hear of no particular depredations from them.

I am very respectfully,
Your obedient servant
Peter Ronan
U.S. Ind. Agent.

June 16, 1880

U.S. Office of Indian Affairs, "Letters Received by the Office of Indian Affairs, 1824-1880," National Archives Microfilm Publication M234, reel 517, frames 678-686.

This gold frenzy among white miners threatened the reservation boundary. However, the rush failed to uncover significant deposits. Maps of the Flathead Reservation drawn before 1880 exist, but they were based on the general lay of the land, not on-the-ground boundary surveys.

The Little Bitterroot River drains the northwest corner of the Flathead Reservation and empties into the Lower Flathead River. It should not be confused with the Bitterroot River south of Missoula.

Flathead Indian Agency, Montana.
June 16th, 1880

The
Hon. Commissioner of Indian Affairs,
Washington, D.C.

Sir:

In my monthly report of March 1st, 1880, I stated, in substance, that intense excitement prevailed in the neighboring settlements bordering upon this reservation in in [sic] regard to an alleged discovery of placer gold mines in close proximity to the western boundary line of the reserve; that miners were passing through the reservation in search of the reported diggings; that I dispatched an employe to ascertain the facts, and that he reported to the best of his knowledge and belief said mines were located some eight miles beyond the Western boundary of the reserve; and inasmuch as I also reported that the Indians claimed that the creek to which the miners were flocking was within the reservation limits, and that the whites claimed that it was not, and that the excitement would tend to gather great numbers of gold-seekers from whom I expected trouble in the spring, and in order to definitely fix the location of these reported mines, and to avoid trouble in the future, I suggested that the reservation boundary lines should be surveyed.

In your reply of April 1st, 1880, you informed me that the records of your office did not show that the boundary lines of the reservation had ever been run and that there were no funds at the disposal of your office applicable to that purpose, and were unable to give me any more definite data with reference thereto than was contained in the treaty of 1855 (12 Stat. 976) which defined the boundaries. It was thought from the quoted description I would be able to ascertain whether the alleged mines were located on the reservation, and in accordance with your instructions to make a thorough investigation as to the location of the mines, and the proper proceedings to take in case I found the mines located within the limits of the reservation, on the 2d day of the present month, accompanied by a guide and my interpreter, I proceeded to carry out your instructions. Following down the Jocko river twelve miles below its Junction with the Pen d'Oreille river we were ferried across the latter stream by an Indian and leaving the river followed a westerly course across Camas Prairie for about thirty-five miles when we entered into Little Bitter Root Valley. At this place I was met by Eneas, chief of the Kootenais, and together we investigated the location of the gulch in question. I found that the creek forms a part of the watershed of and flows into Clarke's Fork, north of a point between the Camas and Horse Prairies, and north as far as to where a line running due East and West through the middle of the Flathead Lake would strike the divide, and therefore report that it is my belief that the creek is not on the reservation. I would also State that it is my belief that no paying mines will be discovered on the creek in question, as I found only three men at work there, the rest of them having abandoned their claims, after giving them a thorough prospecting. While a few colors of gold were discovered in every washing, not enough was obtained to warrant the working of the creek, and it was therefore abandoned with the exception of the three mentioned. The excitement is therefore over, but had the gulch proved rich even though not located on the reservation, is in close proximity to one of the most beautiful and desirable vallies [sic] in the Territory (Little Bitter Root) which is on the reservation, watered as it is with innumerable creeks, cold springs; and also, hot Sulphur springs in which the Indians bathe, and white dwellers in neighboring vallies come to seek health, from their supposed curative qualities. Had the mines in question proved rich the seizure of this valley by settlers would follow, and trouble from the Indians would ensue, but I am now happy to state that I have no apprehension from any influx of miners or settlers to the locality in question, at least for the present season, unless unlooked for developments should take place. As the Indians labored under an impression that the reservation had been surveyed, and claimed that they saw the lines run, I addressed a letter to Surveyor General of Montana in regard to the matter and herewith attach it for your information.

Very respectfully,
Peter Ronan
U.S. Ind. Agt.

Enclosed letter:

Office of the United States Surveyor General, Montana.
Helena, May 31, 1880

Sir:

In reply to your letter of 24th inst, you are respectfully informed that there is no record in this office of the survey of the Flathead Indian Reservation.

Under date of June 11th and 14th, 1875, the Commissioner General Land Office instructed the U.S. Surveyor General for Montana to enter into a contract with Mr. Henry C. F. Hackbusch for the survey of the "Jocko Flathead reservation in Montana," subdividing same into 40 acre tracts; and under date of Sept. 13, 1875, instructed him "that said instructions are superseded by those of the Department of the 10th instant; the sum assigned having been paid to Mr. Hackbusch in satisfaction of a claim arising under his contract of Sept. 8, 1874."

The letters above referred to being the only records in this office relative to the survey of said reservation, I am of the opinion that such survey has never been made.

Very respectfully,
Roswell H. Mason,
U.S. Surveyor General for Montana.

Hon. Peter Ronan,
U.S. Indian Agent,
Flathead Indian Agency,
Montana.

July 28, 1880

U.S. Office of Indian Affairs, "Letters Received by the Office of Indian Affairs, 1824-1880," National Archives Microfilm Publication M234, reel 517, frames 701-706.

Neither the local newspapers nor the letters received by the Commissioner of Indian Affairs in the National Archives give any further information about what became of this group of Nez Perce refugees. It is known that White Bird did not surrender on the Flathead Reservation in 1880 but was killed in Canada by another Nez Perce in 1892.[2] On August 23, 1880, the Commissioner of Indian Affairs recommended to the Secretary of the Interior that if or when the Nez Perce refugees arrived at Flathead they be immediately turned over to the U.S. Army.[3] See also Ronan's letters of July 24, October 6, and November 10, 1879, for more information about this group.

Flathead Agency, M.T.
28 July 1880

Hon. Commissioner of Indian Affairs
Washington, D.C.
Sir:

On the 24th of July 1879 I reported to your Office that ten or fifteen Lodges of Nez Percés (Refugees from White Bird's band of hostiles) were encamped on Tobacco Plains, about forty miles north of the Border, and just over the British Line; — that they Sent a runner here to ask permission to cross the Border, and to live upon this Reservation; that I despatched a messenger to the Nez Percé Camp & informed them that, in accordance with instructions from your Office, dated April 2d, 1879, in case they came in, I would demand of them the Surrender of their arms and horses, and receive them as prisoners, subject to the clemency of the Government.

Under date of October 6th, 1879, I had the honor of addressing a letter to your Office on the same subject; — to which I respectfully refer you for information — and, in answer to said communication I received the following Telegram —

Washington October 23d, 1879.

To Agent Ronan
Flathead Agency, Montana.

In reply to your letter of October 6th, you can say to the Nez Percés, if they choose to come on your Reservation, & be fed, they must do so as prisoners of war, and trust to the clemency of the Government.

(Sgd) E. A. Hayt
Commissioner

Upon receipt of above I held a council with some representatives of the Nez Percés, a full report of which I forwarded to Your Office under date of November 10th, 1879, and, in accordance with arrangements, then made, I gave Tuke-Alix-Shemi (brother of Looking-Glass) a letter, & sent him back to the Nez Percés Camp, but, in the meantime, fearing that they would be made prisoners, & sent to the Indian Territory, the Encampment again Sought refuge with Sitting Bull and White Bird's band, where they remained last winter.

A few days ago a runner came in, Sent by Tuke-Alix-Shemi to inform me that the whole band of Nez Percés, including White Bird, — the Chief with whom they escaped at the surrender to Col. Miles, — were on their way to this Agency for the purpose of Surrendering themselves to me, & throwing themselves on the clemency of the Government.

There are about One Hundred & Forty people, including men, women & children, & they are traveling mostly on foot, having disposed of their horses & guns for provisions for their Starving Women & Children. On their journey here of hundreds of Miles, thro' a mountainous wilderness, the runner informed me, they depend Solely upon their bows & arrows, and fish-hooks for Subsistence,— that they are almost naked and that the once renowned Chief White Bird is utterly broken in Spirit and health, and is perfectly blind. White Bird and his family have not a horse left, & the blind Chief is being led hither on foot. Those unfortunate people will arrive here some time during the month of August, and, as I have no supplies of any kind on hand, either as to provisions or Clothing, I respectfully desire instructions as to what disposition I will make of these people.

They will certainly have to be fed for, at least, one Season, but, if allowed to remain on this Reservation, & assisted with tools and means to farm, next Season they will be in a condition to earn their own living from the production of their farms. As those people, before their unfortunate war, were far in advance in civilizing pursuits, a little assistance in the way of Agricultural Implements, Seed, and Means to fence in farms, will put them once more on the highway to prosperity and civilization. No fears need be entertained, in regard to their Utter and entire Submission, as the misfortunes and miseries, thro' which they have passed since taking up Arms against the Government, have thoroughly Subdued them; and brought them to an understanding of their utter foolishness in undertaking such a cause.

Trusting that I may have some instructions at your earliest convenience,

I remain respectfully,
Your Obedt Servant
Peter Ronan
U.S. Indian Agent.

August 20, 1880
U.S. Commissioner of Indian Affairs, Annual Report of the Commissioner of Indian Affairs *(Washington, D.C.: U.S. Government Printing Office, 1880), pages 231-33.*

Ronan viewed the change from a hunting-gathering economy to one based on ranching and agriculture as a moral question. Tribal members probably saw it more as a practical response to the decline of the buffalo herds and other wildlife resources. Tribal efforts to use agriculture as an addition to the tribal economy, rather than a replacement for hunting, helps explain why tribal members continued seasonal hunting trips when not working on their crops. See, for example, Ronan's letter of December 18, 1880.

Flathead Agency, Montana,
August 20, 1880.

Sir: In accordance with instructions received from your office, I have the honor of submitting my fourth annual report, and in doing so it affords me great pleasure to state that never in the history of this reservation have the Indians enjoyed a more prosperous season. The snug log houses, well-fenced fields of waving grain, vegetable gardens, the thriving stock and permanent appearance of the homes of the industrious portion of the tribes is very encouraging, and has a tendency each year of inducing the more careless and improvident to follow the example of husbandry and thrift. A number of new farms have been fenced in during the past season, and a general tendency to give up their wandering and hunting proclivities for peaceful pursuits has marked the year. The reservation, consisting as it does of 1,433,600 acres of agricultural, grazing, and timber land, well watered by lakes and rivers, and blessed by a temperate climate, where the necessity of irrigation is seldom known, affords facilities for farming not surpassed by any portion of Montana; but it requires time and patience to bring the Indians to a full realization of the blessings which surround them, and the ease with which they can place themselves above want by paying attention to the cultivation of the soil. Encouragement in the way of agricultural implements is one of the chief necessities to this end. Having fenced in a farm, if an Indian cannot procure necessary implements of labor, he becomes discouraged and relaxes to his old habits of the chase and a wandering life, as the amount it would require to purchase a wagon, harness, plow, harrow and other necessary implements is far above the reach of the average Indian.

During the year they have cut and hauled and placed into fence over 60,000 rails and are picking out the most desirable locations in different valleys of the reservation for farms, and instead, as heretofore, of huddling together in villages are spreading out and occupying the land. Last winter was a severe one on stock; hay was scarce and commanded high prices. The Indians have benefited by their experience, and this season are using more energy than they have heretofore displayed putting up hay. On a prairie some 8 miles from the agency, with my employés, I had cut 54 tons of hay for the use of the agency stock. The harvest season is now upon us and the yield will be good. About 25,000 bushels of wheat will be harvested, some 5,000 bushels of oat and barley, besides 6,000 or 7,000 bushels of vegetables. From the agency farm I expect to harvest 300 bushels of wheat, 100 bushels of oats, 400 bushels of potatoes, and 300 bushels of turnips and other vegetables.

Missionary Work.

Under the spiritual guidance of the fathers of St. Ignatius Mission the confederated tribes of this reservation are all professed Catholics. The Indian church at the mission is next to the largest church edifice in Montana, and on Sundays and feast days is hardly capable of holding the throng of Indian worshippers. The choir is composed of Indian school-girls, and their voices, carefully trained by the sisters of charity at the school, are very sweet and plaintive. The laws of the tribes as well as religion strictly prohibit polygamy, and the marriage relations are respected and protected to the best ability of the chiefs and headmen of the nation and their religious teachers.

Indian Education.

The boarding school for boys and girls is carried on in separate buildings, and the progress of the youths is simply wonderful. The girls having the advantage of a boarding school a long time prior to the establishment of one for boys are far in advance of the latter in educational attainments. A few years ago it was a most difficult matter to induce an Indian to allow his boys to be confined to a school-room; but a wonderful change has taken place, and the number of applicants for admission to the school far exceeds the appropriation for feeding, clothing, and taking care of them. The sisters of charity have charge of the school and have competent teachers for boys in fields, mills, and shops, as well as in the school-room. A large number of the children can read and write the English language understandingly, and work in the four first rules of arithmetic. The handwriting of some of the girls are most beautiful specimens of penmanship.

The Sanitary Condition

of the Indians is very good, no deaths having occurred, save from natural causes, and the resident physician has the respect and confidence of the Indians.

Mills and Shops.

At the flouring mill 9,000 bushels of wheat have been ground for Indians; while 100,000 feet of lumber has been cut at the saw-mill for Indian use. The logs are delivered by the Indians, and they also assist in the mill while their bill of lumber is being cut. The blacksmith and carpenter shops every day present a busy scene; and while the Indian apprentice boys receive all the instructions possible in mechanical art, it is very hard to confine them to work, and occasionally some of them take a notion to run away. They much prefer out-door exercise to labor in shops; but patience and forbearance in time may make something out of them, and bring them to a knowledge of the English language and the pursuits of toil.

The Bitter Root Indian Question.

I cannot better present this case to your attention than by furnishing copy of special report written by me to the Indian Office, under date of August 20, 1878, as its direct bearing upon the question has not changed since the date it was furnished.

[Here Ronan quotes his August 20, 1878, letter to the Commissioner of Indian Affairs relative to the Bitter Root land patents which is reproduced above.]

Respectfully submitted,

Your obedient servant,

Peter Ronan,
United States Indian Agent.

The Commissioner of Indian Affairs.

September 17, 1880

U.S. Office of Indian Affairs, "Letters Received by the Office of Indian Affairs, 1824-1880," National Archives Microfilm Publication M234, reel 517, frames 732-733.

Note that the distribution of cattle Ronan proposes here works through the traditional chiefs.

Flathead Agency, M.T.
September 17th, 1880

The
Hon. Commissioner of Indian Affairs,
Washington, D.C.

Sir:

I have two hundred head of stock cattle which were purchased for the Indians, and, from previous correspondence with your office, I was advised that
"said cattle were intended for issue to such of my Indians as in my Judgement
would take proper care of, and not kill or barter them away." As I think the
proper time has arrived to make a partial distribution of the cattle I would
suggest that the most agreeable and satisfactory manner of disposing of them
both as to the Indians and the Agent, (the former head men and chiefs having
fully consulted with me in the matter) would be to turn over one half the band
to the three chiefs of the three different tribes on this reservation and let them
parcel them out to the most deserving of their people — taking a receipt from
every individual, as they are distributed by the chiefs. I would suggest that the
other half of the band be left in the Agent's charge, and a similar distribution
made next year and, from the increase, a distribution made from year to year.

Your Obedt servt,
Peter Ronan
U.S. Ind. Agent.

December 18, 1880

*U.S. Office of Indian Affairs, "Letters Received by the Office of Indian Affairs, 1824-
1880," National Archives Microfilm Publication M234, reel 517, frames 761-65.*

> Ronan's comments about the continued popularity of hunting supports the interpretation
> that many tribal members wanted to use agriculture and ranching to supplement, not
> replace, the traditional economy. See also letter of August 26, 1879, regarding the appren-
> ticeship program.

United States Indian Service,
Flathead Agency,
December 18th, 1880

The
Hon. Commissioner of Indian Affairs,
Washington, D.C.

Sir:

Ever since the promulgation of the order from your predecessor, Mr. Hayt,
to place two apprentices to each mechanic employed at this Agency, I have
striven faithfully to carry out instructions and to nominate and Keep such
apprentices employed; but after a lapse of over a year I find such order, as
applied to this Agency, a waste of time, energy and money and would most respectfully lay the matter before you with the view of correcting this portion of
the service at this Agency at least; for, as I am informed, the Government and
discipline of Indian Agencies vary with circumstances and surroundings, and
where a certain measure or order would be beneficial in one case, it would be
detrimental and pernicious to the good in view by the authority issuing orders
to subordinates, in the other; and, therefore, I submit the case as it pertains to
this Agency.

1st. Although the Indians of this reserve are far advanced in Agricultural and Pastoral pursuits, at certain seasons of the year, after seeding, after harvest and after threshing, every member of a family who can be spared from home is sure to be take himself to the hunting grounds until his labor is needed at home, not only for the spoils of the chase, but for excitement, recreation and to follow the bent of their wild and wayward inclinations; when such parties are fitting out and come to the shops and mills to have grain ground, traps and guns repaired, and create excitement generally in their preparations for departure, around the Agency, is it to be wondered at that the apprentice boy quietly picks ups his blankets and traps and decamps with his relatives for the hunting grounds?

2d. The Agent here, because the Indian[s] are becoming farmers and settlers on their reserve, is forced to be away from the shops and mills and to visit distant portions of the reservation in performance of his duty, and the boys, feeling that they are under no restraint while the Agent is away, are a detrement and source of annoyance to the mechanics, whom they will not obey, but will invariably follow idleness and gambling until the Agent returns.

3d. The Chiefs and parents, invariably, are disposed to discipline the boys, but would rather leave that unpleasant duty to others and find great fault if harsh measures are compelled.

4th. Inspector Pollock, while visiting this Agency last October, was struck by the Expense and trouble of those boys and raised an issue with me, inasmuch as no regular issues are made to the Indians of this reservation, that my accounts in their support would be disputed at headquarters.

5th. One of the most excellent boarding and industrial schools for Indians in the West, is in operation on this reservation where suitable teachers in scholastic attainments, mechanical arts, agricultural Knowledge, — and where strict disciplinarians are employed, whose duty it is to look after and take care of the morals and good behavior of their pupils, and to enforce discipline, and to this institution I would ask to remand the care of those boys for their own good and for the economical benefit of the Indian service on this reservation. I would also state in connection with above, that inasmuch as the apprentice boys at the Agency are allowed beside their clothing and subsistence, five dollars per month, and at the end of each quarter when they receive their pay it is a source of displeasure and Jealousy to the boys at the school, — who perform work in mills, shops and fields, — and they feel that discrimination is made against them. I trust that you will perceive that it will redound to the benefit of the service to at once discharge the boys in question and place them at the Industrial School.

Very respectfully,
Your obedt servt,
Peter Ronan
U.S. Indian Agent.

1881

January 1, 1881
LR 931/1881, RG 75, National Archives, Washington, D.C.

Most of Ronan's monthly reports were not preserved. For some reason, however, a number from 1881 and 1882 survived and are reproduced here. The quality of these reports indicates the missing ones must have contained valuable information about Flathead Reservation life and affairs.

The change from winter free ranging of cattle and horse herds to feeding hay, greatly increased the labor involved in raising stock on the reservation. The increased size of tribal members' herds by 1881, combined with a severe winter, put the survival of the horses and cattle at risk.

United States Indian Service,
Flathead Agency,
January 1st, 1881.

The Hon. Commissioner of Indian Affairs
Washington, D.C.

Sir:

On the commencement of the year 1881, I have to report the continuance of deep snow and furious storms which have prevailed during the whole month, and the snow now lies on the ground fully two feet deep on a level; such storms and deep snow as have prevailed during the past two months are entirely out of the recollection of the oldest Indian inhabitant of This reservation, and great fears are entertained for the safety of stock, as heretofore, the winter ranges were scarcely ever covered and stock throve and fattened without feed of any kind in winter, save the grasses of the ranges, and the idea of putting up hay to feed cattle was scouted at as a useless waste of time by the Indians. Fortunately there are straw stacks in all the Indian fields and by Judicious management and exciting energetic movements on the part of the Indians in caring for their cattle, I trust to "weather the storm" with out serious loss. I had cut and put up for Agency use some fifty-five tons of hay last Summer and I hope to have sufficient for the use of the working stock to carry them through the season. Hay is selling in the White settlements outside of the reservation for thirty dollars per ton, and can hardly be procured at those figures.

The new Threshing machine which was furnished the agency has done good work. It is a railroad horse-power and capable of threshing about twenty five bushels per hour; being small and easily moved and handled I consider it the best machine for Indian use, but one more machine of the same Kind is badly needed here to meet the increasing demand and to facilitate the threshing of Indian grain before winter storms set in; about twenty five thousand bushels of grain of all kinds was raised upon the reservation last year; The Agency farm is not considered a *model farm,* but I was enabled to raise two hundred and fifty bushels of wheat and 197 bushels of Oats the past season. The wheat, (a part of which I convert into flour and issue to the old and indigent Indians and retain seed enough for next season's use,) I have stored in the grannary [sic]. The usual amount of labor has been performed during the month, such as threshing, running saw mill and grist mill, hauling fuel, burning charcoal, hauling hay; and on the first of the week I will start the men at getting out timbers for the building of a bridge across Finley Creek, which is a great necessity for Agency accomodation.

During the month I caused the arrest of two white men on charge of murdering an Indian, a special report of which I will give as soon as all facts are ascertained.

The school is in a very flourishing condition; the boys evincing a great talent for music. At their own expense, the teachers in charge have ordered from California some fifteen brass instruments, and a band will be at once organized among the school boys, with one of the Missionary fathers as musical director.

The taking of the census of the Indians I find to be a most annoying and laborious piece of business, as the Indians are scattered all over the reservation of about a hundred miles square, and some of them are averse to answering questions, being morose and sullen when the long list of (to their ears) complicated questions are asked of them to be answered.

Travel over the reservation, at present, is almost Entirely suspended on account of the depth of the snow and a delay will be caused in the taking of the census.

The Sanitary and School reports are herewith enclosed, giving information on those branches of the service.

Very respectfully
Peter Ronan
U.S. Indian Agent.

January 22, 1881a
LR 2,130/1881, RG 75, National Archives, Washington, D.C.

On February 8, 1881, the Commissioner of Indian Affairs instructed Ronan to work with the District Attorney to secure William Loza's indictment and conviction at the next term of court.[1] Seven people were paid witness fees in the case of Territory of Montana vs. Loso and Asher, presumably in the Justice of the Peace Court.[2] Four pages of testimony and an affidavit, which were probably from the Justice Court trial, were misfiled and have survived in the Missoula District Court Records. The testimony suggests Loza claimed he killed the Indian man in self-defense.[3]

Nothing in the District Court records indicates the District Attorney ever filed charges against Loza in District Court as ordered by the Commissioner of Indian Affairs. The surviving evidence is unclear, but suggests in this case the territorial court system was not able to resolve the case.

No further information was found about defendant Wm. Loza, but Sam Asher died at Horse Plains on January 17, 1882, at about 50 years of age.[4] Washington J. McCormick served a controversial term as Flathead Indian Agent between 1866 and 1868. In the 1880s, he was a prominent Missoula attorney and the owner of Fort Owen in Stevensville.[5] Justice of the Peace Thomas M. Pomeroy came to Missoula in 1865 by way of the California and Idaho gold fields. He died at Deer Lodge in 1882.[6] No information was located about Serg. Fordham. Adolph Lozeau was a farmer near Superior where in 1880 he lived with his wife and seven children.[7]

United States Indian Service,
Flathead Agency, M.T.
January 22d, 1881.

Hon. Commissioner Indian Affairs
Washington, D.C.
      Sir
      In reference to your letter "C.W. Montana, P. 1315-80" enclosing copy of
a report to Hon. Carl Schurz, Secretary of the Interior, dated at Spokan Falls,
Washington Territory, October 26–80, from U.S. Inspector W. J. Pollock, stating
that a wanton and unprovoked murder of an Indian was committed on the 28th
of September last by one Wm. Loza, alias Buffalo Bill, Some thirty miles west of
this Agency, and ordering me to investigate the matter and if possible, obtain
the necessary facts and evidence upon which to institute criminal proceedings
against this man, and place the Same in the hands of the Civil Authorities. I
would respectfully report, that having fully investigated the matter, and procuring necessary evidence, I Swore out a warrant for the arrest of Wm. Loza,
alias Buffalo Bill, charged with the murder of Said Indian, and also for the arrest of one Sam Asher as accessory thereto, both of whom were arrested by the
Sheriff of the County of Missoula, and brought before T. M. Pomeroy, Justice of
the Peace, of the Town of Missoula for a hearing. The District Attorney, whose
jurisdiction extends over three Counties, could not attend the investigation in
Missoula, as Court was then in Session in a distant Town where his presence
was necessary, and he having no deputy in Missoula, I was Compelled to employ Washington J. McCormick to prosecute the case. Although the evidence
against Loza was very strong, the Justice of the Peace Saw fit to discharge both
Prisoners. The following copy of a letter from my Attorney in the case, fully
explains the matter and I herewith append it:

Missoula, M.T.
January 15th, 1881

Major Ronan
U.S. Ind. Agent
Flathead Agency,
      Dear Sir
      In answer to your note of the 9th. inst. in reference to the
Loza murder case investigated by Justice Pomeroy on the 23d.
and 24th. ult. I beg to submit the following reply. The prosecution proved that defendant William Loza (alias Buffalo Bill)
killed an Indian on or about the 28th. day of September A.D.
1880. The proof of the killing was confined to the declarations
of the defendant made to Edwin Johnson and others on the
day of the Killing, and to Lieut. Williams of the U.S.A. and
others subsequently. That the Killing took place on the Mullan Road some four or five miles below Superior City and
about Sixty miles below Missoula. The prosecution Supported
the declaration of the defendant Loza as to the Killing by the
testimony of Serg. Fordham U.S.A. and [Keys?] Teamster to
the effect that they Saw on the following morning at the place
described by the Defendant signs and indication of a difficulty between White Men and Indians, and picked up a Deck
of Cards Covered with human blood.

That about two weeks after the Killing, the dead body of an Indian was found near the Road at the identical Spot where Deft. Loza described the difficulty as having taken place. That the body of the Indian found dead was recognized by Adolph Lozeau, living some Seven miles from the place where it was found, as that of an Indian who had left his house about 1 O'clock, in Company with two other Indians, the Same day that Loza Confessed he Killed an Indian. This is the substance of testimony obtained from fifteen Witnesses examined upon the part of the people.

No Stronger proof as to the Killing and that the Defendant Loza Killed the Indian found dead could be adduced. As to whether the Killing was done in Self-defense can never be determined until all the facts connected with the difficulty are detailed by the other Indians who were present.

This is a fact to be determined by a Trial Jury upon a regular indictment found by a grand Jury. The Government owes it to itself to See that whenever an Indian is Stricken by a White Man without just cause or provocation that he is punished to the extent of the law. And at the June term of the District Court the matter ought to be fully investigated by the Grand Jury, and William Loza indicted and tried for murder. The discharge of Loza by Justice Pomeroy is no bar to an indictment and Trial by the District Court.

Very Respectfully
Your Obt. Servt.
W. J. McCormick

I would respectfully add that the murdered Indian, nor either of the Indians who were in Company with him on the day of the Killing, did not belong to this Reservation, but resided in the Spokan Country. It is possible that I may be able to procure the attendance of the Indians who witnessed the affray before the next Session of the Grand Jury, which meets in June, and I have no doubt but an indightment and arrest of Loza will follow the investigation.

Loza I learn is living on his Ranche again in fancied Security from any other inquiry into this matter.

Very Respectfully
Your Obedient Servt.
Peter Ronan
U.S. Indian Agent.

January 22, 1881b

LR 2,131/1881, SC 55, RG 75, National Archives, Washington, D.C.

The construction of the Northern Pacific Railroad through the reservation was a frequent topic in Ronan's correspondence for several years. Joseph K. McCammon, United States Assistant Attorney General, was sent to the reservation in 1882 to negotiate the purchase of a right-of-way for the railroad through the reservation. A council was held between August 31 and September 2, 1882, and an agreement to sell the right-of-way was signed by 219 male tribal members on September 2.[8]

On May 20, 1881, the Commissioner instructed Ronan to allow the Northern Pacific Railroad "to make the necessary preliminary surveys in order to locate the line of route." He was to assure tribal members that, even though the treaty provided for the right-of-way through the reservation, the land would not be taken without an agreement with the tribes and "fair compensation."[9] Despite these instructions, in March 1882 the Commissioner criticized Ronan for allowing the preliminary surveys.[10]

United States Indian Service,
Flathead Agency,
January 22, 1881

Hon. Commissioner Indian Affairs,
Washington, D.C.

Sir,

As the building of the Northern Pacific Railroad will probably approach this Reservation early next summer, and as the Indians are beginning to evince some feelings of excitement in the event, as it is understood the road is expected to pass through the Reservation, I desire to be fully prepared to act in accordance with your views and to council with the Indians in regard to their rights as viewed by the Honorable Commissioner. It is held by the Indians that no Railroad Company has the right of way through the Reservation unless they (the Indians) sell that right, and from the expressions of some of the head men and Chiefs, difficulties will arise in obtaining the consent of the tribes even if the right of way is paid for unless the matter is attended to in time. I am not aware if it is the intention of the railroad company to run the road through the reservation, but meddlesome persons are giving the Indians a great deal of uneasiness on the subject, going as far as to say that in receipting for an issue of the stock cattle sent here by the Indian Department for distribution among them they would be accepting a small bribe from the railroad company for their land; of course I have eradicated that idea from their minds, and only allude to it to show the necessity of giving me full information and instructions in the matter for my guidance in councils and conversations with the Chiefs and head men of the tribes on the subject.

Very respectfully
Your obedient Serv't
Peter Ronan,
U.S. Indian Agent.

February 1, 1881a
LR 2,692/1881, RG 75, National Archives, Washington, D.C.

United States Indian Service,
Flathead Agency,
February 1st, 1881

The
Hon. Commissioner of Indian Affairs,
Washington, D.C.

Sir:

There has been no cessation during the month of January of the furious snow storms already reported, in fact, the weather has been more severe than during the month of December, and the snow now lies all over the country to a depth of not less than four feet; an occasional gleam of sunshine with a few hours of southerly wind melted the snow on top, and then intense frost set in and now the whole face of the country — mountains, hills and vallies — are encased in one gleaming, glistening crust, shutting out in its cold and dazzling embrace all hope to the starving cattle, horses and wild game. Snow plows were brought into requisition on the Jocko but were found to be utterly useless, owing to the depth of the snow, also the crust on the top and ice on the bottom. I succeeded in getting nearly all of the agency stock and neighboring bands of Indian cattle upon a creek close to the Agency, which is thickly grown with willows, small birch browse and some large cotton-wood trees, which I had felled by axmen, and the ice loosened from the creek to furnish a plentiful supply of water. The calves I separated from the cows, and with the poorest of the cattle, feed upon hay and straw which I have carefully doled out to them. With such precaution the stock could be carried through the rigors of any winter ever before known to the inhabitants of this country. But the intense cold, with unceasing nightly drifting storms are cutting them down in flesh and weakening them to such an extent that they have neither courage or strength to "rustle" for themselves, and already several head have died, and unless a sudden change comes in the weather I fear the worst for the rest. I have about twenty-five tons of hay left at the stack on Camas Prairie, and despite the storm, kept a road open all winter until the 29th inst., and on that day four horses attached to a sled were unable to plow through the drifts to obtain a load of hay; we have since broken the road by shoveling snow ahead of the horses.

I am compelled to employ an Extra hand for this month to assist in breaking roads, hauling hay, and assisting in attending to the cattle.

During the month with Agency employes, I constructed a bridge fifty feet in length across Finley creek and also a smaller bridge across Mill Creek both of which streams were rendered impassable for teams by the gorging of ice. The bridges are constructed in a substantial and workmanlike manner, both streams being spanned with heavy fir stringers and covered with thick pine planks sawed out at the Agency mill.

An unusual amount of sickness prevailed among the Indians during the month, and owing to the non-arrival of medical supplies at this Agency up to present date, the physician labors under great disadvantages in battling with disease. A large quantity of other necessary invoiced articles for this Agency have not yet arrived.

Enclosed please find School and Sanitary reports.

Very respectfully,
Your obedient servant,
Peter Ronan,
U.S. Indian Agent.

February 1, 1881b

LR 2,693/1881, RG 75, National Archives, Washington, D.C.

This request from Ronan emphasizes how few tribal members received supplies from the agency, since most were self-supporting. Ronan's request to distribute supplies as needed was approved by the Commissioner on February 17, 1881.[11]

United States Indian Service,
Flathead Agency,
February 1st, 1881

The
Hon. Commissioner of Indian Affairs
Washington, D.C.

Sir,

I have the honor to request authority to issue supplies to Indians of this reservation who are sick and indigent at such time as they need them without being restricted to regular weekly issues.

The Indians under my charge to a great extent live far from the agency and cannot always be there on Saturdays to procure what they need but come at such times as their necessities compel them. Issues are only made to those who are sick, old, or very poor; no regular rations are given. It seems to them an unnecessary hardship to be forced to wait until a certain day to get what they may need for the sick and poor and so complain to me. In view of these facts I would respectfully ask the authority referred to be granted me.

Very respectfully,
Your obedient servant,
Peter Ronan,
U.S. Indian Agent.

March 1, 1881
LR 4,558/1881, RG 75, National Archives, Washington, D.C.

United States Indian Service,
Flathead Agency,
March 1st, 1881

Hon. Commissioner of Indian Affairs,
Washington, D.C.

Sir:

After a winter, the severity of which has never been known by any inhabitant of Montana, the First of March has dawned upon this reservation clad in the garb of early spring. The snow has disappeared from hills and vallies, the mountain streams have broken their icy bondage, and fresh green grass is springing to the sunlight. Although the cattle herds everywhere in this Territory have suffered greatly and losses will be almost ruinous to many, I feel confident that the percentage of loss on this reservation, when reported, will fall below that of other localities in Montana.

As the Agency hay will be all Expended before plowing season commences, and as none can be procured at any price, and also as the horses have been kept constantly at work all winter and will need a rest, I deem it advisable to turn them out upon the range so soon as a sufficiency of grass appears, and to break the steers for work, received by me under the Power contract for Beef cattle, inasmuch as very little beef has been or will be required here this year owing to the fact that game has been very plentiful during the winter and easily captured and also that the Indians butchered cattle, when it was apparent they could not be saved through the rigors of the winter, and made beef of the same. The Indian horses are small and were poorly fed through the winter, and will be incapable of doing heavy work on a plow, and by breaking the steers mentioned, a great deal of assistance can be rendered the Indians in putting in their crops. Outside of work in mills and shops the Agency employes have been kept constantly busy in hauling saw-logs, wood, and hay, and also in giving attention to cattle which at the First of the month of February looked as though they would be all swept away by the fury of the storms and a lack of feed.

On the 14th ultimo. I sent my head-farmer and an interpreter to the Kootenai camp on Dayton creek (60 miles from the Agency) to take the census of that tribe.

They were compelled to travel on Snow shoes a great part of the distance and to haul their provisions and bedding on tobogans, but succeeded in accomplishing their object in the face of all the obstacles thrown in their way by the elements. The taking of the census has been greatly retarded by the heavy snows which rendered the roads impassable, and the intense cold that made it dangerous to human life to venture out on protracted journeys to the various homes of the Indians on the reservation.

No incident of note occured during the past month that warrants any special mention, and everything pertaining to the welfare of the Indians under my charge seems to be progressing satisfactorily, as I hear of no reports save those of quiet and contentment.

Enclosed please find School and Sanitary reports which give information in regard to those branches of the service.

Very respectfully
Peter Ronan
U.S. Indian Agent.

April 1, 1881
LR 6,132/1881, RG 75, National Archives, Washington, D.C.

United States Indian Service,
Flathead Agency,
April 1st, 1881

The
Hon. Commissioner of Indian Affairs,
Washington, D.C.

Sir:

The month of March has been a very pleasant one at this reservation, as we were visited by no storm of any kind during the whole month, and the grass has sprung up green and luxuriant affording good feed for the cattle that got through the rigor of the winter, which was the severest ever known in this region.

Plowing commenced two weeks go, and the Indians are busily employed in their fields: plowing up land, making new inclosures, and preparing generally for the Spring planting. More farming will be done this season than ever before upon this reservation, as the Indians have been very energetic during the Winter in splitting rails and fencing in new farms.

The prompt arrival of the fine invoice of garden seeds, which I have commenced issuing to those Indians who have garden enclosures, has been very satisfactory and has lent encouragement to their energies.

The mills and Shops have been in constant Employment during the month, grinding wheat, sawing lumber, repairing plows and Wagons and other implements of labor. The present month will be mostly devoted to plowing up land and seeding crops.

Inclosed please find sanitary report and school report for the month of March.

Very respectfully,
Peter Ronan
U.S. Indian Agent.

May 1, 1881
LR 8,239/1881, RG 75, National Archives, Washington, D.C.

United States Indian Service,
Flathead Agency,
May 1st, 1881

The Hon. Commissioner of Indian Affairs
Washington, D.C.

Sir:

The month of April was devoted almost exclusively to plowing, breaking up new land, and planting, and sowing seeds of all kinds, and the Indians have shown marked improvement in habits of industry, and are vying with each other in improving their farms and buildings, and the breaking up and seeding of land. The Excellent quality and varied assortment of garden seeds sent, upon my requisition, by the Department this Spring, arrived on time and has afforded the Indians a great deal of satisfaction, as they are very fond of garden vegetables, and a large number of families have bent their energies towards putting in a kitchen garden as well as raising grain.

The severe weather of last winter, which caused a heavy loss of cattle, has admonished the Indians to be better prepared in the future, and meadow lands where hay can be procured is being carefully guarded from being overrun by stock, and hay in greater quantities will be cut and stacked this season.

Having sowed their crops, the Indians are bringing in their surplus grain to be ground into flour for use until the next Crops are harvested, and the flouring mill is overrun with work. The large Ames' 30 horse power engine, which furnishes the power, consumes an immense quantity of fuel, which requires a great deal of labor to procure.

The Blacksmith is in constant employment sharpening plows, repairing wagons and agricultural implements, while the carpenter's shop presents a busy scene; in fact, all departments of the service here are well attended to, and all that is required of forethought and knowledge of the service is being done for the good management and successful conduct of the service at this Agency.

I herewith Inclose school and Sanitary reports, which give requisite information in regard to those branches of the business.

Very respectfully,
Peter Ronan
U.S. Indian Agent.

May 6, 1881
LR 8,318/1881, RG 75, National Archives, Washington, D.C.

This letter from Chief Arlee to President James A. Garfield appealed to Garfield's interest in Flathead Reservation affairs resulting from his 1872 visit to the reservation and Bitterroot

Valley. Unfortunately Garfield was inaugurated in March 1881, assassinated on July 2, and
died on September 19, 1881.

United States Indian Service,
Flathead Agency,
May 6th, 1881

The
Hon. Commissioner of Indian Affairs
Washington, D.C.
   Sir:
   I enclose herewith a letter from Arlee, Chief of the reservation Flatheads,
to the President of the United States, and respectfully request that it be for-
warded by you to the President.

Your obedient servant
Peter Ronan
U.S. Indian Agent.

Enclosure:

United States Indian Service,
Flathead Agency,
May 6th, 1881

To the
Honorable James A. Garfield,
President of the United States,
Washington, D.C.
   Honored Sir:
   I am sure you will pardon the presumption of an untutored Indian in thus
addressing one who is now our Great father and Chief, and President of the
United States, but as I once held council with you in my own country and
marked the kindness of your heart in dealing with the Indians, and as I feel
sure you do not forget me, I make bold to write you this letter, and sincerely
trust you will not feel it beneath your dignity to answer me, and give me and
my people the encouragement and consolation I desire before the grave closes
over me, as I am now an old man.
   As you will remember, on the 27th day of August, 1872, articles of agreement were made between yourself as special commissioner, authorized by the
Secretary of the Interior, to carry into execution the provisions of the Act approved June 5th, 1872, for the removal of the Flathead and other Indians from
the Bitter Root valley, of the first part, and Charlot, first chief; Arlee, second
chief; and Adolph, Third Chief of Flatheads of the Second part.
   I am Arlee, one of the signers of that agreement, the man that took your
council and induced all the Flatheads that would follow me to remove to the
Jocko reservation, consisting of about one hundred men, women and Children.
The rest of the tribe chose to remain in the Bitter Root valley with Charlot,
First Chief, and Adolph, Second Chief, and unfriendly feelings exist between
the two latter Chiefs in regards to me because I choose to take your council
and obey the agreement entered into between us; but let that pass, I do not
complain of their feelings towards me, but I am only solicitous for the good and
the welfare of all the Indians of the Flathead Nation.
   The Jocko reservation is now our home where we cultivate the Soil, live
in comfortable houses and have herds of cattle and horses around us, and,

although not rich, are happy and contented. We love our homes and country as all men love their homes, but we sometimes fear that we will not be left in possession of our lands, and this fear causes a great many of the Indians of the tribes that occupy this reservation to abstain from improving their homes or of cultivating their lands, saying: "What is the use of trying to make a home — are not the railroad surveyors already commencing to lay off a rail road through our Country — and when the whitemen demand our land we must give it up, and then what can we do to prevent our Children from Starving, but to wander about in quest of game, which is also fast disappearing from the face of the country."

Our Agent, whom we all respect, and who has been here with us four years, informs us that we need not fear that we will be dispoiled of our homes — that the great heart of the American people would not countenance such an act, and advises all to take up land and fence it in and cultivate the soil. Our people need encouragement, and to that end I earnestly beg of you to allow myself, with a chief from each tribe on the reservation including Charlot, from the Bitter Root valley, one interpreter, and the Agent to visit you at Washington, the party to consist of Six persons; and there and then to settle all disputes in regard to the Bitter Root question, which Still remains open as a wound in the minds of some three hundred Flathead Indians that reside there with Charlot; also to settle and set at rest the uneasiness which is daily growing in the minds of our people that if a railroad is permitted to be built through the reservation the whites will immediately take possession of our lands and drive us from our homes; these questions with others of vital importance to us and our future welfare we desire to discuss and to Settle forever. I also call your attention to the fact that although our fathers received and entertained Lewis and Clarke, the first whitemen who ever explored our country, and, to use your own language, in your report to the Hon. Secretary of the Interior, after your visit to us:

"Few tribes of Indians are so intelligent and well-disposed. It is their just boast that none of their tribe has Ever killed a whiteman. Nearly forty years ago, of their own motion, they sent messengers to St. Louis to invite Missionaries to come among them and teach them the Christian religion"; while delegates from nearly every other tribe of Indians have been invited to Washington, no Chief or member of the Flathead Nation, has ever been asked or permitted to see your great Country or to State their grievances and wants in person to the Great Father at Washington, and as you know us, and know that no trifling Excuse would move us to beg this boon, and feeling confident it will be granted

I remain
Arlee his X mark, Chief of Flatheads

Witness to mark:
Henry A. Lambert.

June 1, 1881
LR 10,173/1881, RG 75, National Archives, Washington, D.C.

United States Indian Service,
Flathead Agency,
June 1st, 1881

The
Hon. Commissioner of Indian Affairs
Washington, D.C.

Sir:

The past month at this reservation has been marked by hot sultry days and cold nights accompanied by light frosts, and, although the growing vegetation has not been seriously damaged, it is not so far advanced as it should be at this date.

Since my induction in office as Agent at this reservation, which is over four years, there has been no necessity for irrigating grain fields, but if present drouth continues one week longer, the Indian grain fields will have to be irrigated, but, fortunately, ditches conveying water to nearly every field are already provided, as I foresaw that an emergency of this kind might arise, and an abundance of water can be flooded over the fields. An unusual amount of grain was seeded down this season by Indians in all the different vallies of the reservation, and I am hopeful of an abundant yield. A large number of vegetable gardens are also under cultivation and, as a rule the Indians are thrifty and industrious and are proud of their fields and gardens. The herd of Stock-cattle, which I succeeded in bringing through the rigors of the last winter, I am now issuing to the Indians who are rejoiced with them. I am confining my issues to the old and needy and to those who will take care of them and their increase.

Several Indians are at work delivering logs at the mill which I will saw up into suitable bills for their wants in building and other purposes. In addition to other work by employes, a large pit of Charcoal has been burned, consisting of Some three hundred bushels. All of the Agency buildings are now undergoing a general renovation and are being whitewashed with lime. The usual routine of work is being carried on in mills and Shops, and no event has transpired during the month to mar the good feelings, which exist among the Indians, or to lure them from the pursuits of industry which are beginning to prevail among them.

Enclosed please find School and Sanitary reports which give all necessary information in regard to those branches of the service.

Very respectfully,
Peter Ronan
U.S. Indian Agent.

June 30, 1881
LR 11,861/1881, RG 75, National Archives, Washington, D.C.

United States Indian Service,
Flathead Agency,
June 30th, 1881

Hon. Commissioner Indian Affairs
Washington, D.C.

Sir:

I have the honor to report that the month of June opened with cold, chilly, dry weather, and with occasional frosts at nights, which caused considerable damage to the tender vegetables and plants of the numerous Indian gardens; the grain crops were also backward owing to the same cause, and preparations were being made to commence irrigating the various Indian fields and farms when wet weather set in about the twenty-second of the month and continued for a few days, furnishing warm and refreshing showers, giving life and vigor to the growing crops, and now the fields are waving green and luxuriantly, bidding fair to bless Indian toil with a bountiful harvest.

While the growing crops are maturing, a great many Indians are taking advantage of their time and are delivering logs at the Agency saw mill (one family alone having delivered during the month one hundred prime logs) which I have sawed at the mill into suitable bills of lumber for building purposes, and after harvest time, when the lumber becomes thoroughly seasoned, a large number of new houses will be erected by the Indians. Improvements in the way of building and fencing are very gratifying, and the reservation now is dotted over with thrifty looking farms, snug buildings and well fenced fields, with good crops of grain and vegetables.

For ensuing fiscal year it will be necessary to employ the following list which I have already forwarded for your consideration: viz:

Interpreter whose duties are to report correctly to me all Indian talks and councils also to witness all issues etc.

Physician whose time is almost constantly employed in visiting the sick Indians of the reservation.

Head miller who is employed in the grist-mill and in running the saw mill and shingle machine.

Assistant miller whose principal duty it is to run the thirty horse power engine connected with the mills, acting also as foreman and chopper of fuel.

Head farmer, who has various duties to perform, acting as general foreman, instructor of Indians in their various avocations and farm labors, also assists the Agent in his office duties.

Assistant farmer whose duties require him about the fields and farms, constantly giving instructions in reaping, mowing, planting, fencing, making rails, running threshing machine and all other requirements pertaining to general farm work.

Herder, who has charge of all stock and cattle belonging to the government, and a general supervision over Indian stock.

Blacksmith, constantly employed in the shop, repairing implements of labor, shoeing horses, etc., etc.

Gunsmith, assistant to blacksmith, and is also detailed to do general labor such as hawling wood, burning charcoal et., et.

Carpenter — constantly employed in the shop making doors, sash, coffins, repairing wagons, making harrows, building and doing repairs of all kinds.

The weather at present date is very hot and dry, and a brilliant comet is nightly to be seen in the Northwest.

All Agency employees are kept at work in their various vocations and the Indians are peaceful and contented, and are making rapid advances in civilizing pursuits.

The Grand Jury of the County of Missoula is now in session, and I have presented several cases before them of whisky selling to Indians in the white settlement, and also two murder cases, and as numerous Indian witnesses have been summoned, I am hopeful that several indictments will follow investigation.

Enclosed please find School report, and also report of the Physician, which the necessary information in regard to those branches of the service.

I remain respectfully
Your obedient servant
Peter Ronan
U.S. Indian Agent.

August 1, 1881
LR 14,119/1881, SC 55, RG 75, National Archives, Washington, D.C.

The two white men arrested for selling liquor to Indians were Patrick Farraher and Samuel McKenney. They were accused of providing liquor to two unnamed Indian women in Missoula. Missoula District Court Records suggest the prosecution was dropped because witnesses failed to appear.[12]

The Bitterroot Indian who was arrested for murder was Pierre. According to the court records, he killed Joseph Louis. He was convicted of second degree murder, sentenced to 12 years, and sent to prison at Deer Lodge, where he died on January 10, 1885.[13]

Thomas F. Oakes became Vice President of the Northern Pacific Railroad in June 1881, just after Henry Villard gained control of the company. In 1888, he was named President of the Northern Pacific.[14] After many years experience as an engineer for various American railroads, Adna Anderson was appointed chief engineer for the Northern Pacific Railroad in February 1880. He was in charge of the construction of the railroad through Montana.[15]

United States Indian Service,
Flathead Agency,
August 1st, 1881

Hon. Commissioner Indian Affairs
Washington, D.C.
Sir:
I have the honor to report that the month of July has been a busy one on this reservation.

The severity of last winter, involving as it did a very great loss of cattle, has admonished the Indians of the necessity of providing provender and shelter for their stock, and a large number have been engaged during the month in cutting and stacking hay; others are hawling saw-logs to the mill, which are being cut into suitable bills of lumber, according to their wants. Some of the Agency employees are putting up hay for use of Agency stock, while others are engaged in the usual shop and mill work.

The grain is fast ripening and this week will see the commencement of harvest. The spring was cold and backward and the summer season was very dry, but notwithstanding these drawbacks a fair average crop of grain and vegetables will be harvested.

During this month two white men were arrested and incarcerated in the Missoula County jail for giving or selling whisky to Indians in the town of Missoula. I have succeeded in breaking up the whisky traffic on the reservation, and not a single case of drunkeness has come under my notice or been reported to me during the fiscal year; but when the vicious portion of the Indians visit the towns they are supplied with liquor and get intoxicated, but take good care not to return to the reservation in that condition, as they well know that they will be immediately arrested and punished by the efficient volunteer police force of Indians of the reservation. Vigorous means, however have been instituted by the civil authorities in this county to prevent the sale of liquor to Indians in the settlements, and I think the traffic will eventually be broken up. I also caused the arrest of an Indian, who claims his home to be in the Bitterroot valley, on charge of having murdered an Indian of this reservation; the prisoner is confined in the Missoula County jail awaiting trial.

Several officials of the Northern Pacific Railroad Company have passed through the reservation during the month, among whom was Vice-President [Thomas] Oakes, and I have been notified to expect on the fifth instant General [Adna] Anderson, the Chief Engineer. No locating party has yet made their appearance on the reservation; but I have thoroughly prepared the Indians for that event and no difficulty nor impediments may be anticipated from them in the locating and surveying of the route through the reservation, but when that is done they will expect and ask for a reasonable compensation for the land appropriated by the railroad company.

A large number of Nez Percie Indians arrived here yesterday, claiming to have come from their Agency, in Idaho. They report to me to be on a friendly visit to the Indians of this reservation, and to trade horses for buffalo robes, etc., and expect to return to their reservation in a few weeks.

Enclosed please find physician's report; also report from boarding school for girls. Through some mistake report from the boys boarding school has not yet reached me, but will be forwarded to you in a few days as I have notified the teachers in charge of the school of the non-receipt of said report at this office, and the necessity of forwarding it at once.

Very respectfully,
Your obedient Servant,
Peter Ronan,
U.S. Indian Ag't.

August 15, 1881

U.S. Commissioner of Indian Affairs, Annual Report of the Commissioner of Indian Affairs *(Washington, D.C.: U.S. Government Printing Office, 1881), pages 173-75.*

Ronan equated adopting white American economic activities and values with "progress," but many tribal members supported some economic change to compensate for declining wild game resources. His discussion of how tribal members combined hunting and gathering with agriculture is especially valuable. Ronan pointed out that many tribal members who did not farm engaged in seasonal agricultural and ranch work. He also described how unoccupied reservation land was claimed by tribal members during the nineteenth century.

His report spelled out that in 1881 tribal members routinely traveled off the reservation without passes from the agent.

The tribal census Ronan finished has not survived in the National Archives. See his letters of January 1 and March 1, 1881, for comments on the problems encountered in taking the census.

In the early 1880s, Rev. John B. A. Brouillet, was Director of the Bureau of Catholic Indian Missions which handled relations between the Catholic Indian missionaries and the U.S. Office of Indian Affairs in Washington, D.C. He had previously worked as a missionary to various Indian tribes in the Pacific Northwest.[16]

Flathead Agency, Mont.,
August 15, 1881.

Sir: In compliance with the regulations of the Indian service, I have the honor to submit this, my fifth annual report of the affairs at this agency, and it is a pleasant duty to inform the department of the rapid progress and steady advancement of the Indians in agricultural pursuits, habits of civilization, and moral and religious training. Instead of a wild, waste, and unbroken soil, which only a few years ago marked the scene, the rich and beautiful agricultural valleys are being cut up into farms, with snug houses and well-fenced fields, and the owners have now schools, churches, and a written language. The houses are built by the Indians themselves, who only require the assistance of the agency carpenter as to doors, windows and other matters of finish. Of course the fences are also built by the Indians, who split and haul the rails, and many of whom have become experts with the scythe and grain-cradle, while a few are capable of running mowing, reaping, and threshing machines. When lumber is wanted by an Indian, he delivers logs at the agency mill, where he assists the sawyer in cutting them into the required bill. During the last quarter alone there were 29,000 feet of lumber manufactured as cited above, and delivered to Indians for building purposes, and when the haying and harvesting seasons are over there will doubtless be a lively demand for more.

The cereals raised upon the reservation consist almost entirely of oats and wheat, they being the best adapted to the soil and climate. Considerable corn and beans, however, with some barley, are beginning to be cultivated, while cabbage, turnips, potatoes, and roots of all kinds grow in abundance. Of course we have still a great many thriftless Indians upon the reservation, who prefer to wander about and live a life of vagrancy, but as a rule, they are fast settling down, and the lodge is giving way to permanent habitations.

Education.

The Indian boarding-schools on this reservation for boys and girls are both under contract between the department and the Rev. J. B. A. Brouillet, the boys and girls being taught in separate buildings, and under separate contracts. The former have competent male teachers connected with the Mission of Saint Ignatius, viz, a principal and four assistants, two of whom instruct in farm and garden culture, blacksmithing, carpentering, working in saw and grist mills, cooking, baking, working in printing office, and other useful employments. The pupils are also instructed in the English language in reading, writing, lower mathematics, geography, &c. The girls, who are under the care of the Sisters of Charity, in addition to the English branches just mentioned, are educated in household work of every description, and also in music. The church choir is composed altogether of the girls and boys of the schools, and a band, consisting of a number of the boys, with eight brass instruments, supplemented by drums, fifes, &c., has been formed, and the teachers expect to turn out some very respectable musicians in the course of time. These Indian schools are pronounced by all who visit them, either officially or otherwise, as of the very best in the Indian country, and for results in all the branches taught challenge the admiration of all who take an interest in Indian education. There is a general desire among the Indians to have their children educated, and a large number of applicants to the schools cannot be admitted, as the contract with the government only provides for a limited number.

A New School Industry.

As some of the sisters in charge of the school are practical weavers, I would suggest that a small outlay of some two hundred dollars, for the purchase of a weaver's hand-loom, extra sets of reels and spools, three or four spinning-wheels, some yarn reels, and a dozen or so of hand wool-cards, with one hundred pounds of warp in skeins, would be sufficient to start a new industry at these schools, which would prove of invaluable benefit to the Indians, as the manufacture of cloths in this manner would have a tendency to induce them to destroy their dogs, and raise sheep in place of them.

Sanitary.

Scrofula prevails to a considerable extent among the Indians of this reservation, and it gradually undermines the constitutions of those affected, hastening their passage to the grave. There seem to be no peculiar causes for the affection but those of a character fitted to lessen the energies of the system and to impoverish the blood. The Indians' mode of life may, to a certain extent, account for it. Habitual exposure to cold, insufficiency of nutritious food, with sometimes excesses in eating, want of cleanliness, &c., may have favored the development of tubercles, but, in the great majority of fatal cases of tuberculous disease among them, the original and essential cause would probably be found to be an inherited peculiarity of their organization. Disease of the eye is another affection very common among the Indians, particularly among those of the Kootenais tribe, and to the same causes as those mentioned in connection with the former disease, and to their frequent exposure to smoke in their lodges, it may be attributed. With these exceptions, disease on this reservation is by no means prevalent, and a sanitary report would, I believe compare favorably with one from any other portion of the continent. An hospital here, however, would prove very beneficial to the Indians, by giving them an opportunity of following an appropriate medical course, which is more especially required for chronic diseases, such as those above mentioned. When medicines are given to the Indians to take to their homes, the "direction" is very often forgotten, or, being entirely neglected, the patient uses his own judgment as to the amount or frequency of the doses. Of course drugs cannot be used in this indiscriminate manner, even when comparatively harmless, with any satisfactory results, and to add to the difficulty, Indians neither can nor will diet themselves in a manner appropriate to the treatment or prescription which they receive from a physician. A small hospital, therefore, with a competent nurse, would be a great convenience, and would furnish Indians with the advantage of a comfortable and healthy room while under medical treatment.

Crime

on the reservation is of rare occurrence. With the exception of small faults and delinquencies, to which all races and people are given, I have nothing to report as happening during the past year. Such great crimes as murder or polygamy have been unknown. There is no such thing as the sale of whisky on the reservation, and not a single case of drunkenness or insubordination has come under my notice or been reported to me. But, when the vicious and riotous portions of the tribes visit the towns and settlements outside of the reservation, they are supplied with liquor and get intoxicated, and crimes and debaucheries which are unknown here are then committed. Nevertheless, on account of the miserable few referred to, it would be a great hardship and injustice to the majority of the Indians to prevent, or attempt to prevent, their free trade and uncontrolled liberty to deal with the merchants and traders of the adjacent towns, as a curtailment of such privileges would place those who are now stock raisers and producers to a certain extent at a disadvantage with other producers of the country, and leave them entirely at the mercy of the reservation traders as to the sale of their stock and produce.

As a census has lately been taken, it will perhaps be understood that the replies given to questions contained in the statistical document herewith forwarded should tally therewith and be wholly reliable. But while in a settled white community such would, to a very great extent, be the case, a belief in the absolute exactitude of an Indian census would give birth to very erroneous impressions. It is very well known that in the most enlightened countries census takers meet with no little difficulty in obtaining correct information. What obstacles then are met with in the Indian country, where most of the inhabitants are totally ignorant of weights, measures, yea, even of their own ages, can well be imagined. While, therefore, the census returns are an excellent guide for those who are acquainted with the attending facts and circumstances, and it is believed that in this case, through them, a very close estimate has been arrived at, it is considered necessary to call attention to the following points:

1st. When the total population of the reserve is represented in the census papers as 1,057, it must be remembered that at no season of the year can more than three-quarters thereof be found, a large number being camped in various secluded spots fishing or hunting. In addition to this fact, it should be known that, bordering on the reserve, there is a large plateau known as Horse Plains, which is not only a good fishing-ground but a first rate winter cattle-range. There being very few whites in the neighborhood, Indians will slip across the line, and many are always to be found in that section, while it is often a matter of great difficulty to determine what portion does and what portion does not belong to this agency, as the locality referred to is en route to the lands of the Spokanes, Colvilles, and Cœur d'Alenes, all of which tribes speak the Flathead language. For these reasons the estimate given in the aforesaid document will be found to exceed the population mentioned by name in the census returns by one-fourth, added to the Kootenais and Pend d'Oreilles, there being a correct list of the Flatheads, owing to the fact that they receive regular annuities.

2d. While those only who make a business of farming and "follow it" for a livelihood would, with us, be entitled to rank as farm-laborers, It would lead to a total misconception of the character of the Indians on this reservation were all others denied the credit of doing farm-work. While there are only ninety-six Indians who own farms, there are a great number of their relatives and friends who do a good deal of hunting, but who also assist to cultivate the ground. In fact, while there are very few who can be enrolled as regular laborers or mechanics, there are really a large number who do a considerable amount of work of one kind or another during the year, either for their fellows or in the neighboring settlements.

3d. The census being taken last winter, while yet there was no cultivation of the ground going on, the acreage represented as cultivated to a great extent represents the amount of land under fence, but as such is seldom, if ever, all tilled during any one year, the estimate of cultivated ground now furnished will be found considerably less.

4th. As stated among the statistical replies, there has as yet been no division of ground on this reservation. There being a considerable amount of arable land, any Indian who desires to become a farmer selects from the unoc-cupied parts thereof the location which suits him best, fences as much as he desires, and, being thoroughly independent in connection therewith, proceeds to cultivate.

5th. With respect to dress: Although there are few Indians of this section who have entirely discarded all the outward signs and appendages of their forefathers, there are perhaps still fewer who, in this particular, do not more or less imitate the white man, many to a very great extent.

These remarks being taken into consideration, I believe my report will be found thoroughly reliable, and I think there is nothing of moment to add, with the exception of a statement that, without doubt, these Indians are prosperous and happy; that they are pleased and contented with the treatment they have for some years received from the government, and that there is no reason why this state of affairs should be altered, unless the cupidity of the white race pro-duces a struggle for the land of the red man for which, for the present at least, the former has no necessity.

I have the honor to be, very respectfully, your obedient servant,

Peter Ronan,
United States Indian Agent.

The Commissioner of Indian Affairs.

August 20, 1881a
LR 15,443/1881, RG 75, National Archives, Washington, D.C.

> Telesphore Guillium Demers (1863-1930) was the son of Telesphore Jacques Demers, French Canadian, and Clara Demers, Pend d'Oreille/ French Canadian. For many years he ranched and ran a hotel at Camas Hot Springs on the reservation.[17] See the annotation to Ronan's letter of February 19, 1878, for more information on his father. On September 5, 1881, the Commissioner of Indian Affairs decided Demers' tribal relations did not entitle him to trade on the reservation without a license.[18] See the letter from T. G. Demers, endorsed by Ronan, to the Commissioner on August 14, 1883, for recognition of Telesphore Guillium Demers' tribal membership on the Flathead Reservation.

United States Indian Service,
Flathead Agency,
August 20th, 1881.

Hon. Commissioner of Indian Affairs
Washington, D.C.
Sir

Herewith I have the honor to transmit for your action an application from Guillaume Demers.

Upon inquiry I find the Statements therein contained correct, and believe that both the Character and behavior of the Applicant are worthy of commen-dation.

Should you See fit to grant his request I would, however, respectfully Sug-gest that your approval be accompanied by an emphatic warning against his business transactions on the Reservation being connected with, or interfered with by Outside relatives or friends.

Very Respectfully
Peter Ronan
U.S. Indian Agent.

Enclosure No. 1.
Enclosure:

Flat Head Reservation.
Augst 13, 1881.

Major Peter Ronan
United States Indian Agent
Flat Head Agency.
    Sir
    As I desire to avail myself of the privileges enjoyed by the Indians on the Flat Head Reservation, as to Locating, Trading &c thereupon I beg to state that while my Father is a French Canadian my Mother though not a pure Indian was nearly so & descended on both Sides from Families belonging to the Confederated Tribes.
    Her Father the son of a Frenchman and a pure Flathead Woman was born on the Reserve, while her Mother is a pure Pen' d'oreille whose family has lived within the present lines thereof for Over 20 Years.
    In this manner I claim the right to be treated as an Indian and Exercise the the [sic] forementioned privileges.

Yours Respectfully
Telesphore Guillium Demers.

August 20, 1881b
LR 15,442/1881, RG 75, National Archives, Washington, D.C.

> It is unclear from this letter exactly where J. W. Galbraith wanted to establish his ferry. Ronan's August 1, 1882, letter suggested it would have been at the foot of Flathead Lake. On September 7, 1881, the Commissioner of Indian Affairs rejected Galbraith's application to operate a ferry on the Flathead Reservation.[19] No further information was found about James Galbraith.

United States Indian Service,
Flathead Agency,
August 20th, 1881.

Hon. Commissioner of Indian Affairs
Washington, D.C.
    Sir,
    I have the honor to transmit herewith a letter from Jas. Galbraith in which he requests to operate a Ferry on the Reservation in view of the fact that as the Northern Pacific Railroad is approaching this Section from both East and West, considerable accommodation of that nature will be required by the travelling public.
    While being in a position to recommend to your favorable consideration the character of the applicant I deem it proper to inform you that there are already two ferries, owned and conducted by Indians in the vicinity of the locality where he proposes to establish himself.
    Perhaps, however it may be thought that, on account of the changes, taking place, the accommodations furnished by them will not be Sufficient.

Should Such be your opinion I believe there can be found no more Suitable person that Mr. Galbraith, on whom to bestow a license.

Very Respectfully
Your Obedt. Servant
Peter Ronan
U.S. Indian Agent.

Enclosure:

Missoula M.T.

To Major Ronan
Indian Agent, Jocko Agency
  Sir,
  Owing to the great necessity for a convenient Ferry, both for the Public and for the N. P. R. R. Employees
  I would ask from you the privilege of Establishing and Maintaining a Ferry across the Pen d'Oreille River at or above the Confluence with the Missoula River.
  I will maintain and operate a good and Safe Ferry Boat and Conform to the rules and usages necessary in operating such Ferry Boat, as will give Safety to life and property.

J. W. Galbraith
Aug. 14th, 1881.

August 25, 1881
LR 15,910/1881, SC 55, RG 75, National Archives, Washington, D.C.

> Ronan wanted more instructions from the Office of Indian Affairs regarding reservation timber used in railroad construction. See above for Ronan's January 22, 1881b, letter first requesting instructions relative to construction of the Northern Pacific Railroad through the reservation.

United States Indian Service,
Flathead Agency,
August 25th, 1881.

Hon. Commissioner of Indian Affairs
Washington, D.C.
  Sir,
  In view of the close proximity of the working forces of the Northern Pacific Rail-road to the boundaries of this Reservation, and the danger therefrom that Some of the Tie contractors or others may encroach upon the lands of the Indians, I would respectfully request instructions; especially pertinent to the Situation.
  I have, thus early, the honor of laying the matter before the Hon. Commissioner, as, otherwise, a case for decision might be presented when there may not be Sufficient time to apply for advice.
  For this reason, I would also respectfully request to be informed whether, in the event of the Railroad Company being granted a right of way across the Reservation, Such grant will include a right to appropriate Timber or other material required in Construction; or whether it will be the duty of the Agent to contract, for the Supply of Such materials for the benefit of the Indians, as directed in Section No. 262 of "Instructions to Agents."

Very Respectfully
Your Obedt. Servant
Peter Ronan
U.S. Indian Agent.

August 30, 1881
From George Conford, Depredation Claim 1863, RG 75, National Archives, Washington, D.C.

See the annotation for Ronan's December 9, 1879, report on George Conford's claim for more information. On September 16, 1881, the Commissioner of Indian Affairs awarded George Conford the value of the boat or $400.

United States Indian Service,
Flathead Agency,
August 30th, 1881.

Hon. Commissioner of Indian Affairs,
Washington, D.C.
    Sir
    Referring to your favor 20th Ult. marked "C. Montana R. 900/79," I have the honor to State that the Boat, for which George Conford claims restitution, was taken from a point on the Missoula River, named Superior to the Confluence of that River with Clark's Fork or the Pen d'Oreille River, and thence some Twenty odd miles up the latter.
    In comparing this Statement with that of the Indian Maxime, as contained in my letter of December 9th, 1879; it will be seen that he has made no distinction as to name between the Pen d'Oreille and its Tributary the Missoula; and I therefore enclose a map, more fully to elucidate the matter.
    In reply to your question as to any endeavor on the part of the claimant to recover the Boat, permit me to explain that the Missoula, — from Superior to its mouth, — is composed of a succession of Rapids, down and over which it is possible drop a flat bottomed Boat, but up which it is impracticable, if not impossible to drag one: Hence, no such endeavor has been made. In fact as mentioned in the letter already referred to, no matter what means might have been employed to accomplish it, the return of the Boat would have cost more than it was worth. And, in this connection, I have only further to add that, through use and decay, it has now wholly disappeared.
    To these remarks I am at a loss to add any information that is not fully supplied by the aforesaid letter, and the accompanying affidavits; nevertheless, in the hope that they may be of some Service, I append the conclusions I have myself arrived at. They are — that there is no doubt that the boat was taken at the time, and from the place, as set forth in Conford's Affidavit; that, as to the other articles missing, nothing was taken by Maxime or his companions — except those mentioned in his Statement, and as to the Stove and windows it is impossible to say whether it was by white men or Indians that they were interfered with. Further — that while I have no Suspicion that Warren, who had owned a Ferry about Twenty-five miles above Superior, and very likely lost Some Boats, was not acting in good faith in giving the Indian permission to appropriate such Boats if found, I do not believe the latter would have touched that of Conford, had Warren and Demers been reasonably careful in giving

him instructions as to the property over which they claimed a control: But while holding this belief, of course, it must be admitted that the Indian appears to have taken every advantage of what he apparently construed into an open order; otherwise he would have been less inclined to represent, as tied, — and appropriate, as abandoned; a boat fastened with chains and comparatively new.

I have the honor to be
Very Respectfully
Your Obedt. Servant
Peter Ronan
U.S. Indian Agent.

Enclosed map:

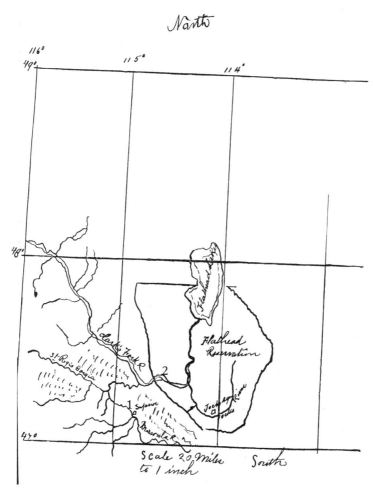

1 – Place where boat was taken.
2 – Place to where boat was taken and left.

September 5, 1881
LR 16,359/1881, RG 75, National Archives, Washington, D.C.

United States Indian Service,
Flathead Agency,
September 5th, 1881.

Hon. Commissioner of Indian Affairs
Washington, D.C.

Sir,

I have the honor to inform you that, for the purpose of furnishing the working parties with Supplies — Chief Engineer Anderson, of the Northern Pacific Railroad, has applied to me for permission to improve the Wagon Road across the Reservation which connects Missoula with Clark's Fork.

As citizens have always enjoyed a right of way thro' the Reservation, for which provision is made in the 3d Article of the Treaty of 1859 [sic] as follows — "And provided, That, if necessary for the public convenience, roads may be run through the Said reservation." And as, after the Railroad is completed, no matter by what route, the wagon road will be less used than now by whites, and therefore the benefits of improvement will also entirely accrue to the Indians. I have conveyed my consent Subject to your approval.

I have had the greatest confidence in taking this action, as, should you be disatisfied [sic] therewith a telegram forbidding the work would reach me before anything is done.

Very Respectfully
Your Obedt. Servant
Peter Ronan
U.S. Indian Agent.

September 16, 1881
LR 17,120/1881, RG 75, National Archives, Washington, D.C.

On September 30, 1881, the Commissioner informed Ronan that Congress had failed to pass an appropriation for the salaries of the Flathead Reservation chiefs for the 1882 fiscal year and no funds were available for that use.[20] See Ronan's letter to Montana Territorial Delegate Martin Maginnis at December 14, 1881, on the same subject. Ronan made another attempt to get salary funds on October 6, 1882.

United States Indian Service,
Flathead Agency,

Hon. Commissioner of Indian Affairs
Washington, D.C.

Sir

I have the honor to acknowledge receipt of your "letter R. 14667,["] dated 2d. Inst. and enclosing "Statement of Funds remitted" for 3d. and 4th. Quarters 1881.

From the latter I find there are no funds appropriated for the payment of the Salaries of the three Chiefs; — Michelle, Chief of Pen d'Oreilles; Arlee, Chief of Flatheads; and Eneas, Chief of Kootenais.

For many years they have been accustomed to receive One Hundred and Twenty-five ($125.00) Dollars each per Quarter, and, as they very much depend upon the payment of this amount to enable them to remain at their homes, and exercise a controlling influence which I believe there is no doubt has always been in favor of the Government, I trust I may be excused for Saying that a cessation of these payments would be very much to the disadvantage of the Indian Department.

Should you however, not approving of my opinion, have decided to discontinue these Salaries, permit me to add that the Chiefs; under the belief that they are to receive them, make prearrangements accordingly, and that therefore So Sudden a Stoppage would be a great misfortune to them, and necessarily cause much disaffection.

Altho' I find the item regularly included in my retained Copy of the "Estimate of Funds" lately forwarded, As I Sincerely trust a clerical error has been the cause of the omission of the appropriation I now enclose that document. And, in event of Such being the case, I earnestly beg that the Honorable Commissioner will be good enough to at once telegraph me authority to Make the regular payments at the end of the present Quarter.

With reference also to the aforesaid "Statement of Funds" I have now the honor to request Authority (by letter) to make use of, during the next Quarter, the amount appropriated to place the New Machinery, now on hand, in the Mill.

Very Respectfully
Your Obedt. Servant
Peter Ronan
U.S. Indian Agent.

Enclosure: *"Estimate of Funds for the 3d. & 4th. Quarters, 188[1], Peter Ronan, U.S. Indian Agent"* which includes $750 for *"Salaries of Indian Chiefs."*

September 20, 1881
The Helena Independent *(daily), September 23, 1881, page 3, col. 4.*

Ronan included in this letter a valuable description of the Jocko River fishery in 1881.

A Monster Trout.
Sent by Agent Ronan to Hon. Martin Maginnis, and What Became of It.

The following letter from Agent Ronan explains itself:

Flathead Agency, Sept. 20th.

To Hon. Martin Maginnis, Helena, M.T.

Dear Friend:— As this is Fair week at Helena, I thought that yourself and friends might like a trout from the Jocko for dinner, and I have procured you a "medium sized" one, weighing, when taken from the water to-day, sixteen and a half pounds. Should any of the trout sharps in Helena persist in calling it a "bull trout" or a "Salmon trout" you may confidently deny the statement and stick to it, and the book and teachings of the graduated disciples of Sir Isaac Waltoh [sic] will bear you out, that this is a common brook trout, a little overgrown I will admit, but such, and even larger ones are common in the Jocko. Trusting that yourself and friends will have a good time discussing his "finny nibs," I am as ever,

Yours,
Peter Ronan.

The above monster was greatly enjoyed yesterday by several friends of Major Maginnis, among them, a portion of the **Independent** staff, several of whom, including a genial shepherd from Meagher County, were eminently qualified to judge of its species as well as its flavor. In looks it might have passed for a lineal descendent of the whale that swallowed Jonah, with teeth like a shark, but its shining speckled crest, as well as its taste when served, proved that our friend Ronan was correct — it was in truth a genuine brook trout — a salmo fontanalis — and no mistake.

November 1, 1881
LR 20,142/1881, RG 75, National Archives, Washington, D.C. No action notation.

> The violence in Stevensville that Ronan referred to in this letter was a case study of the challenge of keeping the peace between the Indian and white communities in the Bitterroot Valley. A drunken argument over a horse sale escalated until one Salish man, Cayuse Pierre, was killed and another, John Delaware, almost died. Two white men, James Morris and Howard Preece, were arrested by the Missoula County Sheriff and jailed in Missoula. Chief Charlo wanted to punish the white men, but finally let the white justice system handle the matter. The Missoula County courts fumbled the prosecution. Preece died in jail after being incarcerated for about six weeks waiting for trial. Morris had trouble raising bail and was in jail for at least three months and possibly eight months waiting for trial.[21]

> The newspaper clipping Ronan enclosed is not reproduced here.[22] *The Weekly Missoulian* article criticized a recent article in the *St. Paul Pioneer-Press* about the killing of Cayuse Pierre in Stevensville.

> Amos Buck was a Stevensville merchant who had previously spent many years as a miner in the Montana gold camps. He took part in the attack on the Nez Perce camp at the Battle of the Big Hole in 1877.[23] Major William H. Jordan, of the Third Infantry, commanded Fort Missoula in the early 1880s. A Civil War veteran, he retired from the army as a colonel in 1892.[24]

United States Indian Service,
Flathead Agency,
November 1, 1881.

Hon. Commissioner of Indian Affairs
Washington, D.C.
   Sir,
   I have the honor to report for the month of October, the usual good behavior and comparative industry of the Indians under my charge. No occurrence has taken place on the Reservation to mar the good feelings or interfere with the advancing Spirit of civilization and progress, which has marked the year to the present date. During the month the Threshing Machine has been kept in constant use threshing Indian Grain, and, altho' the crops are very light, — Some being almost a total failure — the advance in prices, caused by the influx of laborers on the Northern Pacific Railroad Survey, greatly encourages those who have a surplus of Grain, Vegetables, or hay for Sale, and will cause all the industrious Indians to put forth greater energy another season to raise produce for market. For Hay on the Reservation twenty-five dollars per ton is being paid to those who have any to spare; two cents per lb for Oats, and Wheat is bringing eighty Cents p. bushel. The potatoe and other Vegetable crops have almost entirely failed owing to a late cold spring and a dry Summer. A heavy snow storm also commenced on the tenth of October and continued with frost

and Sleet for about twelve days, greatly injuring any root crops which had survived the disadvantageous weather up to that time.

A disease among cattle called "blackleg" has made its appearance on the
Reservation and many head have already died. It Seems more fatal among fat
animals and particularly Calves. It is to be hoped that the early frosts and the
winter Storms will have a tendency to clear this epidemic from the ranges.

Several attempts, during the past month, have been made by trespassers
on the Indian lands, to Secure a foothold thereupon, but I have been enabled
thro' my Indian Police, and my own exertions to prevent any decided encroachment without calling upon the aid of civil law or military force.

During the month of November the Northern Pacific Railroad Company
will send out locating engineers in this vicinity, and this action, doubtless, involves, on my part, the duty of pointing out, as well as I am able the boundaries
of the Reservation. No Survey has ever been made thereof, but a necessity has
now arisen for defining, as nearly as possible, its extent, as the lands are becoming Valuable, and Settlers are clamorous for an establishment of lines.

On the 17th day of October I received the following letter from the Commanding Officer of Fort Missoula

Copy

Fort Missoula, M.T. Oct.

Maj P. Ronan &c. &c.

Mr. A. Buck of Stevensville just arrived here saying that
two Bitter-root Indians were killed yesterday by two Citizens,
— the result of a quarrel about a horse. One Indian Seemed to
have been killed without Sufficient cause, and the other was
killed by the same man — Morris — while the Indians (four
or five) were firing into a saloon in which the man Morris was
at the time. There is great excitement in Stevensville. Charlo
says he must have the men (Morris & Priest) who Killed the
two Indians. Mr. Buck is en route to Missoula to report the
matter to the civil authorities. Mr. Buck Says a runner was
Sent to your Agency last evening to inform the Indians under
Your Charge, and I hope you will do your utmost to prevent
them interfering in the matter. All parties engaged in the row
Should be arrested and dealt with by the Civil Authorities. I
cannot do anything unless I am Satisfied that the proper civil
authorities are unable to keep the peace. I would suggest that
Yourself and a priest go to the town without delay.

Your obedt. Servt.

(Sgd) Wm. H. Jordan
Maj. 3d. Infty

Altho' the matter referred to was not Strictly within my province I immediately repaired to Fort Missoula, as I believed that, from my knowledge of the
Indians &c., My Services would be of Sufficient value to excuse any Slight Step
I might take outside of the bounds thereof. On my arrival I found there was
considerable excitement among the military authorities, there being already
two Companies under marching orders; and arguing from my knowledge of the
Chief Charlo's good judgment, and friendly disposition, that such a display
of force would be more hurtful than beneficial, altho' the Bitter-root Indians
are not within my jurisdiction — they claiming to be, and being recognized as

citizens, — I prevailed upon the Sheriff of Missoula County to proceed alone to the Scene of trouble and try to make the necessary arrests in a legal manner without military aid. This he accomplished and two white men were placed in the County jail, and, at the next term of Court, which Convenes on the 7th inst., will be tried, and doubtless punished according to law for the murder of an Indian; — a crime which according to present information, grew out of a drunken brawl.

In addition to the usual routine of labor performed by the employes, they have assisted the Indians in running the Threshing Machine, having also threshed the Agency Farm Crops, — which afforded a very poor yield — and have completed an extremely good and substantial Carpenter Shop.

Enclosing a Newspaper clipping referring to a highly colored narrative of the fracas at Stevensville published in some Eastern papers, also Physician's and School-teachers' Monthly Report, I have the honor to be

Very Respectfully
Your Obedt. Servant
Peter Ronan
U.S. Indian Agent.

December 14, 1881

LR 21,868/1881, RG 75, National Archives, Washington, D.C.

Ronan lobbied Martin Maginnis, the Montana Territorial Delegate to Congress, in an effort to get the salaries of the three Flathead Reservation chiefs restored. See Ronan's September 16, 1881, and October 6, 1882, letters.

For biographical information on General John Gibbon see the annotation to Ronan's letter of January 10, 1878. Col. Edward Moale was a Civil War veteran who retired from the army in 1902.[25]

House of Reps.
Washington
D.C.

Sir: I am personally cognizant of the facts set forth in this letter and heartily endorse the same. Mr. Ronan is the most capable, honest and intelligent agent that I know of and I hope these statements may reconcile all differences.

Martin Maginnis
Hou. Com.
Ind. Affairs.

Enclosure:

United States Indian Service,
Flathead Agency,
Oct. 21, 1881.

Hon. M. Maginnis
Washington, D.C.
Dear Friend:
While visiting this Agency with Gen [John] Gibbon, Col. [Edward] Moal[e] and other officers last summer, you informed me that all appropriations for the benefit of the Indians under my charge were secure and would be paid by Government as usual notwithstanding the expiration of the treaty. In making

requisition upon the Indian Office I included the usual quarterly payment of one hundred and twenty-five dollars to the chief of each tribe on the reservation, namely Arlee Chief of Flatheads, Michell, Chief of Pend 'd Oreilles, and Enyas, Chief of Kootenais, which was granted them in the Stephens-treaty for the same term of years as the other appropriations. In reply I was informed by the Commissioner of Indian Affairs that no money had been appropriated by Congress for the payment of the Chiefs.

This omission to provide for the support of these three old men who devoted their young manhood and declining age to the interest of their tribes and for the benefit of the Government in bringing the Indians to peacful [sic] pursuits and the cultivation of the soil is very unjust. Of course all or nearly all of the time of the Chiefs has been devoted to the task above cited, giving them but little time to provide for old age, and they well earned the little amount paid to them at the end of each quarter, and now to suddenly cut it off and leave them in want in their old age after a life of devotion to the Indians and to the Government I consider not only unkind but unjust. Of course the honorable Commissioner cannot be blamed in the matter, but I thought I would call your attention to it and ask your assistance in restoring to those poor old chiefs the small amount usually paid to them in the interest of justice and humanity.

Very respectfully
Your obedient serv't
Peter Ronan
U.S. Indian Agent.

1882

January 3, 1882
LR 1,542/1882, SC 55, RG 75, National Archives, Washington, D.C.

United States Indian Service,
Flathead Agency,
January 3d, 1882.

Hon. Commissioner of Indian Affairs
Washington, D.C.

Sir,

As already mentioned in a former communication, a force of engineers have been at work, running preliminary Surveys through this Reservation for the Northern Pacific Railroad Company, for the purpose of determining whether or not to construct the road through a portion thereof.

From verbal information from Said engineers I now learn that it is conclusively Settled that the road will pass through the Reservation, and, in accordance with instructions from Your Office, I have made known to the Indians the purpose for which the Surveys were being made, and the views of the Department concerning the Same, and I also assured them "that the lands necessary for the right of way Should not be taken until after agreement therefor had been duly entered into between the Indians and the United States, and the Indians fairly compensated for the Same."

The locating Surveyors are now at work; and, in furtherance of the promises made to the Indians, I have, of course, notified the Engineers that no work of Construction will be allowed to proceed on the Reserve until Some arrangement is made by the Company and the Indians with regard to payment for the lands, and the Cutting of timber &c. for the necessary construction of said Railroad; And I now therefore respectfully ask for detailed instructions as to the mode of proceedure you wish me to adopt. Begging that you will furnish Such, at your earliest convenience, So as to avoid complications, I am

Very Respectfully,
Your obedt Servt.
Peter Ronan
U.S. Indian Agent.

January 16, 1882
LR 1,843/1882, SC 55, RG 75, National Archives, Washington, D.C.

No further information was found about I. S. P. Weeks.

United States Indian Service,
Flathead Agency,
January 16th, 1882.

Hon. Commissioner of Indian Affairs
Washington, D.C.

Sir,

Under date of January 3d, 1882 I addressed you a communication in regards to an early Settlement between the Indians of this Reservation and the Northern Pacific Railroad Company, as to the purchase of land to constitute a "right-of-way" thro' Said Reservation. In connection therewith I now have the honor of enclosing a Copy of a communication addressed to me on the Subject by the Construction Department of Said Railroad Company. It explains itself and I take the opportunity of again respectfully requesting that the matter receive your earliest consideration, and that I be fully instructed as to mode of proceedure. Further with great deference I would Suggest that a Commission, in which the Indians could have thorough Confidence to appointed to confer with them, or, what would doubtless be still better, an opportunity be afforded a few of the Head Men to visit Washington, and there Settle the Matter directly with the Government.

As the interests, to be attended to, are by no means inconsiderable, — the road, not only passing thro' a number of fields Valuable to individuals, but extending across the Reservation a distance of Fifty Miles, thereby seriously interfering with the plans, habits, and pursuits of the Indians in general, — I am thoroughly convinced that a little extra trouble taken in adjustment now will be well repaid in future.

Very Respectfully
Your Obedt Servant
Peter Ronan
U.S. Indian Agent.

Enclosure:

Copy

Northern Pacific Railroad Co.
Construction Department
Missoula Division Missoula Jan 12th, 1882

Maj. Peter Ronan, U.S. Indian Agent
Flathead Agency
    Dear Sir
    The located line of the Northern Pacific Railroad passes thro the Flathead Indian Reservation.
    It enters the Reservation at the summit of the Coriacan Defile, passes by the valley of Finley Creek to the Jocko. Along the Jocko to the Pend Oreille River, and down the valley of the Pend Oreille, passes out of the Reservation near the Mouth of the Missoula River.
    I understand that by its charter the Northern Pacific Railroad has the Right of Way through all Indian Reservation[s], but that before its actual construction can be entered upon some formal Settlement for the land taken must be made with the Indians.
    The final location will probably be completed in about Six Weeks. Will you please notify me what steps must be taken that a settlement may be made as soon as possible, in order to proceed with the construction of the road.

Yours very Truly
Signed J. I. P. Weeks [I. S. P. Weeks]
Divn. Engr.

February 1, 1882
LR 3,541/1882, RG 75, National Archives, Washington, D.C.

Reports of friction between railroad survey parties and Flathead Reservation tribal members were printed in January 1882 in Missoula and Helena newspapers.[1] A letter from tribal member Duncan McDonald suggested that some of the conflict resulted from damage done by survey parties in the fenced fields of tribal farmers.[2] McDonald was hired by the railroad to assist the survey parties.[3] The Office of Indians Affairs seems to have given Ronan conflicting advice about allowing railroad survey parties on the reservation. See Ronan's March 10, 1882, letter.

At least one Helena newspaper argued that the two 1855 treaties signed by the Flathead Reservation tribes gave the railroad right-of-way access to the reservation and no further consent was needed.[4] Fortunately, the government did not accept this argument and Joseph McCammon was sent to the reservation to negotiate with the tribes.

United States Indian Service,
Flathead Agency,
February 1st, 1882.

Hon. Commissioner Indian Affairs
Washington, D.C.
Sir

I have the honor to report that with the exception of an unimportant and temporary difficulty, the month of January has passed with the usual quiet and good understanding that has hitherto marked the administration of affairs at this Agency. I have lately read some very exaggerated reports in Eastern papers, Stating that great excitement prevailed here, and that the Indians were concentrating and defying the progress of preliminary and locating Surveys by the Northern Pacific railroad Company. While it is true that one Surveying party on the reservation suspended work for a few days on account of Some little opposing demonstration by a camp of irresponsible Indians, without the knowledge or consent of the Chiefs and head men of the tribes, there was no necessity for any excitement in connection therewith, and when the trouble was referred to me, I at once took measures to settle the affair and having gone in person, accompanied by Some of the Chiefs, to the surveying camp, so ordered matters that the work was at once resumed, and it is now proceeding without let or hindrance. While, however, as already stated, the majority of the Indians exhibit a praise worthy friendliness and docility of disposition, I have been kept busy holding councils and making explanations; and, as you will doubtless readily conceive there is a latent uneasiness among them which of course is easily accounted for by their witnessing so much intrusion on their lands. Therefore as intimated in two former communications, it is necessary and politic for Steps to be taken without delay; to have a perfect understanding between the railroad Company and the Indians, as regards a just compensation to the latter for the land constituting the right of way; also for timber used in construction, and damages which will accrue to Indian Farmers through whose enclosures and homesteads the line will run. In connection therewith I beg to call your attention to the fact that Steps Should also be taken to provide for the Surveying of the boundaries of the reserve, as Settlers are crowding thereupon, and it is an impossibility for the Agent when called upon to define the lines with any certainty, without a survey of the Same. This State of affairs gives rise to disputes between Whites and Indians, and all cause for Such, Should in my opinion, be Set at rest by an early Survey of the boundary lines. — I have Secured the Services of a Skilled Mechanic, and the work of putting up the new Mill-burs, changing the bolts and renovating the flouring Mill generally, is in active operation.

Quite a number of Indians are engaged in Splitting and hauling rails, and the coming Spring will mark great progress in the enclosure of Indian fields. Others are hauling logs to the Saw Mill with the purpose of building houses, and the Month has been one of considerable industry.

Small Pox has not yet made its appearance upon the reservation, although Several Cases are reported in various towns and mining Camps of the Territory. In order to Show my faith in the operation I had the Agency Physician vaccinate my own Children in the first place, and explained to the Indians the reasons therefor. The result is that without any trouble children are now being brought to the Doctor's Office by their parents to undergo the Same treatment.

The usual routine of labor in Mills and Shops and about the Agency, is being performed by Employees. The Schools are in a flourishing condition, and I herewith enclose Monthly reports of Same, also report of Agency Physician.

I am very Respectfully
Your Obedient Servant
Peter Ronan
U.S. Ind. Agent.

February 6, 1882
LR 3,838/1882, RG 75, National Archives, Washington, D.C.

> The meadow Ronan referred to here is in the area now known as Evaro between the Missoula and Jocko Valleys.

United States Indian Service,
Flathead Agency,
February 6th, 1882.

Hon. Commissioner of Indian Affairs
Washington, D.C.

Sir,

On the Southern Border of the Flathead Reservation, and adjoining a locality now becoming thickly Settled by White People, is a meadow called "Camas Prairie," where I have heretofore Secured hay with which to feed Agency Stock. There is no other convenient place on the Reservation where hay can be procured for the Agency, and, in view of the fact that a road runs through the prairie which, during the coming Season, will be daily lined with teams conveying supplies to the Construction Parties of the Northern Pacific Railroad Company on the Clark's Fork Division, and that no method, outside of a military force, in my opinion, can prevent freighters from encamping on the meadow, and thereby destroying the hay, I would Suggest, as a matter of economy, and to prevent trouble and annoyance, that I be authorized to hire "Irregular Employes" (which would probably be the cheapest plan) or to advertise a contract, to be let to the lowest bidder, to build a good Substantial fence around Said prairie to protect the Hay Crop for use of Agency Stock and for the benefit of the Indians; — Said Contract not to exceed the sum of Five Hundred ($500.00) Dollars. I had hoped to be able to detail Some of the "Regular Employes" to perform this work, but the increased desire of the Indians to become civilized results in So many demands for aid that the "Hands" at the Agency are kept more than fully employed.

As Hay on the Reservation and on the adjoining White Settlements is now Selling as high as $40.00 per Ton, it will be readily Seen by the Honorable

Commissioner that the expenditure of the amount necessary for constructing fence around the meadow in question would be a matter of Strict economy, and would be of great benefit to the Indians and to the Agency.

I am, Very respectfully,
Your Obedt. Servant
Peter Ronan
U.S. Indian Agent.

March 10, 1882
LR 5,417/1882, SC 55, RG 75, National Archives, Washington, D.C.

On May 20, 1881, the Commissioner had instructed Ronan to allow the railroad to conduct preliminary surveys on the reservation.[5] Ronan was surprised then in March 1882 to be criticized for allowing the surveys. No action was taken against Ronan, so this explanation answered the criticism.

United States Indian Service,
Flathead Agency,
March 10th, 1882.

Hon. Commissioner of Indian Affairs
Washington, D.C.
Sir,
I have the honor of acknowledging receipt of your communication "L. 3541" dated 28th Ult. in which you State that "the Surveying operations of the Northern Pacific R. R. Co. Should not have been permitted in the first instance until consent of the Indians, and order of the Department had been obtained."

As I, of course, very much desire to avoid furnishing any occasion for your disapproval I respectfully ask your attention to your letter of May 20th, 1881, in which you directed me to "impress upon the Indians that the Northern Pacific R. R. Co. is empowered to make the necessary "preliminary Surveys" through the Reservation, to prepare them for the Same, and to "inform them that the Surveying parties must not be molested." These remarks led me to conclude — perhaps hastily — that any interference of mine with the Surveying parties, as long as the regulations of the Department were not infringed, would be an unwarrantable exercise of Authority; and that my action in the matter was expected to be confined to Seeing, as far as possible, that the Indians did not obstruct the Surveys, and that their feelings of dissatisfaction were allayed by your promise that they should "receive a fair compensation" for any land that might be required of them.

Under this belief I called a council of the Chiefs, and laid before them the Subject of your letter, and otherwise followed your instructions; and the result was that they gave their united Consent to Said preliminary Surveys being made, and promised to use their influence to prevent any opposition thereto. From this position they have not receded, for, altho, as detailed in my monthly Report for January, one Surveying party met with Some annoyance from a few irresponsible Indians, the Head-men, who quickly put a Stop to it could no more be held blamable therefor than could our own Government for Several well-known illegal raids of a few of its Citizens into the Territory of our Neighbors.

With regard to the uneasiness mentioned, which is felt by a majority of the Indians, — in a great measure occasioned no doubt by their inability to grasp the Situation, — and which increases as time passes, and their patience as to what is to be done, diminishes, you can certainly comprehend it thoroughly, without my troubling you with a lengthened explanation.

More especially was I convinced that my conclusions were correct from the Circumstance, that I wrote, — without eliciting any further orders on the Subject, — as follows, addressing you on the 25 of August last,

"In view of our Close proximity of the working forces of the Northern Pacific R. R. Coy to the boundaries of this Reservation – – – – I would respectfully request instructions especially pertinent to the Situation."

and on the 1st of November 1881

"During the month the Northern Pacific R. R. Coy will Send out locating Engineers in this vicinity, and this action doubtless involves the duty, on my part, of pointing out, as well as I am able the boundaries of the Reserve" &c.

Hoping that this presentation of the case will be considered Sufficient excuse for any mistake I may have made in the matter,

I am, with much respect
Your obedt Servant
Peter Ronan
U.S. Indian Agent.

March 20, 1882
LR 5,938/1882, RG 75, National Archives, Washington, D.C.

> In this letter Ronan defended the value of services provided by agency employees to tribal members and pleaded for funds to continue their work. Apparently the Washington, D.C., Office of Indian Affairs made a mistake in their budgeting for the Flathead Agency and only discovered the shortfall during the last quarter of the fiscal year. On March 31, 1882, the Commissioner telegraphed Ronan and ordered him to lay off five agency employees on April 1. This left the Flathead Agency with an agent, miller, farmer, carpenter, and blacksmith for the last quarter of the year.[6]
>
> On the same day Ronan wrote this letter to the Commissioner of Indian Affairs, he also wrote the Bureau of Catholic Indian Missions in Washington, D.C., asking them to lobby the Indian Office to fund all the Flathead Agency employees. The Bureau of Catholic Indian Missions replied on May 9, 1882, that Congress' small appropriation for the Bureau of Indian Affairs meant there was no way the Flathead Agency funds could be restored.[7]

United States Indian Service,
Flathead Agency,
March 20th, 1882.

Hon. Commissioner of Indian Affairs
Washington, D.C.

Sir,

I have the honor of acknowledging receipt of your communication of 6th. Inst. accompanying "Statement of Funds" allowed this Agency for First and Second Quarters of 1882. By it I find with much dismay and anxiety that the allowance for pay of Employés is curtailed by $1458.73, and I therefore hasten to enter a protest thereto. I desire to do so in the Strongest terms compatible with the respect due you, and am afraid that in So doing I will be unable fully to represent the injustice and unhappy results of the reduction, Should it be insisted upon.

In the first place, I would respectfully call your attention to your communication of June 16th, 1881, in which you distinctly inform me that the amount allowed at "this Agency for all employés (except Indians and Interpreter and School employés) for the fiscal year ending June 30, 1882 is $7420.00," and you further direct me as to the positions to be filled, and the salaries applicable to each. In Conformity with this unconditional authorization, and the instructions connected therewith I have Conducted the Affairs of the Agency for very nearly three Quarters of the period referred to, and — altho' often much in need of extra assistance, — have done as best I could without applying to the Department until the 6th Ult., when, — in requesting permission to fence a Hay Meadow, — I made the following remark — "I had hoped to be able to detail some of the regular employés to perform this work but the increased desire of the Indians to become civilized results in So many demands for aid that the "Hands" at the Agency are kept more than fully employed." Now the amount deducted necessitates the discharge, — during the whole of the ensuing quarter, — of every mechanic and laborer attached to the Agency, and you will excuse me for Saying that, under the circumstances, granting the Requisition as to fencing is equivalent to presenting a Cup of Coffee to a hungry man, and depriving him of Solid food after his request for the beverage to assist in the mastication of the latter.

Of course, I understand that any complaint as to a change in what I was led to expect might receive Slight attention, were it not supplemented by arguments that such change would be prejudicial to the interests of the Service, and I will therefore furnish Some which I believe conclusively prove the correctness of Such a position.

Principally among them is the fact that the discharge of the employés means the almost total withdrawal of Government aid to the Indians. The Amount of "Annuity Goods and Supplies" furnished this Agency, — if equally distributed, — is not sufficient to provide each Indian with Three Dollars worth per annum, and is therefore a Small factor in preserving that influence over them, which is desirable both for their own good, and that of the Government.

On the contrary the Mills, Shops, and work of the farmers are of great value to them and their appreciation is well evidenced by the over-abundance of work asked for. At the present moment the open ground in front of the Sawmill is covered with logs hauled there by Indians, to whom, — following the express urgings of the Department, — I have given every encouragement to build; the Blacksmith is obliged to call upon those waiting to have a job completed to "blow" and "Strike," and complains that he has always a month's work ahead; the Carpenter is in a similar predicament; the Grist-mill (Still undergoing repairs) is full of wheat, and cannot be run without a Miller, fireman, and men to Supply fuel; and, — as the plowing season is just opening, — there is more farm work than hands to perform it.

Had the amount now with-held been deducted from money used in purchasing goods no complaint would have been made; or, had it even been deducted from the pay of employés at the commencement of the fiscal year, I Should have considered it my duty to acquiesce without a murmur — no matter how Short Sighted I considered the economy; different arrangements would have been made, and any entanglement avoided; but now, Should your decision be irrevocable, there will not be sufficient white men left on the place to witness what few issues are made — the log-hauling of the Indians will be work thrown away; — their sacks of grain will require packing elsewhere; their plows, now lying at the Smithy for repairs, will, I am afraid, remain for the year, in idleness; the timothy Seed, which you have been good enough to furnish, must remain un-Sown; and, — without further enumeration, permit me to repeat, generally, that most assuredly more damage will result to the interests of the Service, than can be balanced by an outlay of many times the amount proposed to be unexpended.

More especially would it be impolitic to take Such action at this time when on the eve of an agreement as to lands &c. required by the Railroad. A three months virtual closing of the Agency, combined with the irritation which would be caused by the Stoppages I have described, at the very time when the Indians will be asked to bargain away their lands will produce such a want of confidence as no words will explain away.

Added to this I would respectfully inform you that, on account of the Railroad "excitement," common laborers are now receiving from $50.00 to $60.00 per month with board, and that therefore, Should this Agency be in need of hands three months hence, the Department will require to compete with these rates, or otherwise place Such men in the vacant positions, as will be unfit therefor, and a disgrace to the Service. If the question is put as to how the Agency is so well Supplied at present, I can explain that the employés now engaged are nearly all old hands, who are acquainted with the necessities of their positions; who are also acquainted with, and friendly to the Indians; and, who, already having cooking utensils, and other requisites, and having discovered that there is no temptation to Spend money foolishly, are willing to retain what they consider Steady employment. Such men can easily secure positions elsewhere, but cannot be picked up every day, nor will they again be had at the wages at which they are now retained.

With regard to retrenchment, as far as this Agency is concerned, while I often believed that I could have used an increase of means to the great advantage of the Service, I hope that I have economically used what has been allowed; — at least the State of affairs here has met with many encomiums from various Sources, in addition to your approbation; — as expressed in my reappointment — of which I have already assured you I am justly proud. And, furthermore, permit me to add that I have been so careful of over-running appropriations that there has always been a balance returned at the end of the Fiscal Year.

Hoping that these remarks, though made at length, will not be considered tedious or inapt, and assuring you that they fall short of representing the injury that will accrue from the withdrawal of the Employé force as described, I have the honor to be

Very Respectfully
Your Obedt. Servant
Peter Ronan
U.S. Indian Agent.

March 21, 1882
LR 5,546/1882, SC 55, RG 75, National Archives, Washington, D.C.

> Ronan lobbied Martin Maginnis, the Montana Territorial Delegate to Congress, to push the Office of Indian Affairs to negotiate with the Flathead Reservation tribes about selling a railroad right-of-way through the reservation.

H. R.

March 21. [18]82

To the Hon
The Com. Ind Affairs
    Sir:
    I have the honor to recommend that a delegation of the Flathead Indians be ordered to Washington to enter into negotiations for the sale of a right of way thro' their reservation to the N.P.R.R. Company — None of these Indians have ever been East or had any chance to see the power of the nation or the achievements of Civilization. Other questions in regard to their reservation — to the adjudication of rights in the Bitter Root valley etc. ought to be considered. I have understood for some time that the Dept had this in consideration. I think that this is a favorable opportunity to carry out these intention and would recommend that the agent and chiefs be ordered here.

Martin Maginnis

Enclosure:

United States Indian Service,
Flathead Agency,
March 9, 1882.

Hon. M. Maginnis, M.C.
Washington, D.C.
    Yours had been received, dear friend, and I send many thanks for your suggestion as to communicating with you about the N P. Railroad business, and your offer in regard to seeing the Commissioner with the view of my being ordered up to Washington.
    Up to the present a general resume of the matter is that: on the 22d of January, 1881, I asked for instructions as to my action in order to prevent the Indians becoming too restive under a suspicion that they were about to be goreged [sic] out of their lands. In reply on May 20th, I received a long letter from the Department, informing me that the preliminary surveys must be allowed but directing me to "assure the Indians that the lands should not be taken from the Indians until after agreement therefor had been duly entered into between the Indians and the United States, and the Indians fairly compensated for the same."
    Since then there have been in more or less cases in connection with railroad affairs a great number of men on or passing through the Reservation occasioning as you may have seen thro' garbled newspaper accounts considerable uneasiness among the Reds; however thro' the confidence with which I have happily been able to inspire them, and by taking matters cooly, there has been no disturbance and no trouble worth mentioning. Here let me interpolate — In the report of the Commissioner of Indian Affairs page 28 I find the following statement: "It is gratifying to remark that the Indians have offered no opposition to the passage of railroads over their reservations; on the contrary they hail their construction with every evidence of satisfaction." Why one

would suppose they were anxious to donate their lands to a railroad company; now I may have been totally misinformed or glaringly misled with regard to other Indians, but I wish it to be understood that as far as these Indians are concerned they have the strongest objections to having a railroad pass thro' their lands, and that it is only their intelligent consciousness of their weakness that prevent physical opposition, and that even such knowledge would not prevent the more daring and reckless from an armed protest, were not much trouble, and if I may say so, good management used to allay the bitterness of their feelings.

Without troubling you with intermediate correspondence, I will now furnish you with a few extracts from letters lately written on the subject:

Missoula, Jan. 12, 1882.

Major Ronan &c.,

I understand that by its charter the N. P. Railroad Company has the right of way thro' an Indian Reservation, but before its actual construction can be entered upon, some formal settlement must be made with the Indians. The final location will probably be completed in about six weeks. Will you please notify me what steps must be taken that a settlement may be made as soon as possible in order to proceed with the construction of the railroad &c., &c.

Yours etc.,
Signed. J. I. P. Weeks [I. S. P. Weeks],
Division Engineer.

Flathead Agency
Jan. 16, 1882

J. I. P. Weeks, Esqr. &c., &c.

x x x x x Permit me to state that I have laid the matter before the Hon. Commissioner of Indian Affairs from whom I expect instructions.

Signed Peter Ronan
U.S. Ind Agt

Flathead Agency
Jan 16, 1882

I now have the honor of enclosing a copy of a communication addressed to me by the Construction Department of the N. P. Railroad Company. It explains itself and I take the opportunity of again respectfully requesting that the matter receive your earliest consideration, and that I be fully instructed as to mode of proceedure. Further, with due deference I would suggest that a commission, in which the Indians would have thorough confidence be appointed to confer with them, or what would doubtless be still better, an opportunity be afforded a few of the head men to visit Washington and there settle the matter directly with the Government" &c., &c.,

In my reports for January and February I again urge that early measures ought to be taken looking to an adjustment of the matter but as these communications all much in the same terms as the foregoing (only differing in mentioning some acts of the Indians which exhibited both uneasiness and displeasure at their [sic] being so much delay in coming to an understanding).

I think it unnecessary to do more than add that Division Engineer having wrote to Chiefe engineer Anderson to urge a movement at Washington, such action is probably being taken now, and if so it will afford you an opportunity of presenting your views.

Should they (the authorities) conclude to have me go, I would much like to have it left to my option or perhaps, I might say to the option of the tribes as to who should be their representatives.

Thanking you again for your many marks of friendship I have the honor of subscribing myself

Your friend
Peter Ronan
U.S. Ind Agt.

July 18, 1882

LR 13,107/1882, telegram, SC 55, RG 75, National Archives, Washington, D.C.

> On July 13, 1882, the Commissioner of Indian Affairs telegraphed Ronan that the Commissioners to negotiate for the railroad right of way through the Flathead Reservation would be on the reservation soon: "If entirely Satisfactory to Indians may commence grading before Commissioners arrive."[8] Ronan's reply indicated the Indians would not agree to the railroad work starting on the reservation before the negotiations were completed. On July 19, 1882, the Commissioner replied to Ronan: "Allow nothing to be done by Rail Road Company on reservation without full consent of Indians. This is absolute."[9]

July 18 18
Flat Head Agency Mont

Commsr Indian Affairs
Washn DC

Indians not satisfied that work proceed until commissioners arrive and settle right of way. I think it imprudent to let work go on before.

Ronan Agt.

July 27, 1882

Thomas C. Power Papers, MS 55, box 117, folder 1, Montana Historical Society Archives, Helena, Montana.

> T. C. Power & Brother had the government contract to supply grain for the Flathead Agency, and Ronan suggested that they purchase the grain from reservation farmers. Thomas C. Power, one of the principal merchants in Montana in the 1880s, was headquartered at Fort Benton, the head of shipping on the Missouri River. He had extensive interests in freighting and merchandising across the territory. He secured many supply contracts from the Office of Indian Affairs. In 1890 he was elected to one term in the United States Senate and he died in Helena in 1923.[10]

United States Indian Service,
Flathead Agency,
July 27th, 1882.

Messrs. T. C. Power & Bro.
Fort Benton

Gentlemen,

In reply to your favor of the 16th. Ult; I may inform you that Eddy, Hammond & Co conduct a Trading Post in close proximity to the Agency, and, as they trade with the Indian and Half-breed Farmers, have it in their power to Supply Grain at this place cheaper than any-one could possibly haul it from the Surrounding Settlements. Beyond this information however I would very much object to go in the way of Suggesting with whom you Should deal in the matter of filling Your Contracts and I beg you to understand that my only reasons for my previous reference to the subject were a friendly desire that you Should be made aware that Circumstances had altered prices, and an anxiety that there Should be no hitch as to prompt delivery.

With regard to delivery of Wagons & other goods I wrote you very explicitly on June 19th, but have not been honored by a reply. — Are they or are they not on their way? — I ask a reply by Telegraph and will await therefor eight days from date.

I am compelled to assume this position as the indifference with which you have treated both my requests and demands are the reverse of Courteous.

Yours Obedtly
Peter Ronan
U.S. Indian Agent.

August 1, 1882

LR 14,921/1882, RG 75, National Archives, Washington, D.C.

> On September 18, 1882, the Commissioner of Indian Affairs approved the sale of Revais' ferry on the Lower Flathead River, provided it was sold to another tribal member.[11] See Ronan's August 20, 1881, letter for an earlier proposal to establish another ferry across the Flathead River. For biographical information on Antoine Revais, see Ronan's letter of December 29, 1879, and annotation. No further information was found about James Galbraith.

United States Indian Service,
Flathead Agency,
August 1st, 1882.

Hon. Commissioner Indian Affairs,
Washington, D.C.

Sir:

Under the date of August 20th, 1881, I had the honor to transmit a letter to you from James Galbraith; in which he requested to operate a Ferry on the Reservation. I also stated in my remarks "that as the Northern Pacific Railroad is approaching this section from the East and West, considerable accomodation of that nature will be required by the traveling public."

In your reply, dated September 17th [i.e., 7th], 1881, occurred the following remarks: "I see no reason for a Ferry by a whiteman, the effect of which would probably be to break up, or seriously interfere with the occupation of Indians, who should be encouraged in utilizing every legitimate avenue to prosperity, especially on their own Reservation. I suggest whether such encouragement and assistance as you may be able to give the Indians may not put them in condition to meet the necessities of the traveling public both present and prospective. It occurs to me that this might be done and the introduction of a white man on the Reserve be thus rendered unnecessary."

Upon receipt of the above letter I furnished the then principal Ferryman, an old Indian named Antwoine Revias with lumber to build a larger boat suitable to the increasing travel, and up to present date he has been operating it. He however was obliged to incur for wire rope &c., considerable personal expense and now desires to sell the Ferry, giving as a reason that he is too old to run it, that he is in debt on account of it and desires to settle, and that he wishes to invest the money in stock. The necessity of having the Ferry conducted in a more efficient and systematic manner has been repeatedly urged upon me by the officers of the N. P. Railroad Company, and now it is expected that a mail route will be established connecting the East and West ends of the Railroad, over which a line of coaches will be run, and the Ferry will require to be operated in a manner that will better accomodate the traveling public. Unless the Indian Revais is allowed to dispose of his boat, the Northern Pacific Railroad Company will certainly ask and probably get permission to establish a Ferry, as Revais on account of age and lack of business qualifications is totally unfitted to meet the requirements of the case. Should another Ferry be allowed, and Revais prevented from disposing of his, of course it will break up his business and leave the old man penniless and in debt. I therefore recommend that permission be granted him to sell his boat and that a license or permit be issued to the purchaser to conduct the Ferry business.

Respectfully Yours
Peter Ronan
United States Indian Agt.

September 4, 1882

U.S. Commissioner of Indian Affairs, Annual Report of the Commissioner of Indian Affairs *(Washington, D.C.: U.S. Government Printing Office, 1882), pages 102-104.*

Between August 31 and September 2, 1882, Joseph McCammon, United States Assistant Attorney General, negotiated with Flathead Reservation tribal members for a railroad right-of-way through the reservation. Tribal leaders complained about possible negative impacts from the railroad and wanted it to proceed west from Missoula to avoid the reservation. In an effort to keep the railroad off the reservation, the chiefs asked for a million dollars for the right-of-way. Kootenai Chief Eneas stated that the reservation was "a small country; it is valuable to us; we support ourselves by it; there is no end to these lands supporting us; they will do it for generations."[12] Salish Chief Arlee argued, "You seem to like your money, and we like our country; it is like our parents."[13] McCammon offered $15,000 or $10 an acre and finally proposed $16,000. McCammon's condescension was palpable in the transcript as he pressured and threatened the chiefs to force an agreement.

The chiefs finally agreed to sell the right-of-way but insisted on getting the payment in cash rather than annuities. They complained that the tribes had not gotten many of the goods and services promised in the 1855 Hellgate Treaty. The chiefs also made McCammon agree to use his influence to get the northern boundary of the reservation moved to the Canadian border. McCammon presented the proposed boundary move to the Commissioner of Indian Affairs in a November 21, 1882, letter reproduced below. A year later, when Senator G. G. Vest visited the reservation, the chiefs and headmen had changed their minds, fearing that any adjustments in the boundary might be manipulated against the interests of the tribes.[14]

The written terms of the right-of-way sale agreement signed by 219 tribal members on September 2, did not agree with the verbal agreement reached during the negotiations. According to the transcript, the railroad was getting use of the land, not full title. Pend d'Oreille Chief Michelle stated, "It is like the railroad borrowing the strip of land." McCammon agreed, "It is just buying the use of the strip of land." The written agreement, however, provided that the tribes "do hereby surrender and relinquish to the United States all the right, title, and interest" they had in the right-of-way land.[15]

Emotions ran high at the negotiations and, according to Duncan McDonald, one young tribal member attempted to assault one of the government negotiators.[16] See the annotation to Ronan's letter of July 28, 1884, for more information about the delay and controversy surrounding the final payment for the right-of-way and timber cut on the reservation by the railroad company.

Joseph K. McCammon, a lawyer born in Pennsylvania, was Assistant Attorney General between 1880 and 1885. Before coming to Flathead in 1882, he had investigated the Indian service and negotiated with the Bannock and Shoshone Indians for a right-of-way through their reservation. In 1884, he entertained Charlo and the Bitterroot Salish delegation in Washington, D.C. He died in 1907.[17]

Flathead Agency, *September 4th,* 1882.

Sir: As directed, I have the honor to submit my sixth annual report from this reservation, which is occupied by the confederated tribes of Flatheads, Kootenays, and Pend d'Oreilles. The reservation covers a considerable area of arable land, which is capable of yielding large crops of wheat, oats, barley, and corn, as also of vegetables of various kinds, and fruits of the hardier sorts. There are extensive forests of pine, fir, and tamarac, with some other useful timber on the mountain sides, and the valleys are cut by rapid rivers, clear brooks, and beautiful lakes, which lend a peculiar charm to the scenery; the whole furnishing homes for the Indians unsurpassed in all the broad domain of the great Northwest. It cannot therefore be a matter of wonder that this country is now looked upon with covetous eyes by advancing settlers, who are drawn hither by the construction of the Northern Pacific Railroad, which has been located, and is now about to be built through the reservation.

A fierce spirit of opposition still prevails on the part of many of the Indians to the construction; they regarding the road as fatal to their interests, and the sure precursor of the abandonment of their homes and lands to the whites. On the 2d day of September, 1882, Joseph K. McCammon, Assistant Attorney-General of the United States, entered into an agreement with the confederated tribes resident on the Jocko or Flathead reservation:

That for the consideration hereinafter mentioned the said confederated tribes of Flatheads, Kootenays, and Upper Pend d'Oreilles do hereby surrender and relinquish to the United States all the right, title, and interest which they now have under and by virtue of the treaty of July 16, 1855, in and to all that part of the Jocko (or Flathead) Reservation situated in the Territory of Montana, and described as follows, namely: A strip of land not exceeding two hundred feet in width, that is to say, one hundred feet on each side of the line laid down on the map of definite location hereinbefore mentioned, wherever said line runs through said reservation, entering the same at or near the summit of Coriacein Defile, passing by the valley of Finley Creek to the Jocko, along the Jocko to Pend d'Oreille River, down the valley of the Pend d'Oreille, and passing out of the reservation at or near the mouth of the Missoula River; said strip of land being intended to be used by the Northern Pacific Railroad Company, its successors, or assigns as a right-of-way and road-bed, and containing thirteen hundred acres. An official copy of said map of definite location was on the day of the date hereof produced and shown to said Indians, in counsel assembled, was fully explained to them, and is attached to and made part of the agreement. Also the several pieces or parcels of land situated along and adjoining the said strip of land hereinbefore described, as the same are delineated on the five several plats or maps thereof, also produced and shown to said Indians, containing, exclusive of the strip of land hereinbefore mentioned, one hundred and thirty acres, the same being intended to be used by the said Northern Pacific Railroad Company for the purposes of station-houses, depots, sidings, &c. In consideration of such surrender and relinquishment of lands as aforesaid, amounting in the aggregate to fourteen hundred and thirty acres, the United States stipulates and agrees to pay to the said confederated tribes of Flathead, Kootenay, and Pend d'Oreille Indians the sum of sixteen thousand dollars, being at the rate of eleven and $^{18}/_{100}$ dollars per acre, to be deposited in the Treasury of the United States, to the credit of the said confederated tribes, upon ratification of this agreement by Congress and necessary appropriations made therefor; the sum aforesaid to be expended for the benefit of said Indians in such manner as the Secretary of the Interior may direct.

And for the considerations aforesaid the United States further stipulates and agrees, upon ratification of this agreement by Congress, and necessary appropriations therefor, to pay to the individual Indians, members of said confederated tribes, whose names appear on the schedule marked with the letter "K," the several sums set opposite their respective names, as full compensation for any damages to improvements or fenced or cultivated fields which they may sustain by reason of the surrender and relinquishment of said lands, or any part thereof, as aforesaid; such compensation to be expended for the benefit of such individual Indians, or paid to them in cash, in the proportions to which they may be severally entitled thereto, appearing by said schedule, as the Secretary of the Interior may direct. All provisions of existing treaties with the confederated tribes of Flathead, Kootenay, and Upper Pend d'Oreille Indians not affected by this agreement to remain in full force and effect, and this agreement to be subject to ratification by Congress.

As the chief incentive to signing the foregoing agreement, the Indians received the promise of the honorable commissioner, Joseph K. McCammon, that he would urge upon the government the propriety of granting a desire, which they entertain very strongly, viz, that they should have ceded back to them that portion of the national domain lying between the present northern boundary of this reservation and the forty-ninth parallel, or what is generally known as the British line. It is a tract of country very mountainous, with numerous streams, having even the narrow valleys so densely timbered that there is very little probability of any desire being exhibited for many years on the part of the whites to occupy it to any appreciable extent. At present, on the whole tract, as far as I can learn, there are not more than eight bona-fide white settlers, perhaps not so many, and they are confined to one spot at the head of Flathead Lake. The Indians mentioned this state of affairs in support of their prayer that the grant should be made, saying, as above stated, that, with the exception of the open country at the head of Flathead Lake (which is a very small portion of the whole), the area asked for is unfit for white settlement, but, being fair trapping and fishing grounds, is well adapted to the wants and for the homes of Indians. Added to this, as there is scarcely any white travel through that portion of the country, they argue that they would be much more liable than now to be allowed to rest in peace.

The year has been a prosperous one for the Indians, as large yields have followed their tillage of the soil, which has been much increased over previous years, the plows and other agricultural implements furnished by the department having been in urgent demand.

The sanitary condition of the Indians is at present good, but during the year there has been some increase in the percentage of deaths. Many consider that their change of modes of living, from lodges to houses, and from their hitherto simple food to the more complicated cookery of the white man, has an injurious effect on their health. Probably such is the case, as consumption is certainly the only disease with which they are much afflicted; but the decision of this question I am willing to leave to more scientific inquirers. Rumors prevail that small-pox has made its appearance in the town of Missoula, situated on the eastern border of the reservation. Should the disease spread, I fear the Indians here will greatly suffer, especially as the resident physician has intimated an intention of handing in his resignation at the end of the present quarter, on account of the late reduction of salary, which is now inadequate for the support of himself and family, and I very much doubt if I can well replace him for the amount now allowed by the department.

The missionary work on this reservation, as in the past, is conducted by the Jesuit priesthood of St. Ignatius Mission, and their efforts and exertions need no comment; from me, as to them, to a very great extent, are due the peacefulness, good conduct, and prosperity of the Indians under my charge. Under the supervision of these fathers and the good Sisters of Providence, the industrial schools for boys and girls in connection with this agency have steadily improved, and for results will, I believe, compare favorably with any other institution of learning of a like kind, more especially if the amount of government assistance furnished is taken into consideration.

Very respectfully, your obedient servant,

Peter Ronan.
United States Indian Agent.

The Commissioner of Indian Affairs.

September 25, 1882
Thomas C. Power Papers, MS 55, box 117, folder 1, Montana Historical Society Archives, Helena, Montana.

Ronan exchanged government issues of wagons and other farming equipment for Indian labor in putting up hay for agency stock.

In the 1880s, Andrew B. Hammond was a major businessman in western Montana. He supplied lumber and ties for the construction of the Northern Pacific Railroad in 1883 and controlled an empire stretching from lumbering, merchandising, banking, transportation, to land development. See Ronan's October 23, 1886, letter which mentioned Hammond owning a trading post on the Northern Pacific right-of-way near Arlee. He died in 1934.[18]

United States Indian Service,
Flathead Agency,
Septr. 25th, 1882.

T. C. Power Esq.
Helena
Dear Sir,

Referring to your favor of 25th Ult. I beg to advise you that I gave a letter of introduction to an Indian, who having business in Helena proposed to bring down Some of the Wagons in your hands for this Agency. I have learned Since, however that two of his horses have become sick, and I therefore See no other way of getting the wagons here than thro' means employed by you.

While thanking you for your kindly mention of my patience &c. I greatly desire that you would exert yourself in this matter, as Said patience has been Sorely tried. My force of employes has been very Considerably reduced, and I have been ordered by the Department to require a certain amount of work from the Indians in return for the goods Supplied. Had I had the wagons in question my Hay & wood would have all been hauled by this time, but while the Indians are waiting for the wagons I am waiting for the work, and am liable to have the Hay spoiled as well as being placed generally behind hand.

With regard to other freight I have to inform you that I have received Bs/Lg from the U. & N. R. R. Terminus, which State that the good are "to be delivered to me on payment of freight." Now this wording may cost some one trouble, as I have already received a load delivered by the Teamster under protest, as he expected to be paid here, and was certainly according to the printed Contract entitled to retain the goods until a Settlement was made.

With regard to wheat and Oats I already wrote you that if you received them at 3¢ I believed you would be fortunate. I also wrote that I was in great need of them, but have learned nothing further on the Subject.

Hammond, I understood to tell me that you informed him there was no necessity to furnish Sacks. Now the Copy of the Contract which has been Sent here distinctly includes Sacks, and as I will require to Carry them on my Papers, I cannot, as you will See, Sign any receipt unless they are Supplied, or I have other instructions.

Pray give your attention to this letter in detail and so permit me to retain the credit which you give me for patience, as I presume you do not desire to be accused of taking advantage thereof.

Yours truly
Peter Ronan
U.S. Indian Agent.

Note added to bottom of above letter:

Ans.

Joe Please attend. PR is right about the grain on referring I have to furnish the Sacks. Is Jno McCormick filling the grain. Please write. Morse & Joselym are the forwarders at Silver Bow. they bought our [* * * *] & tell them what to do about paying wagon freight & have them act prompt in getting the goods through during good weather.

T. P.

10/1/82.

October 1, 1882

LR 18,557/1882, RG 75, National Archives, Washington, D.C.

A newspaper report mentioned one case where a tribal farmer objected to railroad contractors destroying his fences.[19] Tribal members had not yet received any compensation for their land or improvements disturbed by the railroad construction.

As Ronan mentioned in this report, smallpox broke out in Missoula and the Bitterroot Valley during September 1882. Father Jerome D'Aste of St. Mary's Mission vaccinated many Bitterroot Salish, but four died of the disease. Charlo and a party of Salish left the valley on September 25 to hunt buffalo and avoid the infection. This was their last buffalo hunt.[20] One of the white smallpox victims in Missoula was a bank cashier, Ferd Kennett. A newspaper report blamed the spread of the disease to the Bitterroot on a priest who had visited an ill patient at the Missoula pest house.[21]

United States Indian Service,
Flathead Agency,
October 1st, 1882.

Hon. Commissioner of Indian Affairs
Washington, D.C.

Sir,

All is quiet on the Reservation and the Northern Pacific R. R. Employés are pushing forward their work of clearing the "right of way" and grading without molestation. The disturbers and mal-contents of the Tribes, who Sought occasion to make trouble while the council, arranging for the Railroad Right of way, was in Session, are Silenced, and the advice of the real friends of the Indians has prevailed, and I now have no expectation of any act of hostility on the part of the latter.

I am however Subjected to very considerable annoyance thro' white tresspassers, who attempt to take advantage of the present necessary open State of the Reservation, and from Railroad Employés, whose every petty Cause of Complaint against the Indians is immediately reported to me, and I am expected at once to drive to the scene, and Settle the most triffling matters of dispute. Added to this the constant watchfulness and attention required to prevent whisky trading on the Reserve is sufficient to keep me actively employed, and Seriously interfere with the Clerical duties of my position.

Small-pox, as I already had the honor of reporting, is in existence in the neighboring town of Missoula, and four cases are now reported among the Flathead Indians of the Bitter-root Valley. No case has as yet appeared upon the Reservation, but the Indians are thoroughly frightened, as they are well aware of the fatal character of the disease; the tribes some eighty years ago having been almost annihilated by it; — and they are now betaking themselves to the mountains, away from the Settlements, and from contact with the Railroad Employés, with the hope of escaping contagion.

I have no hospital, nor means of taking care of the Indians Should the disease Spread among them, and the Agency Physician's resignation is forwarded today, on account of the Reduction of his Salary. I will try to procure another as Soon as I can leave the Reservation for the purpose.

The Agency Threshing Machine is now engaged on Indian Grain and my Small force of employés have been Kept very busy in harvesting the Small Crop in connection with the Agency and in aiding the Indians with theirs.

I herewith enclose the Physician's Report, and also Reports referring to Schools Employés and Funds, and have the honor to be

Very Respectfully
Your Obedt. Servant
Peter Ronan
U.S. Indian Agent.

October 6, 1882
LR 18,923/1882, RG 75, National Archives, Washington, D.C.

> See September 16 and December 14, 1881, for Ronan's previous requests for funding for salaries for the chiefs. This letter has written on it: "No funds."

United States Indian Service,
Flathead Agency,
October 6th, 1882.

Hon. Commissioner of Indian Affairs
Washington, D.C.

Sir,

On September 16th, 1881, I had the honor to address you with reference to the discontinued payment of Salaries to the three Indian Chiefs of this Reservation.

Being urged by them So to do, I also asked Hon. Martin Maginnis to use any influence he possessed in furtherance of the renewal of the payments.

In acknowledging my communication that Gentleman was kind enough to forward your reply to him, in which you write, — "I have to advise you that, owing to the language of the act making appropriations for the Support of the Flatheads for the Current fiscal year" (1881-2) "the sum provided can only be used for their Support, and for pay of employés, but that Steps will be taken by this office to remedy the defect, in the bill to be acted upon by Congress for the Support of Said Indians for the fiscal year ending June 30th 1883."

Taking this Statement into Consideration, I felt at liberty to give the Chiefs Some encouragement in the matter, but felt averse to trouble you further until

I was advised that the "Steps" Spoken of had been successful. In the absence of further information I also had a delicacy about including the necessary amounts in my late Requisition for funds, but am now compelled again to call your attention to the Subject, as I am unable an longer to allay the impatience of the Chiefs, and have been obliged to promise them that I would request you to favor me with definite instructions.

I therefore now have the honor to beg that you will furnish me Such, and — Should it unfortunately happen that the salaries cannot be renewed — that you will provide me with an authoritative Statement to make to the Applicants.

Very respectfully
Your Obedient Servant
Peter Ronan
U.S. Indian Agent.

November 1, 1882
LR 20,702/1882, RG 75, National Archives, Washington, D.C.

On November 17, 1882, the Commissioner of Indian Affairs informed Ronan that the Commissioner was requesting the War Department to "detail a sufficient military force to cooperate with you in maintaining such orders and instructions as are given to you from this office." The Commissioner also instructed Ronan to only permit a limited number of "venders of legitimate supplies" to trade with the railroad construction crews while on the Flathead Reservation.[22] A St. Paul, Minn., newspaper interpreted the affair as an attempt by Ronan to personally control and profit from the trade with the construction crews while on the Flathead Reservation. The charge was publicly rebuked by General John Gibbon.[23]

No further information was located about J. L. Hallett, the railroad construction contractor. Dr. Louis Terry was Flathead Agency physician between 1862 and 1865 and again between 1883 and 1884. He maintained a private practice in Missoula while employed on Flathead. His career was notable for short stays in many different Montana, California, and Nevada towns.[24] For biographical information on Dr. L. H. Choquette see annotation to Ronan's August 8, 1879, article.

United States Indian Service,
Flathead Agency,
November 1st, 1882.

Hon. Commissioner of Indian Affairs,
Washington, D.C.,
  Sir: —
  October has passed in the usual quiet and orderly manner on this reservation.

As remarked in a former communication to you, a large majority of the Indians have gone into the mountains to hunt and will probably be out until Christmas. The cause of such an unusual proportion of the Indians leaving for the chase is their Great dread of small pox, as a few cases stil[l] prevail in surrounding settlements although no case has yet appeared on the reservation.

The immense crew of railroad constructors now at work West of the reservation, in charge of J. L. Hallett, consisting of seven thousand four hundred men! with camp followers, gamblers, ex-convicts, lewd women, &c., are rapidly advancing to the borders of the reservation, accompanied by portable saloons, gambling houses, etc., Merchants and traders of all description also advance with the construction party, and when the border of the reservation is reached the question will arise whether this trade can be continued in an Indian Country. I will require from your office some instructions as to any modification, should you propose such in regard to intercourse laws. It is evident that this vast army of laborers must be supplied while at work on the reservation, and if your instructions imply a strict conformity to the intercourse laws governing Indian reservations, the two regularly licensed traders of the reserve should have timely notice to provide supplies which will meet the exigencies of the case.

It will, at all events, require a Military force to keep back the traders, shop keepers, saloons, etc., who have followed up the construction party named, if decided that the Agency licensed traders alone shall be allowed to do business on the reserve. With a military force I apprehend no danger or difficulty in keeping the whisky traders off the reservation, but in regard to the prohibition of the sale of clothing and necessary supplies by the shopkeepers now advancing with this army of working men, you will please give the necessary instructions, and I will follow them, and perform my duty to the best of my ability.

With the limited force of employes now at this Agency, work progresses slowly. The grist mill is full of Indian wheat; the saw mill yard is piled up with logs awaiting to be sawed into the required bills of lumber for Indians desirous of building. The carpenter's shop is filled with broken wheels and other articles requiring repairs, while there are orders for many sashes and doors from Indians constructing houses, etc. The blacksmith shop is crowded with work of every description, while the blacksmith is now in the woods burning a pit of charcoal with which to perform his work, and I have no other detail to take his place at charcoal burning.

Dr. [Louis] Terry has reported for duty and will take the place of Dr. [L. H.] Choquette.

Enclosed please find the usual monthly reports with the exception of that of the Physician, which is not included as for the last month there has been no doctor at the Agency,

I remain respectfully
Yours
Peter Ronan
U.S. Indian Agent.

November 10, 1882
LR 21,012/1882, SC 55, RG 75, National Archives, Washington, D.C.

> This letter is more evidence of Ronan's dependance on the traditional chiefs to approve sales of reservation timber and maintain peace on the reservation. See the annotation to Ronan's letter of July 28, 1884, for more information about the delay and problems associated with the payment for timber cut by the railroad on the Flathead Reservation.

United States Indian Service,
Flathead Agency,
Nov. 10th, 1882.

Hon. Commissioner Indian Affairs
Washington, D.C.

Sir:

I have the honor to acknowledge receipt of your letter L-19314 – 1882, dated October 26th, 1882, and also your telegram of same date, with reference to the application of the Northern Pacific Railroad Company to the Department of the Interior to cut timber on this reservation, and to the authority granted by the Department to the said Company to take such timber from the Flathead reserve as might be necessary for the construction of its road, subject to the consent of the Indian occupants being obtained.

Without delay I called the principal Chiefs together (the greater portion of the Indians having gone on hunting expeditions, chiefly urged thereto by fear of small pox as before reported to you) and fully explained the matter to them, with the terms submitted to the Company by the Department for acceptance. The chiefs in behalf of the tribes accepted the conditions named, but were a little cautious as to how the Compensation should be paid, demanding quarterly settlements in cash. This matter, of course, I informed them would be settled by the Department, and I promised that their request would be properly laid before you for attention.

> I am very respectfully,
> Your obed't serv't.
> Peter Ronan,
> United States Indian Agt.

November 21, 1882
LR 21,056/1882, SC 55, RG 75, National Archives, Washington, D.C.

> Ronan reminded McCammon of his promise to relay to the President the request of tribal leaders to have the upper Flathead Valley added to the reservation, possibly in exchange for giving up tribal claims to the Jocko Valley. In September 1883, however, they decided that it was preferable to leave the boundaries as they were set out in the 1855 Hellgate Treaty. See Ronan's October 1, 1883, letter.

> Department of the Interior.
> Washington.
> November 21, 1882.

Hon. Hiram Price,
Commissioner of Indian Affairs:

Sir:

I am in receipt of a letter from Peter Ronan, Esq., U.S. Agent at the Flathead Agency, Montana Territory, in relation to the expressed wishes of the Indian chiefs on that reservation that the boundaries thereof be extended so as to include all that portion of country lying north of that reservation to the British line, and requesting me to forward to you a copy of the letter addressed to me — which I now do.

It is my purpose, as soon as I am enabled to make a full report of the result of my visit to the Flathead Reservation, in September last, to present the matter of which Agent Ronan writes for the consideration of the Department. However, it will not be improper for now to state briefly that it seems to me to be a matter of considerable importance to the Indians that the northern boundary of the reservation be extended to the British line. My belief is that, so long as the reservation system is kept up, it will be better for these Indians to be as far out of the reach of white settlers as possible; and this can be best accomplished by moving, as it were, the reservation northward about thirty or forty miles.

This expression of opinion is, as I have stated, only preliminary, and is made only because of the propriety of my expressing some opinion when I forward to you a copy of Agent Ronan's letter.

Very respectfully,
Jos. K. McCammon
Asst. Atty. General.

Enclosure:

United States Indian Service,
Flathead Agency,
Nov. 7th, 1882.

Hon. Jos. K. McCammon
Assistant Attorney General
Interior Department,
Washington, D.C.

Sir: —

You will remember that at the general council held at the Flathead Agency, and which was concluded by you on the 2d. day of September, 1882, the Indian Chiefs urged in the most strenuous manner that the boundaries of their reservation be extended so as to include all that portion of country lying North of said reservation to the British line; Said strip of country from the best information I can obtain from parties who have traversed it, is of no value whatever save as for hunting and fishing grounds for Indians, as it is a wilderness of rock, forest and streams, abounding in game and fish, with the exception of that small portion which lies at the head of Flathead lake, where there are now a few settlers engaged in stock raising. The Chiefs have a perfect understanding of what you promised in regard to the extending of their boundaries, which in effect was that you would use your influence at Washington to have their wishes complied with; but the young men and malcontents have been sowing the seed of discontent by claiming that you made a distinct promise that the country would be given to the Indians provided they agreed to your proposition in regard to the Northern Pacific Railroad right of way, and have been warning settlers at the head of the lake that the country belongs to them and to stop making improvements there. A few days ago I was waited upon by the Chiefs and the matter was fully discussed and I promised to lay the case before you. I tried to impress upon the Indians the folly of urging a proposition upon the government which would involve the ceding to them of thousands of acres of land while it seems to be the policy to cut down instead of enlarging Indian reservations. To this they answered that a very short time ago the country was all their own — that in begging back this strip of wild country, which is unfitted by God and nature for any other purpose than hunting and fishing grounds for Indians, they were actuated by not altogether selfish motives for their own tribes, but that it would be a great benefit to the western Indians, who are being pushed aside by advancing settlers, and who would be welcomed to a home upon their reservation should the boundaries be extended to the British line.

I furthermore represented to the Chiefs that in all probability the government would ask in return for the cession of the land asked for by the Indians all
that tract now belonging to them lying some fifty miles along the Pen d'Oreille
river to Horse Plains. To this suggestion the Chiefs replied that they would ask
for the extension of their boundaries without giving any land in return; but if
they could not get it in that way they were willing to talk about and negotiate
a trade with any Commission who may be empowered to negotiate with them,
and chainge [sic] and establish boundaries. It is my humble opinion that the
extension of the boundaries of this reservation to the British line and the curtailment of the reservation along the line of the Northern Pacific Railroad, and
the removal of the Indians from this great line of travel, will redound greatly
to the benefit of the Indians as well as to the white settlers. At the request and
urgent solicitations of the Chiefs of the tribes occupying this reservation, I lay
the matter before you, and trust you will give me an early answer as to whether
or not any steps will be taken in the matter looking to a settlement of the question so that I can inform the Chiefs who will look for a reply from you.

With great respect I remain
Your obedient Servant,
Peter Ronan,
U.S. Indian Agt.

December 1, 1882
LR 22,205/1882, RG 75, *National Archives, Washington, D.C.*

Ronan reported that Flathead Reservation tribal members had secured wage and contract
work in the construction of the Northern Pacific Railroad through the reservation. Unfortunately neither Ronan's letters nor the other historical sources tell which tribal members
benefitted economically from the construction or how much money they made.

In this letter Ronan mentions the upcoming trial of Koonsa Finley for the June 21,
1882, murder of Frank Marengo on the reservation. Ronan's report to the Commissioner of
Indian Affairs on this murder has not been found. It may have been part of one of Ronan's
monthly reports which were not preserved. Koonsa was the 25 year old son of Basson Finley.
Koonsa had been captured by a Blackfeet war party in 1867 and spent most of his early
life with that tribe.[25] Marengo was shot by Koonsa during a drinking party at the house
of Peter Finley on the reservation.[26] When Ronan finally arrested Koonsa and transported
him to jail in Missoula, Chief Arlee argued that the white man who sold the alcohol was
the real criminal. Arlee and Chief Michelle took Koonsa's horses as punishment for his part
in the murder.[27] In December 1882 Koonsa was released by Judge William Galbraith of the
U.S. District Court in Deer Lodge because he had already been punished for the crime "in
accordance with the customs of the tribe." A trial in U.S. Court would mean Koonsa would
have been tried a second time for the same crime.[28] *The Weekly Missoulian* railed against
the decision.[29] This was the opening round of a long-running battle between Ronan and the
traditional chiefs over control of law enforcement on the reservation. See also Ronan's letter
of February 1, 1883, for more about his disgust at the court's decision. Koonsa was killed on
the Jocko River by a Kalispel Indian named Pial in September 1888.[30]

United States Indian Service,
Flathead Agency,
December 1st, 1882.

Hon. Commissioner of Indian Affairs
Washington, D.C.

Sir,

I have the honor to report the usual good order upon this Reservation during the month of November, and that Indians who desire employment are now receiving good wages from the Northern Pacific Rail-road Company in various Capacities. — Several Indians have taken Contracts from the Division Engineer for the delivery of Piles at points where it is necessary to build bridges on the Reservation, and the Wagons and Harness, furnished by the Indian Department have become a great Source of revenue to them, as they can get plenty of employment for their teams at more than a fair remuneration. This encouragement tends to conciliate the Indians as the passage of the Railroad thro' the Reserve, and has a good effect in Stimulating them towards independence and Self-Support.

The large force of Constructors, mentioned in my last Monthly Report, under charge of J. L. Hallett, is now at work about twenty miles from the Western border of the Reservation on the Pen d'Oreille River, and his next head-quarters will be on the border of the Reservation where he will in all probability be located next month.

When the removal takes place it will be the proper time to invoke military aid to keep back the lawless horde of Camp followers and generally to follow your instructions as contained in your communication of the 17th. Ult.

I have already notified Mr. Hallett of your views by forwarding to him a copy of your instructions, as aforesaid, and upon hearing from him, will furnish the names of those Traders who apply for a special license, and will be as careful as possible that none but respectable persons will be recommended therefor.

I have been summoned to appear before the United States Court at Deer Lodge, — to be held on the 4th day of this Month to testify with reference to the Indian murder which occurred on this Reservation in June last, and will leave for that place to-morrow, leaving a competent man to act during my absence.

If possible more than the usual amount of work for Indians is being done in the Shops and Mills, and all Classes of business, pertaining to the Service Seems to be in an encouraging and Satisfactory Condition.

I herewith have the honor to enclose School, Medical, Fund and Employé Reports, and am

Very Respectfully
Your Obedient Servant
Peter Ronan
U.S. Indian Agent.

1883

January 6, 1883

LR 1,226/1883, RG 75, National Archives, Washington, D.C.

Alexander C. Botkin, United States Marshall for Montana Territory between 1878 and 1885, had a long career in journalism before his appointment. He was crippled by paralysis in 1879 but continued to be active for many years in Montana politics. In 1882 he ran against Martin Maginnis for Territorial Delegate to Congress. He lost in the midst of allegations of voter fraud.[1] Mr. Smith, the timber inspector, was not further identified.

> United States Indian Service,
> Flathead Agency,
> January 6th, 1883.

Hon. Commissioner of Indian Affairs
Washington, D.C.

Sir,

I have the honor to acknowledge receipt of your communication of 21st. Ult. conveying the information that a Complaint had been made to Marshal [Alexander C.] Botkin that wood is being cut on this Reservation for purposes other than Railroad construction: Also that I would not forward the Complaint.

In order thoroughly to corroborate my belief that the complaint was unfounded as I know the Statement to be that I would not forward it, I have for a few days delayed a reply. — Having now however made Searching enquiry I beg respectfully to State that I am still as much as ever at a loss to discover even a foundation for the Charges made. With the exception of Squared timbers, piles and ties which the Railroad Company is having Cut Strictly in conformity with the Agreement entered into, and, in such Cutting the Engineers have taken particular pains to have the Indians engaged, there is nothing of the kind being done on the Reservation, with the added exception that the Company is having the brush and felled timber, which lay on their "right of way" cut up, So as to be of use to the construction trains when they come along.

To find fault with such action I Should consider quite beyond the Scope of my duty, nor can I suppose that any one could See therein cause of Complaint, as, — not to enter into the question as to whether or not the brush and timber on the "right of way" are considered by you, the property of the Railroad Company, — it is evident that the Cutting down thereof was a necessity, and, that having been cut down, the removal is a benefit. — I have only to add that, in Support of this rendering, I am glad to be able to inform You that within the last few days, and while I was engaged on this Subject, Mr. Smith, U.S. Timber Inspector, has Crossed and recrossed the Reservation; that I took the liberty of laying before him Your Communication & requesting him to pay particular attention to the matter, and that he fully agrees with me as to the baselessness of the Complaint.

> Very respectfully
> Your obedient Servant
> Peter Ronan
> U.S. Indian Agent.

February 1, 1883
LR 3,757/1883, RG 75, National Archives, Washington, D.C.

> See the annotation to Ronan's December 1, 1882, letter for details about the trial of Koonsa Finley for the murder of Frank Marengo. Judge William Galbraith held that an Indian could not be tried in U.S. Court for a crime if he had already been tried and punished by his tribe. The U.S. Constitution protects people from double jeopardy. Ronan's description of the "trial" of the white bartenders for serving liquor to Indians was similar to the report in *The Weekly Missoulian*.[2]
>
> William J. Galbraith was appointed U.S. District Judge in Deer Lodge in 1879. He was a Civil War veteran and practiced law in Pennsylvania, Nebraska, and Iowa before coming to Montana.[3] No further information was found about F. M. Eastman, U.S. District Attorney in 1883.

United States Indian Service,
Flathead Agency, Montana
Feby 1st, 1883.

Mr. Eastman
U S District Attorney
Fort Benton
    Sir,
    In answer to your telegram of 26th of Jany, I would state that it is not my intention to prosecute Francois for the recent murder committed on this reservation, in the face of Judge Galbraiths decision in the Koonsa case.
    The Indians placed Francois in jail and Kept him there for a few days and then turned him loose, simply I suppose, to shield the culprit from a trial before the United States Authorities and should I arrest the Murderer it would end in a farce, and leave me personally out of pocket, as did the recent case of Koonsa, and also give the Indians another chance to laugh at and ridicule the law as administered against them.
    I had a whiskey case tried in Missoula last week the result of which has sickened me in the hope of securing *any conviction in any Indian case*:
    The particulars of which I give you as an illustration of American Jurisprudence in this portion of Montana.
    On Sunday the 14th of January Arlee Chief of the Flatheads came to the Agency and informed me that his Step Son came to his house on the previous night with several bottles of Whiskey; that he was very drunk and boisterous, and that he (Arlee) ordered the drunken boy out of the house, and that the boy drew a knife on him and threatened to kill him, and would probably have done so but for the interferance of an Indian who was present. Upon making this statement Arlee asked what could be done to prevent the sale of liquor to Indians, I told the old man that on several occasions I had parties arrested for that offense, relying upon Indian evidence, but invariably when the offender was brought into Court, instead of prosecuting, the evidence tended to shield the culprit and all cases resulted in a dismissal.
    Arlee then stated that he would furnish money to two trusty Indians and send them out to the suspected place to purchase whiskey and fasten the crime against them so that the punishment would be an example to others. The Chief carried out his plan — the Indians sent by him not only drank at the bar but

bought a bottle of whiskey which they brought to the Agency. The parties were arrested on complaint of the Indians and tried before a Justice of the Peace in Missoula. I was present and seeing the defense were liable to have matters their own way in the absence of a District Prosecuting Attorney, I employed Mr. Woody at a personal expense (unless the Indian Office may see fit to allow the account) to prosecute the case.

The evidence for prosecution given by said Indians was straight forward truthful, and to the point, — that on sunday Jany 14th they drank at the bar of a saloon Kept by one Kibble and a woman named Belle Ross alias Calamity Jane, whom they pointed out to the Sheriff for arrest and afterwards identified in court; that they paid said parties for the drinks at the bar and also purchased whiskey which was put into a bottle, safely corked, and produced in court, and the bottle identified by a certain mark.

In the face of this evidence, the defence produced a railroad "rounder" who testified that he was in the saloon Kept by Kibble and Calamity Jane during the day and evening of 14th of January and that no Indian came upon the premises nor did any Indian purchase whiskey in that saloon on that day or evening.

The Justice discharged the Prisoner, and Calamity Jane overwhelmed him with thanks for his good office.

I have no comments to make except experience has taught me to act very prudently in bringing up Indian matters before the Courts.

Yours Truly
Peter Ronan
U S Indian Agent.

Respectfully referred to the Comr of Indian Affairs for his information.

F. M. Eastman
US Atty

March 10, 1883

LR 4,862/1883, RG 75, National Archives, Washington, D.C.

> See Ronan's letter of November 1, 1882, for his request for military assistance to maintain order during the railroad construction on the reservation and the Commissioner of Indian Affair's response.
>
> First Lieutenant Melville C. Wilkerson was stationed at Fort Missoula in 1883. A Civil War veteran, he was commended for gallantry in Idaho during the Nez Perce War. He was killed in 1898, fighting Indians in Minnesota.[4] For Major William H. Jordan, see annotation to Ronan's letter of November 1, 1881.

War Department,
Washington City,
March 10th, 1883.

Sir:

I have the honor to transmit herewith for your information a copy of instructions issued under date of the 19th. ultimo, by the Commanding General of the District of Montana, to the Commanding Officer at Fort Missoula, Montana Territory, with a view to the protection of the Flathead Indian Reservation from illegal intrusion during the construction of the Northern Pacific Railroad through said reservation.

A copy of a letter on the subject, dated the 12th. ultimo, addressed to the Commanding Officer at Fort Missoula by Mr. Peter Roman [sic] United States Indian Agent, Flathead Agency, is also transmitted herewith.

Very respectfully
Your obedient servant,
Robert T. Lincoln
Secretary of War.

The Honorable
The Secretary of the Interior.
Enclosure:

Copy

Northern Pacific Railroad Company,
Western Division,
Office Sup't of Construction,
At the Front, February 5, 1883.

The Post Adjutant
Fort Missoula, M.T.
   Sir:

"Extract"

I have the honor in accordance with letter of instructions of date January 30, 1883, to inform you that Mr. Hallett, Supdt. of Construction informs me that on the 3d. instant, there were one (1000) thousand men of his force at work upon the Flathead Indian Reservation, that in a few days there would be at least two (2500) thousand five hundred, and also that the track layers will be at work upon the Reservation by the 25th inst.

I have also to inform you that Agent Roman [sic] is clearly of opinion that the best operating military force that can be used upon the Reservation for the purpose contemplated will be a small mounted one under command of an officer.

I have also to inform you that I will be able to complete the duty assigned me in conformity with the letter of instructions to which this is a reply on the 8th instant.

* * * * * * *

Very respectfully,
Your obedient servant,
(signed) M. C. Wilkinson
1st Lieut. 3d Infantry.

Enclosure continued:

United States Indian Service,
Flathead Agency, February 12, 1883.

Major Wm. H. Jordan
Fort Missoula, M.T.
   Dear Sir:

In reply to your communication of the 24th ultimo, in which I am notified that, on making to you the necessary representation, such a military force as may be requisite to protect this reservation from illegal intrusion during the construction of the N.P.R.R., thereupon will be furnished; I beg to inform you that, as a large Railroad Camp has now been established within a mile of the Western boundary of the Reserve, and as construction parties of several thousand men will enter it within the next ten days, I believe the time has arrived to request the assistance referred to, seeing that, should no preventive measures be adopted, the saloons and other objectionable following of the working forces will doubtless accompany them across the boundary.

In my estimation a small command, say of fifteen mounted men, acting as a patrol from quarters established in proximity to the main camps, formed by the construction parties, would meet the necessities of the case, and be more efficient than a larger number of Infantry.

Of course I recognize that your own judgment will be the best guide on the matter, and I beg you will excuse my offering an opinion.

In conclusion permit me to add that the delay in answering your communication arose from an anxiety on my part, to give you as little trouble, and to occupy as little of your time as possible in this connection.

I have however carefully watched the advance of the elements we desire to oppose, and now conclude that I am no longer justified in assuming that my personal influence is alone sufficient to maintain peace, and security on this reservation.

Very respectfully,
Your obedient servant,
(signed) Peter Roman
U.S. Indian Agent.

Enclosure continued:

Headquarters District of Montana,
Helena, Mont. Feby. 19, 1883.

Commanding Officer,
Fort Missoula, M.T.

Referring to your communication and letter of the 12th instant, from U.S. Indian Agent Roman addressed to you, the District Commander directs that you send a sufficient force, under a discreet officer, to the Flathead Indian Reservation, to the immediate vicinity where working parties engaged in the construction of the Northern Pacific R.R. will enter upon the reservation from the west, but such force not to be confined to the particular locality mentioned, but to go wherever the performance of the duty specified below can be best performed.

The duty to be performed will consist, *first*, in expelling on request of the Indian Agent, those persons designated by him who may come upon the reservation in violation of law. *Second*, in expelling those who may be on the reservation and not having proper authority to remain, have been ordered by the Agent to leave the reservation and do not go. *Third*, in making arrests within the limits of the reservation of those who having been expelled shall thereafter return to the reservation without proper authority, and of those found within the limits of the reservation in the act of introducing therein ardent spirits in violation of Section 2139 Revised Statutes. *Fourth*, in making search as occasion may seem to require, for and destruction of ardent spirits that may be introduced into the reservation in violation of Section 2139, Revised Statutes and seizure of property as provided in Section 2140 Revised Statutes.

In case of arrest of any person or seizure of property, such person or property shall be delivered to the Civil authority as provided in sec. 2150 Revised Statues.

Have the force sent properly provided for cold weather, and if mounted men are sent, which is desirable, send also a part of the force a sufficient number of men, not mounted, for camp guard, to permit sending all the mounted men from the camp.

The force sent will remain upon the duty indicated until further order or until the Indian Agent shall say it may be dispensed with. Your attention in connection herewith is called to communications heretofore sent you relative to the general subject of the employment of a Military force to aid the Indian Agent in preventing illegal intrusion and traffic upon the reservation whilst construction of the railroad across the reservation shall be in progress. It is desirable that the officer in command of the detachment have, when practicable, the written request of the Indian Agent for the use of the troops in each instance. Furnish the officer in command with copies of the Sections of the Revised Statutes to which your attention is invited. Also of Sections 2133, 2147, 2148, 2149, 2151.

> (signed) Turner
> A.A.A.G.

Official copies respectfully forwarded to the Adjutant General Department of Dakota, Fort Snelling, Minn.

In the absence of the District Commander:

> (signed) G. L. Turner
> 2d Lieutenant 18th Infantry,
> Acting Assistant Adjutant General.

> Headquarters Department of Dakota,
> Fort Snelling, Minn. Feby. 27. 1883.

Official copy respectfully forwarded to Headquarters Military Division of the Missouri.

> (Signed) Alfred H. Terry
> Brigadier General
> Commanding

> Endorsement.
> Headquarters Military Division of the Missouri,
> Chicago, March 5. 1883.

Respectfully forwarded to the Adjutant General of the Army.

> (sd.) P. H. Sheridan
> Lieut. General
> Commanding.

May 2, 1883
LR 9,360/1883, RG 75, National Archives, Washington, D.C.

No further information has yet been located about the killing of an unnamed Indian by a Flathead Reservation Indian named Francois or the Salish theft of Blackfeet horses. It is interesting to note that in 1883 Ronan depended on the chiefs and headmen to punish tribal members. Ronan also mentioned the Francois murder case in his February 1, 1883, letter.

Suasa, the Flathead who stole the horses from the Blackfeet, later settled down, married Chief Arlee's granddaughter, and inherited Chief Arlee's farm when he died in 1889. He became a successful cattleman and grain farmer. In 1895, a group of Jocko Valley Indians forcefully interfered with Agent Joseph Carter's arrest of Judge Louison in a dispute over an Indian dance. Suasa and two others were jailed in Missoula until Duncan McDonald hired a lawyer and got them released on a writ of habeas corpus.[5] No further information was located about Peell, the Pend d'Oreille involved in the horse theft. John W. Young, was Blackfeet Agent between 1876 and 1884. He was a Methodist minister and involved in a bitter feud with the Jesuit Catholic missionaries to the Blackfeet. He was agent during the starvation winter of 1883-1884 when the federal government failed to provide rations to make up for the extermination of the plains buffalo herds.[6]

United States Indian Service,
Flathead Agency,
May 2, 1883.

Hon. Commissioner of Indian Affairs
Washington, D.C.

Sir,

I have had the honor of receiving from you two communications with reference to Indians of this Reservation accused of crimes — one marked "C. 3757" of March 8th referring to the killing of an Indian by another named Francois, and directing me to make a full report of the case. This I regret to Say I have not yet been able to do, as, while I have procured the Story of the Father of the deceased, I have not that of the other Side, as the youth who committed the act, with his Father and an old woman / the only other witness, has been off in the mountains for some time. They are now expected daily and, as as soon as they arrive I Shall have the honor of furnishing Such an account, as, I hope will warrant the U.S. Prosecutor in forming a decision.

The other communication refers to the Stealing by Some of the Flathead and Pen d'Oreille Indians of Horses from the Blackfeet and is of April 21st and marked "C. 7296-1883."

As evidence that I was not indifferent to the importance of the subject I may State that I received Agent Young's notification of the theft on the 7th Ult, and that, on the Same day I made enquiries of the Indians resulting in the information that a Flathead named Suassa and a Pen d'Oreille named Pe-ell had Stolen a band of Horses in the Blackfeet Country. What number the band consisted of I could not learn, nor, as Mr. Young wrote me, — could he. I then addressed a letter to the Deputy Marshall at Deer Lodge, and in the absence of Such an official at Missoula, — another to the Sheriff there, enclosing to each a copy of Agent Young's communication, and furnishing all the facts I myself had gathered, managing to get the same conveyed to Missoula Still on the same day.

By these means I had great hope of having the culprits in a position to be prosecuted before reaching this Reservation, and So, of escaping the unpleasant dilemma of being expected, without having the power to mete out punishment to those who richly deserved it. For, — while I hold, — as I believe my records will Substantiate, — that the Indians, under my charge, are, as a people, extremely well-behaved, and also that I can and do exercise considerable influence over them — to expect they themselves to punish the thieves, in Such a case as this, in which they regard the acts committed as an honorable and to some extent meritorious reprisal is asking a step in advance of their present Code of Morals. And, of course, in opposition to the views of the Chiefs and headmen I can only look for correction to be applied by the civil authorities.

The results of my actions, and some additional views are Stated in my last letter to Agent Young, a copy of which I have the honor to enclose, and, to which, in order to avoid repetition I beg respectfully to refer, as I believe you will thus have all the leading facts connected with the Case.

Before concluding, however, permit me to recall to your attention the paragraph entitled "Laws for Indians" on page 18 of your Report for 1882, as I find the remarks you therein make bearing exactly on my present situation as well as more concise and to the point than any I can otherwise offer.

Owing to the opinions expressed I am happy in knowing that you are aware of the obstacles with which I have now to contend, and await, with due deference any instructions which you may deem advisable in order to enable me to Surmount them.

Very respectfully
Your obedient Servant
Peter Ronan
U.S. Indian Agent.

Enclosure:

United States Indian Service,
Flathead Agency,
May 1st, 1883.

Major John Young
U.S. Indian Agent
Blackfeet Agency, M.T.

Sir,

On the 12th Ult. I wrote you with reference to your communication of March 28th, informing you that one of the Indians who Stole the horses of which you made mention was arrested and awaiting charges in Missoula and requested that you would at once take measures to have him prosecuted, as Should he reach this Reservation the difficulty of having him punished (as you must know from your own experience) would be greatly increased. That I have received no reply has greatly astonished me, more especially as the Sheriff of Missoula County informs me that he also notified you of the circumstance, and I regret to Say that I fear the want of action will disadvantageously complicate matters.

On the 24th ult. I received a letter from the Justice of the Peace of Missoula in which he States that having heard nothing from you or Judge De Witt he had released the prisoner, who, with his companion in the crime is now on this Reservation, where they can at any time be arrested by the United States Marshal on proper steps being taken to prosecute.

As you must be well aware however I have no power within myself to pun[i]sh or have punished a culprit of the Reservation, and, in a case of the present Kind must depend for results on the decisions of the Head-men and majorities of the Tribes, and on my personal influence over them.

In So doing I have Succeeded in having Arlee and his lieutenants take possession of 17 Horses, which are those or of those taken from the Blackfeet, but unfortunately he uses exactly the same argument expressed in your letter of August 14th, 1882 when you wrote of Horses then in possession of your Indians, stolen from Flatheads who were not accused of being thieves "My Indians admit Still holding six (Horses)" "but authorize me to express their willingness to give them up on the return of theirs, a description of them is enclosed."

In other words, he with the rest of the Indians here, insists that your Indians were the first aggressors, and that they have now more of the Flathead and Pen d'Oreille Horses, Stolen within the last few months than the number of Blackfeet animals now in his possession, and therefore he demands an exchange take place.

Referring to the same letter you also write "I look on it as making a difference where the theft is committed. My Indians are not accused of going on your Reservation, and making the theft. Yours it's not denied came here." Now I am very anxious to have the Indians of this Reservation remain thereon and I flatter myself that year by year I succeed the better in lessening their roaming propensities, but, by referring to a copy of "Revised Treaties" you will find them guaranteed the right of visiting the Eastern side of the Rockies.

These provisions they are well acquainted with and it would be difficult to convince them that they are less entitled to the possession of their ponies on the East than on the West Side.

It is worse than useless however for us to follow up this train of argument. Stolen property ought to be delivered to the rightful owner wherever found, and the thief punished; and, only thus will cause for reprisals be done away with. Now we have two thieves, of whom to make an example if the means are to be had, and as I have not the power necessary, I can only suggest that you as complainant procure the assistance of the United States authorities.

Yours Obedtly,
(Sigd) Peter Ronan
U.S. Indian Agent.

May 19, 1883
LR 9,212/1883, SC 55, RG 75, National Archives, Washington, D.C.

> Ronan's appeal to McCammon, which is quoted in this letter, is another example of Ronan's need to go around his immediate superiors in the Office of Indian Affairs to get action for the Flathead Reservation tribes. Ronan needed to deal with tribal complaints about the delay in the payment for the right-of-way, but the officials in Washington got hung up on bureaucratic procedures and rules.

Dept. of the Interior
Office of the Secretary
May 19, 1883

Respectfully referred to the Commissioner of Indian Affairs who will communicate to Agent Ronan for the purposes herein requested the causes of delay in the payment of the amounts agreed upon for right of way to the Northern Pacific R. R. Co., through the Flathead Indian Reservation; furnishing him at the same time with a copy of Ex. Doc. #44 of 47th Cong. 2nd Sess. on the subject.

As a rule, the consideration stipulated in such agreement should not be received by the Department until the agreements shall have been ratified by Congress.

As the Railroad Company in this case however has been permitted to proceed with the building of the road through the reservation I think that the proper officer should be called upon to pay the amount agreed upon as compensation to the individual Indians for damages to improvements, &c., and payment thereof be made to the respective claimants named in the award.

H. M. Teller
Secretary

Enclosed letter:

Department of the Interior,
Washington,
May 19, 1883.

Hon. H. M. Teller,
Secretary of the Interior:

Sir:

I am in receipt of a personal letter from Peter Ronan, U.S. Agent for the Flathead, Kootenais and Pend d'Oreilles Indians, residing on the Flathead Indian Reservation, in the Territory of Montana, of which the following is an extract:

"Of late, I have been worried by the Indians making demands on me to tell them why they have not been paid for the right of way of the Northern Pacific Railroad across the reservation, as agreed upon between yourself and them in the council of September, 1883 [i.e., 1882]. Troublesome white men point out the fact to the Indians that the railroad will soon be finished through their country, and the company will then let them whistle for their money. You will confer a great kindness on me if you will write the cause of the delay, and explain something about the time you think a settlement will be made, so that I can read the letter to the Indians and satisfy them."

Deeming this matter of sufficient importance to demand your attention, I take this method of bringing the extract to your notice.

Very respectfully,
Your obedient servant,
Jos. K. McCammon
Asst. Atty. General.

July 19, 1883
LR 13,683/1883, RG 75, National Archives, Washington, D.C.

Ronan explained the legal gyrations within the white political system that attempted to justify moving the Bitterroot Salish Indians to the Jocko or Flathead Reservation. From the viewpoint of Chief Charlo and the other Salish leaders however, a fair and honest interpretation of the 1855 Hellgate Treaty provided for a Bitterroot Valley reservation for the tribe.[7]

United States Indian Service,
Flathead Agency,
July 19th, 1883.

Hon. Commissioner of Indian Affairs
Washington, D.C.

Sir,

I am unofficially informed that a Commission, Consisting of five Senators and three members of the House, was appointed by the last session of Congress, to visit Montana this Summer to Study the Indian question, by a consultation directly with the tribes at their various Agencies, and as this body of eminent Statesmen may not have the time or opportunity, in a hurried visit to an Agency to look carefully into important matters connected with the welfare of the tribes, I take the liberty of addressing you in regard to the Status of the Indians of the Flathead Nation, with a view that attention may be directly drawn to the condition of their affairs.

I will merely call your attention to the Garfield Agreement, made on the 27th day of August 1872, and to the provisions therein agreed upon; and State that a very few of the Bitter Root Flatheads received any benefit from the arrangements, outside of the few connections and followers of Arlee, third Chief of Flatheads, who removed from the Bitter Root Valley under the Garfield agreement to this Agency, and profited thereby at the expense of the majority which refused to follow him.

By act of Congress approved June 5th, 1872, entitled "an act to provide for the removal of the Flathead and other Indians from the Bitter Root Valley in the Territory of Montana" it is provided "That is [sic] shall be the duty of the President as soon as practicable, to remove the Flathead Indians (whether of full or mixed bloods,) and all other connected with said tribe, and recognized as members thereof from Bitter Root Valley, in the Territory of Montana, to the general reservation in Said Territory, (commonly Known as the Jocko reservation,) which by treaty concluded at Hell-Gate, in Bitter Root Valley, July 16th, 1855 and ratified by the Senate March 8th, 1859, between the United States and the confederated tribes of Flatheads Kootenai and Pen d'Oreille Indians, was Set apart and reserved for the use and occupation of said confederated tribes"; that "the Surveyor General of Montana Territory shall cause to be Surveyed, as other public lands of the United States are surveyed, the lands in the Bitter Root Valley lying above the Lo-Lo Fork of the Bitter Root river"; and that "any of said Indians, being the head of a family or twenty one years of age, who Shall, at the passage of this Act, be actually residing upon and cultivating any portion of said lands, shall be permitted to remain in Said valley and pre-empt without cost the land So occupied and cultivated, not exceeding in amount one hundred and sixty acres for each of Such Indians, for which he shall receive a patent without power of alienation; *Provided*, That Such Indian Shall, prior to August first, eighteen hundred and seventy two, notify the Superintendant of Indian Affairs, for Montana Territory that he abandons his tribal relations with Said tribe; and intends to remain in Said valley; *And provided further,* That said Superintendent shall give Such Indian at least one month's notice prior to the date last above mentioned of the provisions of this act and of his right to remain as provided in this Section of the act."

In accordance there was deposited in the General Land Office of the United States an order for the Secretary of the Interior, dated October 21st, 1873, granting patents to individual Indians, under the provisions of said act, to the number of fifty one. Upon assuming charge of the Jocko Reservation, I found among the papers of the office said patents, and under instructions from Commissioner of Indian Affairs, dated at Washington, August 23d, 1877, I proceeded to the Bitter Root Valley to deliver the said patents to the Indians and take their receipts properly witnessed therefor, they refused to accept them, a report of which will be found on page 110 in my annual report to the Commissioner of Indian Affairs for 1880.

The Indian land claims of the Bitter Root Valley are sadly mixed. A number of Indians in whose names claims were located and for which patents were issued are now residents on this reservation.

There is another class of Indians in whose names claims were located and patented, who are dead and have left no Known descendants or heirs. All of the above described classes of claims are vacant and are amongst the best lands in the valley. No other person or persons can gain any right or title thereto.

There is still another class of Indians in the Bitter Root Valley (Flatheads) for whom no claims were located — and also Some for whom claims were located — that are now living on and occupying public lands of the United States, to which they have no right, but claim the Same to the exclusion of the white settlers, while a large number of the actual Indian claims in the valley are unoccupied.

In regard to the future welfare of the Flathead Indians, both moral and temporal, it is my impression that they should be removed from the Bitter Root valley and provisions made to settle them permanently on the Jocko reservation for the following reasons.

1st. Under the law they cannot remain in the Bitter Root valley but by becoming citizens of the United States, severing their tribal relations and complying with the rules imposed by the laws of this country upon all citizens; but these Indians until a few years ago, having nourished a contemptious resentment for the white race, remained obstinately attached to their customs; did not care to acquire the English language (and how could they, having had no School established among them) and refused to be instructed in the ways of the whites, So that they are not now ready to become citizens, to any advantage for themselves or the community.

2nd. The only hope of changing the ways of these Indians is in raising a new generation, by establishing schools for their children in which they may learn the English language and be trained to work; but this requires a boarding School for both sexes which it would not be so easy to establish in the Bitter Root valley for them, but which exists and is in a flourishing condition on the Jocko Reservation.

3rd. By the Garfield agreement only a small portion of these Indians were provided with lands under Government patent, and not a few among them being absent at the time of the meeting, on their hunting expeditions, and therefore unable to manifest their intention in the matter, have been forgotten and deprived of the privilege of getting land in the valley; and in the way that land has been taken up in the valley by white settlers, since the Garfield agreement was made, it would be next to impossible to provide these Indians with homes, consequently they with their families would continue their roving life and become a burden to those who Secured land, upon a return from their tramps to the Bitter Root valley.

4th. Were the conditions of the Garfield agreement to be carried out rigourously not many of the Indians for whom lands have been surveyed could be able to hold said land, for reason that Some of those for whom land has been surveyed and patented, removed to the Jocko and got their share of the money granted in the stipulation; many more for whom land has been surveyed never Knew where the land is situated which had been surveyed for them So that they never had any improvements and others again traded off the land Surveyed for them and bought or Settled upon other land to which they hold no legal right. Hence complaints bad feeling and actual wrong would be the result of the rigourous carrying out of the Garfield agreement.

5th. A large number of the young men have grown up indulged in their lazy inclinations, and there is very little hope that if left to themselves by becoming citizens, they will settle down and farm even in case land would be provided for them and means furnished to them to Start a farm. But these very Indians, far from the influence of demoralizing surroundings and whiskey trading whites, on the Jocko reservation, where a good many of their race and blood have already good farms, might easier be induced by the example of others and the help they will then receive from the Government, to settle down; on the contrary, remaining in the Bitter Root valley, Surrounded on every Side by new Settlers, Some of whom are inclined to take advantage of their ignorance, and in fault of activity of the Indians, they cannot with any advantage compete with their white neighbors.

There are however many difficulties in my judgment against this removal.

1st. The natural and I may say traditional attachment to their land.

2nd. The Stubbornness their hereditary Chief Charlos founded on his never having consented to the opening up of Settlement of the Bitter Root Valley or the Sale of the lands; and also on account of the fact of most of the Flatheads having been deprived of the fruits of the Sale of their land on behalf of only a few who removed to the Jocko reservation.

3rd. The prejudices the Flatheads entertain against the Pen d'Oreilles and Kootenais.

4th. Their repugnance to have Henry or Arlee as their chief, instead of Charlos.

5th. The idea entertained by some of them, that they will again be removed even from the Jocko reservation make room for white Settlers, and this idea is intensified by whites who tell them plainly that this is the determined policy of the Government.

6th. The fear of being entirely shut up on the reservation and prevented from hunting outside the limits of the Same.

To overcome these difficulties the Government should make generous appropriations and offer to these Indians in the way of establishing them on farms, with implements of labor and Stock. Those who have improvements in the Bitter Root valley should be allowed to sell them and receive prices according to their value. The Indians should be made to understand that the Government will help them on the Reservation, with the necessary implements and means according to the disposition Shown by each of them, and the need they stand in; that if they settle down on the Reservation and the land be divided among them in severalty they will not be removed at least for many years. They should be encouraged by proposing to them the advantages of a good school for their children.

The Indian Department and the Commissioners should also be reminded of the constant good behavior of the Bitter Root Indians through very adverse circumstances. That the Garfield treaty or agreement has been carried on to present date without the consent of the hereditary Chief of the Flatheads — Charlos — although his name appears appended to the agreement; and resulted to the benefit of a few families who removed to the Jocko reservation, while the greater portion clung to Charlos and his poverty and remained in the Bitter Root Valley; that the Flatheads Showed their fidelity to the Government in a wonderful way, during the Nez Percé War, when Joseph and his band marched triumphantly through the Bitter Root Valley. Instead of joining the hostiles, who were their friends, both by marriage ties and former alliances, and flushed at the time with apparent success, none of them either joined or helped them, and by their behavior and bravery Saved the Bitter Root Settlement from Slaughter and devastation.

I am of the opinion that it will not be a difficult task to induce the Indians, of their own accord, and without forcible measures to remove from the Bitter Root valley to the Jocko Reservation; they see themselves Surrounded on all Sides by white Settlers only too eager to take advantage of their ignorance; they see their chances of making a living in competition with the white Settlers deminishing, and if they be asked their opinion individually, (not making the Chief their mouthpiece) a large majority will be willing to remove to the Jocko Reservation providing suitable arrangements can be made for their future welfare.

In regard to the Jocko Reservation, I claim that the Indians are making fair progress towards civilization and self support, and that their condition and surroundings will compare favorably with any other Indians outside of the civilized tribes of the Indian Territory. However of that the Commission will be able to judge for themselves and I have no Suggestions to make, Save to here give copy of a letter addressed by me to Hon. J. K. McCammon, Assistant Attorney General of the Interior Department, Washington D.C. which will explain itself, and Save going over the same ground.

[Here Ronan copied his November 7, 1882, letter to Jos. K. McCammon which was reproduced above as an enclosure under date of November 21, 1882.]

Respectfully Submitted,

Peter Ronan
U.S. Indian Agent.

July 26, 1883
LR 14,283/1883, RG 75, National Archives, Washington, D.C.

See Ronan's August 20, 1883, letter for his report on his trip to the Kootenai village at Elmo and the northern boundary of the reservation.

United States Indian Service,
Flathead Agency,
July 26th, 1883.

Hon. Commissioner of Indian Affairs
Washington, D.C.

Sir,

I have the honor of informing you that on the 7th inst; when at this Agency, Mr. S. S. Benedict, U.S. Indian Inspector, gave me written instructions to visit at my "earliest convenience the Bitter Root Country on this Reservation and warn all intruders, whether holding Cattle or otherwise, off this Reservation" with Some additional directions as to my mode of procedure. Awaiting information (in order to enable me correctly to locate the boundary) which Mr. Benedict expected to Secure in Helena, and which I received about ten days ago, I concluded that it would be better to delay the trip until my Second Quarter's Papers were made out and until some other Official business was disposed of. Such will be the case in a few days and I have now respectfully to ask your approval of my absence from the Agency for the purpose referred to, for Twelve days commencing on the 2d of August when I Shall have mailed my Reports for the month of July.

And, in this connection I also respectfully ask permission to hire at Two and a half ($2.50) Dollar each per diem, — for ten days, — two temporary employés, — one as Herder and Interpreter, and the other (an Indian who saw the boundary Surveyed Eleven years ago) as Guide and Packer.

I expect to meet with Some trouble in finding the Surveyors Posts and mounds, and as the work will require to be done on foot and horseback I Shall require to have Some one to look after the Horses while I with the guide are Searching for them. Add to this that I cannot procure a guide who can Speak English and I hope you will agree with my believe [sic] that I cannot properly accomplish the task more economically especially when it is taken into consideration that the men employed will be required to furnish their own Riding animals, the demands at this season on our Small Agency force of Men and Horses being Such that none of the former and not Sufficient of the latter can be spared for any extra duty.

Very Respectfully
Your Obedient Servant
Peter Ronan
U.S. Indian Agent.

Attached undated note in pencil:

"Tell Ronan to submit an itemized account of expenses of trip — upon his return, for approval accompanied by a copy of his orders from Benedict, and a *[rest of note illegible]*.

August 13, 1883a

U.S. Commissioner of Indian Affairs, Annual Report of the Commissioner of Indian Affairs *(Washington, D.C.: U.S. Government Printing Office, 1883), pages 157-59.*

> Ronan emphasized changes in the tribal economy from hunting and gathering to ranching and farming. His prejudices saw the new economy as morally virtuous and the old tribal economy as bad. Skills taught at St. Ignatius Mission schools were not just economically practical, but morally superior.
>
> Note his discussion of tribal employment opened up by the construction of the railroad through the reservation. Ronan used U.S. Army support to arrest and send home Indian visitors from the Lower Columbia Country.[8]

Flathead Agency, Mont.
August 13, 1883.

Sir: In compliance with your instructions, I now have the honor of submitting this my seventh annual report.

I much regret to record the fact that the inclemency of the weather during the month of May had a very injurious effect on seeds planted, many of the more tender vegetable seeds, such as beans, corn, melons, squashes, &c., having been entirely destroyed by frost. Again, the cold and constant rains of the spring were followed by scorching heat, and the grain harvest will be extremely light.

Quite a number of Indians are at present engaged in putting up hay, a fact which will doubtless be considered a stronger evidence of their advance towards civilization than the harvesting of their grain, which has also now commenced. During the present year a large increase of acreage has been sown, and were the results, which, of course, can only be approximated in the accompanying statistical report, such as to repay them with an abundant harvest, the Indian farmers would have been greatly encouraged as to future efforts. I fear, however, no retrogression, as the inhabitants of this reservation have evidently proved to themselves that farming, even with light crops, affords them a more comfortable and reliable, if not more pleasant, livelihood than hunting and trapping; and nothing has so much conduced to this end as the distribution by the Department of agricultural implements.

In connection with education, there are two schools — one for boys and one for girls — located some 18 miles north of this agency, at St. Ignatius Mission. These are conducted according to a contract with Rev. J. B. A. Brouillet, director of the Catholic Indian missions, and under the present management are in a flourishing condition. Still better results, however, may henceforth be expected, for, as appropriations have been increased, attendance will be increased accordingly, seeing that ample provisions are now being made for the accommodation of children; and I have no doubt that our schools, as institutions for the industrial education of Indian children, will continue to bear, as I believe they have heretofore borne, a favorable comparison with those of any other agency.

Two new school-houses are now in course of construction, one of which, being for boys, the missionaries at Saint Ignatius are building, entirely at their own expense, while the other, for girls, is being built by the Sisters of Providence, those parties having the educational charge of the children. The new building for boys is in the shape of an L, each arm being 66 feet in length and 22 in width or depth. There are, besides, an addition of 14 by 14, and a two-story porch or veranda 14 feet wide and 90 feet long. The main building is to be three storied, of which the first floor is to consist of a chapel 39 by 22, a recreation-room 27 by 22, two class-rooms 22 by 22 each, and an infirmary 14 by 14; the second floor of two class-rooms, each 22 by 22, a museum 27 by 22, two private rooms each 12½ by 22, and a clothes-room 14 by 36; and third floor of a dormitory 110 by 22. For safety in case of fire it has been determined to erect two staircases, one at each end of the building, which, when completed, it is computed will cost not less then $7,000. The new structure in connection with the present school for girls is also to be a building of three stories, 50 feet in length by 45 in breadth, while in height the first story is to be of 10 feet, the second of 11, and the third of 10. A corridor 6 feet in width, and having three rooms on each side, will bisect the first story, the six rooms composing a parlor, a sewing-room for the girls, and four apartments for the use of the Sisters. The second story will likewise be divided by a corridor, having on one side a chapel, and on the other a dormitory, while another large dormitory will form the third story. The two lower stories will be connected with the school-house, now in use, by passages 15 by 15, when the whole will present a commodious and healthy institution.

With regard to missionary work, which is under the supervision of Rev. L. Van Gorp, S.J., of Saint Ignatius Mission, everything appropriate is being done for the spiritual welfare of the Indians, who, added to this, have gained much in temporal matters through the aid, precept, and example of their spiritual advisors. Several priests and brothers of the order of Jesuits are stationed here, the Mission being one of the oldest in the Territories, having been established under the Apostlelate of Father [Pierre] De Smet, whose zeal and perseverance have, here at least, been well emulated. Several Sisters of Providence have also established themselves at Saint Ignatius Mission, and it would only be an unnecessary repetition of words to try to portray the great and lasting benefits conferred by their Christian teachings, their physical and moral cleanliness, and their habits of industry, or to describe the civilizing influence wielded by them over the Indian girls who are so fortunate as to be placed under their gentle and charitable care.

With reference to industrial pursuits, in addition to the cultivation of land and the erection of a number of houses, many Indians have been engaged in furnishing piles, ties, and cord-wood for the Northern Pacific Railroad Company, and have been well pleased by the fair wages paid them, and the means thus opened to procure the necessaries and some of the comforts of existence. These Indians are excellent herdsmen, and pay great attention to their stock, each owner of any number having his own brand, which is respected quite as much as is the case among white herdsmen. The high prices lately paid by beef contractors connected with the railroad afforded the Indians an excellent market for surplus steers, but very few were induced by the most tempting offers to part with their cows.

Of the Indians under my charge, it is undeniable that there are some who still prefer to lead more or less of a nomadic life; but even of these very few are criminal, and very few are paupers. With regard to criminals, I think there are few populations in which, compared in number, a smaller number of offenses against law occurs; and as to paupers, I believe that if the amount of assistance afforded these Indians by the United States Government be compared with the poor rates of many of the States, such a comparison will not prove unfavorable to the Indians. On the other hand, there are a few whom it is almost impossible to prevent from wandering about the country, leading vagabond lives, seeking for opportunities to drink and gamble, and of such I have just had a vivid experience.

While away from the agency, under orders to locate the northern limits of the reservation, some forty Indians arrived from the Columbia River country, consisting of Spokanes, Lower Calispels, Umatillas, and Nez Percés, who evidently visited this region on a gambling excursion and for a spree. Having induced five young men of this reservation to join their carousals, they encamped just across the southern border of the reserve, where, having procured whisky, of which they imbibed freely, they proceeded to terrorize a few railroad employés, threatening death and destruction if their wishes, which seem chiefly to have been centered on fire-water, were not complied with. A traveler also was halted by three Spokanes and three Nez Percés, and compelled to yield up his pocketbook, containing $210. As soon as the news, which was conveyed by startling telegrams, reached me, not knowing the extent of the *emeute*, I sent a dispatch to Major Jordan, at Fort Missoula, for assistance, and started for the scene of action. On my arrival there I placed under arrest, for selling whisky to Indians, a white man, who, having done so off of the reservation, Was turned over to the county authorities. With the military command which had come at my request, I then followed the Indian offenders to the reservation. Those, however, who had been engaged in the robbery, made their escape; but I went with the soldiers and "rounded up" all of the alien Indians on the reservation, and, under a penalty of imprisonment in case of disobedience, I ordered them to their homes. They left without delay. Peaceful pursuits followed the departure of the "visitors," and perfect quiet now prevails.

Before concluding, permit me to make, in connection with the foregoing, the following comment. While not being surprised that strangers on the ground would become excited and create unnecessary commotion, on account of such behavior on the part of a few drunken Indians, and while being still further from having any desire to palliate such actions, I desire to call attention to the fact that such a disturbance might at any time take place in a town of medium size and scarcely be heard of in the next street, while, on the other hand, judging from past experience, occurring as it did, to some extent at least, in connection with an Indian agency, there is a probability of more or less attention being attracted thereto over the length and breadth of the land, and of occasion being taken therefrom to criticise, in not the most complimentary terms, the Indian Department, its servants, and their charges.

As a proof that the Indians of this reservation, while undoubtedly brave, are also law-abiding, I refer with pride to the fact of the completion of the Northern Pacific Railroad through their lands, and against their strongest wishes, without any annoyance or opposition being offered to the railroad company that for a moment could be termed serious.

Very respectfully, your obedient servant,

Peter Ronan,
United States Indian Agent.

The Commissioner of Indian Affairs.

August 13, 1883b
LR 15,873/1883, RG 75, National Archives, Washington, D.C.

> On September 5, 1881, the Commissioner had determined that Telesphore G. Demers was not entitled to trade on the reservation without a license. (See Ronan letter of August 20, 1881a.) On October 13, 1883, in response to this letter, the Commissioner decided that T. G. Demers and his brothers and sisters were entitled to all the rights of any mixed blood Indian on the Flathead Reservation.[9] In 1883 only full blood Indians were exempt from having to get a license to trade on a reservation.

Missoula, Montana
August 13"/ 883

To the Honorable the Secetary of
Interior of the United States
    Sir,
We herewith submit for decision by your Honorable department whether the following persons are entitled to be received upon and enjoy the same privileges of the other indians belonging to the Flat head indian agency and reservation "towit" Telesphore G. Demers Alphonsine P. Demers Delema Demers Hemine Demers Louis Antonine Demers who are the children of the daughter of Antoine and Emilie Rivais who are and have been since the establishment of the Flathead agency members of the tribe and have at all times been on the reservation and under the charge of the United States Indian Reservation, and Agents. The above named Telesphore G. Demers Alphonsine P. Demers Delima Demers Hemine Demers Lewis Antoine Demers are and have been at all times recognized by the following chiefs "towit" Michele Chief of the Pond de

Reille, Allee chief of the Flatheads and Ignious [sic] chief of the Kootinai as belonging to the tribe and have quite recently so expressed themselves in the presence of Maj Ronan the present agent on the Flat head reservation.

Their mother Claris was born and raised on the reservation. Their Grand Father & Mother above referred to are still living on the reservation their mother is not living.

The parties named other than myself are my brothers and sisters.

Your early attention to this matter will much oblige.

Your Humble Servant
Telesphore G. Demers.

The foregoing statement is true to the best of my knowledge and belief.

Peter Ronan
U.S. Indian Agt.

Flathead Agency
August 14, 1883

August 20, 1883

LR 15,923/1883, RG 75, National Archives, Washington, D.C.

> The 1855 Hellgate Treaty located the northern boundary of the Flathead Reservation "half way in latitude between the northern and southern extremities of the Flathead Lake." During the annual spring runoff, however, the lake flooded wetlands to the north, causing the halfway point to move with the seasons. The Kootenai located the northern boundary on a small range of hills just north of the surveyed boundary. An 1872 survey of the southern boundary of the public land in the Flathead Valley and finally an 1887 survey of the reservation boundary by U.S. Deputy Surveyor Edmund Harrison placed the boundary south of the natural boundary observed by the Kootenai. In 1965 the U.S. Court of Claims determined that the 1887 boundary survey had been in error and should have been 820 feet further north. As a result of the mistake, over 4,200 acres of land and water were excluded from the reservation.[10] See Ronan's two letters dated October 31, 1890, about his problems with the survey, and his request that the northern boundary be set at a row of hills just north of Harrison's survey which the Kootenai had considered the northern boundary since 1855.
>
> Since the northern boundary of the reservation was not fenced, the lack of a natural barrier to keep neighboring cattle off the reservation led to years of conflict. As Ronan mentioned in this report, some of the cattlemen paid Kootenai Chief Eneas for use of the reservation pasture.[11] No direct evidence has been found indicating why Harrison made the surveying error, but it is known that Eugene McCarthy, who worked on the survey, returned to establish a homestead claim on the reservation land that had been erroneously located in the public domain.[12] For biographical information on McCarthy see the annotation to Ronan's July 25, 1892, letter.
>
> In 1886, Crossen & Cummings paid $406.28 in taxes to Missoula County.[13] Hugh Crossen at various times raised cattle in the Flathead Valley and mined for gold and silver at Cedar Creek, near Superior, and Horse Plains.[14] Daniel O'Sullivan was selling cattle and living in Horse Plains in 1885, and in 1888 had "a herd of several hundred cattle and one of the choice places upon the Little Bitter Root creek."[15]

Flathead Agency,
August 20th, 1883.

Hon. Commissioner Indian Affairs
Washington, D.C.

Sir:

I have the honor to report that having made the examination of the Northern Boundary of the Reservation, directed by Mr. Inspector Benedict, as mentioned to you in my communication of July 26, 1883, I found certain land marks designating the same thro' the assistance of surveyor's notes sent me from the Surveyor General's Office in Helena.

Up to this time I was unaware of any such — having been informed that there was no marked boundary by the Indians, who, on close inquiry resulting from my present discoveries, I find do not recognize as correct the survey referred to, claiming that the treaty boundary lies still further North, and I was the more convinced of the absence on account of a communication from the Department marked "L" — Montana — R. 266 — 1880, and dated April 1st, 1880, in which the statement was made that "The records of this office do not show that the boundary lines of this Reservation have ever been surveyed." However, acting upon Mr. Benedict's instructions, I also found that there were grazing more or less upon the Reservation four herds of cattle, the owners of which must be considered as trespassers although each and all had made payments to the Indians for the privilege, which accounts for the acquiescence of the latter in these cases.

On my return I immediately issued the following circular:

"Flathead Agency
August 12, 1883

"Sir: Having received new and imperative orders to personally attend to the strict enforcement of the following laws and regulations, I have now to inform you that, hereafter any infringement thereof cannot possibly be overlooked, and that at the end of thirty days, any stock trespassing on this reservation will be taken in charge by a U S Marshal, and I am particularly directed to notify trespassers that no payment made to any Indian or Indians can be held as conferring any right of location or otherwise on a Reservation.

"Under Section 2118 U.S. Revised Statutes every person who makes a settlement on any lands belonging, secured or granted by treaty with the United States to any Indian tribe is liable to a penalty of one thousand dollars.

"All persons who cut or attempt to cut timber or hay upon Reservations are intruders and criminals subject not only to apprehension and removal but to fine and imprisonment for such trespasses.

"Agents in case of Stock grazing on Reservations belonging to unauthorized persons will notify such persons, and in case such stock is not removed within thirty days, the names of such persons, together with the names of witnesses must be reported to the Indian Office, that proper legal action may be taken in the premises.

"No further notification need be expected.

Respectfully
Peter Ronan
U.S. Indian Agent."

As a result I have been informed that Mr. Demers has laid his case before
the Honorable Secretary of the Interior, while I have received the following
communication from Cummings, Crossen & Co. consisting of three partners,
namely Mr. Cummings, H. Crossen, and Daniel O'Sullivan, which I respectfully
present in full, as I deem it my duty to allow them to submit their petition,
while I desire to be relieved of personal responsibility.

"Little Bitter Root,
August 17th, 1883.

"Peter Ronan
U.S. Indian Agent,
Flathead Agency, Montana
      "Sir
      "In reply to your letter of August 12th, 1883, informing us
that after a personal visit to the Northern border of the Flathead Reservation, you were convinced that our herd of cattle
was grazing upon the Indian Reservation, and that therefore
we were trespassers, and ordered our band of cattle driven off
under penalty of prosecution before the Courts. We humbly
call you attention to the following facts:
      "For several years past we have herded and grazed our
band of cattle at a point on the extreme Northern border of
the Reservation, which we always considered as being outside
of the line and on public domain. The range is on a tributary
of a stream called Little Bitter Root, where there are no Indian habitations within twenty miles of our herd, nor do the
Indians ever visit this place except early in Spring, when a
few come to dig camas and Bitter Root. In order that there
should be no cause of complaint, and that no injustice should
be done, should our herd stray over the border, we have paid
to the chiefs and head men, for the benefit of the tribes three
hundred dollars a year. This amount we paid more for their
good will and friendship then in consideration that our cattle
were trespassing upon their lands, as we were totally ignorant of the points designated as treaty boundaries, but from
our interpretation of the treaty believed ourselves on public
domain.
      "Now to summarily eject us from the range we occupy at
this late season, will work ruin to us, as the haying season is
past and no time is left to provide for winter provender. We are
living outside of the lines you designated as being the Northern
Boundary of the Reservation, according to Territorial survey,
but we cannot disguise the fact that our cattle stray across it,
and it is a matter of impossibility for us to prevent their so
doing. We have paid the Indians three hundred dollars for this
privilege for the current year, and we are willing to pay that
or any reasonable sum for each succeeding year, should we be
able to make such an arrangement, and will bind ourselves not

to allow any of our herd to stray further over the reservation line than the junction of Warm Spring creek with Little Bitter Root creek, a place on the extreme North of the Reservation, which as we stated before is totally unoccupied by Indians. We hope that you will be able to consider our proposition as one of benefit to the Indians, and that we won't be unnecessarily compelled to suffer a ruinous loss, and are

Yours respectfully
Signed Cummings, Crossen & Co."

While being able to endorse the statement that the granting of the privilege asked for would be a benefit and not a detriment to the Indians, as they would receive payment for what they do not require, and do not use, and the selling of which would produce no hurt hereafter; and believing that any representations to the contrary could only arise from personal enmity to the Indians or the petitioners, I still would not take the liberty of troubling you with the matter had I not lately observed that such leases had been approved in connection with other Reservations, and did I not find in my copy of instructions to Indian Agents Sec. 269, that white persons will not be permitted to graze cattle upon Indian Reservations without consent of the Indians, and the approval of the Agent thereto, and in such cases only upon such terms and conditions and subject to the payment of such rate of compensation for the privilege as may be prescribed by the Agent, with the approval of this department.

Before completing this report I would respectfully request information as to your views with regard to those whitemen who have for years precedent to my taking charge here, had a home and been recognized as inhabitants of the Reservation. As those men are not in the common acceptation of the word Squaw-men, having married Indian women many years ago when there were no whites in the country and having raised families respectably, as I found them established here on on [sic] my arrival, and as their removal would either necessitate the separation of a father from his wife and children or the pecuniary ruin of all. I have hitherto had no thought of disturbing them and considered it unnecessary to call attention to the subject. Having had occasion however to believe that cause has been sought for fault finding with mat[t]ers under my jurisdiction I most respectfully ask instructions on these questions sufficiently full to enable me to meet your wishes.

I remain respectfully
Peter Ronan
United States Indian Agt.

September 5, 1883
Samuel T. Hauser Papers, MC 37, box 18, folder 34, Montana Historical Society Archives, Helena.

Ronan's letters to Samuel T. Hauser, a Helena banker and longtime friend, document how productive a fishery the Jocko River was before the irrigation construction and pollution of the twentieth century. See also Ronan's October 5, 1883, letter to Senator G. G. Vest and his October 8, 1883, and August 18, 1884, letters. For more information about the visit of U.S. Senator G. G. Vest, Montana Governor John Crosby, and Montana Delegate Martin Maginnis to the Flathead Reservation see Ronan's report of October 1, 1883.

Samuel T. Hauser was a prominent banker, financier, and politician in Montana Territory in the 1880s. He got his start as a gold miner in Alder Gulch in Helena and built an empire including silver and coal mines, railroads, toll roads, and reclamation works. In addition to his bank in Helena, he also financed banks in Butte, Fort Benton, and Missoula. In 1885 he was appointed Governor of Montana Territory and served for several years in that position.[16]

United States Indian Service,
Flathead Agency,
September 5, 1883.

S. T. Hauser,
President First National Bank
Helena, Montana.
Dear Sir,
To-day I send you by express five trout taken from the Jocko river this morning. I do not think any one of them will exceed ten pounds. They are rather "small fry" for this part of Montana, and I probably would have succeeded in a heavier catch but that after making a few casts and succeeding tolerably, I was overwhelmed by a telegram from Helena, announcing that Senator Vest of Missouri, Governor Crosby and Major Maginnis of Montana were speeding on their way to the Agency on Special train, and expected me to meet them with a delegation of Indians, with whom they expect to hold a Council. Well, I trust at the driving of the gold spike of the Northern Pacific Railroad you will assist, with other citizens of Montana, in entertaining Mr [Henry] Villard and other magnates of the road, and if I cannot be there in the flesh permit an old timer and friend to be represented in the "fish!" In brief here are your big trout, and I expect you to furnish the lies.

Yours truly
Peter Ronan.

October 1, 1883
LR 18,829/1883, RG 75, National Archives, Washington, D.C.

Senator G. G. Vest and Delegate Martin Maginnis reported on their visit to the Flathead Reservation in "Report of the Subcommittee of the Special Committee of the United States Senate Appointed to Visit the Indian Tribes of Northern Montana."[17]

Note that Chief Michelle was selected as spokesman for the tribes and a two day council was held to determine tribal policy ahead of time. The tribal members changed their mind about altering the reservation boundaries. The year before they had asked Joseph McCammon to support moving the reservation further north away from Missoula and the new railroad.

In this letter Ronan failed to mention Chief Arlee's complaint about the St. Ignatius Mission schools. According to Vest's account, Arlee was upset because his son had been put to work farming while a student at the school. Ronan also omitted Chief Eneas' complaint about the survey of the northern boundary of the reservation.[18] Senator Vest was impressed by conditions on the reservation and returned for several other visits. He became a key congressional supporter of the St. Ignatius Mission schools.

After the last spike ceremony completing the railroad, Northern Pacific Railroad President Henry Villard and his party stopped at Ravalli and hiked the Mission Mountains. The excursion, including a specially built trail, was arranged by tribal member Duncan McDonald, who had worked for the railroad during the construction.[19]

Senator George G. Vest of Missouri had been a representative and senator in the Confederate Congress during the Civil War. He was in the United States Senate between 1879 and 1903 where he opposed high tariffs and the acquisition of American colonies. He took a special interest in the Rocky Mountain West and especially Montana and Yellowstone National Park.[20] Montana Governor John S. Crosby was a Civil War veteran from an aristocratic New York family. He was territorial governor for less than two years in 1883 and 1884. Some Montanans found him abrasive, but he worked to build up the Republican party and personally invested heavily in the territory.[21] Henry Villard was born in Germany and spent much of his career as a newspaper journalist in America. In the 1870s, he gained control of a series of Pacific Northwest railroads and steamship lines. Between 1881 and 1884, he was President of the Northern Pacific Railroad.[22]

> United States Indian Service,
> Flathead Agency,
> October 1st, 1883.

Hon. Commissioner of Indian Affairs
Washington, D.C.

Sir,

Having now the honor to Submit my report for September I may state that the chief occurrence during the month was the visit paid this Reservation by the Special Congressional Commission as represented by Senator Vest and Delegate Maginnis, who were accompanied by Governor Crosby of this Territory. On the 5th day of September a Council was held here, at which whatever of moment took place might be condensed as follows:

Senator Vest, — having first informed the assembled Indians, of whom there were Several hundreds, that the Commission was not Sent to bargain for their lands or do anything injurious to their interests, but to inquire into their Condition and find out what they themselves desired, — proceeded to State that it was understood that they wanted to make an exchange of the Strip of land, thro' which the Railroad is now running, for other land further north; also that their views as to the Bitter-root Flatheads being brought upon their Reservation were desired, and their opinions as to their each taking up 160 acres of land.

The Senator also explained that it was on account of the adjournment of Congress before the money for the "right of way" was paid by the Railroad Company, that the payment to the Indians had not already taken place; and concluded his remarks by telling them that immediate replies to his questions were neither expected nor desirable, but that they had better have an interchange of opinions among themselves, and when Conclusions were arrived at the Commission would again meet them.

Michelle Chief of the Pen d'Oreilles immediately arose, and, having Stated that he had been chosen as the mouthpiece of all the Indians, Said — Your questions will not take a long time to answer. Some days Since you Sent us word that you were coming, We gathered to-gether and have been in Council for the last two days, and already know what we want to Say.

We never expect to move our boundary lines. — Our children were born here and we love our country. — Our great father promised that we Should always have it, and we depend on that promise. As to the Flatheads they are our people and our friends, and, we will be glad if they come and live with us. — We don't want to take, each, 160 Acres of land and Sell the rest. — With regard to the Railroad money we are glad to have your explanation, and are Satisfied with it.

Major Maginnis then asked if they would not rather have more cattle and money and less land. To which the Chief replied — If I had much and good land, and a few cattle and a little money I would be glad. — The reverse would not please me because my Children are yearly farming more and more and so get money.

Major Maginnis further enquired how they would like to sell their ponies, and buy cattle, and was informed that "that was what they were always doing and that hence it was so many Indians had Cattle."

Questions were then put as to how the parents and Children were satisfied with the Schools, which were answered by the assertion that the parents were Satisfied because they wanted their Children to learn, and were therefore pleased to have them taught. It was Stated that Some of the Indians would prefer to have the Schools at the Agency but upon further examination into the subject the fact was elicited by Senator Vest that the present location is much more central.

Senator Vest then repeatedly enquired if any other Indian desired to offer any remarks, also if any of them had any grievance.

With regard to the first question he was Simply told that what Michelle Said was in the hearts of all his people; and to the Second Michelle at last replied — I will tell you what I don't like — Liquor Sometimes comes on the Reservation leading to gambling and other offenses. We can't tell where it comes from and I want you to help me to Stop that. White people are strong enough and smart enough to do what they choose. Why don't they Stop that?

To this the Senator replies — that White people were neither strong enough nor Smart enough to stop drinking or gambling even among their own people; that many laws were enacted for the purpose, but that bad men managed occasionally to break laws and escape punishment.

Senator Vest then concluded by informing the Indians how pleased the Commission was to find them doing so well and so well contented, and the Council was finally brought to a close by Some remarks made by Governor Crosby of a nature So complimentary to the Agent, that I may be excused from further alluding to them.

In connection with the foregoing the only comment necessary is in explanation of the radical change in the wishes of the Indians as exhibited in their Statement that they now desire no alteration with regard to the lines of the Reservation. Upon investigation I find that this change has been caused by their arriving at the Conclusion that the present Southern boundary is better adapted, than any other would be, to prevent the encroachment of trespassers. It runs along the backbone of a ridge of Mountains, and, they being thickly wooded, no Settlement is possible for Several miles on either Side of the line. On the Contrary any change would necessitate a line running, during some portion of its length, thro' an open country, and thus whisky Shops &c. might be placed within a few yards of an indian ranch. It is evident therefore that one this matter, the judgment of the Indians deserves much commendation.

In addition to this argument is another, which arises from a suspicion on their part that Should they accept an alteration of boundary now, in their own favor, the fact might be used, in the future, as a precedent, to make a change to their disadvantage, and, here again, I must admit I, to Some extent concur in their reasoning.

The bridle path regarding which the Northern Pacific R. R. Coy received your permission to make for the purpose of obtaining a view from Mc Donalds' Peak, has been completed and, on the 29th Ult., was taken advantage of by a portion of the party, which lately crossed the Continent with President Villard, who detained the Special cars, used on the occasion, some 18 or 20 hours on the Reservation for that purpose.

On Wednesday last I was informed that there were several lodges of Indians belonging to Alien tribes camped some 15 miles west of this and that the members were drinking and gambling. I thereupon notified them that if they did not at once depart they would be arrested and having just received another complaint with regard to them, will immediately proceed to put the threat into execution, as determined measures are necessary to break up this constantly recurring incursion of vagabonds, of which I have lately had So much occasion to write.

My action and its result I shall report in due course; meantime I have the honor of Submitting herewith Medical, School and Fund Reports, with Statement of Indebtedness on account of employés; Also a note from the Principal of the Boys Boarding School, explaining why the Statement of Expenditures in connection there with is not now transmitted, and I respectfully await your decision as to how far his view is correct.

Very respectfully
Your obedient Servant
Peter Ronan
U.S. Indian Agent.

October 5, 1883

Excerpt from G. G. Vest, "Notes of the Yellowstone Trip," Forest and Stream, *vol. 21, no. 15 (Nov. 8, 1883), page 282.*
[Major Peter Ronan, private letter to Vest dated October 5, 1883:]

Yesterday an Indian caught thirteen trout, the largest of which weighed fourteen and a half pounds, and the smallest six pounds and three-quarters. The weather is now cold enough to ship trout East, and if you so desire, I will send a specimen of these fish to your address, and after an examination, and discussion of their merits at the dinner table, I trust you will inform me if I am in error in still clinging to the opinion that these overgrown Jocko fish are real and genuine trout.

October 8, 1883

Samuel T. Hauser Papers, MC 37, box 18, folder 34, Montana Historical Society Archives, Helena, Montana.

> Samuel Hauser's gift of mining company shares to Ronan would not be considered ethical in the twenty first century. Ronan speculated in mining stock and claims during his entire

tenure as Flathead Agent. This letter included more evidence of Jocko River fisheries during the 1880s.[23]

United States Indian Service,
Flathead Agency,
October 8th, 1883.

S. T. Hauser,

Helena, Montana

    Dear Friend,

    I scarcely know how to express my thanks to you for your thoughtful generosity in sending to me a certificate for one hundred and fifty shares in the Helena Smelting and Mining Co. B[e]lieve me I sincerely appreciate the favor, and hope some day to be able, in a measure, to return your many acts of Kindness to me.

    I forwarded to your address on Saturday night two Jocko trout. I think the largest one weighed fourteen pounds. Soon as I learn of Senator Vest's arrival a[t] Washington I intend to express him a couple of Jocko trout. Vest claims I am mistaken in calling them trout and the dispute is to be settled in Washington over a dinner from one of the fish.

I remain your friend
Peter Ronan.

October 9, 1883

LR 19,115/1883, RG 75, National Archives, Washington, D.C.

On October 3, 1883, orders were issued at Fort Missoula for Second Lieutenant Frank P. Avery and fifteen enlisted men to proceed to the Flathead Reservation and remove "all renegade indians pointed out . . . by the agent."[24] Chief Michelle of the Pend d'Oreilles had requested the removal of the outside Indians from the reservation.

United States Indian Service,
Flathead Agency,
October 9th, 1883.

Hon. Commissioner of Indian Affairs

Washington, D.C.

    Sir,

    As I had the honor of Stating in my Report for September certain Indians on this Reservation have been so conducting themselves as to necessitate peculiar action on my part, of which, as I then informed you I would Submit a detailed account.

    In order to do so I believe I can do nothing better than offer a copy of a Report which I have been called upon to furnish to the Military Commander of the District of Montana, and which was worded as follows —

Flathead Agency October 9, 1883

        Col. [Thomas] Ruger

        Commanding Dist. of Montana — Helena

            Sir

            Having the honor of acknowledging receipt of your telegram of 7th inst., in compliance with the tenor thereof, I have to report, of the Indians placed under arrest by the Military Detachment, as follows —

On the 24th. Ult. I was informed that Several lodges of alien Indians (Chiefly Nez Percés) were camped on the Jocko River on this Reservation at a point some 15 miles west of this Agency, and that some of these Indians were picking quarrels with members of the Pen d'Oreille tribe. Again on the 26th the Pen d'Oreille Chief of Police complained that these people were drinking and gambling and demoralizing the young men of his own tribe; that, upon being admonished and requested to leave they treated his advice with contempt, asserting that they recognized no authority; and that, as there were Several desperate Characters among them who would forcibly resist arrest by Indians; his own men declined to act in the matter, as they believed, Should they do so, bloodshed would result. On this presentation I notified the parties, complained of, that if they did not remove from the Reservation before the 30th they would be arrested.

On the 1st Inst. I received the following

                                            Septr. 30th, 1883

Major P. Ronan &c, &c,
    Sir
    I wish to inform you that there are a
    number of Cayuse Indians near Duncan Mc-
    Donald's Store who are drinking & fighting,
    & it will not be many days before there will
    be regular fighting & bloodshed. They are to
    move to-day to the mouth of the Jocko. I wish
    you could drive them out of the Reservation
    as soon as possible, & also two Spokane Indi-
    ans who are with them Quats-ah-kas-an and
    Ins-chew-sti, who are bad Indians. They are
    well known as Such.

                                  Respectfully &c.
                        (Sgd.) Michelle — Chief of Pon
                                          d'oreilles

Believing that my duty demanded a decided course of action, on receipt of this letter, I immediately applied in person to Col. [George] Gibson commanding at Fort Missoula and, on Wednesday, the 3d Inst, a detachment of Soldiers was placed at my disposal; Proceeding with it to Ravalli Station, in the immediate neighborhood of which the offenders had been camped, I found they had left; (but only on that morning) and, on going a few miles to procure further information, I Saw their camp in the distance; they having only moved some 6 or 7 miles to evade the Soldiers, but with no intention of leaving the Reservation.

I then returned to the Detachment and, on a dark rainy night, marched therewith to within a Short distance of the lodges, which were Surrounded at early dawn, and the following mentioned occupants were placed under arrest and conveyed to Fort Missoula —

Aich-keh-keh-pilp, Lose-a-coos-tin, Wet-a-shil-pilp and Wee-ów-a-seest-kan, four Nez Percés who left White Bird's Camp, in the neighborhood of Fort McLeod, Some three years ago, and have Since, as I am informed, been floating about in the North-west, gaining a living by hunting and working for other Indians;

Ols-ols-Stute-lum a half Nez Percé and half Flathead, who left White Bird's Camp with those just mentioned, and who is a professional gambler;

Wah-tah-wah-tah-owlish, a Nez Percé lately arrived from Fort McLeod;

Ees-ha-meh-ya, an old Nez Percé from Lap-wai, who has taken up a Small ranch on Flathead Lake.

Weh-tah-see-cow-neh, a Walla-walla Indian and a gambler, lately arrived here;

Yeh-meh-wet, a half Nez Percé and half Cayuse lately from Walla-walla, & also a gambler;

and Skulseh, a Kootenay, who arrived in the camp on the previous day, and who had Seven bottles of whisky in his possession.

There were others of whom complaint was made, and who were, I believe, more objectionable as to character than any of those enumerated, but, on account of this very fact, they took care to avoid Capture.

With regard to those now in Confinement, I have no more definite Complaint to make than is contained in this Statement. No matter how much an Indian may annoy or even injure his brethren, my experience is that as soon as the Culprit is in the custody of white men his people Shrink from assisting in his prosecution and exhibit a vast amount of Sympathy in his misfortune.

I have already referred to this matter in a communication addressed to the Honorable Commissioner of Indian Affairs, and will forward a Copy of this Report; and have only to add that, if permitted, I would Suggest that the prisoners be Sent to their own Reservations.

Respectfully &c.
(Sgd.) Peter Ronan
U.S. Ind. Agent

Hoping that my action may meet with your approval, and awaiting any instructions which you consider applicable to the present case, or may deem necessary for my guidance in the future I am,

Very respectfully
Your obedient Servant
Peter Ronan
U.S. Indian Agent.

November 8, 1883
LR 20,926/1883, RG 75, National Archives, Washington, D.C.

This letter was the beginning of arrangements for the early 1884 visit to Washington, D.C., by Chief Charlo and a delegation of Bitterroot Salish leaders. The delegation resulted from the recommendation of Senator G. G. Vest, who had visited the Bitterroot Salish earlier in 1883. Ronan's letters to his wife Mary, describing the events and experiences of the trip, are reproduced below.

Michel Revais, the longtime interpreter for the Flathead Agency, was blind but spoke several languages. See the annotation to Ronan's May 1, 1878, letter for biographical information on Michel Revais.

United States Indian Service,
Flathead Agency,
November 8, 1883.

Hon. Commissioner Indian Affairs
Washington, D.C.
Sir:

I have the honor to to state that owing to the fact that the telegraph station at Arlee is four miles from this Agency, your telegram of the 6th inst did not reach me until this morning. In reply to your question if I could act as interpreter for Charlos in case he is ordered to Washington, I would respectfully inform you that my knowledge of the language would not admit of my assuming to do so. The official interpreter at this Agency, Michel Revis, is one of the most efficient men I know of and has the confidence of both whites and Indians, wherever he is known. I would respectfully suggest, however, and I think if you consult the sub-committee who counciled with Charlos, they will bear me out in the statement that in order to make any satisfactory terms with Charlos, it will be necessary to have several of the head men of the Bitter Root Flatheads to represent their people, in addition to Chief Charlos.

Very respectfully
Yours
Peter Ronan
U.S. Indian Agent.

November 12, 1883
LR 21,276/1883, RG 75, National Archives, Washington, D.C.

United States Indian Service,
Flathead Agency,
November 12th, 1883.

Hon. Commissioner of Indian Affairs
Washington, D.C.
Sir,

Having the honor to acknowledge receipt of your communication of 25th Ult; making inquiries as to a school herd, I beg respectfully to State that I deemed it unadvisable to furnish replies until I had visited the Schools and procured reliable information on the Subject.

This I have now done and, premising that there is at present no herd of that description have the honor to State that, Should one be furnished it can be taken care of by the School Children without expense to the Government, provided that there are no requirements or regulations to be attended to in Connection therewith other than are customary with the private Stock-raisers of the country. The business of the latter is considered, — in fact known to be, — very profitable, and I have no hesitation in Saying that a School herd could and would be So managed as to Show results which would compare favorably with theirs, but it must be understood that pastures are not fenced that no housing is provided and but little hay used in comparison to what is considered, and probably is, necessary in the East.

The number of children now is — in the Boys' School Fifty-one (51); and in the Girls' School Fifty-two (52).

I am
Very respectfully
Your obedient Servant
Peter Ronan
U.S. Indian Agent.

November 13, 1883
LR 21,278/1883, RG 75, National Archives, Washington, D.C.

United States Indian Service,
Flathead Agency,
November 13th, 1883.

Hon. Commissioner of Indian Affairs
Washington, D.C.

Sir,

I have the honor to acknowledge receipt of your communication of 6th Inst marked "F," and in connection therewith to State that on the 8th I received your telegram of the 6th; as follows — "If Charles Should come to Washington Could you act as interpreter or must Some one else come as interpreter Send your letter this day." I therefore Concluded that a reply was not desired by telegraph and accordingly immediately despatched by mail an answer to the effect that the Slight acquaintance I have with the Flathead language would not enable me to act as interpreter, adding thereto that I believed if Several of the Head-men of the Bitter-root Flatheads were called to Washington a more Satisfactory result would follow than if Charlos alone was taken.

Referring now to your communication of the 6th I have only respectfully to add that I consider your Suggestion as to bringing the Agency Interpreter (Michael Rivais) the best, which could be put into execution; that, if necessary, the person whom I propose to leave in charge will be able to get along without an Interpreter for a Short time, but I would venture to State that if you would permit the issue of a wagon (of which there are a number here) in return for the Services of Some half-breed to act as Interpreter during the absence of Rivais the business of the Agency could probably be conducted with greater Satisfaction to yourself and the Indians and without entailing any extra expense to the Department.

I take the liberty of making this Suggestion as the regular indian Employé here understands very little English and the knowledge any of the white employés have of the Indian languages is very meagre, and I prefer seeing all Indians and Half-breeds on their farms to encouraging them to hang about the Agency.

Very respectfully
Your Obedient Servant
Peter Ronan
U.S. Indian Agent.

November 24, 1883
LR 22,106/1883, RG 75, National Archives, Washington, D.C.

Inspector S. S. Benedict's July 10, 1883, report criticized the St. Ignatius Mission schools on the reservation. According to Benedict, "Many of the leading men of the nation do not patronize the school and have a strong prejudice against its management. Among them is Chief Arlee, head chief of the Flatheads. Although a Catholic by profession, he says he wants his people to be taught something besides how to pray." Benedict suggested that government aid for the schools be limited, because with its farm, shops, and cattle herds, "The Mission as managed is a money making institution." The inspector was reporting the views of Chief Arlee, a longtime critic of Flathead Agency and St. Ignatius Mission operations. Benedict's personal views about the Roman Catholic Church seem to have been bigoted: "The quarters of the priests [at St. Ignatius] were dirty and ill kept as bachelors quarters always are . . . it seemed a relief to leave the place. The surrounding atmosphere seemed as mouldy as a cloister of fifteenth century."

Ronan gave his views on the subject in this letter and one dated December 26, 1883. See also Ronan's August 20, 1883, letter for Benedict's suggestions regarding the long-troubling northern boundary of the reservation.[25]

United States Indian Service,
Flathead Agency,
Nov. 24th, 1883.

To the Hon. Commissioner of Indian Affairs
Washington, D.C.

Sir,

I have the honor to reply to our communication marked "Accounts 13058" of October 13th having deferred until I was in a position to do so in a satisfactory manner.

In order to attain this end & avoid extra expense I requested one of the employés of the N. P. R. Co to inform me as to the probable cost of repairs needed by the Agency Boiler as pointed out to inspector Benedict, and reported upon to you by that Gentleman. After some correspondence from which it was determined that no reliable estimate could be given without inspection by a competent mechanic the Supt of machinery was so very Kind as to send his "Foreman Boiler maker" from Washington Territory to make a personal examination.

The conclusion just arrived at by the latter is that the patch which I had put on by the Agency Blacksmith and Miller for the fall work could not be of a nature such as to render the Boiler secure for any length of time; that in addition to some lighter repairs a new crownsheet is required; & that as in order to place one in proper position a thoroughly competent workman is necessary (such a one as can not probably be got nearer than Portland, Oregon, the job, including wages & material would cost about Two Hundred & Ten Dollars, and I have now the honor to forward herewith in the usual form an application for authority to expend this amount.

Before leaving this subject permit me to add that the Gentleman for whose advise I was indebted particularly impressed upon me that the reliability of his estimate depended upon my getting one of the best mechanics, as by such a one the work could be done in eight to ten days, while a poorer workman at smaller wages might easily expend three weeks entailing less satisfaction & greater cost.

With regard to the Agency Farm being used as a meadow I have the honor to submit that following the views of the Department I have long avoided any attempt to raise cer[e]als or vegetables in any considerable quantities but have applied myself to the increase & encouragement of Indian Farming.

On a considerable portion of the Agency field I have already sown Timothy & will do my best to increase the amount thereof, but I fear that, owing to the dry & sandy nature of the soil, the result will not be one of which to be proud, & owing to the encouragement spoken of there is no vacant land in the neighborhood of the Agency at all suited for the formation of a meadow. On a small portion of the field I have been in the habit of sowing a little oats & planting some potatoes & as this has been done entirely without expense to the Government, while affording me an opportunity to give a little employment to Indians either too old or too poor to conduct a farm on their own account, in addition to providing something available for issue to such persons without applying to the Department therefor I have considered the course quite a beneficial one.

In commenting upon Mr Benedict's recommendation that "Education facilities be extended" it will be appropriate to include in my remarks, opinions as to that Gentlemans views as quoted in your communication regarding the present schools. That the Indians of this Reservation appreciate the benefit of tuition I have on many occasions had the honor to report, & that an ordinary school would be filled to overflowing is proved from the fact that at present in the schools at St. Ignatius Mission there are over one hundred Indian children, while admission to a number of applicants has been delayed until the new schools now in course of erection, are completed. On these grounds I cordially agree that an extension of educational facilities would produce the best results. On the other hand, however, while having a great objection to criticise Mr Benedict's opinions, it is necessary to admit that I cannot coincide with some of his apparent conclusions. These, I believe, might have undergone some alteration had he honored me with information as to the data on which they were based. I was of course, aware that he was receiving statements from certain persons but could not presume to make any comment thereon. Nevertheless had he invited my views I am thoroughly convinced that I could have presented him with proofs that he was in danger of forming what he considered correct opinions from prejudiced sources.

That many of the leading men of the nation do not patronize the school is a statement which greatly surprised me & into which I have inquired in case that I had been unwittingly in the dark. In corroboration thereof I can certainly find no evidence.

There is one chief (Arlee) — doubtless the same who told Mr Benedict he desired his people taught something beside praying — who had his only child of school age at the school for some time & who removed the lad on account of his being required to assist with the other boys in attending to the school farm — a method of teaching of which I believe you highly approve. This man is, as far as I can learn, the only one of the headmen who, having children of school age, does not patronize the School, &, subject to correction my belief being only founded on suspicion as to who was Mr Benedict's chief informant, the latter had his only child at school until her death.

That much stress should be laid on general complaints from Indians that they lack educational advantages, or other things, I hardly believe, as they sometimes seem to be afraid that if they do not ask enough they will get nothing.

Their awakening to the benefits of education has been a very recent occurrence, & until quite lately no applicants for tuition have been refused. This state of affairs however is undergoing a change &, in order to meet it, both the Fathers & Sisters are putting up school buildings which will be highly creditable structures. I therefore would respectfully submit that any additional educational facilities which you may propose to afford can be utilized to better advantage thro' the parties at present employed than by any other means. The Missionaries have already expended sums in this direction very greatly in excess of any aid provided by the Government & have thereby shown their unselfish interest in the work, while, if others were employed, in addition to such action requiring a large outlay for the erection of suitable buildings, I fear it would be extremely difficult to find persons so anxious as to favorable results.

In commenting upon Mr Benedict's recommendation "That part of the sum used in purchase of annuity goods be used in labor about the mills" I beg to state that I have on several occasions had the honor of making such a representation & without repeating arguments used in support thereof, will simply quote from my letter of April 22nd/82 as follows — "I am thoroughly convinced that the benefits derived by the Indians, & per consequence by the Service from the labor & aid of the employés, exceed those from all other assistance furnished the Indians by the Government."

Referring to the recommendation "that four wagons that are not necessary for Agency use be immediately issued to deserving Indians" I beg respectfully to reply to my letter of August 14th/83 in which I requested permission to dispose of wagons in the manner Stated & to your reply, marked 15604 Aug 27th/83, action on which has been already taken & will be found duly entered in my accounts for the current quarter. — I would however again respectfully urge upon your notice the arguments then used in support of a request to be allowed to issue surplus wagons on account of such benificial work as I am enabled to map out, viz that the wagons are here without protection from the weather & unless otherwise than for issue, and that there is no freighting to be done thro' which the Indians could acquire them.

I am
Very Respectfully,
Your Obedient Servant,
Peter Ronan.

December 26, 1883
LR 595/1884, RG 75, National Archives, Washington, D.C.

See Ronan's letter of November 24, 1883, and annotation for more information about Inspector S. S. Benedict's report on the St. Ignatius Mission schools.

United States Indian Service,
Flathead Agency,
December 26th, 1883.

Hon. Commissioner of Indian affairs

Sir,

Having the honor to acknowledge receipt of your communication "A 13058/22106" of Dec 8/83 in which it is stated that my explanations in reference to report of Inspector Benedict were partially satisfactory I ask to be allowed the hope that the chief cause they were not more so was that I was not then informed of the subjects now chiefly demanding consideration. With regard to the employment of Indians, the amounts of Hay, Grain & vegetables resulting from their labor have always appeared on my returns, & the supplies received by them have, of course been regularly entered on the issue sheets.

As to the sanitary condition of the schools a change has very lately been made in the Director, and I have been promised that the cause of complaint in this connection will be removed. Concerning any want of confidence in the schools on the part of the older Indians, as I have already had the honor to advise you, I am ignorant; but the Hon Commissioner will recognize the utter impossibility of thoroughly pleasing every individual member of a large community.

The Horse which Mr Benedict recommends be Killed is quite passed service, &, although doubtless there are Indians who would accept him & force him to do some days' or months' work, I should not advise that he be issued, as such a course would be, by no means, a good example of gratitude on the part of white men for Indians to pattern after. The Horse in question has served the Department well & faithfully for twelve years (under my own control for seven) &, while sentiment may be out of place, I acknowledge that I should be willing personally to give more than he is worth, for his life. There are a number of articles now at this agency unfit for use of which, upon General Howard's advice, I shall soon forward a list asking for a "Board of Survey" & would suggest that the old Horse be included among any property it may be determined upon to offer for sale.

My attention is now attracted to a portion of the Inspector's report necessitating, in self defense a plain statement. I will therefore now express definitely, what I formerly only hinted at, viz that I am convinced that he received his information entirely from Duncan McDonald — a halfbreed — & chief Arlee — not given for the good of the Reservation, not for the benefit of the Indians, but simply for personal & unwarrantable ends. The complaint now received in connection with the running of the mills has convinced me of the correctness of my belief, with regard to McDonald who, for many years has conducted a store on the Reservation & who, on several occasions, has made application to have milling done in a manner which I considered would be unjust to the other Indians. In other words he desired to be enabled to induce Indians to sell him all their wheat (which he could easily do by advancing goods before the Crops were harvested) & then have the whole ground for himself personally; where he would be in a position to sell it back to the growers in Flour; thus monopolizing the benefits of the mill & employés, & discouraging Indian Farmers, who, if they were anxious to sell surplus grain, would not be likely to get from McDonald any increase over the regular market rates.

Respectfully asking your attention to page 5 of your communication I beg to assert that no Indian was ever required to assist in any manner in getting a bushel or many bushels of wheat ground, nor has any obstacle been placed in the way of any of them having all of the wheat which they have raised ground free of expense or labor. On the other hand, while the statement is incorrect (to say the least) that to get a log sawed, Indians are obliged to furnish assistance, I treat the operations of flouring & sawing in somewhat of a different manner.

In flouring three men are occupied — the Miller, the engineer or fireman & a man hauling wood to Keep up steam. The last operation I believe I might require performed by those wishing the work done without detriment to the Indians, & in compliance with general instructions i.e. with the approval of the Department.

As just said however I have not done so; but, in sawing, not less than five men are necessary &, as reported by me at various times in both monthly & annual Reports, I have been in the habit of requiring those desirous of procuring lumber to supply from two to three hands. This more especially since the employé force here was so much reduced, & it will easily be understood that were such not the case a few half-breeds who have been building extensively, would occupy the time of every employé allowed.

That the mills are not of more benefit to the members of the Reservation arises from the fact that they are not located in a sufficiently central position but so as to cause the trouble & expense of the hauling to & fro to more than offset the benefits of their use with a majority of those requiring their employment, & not from their method of management.

I have no desire to find fault with Inspector Benedicts on account of receiving information from whatever source he chose, but I do think he might have given me an opportunity of presenting my side of the case. I should then have informed him that; with regard to the grinding of wheat bought for speculation by Duncan McDonald; I had informed Duncan's father not long before that, if my course was objected to, you were the authority to whom to apply for relief &, with regard to sawing, that for the same man (Duncan) during the year, I had sawed over 60,000 feet of lumber — he furnishing assistance such as referred to — a portion of which, as I afterwards learned he had sold, & I am strongly convinced that Mr Benedict would have agreed with me that the position I have taken is a correct one.

It would be a very easy matter for me to enroll among my warmest supporters such men as Arlee & McDonald who can each easily be estimated as worth $10,000; are fond of money & thoroughly selfish in acquiring it; but I believe it is my duty to afford greater help to those not so capable of helping themselves, &, from those, I have heard no complaint as to the amount of assistance required in the sawmill or elsewhere.

With regard to the wash-tubs in use about the Agency, altho they were not being hurt for issue & were, I considered in Government employ, I can only say I will be more Careful in future And as to Cattle, I shall attend strictly to your instructions.

Very respectfully
Your obdt Servant
Peter Ronan
U.S. Indian Agent.

1884

January 9, 1884
LR 444/1884, telegram, RG 75, National Archives, Washington, D.C.

> The Office of Indian Affairs finally approved a delegation to Washington, D.C., of five Bitterroot Salish leaders, an interpreter, and Ronan. See excerpt from Ronan's book about the delegation at January – February 1884.

Jan 9 1884.
Flathead Mont via Arlee Mt

To Comer Indian Affairs, Washn, D.C.

Met Charlos at Bitter-Root arranged to have indians at Missoula on Sixteenth Charlos urges in strongest terms that he does not want to take responsibility of wholly settling question with only two other indians & desires that three more be added that all factions may be represented. His demand seems just & would advise that one at least be added to the delegation awaiting transportation and instruction.

Ronan
Agent.

January 15, 1884a
LR 1,589/1884, RG 75, National Archives, Washington, D.C.

> The 1883 murder of a Chinese man at Martina, near Frenchtown, west of Missoula, by a party of Flathead Reservation Indians was detailed in *The Weekly Missoulian*. According to the newspaper article, Koonsa Finley was involved.[1] No further information has been located about the other murders Ronan mentioned in this letter.
>
> Due to the constitutional prohibition against double jeopardy, the white courts could not try Indians who had already been punished under tribal law. On March 3, 1885, the U.S. Congress ended tribal jurisdiction over major crimes when it passed a law specifically giving jurisdiction to federal courts over Indians accused of murder, manslaughter, rape, assault with intent to kill, arson, burglary, and larceny.[2]
>
> About this same time the Flathead Reservation Indian police tried to arrest an Indian man and woman who had eloped and fled off the reservation to Missoula. Missoula law officials intervened and refused to recognize the jurisdiction of the Indian police to act within the town.[3]

United States Indian Service
Flathead Agency,
January 15th, 1883 [sic, 1884]

Hon. Commissioner of Indian Affairs
Washington, D.C.

    Sir:

    In compliance with your directions I have the honor to submit the following. On my return from California I learned of two murders having been committed on this Reservation. One being that of an Indian woman by her brother-in-law (a Kootenais of the Confederated tribes) on account of the victim slightly interfering by word in a quarrel between the culprit & his wife; the other being that of a Pen d'Oreille by his brother, they having found some whiskey secreted by another Indian, become intoxicated & quarrelled as to the treatment of the owner of the liquor.

These two murderers with two others — one accused of Killing & robbing a chinaman in a mining camp in Missoula Co — the other (an alien Indian) accused of Killing several Indians in Missoula, the Spokane Country & else-where & suspected of murdering white men, were placed in the Reservation jail & I held a council with several of the Headmen of the Confederated tribes, showing them that the Criminals merited the severest punishment & obtaining their promises that the prisoners would not be dealt with according to tribal laws, but on demand, would be delivered to the civil Authorities. I thereupon telegraphed to you the main particulars &, on receiving your instructions to hand over the murderers to the Territorial Authorities proceeded to have the promises executed. I was then informed that the rest of the Indians had held a council, determining that they would still retain their tribal customs & there-fore the Culprits, thus disabling the men who made the promises from Keeping them. I was of course very much disappointed & chagrined at this result, but seeing that there is little danger of not being able to find the criminals at any time that it is so desired, & that I am under your orders shortly to report in Washington, I considered it was better not to call for Military aid or take any other violent steps on my own responsibility.

I have however taken occasion to state the case verbally to the Sheriff in Missoula & also to the U.S. Deputy Marshal at the same place offering to afford them every facility & assistance in my power to take the prisoners & furnish witnesses, for trials before the civil Authorities. Deputy Marshal Smith made some apology for not acting immediately stating that he would refer the matter to his Superior, Marshal [Alexander] Botkin at Helena, but up to the present date I have not been apprised of any decision as to the case.

I have merely to add that — the having noticed recent decisions in U.S. Courts, — one in California & one in Dacotah with reference to the Red Cloud murder — as to the inability of U.S. judges to try such criminals as the two first mentioned, — has convinced me of the necessity of moderation as to any action of mine, & of the great necessity of a change in the present laws.

Very Respectfully
Your Obedient Servant
Peter Ronan
U.S. Indian Agent.

January 15, 1884b
LR 1,817/1884, RG 75, National Archives, Washington, D.C.

The full text of C. H. Howard's report on Flathead Agency is available in C. H. Howard to Secretary of the Interior, December 4, 1883.[4] See Ronan's August 20, 1883, report on the Cummings & Crossen cattle on the reservation. Ronan reported in this January 15, 1884, let-ter that Cummings & Crossen had 800 cattle on the reservation, but one newspaper report indicated they had 2,500 head on the reservation.[5] The report on T. J. Demers' status on the reservation is at August 13, 1883, rather than October 1, 1883, as indicated by Ronan in this letter. In April 1877, John A. Fredline married Philomene Couture, a mixed blood tribal member. In 1880 the couple lived in Missoula with their one year old daughter and the wife's brother, Louis Couture. By 1885, he had "a good location in the Flathead country" and owned "considerable stock."[6]

The problem with the location of the Flathead Agency was frequently mentioned during the nineteenth century but no change was made due to lack of funds.[7]

Ronan vigorously objected to Chief Arlee's complaints, but unfortunately Arlee's side of the conflict was not recorded. It is interesting that Louison and Thomas McDonald supported Ronan. Dandy Jim was killed in a fight at a January 1888 dance near St. Ignatius Mission.[8] Thomas McDonald, half Nez Perce and half Scottish, was about 26 years old in 1884. He married into the Pablo family in 1894 and suffered a painful accident from a runaway team of horses in 1899.[9] Robert McGregor Baird taught in one of the first schools in Missoula in 1872. In 1876 he and Duncan McDonald went prospecting for gold in the Upper Flathead Valley and by 1877 he was in charge of T. J. Demers' businesses in Frenchtown. In 1880 he was living at Flathead Agency and listed his occupation as "bohemian." After working for Ronan as farmer or clerk in the early 1880s, in December 1884, he took a pack train to the Kootenai Valley of British Columbia for T. J. Demers. He was murdered in Canada by someone named "Bull Dog Kelly."[10] Dr. W. R. Adamson was Flathead Agency physician in 1883-1884.[11]

The Office of Indian Affairs must have been satisfied with Ronan's explanations as the action notation on the letter is "File."

United States Indian Service,
Flathead Agency,
January 15th, 1884.

Hon. Commissioner of Indian Affairs
Washington, D.C.

Sir:

Having delayed a reply to your communication "A 22936" of Dec. 20th., referring to report of Inspector [C. H.] Howard, until I could ascertain, as nearly as possible, the number of cattle, belonging to *"Whites,"* on this reservation, and — having now done so, I have the honor to State that there are eleven herds, which belong, or have been Said to belong to white men, and these are the Cattle of

> Cummings & Crossen – numbering 800 head
> D. O. Sullivan – numbering 160 head
> T. J. Demers – numbering 1250 head
> St. Ignatius' Mission – numbering 800 head
> John Fredline – numbering 50 head
> Angus McDonald – numbering 700 head
> Joseph Couture – numbering 60 head
> Camille Dupuis – numbering 130 head
> George Ledoux – numbering 200 head
> David Polson – numbering 160 head
> Joseph Aslin – numbering 9 head

With regard to the herds of Cummings & Crossen and D. O. Sullivan I had the honor to make a full report on Aug 20/83, when I conveyed the information that, while they lived not on the reservation, their Cattle Strayed thereon; and an application from them to be permitted to pay an Assessment therefor; And, from your Communication of Decr. 8th, I learn that the Subject is Still under consideration. In addition I have learned that Mr. Sullivan has lately assigned his Cattle to an Indian relative, but, not having personally seen him for Some time, I cannot vouch for the truth of the Statement.

With regard to the herd, Spoken of as belonging to T. J. Demers, I had also occasion to report at length, which I did on the 1st of October [sic, August 13], and, referring thereto, you directed me to recognize the claims of the Indian children of Mr. Demers to the privileges of the Reservation. Since then Inspector Howard, calling attention to the fact that the assignment of Cattle, made by Mr. Demers, would be worthless unless recorded, instructed that an examination be made as to whether or not it had been done. Having investigated this point I am now in a position to answer the question in the affirmative.

With reference to the Mission herd I have already had the honor of expressing my views to the effect that it would have been equally logical to have deprived Peter Cooper of his working Capital and expected the enjoyment of his charities, as it would be to deny the Priests of St Ignatius' Mission the means of producing a Revenue, and expect them to continue the expenditure of that revenue for the benefit of the Indians, as they have done.

Concerning the Cattle, Said to belong to John Fredline — (a man living in Missoula), — they were driven here by his brother-in-law, — a half-breed of this reservation, — who asserts he purchased them. Information as to their advent was given on the day thereof, in my absence, to my representative, — R. M. Baird, — in presence of Inspector Howard. Baird, turning to the Inspector, — Said "General I am glad this has occurred while you are here. — The Agent's greatest trouble arises from Cattle trespassing, and, while there is not a great deal of it on this Reservation, he finds it a difficult matter to handle. I am ready to call upon the Marshal to make seizures, or to take any other Steps under your Guidance. To which the Inspector replied — "Well but perhaps these men may have been Smart enough to give and take a Bill of Sale," And, — when told that such was extremely probable, — added — "in that case I don't see what can be done.["]

Not to be too tedious in connection with the remaining Six white owners of Cattle mentioned, I would respectfully refer you to page 9 of my report of August 20th; — merely Stating that they are old residents, whom I found located here, all of them having Indian families, to whom they Claim their herds belong.

With reference to the Inspector's recommendation of a change in the location of the Agency, I most fully concur. As you are aware that it is at present Situated at the extreme verge of the Southern habitable portion of the Reservation. I already have had the honor of representing that this to a great extent, nullifies the benefits which the Indians are expected to gain, as many of them, — to have wheat ground at, or to procure lumber from the Mills are necessitated to haul or pack these articles fifty Miles and even further, thus causing the cost of freighting to exceed the value of the articles, and naturally this State of affairs not only prevents the erection of houses but also discourages farming. There are very few residents of the Jocko Valley, (in which the Agency is now Situated) but these are well Supplied with houses and barns — the result of contiguity to the Mills, — and they would therefore Suffer little by a removal, while the Great body of the Indians would gain immensely. As I have often had the honor of Stating, I am convinced that, on a Reservation, there is nothing so Conducive to the progress of Civilization as Mills, Shops and Mechanics.

When the Agency was built it was probably placed here in order to be within a reasonable distance of Missoula, where was then the nearest Post Office, and where nearly all goods and Supplies were bought in open market. Whether the end justified the means I very much doubt, but no Such reason could now be given, — for a central location can be chosen, not more than a mile or So further than the present agency from a Post Office, and within ten or twelve miles from a Railroad Station. And, in this connection I would remark, — and I respectfully ask attention to the subject — that, Should a change be deemed advisable transportation Contractors ought to be notified that the point, at which goods would be landed from the Cars, would be "Ravalli" — a Station some eight miles west of "Arlee."

As to the Complaints with regard to Wagons &c. being Scattered about and not Sheltered — while I ask the liberty of Stating that the wagons, not in use, were and are placed together, — I cannot better defend myself than by asking attention to the fact that I have myself reported as to the want of proper Shelter for Such articles. The amount of Storage room required to Shelter 20 wagons is large. It was not provided at this Agency before my arrival and I have not had Sufficient force to Supply Such a desideratum, nor have the appropriations been Such as to enable me to do So thro the labor of temporary employés. The Agricultural implements, mentioned by the Inspector, were placed in an open Shed; the only available place of Shelter, — and Stock occasionally entered, but having been well Sheltered and Stowed have Sustained no damage.

As to the condition of the Store-room the goods had but lately arrived, and were even then undergoing examination, and owing to my absence and the many calls on the time and attention of the person left in charge, neatness was doubtless somewhat neglected.

With reference to the Statement that "Indians complain that Mr. Cummings branded Some of their Cattle &c. &c." I am assured that Such is not a correct presentation of the case. On the contrary I am told that *one* Indian — "*Arlee*" Said that he had heard another Indian — Dandy Jim — make one or all of the accusations preferred. I am further informed that the following day, Louison, one of the most independent, highly respected and influential Indians of the Reservation, called upon General Howard, and premising that he did so because his heart was sore on account of learning that a man in the position of a chief lied about their Agent, accounting therefor by Arlee's Senility — informed the General that his (Louison's) Cattle ranged with the Agency herd; that he was constantly among them, and that no one would have Known as well as he had any of the latter been misappropriated.

Thereupon R. M. Baird — the Agency Farmer — who was in an adjoining room, approached Louison, and excusing himself for the interruption, told the latter that he was much pleased to See that I had at least one Indian friend to uphold my character in my absence and that he wanted all the Indians to be made aware of what Arlee had Said, So that they might have an opportunity to Support him or otherwise.

On the day Still following Arlee paid another visit to the Inspector, when he stated that he had made a great mistake in reporting an idle rumor which he did not believe. Further that he greatly regretted So doing and that he was convinced their Agent had never defrauded the Indians of a dollar. In this connection Mr. Baird desires, in order to avert possible misapprehension, to State emphatically that neither he nor any white man attempted to influence or even held the Slightest conversation with any Indian on the Subject, — other than as above Stated. After branding the accusations as malicious falsehoods Mr. Baird asked General Howard if there was any information or evidence desired to be procured adding that it would be an act of injustice to repeat a calumnious Rumor, that was even denied by its reporter, especially Seeing that my being a perfect Stranger to the Honorable Secretary of the Interior, Such a repetition would produce an injurious impression, almost impossible to eradicate. General Howard then Stated that he would reserve a report on the Subject in order to give an opportunity to procure an affidavit from the man Said to have first given occasion for Arlee's Statement, telling Baird he could himself attest said Affidavit.

To this Baird replied — "No, I am acting for the Agent and my motives and actions may be Subject to your Suspicions. I Should prefer to have affidavit differently attested."

"Well," said General Howard, "have Dr. Adamson witness it and it will be perfectly Satisfactory."

Such an Affidavit was got, and, with it, another from one of the very best Cattle men in the Country, (a brother of Duncan McDonald, who happened to be present and made a Voluntary Statement) but, before a letter was written to General Howard as an accompaniment your communication was received, and the affidavits were retained to be enclosed herewith.

In this connection I have only to add that, at their Christmas Gathering at St Ignatius' Mission, the Indians fully discussed the foregoing Subject. Arlee was publicly accused by the headmen of that Section, of maliciously lying about their Agent, they telling him that their people often visited Little Bitter Root, Some of them living there and that they would know if there were any Indian Cattle driven to the neighborhood. The darkest cloud has a Silver lining and I Shall never again hold the opinion that Gratitude and appreciation are entire Strangers in the breast of an Indian.

With regard to irregular issues I cannot well understand how General Howard could expect to find regular or Systematic issues at an Agency where only occasional or irregular issues are allowed. Those made are Strictly in conformity with your instructions, viz for Some beneficial act performed or to the very old or Sick, I having long Since convinced loafers and vagrants that assistance is not for them.

It is extremely disappointing that — while (as in my own defense I may be excused for Saying) I have Succeeded in gaining encomiums, — many of which have appeared in Some of the leading Newspapers of the Country — from men employed to report to the public, — men often Strongly prejudiced against Indian Agencies; while I have received from others high in position; and, while I have acquired the confidence and gratitude of those most directly interested in my course, and those usually most prone to Suspect unfair dealing — the Indians — I learn of nothing but fault-finding from Inspectors, from whom, being Superior Officers in the Same Department, I would naturally expect an occasional expression of Sympathy and encouragement.

Very respectfully
Your Obedient Servant
Peter Ronan
U.S. Indian Agent.

Enclosure:

United States Indian Service,
Flathead Agency,
December 18th, 1883.

I hereby solemnly swear that I know of no Agency or Indian Department cattle having been branded with Major Ronans brand or appropriated by him; and further that I am not aware of his disposing of for his own benefit or Selling any Indian Department Bacon or other Indian Goods; and that I never made contrary Statements to Arlee.

Witness W. R. Adamson

Dandy (His X Mark) Jim

Flathead Agency Decr. 18th, 1883

I hereby solemnly Swear that I have repeatedly ridden through Cummings and Crossens' herd of Cattle on "Little Bitter Root" examining brands as I was hunting for Stock and that I am convinced that there have not been any Indian Department Cattle there with Major Ronan's brand upon them; and further that I believe any report to the contrary originated from the fact that a few head which belonged to the Major personally and which I understand he Sold to Cummings and Crossen are running in the herd referred to.

Witness W. R. Adamson

Thomas McDonald

Subscribed and Sworn to these Affidavits of Dandy Jim and Thomas McDonald, before me this Eighteenth Day of December 1883.

Robert M. Baird.

January – February 1884
Peter Ronan, Historical Sketch of the Flathead Indian Nation from the Year 1813 to 1890 *(Helena, Mont.: Journal Publishing Co., 1890), pages 67-70.*

The 1884 delegation to Washington, D.C., with Ronan, Michel Revais, Charlo, and the other Bitterroot Salish leaders has been richly documented in the historical record. Ronan described the visit in his 1890 book; many of his letters home to his wife describing the trip were transcribed in his daughter's 1932 master's thesis; and his letters documenting the party's expenses to the U.S. Treasury Department have survived in the National Archives. The experience must have been an exciting and bewildering adventure for the visitors from Montana.

The trip was arranged by Senator G. G. Vest after he returned to Washington from Montana in 1883. Vest verified that Chief Charlo never signed the 1872 agreement with Congressman James A. Garfield and hoped that a visit to Washington might persuade Charlo to remove to the Jocko Reservation. As it turned out, Charlo still insisted on the treaty right of the Salish to live in the Bitterroot Valley. He spurned offers of money, aid, and honors in favor of staying in the valley he loved.[12]

The time in Washington included a bewildering flurry of social events and new experiences. Newspaper accounts describe the Salish tasting ice cream; and they even witnessed a colorful masquerade by Washington school children.[13] The Salish visited the President at the White House and were popular guests at a variety of dinners and receptions. Charlo and

Michel Revais, the interpreter, even had eye operations while in Washington. The operation was successful in restoring Charlo's eyesight but not Revais'.[14] Charlo was grateful to have his eyesight restored, but still did not agree to move to Jocko.[15]

Member of the delegation, Antoine Moiese was the son of Chief Moise, the second chief of the Bitterroot Salish in 1855. As a young man in 1878, he got drunk at a horse race near Stevensville and accidentally killed Narcisse, a prominent Salish farmer. On sobering up, Antoine was whipped by Chief Charlo. Later he matured into a leader in the tribe. After he returned from Washington, D.C., in 1884, he accepted Ronan's proposal to remove to the Jocko Valley where in 1885 he had ten acres under fence and had raised 100 bushels of wheat and barley. He was a judge on the reservation Court of Indian Offenses between 1892 and 1899 and attended the Omaha Exposition in 1898.[16] Louis Vanderburg was a respected leader among the Bitterroot Salish in the 1880s. In August 1883, he helped keep drunks away from the St. Mary's Mission. According to Martin Charlo, it was Vanderburg who convinced Charlo in 1889 to finally move to Jocko. When the Salish arrived at the Jocko agency in 1891, he declined to join most of the other Salish at a church service at the Jocko church.[17] John Hill, Delaware and Nez Perce, lived in the Bitterroot Valley and was a member of Charlo's band. He was a Civil War veteran and seriously injured a hand in the fighting. He was arrested in 1877 during the Nez Perce scare and held prisoner for a period at Fort Missoula. In June 1894, he was arrested in Missoula for drinking and fighting.[18] Thomas Abel Adams was born in the Bitterroot Valley in 1855. He was part of the 1884 delegation to Washington, D.C., and seems to have moved to the Flathead Reservation in 1887. In 1895, he was part of a delegation of Salish leaders, including Charlo, who visited Deer Lodge and Helena to request a pardon for two young tribal members who were held at the penitentiary.[19] For biographical information on Michel Revais, the interpreter, see the annotation to Ronan's May 1, 1878, letter. Henry Moore Teller, the Secretary of the Interior in 1884, had been a lawyer in Denver and a longtime senator from Colorado. One of his principle causes in the Senate was expanding silver purchases by the government.[20]

Charlot's Trip to Washington.

On the 16th day of January, 1884, the United States agent for the confederated tribes of Indians living upon the Flathead or Jocko reservation, in accordance with instructions of the honorable commissioner of Indian affairs, took his departure from Missoula, Montana Territory, for the city of Washington, accompanied by the following named delegation of Charlot's band of Bitter Root Flathead Indians:

1. Head Chief Charlot — Slem-Hak-Kah. "Little claw of a grizzly bear."
2. Antoine Moise — Callup-Squal-She. "Crain [sic] with a ring around his neck."
3. Louis [Vanderburg] — Licoot-Sim-Hay. "Grizzly bear far away."
4. John Hill — Ta-hetchet. "Hand Shot Off."
5. Abel or Tom Adams — Swam-Ach-ham. "Red Arm."

And the official interpreter, Michel Ravais, whose Indian name is Chim-Coo-Swee. "The Man Who Walks Alone."

The object of ordering the Indians to Washington was in accordance with the recommendations of Senator Vest and Major Martin Maginnis, the subcommittee of the United States senate committee, and was to try to secure

Charlot's consent to remove with his band from the Bitter Root valley, and to settle upon the Jocko reservation. Nearly a month was spent at the national capital, and during that time several interviews were held by the Indians and the agent with the secretary of the interior, Hon. H. M. Teller, but no offer of pecuniary reward or persuasions of the secretary could shake Charlot's resolution to remain in the Bitter Root valley. An offer to build him a house, fence in and plow a sufficiency of land for a farm, give him cattle and horses, and seed and agricultural implements, and to do likewise for each head of a family belonging to his band. Also a yearly pension of $500 to Charlot, and to be recognized as the heir of Victor, his deceased father, and to take his place as the head chief of the confederated tribes of the Flatheads, Pend d'Oreilles and Kootenai Indians living on the Jocko reservation, had no effect. His only answer to those generous offers was that he came to Washington to get the permission of the Great Father to allow him to live unmolested in the Bitter Root valley, the home of his father and the land of his ancestors. He asked for no assistance from the government, only the poor privilege of remaining in the valley where he was born, and where the dust of his tribe who lived before him was mingled with the earth. If any of his tribe desired to accept the bounty of the government and remove to the Jocko reservation they were at liberty to do so, and he would offer no objection; but it was his own and individual wish to live and die in the Bitter Root valley.

At the last interview held with the secretary of the interior Charlot was told if he desired to live in the Bitter Root valley, he could do so as long as he remained in peace and friendship with the white settlers. No promise of assistance was given the chief or his band by the secretary so long as they remained in the Bitter Root valley. After an interview with President [Chester] Arthur, arrangements were made for departure to Montana, without having accomplished anything whatever looking to the removal of the chief and his band to the Jocko reservation.

Before departure from the capital, the secretary of the interior held a special interview with the agent, none of the Indians being present, and after patiently listening to his recital of the extreme poverty of Chief Charlot and his band, who received no aid or assistance from the government, the secretary gave the agent verbal instructions to proceed to the Bitter Root valley, as soon as practicable after his return to the Jocko reservation, and report to him through the commissioner of Indian affairs the wants and necessities of this unfortunate tribe; and also to give his views in detail as to the most practicable method for the department to relieve their wants, which should have consideration, and also to encourage them to remove to the Jocko reservation.

On the evening of the 7th of March, 1884, the agent arrived in Missoula, Montana, from Washington with the Flathead Indian delegation, where he procured wagon transportation and sent them to their homes in Bitter Root valley. The members of the Flathead tribe were in the mountains hunting for game with which to support their families, as they had no other resource for food in the winter season. The agent sent out runners to call them in, so that he could proceed according to verbal instructions given to him by the secretary of the interior, on the 1st day of March, 1884, at his office in the interior department at Washington, which was in effect, to go to the Bitter Root valley and report as to their necessities and wants and to their affairs generally. Previously the agent had but very little intercourse officially with Charlot's band of Indians, but from conversation with the secretary of the interior he became convinced that his relations with them afterward would become of a closer character.

January 23, 1884 — January 29, 1884

Margaret Ronan, "Memoirs of a Frontiers Woman: Mary C. Ronan," unpublished masters thesis, State University of Montana, Missoula, 1932, pages 355-358. Some footnotes have been omitted.

Ronan's letters to his wife in Montana describing his experiences with the Bitterroot Salish delegation in Washington were included in his daughter Margaret's 1932 master's thesis at the State University of Montana in Missoula. The original letters have not survived in any archive, making Margaret's typescripts especially valuable.

John Mullan, who entertained the Salish delegation, first met the tribe in 1853-1855 as part of Governor I. I. Stevens' railroad survey through western Montana. He wintered in the Bitterroot Valley and traveled with the tribe. Between 1859 and 1863 he supervised the construction of a military road between Fort Benton and Walla Walla. In 1884, he was a lawyer in Washington, D.C. Between 1884 and 1886 he was also Commissioner and later President of the Bureau of Catholic Indian Missions which lobbied in the capital for Catholic Indian missions. See Ronan's letter of February 12, 1885, for problems that developed from Mullan's mistaken suggestion that 100 patents had been issued in the 1870s by the General Land Office for Salish farms in the Bitterroot Valley.[21]

For a description of the reception hosted by T. A. and M. C. Bland at the "Council Fire" residence in Washington see "Our Latest Reception to Indians."[22] Ronan gave a talk on Salish history and Charlo spoke about why he wanted to remain in the Bitterroot Valley.

> Willard Hotel,
> O. G. Staples, Proprietor,
> Late of Thousand Island House
> Washington, D.C., Jan. 23, 1884.

My Darling Wife:

At eleven o'clock last night we arrived in Washington. Commissioner [Hiram] Price had a man waiting for us at the depot; and [Martin] Maginnis, Hugh McQuaid and Al Hamilton were also there to meet us. The Indians were provided for at the Tremont House and I was taken to Willard's Hotel, where Major and Mrs. Maginnis have always had rooms since Maginnis resided here as delegate.

Of course I was tired after the long journey, but this morning I was up with the lark, and after a nice bath and shave felt fresh as a daisy. After breakfast in company with Maginnis, I reported to Commissioner Price, who received me very cordially and informed me that the President and Secretary [Henry] Teller were both out of town and would be gone for several days, and to show the Indians the sights and enjoy myself as well as I could as no business would be done until their return. I was then introduced to the Indian office clerks and visited Mr. [Joseph K.] McCammon, who really exhibited both friendship and pleasure at our meeting, and inquired very particularly about you and the children.

From Mr. McCammon's Maginnis and myself went to the Senate Chamber and met Senator [G. G.] Vest, who received me in the most cordial manner.

Tomorrow Maginnis, myself and other guests are invited to dinner at the Senator's residence. The dinner is to be given in honor of the Indian Delegation and Charlot and all the Indians are to be present.

Today I took the Indians to call upon Father Brouilett [J. B. A. Brouillet], but we could not see him, as he was not expected to live through the night. On Friday we are to be escorted through the halls of Congress and all the public buildings. Saturday's program is not yet laid out; but the program for Sunday is, which is no less a treat, than to have seats reserved for us in the church for Mass and to listen to a sermon from Monsignor Capel, who is now in Washington. I anticipate my greatest pleasure on Sunday is listening to the great Catholic prelate.

I took Michel and Charlot to a doctor today, who says there is a chance, and only a chance, of restoring Michel's sight. Charlot he says will, in the course of a year, be as blind as Michel if an operation is not performed on his eyes. After the return of the President and the Secretary, when their business is settled, I will see what can be done for them.

Major and Mrs. Maginnis. . . are out to a party tonight, given by a congressman whose name I forget just now. I had an invitation but I concluded rather to retire to my room and scratch off a few lines to sweetest love — my darling wife, and my dear little children. . . .

Before I close I must tell you what Senator Vest said about my standing in the Indian Department, for I know it will please you. He said, in a conversation with Commissioner Price, that gentleman told him that there were only three Indian Agents in the Service, that were up to the standard of what he considered fit men for their positions and that I was one of the three and stood at the head of the class. . . .

* * * * * *

Willard Hotel, January 27, 1884.

. . . . This being Sunday morning I arose early to write first to you, and then to prepare myself and the Indians for Mass at the Jesuit Church of Saint Aloysius. . . . I am just beginning to get uneasy and restless to hear from you. . . .

President [Chester A.] Arthur and Secretary Teller returned from New York last night, and I expect my Indians and their affairs will be brought before them on Monday. In the meantime I have been enjoying myself immensely.

Just now (I suppose for lack of other beasts) Agent Ronan and his Indians are the lions of Washington. I am actually over-run with invitations for myself and the other animals. Senator Vest, on account of the rush on me, postponed his entertainment until yesterday, when we spent a delightful day with the Senator, his family and invited guests, among them were Major Maginnis and other acquaintances of mine. I attended a garden party, a hop at Willard's, a masquerade, and Senator Vest's dinner party since I wrote you, and my memorandum book is filled with engagements up to Saturday next, when we dine with Captain Mullen [John Mullan], who has taken the place of General Ewing at the head of the Catholic Indian Bureau. . . .

* * * * * *

Willard's Hotel, January 29, 1884.

. . . . In company with Major Maginnis and Senator Vest I had an interview today with Secretary Teller, and tomorrow I will bring Charlot and the Indians before him to talk business. With filling engagements and visiting with the Indians my time is constantly occupied. This evening I took them to Ford's Opera

House to witness a grand performance by a troupe of "sure enough Negroes," and the Indians enjoyed it very much. They are all well and Charlot is in the best of spirits. Tomorrow night I must take them to the "Council Fire," residence of a Dr. and Mrs. [T. A.] Bland, where we are to have a reception. I know this will be an infliction — but as I am on the rounds with the Indians I cannot afford to act discourteous with anyone. . . .

January 29, 1884
LR 2,203/1884, RG 75, National Archives, Washington, D.C.

Washington, D.C.
January 29th, 1884

Hon. Commissioner Indian Affairs
    Sir:
    I respectfully request for authority to purchase for Chief Charlos and five Indians of the Flathead Nation, now in Washington under orders from the Interior Department, the following articles of clothing, of which they are greatly in need of, viz:
    Six pair of Shoes; one dozen pairs of Shaker socks; six pairs of pants; six pairs drawers[;] six vests; six coats or blouses; one dozen woolen over shirts; one dozen under Shirts; three hats.
    I also respectfully ask authority to advance Chief Charlos the sum of twenty-five dollars, in money, to be expended for the support of his family while away from home as they have no means of dependence in the absence of Charlos.
    I would also add that the other Indians composing Charlos' Delegation have families in Bitter Root Valley, Montana, dependant upon their efforts for support but they have not requested any advancement.

Very respectfully
Your ob'dt se'vt
Peter Ronan
U.S. Indian Agent

Flathead Agency, Montana.

February 1, 1884
LR 2,225/1884, RG 75, National Archives, Washington, D.C.

Washington, D.C.
Feb. 1st, 1884

Hon. Commissioner Indian Affairs
    Sir:
    I have the honor to state that I expended twenty-five dollars in procuring necessaries for Chief Charlot, and for supplies for the support of his family, while the Chief is in Washington, pursuant to orders from the Honorable Secretary of the Interior, and beg that authority be granted for such expenditure.

Very Respectfully
Peter Ronan
U.S. Ind. Agt.

Flathead Agency
Montana, Ter.

February 3, 1884 — February 8, 1884

Margaret Ronan, "Memoirs of a Frontiers Woman: Mary C. Ronan," unpublished masters thesis, State University of Montana, Missoula, 1932, pages 358-361. Some footnotes have been omitted.

More information about the reception at the White House attended by Ronan and the Salish delegation can be found in "The President's Public Levee."[23] A detailed story about the burial of Father John Baptist Abraham Brouillet, which Ronan and the Salish attended, can be found at "Obituary," *The New York Freeman's Journal and Catholic Register.*[24]

The operation on Charlo's eyes was successful and restored his eyesight. Unfortunately the operation on Michel Revais' eyes did not restore his eyesight.[25]

February 3, 1884.

. . . . I feel as gay as a young colt. . . .

Darling, you ought to have seen your dude of a husband yesterday at Mrs. [Mary Arthur] McElroy's reception at the President's house. He was compelled by force of circumstances to order two suits of clothes; one an evening dress suit — "claw hammers" coat, white kids, white satin necktie, a beaver hat, etc., etc. The other is an afternoon calling suit — a four button cut-away coat with everything else to match, and if you think I have had an idle moment since I arrived here you are mistaken. Every night I have to make a list of engagements for the next day and evening.

Yesterday I took the Indians to the Smithsonian Institute where we were all photographed in groups and singly. I say "we" because an order was issued from the Secretary's office for me to have my photograph taken with the group. I have been informed that I will be supplied with a dozen copies of each of the pictures. After that was over I had an interview with the Secretary, then an interview with the Commissioner of Pensions, and then made my call with Major and Mrs. Maginnis at the President's, and in the evening took dinner with Captain John Mullen and his interesting Catholic family in their magnificent mansion. So you see how yesterday was. The day before I had a similar round and wound up with a dinner party at Mr. McCammon's, where I met a young Frenchman who is a great grandson of Lafayette. He conversed in French with Michel and was delighted with the Indians at the McCammon's table, who ordered fish for dinner because it was Friday.

On Monday we are to have a final talk with the Secretary and make a call on the President. I do not know how Charlot's business will turn out. He has had most tempting offers to remove to the Jocko, but he still clings to his wish to remain in the Bitter Root. However it will terminate, the visit will result in great good to the Indians and most beneficially to me, as I have been thrown among and formed a personal acquaintance with all the officials in the Indian Department, who, from the mightiest to the lowest, have treated me in such a marked and courteous manner, that I have excited the curiosity of Inspectors Benedict and Howard who are both here settling their accounts. . . .

Besides other engagements on Monday, I am going calling with Mrs. Maginnis, in a carriage which has been placed at my disposal by the Indian Office. Oh! they do things up here in shape, and a government official is "some pumpkins," but I am afraid you will think I am drifting into the same groove with the Virginian who held a position here, and was so elated over his honors that he wrote to his friends that he was "a bigger man than old Grant.". . .

I feel happy because I stand so well with my superiors and because my present position, humble as it is, seems to me to have opened up a bright and prosperous career, and will enable me to educate and bring up our little darlings and fit them for a life of usefulness and morality. . . .

. . . . Our expenses here will fit us something like forty dollars a day, but as they are all paid here by the Government, and as it seems to be the disposition of the Department to give me plenty of time, and to go to the trouble to inform me that as far as I am concerned time is not pressing! . . .

I had a letter from my sister Theresa enclosing a letter of introduction to Congressman [Patrick] Collins of Boston, who is the brightest man in Congress.

★ ★ ★ ★ ★ ★

February 5, 1884.

. . . . I will have to remain East some three weeks longer to have operation[s] performed on Michel's and Charlot's eyes. . . . I have only time to write a few lines this morning, as I am very busy today. At eight tonight Maginnis and I will attend the President's reception, accompanied by the Indians.

★ ★ ★ ★ ★ ★

February 6, 1884.

. . . . It is strange that it takes a letter three days longer to reach here than a traveler. . . . I assure you that I have either written or sent you marked newspaper notices of my movements every day since my arrival here.

I attended the President's reception last night and was required to bring the Indians along. Our position was opposite the President and Mrs. [Mary Arthur] McElroy and the ladies of the Cabinet, who assisted in receiving. We were placed there by wish of the President so that we could hear each name pronounced as introduced and view the callers as they passed. The night was oppressively hot, and after an hour's gazing upon the most gorgeously dressed and beautiful women, and fine looking gentlemen, that I ever saw congregated together, I made my exit followed by the Indians, who received a perfect ovation.

Charlot is the hero of the day, and although there are four other Indian Delegations now in the city, he and his people receive most exclusive attention from the government officials and citizens. Most of this has been brought about through the courtesies shown them by Maginnis, McCammon, Captain John Mullen, Major Blacke, Captain Clarke, and a host of others, who have been in Montana, and have social influence and standing in Washington.

The operation which was to have taken place on the eyes of Charlot and Michel has been postponed until tomorrow, on account of lack of accommodation in the hotel and they will be transferred to Providence Hospital tomorrow, where they will be operated upon. Chloroform will be administered, and Charlot has particularly requested that I be present. In a day or two after the operation I will go to Boston and leave the Indians here. I will stop there a few days with my mother and then return here. It will probably be three weeks from date before I can leave for home. . . . This city, with all its charms and gaities [sic] of society possesses no nook or corner in my heart and I long for my quiet home. . . . Tell Michel's wife that he will soon be home and I trust with his eyesight restored, at all events he will not lack for skill and money.

★ ★ ★ ★ ★ ★

February 8, 1884.

. . . . Yesterday the operation was made on Michel's eyes and also on Charlot's, and of course I had to be with them. Today with the other Indians I attended the funeral of Father Brouilett at the Church of St. Matthew and witnessed one of the grandest pageants of the church. I will not attempt to describe it, as it will be published. After service myself and the Indians in a carriage attended the funeral to the cemetery. . . . Our carriage was placed next to the hearse. I will send you the full account as soon as it is published.

Now that the operation has been made the Indians will be kept in a dark room for about two weeks and then we will return home. . . . I attended a brilliant party tonight at Willard's, and tomorrow I will attend Mrs. McElroy's reception.

February 9, 1884
LR 2,659/1884, RG 75, National Archives, Washington, D.C.

Washington, D.C.
Feb. 9th, 1884

Hon. Commissioner Ind Aff'rs
Washington
  Sir:
  I would respectfully state that in accordance with permission granted to me from your office and the office of the Hon. Secretary of Interior, I will visit Boston on Monday. Inasmuch as I have been put to daily personal expense for Indians and for myself since leaving home which will not be allowed if put into my accounts, I am satisfied from former experience. I respectfully ask as a matter of justice that I be ordered to Boston in my capacity as an Indian Agent, in order that my necessary traveling expenses may be covered.

Very respectfully
Peter Ronan
U.S. Ind. Agent
Flathead Agency, Montana.

February 10, 1884 — February 12, 1884
Margaret Ronan, "Memoirs of a Frontiers Woman: Mary C. Ronan," unpublished masters thesis, State University of Montana, Missoula, 1932, pages 361-62. Some footnotes have been omitted.

February 10, 1884.

. . . . I must tell you what I have done since my last. Saturday morning I visited Michel and Charlot, who are in a darkened room. Charlot will be entirely restored to sight, but there is only a hope that vision will be restored to Michel in one eye, sufficient to go around without being led. I then visited the Indian office and then went out with Mrs. Maginnis to make some little purchases . . . for you and the children, which will be forwarded . . . tomorrow. I then attended Mrs. McElroy's reception, and in the evening went to the theatre with Major Maginnis. Today I attended mass with the Indians at St. Matthew's church and listened to the finest music and finest sermon you can imagine. . . . After luncheon I was invited to drive around the city with Mr. and Mrs. Maginnis. After dinner I retired to my room and here I am for the night.

* * * * * *

February 12, 1884.

.... Tomorrow night I expect to be in Boston with my mother.... You may depend upon it I will start for home the very next train after the doctor informs me that the Indians can travel.

February 18, 1884

LR 4,019/1884, RG 75, National Archives, Washington, D.C.

> Problems resulting from the location of the Flathead Agency on the southern extreme of the reservation were discussed for many years in the nineteenth century, but no action was ever taken.
>
> This letter was actually signed by "R. M. Baird, Farmer in Charge," but in Ronan's annual report for 1884 (August 12, 1884) Ronan refers to this as "my report."

United States Indian Service,
Flathead Agency,
February 18, 1884.

Hon. Commissioner of Indian Affairs
Washington, D.C.

Sir:

I have the honor to inform you that it has been intimated to me that, if I agree in the views So often expressed by Officials and others as to the propriety of a change of location of this Agency, I Should through you, present a Report on the Subject to the Honorable Secretary of the Interior.

Should you consider Such an intimation Correct, I would respectfully ask you to Submit, to the Honorable Secretary, the following Statements.

The Agency is, at present, Situated at the extreme end of the Southern habitable portion of the Reservation; a fact which will be readily admitted when it is known that not a Single farm or even Indian lodge is in existence between it and the Southern boundary. It is also placed at the immediate foot of the Mountains, forming the Eastern line, thereby precluding any Settlement in that direction.

On the other hand, to the North and West, there are farms extending, in the one case to a distance of 40 and, in the other, to a distance of at least, 60 miles.

Owing to this State of Affairs, it will be evident that the use of the Mills and the Services of the Mechanics, connected with the Agency, cannot be utilized by the great Majority of the Indians, except at considerable Cost and inconvenience; and, — per consequence, — that they have not the encouragement, which it is the intention of the Government to Afford them, to follow civilized pursuits.

This is especially apparent in connection with building and grain raising, — two matters to which attention is most Strongly urged by your Department. Seeing that the transportation by wagon, of Lumber or Wheat, for any considerable distance, exceeds the value of the article itself.

An argument in favor of the removal is also furnished through the closer relations in which the Agent and employés would be placed with those who it is their duty to Assist and direct.

In opposition, no valid objection, — with the Sole exception of the expense, — can possibly be raised to a removal.

As already I had the honor of Setting forth, a central Site Could be Chosen, which would not appreciably increase the present distance from a Railroad Station and from a Post-Office, and, as to the very few inhabitants of the Reservation, who would then be more remote from the Agency, the Majority consists of half-breeds, who have had, for years, the benefits of Contiguity, and are proportionably well off, while the remainder are Indians in a like condition.

That "what is worth doing is worth doing well," is, of course, a universally accepted axiom, and, — permit me to repeat, — that the benefits the Government expects the Indians to gain from the appropriations for the Mills, Agricultural Machines &c., cannot be fully derived, in the present Situation, is unanswerable.

The Subject therefore is resolved into a matter of Cost. — This, I believe would, if well managed, not exceed Thirty thousand Dollars, and, in that Sum would be included amounts for a planing and matching Machine, a Turbine wheel (to do away with the expense and inconvenience of a Steam engine) and all other improvements which I deem necessary and appropriate.

In order to be within this limit however it would be requisite to proceed with judgment.

For instance were the removal to be made, I Should advise that the Site be immediately Chosen, — that a ditch (which will prove an important factor in determining the total Cost, and the expense of which Cannot be estimated until a location is made) be built; — that a Turbine wheel and other accessories needed for the Saw-mill be procured, and that the Mill itself be Set in motion without delay, to furnish the necessary lumber. The foregoing is presented as the more Salient features in connection with the Subject; and

I am
Very respectfully
Your obedient Servant
R. M. Baird
Farmer in Charge.

February 26, 1884

Margaret Ronan, "Memoirs of a Frontiers Woman: Mary C. Ronan," unpublished masters thesis, State University of Montana, Missoula, 1932, pages 362-363. Some footnotes have been omitted.

On March 1, 1884, Charlo, Ronan, and the Salish delegation paid a farewell visit to President Chester Arthur and left the East Coast for Montana.[26] Charlo still refused to move to the Jocko Reservation, but he agreed to let each Salish family choose for themselves between the Bitterroot and Jocko Valleys. Charlo probably did not know yet that Interior Secretary Henry Teller had decided to provide subsistence and agricultural assistance to those Salish families who remained in the Bitterroot Valley. See below for Ronan's letters describing how the negotiations in the Bitterroot Valley played out during the months following the delegation's return to Montana.

See also Ronan's letter of April 2, 1884, justifying some of his expenses while in Washington for more information about the activities of the delegation.

Washington, D.C.
February 26, 1884.

I found the Indians, Charlot and Michel, with their eyes still bandaged and the doctor told me they could not travel for at least four days. What a disappointment, for I hoped that I could take the train at least one day after my arrival here and speed away for home. What a dull and heavy thing it is to be homesick. Here I am tonight in the great city of Washington — with all its glare and amusements — actually sad and homesick — within a block of where the great Italian opera troupe holds forth and I have no wish to attend. In fact I did not go the opera since I came East and only attended the theatre three times — once in Washington, to see Florence, once in New York to see Mrs. [Lillie] Langtry, and once in Boston to see [Edwin] Booth in *Hamlet*, but tomorrow night I expect to go and hear Neilson, as it will be the last chance I will have.

The Indian matters are virtually settled. The Flatheads will occupy their lands in the Bitter Root. Plows, harrows, wagons, etc., will be issued to them, at least are promised, and I will have charge of their affairs. I will not go into details as I will start for home probably — yes, early on Saturday, and will reach there a few days after this reaches you. Do not let anything trouble you about my affairs. It is enough to say that I am assured by Secretary Teller, himself, that I stand in the highest notch in the Indian Department. I will tell you when I get home why those inspectors came so thick — it has all been explained — one reason was to give them a chance to spend all of last year's appropriations — so that no money would go back into the treasury from that fund. Their going to the Agency was connected in no way with any distrust or suspicion of mismanagement at the Agency. I have learned a great many useful things here, and one of them is that the visit of an Inspector at the Agency again will neither give me concern nor annoyance any more. . . . I will telegraph about the day of my arrival at Missoula, and if you can, take the baby and meet me, telegraph to the Arthur house to reserve nice rooms for us.

March 11, 1884
LR 5,489/1884, RG 75, National Archives, Washington, D.C.

> In this letter, Ronan discussed the alcohol problem on the Flathead Reservation in 1884. He argued that many tribal members did indulge, but the problem was limited, and there was actually little the agent could do to totally eliminate it. The Office of Indian Affairs accepted Ronan's arguments and filed his report.

United States Indian Service,
Flathead Agency,
March 11th, 1884.

Hon. Commissioner of Indian Affairs
Washington, D.C.

Sir,

Having had the honor of receiving your communication marked "C 1465/1589" of 25th Ult., in which, referring to crimes committed on this Reservation, you inform me that, "from reports," intoxicating liquors appear to be largely indulged in by these Indians, and are the occasion of Said crimes.

That there is Sufficient foundation for Such a belief as to cause regret, I will not dispute, but Still, I hope, you will excuse me for Stating that, without doubt, the reports have been highly colored.

During eight years there have been four persons Killed on this Reservation, and of these, the deaths of two were plainly attributable to Whisky, while the others were caused by Jealousy and a refusal to discharge a debt.

With regard to Indians, who have brought liquors on the Reservation, while I have Suspected a number, I have been unable to find proof against any except those of other tribes, who have either been punished and Sent away, or been frightened off as reported at various times.

In relation hereto, as Showing the difficulty of obtaining the proof desired I may mention that Some months ago, having a conversation with one of the "headmen," (a Sober industrious and responsible Indian) I urged that he, — being a leader and having the good of his people at heart, and being in a position to easily bring the guilty to punishment, — purchase Some whisky and furnish evidence to convict.

In reply, Smiling, he told me that, when young, he liked himself to take a drink occasionally, and that he could not act the hypocrite, to get into trouble, others, who are now as he was then.

As to Indians who drink liquor — while, of course, I do not See it done, I believe that, if your question is to be literally interpreted, almost every adult Indian in the country might be included in an affirmative reply; while, if reference is made, as I presume is the case, to those who habitually use intoxicants, I am glad to Say that I do not Know of a Single individual — and, furthermore, I do not believe there is one.

Altho' I am very particular as to not affording assistance or making issues to Indians of loose character it is necessary to remember that the small quantity of "Annuity Goods" furnished for these Indians, if equally distributed, would not exceed, in value, five dollars p. annum for each individual. They must therefore be looked upon as an evidence of friendliness on the part of the Government, and as a Slight encouragement towards civilization, but any threat, to with-hold them, would be, by the majority, received with contempt, and merely arouse a Spirit of enmity and rebellion, without producing any good result.

Again assuring you that the reports you mention were evidently calculated to create a false impression, as I have every confidence in Stating that we have here a community, which would be deemed eminently Sober in any part of the Globe, and this in the face of the undeniable fact that, outside of the Reserve, any Indian can easily procure all the Whisky he wants, for which he has the money to pay, I have the honor to be

Very respectfully
Your obedt Servant
Peter Ronan
U.S. Indian Agent.

March 17, 1884

LR 5,301/1884, telegram, RG 75, National Archives, Washington, D.C.

On March 17, 1884, the same day Ronan sent this telegram, the Northern Pacific Railroad office in New York City, telegraphed their General Manager at St. Paul, Minn., to give the twenty Crow Indians passes to return to their reservation.[27]

March 17 1884
Flat Head Agency Mont.

To Commissioner Indian Affairs, Washn, D.C.

Twenty Crow Indians here who came over Northern Pacific Railroad without pass Attempted to go back on train to their reservation & were put off what shall I do with them?

Ronan Agent.

March 27, 1884
LR 6,629/1884, RG 75, National Archives, Washington, D.C.

This report on the status of Salish agricultural development in the Bitterroot Valley in 1884 indicated that the Salish could make good use of farming equipment and subsistence from the government. Ronan had an interesting description of the council where 21 Salish families agreed to accept the government offer of assistance if they removed to the Jocko Reservation. Unfortunately we do not have Charlo's version of the negotiation to compare to Ronan's. Some Salish who had removed to the Jocko Reservation in the 1870s owned patented land in the Bitterroot Valley which could not be sold. Even more important was providing for those Salish who had no land or had improvements located on land that was not patented to them.

On April 29 and May 5, 1884, Ronan had to write again petitioning for funds and official permission from Washington to fulfill his promises to the Bitterroot families who had agreed to move to the Jocko.

On April 9, 1884, the Commissioner of Indian Affairs requested an appropriation of $21,000 to assist the Salish who removed to Jocko and those who remained in the Bitterroot Valley.[28] The $21,000 was included in the Indian Appropriation Bill which became law on July 4, 1884.[29] By the time Ronan was finally authorized to spend the money for the Salish, only 20 families were still willing to remove to Jocko. See Ronan's letter of August 16, 1884.

United States Indian Service,
Flathead Agency,
March 27th, 1884.

Hon. Commissioner of Indian Affairs
Washington, D.C.

Sir,

I have the honor to inform you that, in compliance with Verbal instructions, received from the Hon. Secretary of the Interior — given on account of the failure of the late visit to Washington of Charlos, Chief of Flatheads, with four of his headmen, to accomplish its object of gaining his and their Consent to the removal of the Bitter-root branch of the tribe to this Reservation, — I have, owing to the fact of their having been engaged in hunting in the Mountains and requiring to be gathered thence, — just Completed a thorough investigation into the Condition, necessities and desires of these people, and beg Respectfully to Submit, thro' you, to the Honorable Secretary the following Report.

Of the whole number of families, (ninety-five in all) I found there were only five So provided with agricultural implements and other requisites as to enable them to make a living by farming. The remainder may be Said to be perfectly destitute having had, for months, neither flour nor vegetables, and only what meat resulted from their efforts in hunting. Among them are only three wagons and five plows, with a like dearth of all other aids to tillers of the Soil. Still they have Some forty dwellings Surrounded by enclosed farms, and, in addition, about twenty Small fenced fields. These they are not only willing but anxious to Cultivate, — having a very fair knowledge of farming gained by hiring to their white neighbors during Seeding and harvesting times, — but have been unable to procure the necessary materials, their pressing and daily wants consuming all their earnings, and preventing the Saving of Sufficient to enable them to "make a Start."

In accordance with the views of the Honorable Secretary I ascertained that Wagons, plows, harness and Seeds can be purchased in Missoula, and promised that the three last mentioned articles would be furnished them, with a few of the first if it were possible; Also that Sufficient issues of food would be allowed to enable them to Subsist while planting.

During my visit and Council, which lasted five days, as I found that the ends in view could be best Subserved by Separate interviews with the heads of families, I was (on account of the fact, already Stated, that they were entirely dependent, for their living, on hunting, from which I had to Call them) obliged to Supply them with Subsistence. The expenditure will, of course, appear in my regular accounts, but I refer to it here in order that I may respectfully ask approval of the Same.

I will now proceed to give an account of my exertions with regard to procuring removals to this Reservation.

When the Council first opened, Charlos, doubtless fancying that very few of his people would take advantage of his remarks, and possibly desiring to create in my mind, a favorable impression, informed the Indians that all who So chose might go, and that he would make no attempt to hinder them. Finding, however, that under Such circumstances, a large number were willing to remove, he withdrew his permission and Commenced to offer adverse criticisms.

He Stated that he had been told that there were 103 or 4 land patents issued, while I Said there were only 51, and that, if he had Sufficient money he would return to Washington and ask the Honorable Secretary if his words were to be depended upon. I informed him that it was a private and unofficial Gentleman who had made the Statement, and that the necessary data, not being immediately at hand neither the Hon. Secretary nor myself were then in a position to contradict it; but that I had advised that the matter be examined into, and, that, as a result, I had a letter with the Hon. Secretary's own Signature, which was equivalent to his own Spoken words, and that therein I was notified that fifty-one was the correct number.

I then produced the letter, which was read by a few of the tribe Capable of So doing, having, in addition, my remarks Sustained by the rest of the delegation which visited the Capital, And this matter was permitted to drop.

The next difficulty, raised, proved a more Serious one. — Charlos informed his people that he was promised that, in case of a removal, the old Stevens Treaty would be duplicated; i.e. that thirty-Six thousand dollars would be expended for their benefit during the first year, twenty-four thousand during the next four years &c. &c.

A number of Indians, who had proposed to remove Said — in that case, I should promise likewise, or they would remain where they were. — I again Called upon the others who had been at Washington to Corroborate my denial that the Honorable Secretary had made any Such proposition. The offer, as they Stated, was made in the Tremont Hotel by Captain Mullan, who, as I understand it, inquired if any offer of that nature would induce them to remove, but, without doubt, made no promise.

However it proved a difficult matter, — and one, in which I did not entirely Succeed, — to eradicate the disadvantageous impression produced, And is but another proof of the many I have had, of the desirability and necessity of not allowing any chance of a misunderstanding by Indians of any of the bearings of a case in which they are interested.

The final result of the council, for the present, was that twenty-one heads of families concluded to remove, and, to them, following the views of the Honorable Secretary of the Interior, as expressed to the Indians in Washington, I promised to each —

1st. A Choice of 160 acres of unoccupied land on this Reservation.

2d Assistance in the erection of a Substantial house.

3d Assistance in fencing & breaking up of a field of at least ten Acres.

4th The following Gifts —

Two Cows

A Wagon and harness

A plow with other necessary Agricultural Implements.

Seed for the first year & provisions until the first crop was harvested.

Taking into consideration the very kindly & just expressions made use of in connection with the deserts of these Indians, by the President and the Honorable Secretary, I could but have made an unfavorable impression by offering less. I therefore trust it Shall be considered that I have been Sufficiently moderate, but I would add that, even after the first year, they will depend Somewhat on the generosity of the Government to uphold their hands in Striving for a Civilized independence, and a Sustained well-doing. Should my actions meet with approval and I be allowed to carry out the programme, as inaugurated, I am confident that, in course of time, the whole tribe, with the exception of Charlos and his family, will remove.

In event of gaining Said approval, I respectfully offer the following Suggestions, based on the facts here presented, and ask your attention to the accompanying requisition, without the granting of which, it is needless to Say, my hands would be tied.

Where as a large number of the Indians, to whom patents were granted for lands in the Bitter-root Valley, have removed, and will eventually remove to this Reservation, and will make a permanent home here, and, as the lands that have been granted to them in the Bitter-root Valley will become unoccupied, and will still continue to be owned by them, they holding Said lands under patents containing a clause preventing them from alienation, I would Suggest that a special act of Congress be passed, providing that any Indian, who has received a patent for any lands in the Bitter-root Valley, may be allowed to Sell and convey the Same to any person, provided the Indian Shall have first removed to and permanently established him or herself upon what is now Known as the Flathead Reservation.

This would confer a benefit on the Indian Selling by giving him a sum of money which he might invest in Cattle or other property Calculated to promote his welfare. It would also be a benefit to the white Settlers and to the Community at large, by Settling up Certain valuable tracts of land now lying vacant, And which must continue to be unoccupied unless something of this kind is done.

In this Connection I would also Suggest that, as a number of these Indians are residing on Public lands of the United States, and not upon the lands, Surveyed for, & patented to them, — if found practicable, the original patents issued be recalled & cancelled and patents be issued to them for the lands upon which they are actually residing.

I respectfully ask that I be authorized to procure the opinions of a competent lawyer, Should there be any disputes between whites & Indians as to claims and I would earnestly recommend that a reliable Civil engineer be employed to Survey & establish the lines & corners of the land claims referred to, in order that the Indians may Know exactly where their lands are, and to prevent the whites from encroaching upon them.

I think if these Suggestions are carried out, — taking it for granted that it is possible so to do, — it will be greatly to the advantage of the Indians, & also of the Whites.

Further, I would respectfully ask that I be informed by telegram, in case it is determined to carry out the views now Submitted, as, by taking the preliminary Steps at once, I believe there is yet time, — Should purchases be made in open market in this Country, — to have Some crops raised by those Indians remaining in the Bitter-root Valley.

Permit me, before closing, to specifically direct your attention to my remarks, in the enclosed requisition, concerning a needed clerk, So that an authorization to engage one, on whom I could depend, may not be delayed, in event of my being ordered to employ myself in the affairs of the Indians aforesaid.

Very respectfully
Your obedient Servant
Peter Ronan
U.S. Indian Agent.

April 2, 1884
LR 6,885/1884, RG 75, National Archives, Washington, D.C.

United States Indian Service,
Flathead Agency,
April 2nd, 1884.

Hon. Commissioner of Indian Affairs
Washington, D.C.

Sir,

Having the honor to acknowledge receipt of your communication "F" 23911 of 22d Ult, I beg to State that, having received from the Second Comptroller a communication of the same purport, vis — a request to furnish explanations as to certain charges made by the Proprietor of the Tremont Hotel, I have to-day addressed to that Gentleman the following letter —

Sir,

Having the honor to acknowledge your communication of the 25th Ult., I beg to inform you that among the Flathead Indians, lately in Washington, under my charge were two (Charlos, the Chief and Rivais the Interpreter) who were blind, or very nearly so, and that the Honorable Secretary of the Interior ordered an operation to be performed on their eyes.

Dr. [William V.] Marmion, whose Services were engaged for the purpose, for professional reasons, desired the removal of the patients, for a time, to Providence Hospital, and I, in pursuance of general instructions given by the Honorable Secretary of the Interior, gave directions at the Hotel to have them conveyed to, and when it Suited, the Doctor's views; conveyed from the Hospital; as also to furnish, after the return of the invalids to the Hotel and during my absence, by permission, in Boston, — any medicines or delicacies which might be required.

With reference to the amount for transportation to and from the Mount Vernon boat — Captain Blake of the Steamer "Corcoran" extended to the Flatheads an invitation to take a trip thereon, at his expense. They being ignorant of localities at Washington, I gave Similar instructions, to those already described, with regard to their conveyance to and from the vessel; And, in both cases, requested that the charges would be included in the general Hotel Bill.

There is a great mistake in any Statement that any money was advanced to me, which I can only account for by Supposing Some misapprehension of information given.

Taking into consideration that my business precluded the possibility of procuring Separate Vouchers for every Small item of expense, I was convinced of the propriety of, and believed that my action was quite in accord with the intent of the instructions received from the Honorable Secretary of the Interior. Still, as a guaranty to the Hotel Proprietor, when giving the directions, I said that, if the items were not approved, the bill might be sent to me personally.

This may have occasioned a Statement that Such expenses were incurred on my personal account, or that the money was advanced for me, which, of course, was not the case.

This is certainly the only explanation I can offer and hoping that it may prove Satisfactory.

I have the honor to be &c,

(Sgd.) Peter Ronan

Trusting that this presentation may also meet with your approval,

I am, Very respectfully
Your Obedient Servant
Peter Ronan
U.S. Indian Agent.

April 18, 1884
The Bozeman Weekly Chronicle, *April 23, 1884, page 3, col. 5.*

The 1884 murder of two Salish Indians near Bozeman generated considerable comment and even a $300 reward, but was apparently never solved.[30] Incidents such as this emphasized how ineffective the nineteenth century Montana justice system was in protecting peaceful Salish Indians. Nels Murray, a white friend of the two murdered Indians, arranged to have the bodies buried on his farm in the Gallatin Valley.[31]

The Bitterroot Indian who was killed was named Peter and may have been seventeen years old in 1884.[32] Frank Enos may have been the Francis, son of Ignace (metis Flathead) and Julia, who was baptized at St. Ignatius Mission on July 12, 1865, at three months of age. That would have made Frank Enos nineteen years old in 1884.[33]

Those Two Indians
<hr>

Flathead Agency, April 18, 1884.

Hon. S. W. Langhorne: —
Dear Sir: —
I received a marked copy of your paper dated the 14th inst., which gives an account of the cruel murder of two unoffending Indians, who were on their way home to this agency from Bozeman, and I trust the good citizens of your town and the officials of your county will use every effort to trace up and bring to justice the perpetrator of this foul and unprovoked murder — for such it seems to be.

In this connection I wish to give you a statement of some facts with regard to some six or seven lodges of Bitter Root Flatheads, who have been camped in the vicinity of Bozeman, which may be of use in the investigation of this matter.

The Indians, in question, left Bitter Root valley, where they reside, last fall, and are a portion of Charlo's Band, which refuses to remove to this reservation. Their object in going to Bozeman was to spend the winter in hunting in the mountains in that locality. Upon learning of my return from Washington with their chief, and that I was to hold a council at Bitter Root under instructions from the honorable Secretary of the Interior with the view of gaining a consent to a removal of these Indians, eight in number, determined upon attending the council.

A few days previous to this determination, two Flatheads; also Charlo's Band, arrived in their camp with a number of stolen horses. The thieves turned these horses among the Indian ponies of the camp and took the train for Missoula, with the eight Indians referred to, who left at the camp one old, crippled Indian, with the squaws and children composing their families.

In their absence a party of white men arrived and finding the stolen horses among those of the Indians, drove off the whole band, including the Indian ponies.

The two thieves arrived in the Bitter Root valley and as I am informed remained there, and can there be found, while the eight men belonging to the camp near Bozeman returned thither.

Meantime Frank Eneas, the half-breed, and the Flathead who were so cruelly murdered, as related in your paper, and who, with three other Indians, some time since, left this place to visit the Crows. On their way back here, through Bozeman, were arrested on suspicion of their being the thieves.

After an incarceration of some days in jail, it is related here by Indians, the three last mentioned (whom I should have mentioned were also imprisoned) were discharged and returned home, while the authorities kept Frank Eneas, who spoke English well to interpret, should the thieves be caught, and with him a companion — the other man since murdered.

It appears they also were soon allowed to depart and met their death at the hands of one or more murderers, while on their way to this reservation.

Will you be kind enough to let me know by letter what disposition was made of the thirty ponies these Indians were driving when murdered, and any other facts in connection with this crime which you may be able to gather.

Your obedient Servant,
Peter Ronan
United States Indian Agent.

April 29, 1884
LR 8,565/1884, RG 75, National Archives, Washington, D.C.

See also letters of March 27, 1884, and May 5, 1884.

United States Indian Service,
Flathead Agency,
April 29th, 1884.

Hon. Commissioner of Indian Affairs
Washington, D.C.

Sir,

Under date of March 27th 1884, I had the honor of addressing you a report of my visit to the Flathead Indians of the Bitter Root Valley under Chief Charlos, which was made according to verbal instructions from the Secretary of the Interior. Believing I had made preliminary arrangements with these Indians which would lead to a speedy and satisfactory removal of the tribe to this reservation, and a settlement of that vexed land question in the Bitter Root Valley, I hoped to have a reply to my communication which would be a guide to my future movements and promises in the case.

Five families removed here under my representations and have been receiving supplies for their support out of the scanty store at the Agency, ten other families are awaiting in the Bitter Root for an invitation from me to come here, and others will follow if encouraged. This I believe was the desire of the Indian Office when I left Washington.

Please inform me if I will be justified in bringing any more families to this Reservation by reiterating the promises contained in my report of the 27th, or any other promise, and if I will be allowed to furnish supplies any longer to the families who have already come to make their homes here. In case no encouragement can be given to the Indians to remove here as indicated in said report it would be well for me to let the Indians understand it at once so as to save further complications.

Very Respectfully,
Your obt. svt.
Peter Ronan
U.S. Indian Agent

May 5, 1884
LR 8,856/1884, RG 75, National Archives, Washington, D.C.
Hon. Commissioner
Indian Affairs, Washington
    Sir:
    I have the honor to forward forgoing letter from the Missioner in charge of the Bitter Root Flathead Indians, which will indicate the pressing necessities of Charlot's band. As I have written you fully upon this subject, I deem it unnecessary to add any further comment.

Most respectfully
Your obdt servt
Peter Ronan
U.S. Ind. Agt.

Enclosure:

Stevensville, May 1st 84

Maj. P. Ronan
U.S. Indian Agent
    Dear Major,
    Excuse me if I bother you again. But I think I am bound by charity to let you know that if these Indians do not receive from the Government some help, now, we will have some deaths of starvation. Just yesterday I had to give 100 lbs flour, 50 of which to the chief, because they have nothing to eat. The chief had prepared two fields to put in crops, but all he could get have been two sacks of wheat. The very roots, this year, are scarce, most of the places where they used to dig them having been fenced in, or being rooted out by hogs who are roaming abroad every where here in the valley.
    I hope you will try to do soon some thing to help them.

Yours Respectfully
J. D'Aste S.J.

June 11, 1884
LR 11,732/1884, SC 55, RG 75, National Archives, Washington, D.C.

> The failure of the Northern Pacific Railroad Company to pay compensation for tribally owned stock killed by trains on the newly constructed railroad through the reservation was particularly galling to tribal members. The tribe had still not been paid for the right-of-way and tribal members who lost improvements to the railroad construction were still unpaid. In this hostile environment the railroad originally took a legalistic and parsimonious approach to the damage claims. Ronan argued that it was in the railroad's best interest to settle the damage claims fairly and generously. The Commissioner replied that even though Congress had not completed action on the bill confirming the tribal agreement with the Northern Pacific Railroad, there was no reason the company could not go ahead and settle the damage claims.[34]
>
>   William H. Dewitt received his law degree in New York City in 1878 and came to Helena in 1879. In 1881, he moved to Butte and continued to practice law into the twentieth century. Between 1883 and 1885 he was United States District Attorney for Montana and later served one term on the Montana Supreme Court beginning in 1889.[35]

Ronan's August 30, 1884, letter below also addresses the damage claim problems and includes a list of the stock killed and injured by the railroad. His September 12, 1884, letter spoke of the tribal anger over their treatment by the railroad company. Some of the hostility spilled over into vandalism.

The railroad claims agent finally settled for the losses in November 1884. According to press reports, the stock owners were satisfied with their compensation. Ronan's report to the Commissioner of Indian Affairs about the final settlement has not survived in the National Archives.[36] The claims agent, D. K. Ford, gave an account of his Flathead Reservation visit to a St. Paul, Minnesota, newspaper.[37]

United States Indian Service,
Flathead Agency,
June 11th, 1884.

Hon. Commissioner of Indian Affairs
Washington, D.C.

Sir,

As I have had the honor of informing you, considerable correspondence has passed between the Officials of the Northern Pacific R. R. Company and myself as to Cattle Killed by R. R. Cars on this Reservation, and Some anxiety and much worry has been occasioned by the difficulty of convincing the Indians that the delay in making Settlements does not owe its existence to a high-handed and cruel indifference to their rights.

From at first confining themselves to complaints against the Company they have proceeded to include the Government in their arraignment. They now Say, "We would never have admitted the Railroad Company upon our Reservation on its own account, but the Government Compelled us So to do, Sending Chiefs here to tell us it would do us no harm, and that any damages we might Sustain would be well paid for. — Now here are our Stock Cattle being Killed. The Railroad men won't pay for them. Why does He, who pretends to be our Father, and who placed us in this position [not] protect us?"

The immediate cause of my addressing you to-day is the reception of a letter from the Territorial U.S. Attorney, requesting information on this Subject. I have the honor to enclose a copy thereof, as also of my reply, and would respectfully request that my request for instructions be Submitted to the Honorable Secretary of the Interior.

Asking also that my views on this matter, as contained in my Monthly Report for May, of the current year, may receive Such attention as they may merit,

I am
Very Respectfully
Your obedient Servant
Peter Ronan
U.S. Indian Agent.

First enclosure:

Copy

Butte, Montana, June 7th, 1884

Major Peter Ronan
U.S. Indian Agent

Sir,

I have received from the Dept. of Justice a Copy of the law relating to damages done to the Cattle of Indians on your Reservation.

I inclose you a copy of the Sec. of the law which relates to said matter. The Claim Agent of the N. P. R. R. has written to me about Some losses that he wishes to adjust. You probably Know the Status of the Cases, and perhaps can advise me of any Step which Should be taken in the matter.

Respectfully

(Sgd) William H. DeWitt

U.S. Att'y Montana.

A typescript of "Sec. 3" of an unidentified law was attached.
Second enclosure:

Copy

United States Indian Service,

Flathead Agency,

June 11th, 1884.

William H. DeWitt, Esq.
U.S. Attorney
Butte, M. T.

Sir,

Replying to your favor of 7th. Inst: permit me to Say that, if I am not misinformed, the law relating to Cattle, Killed by the R. R. Compy. on this Reservation, is not yet a completed one, there having been made thereto certain amendments, upon which final action has not yet been taken.

The matter, I think, requires the personal Supervision and direction of the Honorable Secretary of the Interior, and I have, therefore, thro' the Honorable Commissioner of Indian Affairs, applied for instructions as to my Course, upon receiving which I Shall be in a position to afford authoritative information on the Subject.

Respectfully

(Sgd.) Peter Ronan

U.S. Indian Agent.

July 28, 1884

LR 14,753/1884, RG 75, National Archives, Washington, D.C.

During the August and September 1882 negotiations over the sale of the railroad right-of-way through the Flathead Reservation, the chiefs made a point of insisting on getting the payment in cash. Too many of the goods and services promised by the government in the 1855 treaty and other agreements had failed to arrive.[38] On July 15, 1884, however, the Acting Secretary of the Interior advised the Commissioner that he wanted the money spent by the government for the benefit of the Indians rather than distributed as a per capita payment.[39]

The payment for improvements owned by individual tribal farmers displaced by the railroad had been made in July 1883, apparently in cash.[40] The money from the railroad for the right-of-way and timber cut was finally distributed as a cash per capita payment during January 1885 — two and a half years after the sales agreement was signed. Each tribal member got a check for $14.21.[41] Some controversy arose about how much of the money

was used for drinking and gambling.[42] Ronan's account of the per capita payment was probably in one of his monthly reports which did not survive in the National Archives.

United States Indian Service,
Flathead Agency,
July 28th, 1884.

Hon. Commissioner of Indian Affairs
Washington, D.C.

Sir,

Having the honor to acknowledge your communication marked "L. F. 13427/84" of 19th Inst. I ask the liberty of quoting from my Report of April, in which, after an explanation as to how delays in Settlement had aroused, among the Indians, Suspicions of unfair dealing in the matter of payment of the Indians of the amount due them by the Northern Pacific R. R. Company, I wrote as follows — "In this State of affairs I beg to repeat that the only manner of Satisfactorily handling it" (the Sum due) "is by giving the amounts in money as no quantity of goods, issued to them, will convince the Indians that they have been honestly Settled with. On the other hand, with your advice and direction, I have no doubt but that Such arrangements can be made for a Cash payment, as would meet the approval of the Department and the Indians. Also that, with exceptions Such as would be present in any community, the money would be judiciously expended."

Since the receipt of your instructions, now, referred to, I have held consultations with the Chiefs and Some of the head-men with the purpose of obtaining their views as to what articles would be of most benefit to their Tribes, and most acceptably received. I find, however, that they are, as firmly as ever opposed to any Settlement otherwise than thro' a Specie payment. They Say — "We were compelled to enter into the treaty and to accept a Sum which we considered a wholly inadequate recompense, and now it is demanded that we be pleased to receive whatever it is Chosen to give in lieu thereof."

In fact, I regret to Say, Some have gone Still further, adding — "We were compelled to accept the treaty, but you can't compel us to take the goods and we won't."

They further represent that they have, from the beginning, expressed their desire to be paid in cash; that, while Mr. McCammon Stated his instructions relative to the matter being in the hands of the Hon. Secretary of the Interior, they were assured there would be little difficulty in having their wishes on the Subject met. Also that while the Congressional Committee were here, the Subject was again mooted, and that Senator Vest gave like assurances.

Such are a few of the Statements which have been made to me by the Indians, And will now, respectfully Submit my own opinion.

Of course it would be a Simple matter to inform these people that certain goods were to be offered them, which they could either take or let alone, and that, if thro' any rebellious Spirit, they committed offenses, they would be Severely punished. The question arises, however, would the good accruing from the expenditure of the Sum under consideration, according to the better judgment of the Honorable Secretary of the Interior, Sufficiently exceed the benefits derived by the Indians from the outlay in accordance with their own desires, to offset the evils which will arise from exciting the enmity of these Tribes.

They are, I believe, at present, a Credit to the administration of your Department, being, as you are fully aware, almost Self-Supporting, And, in this fact alone, there is Strong presumptive evidence that they are not unacquainted with the proper use of money.

Again there are individuals in the Tribes, who, to a great extent, Stand alone, neither having dependents, nor depending on others. Each of these considers himself or herself entitled to, And expects to receive a proportionate Share of the Amounts promised. To meet Such an expectation (by no means an unreasonable one) would be utterly impossible were wagons, Cattle And Such things purchased. Indeed every Single individual from the age of ten, upwards, has looked forward to the reception of a particular Share, and in no case could a just apportionment be made. A family of three could not be presented with a cow, nor a family of five with a wagon without reducing the payments, due others, while a family, the number of which would entitle it to Such issues might probably not be in need thereof.

Without further expatiation, I would respectfully request that these views be laid before the Honorable Secretary of the Interior, and that his attention be asked to the fact that the Tribes on this Reservation have a very Keen perception of the value of dollars — learned to a great extent from the free competition of Traders for their custom.

I have only to add that in event of this communication not having the hoped for weight with the Honorable Secretary I respectfully agree with you as to propriety of buying Stock Cattle And Agricultural Implements. But, as to work cattle, I think they would be comparatively useless as the Indians are unacquainted with the method of handling them, And, I believe, are not yet adapted for instruction concerning it, as they know and prefer the quicker movements of the horse.

Very respectfully
Your Obedient Servant
Peter Ronan
U.S. Indian Agent.

July 29, 1884
LR 14,754/1884, RG 75, National Archives, Washington, D.C.

United States Indian Service,
Flathead Agency,
July 29th, 1884.

Hon. Commissioner Indian Affairs
Washington, D.C.

Sir:

Referring to your letter C. 6629–1884, dated July 17th, 1884, I respectfully submit that immediately upon receipt of same I proceeded to the Bitter Root Valley, in order, as instructed to obtain information as to the number of Indiains [sic] who are determined to remain in the Bitter Root Valley, and the exact number of those who are willing to remove to the reservation.

I found upon my arrival at Charlot's camp, the Indians, with exception of a few families, were out in the mountains gathering berries, hunting and fishing in order to obtain sustanance [sic], and I sent a runner to inform them of my business and to gather them together at St Marys Mission. It will be impossible to collect a majority of the band together before the 12th of August, and upon that date I arranged to meet them.

I would respectfully ask if I will renew my promise to the Indians who are determined to remain in the Bitter Root Valley of assistance in the way of Agricultural Implements, seeds etc., for next season.

Very respectfully
Peter Ronan
United States Ind. Agt.

August 12, 1884

U.S. Commissioner of Indian Affairs, Annual Report of the Commissioner of Indian Affairs *(Washington, D.C.: U.S. Government Printing Office, 1884), pages 155-158.*

> Ronan had a tendency to become philosophical in his annual reports which emphasized his bigotry and prejudices. Like most nineteenth century white Americans, he saw white economic activities, such as farming, as civilized and good. Traditional Indian economic activities, such as hunting and gathering, were savage and bad. Many tribal leaders supported Ronan's efforts to encourage the development of farms and ranches on the reservation, but, for the tribes, the new economic activities were practical necessities, not moral imperatives.
>
> Ronan outlined the negative impact undermining the traditional chiefs and tribal moral codes had on law and order on the reservation. His recommendation, however, was for tribal punishments to be totally eliminated and the white court system be given full control.

Flathead Agency, Montana,
August 12, 1884.

Sir: In submitting my eighth annual report it is gratifying to be able to state, without fear of successful contradiction, that the Indians of this reservation have steadily advanced during the past year in all the civilized pursuits which are necessary to a self-reliant and self-sustaining community, and in reply to the signified disbelief and sneering remark contained in last year's report of a certain agent, that "it is interesting to read agents' reports of how their good Indians love to work, and how they are *rapidly becoming self-sustaining,* &c.," I may be pardoned if I quote a paragraph from the report of the subcommittee of the special committee of the United States Senate appointed to visit the Indian tribes in Northern Montana last summer, and it, I think, ought to go far to silence in an effectual manner the implied "fling" at representations made to you from agencies, of the condition of which the writer referred to has evidently no conception. Alluding to this reservation, the following remarks are to be found in the report:

> The general condition of these Indians, however, is so good that we feel justified in reporting that in a very few years they will be as useful and prosperous a community as any in the far West. They are kindly, intelligent, and anxious to learn. Their relations with Major Ronan, the agent, are of the most satisfactory character, and, more than all, they appreciate the new order of things and the necessity of self-support by hon-

est industry. Many of them are cutting wood for the railroad, and many cut logs and haul them to the agency saw-mill to procure lumber for their houses. In no tribe is there such an opportunity for testing fully the capability of the Indian for the modes and arts of civilized life, and their progress so far demonstrates that this unfortunate people have a future other than barbarism or ultimate extinction.

As germane to the above statement, I will here mention that within the last two months there were delivered at the agency saw-mill by male members of fifteen Indian families 379 pine logs, which were cut, loaded, and hauled by the Indians with their own teams, and were sawed into 128,000 feet of lumber of various dimensions, suitable for the erection of dwellings and outhouses, the only assistance furnished by the Government being the loan of trucks and logging chains and the services of the agency sawyer. This lumber has now been hauled off, and has been carefully piled upon the farms of the owners, where it will remain until after harvest, when these same Indians will construct with their own labor and by their own ingenuity the buildings for which it is intended, assisted by a very little aid from the agency in the way of glass, nails, hinges, and, in some of the more helpless cases, doors and sashes, and this in addition to 18 new dwelling-houses, which have already during the year been put up on this reservation by the Indians and for the Indians. I would also add that the surroundings of these houses and others of longer standing — the vegetable gardens and waving grain, the latter of which is now beginning to fall before the grain-cradle wielded by stalwart Indian arms, as well as before not a few reaping machines run by Indians in their own fields and paid for by Indian toil and thrift — to my mind tell a story of advancing civilization which cannot be successfully jeered at.

Such are facts in this case, and for many who cannot be personally cognizant of them I am proud to have in at least their partial support the evidence of the eminent statesmen who composed the committee aforesaid. Still there are doubters and doubters and for those I have still an argument left — a fact which incredulity can neither overcome nor even combat. In the list of appropriations for Indians for the fiscal year 1883-'84 those who run may read:

For subsistence and civilization of the Flatheads and other confederated tribes, including pay of employés, $13,000.

That this munificent sum was not exceeded can be verified at your office. Therefore it will be evident that had the amount expended in their behalf been equally distributed among the 1,700 Indians of this reservation, each would have been benefited to the extent of nearly $8. It is unnecessary to explain that a wagon, for instance valued, let us say, at $80, could not well be distributed in ten equal parts; and that when one Indian of necessity, became the recipient of the vehicle the portions of the appropriation assigned others were correspondingly reduced, nor will it be requisite to prove that even had each received the full sum of $8 the amount would scarcely suffice during a twelvemonth for "subsistence and civilization." I shall therefore allow the fact itself to work its own way toward a proof that the Indians of the Flathead Reservation are rapidly learning to work according to the methods of the white man, which indeed, is about the only manner they now have of supporting themselves, and that they are *"rapidly becoming,"* if they may not already be considered, *"self-sustaining,"* &c.

Again, in connection with the Indian schools of this reservation, in order that I may escape any accusation of originating rose-colored statements regarding them, I will quote from the committee report already made use of:

> The schools have now 100 scholars, about equally divided between the two sexes, and the Government pays $100 annually for the board, tuition, and clothing of each scholar to the number of 80. The boys and girls are in separate houses, the former under a corps of five teachers (three fathers and two lay brothers) and the girls under three sisters and two half-sisters, Father Van Gorp being at the head of the institution. The children are taught reading and writing, arithmetic, grammar, and geography and their recitations, all in the English language, are equal to those of white children in the States of the same age. The mission has a saw and grist mill and planing and shingle machine, worked by the boys, several hundred head of cattle and horses, and 300 acres of land belonging to the mission, cultivated successfully by the male scholars, the product being sufficient to furnish enough wheat and oats and vegetables for all purposes. The girls are also taught by the sisters, besides the branches we have mentioned, music, sewing, embroidery, and housekeeping. For a time the school was only for females and the result was that the young women, after being educated, married ignorant half-breeds or Indians and, unable to withstand the ridicule of their companions, relapsed into a barbarism worse, if possible, than that of the husband and tribe. Now, after the establishment of the department for males the young people, when they leave school, intermarry, and each couple becomes a nucleus for civilization and religion in the neighborhood where they make their home, the fathers and agent assisting them in building a house and preparing their little farm for raising a crop. We cannot sufficiently commend this admirable school and we do not envy the man who can see only a mercenary object or any but the highest and purest motives which can actuate humanity in the self-sacrificing devotion of the noble men and women, fitted by talents and accomplishments of the highest order to adorn any walk in life[,] who are devoting their lives to the education of these Indian children.

On this topic I will only further add that the beneficial results of those schools are now still more apparent than when the above report was written, nearly a year ago; that two new and commodious school-houses, described in my last annual report as in course of erection, have lately been completed and are of the greatest credit to the reservation, and that by recent contracts entered into by your Department the number of scholars which may be paid for by Government funds has been increased to 100, and it is to be hoped that hereafter Congress will grant such appropriations as will enable an increase to be made from year to year of the number of scholars at this as well as every other boarding-school for Indian children.

Referring to the subject of crime, I desire to say that while I am too practical a believer in the "survival of the fittest," and have suffered too many annoyances personally from objectionable traits of the Indian character to permit of my being much of a sentimentalist on the Indian question, I still am prepared to indorse what I have hither to reported, viz, that, upon this reservation at least, the behavior of Indians will compare favorably with the conduct of any community of a like size in any locality of which I have any knowledge; and here permit me to intrude the remark that what little success I may be accredited with in my treatment of these people is, to a great extent, I believe, due to my readiness to admit that even "red devils," like others, are not so bad as they are painted. Indians are extremely good judges of the feelings of others; they are naturally thoroughly independent, and full of, if not pride, at least vanity. It is by no means strange that such characters (comparatively easily led, but almost impossible to drive) should meet contempt with aversion and dislike with hatred.

With this digression I will proceed to state that while crimes here are of rare occurrence, I consider that they, with offenses of a nature less grave, might be easily reduced by the enactment of laws rendering Indians amenable to the same regulations and penalties as those to which their white neighbors are obliged to submit. I know, and I regret that it is so, that in this opinion I am at variance with some of the brightest minds of our legislators; with men who have a true friendship and a Christian sympathy for a race much in need of their powerful aid; but I feel compelled to record my belief that their efforts in this particular are misdirected, and with this view I can find many of our best Indians who coincide. It has been the policy (I believe, a good one) of the Government to abolish tribal relations and annul the power of the chiefs, but by these means the unruly spirits of the tribes were heretofore controlled, and when such means are destroyed we should be prepared to offer something better as a substitute.

True, the establishment of Indian courts has been proposed and may be of great service, but it can hardly be expected that such tribunals would deal out capital punishment for capital crimes, or take very severe views of the theft of horses from supposed enemies. In fact, the transition from an autocratic to a republican form of government is too sudden. We have deprived these people of their pillars and should be prepared to support them. We treat them as children, and should be prepared to protect, guide, and control them. I repeat, and with emphasis, that, while guided and controlled they should also be protected, for, while many of the headmen have expressed their desire that their rebellious brethren be made to succumb to the white man's laws, they have also expressed a fear that such laws would be enforced in different manners as against the red and the whiteman; a fear, which I regret to say knowledge and experience do not tend to allay. It has been urged that Indians should not be punished for breaking laws they do not understand, but I would submit that all Indians, at least all of whom I have any knowledge, have codes of morals not at all dissimilar to our ten commandments. Their consciences are pretty fair guides as to what is right and as to what is wrong, and it will be found that a good Indian among Indians would be considered a pretty good man in any community. Our penalties for crimes and methods of punishment are doubtless somewhat different, but, when not already known, I have no doubt that a couple of months would be sufficient to convey to the tribes, at least of which I write, a clear understanding thereof. I have three murderers roaming at will on this reservation, who, having escaped the vengeance of relatives of the slain, know full well they have no other punishment to fear, and yet as fully know that white men in their position would be liable to be hanged. While, therefore, not presuming to suggest, I still hope that some code, a simple one if necessary, will be enacted through which the lawless natives of Indian reservations may be held in check. That with the clear understanding of many of the people of their immunity from punishment their crimes should be so few is the highest evidence in favor of their behavior and dispositions.

I will only further touch, and that slightly, upon my endeavors, directed by the honorable Secretary of the Interior and yourself, to have the Flatheads, now residents of the Bitter Root Valley, remove to this reservation. The visit to Washington during the current year of a delegation from that band is too recent an occurrence to require recital here. Suffice it to say that, in the face of Chief Charlos' determined opposition, and notwithstanding the proverbial Indian love for the soil of his nativity, I have, as has been fully reported to you, induced the heads of twenty families to agree upon a removal, upon the condition that they will be aided in establishing themselves in their new homes (appropriations therefor having already been granted), and that they will enjoy in the future the protecting arm of the Government. In order that this aid and the necessary accompanying supervision may be rendered efficiently and economically, it is absolutely requisite that the agency be removed from its present position on the verge of the reservation to a more central one, within a reasonable distance of where these people will require to locate; but this subject was fully dealt with in my report of February 14 [i.e., 18], 1884. That such removal of the families mentioned will only be the commencement of the immigration hither of the great majority, if not the whole band, I firmly believe, and to this end expect to direct my exertions.

Very respectfully, your obedient servant,

Peter Ronan,
Indian Agent.

The Commissioner of Indian Affairs.

August 16, 1884
LR 16,228/1884, RG 75, National Archives, Washington, D.C.

See Ronan's March 27, 1884, letter for more information about the funds to assist the Salish who removed to Jocko and those who chose to remain in the Bitterroot Valley. The funds were included in the Indian Appropriation Bill which became law on July 4, 1884.

United States Indian Service,
Flathead Agency,
August 16, 1884.

Hon. Commissioner of Indian Affairs
Washington, D.C.
Sir,
In accordance with views expressed in my letter of 29th Ult. in reply to your communication "C 6629 1884" of 17th Ult., I have the honor to report that on the 12th inst. I met Charlos' band of Bitter-root Flatheads at St. Mary's Mission.

After making a thorough canvass with reference to their numbers, desires as to location &c., I found the following result

Of Married men there are	79
Of Unmarried Males above 16	25
Boys under 16	<u>68</u>
Total number of Males	172

Of Married Women there are	100
Of Marriageable Girls	9
Of Girls under the age of puberty	<u>61</u>
Total number of Females	170

or, in all, 342 individuals of whom 101 are heads of families, who are either now married or have been So.

The number of families who expressed to me their willingness to remove during the present Season, to the Flathead Reservation, is twenty comprising an aggregate of Sixty-one persons. These, in the face of the opposition of Charlos, agreed to follow my advice; provided that I was enabled to carry out the promises I made last Spring, in their behalf, under the direction of the Honorable Secretary of the Interior; And, as I am advised by you that the necessary appropriation has been granted, I See no cause to doubt that their removal will be Speedily accomplished, nor that, after they are comfortably Settled, others will Soon follow; And that, in the Course of a limited period, the greater portion, if not the whole tribe, will become inhabitants of this Reservation.

As the families, which have elected to remain in the Bitter-root Valley, are also in urgent need of aid, as indicated in my Report and Estimate of March 27th 1884, I trust that the articles, which are to be distributed among them will be Shipped to Missoula at an early date, with the necessary directions regarding transportation to the locality of the homes of the intended recipients, — a distance of Some thirty miles — and with full instructions as to distribution.

The Supplies requisite for those who Settle here in accordance with promises given and received, it is hardly necessary to State Should be delivered at this Agency.

As I have not, as yet, been favored with any Special views you may entertain as to the expenditure of the Appropriation granted for the furthering of the matter now under Consideration, I have nothing more, on which to report at present, but have the honor to be

Very respectfully
Your Obedient Servant
Peter Ronan
U.S. Indian Agent.

August 18, 1884
Samuel T. Hauser Papers, MC 37, box 18, folder 34, Montana Historical Society Archives, Helena.

Another Jocko River trout shipped to Samuel Hauser in Helena. See also Ronan's September 5 and October 8, 1883, letters to Hauser, and his October 5, 1883, letter to Senator G. G. Vest.

United States Indian Service,
Flathead Agency,
Aug. 18th, 1884.

S. T. Hauser,
Helena, M.T.

    Friend Sam:

    One weeak [sic] ago last Saturday night, a half-past nine, I put a spotted trout into a box drip[p]ing from the Jocko, and placed it in charge of Wells Fargo & Co's messenger, with expectation that it would be delivered in time for the Hauser Family to enjoy a good Sunday dinner. As the trout weighed on the scales just fourteen pounds and three quarters and was a "speckeled beauty," I am just a little anxious to know if you received it all fresh and nice as I thought you would.

Yours as ever
Peter Ronan.

August 29, 1884
LR 16,849/1884, RG 75, National Archives, Washington, D.C. Penciled note filed with letter in National Archives: "Usual letter 'Do the best he can' no funds."

> In this letter Ronan clearly spelled out the limits to his powers as agent in 1884. He explained that on a non-ration reservation he had "with the exception of Some moral force, but little real power over them."

United States Indian Service,
Flathead Agency,
August 29th, 1884.

Hon. Commissioner of Indian Affairs
Washington, D.C.

    Sir,

    While I have the honor to enclose the accompanying receipt I beg to inform you that a compliance with the instructions, to which it refers is a Simple impossibility, except at the expense of attention to duties of the utmost importance, in connection with my position, unless a Sum necessary for the remuneration of temporary employés to perform the work is placed at my disposal.

    It is almost unnecessary to call your attention to the fact that, if possible, my individual time and efforts, are more fully called into requisition from the present date until the end of the year in receiving Consignments, attending to the grinding of Indian Grain, making issues &c., in addition to which I expect to be busily employed in Connection with the removal of Bitter-root Flatheads to this Reservation.

    My regular employés will also have their hands more than full, And, of them, the only one, to whom, in case of absolute necessity, I could intrust the business at hand, has notified me that, in expectation of bettering himself, he will resign on the 1st proximo.

    You clearly understand that there are no regular issues at this Agency, and that donations, except to the Sick or aged are only made in return for work. The Consequence is that, as I have often pointed out, I, as your Agent, can offer to the Indians no very tangible inducement to act contrary to their inclinations, and have, with the exception of Some moral force, but little real power over them.

    Many Indians belonging to this Reservation do not report at this Agency more than once a year, — perhaps not So often — the "Gifts" I am enabled to offer being no inducement towards a journey of Say one hundred miles.

For these reasons, and taking into consideration the fact that, even in So called civilized white communities, Census-takers meet with many difficulties, it will be understood that the instructions referred to cannot be carried out unless every nook and corner, where there may be an Indian Lodge or Cabin of this Reservation be visited, And means taken to explain the why and wherefore thereof.

To do So will necessitate the employment of one intelligent man as Census-taker, with a Half-breed as Interpreter and three horses, which with the exercise of the utmost economy, I believe can be Secured for the necessary time (about one month) for Two Hundred and Twenty ($220.00) Dollars, and for this sum I hereby respectfully apply.

Very respectfully
Your Obedient Servant
Peter Ronan
U.S. Indian Agent.

August 30, 1884

LR 17,163/1884, SC 55, RG 75, National Archives, Washington, D.C.

> Here Ronan continued his pleas for the railroad to settle damage claims with tribal stock owners.[43] His list of stock killed and injured by railroad trains indicated widespread stock ownership among tribal members. A few mixed bloods, such as Charles Allard, seem to have had especially large herds.

United States Indian Service,
Flathead Agency,
Aug. 30th, 1884.

Hon. Commissioner of Indian Affairs
Washington, D.C.

Sir,

Having now the honor to refer to your communication "L["] 11732–1884 of 2d Ult. receipt of which was acknowledged 12th Ult. and explanation submitted as to the necessity of a delay in Complying with your requisition for a list of Indian claims against the Northern Pacific Railroad company, I beg to infor[m] you that the results of my application to the company for a return of memoranda loaned them was a discovery that portions thereof had been lost. This obliged me to form a new list which after considerable trouble in gathering information I have just completed and have the honor to forward herewith.

While I have exerted myself to do as well as possible under the circumstances the list is not compiled as I could wish, and with regard to the exact dates &c of the Killing of some of the animals, the data which can now be furnished are neither so precise nor full as might be desired, but the officials of the company are the parties responsible therefor, both on account of their tardiness in dealing with the matter and on account of the aforesaid loss of information already supplied.

However as they have repeatedly given assurances that they are not only willing but anxious to treat the Indians with justice, I presume, when in support of these claims proofs are offered which would be considered sufficiently good in equity, no technical objections will be urged by these gentlemen.

Such proofs however cannot be supplied to persons remaini[n]g at a distance and for this reason the only practicable or satisfactory manner in which these claims can be adjusted is by having Agents clothed with authority necessary to examine and settle them on the ground and within reach of evidence concerning them.

To this end I have repeatedly offered my personal services in aid of any representative who might be detailed by the company for this work, being urged thereto more especially by remarks occasionally appearing in correspondence on this subject.

Clearly to illustrate my meaning I ask your attention to the following quotations

St. Paul July 6 – 84

Major Peter Ronan
U.S. Indian Agent

– – – – – a large portion of the claims presented are not verified. We simply have in these cases the statements of the Indians to the effect that their stock was Killed. We cannot, merely on grounds of policy, settle any of these Indian claims – – – –

(Sgd) D. K. Ford
Gen'l Claim Agent

* * * * * *

Flathead Agency
June 11 – 84

D. K. Ford Esq.
Genl Claim Agt &c.

– – – – –The reason doubtless of the lack of verification of certain claims is indifference thereto on the part of your employes or, perhaps, their interest in concealing accidents. And the lack will probably exist until some action is taken to obviate it. I have repeatedly offered assistance to such an end.

Why you write that you "cannot merely on grounds of policy settle any of these Indian claims" you will pardon me for being unable to understand. I have argued in this matter (as some do with regard to all concerns), that it would be politic to do rightly i.e. for the Company to settle these just claims fairly and without all this delay. I certainly have not a[r]gued in favor of, and would not uphold on any grounds, the settlement of an unjust claim, of which nature I have not the slightest suspicion you will find one, nor do I believe that the mere fact of your being without verification for which, — from the clai[m]ants, at least, — you have not sought — will support such an inference. If the Indians are interviewed I believe they will convince, of the justness of their claim, any person who may be employed to conduct the operation.

(Sgd) Peter Ronan
U.S. Indian Agent

I would merely add in this connection that in the case of these Indians it can hardly be accepted as a valid excuse, for non-payment by the company, the absence of proofs, — of the Killing of cattle, — in the hands of the latter when no opportunity has been given the Indians of presenting them.

Very few marks of hostility to the company have as yet been exhibited by the Indians but the Keeping such in abeyance has been no light task and I desire to record with you, as I have done with the Company, my protest against any responsibility on my part, should such occur, unless these claims receive honest and speedy attention.

Very Respectfully
Your obedient Servant
Peter Ronan
U.S. Indian Agent.

Enclosure. This handwriting was particularly hard to read, especially for names. This is the best transcription the editor can give:

[List] 1

Animals Killed and crippled by N.P.R.R.

August '83

One red steer Killed near the Ferry which Antone Rivais ran during construction of N.P.R.R. P. Corcory who is now believed to be stationed at Arlee examined and buried the animal. Big Leo Owner. Value $50.00. Interview D. McDonald for particulars.

Leon Sayti, one two year old steer Killed in August.

Antone Rivase one cow Killed August 2d 1883.

Antone Rivaise one steer, Aug 30. Ravalli.

September 83

A McSumes & Son one horse crippled for life damages $5.00.

Jos. Finlay, owner. Two yearling cattle Killed.

Two horses belonging to Pi-Ell-Ee-nyme. Killed at Little Salmons ranch branded *ℓ* on right hip. Witness Little Salmon and Pierre Matte. Killed either on night of 11th or morning of 12th of September. Value @ $30.00 — $60.00.

A white milch cow branded Q. R. on left hip Killed on night of 13th September about 3 miles below Jocko Station. Supposed to have been Killed by passenger train. Owner Octave Rivais. Witness A. Rivais. Value $60.00.

6 year old milk cow Killed by [up ?] passenger train below Duncan on Sep 28th. Seen by Section hands who took the meat value $60.00. Dominic owner.

Killed near T. Finlay's house one calf. Witness Mrs. [Tremon T. Matrus ?]. Value $20.00. about 29th. owner Antoie Finlay.

One cow and calf Killed about ¾ of a mile below Aix Morrizuiu's house. Cow branded ⱽ. Calf branded ⌀. Supposed to have been Killed by passenger train about 9 P.M. on 7th Sept. Witnesses Pend Orelle Jim and Sam. Owner Curtois Finlay. Value both animals $70.00.

Killed on 29th Septr. a calf belonging to T. Finlay at his house, Six miles west of Arlee. Wants $20.00.

Novr. 83

One 1½ year old hiefer one mile east of Arlee. Skinned by Louis Vielly. Value $25.00. Owner Chas Allard.

Decr. '83

Alick Morrigeau two large cows.

Killed on morning of 11th by down train one black work horse below the bridge crossing the Pend Orielle. Owner Widow Theresse. Witness Deaf Usel ah and Section hands. Value $50.00.

One heifer below Duncan. Witnesses Antone and Vitteel. Value $30.00. Owned by C. Allard.

One 3 year old steer near Antone Rivais house. Witness Anton and Vitteel. Value $40.00. Owned by C. Allard.

Dec. 24 below and near Duncan one cream work horse. Owner Jos. Soo chek. Witness Section foreman. Value $80.00.

Jany '84

On 7th one milk cow Killed by Pay Car, causing loss of 2 mos. calves, below Ravalli. $55.00. Owner C. Allard.

On 20th at Pete Matte's place one 3 year old milk cow badly crippled and one calf Killed. Also one cow Killed. Value $85.00. Owned by Chas. Allard.

In-to-Kall Lame man 5 head of horses Killed.

A. Rivase one cow in Jany.

Alick Morregeau one large cow.

February '84

Killed 29th by eastern bound passenger train at 4 o'c P.M. in the owners field. One work horse belonging to Isadore Laderooutes 4 miles below Arlee. Seen by section hands. 1000# work horse. Value $75.00.

One steer crippled at Isadore Laderooutes. Required carrying feed, water &c. Damage $15.00. Supposed to be in Feby. '84. Owner C. Allard.

March '84

Killed two horses and crippled one. One valued at $100.00. Another at $60.00. Damages cripple 10. Total $170.00. Gustin owner.

Milk cow Killed by train about 9 o'c P.M. about two miles east of Duncan belonging to Rivais. Value $55.00.

White cow branded A. R. owner A. Rivais valued her at $60.00. Note Reported that The agent at Duncan notified Indian who owned the cow that he (the agent) would sell the meat to chinamen from which he thought he could realize twelve (12) dollars and that that sum would be tendered to owner and if not accepted would probably be the only recompense offered. Noted for further investigation.

Killed on 19th of March near Duncan after Sun down by West bound passenger train one spotted cream 3 yr old gentle milk cow at Maximes house and owned by him. Dragged by cars. Value $60.00.

Belonging to Chief Arlee one milk cow was Killed on Tuesday evening March 11 – 84 above Arlee Station about one mile from depot. valued at $50.00. Arlee also had a yearling steer Killed on same night that Deaf Louis had steer Killed which failed to be reported.

Jos. McSeems Son one cow Killed.

Ki Mi, P. Mattes father in law yearling steer.

A. Porrier one cow crippled for life damage $20.00.

One 3 yr. old steer Killed one mile below Jocko. C. Allard owner $40.00

Killed one yearling heifer at 8 o'c on Mar 17 by Ft. train. Owner C. Plant.

George [Chim Kamie ?] owner. Killed on Tuesday night Mar 11 near mouth of Missoula River. One large brown American horse (Stud) brand on right shoulder ⌐𝒪. Valued at $100.00. Also two mares one of Large size the other small. Valued at 25 each, $50.00.

Killed on same night and at same place two large mares at $45.00 each belonging to Penama wife of George [Chim Kamie ?]. Reported Mar. 13/84.

April '84

Usetah one horse.

Usetah two horses.

C. Plant heifer Killed.

May 10th 1884

About 10th Killed in Allards field.

One roan Amr. mare with foal $25.00.

One Iron grey hf breed horse $75.00.

One yearling Amr. Colt $50.00.

All owned by C. Allard.

June '84

One milk cow Killed in the beginning of June. Witness Mr. Winston R. R. contractor. Mr. said to have noted down particulars soon after Killing. value $50.00. Alick Morregeau supposed owner.

One riding horse belonging to Alex Decron. Value $40.00.

* * * * * *

[List] 2
Animals Killed and Crippled by N.P.R.R. Second list.
December '83

On 2d one heifer just below Duncan and one steer near Antone Rivase. Killed. Witness Antone & Vieteel. C. Allard owner.

Same date as above one cow four year old belonging to Alick Morregeau. Killed. Witness L. Brown.

January 84

On 10th or 11th one 3 year old gentle cow belonging to David Couture. Killed by Frt train going east about 11 o'c near Arlee Station. Witness Esparnot and Peter Ving.

One cow Killed a little below Arlee by same train as above. On 7th. C. Allard owner.

Killed on 7th milk cow (causing loss of calf) belonging to C. Allard by pay car (engineer of which is accused of Killing several. Not trying to decrease speed.[)] Reported by section hands below Ravalli. $55.00.

One Cow belonging to Alick Morregeau at his house Killed on 11th by freight train going east before noon.

One of C. Allard's was Killed at Jocko on 11th. Same train as above.

Cow reported Killed on 9th 4 miles west of Arlee. Owners name could not be ascertained by section boss. Killed by train going west 6.40 o'c P.M. Valued at 40.00. On shaws memoranda and list reported.

Killed for Ki Mee one steer see D. McDonald for particulars.

February 84

Alick Matte owner. In his field on 13th 6 year old milk cow by engine going west with car and caboose. Value $60.00.

Also owned by A. Matte badly crippled at same place as above one young cow. Damage $25.00.

On 23rd one mile below Victor a white horse belonging to Usetah Ex chotshim for which he was offered by Lareau $100.00.

Lately this Usetah &cs brother named April lat-tioni-veie had his leg broken. Below Paradize.

On 18th Killed in A. Poildeus field and dragged on cow catcher to Jocko Station a cow belonging to Alick Morregeau. Supposed to be by freight train at 6 o'c in morning.

March '84

On 1st to the south of the Morie trestle by train coming west a little after dark. One work horse belonging to Big Sam and one work horse rendered useless. Value $120.00.

May '84

Crippling her badly and Killing her calf a gentle milk cow belonging to Alex Matt about two miles east of Arlee on May 4th by local passenger train going west, say at 5 o'c P.M. Value $30.00.

Supposed to have been Killed May 24th by local passenger train going west about 6 P.M. One horse belonging to Arlee some six miles west of Arlee Station. Witness Te-nomue.

Jos. La pinos Whea Gein damaged two ribs broken. An ankle broken and one unjointled & crippled for life. Letter D. McDonald.

August '84

On Sunday 10th Aleck Morregeau lost a three year old steer below his house.

On monday 11th Killed by a western bound freight train (3 miles below Duncan Station) one pinto work horse branded "M" belonging to Eneas-In-cha-chi-aken. Value $70.00.

At same time and place and same owner as above one colt. Value $10.00.

Evening of 22d one large horse Killed belonging to Felicite (Ales Roman Noze) for value &c see Duncan McDonald.

September 6, 1884
LR 17,394/1884, RG 75, National Archives, Washington, D.C.

United States Indian Service,
Flathead Agency,
September 6th, 1884.

Hon. Commissioner of Indian Affairs
Washington, D.C.

Sir

While having the honor to acknowledge receipt of your communication "L. 6629 14589 Auth. 8366/ 84" of 29 Ult., I beg to State that I am not clear as to my understanding of your wishes as Contained therein, and therefore beg an explanation.

Authority is granted me to expend a Sum of Three thousand dollars in the purchase of flour, oats, wheat and potatoes to be "delivered on the Reservation."

The inference, therefore, is that this Amount is to be applied Solely for the benefit of Flatheads, who remove hither from the Bitter-root Valley, but as the Honorable Secretary of the Interior expressed his intention of also aiding those Indians who decided to remain in Bitter-root, and as I am, of course, very anxious to avoid any mistake, I request information as to whether Such inference is correct.

Any Supplies to be bought for the last mentioned people will require purchase and deliver in the neighborhood of Stevensville, Missoula County — such being much the most economical method.

The "list of articles" mentioned in your letter as enclosed therewith, I regret to Say, — as it might have elucidated the question, — was not So enclosed.

While writing on this Subject permit me the liberty of Stating that I consider it will be the better plan to make the purchase referred to, as Soon as possible after the completion of harvesting both in order to avoid any increase in price, which generally takes place in Spring, and for the Still Stronger reason that I Shall be in a position to Say to the Indians (who, from the necessary delay in action, have exhibited Some want of confidence) — "there are the Seeds &c., provided for you by the government, and ready to be distributed when you are prepared to make proper use of them; — now Settle down and Show your anxiety and will to raise crops."

Still, I believe that the issues of Oats, wheat and Some other Articles Should not be made until Spring, or until proof is given that they will be used as intended and not Sold to gratify temporary desires.

Again, as the grain and potatoes will probably be purchased in Small lots from farmers, who, from ignorance or otherwise, would object to the acceptance of Certified Vouchers, I respectfully request your views as to my being placed in funds for the purpose of making Cash payments.

Very respectfully
Your Obedient Servant
Peter Ronan
U.S. Indian Agent.

September 12, 1884
LR 18,029/1884, RG 75, National Archives, Washington, D.C.

> The failure of the railroad company to settle damage claims on the reservation led to vandalism against railroad property.[44] Ronan continued to lobby for quicker settlement of the claims. They were finally paid during November 1884.
>
> Ronan called on the U.S. Army at Fort Missoula for assistance in forcing a group of Spokane Indians off the reservation.[45]

United States Indian Service,
Flathead Agency,
Sep. 12, 1884.

Hon. Commissioner of Indian Affairs
Washington, D.C.

Sir:

For your information I have the honor herewith to enclose copy of a letter addressed to J. B. Cable, Division Superintendent of the Northern Pacific Railroad Co. in response to a letter of inquiry from him in regard to Indian depredations on the line of the Northern Pacific Railroad through this reservation.

Very Respectfully
Your Obedient Servant
Peter Ronan
U.S. Indian Agent.

Enclosure:

United States Indian Service,
Flathead Agency,
Sept. 12th, 1884.

J. B. Cable
Division Supt. N. P. R. Railroad
Missoula M.T.

Dear Sir:

In reply to your favor of the 9th, I would state that I am of the opinion after an examination into the circumstances attending the burning of your wood shed at Jocko Station, that it was not set on fire by any camp of Indians, as there was no encampment near that place on the night of the fire. This fact I am informed of by an old Indian named "Stanislaus" who has a little ranch near the Jocko Station and lives there with his family. I consider from years of dealing with Indians, that the old man and family are reliable and feel assured he would let me Know if suspicion attached to any Indian. I therefore am of the opinion if the shed was set on fire it was done by a secret enemy, but not done as any open hostile act by the Indians of this reservation. As stated by your Agent at Arlee, I have no doubt but some Indians smarting under what they consider a great wrong on the part of the Company in delaying or refusing to pay for their stock which are being Killed by trains, have uttered threats and unless the Company see fit to amicably adjust those claims, some of which are standing for two years, I see no way morally or physically to prevent such threats. My correspondence with the Claim Agent of the company has been evasive on his part and unsatisfactory to the Indians and I have laid the matter before the Commissioner of Indian Affairs and the Secretary of the Interior, partly in justice to the Indians and partly to relieve myself from responsibility should anything occur from neglect of the Company to adjust the proper claims of the Indians for stock Killed by the Company's trains upon their Reservation, which was distinctly promised to them, not only by the Company's Attorney, the commissioner from Washington, but by the Governor of the Territory in a speech to the Indians in August of last year. I think however your Agent at Arlee is wrong if he states that Chief Arlee made any hostile threats. That old man is now out at the head of the Jocko hunting and was in the mountains two weeks before the fire and consequently could have had nothing to do with it. Further I would state that the new settlement of claims above alluded to worries the old man who feels that uncontrollable young men, exasperated by the loss of their stock for which they get no satisfaction from the company may commit some act which will involve his people in trouble. This reflection I repeat worries the old man and he might have said some hasty thing to your Agent, but I assure you that he seconds me in every way in his power to Keep the Indians from doing an overt act, and councils them to patience and forbearance until their losses are looked into by the Hon. Commissioner of Indian Affairs, to whom they have appealed. And now I trust you will excuse me if in this connection I again refer to the demoralizing effect which the carrying to this reservation and dumping off here by your trains, drunken outlaws and gamblers from the lower country tribes, which is daily being done notwithstanding I have been assured a stop would be put to it and none allowed to travel unless they had a proper pass, or were Indians of character who travelled for legitimate purposes and paid their way. Those reprobate Indians after being dumped off here, are refused passage back unless they hold a pass from me which I give them in order to get them away from this reservation and back to the country they came from: but they tell me they have no trouble getting back here. Only yesterday I had an illustration of this: Two strange Indians asked me for a pass to go beyond Spokane and asked how they got up here. One of the Indians exhibited a piece of paper on which was written in pencil a recommendation to railroad men for the Indian and asking for him their good offices and signed "Dick the Tough." The Indian said he got to Spokane from Ainsworth on that paper but was compelled to pay to get from that place here. This is the first instance of paying fare I have heard of among the numerous arrivals here, but trust it will be enforced hereafter. If the lower country Indians are prohibited from coming here without proper passes it will Keep them at home, and I will have very little trouble in controlling the legitimate Indians of the reserve if the company will see they they [sic] are paid for stock Killed on the reservation.

Of course you are aware that I was compelled last week to call upon the commanding officer at Fort Missoula to assist with soldiers to run off or arrest a drunken set of Indians from the Spokane country who murdered an Indian of this reserve in one of their brawls. Your shed was burned the night after said brawl, which occurred on the Jocko seven or eight miles above the station where the fire occurred, and it was my theory that incencensed [sic] at your train men for not taking them back without passes, after delivering them here, they might have set fire to the shed; however of this I have no proof, and only give it as a suspicion. The old Indian before spoken of who lives near the station claims the fugitives did not stop there when making their escape and consequently did not fire the place.

Yours Respectfully
(Sgd) Peter Ronan
U.S. Indian Agent.

October 20, 1884
LR 20,677/1884, RG 75, National Archives, Washington, D.C. The plans and esti-mates Ronan refers to were not filed with the letter.

United States Indian Service,
Flathead Agency,
Oct. 20th, 1884.

Hon. Commissioner Indian Affairs
Washington, D.C.

Sir:

Reffering [sic] to your communication of Oct. 7th {F19011} I have the honor to transmit herewith plans and estimates for the erection of the buildings needed for the Bitterroot Flathead Indians who have recently removed to this reservation; In this connection I would respectfully state that inasmuch as the labor of the Indians will be required in conveying the irrigating ditch upon the plateau selected by them for occupation, and of the Agency employés in their necessary duties I can hardly see how I can employ them also at the erection of the buildings in question but will assuredly make the most of their services in the premises. I therefore respectfully submit that the most economical plan would be to contract for the erection of the same and should the Hon. Commissioner deem it proper to approve of the plans etc enclosed that he grant me the necessary authority to commence operations at once as winter will rapidly close in. I would add however that for the present it will only be necessary to erect homes for the families already removed here, say ten in all, the balance to be built at such time as the Hon. Commissioner may deem most appropriate after the arrival of the expected additional families.

> Very Respectfully
> Your Obedient Servant
> Peter Ronan
> U.S. Ind. Agt.

November 22, 1884
LR 22,714/1884, RG 75, National Archives, Washington, D.C.

> On December 5, 1884, the Commissioner of Indian Affairs granted Ronan authority to issue monthly rather than weekly rations to the Bitterroot Salish.[46]

> United States Indian Service,
> Flathead Agency,
> November 22d, 1884.

Hon. Commissioner of Indian Affairs
Washington, D.C.
Sir,

I have the honor to submit that in my opinion it would be a matter of economy and advantage to issue rations to the Bitter Root Flatheads monthly instead of weekly as has been my practice, by making such issues I could readily collect the heads of all the families, supply them with their proportion of the articles furnished for them, and save valuable time in reducing the number of days occupied in such business to one per month and necessarily the expense incident to the reduced number of visits, and therefore respectfully ask the Hon. Commissioner for the necessary authority in the premises.

> Very Respectfully
> Your obt. svt.
> Peter Ronan
> U.S. Indian Agent.

December 30, 1884
LR 274/1885, RG 75, National Archives, Washington, D.C.

> Ronan continued to lament the negative law and order effects of the policy of undermining the chiefs and traditional tribal social controls. He claimed the Christmas 1884 general council of tribal members supported his call for a strengthened tribal police and court system under the agent's control. Unfortunately we have no Indian sources to confirm this.[47] The new police force and judges were soon involved in a power struggle with the traditional chiefs. For more about the case of Koonsa Finley see the annotation to Ronan's December 1, 1882, letter.

> United States Indian Service,
> Flathead Agency,
> December 30th, 1884.

Hon. Commissioner of Indian Affairs
Washington, D.C.

Sir,

Up to present date, I have tried to control matters on this reservation, by the aid of a volunteer force of Indian Police, and until the advent of the railroad, found it very efficient, but there is now a change in the condition of things which require constant vigilance in order to hunt down and punish Indian depredators from other reservations, as well as the outlaws of the tribes of this reserve. Every Spring and Fall brings a gang of Indian outlaws from Spokane, and the lower Columbia who come for no other purpose than to gamble with the Indians of this place for horses or any other property, and indulge in wild carousals, whiskey is obtainable in every town and village from off the reservation, and the Indians while under its influence are liable to commit any crime. Every year I have been compelled to call upon the military authorities to aid in driving this class off the reserve, but as there seems to be no other punishment but to expel them, they return. If I make prisoners of them, and turn them over to the County Officials, they are released on the plea of non-jurisdiction over Indian reserves, if I turn them over to the military authorities, there is an order from the Commandant of the District prohibiting their confinement in the military guardhouse. If I arrest a murderer, as in the case of Koonsa, as fully reported to you at the time, the redhanded murderer is turned loose upon the reservation, but a decision of a judge of the United States Court, "That the criminal had been tried by tribal law" and therefore "was not amenable to the laws of the United States." The said tribal law would probably give to the relations of the murdered man a horse or a gun, and the murderer roams over the reservation a terror to peaceable Indians, as well as to the Agent and his Employes, as Koonsa the murderer is doing to day.

Recently outrages were committed along the line of the Northern Pacific R. R. on this reserve; in one instance a switch was thrown open, or left open by carelessness, and a train ditched, causing no loss of life, but great trouble and expense to the company; a large wood shed was also burned down, and petty annoyances such as shooting insulators off the telegraph poles and the throwing of stones at passing trains, the latter is Known to have been done by Indian boys, and the shooting of telegraph insulators by Indians and also by passengers on Emigrant trains, who were seen by employes of the Company amusing themselves in that way, while the trains were delayed or side tracked on the Reservation.

But as to the opening of the switch, or the burning of the shed, although I devoted my time to a thorough investigation, I failed to learn anything which would convince me of the probable guilt of either Whiteman or Indians. The Company Sent detectives here to unravel the matter, and they Stated to me that they had the evidence from the Missioner in charge of St. Ignatius Mission which would prove that Indians burned the shed. I communicated at once with that gentleman, and herewith attach correspondence.

At a General Council of the Indians which was held on Christmas Day, the whole matter was fully discussed, and the Indians as a Nation deplore the outrageous actions of individuals and pledged themselves to aid me in every way in the suppression of such acts. They are now willing to disband their volunteer force, and ask me to organize a regular force of uniformed and paid police, who will obey my orders, and do everything in their power conducive to friendliness towards the Railroad Company, who have So justly and honorably treated them in the Settlement of all claims, and the privilege of free transportation over certain limitations of their line.

They also desire to be in a position to arrest Indian gamblers and outlaws who come here yearly as before stated, and compel them to return to their homes, without calling in the aid of the military authorities; and to preserve peace and good order among the tribes.

In order to carry out these plans in an efficient manner, I desire authority to form a police force of at least nine privates and three officers with whatever pay, clothing and rations the Hon. Commissioner may judge proper to allow, as the Indians and half breeds whom I will Select for this duty will be chosen from among the best characters, who have families to support, it is to be hoped that they will be dealt with liberally in order that a good portion of their time can be given to their duties.

Very Respectfully,
Your obt. svt.
Peter Ronan
U.S. Indian Agent.

First enclosure:

United States Indian Service,
Flathead Agency,
December 15th, 1884.

Rev. L. Van Gorp, S.J.
St. Ignatius Mission
    Dear Friend
    On Sunday night last two young men who claim to act as detectives and sent out by the R. R. Company, to look up depredations on the line, informed me that they had positive information that Indians burned the wood shed at the Jocko last summer. At the time of that occurrence I made as thorough an investigation as I could and found no evidence leading to the conviction of Indians, and reported that while Indians might have done it, the fire might also have been caused from sparks from the engine in that very dry season, or the work of incendiarism might as well have been perpetrated by tramps of whom there were many going down the road, at all events so far as I was concerned I could not unravel the mystery.

The Young men alluded to, asserted, as stated, that it was positively Known who set the place on fire, that Father Van Gorp had so stated, and of course could say who the Indians were. As I fully determined to do all in my power to bring any depredators of the road to justice, and to demand their delivery to me by the tribes for punishment by Territorial law, I trust you will furnish me any information you may have which will lead to the arrest of the guilty parties.

Very Respectfully,
Your obt. svt
(Sgd) Peter Ronan
U.S. Indian Agent.

Second enclosure:

Copy.

St. Ignatius Mission, Decr. 17th 1884.

Major P. Ronan

Dear Friend,

Yours of the 15th inst. duly received I can say nothing about the burning of the shed except that it was reported in the camp here that it was done by Indians, some attributing it to the murderers of Joseph, others to saying it was done by Indians who were mad with the R. R. for allowing those roughs to travel up and down, carrying whiskey, which led to the fighting etc and Killing of Joseph.

Respectfully Yours
(Sd) L. Van Gorp, S.J.

The Bitterroot Salish delegation to Washington, D.C., 1884: *back row, left to right,* John Hill, Peter Ronan, and Michel Revais; *middle row,* Antoine Moiese, Chief Charlo, and Louis Vanderburg; *front,* Thomas Abel Adams.
Photograph by John K. Hillers.
Montana Historical Society Photograph Archives, Helena, Montana, negative 954-526.

Photographic Tour of the Flathead Reservation, 1884

Photographs by F. Jay Haynes

In 1884, F. Jay Haynes toured the Flathead Indian Reservation and compiled a portfolio of reservation scenes. His work included many scenic views as well as shots of St. Ignatius Mission, the Flathead Indian Agency, and Indian farms. Fortunately Haynes' photograph collection has been preserved in the Photographic Archives of the Montana Historical Society in Helena and provides us with a unique visual tour of the Flathead Indian Reservation during Peter Ronan's term as agent.

During the 1880s, F. Jay Haynes was the official photographer for the Northern Pacific Railroad Company and the Yellowstone National Park Company. Based in Fargo, North Dakota, he traveled the railroad and surrounding area in a specially designed studio railroad car to take promotional photographs for the Northern Pacific publicity department. The railroad used Haynes photographs to attract passengers and, especially, settlers to the towns, mines, and agricultural areas around the Northern Pacific Railroad line.

Haynes made his living selling copies of his photographs to the public, and he left a legacy of many of the earliest views of the Pacific Northwest. In 1884, photographic equipment and supplies were bulky and fragile. Haynes had to haul his camera, photographic plates, and supplies across the reservation by stage or wagon. The resulting record of life on the Flathead Indian Reservation in 1884 provides us with unique and valuable historical evidence.

Haynes photographs of scenic features on the reservation are not reproduced here. The editor has selected views of reservation landmarks and life. All photographs in this section were taken by F. Jay Haynes and are reproduced courtesy of the Montana Historical Society Photograph Archives, Helena, Montana.

References: Freeman Tilden, *Following the Frontier with F. Jay Haynes: Pioneer Photographer of the Old West* (New York: Alfred A. Knopf, 1964); Montana Historical Society, *F. Jay Haynes, Photographer* (Helena, Montana Historical Society Press, 1981).

Flathead Indian Agency, Jocko, Montana.
(MHS H-1271)

Major Peter Ronan and family. Indian agent's residence, Jocko, Montana.
(MHS H-1333)

Mt. Ronan, Mission Range. Peter Ronan standing at left. (MHS H-2011)

Above: Flathead Agency sawmill with Indian crew. (MHS H-1334)
Below: Flathead Reservation Indian farm (MHS H-1341).

A band of Flathead Indian ponies. (MHS H-1340)

Jocko Valley, Flathead Reservation. (MHS H-2009)

Above: Indian farmer, Flathead Reservation. (MHS H-1335).
Below: Flathead Indian chief and family. (MHS H-1337).

Above: St. Ignatius chapel, exterior. (MHS H-1346).
Below: St. Ignatius chapel, interior. (MHS H-1347).

Above: St. Ignatius boys school. (MHS H-1348).
Below: St. Ignatius girls school. (MHS H-1349).

Flathead Indian band, St. Ignatius Mission. (MHS H-1350).

Above: Trader's residence (Alex L. DeMers). (MHS H-1352).
Below: Trader's store, St. Ignatius Mission. (MHS H-1351).

Mission Valley, Flathead Reservation. (MHS H-1345)

Above: Flathead Lake, looking north. (MHS H-1360).
Below: Trader's store, Foot of Flathead Lake. (MHS H-1365).

1885

February 12, 1885a
LR 3,554/1885, SC 190, RG 75, National Archives, Washington, D.C.

Charlo felt betrayed when he learned that the Bitterroot Salish would only receive the 51 land patents that had been issued under Congressman James Garfield's 1872 agreement. During the negotiations in Washington, D.C., in early 1884, he had understood the Salish were to receive 103 or 104 patents for farms. The confusion could not help but add to his disgust at the mistreatment the Bitterroot Salish received from yet another government representative.

The Commissioner of Indian Affairs decided on May 8, 1885, that land patents made out to the Salish who had moved to Jocko or had died without heirs could not be reassigned without Congressional action. See Ronan's letter of November 6, 1885, for more detail about the Salish Bitterroot land patents.

In his reply to Ronan's report, the Commissioner did suggest that arrangements be made to file Indian homestead claims on Salish farms that were not protected by the 51 patents already issued. No record, however, has been found indicating any Indian homestead claims were ever filed in the Bitterroot Valley.

The Commissioner's decision regarding Bitterroot Salish liability for Missoula County taxes was an example of the bureaucratic double talk that frustrated Charlo. In Washington, D.C., the Secretary of the Interior had assured Charlo that the Salish would not be forced to pay taxes. The Commissioner reinterpreted this promise to mean the Salish would be exempted from taxes only on their land — not on their personal property such as cattle, horses, and equipment.[1]

The white man who filed a homestead claim in 1885 on land farmed by a Bitterroot Indian was Peter M. Lafontaine. In the 1870s and 1880s, he operated a flour mill in the Bitterroot, but in the 1880 census he gave his occupation as farmer.[2]

United States Indian Service,
Flathead Agency,
February 12th, 1885.

Hon. Commissioner of Indian Affairs
Washington, D.C.

Sir,

I herewith have the honor of enclosing a petition sent to me by Charlos, Chief of Flathead Indians, now residing in the Bitter Root Valley. It will be seen that Charlos still retains the idea that he was promised one hundred and four patents for lands, instead of the number surveyed for his Indians, fifty one, which I Still hold. In a letter addressed to you bearing date March 12th, 1884, I had the honor of alluding to this matter as follows:

"At one of the meetings at the office of the Hon. Secretary of the Interior, I stated that it was my opinion that the fifty one patents in my possession, were all that has been issued, but information was then offered that there had been issued one hundred and three or four, and that if they were not all in my possession, some would be found in one of the Departments at Washington. The Indians naturally returned with the impression that this information was correct, and it will require considerable tact to eradicate the idea."

Again in my special report in regard to a Council held with Charlos and his band of Bitter Root Flatheads, bearing date March 27th, 1884, that Chief stated in the Council that he "had been told that there were 103 or 104 land patents issued, while I stated there were only 51, and that if he had sufficient money he would return to Washington, and ask the Hon. Secretary if his words were to be depended upon, I informed him that it was a private and unofficial gentleman (Captain John Mullin [Mullan]) who had made the statement, and that the necessary data, not being immediately at hand, neither the Hon. Secretary nor myself were then in a position to contradict it, but that I had advised that the matter be examined into, and that as a result, I had a letter with the Hon. Secretary's own signature, which was equivalent to his own spoken words, and that therein I was notified that 51 was the correct number. I then produced the letter which was read by a few of the tribe capable of So doing, having in addition my remarks sustained by the rest of the delegation which visited Washington."

The letter above alluded to bears date at the Office of the Secretary of the Interior March 1st, 1884.

In regard to the wishes of Charlos, as stated in his petition I will offer a few suggestions.

1st. As the Indians desire to accept the patents in my possession, a proper map of the Bitter Root Land District should be furnished, so as to be able to properly show the boundaries of the same, and if the original patentee is dead the next of Kin, or in case no heir survives, then the patent be transferred to any Indian, being the head of a family, whom a majority of the Indians of Charlos Band may select, with the consent of the Department or Agent whichever may be deemed most advisable.

2nd. Charlos is correct in stating that under the Garfield Agreement several Indians removed to this reservation, abandoning their right to the Bitter Root patents and have made permanent homes here, and the lands that have been granted to them in the Bitter Root Valley is [sic] now unoccupied and will still continue to be owned by them, they holding said land under patents containing a clause preventing them from alienation. It would in my opinion be well to transfer such lands to any Indian of Charlos' band who might select to live upon and cultivate the same.

3rd. In connection with Circular #133, dated Washington July 28th, 1884, published for the information and guidance of Indian Agents in relation to the appropriation of $1000.00 "to enable Indians to make selection of homesteads and the necessary proofs at the proper land office" without payment of fees or commissions on account of entries or proofs, I respectfully submit, that in as much as the Register and Receiver of the Land Office are located at Helena, 150 miles distant from the Bitter Root Valley, and the Indians desirous of entering homesteads as provided in said act of Congress are poor and unable to defray the expenses of such a long journey, it would be a matter not only of justice in aiding them to take advantage of its beneficent provisions, but of economy (as the Indians would look to the Government to defray such travelling expenses for the reasons stated) that such entries and proofs be made either before some attorney authorized by the Land Office to perform such duties at Stevensville, in the Bitter Root Valley, or before the Clerk of the U.S. Court at Missoula, and a sum sufficient to defray the actual expense thereof be placed to my credit in order to accomplish the same, and upon presentation of the proper vouchers the expenditure of said sum be allowed.

4th. While at the office of the Hon. Secretary of the Interior, last winter, in conference with Charlos Band, complaint was made by the Indians to the Hon. Secretary that each year they were annoyed by the County Commissioners, and other officers of Missoula County, who claimed that the Indians of the Bitter Root Valley were amenable to taxation, and that said tax would be levied and payment of same enforced. The Hon. Secretary stated emphatically to the Indians that they would not be forced to pay taxes, and I trust this matter will be carefully looked into that I may be advised how to proceed should the county officers attempt to force payment of taxes from Indians living in Bitter Root Valley.

In conclusion I would state thirteen families of Charlos' Band have already removed to the Agency in compliance with arrangements made by me, under instructions from the Hon. Secretary of the Interior, and that houses are now under course of construction for them, and I expect to have them comfortably settled and cultivating the soil of the Reservation this season, and that more families will continue to follow until a large majority, if not all of the tribe will finally settle here. But I would suggest that the petition of Charlos be acted upon so that the Indians will have nothing to complain of in the future, in regard to their rights to the lands of the Bitter Root Valley. It is my humble opinion that this course will have a tendency to show the Indians that they can place reliance upon the promises and good will of the Indian Department and its servants, and when their rights in the Bitter Root are secured, they will be prepared to dispose of the same as the Department may direct and remove to the Reservation.

Very respectfully
Your obt. svt.
Peter Ronan
U.S. Indian Agent.

Enclosure in handwriting of Jerome D'Aste, S.J.:

Stevensville, Feb. 7th, 85

Major P. Ronan
U.S. Indian Agent
    Major

    Last winter I and some of my Indians came back from Washington to Bitter-Root valley with our hearts gladdened thinking we had secured for our families and tribe a home, in this valley, having been promised by the Government one hundred Patents. But we have been Sadly disappointed when, after coming home we heard from you that only fifty one Patents were offered to our people. Waiting in vain for the fulfillment of the Government's promise, I refused until now to receive the Patents already issued for some of my people. I felt bad in thinking, that by receiving those Patents I would exclude a good many of my people from having land in this valley, and that for the only reason that they were not here to give their names as willing to remain here, at the time of Garfield's treaty, and thus secure a farm. But now that I see that not only we are refused what we have been promised, but that white people are trying to take from my people even the few farms we are in possession of in this land of our forefathers, I beg of you to protect us in our rights. Knowing that you have taken so much interest in the welfare of the Indians under your charge, I hope that you will be willing to make the Government acquainted with our needs and wishes.

1. I with my people came to the conclusion to accept the Patents issued so many years ago for some of us. But the lands so patented having been surveyed when most of the Indians were off on the Buffalo hunt, only a few Know where the lines of their respective farms are. Hence I ask that the Government appoint some trusty man to find out for us the lines of such lands, not leaving the whites to take advantage of our ignorance.

2. In the second place we ask, that since we see very little hope of getting the other Patents promised in Washington, last year, at least, the Patents issued for those Flat-Heads, who agreeably to Garfield's treaty, moved to the Jocko, be turned to some of our people who got no land, because they were not here to represent their lands at that time.

3. In the third place I ask that some of our people who for several years are farming on lands which were not surveyed for them, be by the Government protected against those greedy whites, who having come here only lately are trying to jump these lands, though the Indians are living and have improvements on them. There is a case in particular, on eight-mile creek, where a white man, P. Lafountain, pretends by force to take the land from an Indian who has been farming several years and has a house on it. I would ask that the Government would send some trusty man to inquire into the matter, and if found that the Indians have the first right to those lands, that said lands be surveyed for the Indians and Patents issued to them.

4. In the fourth place, since I have been promised, in Washington that we would be exempted from paying taxes, we ask that the Government should look in this matter and see that we be not bothered by County Officers, as they began to do with some of our people.

Thanking you for the help you obtained for our people by getting them wagons, plows, harnesses and provisions, and hoping that you be willing and able to assist us in our present needs, I am with all my people in whose name I send this petition.

Yours Respectfully
Charlos Chief of the
Flat-Head Indians
His signature +

February 12, 1885b
LR 3,725/1885, RG 75, National Archives, Washington, D.C. The proposed "Rules governing the Court of Indian offences" were approved by the Secretary of the Interior on March 2, 1885, and are now filed in the National Archives with 4,436/1885 from the Secretary of the Interior to the Commissioner of Indian Affairs.

> Both this report to Washington and a February 6, 1885, article in *The Weekly Missoulian*, which was probably based on information from Ronan, specified that the judges and the "Rules governing the Court of Indian Offences" were approved by a general council of tribal

members in early February 1885.[3] The new Indian court and police force, paid by the government and under Ronan's control, sparked a power struggle between the new judges and the traditional chiefs.

Of the new judges, Joseph Et-sua-sua-la could not be identified in other sources because Joseph was a common Christian name and several judges named Joseph served overlapping terms. Ronan wrote in March 12, 1885, that the nomination of Francois Chemloo was a clerical error and nominated Louison Quil-quil-sceu-na as the third judge. See the Biographical Sketches for more information about Louison. Baptiste or Partee Kakashee was the leader of the St. Ignatius Mission Indian community for much of the late nineteenth and early twentieth centuries. He was judge in 1885-1889, 1890-1892, 1893-1897, and 1900-1908. He was discharged in 1889, 1892, 1897, and 1908. In his August 1885 annual report, Ronan credited Kakashee with having 100 acres under fence in the Mission Valley and a crop of 300 bushels of wheat and oats. In December 1885, Chief Arlee complained that he had "appointed" Kakashee and the other judges, but the judges had since usurped the authority of the traditional chiefs. According to Arlee, Kakashee was a Flathead who lived with the Pend d'Oreille. In June 1891, Kakashee and the Indian police stationed at St. Ignatius went to Elmo to stop a traditional dance there. Kakashee was the church chief responsible for keeping order at church services in St. Ignatius Mission. In the early twentieth century, he frequently borrowed money from Father Jerome D'Aste and paid it back. In March 1902 he had an argument with D'Aste over the white men hired by the mission as laborers. He apologized to D'Aste the next day. D'Aste was disgusted with Kakashee's encouragement of the 1904 Fourth of July Powwow at St. Ignatius. In 1907, he joined the other reservation chiefs in objecting to the sale of reservation land to white homesteaders. He died in 1922.[4]

The new "Rules" criminalized Indian dances and ceremonies, persecuted traditional healers and spiritual leaders, and went out of the way to protect the property of the Northern Pacific Railroad on the reservation. Ronan was trying to expand the powers of the government agent. He was careful, however, to select judges and policemen who were respected in the tribal community. See Ronan's February 14, 1885, letter.

In this context see Ronan's February 16, 1885, letter requesting funds to erect new jails at St. Ignatius and the Jocko Agency.

United States Indian Service,
Flathead Agency,
February 12th, 1885.

Hon. Commissioner of Indian Affairs
Washington, D.C.

Sir

I have the honor to transmit herewith a code of laws adopted at a Council of the Indians held at this Agency at the organization of the Police force and selection of Judges for the Court of Indian offences, as authorized in your communication marked "A" 274/85, dated Jan'y 12th 1885, in this connection I would respectfully invite the attention of the Hon. Commissioner to the fact that with the exception of the few families of Carlos Band of Bitter Root Flatheads, the Indians of this reservation receive no rations or supplies, except in

return for labor performed, and to the aged and infirm, the withdrawal or withholding of rations necessarily could prove of no benefit, hence other modes of
punishment have been adopted.

I would further respectfully submit that in order to suppress gambling, intoxication, shooting of cattle, and depredations along the line of the Northern
Pacific R. R. Co. the Council adopted rules for the punishment of such crimes
which they have incorporated into the rules already established, no provision
having been made therefor, and I trust the same will meet with the approbation of the Hon. Commissioner.

Very Respectfully
Your obt. svt.
Peter Ronan
U.S. Ind Agent.

Enclosure, which is now filed with 4,436/1885 in the National Archives:
Rules governing the Court of Indian Offences [sic]

1. There shall be established at the Flathead Agency, a tribunal Known as
the "Court of Indian Offences" and the three members of said Court shall be
styled "Judge of the Court of Indian Offences"

The Board of Judges shall consist of:

Joseph

Baptiste Ka-ka-shee

Francois Chem-loo

The Judges herein provided for shall receive no money consideration of
their services in connection with said court.

2. The Court of Indian Offences shall hold at least two sessions in each and
every month, the time and place for holding said sessions to be agreed upon by
the Judges, or a majority of them, and approved by the Agent.

3. The Court as above organized shall hear and pass judgment upon all
such questions as may be presented to it by the Agent or by his approval, and
shall have original jurisdiction over all "Indian Offences" designated as such
in Rules 4, 5, 6, 7 and 8 of these rules. The judgment of the Court may be by
two judges; and that the several orders of the court may be carried into full
effect, the United States Indian Agent is hereby authorized and empowered to
compel the attendance of witnesses at every session of the Court, and enforce,
with the aid of the police, if necessary, all orders that may be passed by the
Court or a majority thereof; but all orders, decrees or judgments of the Court
shall be subject to approval or disapproval by the Agent, and an appeal to and
final revision by the Indian Office; provided that when an appeal is taken to
the Indian office, the appellant shall furnish security satisfactory to the Court
and approved by the Agent, for good and peaceful conduct pending the final
decision of the Indian Office.

4. The "sun-dance" the "war dance" the "scalp dance" and all other so
called feasts assimilating thereto, shall be considered "Indian Offences" and
any Indian found guilty of being a participant in any one or more of these offences shall, for the first offence committed, be punished by withholding from
the person or persons so found guilty by the Court all annuities, at the option
of the Agent, and if found guilty of subsequent offense, shall be incarcerated
in the Reservation prison not exceeding thirty days.

5. Any plural marriage hereafter contracted or entered into by any member of the Indian tribes of this Reservation shall be considered an "Indian

Offense" cognizable by the Court of Indian Offenses, and upon trial and conviction thereof by said Court the offender shall pay a fine of not less than twenty dollars or work at hard labor for a period of twenty days, or both, at the discretion of the Court, the proceeds thereof to be devoted to the benefit of the tribe to which the offender may at the time belong; and so long as the Indian shall continue in this unlawful relation he shall forfeit all right to receive annuities from the Government. And whenever it Shall be proven to the satisfaction of the Court that any member of the tribes fail, without proper cause to support his wife and children, no Government aid in way of Agricultural implements or other articles will be issued to him until such time as satisfactory assurance is given to the Court, approved by the Agent that the offender will provide for his family to the best of his ability.

6. The usual practices of so called "medicine men" shall be considered Indian Offences cognizable by the Court of Indian Offences, and whenever it shall be proven to the satisfaction of the Court that the influence or practice of so called medicine men operates as a hindrance to the civilization of a tribe, or that said medicine man resorts to any artifice or device to Keep Indians under his influence, or shall adopt any means to prevent the attendance of children at the Reservation schools, or shall use any arts of a conjurer to prevent the Indians from abandoning their heathenish rites and customs, he shall be adjudged guilty of an Indian Offense, and upon conviction of any one or more of these specified practices, or any other, in the opinion of the Court of an equally anti-progressive nature, shall be confined in the Reservation prison for a term not less than ten days, or until such time as he shall produce evidence satisfactory to the Court, and approved by the Agent, that he will forever abandon all practices styled Indian Offenses under this rule.

7. Any Indian of this Reservation who shall wilfully destroy, or with intent to steal or destroy, shall take and carry away any property of any value or description, being the property free from tribal interference, of any other Indian or Indians, shall without reference to the value thereof, be deemed guilty of an Indian offense, and, upon trial and conviction thereof by the Court of Indian Offenses, shall be compelled to restore the stolen property to the proper owner, or, in case it shall have been lost or destroyed, the estimated full value thereof, and in any event the party or parties so found guilty shall be confined in the Reservation prison for a term not exceeding thirty days, and it shall not be considered a sufficient and satisfactory answer to any of the offenses set forth in this rule that the party charged was at the time a "mourner" and thereby justified in taking or destroying the property in accordance with the customs or rites of the tribe.

8th. Any Indian or mixed blood who shall pay or offer to pay any money or other valuable consideration to the friends or relatives of any Indian girl or woman, for the purpose of living or cohabitating with said girl or woman, shall be deemed guilty of an Indian Offense, and upon conviction thereof shall forfeit all right to Government aid for a period at the discretion of the Agent, or be imprisoned at the Reservation prison for a period not exceeding sixty days; and any Indian or mixed blood who shall receive or offer to receive any consideration for the purpose hereinbefore specified shall be punished in a similar manner as provided for the party paying or offering to pay the said consideration; and if any Whiteman, Chinaman or Negro shall be found guilty of any of the offences herein mentioned he shall be immediately removed from the Reservation and not allowed to return thereto.

9th. In addition to the offenses hereinbefore enumerated the Court of Indian Offenses shall also have jurisdiction (subject to provisions of Rule 3) of misdemeanors committed by Indians belonging to the reservation, and of civil suits wherein Indians are parties thereto; and any Indian who shall commit any act of outrage along the line of the Northern Pacific Railroad, through the reservation, such as displacing switches, placing obstructions on the track, Shooting at telegraph insulators, cutting the telegraph wire, camping along the right of way at or near the stations reserved to the company by agreement for right of way, or throwing missiles at the trains, shall be punished by imprisonment in the Reservation Jail for not less than twenty days, nor more than ninety days, or by the withholding of all Government aid in way of Agricultural implements or supplies, at the option of the Agent; and any Indian or mixed blood who shall be found intoxicated, or shall sell, exchange, give, barter or dispose of any spirituous, vinous or fermented liquors on the reservation shall be punishable by imprisonment for not less than thirty days nor more than ninety days, or by withholding government aid at the discretion of the court and approval of the Agent; and any member of the tribe who may steal horses or other animals from whites or Indians and drive the same upon the reservation, shall be punishable by imprisonment in the Reservation Jail for a period not less than thirty nor more than ninety days, or by the withholding of government supplies and implements of labor therefrom, at the discretion of the Court and approval of the Agent. Said animals to be advertised in neighboring newspaper, and delivered to the proper owner without delay, when said owner is found.

It shall also be the duty of the Court to suppress gambling, burning of grass, caching horses of travellers or others with a view of extorting money; Killing of stock in revenge for stock breaking into fields poorly protected or fenced in; catching horses not belonging to them and riding such horses a distance more or less great and then letting them go, thus endangering the loss of the horse to the owner. All of the above will be considered Indian offenses and shall be punishable by imprisonment in the Reservation Jail for a period of not less than ten days nor more than thirty days or by the withholding of agricultural implements and government supplies therefrom at the discretion of the Court and approval of the Agent.

The civil jurisdiction of said court shall be the same as that of a justice of the Peace in the Territory of Montana, and the practice in such civil cases shall conform as nearly as practicable to the rules of government of the practice of justices of the peace in said Territory, and it shall also be the duty of the Court to instruct, advise and inform either or both parties to any suit in regard to the requirements of these rules.

Respectfully submitted with the approval of
Peter Ronan
U.S. Indian Agent.

February 14, 1885
LR 3,766/1885, RG 75, National Archives, Washington, D.C.

Note that Ronan made a point of nominating Indian police and judges who were already influential. Ronan was working to change the tribal economy and social structure, but he realized the importance of promoting new tribal leaders who were accepted and respected by other tribal members. Since the police were mature and prominent in their own right, Ronan could not force them to obey orders which would threaten their status in the community.

Ronan nominated ten men as Indian police at Flathead. Those policemen who were identified only by Christian names could not be traced in other records. Of the mixed bloods who were listed with family names, only Peter Finley had further information available. According to Ronan's August 17, 1885, testimony, Finley had 20 horses and 60 cattle. Ronan's August 1885 annual report added that he had 100 acres under fence and produced 100 bushels of wheat and oats in the Mission Valley. In 1889 Peter Finley was granted custody of the mixed blood children of Frank Decker, the deceased agency miller.[5] In 1891 his first wife, Lucy, divorced him in a Montana state court and in 1894 he married Mary Louisa Bouche.[6] Finley was active in horse racing circles in Kalispell and was injured in a racing accident in 1892.[7]

United States Indian Service,\
Flathead Agency,\
February 14th, 1885.

Hon. Commissioner of Indian Affairs\
Washington, D.C.

Sir,

I have the honor to submit for your approval, in connection with the descriptive statement of nominations for the police force authorized in communication from Office Indian marked "A" 274/85 enclosed herewith, the names of the following persons selected to act as Judges of the Court of Indian Offenses, viz;

> Baptiste Ka-Ka-shee\
> Joseph Et-sua-sua-la\
> Louison Quil-quil-sceu-na

I would respectfully state that the indians whose names are submitted for your approval to fill the important office of Judges, are among the most influential best behaved reputable and reliable of the Indians of this reserve.

Very Respectfully,\
Your obt. svt.\
Peter Ronan\
U.S. Ind. Agent.

Enclosed was a form, "Reports Changes in the U.S. Indian Police Service," dated February 11th, 1885, for Flathead Agency. In the original document the information was in tabular form but it has been reproduced here as text:

Pierre, Ind, Officer, Flathead Nation, Pen D'oreille Tribe, born in Montana, married, 3 in family, age 35, 6 feet 1½ inches tall, 204 pounds, 42½ inch chest with lungs inflated, 39 inch chest with lungs not inflated, compensation $8.00 per month.

Salin, Ind, Private, Flathead Nation, Flathead Tribe, born in Montana, married, 5 in family, age 51, 5 feet 9½ inches tall, 250 pounds, 46 inch chest with lungs inflated, 42 inch chest with lungs not inflated, compensation $5.00 per month.

Alex Aslin, HB [Half-blood], Private, Flathead Nation, Pen D'oreille Tribe, born in Montana, married, 2 in family, age 22, 5 feet 8 inches tall, 175 pounds, 41 inch chest with lungs inflated, 38¾ inch chest with lungs not inflated, compensation $5.00 per month.

Modeste Pichet, HB, Private, Flathead Nation, Pen D'oreille Tribe, born in Montana, married, 4 in family, age 29, 5 feet 9½ inches tall, 168 pounds, 41 inch chest with lungs inflated, 38½ inch chest with lungs not inflated, compensation $5.00 per month.

Peter Finlay, HB, Private, Flathead Nation, Flathead Tribe, born in Montana, married, 2 in family, age 36, 5 feet 9 inches tall, 175 pounds, 40½ inch chest with lungs inflated, 37½ inch chest with lungs not inflated, compensation $5.00 per month.

Augustus, Ind, Private, Flathead Nation, Pen D'oreille Tribe, born in Montana, married, 2 in family, age 43, 5 feet 11 inches tall, 158 pounds, 40 inch chest with lungs inflated, 37 inch chest with lungs not inflated, compensation $5.00 per month.

Leo, Ind, Private, Flathead Nation, Pen D'oreille Tribe, born in Montana, married, 2 in family, age 58, 6 feet tall, 160 pounds, 40 inch chest with lungs inflated, 37½ inch chest with lungs not inflated, compensation $5.00 per month.

Paul, Ind, Private, Flathead Nation, Pen D'oreille Tribe, born in Montana, married, 2 in family, age 48, 5 feet 10½ inches tall, 156 pounds, 40 inch chest with lungs inflated, 37 inch chest with lungs not inflated, compensation $5.00 per month.

Johnny, Ind, Private, Flathead Nation, Pen D'oreille Tribe, born in Montana, married, 2 in family, age 46, 5 feet 8½ inches tall, 130 pounds, 39½ inch chest with lungs inflated, 36½ inch chest with lungs not inflated, compensation $5.00 per month.

Eneas, Ind, Private, Flathead Nation, Pen D'oreille Tribe, born in Montana, married, 2 in family, age 37, 5 feet 8½ inches tall, 135 pounds, 39 inch chest with lungs inflated, 36¾ inch chest with lungs not inflated, compensation $5.00 per month.

All can speak the Flathead Pen D'oreille and Kootenais tongues, are men of influence, and possess all the qualifications demanded to make good and efficient members of the police force.

February 16, 1885
LR 3,874/1885, RG 75, National Archives, Washington, D.C.

> The need for new jails followed naturally from a new Indian court and police force. On February 25, 1885, the Commissioner replied that construction funds had been exhausted but "there is no objection to building it [the jail], if it can be done without the expenditure of money."[8]

United States Indian Service,
Flathead Agency,
February 16th, 1885.

Hon. Commissioner of Indian Affairs
Washington, D.C.

Sir,

I have the honor to request that I be authorized to expend a sum not exceeding $300.00 and that the said amount be placed to my credit should it meet with your approval, for the purpose of erecting a new jail at the Mission, the most central point on the Reservation, for the safe Keeping of such prisoners as may be sentenced thereto in accordance with the rules for the government of Indian Courts for the punishment of offenses, my reasons for making this request are, 1st the insecurity of the present jail, being absolutely useless for the safe confinement of any culprit and 2d the inadequate accomodations thereof, even where [sic] it secure.

I would also respectfully request that authority be granted for the erection of a suitable building at the Agency for the temporary confinement of any persons found guilty of any of the offences enumerated in my "Rules for the government for the Court of Indian Offenses["] submitted with my communication of the 14th inst. this structure will need no expenditure of money, the timber and other materials necessary can be furnished from the Agency, and the labor performed by the employes.

> Very Respectfully,
> Your obt. svt.
> Peter Ronan
> U.S. Indian Agent.

March 12, 1885

LR 5,760/1885, RG 75, National Archives, Washington, D.C.

> United States Indian Service,
> Flathead Agency,
> March 12th, 1885.

Hon. Commissioner of Indian Affairs
Washington, D.C.

Sir,

Referring to your communication of March 5th 1885, marked Land E. 3725/4436 — 85 I have the honor to state that the name "Francois["] in Rule I of rules for government of Court of Indian Offences was inserted through a clerical error, and that the Indian, Louison, who was appointed and commissioned is the proper party whose name should appear and does so appear upon the records of this office.

> Very Respectfully
> Your obt. svt.
> Peter Ronan
> US Indian Agent.

March 13, 1885

LR 5,582/1885, SC 55, telegram, RG 75, National Archives, Washington, D.C.

According to newspaper reports, the new Indian police accompanied Ronan to the Horse Plains area and arrested four unnamed Indians who had obstructed the railroad tracks while drinking whiskey. They also arrested a white railroad employee in Horse Plains who was accused of attacking an Indian woman.[9]

Mar 13, 1885

Dated Arlee, Mont
To Secy Interior Washn D.C.

I arrested the Indians with Indian police & have them in indian Jail. I am in receipt of following telegram. Peter Ronan, we congratulate you on the Success of your trip & thank you for the very prompt manner in which you have dealt with the offenders, J. B. Cable, Supt N P R R. The Indians found a barrel of whiskey in the river lost by freighters three years ago, resulted in a drunk which caused disturbance. I found whisky & destroyed it, will report by mail, no trouble now.

Ronan Agt.

May 2, 1885
The New North-West *(Deer Lodge, Mont.), May 8, 1885, page 3, col. 4.*
The Suit Against Agent Ronan.
An Exhibit Showing That the Account Was Balanced Last Year.
(That the matter my be fully understood, we give the following correspondence entire. — Ed. N. N-W.)

United States Indian Service,
Flathead Agency, May 2, 1885.

James H. Mills, Deer Lodge, M.T.:
Dear Sir: the appearance of my name as defendant in a suit brought by the United States against me at two different terms of Court, would, under ordinary circumstances, be annoying, but when my accounts are definitely settled (as per letter enclosed) under my old bond, it is more than annoying to see the same published. Of course I do not lay any blame at your door, but whoever is to blame for thus making me appear as a defendant in a case with the United States, where there is no cause for action, is doing me an injury. Would you please publish a synopsis of enclosed letter in relation to the matter?

Peter Ronan

———

Treasury Department,
Second Auditor's Office.
Washington, D.C., July 18, 1884.

Sir: Your account as Indian Agent under bond of April 6, 1878, showing a balance due United States of $241.65, on which suit in process of commencement, having been reopened by order of the Secretary of the Treasury, in connection with evidence filed by you in regard to property charged as unaccounted for, has been readjusted, and on deposit by you of the $16.50 suspended in the cash account, this office will restate the same, crediting you with the amount of property charged $225.15, thus balancing and closing the account under above bond. Please deposit and transmit vouchers therefor as early as practicable referring to the letter.

Respectfully,
[Signed] O. Ferris, Auditor.
Per C. C. S.

Peter Ronan, Indian Agent,
Flathead Agency, Montana.

June 20, 1885
LR 14,292/1885, RG 75, National Archives, Washington, D.C.

> The human tragedy of mental illness in the nineteenth century touched the Flathead Reservation. Ronan's November 5, 1885, letter on this subject enclosed a letter from tribal member Lorette Pablo arguing that his wife was insane. Whatever combination of mental illness and marital strife Pablo's case represented, there were no mental health facilities on the reservation and the State of Montana was unwilling to bear the cost of treatment. The Commissioner finally replied on November 23, 1885, that there were no facilities available to treat tribal members with mental problems. Ronan had to "make such provision for the care of these people as you are best able."[10] See Ronan's letter of July 25, 1888, about his efforts to deal with another case of mental illness on the reservation.

United States Indian Service,
Flathead Agency,
June 20th, 1885.

Hon. Commissioner of Indian Affairs
Washington, D.C.

Sir,

Referring to your communication of 2d inst. marked C. and E. 12071/1885 relating to the Safe Keeping of demented Indians, I have the honor to enclose herewith copy of correspondence had with Dr C. F. Mussigbrod in charge of the Insane Asylum, as also with Hon. B. P. Carpenter, Governor the Territory, from which you will perceive no arrangements have been effected with them: I would therefore earnestly request that the Hon. Commissioner either make the necessary arrangements for the prompt safe Keeping of the Indians alluded to or issue such authority and instructions as will justify me in doing the same, and would further respectfully state that until I am aware of the point where these Indians will be placed, I can form no idea of the amount needed for their transportation and the cost for their care support and medical attendance.

In relation to the preliminary steps for the commitment of the demented Indians, I have the honor to state that the Territorial laws state explicitly the manner of procedure, but whether they would apply in these particular cases, is, judging from the Governor's letter, a question I cannot, and would rather not attempt to decide.

Very Respectfully,
Peter Ronan
U.S. Indian Agent.

First enclosure:

Warm Springs Asylum
Deer Lodge County, M.T.
Warm Springs, Mont., June 11th, 1885

Mr. P. Ronan Esqu. Flathead Agency

Dear Sir:

In Reply to yours of the 9th I have to state that we have to Receive every one who has been declared insane under the statu[t]es of the Terr. and that the Territory pays for all the patients, for maintenance, care, and medication 8.00 per week or capita. Private patients (insane) we do not admit. If Indians would come under the statu[t]es of the Terr. or not, I do not Know, and I think that you better cor[r]espond with the Governor of the Territory about it.

very Respectfully
Chs. F. Mussigbrod, M.D.

Second enclosure:

Territory of Montana
Executive Department
Helena, June 15, 1885

Hon. Peter Ronan
US Indian Agent
    Dear Sir:
    I have the honor to acknowledge the receipt of your favor of the 13th inst, & thus reply.
    Only persons adjudged insane under the laws of this territory may be cared for in any asylum provided by the Territory, & the Territory is prohibited from asking or receiving any compensation therefor. Revised Statutes M T p. 559, Laws of 13th Session p. 112. Indians dwelling on reservations, & subject to the tribal system of government, do not ordinarily come within the jurisdiction of our courts, & no Insane Asylum has been provided for them by the Territory.

Very respectfully
B. P. Carpenter
Governor.

August 1885

U.S. Commissioner of Indian Affairs, Annual Report of the Commissioner of Indian Affairs *(Washington, D.C.: U.S. Government Printing Office, 1885), pages 126-29.*

Ronan tended to get philosophical in his annual reports laying out his prejudices about traditional Salish and Kootenai economic and cultural activities. Many tribal members did not agree with Ronan's value judgments but did support his efforts to expand reservation farms and ranches and protect tribal economic independence. His 1885 annual report included a valuable survey of the acreage and grain production from tribal member farms. For a survey of stock owned by tribal members in 1885 see the table Ronan included in his testimony on August 17, 1885. Most tribal farmers had individually fenced plots and a system of brands had been developed to identify cattle ownership. The Kootenais at Dayton Creek had a large community farm that produced wheat and various vegetables. Unfortunately this promising experiment in cooperative tribal farming offended the sensibilities of nineteenth century American whites and was opposed by Ronan and other government employees.

In the middle 1880s the government was providing economic assistance to the Bitterroot Salish who removed to the Jocko Reservation and those who chose to remain in the Bitterroot Valley.

Ronan noted that in January 1885 the tribes were finally paid for the right-of-way and timber used in constructing the Northern Pacific Railroad through the reservation. It had taken almost two and a half years for the tribes to receive the money they were promised in September 1882. At tribal insistence the payment was made in cash rather than goods.

One of the earliest irrigation ditches on the reservation was under construction in the Jocko Valley. Ronan's November 21, 1884, letter to the Commissioner relative to the Jocko Valley irrigation ditch, which he refers to in this annual report, is not included in this publication because it was missing from the National Archives files.

Flathead Agency, Montana Territory, *August*, 1885.

Sir: In compliance with instructions from your office, I have the honor herewith of submitting my ninth annual report from the Flathead Indian Agency, which is situated at the head of the Jocko Valley, on the line of the Northern Pacific Railroad, and within ten miles of the southern boundary of the reservation, adjoining the county of Missoula, in the Territory of Montana. The reserve has never been surveyed, but is supposed to have an acreage of 1,300,000, and is described as follows:

> Commencing at the source of the main branch of the Jocko River; thence along the divide separating the waters flowing into the Bitter Root River from those flowing into the Jocko to a point on Clarke's Fork between the Camas and Horse Prairies; thence northerly to and along the divide bounding on the west the Flathead River to a point due west from the point half-way in latitude between the northern and southern extremities of the Flathead Lake; thence on a due east course to the divide whence the Crow, the Prune, the So-ni-el-em, and the Jocko Rivers take their rise; and thence southerly along said divide to the place of beginning.

There are different classes of Indians on this reservation, composed as it is of three different tribes, the Flatheads, the Pen d'Oreilles, and the Kootenais. Some have made great strides towards civilization; others not so much, but have made a good beginning; and still a few others who are loath to change the wild freedom born of their savage nature. A large majority have advanced greatly in all the arts of peace in matters of religion, education, agriculture, mechanism, as also in commercial pursuits. A great majority are also owners of herds of cattle and horses, and take as good care of them and have as much pride in the ownership as the average white farmer or stockman. They use their own brands and marks, have their regular "round ups" and the property of individuals is respected and protected. The attention of those Indians is turned to stock-raising, agriculture, education, and religion, and every inducement should be held out to them to continue in such pursuits. They are attached to their homes, and are beginning to learn that by pursuing a peaceful and industrious life they can surround themselves with plenty and are able to support themselves without resorting to the hunt except for recreation and sport, as in the case of our own race.

In order to give an illustration of the advancement of the tribes of this reservation, I will here cite the names of some of the prominent Indian farmers, with an estimate of their grain crops, which are now being harvested. In addition to the grain crop each farmer raised a small patch of vegetables, such as potatoes, turnips, cabbage, carrots, parsnips, onions, &c., sufficient, perhaps, for family use.

Name	Under fence. Acres.	Wheat and oats produced. Bushels.	Name	Under fence. Acres.	Wheat and oats produced. Bushels.
Jocko Valley			John Solee	160	150
Arlee, chief of Flatheads	160	800	Deaf Louis	160	300
Antoine, Kicking Horse	100	200	Francois	50	100
Lassah	100	150	Pierre Eneas	50	60
Big Sam	100	200	John	100	150
Louison	100	300	Adolph	50	80
Tawa	50	150	Michael Colville	160	800
Alex See	50	100	Eneas Pierre	50	60
Eneas Lorette	50	200	Nicholas	160	400
Partee	50	100	Frank Camille	100	500
Alexander Morrijeau	160	1,200	Dandy Jim	160	500
Joe Finlay	100	400	Koosack Matte	100	300
Charley Plant	160	1,500	Joe Guardapuis	100	400
Alex Poirrier	160	800	Alex, the Snake	160	700
Isadore Laderoute	160	1,600	Pierrish (See-You)	100	250
Frank Finlay	160	300	Big John	100	400
Louis Valle	160	500	Louie La Rose	180	600
Adolph Finlay	160	800	Clatch-Kee-Lasa	50	100
Espanol	160	800	Angus McDonald	300	‡
Mary Finlay (widow)	50	200	Charley Moolman	160	300
Alex Matte	160	200	Pierre Moolman	160	150
Mat. Coture	160	⋆	Louie Moolman	160	300
Joe Coture	160	800	Alexander Bonaparte	100	200
Octare Rivais	160	⋆	Red Mountain	50	60
Joe Tuion Finlay	100	500	Isaac Chel-Kau-See	50	60
Courtois Finlay	60	300	Philip Stel-sa-Kau	60	80
Pierre	100	400	Michelle, Chief of the Pend d'Oreilles	160	250
Joe Barnaby	20	200	Artemus Tallman	100	250
Antoine Moise	10	100	Ooyste Finlay	160	500
Louise (widow)	10	50	Grand Joe	100	250
Samwell	10	100	Joseph Finlay	160	500
Thomas	10	100	Abraham Finlay	200	1,200
Adophe	10	100	Dupee	200	1,000
Antoine	10	100	Joseph Aslin	160	800
Eneas	10	100	Lorette Pablo	160	800
Michelle	10	100	Jim Michel	100	400
Aneas	10	100	Philip Iandra	60	100
Antoine Partico	10	100	Michelle Pablo and Charles Allard	300	†
Timothy	10	100	Slone	200	⋆
Joseph Coolmanie	10	100	Peter Finlay	100	100
			Baptiste Eneas	100	400
Mission Valley			Polson	100	200
Joseph	160	450	David Finlay	100	⋆
Charloanie	100	500			
Partee	100	300	**Pend d'Oreille River, Mouth of Jocko**		
Lowman (son of Joseph)	200	400	Paul and Samwell	200	500
Vetal	100	300	Pe-Arlee	300	300
Petell Halks	50	150	Little Salmon	50	60
Joseph (Qui-Quil-Cha)	100	200			
Felix	160	400			

Name	Under fence. Acres.	Wheat and oats produced. Bushels.	Name	Under fence. Acres.	Wheat and oats produced. Bushels.
Peter Matte	100	500	Big Head, Chi-ka-kee	100	150
Kaimee	100	250	Norbert Seepa	200	100
Baptiste Eneas	200	200			
Spokan Jim	60	100	**Camas Prairie**		
Pierre Paul	50	150	Joseph Who-lem-too	100	100
Adrian	50	300	Benway & Son	150	300
Sin-Cla Stanislaus (blind)	50	100	Louie Pierre	50	100
Pierre Qui-ma (blind)	50	100	Michelle Yolt-em-mee	100	250
Marceal	100	150	Big Semo Sinta	100	400
Benwa Nenema	60	50	Chita-masca	100	300
Antoine Rivais	300	200	Gregoire Che-took-tah	50	100
Isaac	100	200	Nichola	150	300
McSeem	160	250	Joseph Eu-cootle-stoo	100	300
Dominick Rattlesnake	50	50	Joseph Morrijeau	50	100
Big Lee	60	150			
Petall	50	50			
Charles Skieshen	50	60	* No crop.		
Eustah	60	40	† For pasture for their cattle.		
George Chumkanee	50	60	‡ For hay only, 380 tons produced.		

Dayton Creek. — Eneas, chief of the Kootenais, 200 acres fenced for use of tribe, about 1,000 bushels of wheat raised in common, besides potatoes, turnips, cabbage, onions, carrots, parsnips, peas, &c.

There are several other small garden patches in different portions of the reservation under cultivation, and not a few other Indians have located their farms with a view of fencing in the same, the coming winter.

Charlos' Band of Bitter Root Flatheads.

The visit of Charlos, the hereditary chief of the Flathead Nation, to Washington, accompanied by myself and a party of his Indians, resulted in a failure to induce that chief to abandon the Bitter Root Valley, and remove with his tribe to the Flathead Reservation on the Jocko. In compliance with verbal instructions from the honorable Secretary of the Interior, a full report of which I furnished the Indian Office under date of March 27, 1884, I made certain propositions to individual families to remove from the Bitter Root and settle at the Flathead Reservation, and the result was that twenty-one heads of families concluded to remove, and to them, following the views of the honorable Secretary of the Interior, as expressed to the Indians in Washington, I promised to each (1) a choice of 160 acres of unoccupied land on the reservation; (2) the erection of a suitable house; (3) assistance in fencing and breaking up ten acres of land for each family; (4) the following gifts: two cows, a wagon, set of harness, a plow, with other agricultural implements, seed for the first year, and provisions until the first crop was harvested.

Taking into consideration the very kindly and just expressions made use of in connection with the deserts of these Indians by the President and honorable Secretary, I could have made but an unfavorable impression by offering less. I would add that even after the first year they will depend somewhat on the generosity of the Government to uphold their hands in striving for a civilized independence and a sustained well-doing. My action met with the approval of the Government, and I have been enabled to carry out every promise made to the Indians. Ten families reported at the agency, and for them I erected ten houses, fenced in their fields as agreed upon, and to-day they are harvesting their crops. Three other families followed after I sent in estimates for the first ten, and to them I assigned land, but could not fence or build, although I provided them with fields, which I plowed inside of Government and other inclosures, where they raised crops this year. These additional three families have been provided with cows, as well as the original ten for whom houses were erected. Two more families soon followed the thirteen mentioned, and this week I have been notified by three other families that, they will remove here at once. I have no hesitation in saying that if the same policy is carried out in the future as in the past year, it will be only a brief matter of time until Charlos band, with exception of that chief and a few of his relatives, will be settled on the reservation.

Fears were entertained that by the issue of agricultural implements, provisions, and seed, which were supplied by the Government last year for Charlos band remaining in the Bitter Root Valley, it would be an inducement and an incentive to them to refuse to remove to the reservation. On the contrary, it has encouraged and given these poor people faith in the promises and fostering care of the Government should they leave their homes and remove to the reserve.

The Police Force.

For several years a volunteer force of Indian police used their best energies to keep peace and good behavior among the tribes, but the building of the Northern Pacific Railroad through the reservation changed the condition of affairs, and caused so much lawlessness along the line that I deemed it best to disband the old force and organize a paid force under immediate control of the agent.

The Indians now have their own judges, three in number, a code of rules governing the court of Indian offenses, and the laws are enforced by imprisonment, hard labor and fines. The administration of the laws in all respects are borne out with good judgment and dignity. I would recommend, however, that the judges of the court be paid as well as the police, as upon them principally rests all the good that police can perform upon the reservation, and they should be encouraged. Since the organization of the paid force of police and the adoption of the rules governing Indian offenses, we have had scarcely any trouble upon the reserve, and I trust good encouragement in the way of equipments, food, and clothing, in addition to pay, will be granted them.

Pay of Indians for "Right of Way" Through and "Timber Cut" on Reservation.

Early in the month of January I commenced and concluded the payment per capita to the Indians of the reserve for the right of way of the Northern Pacific Railroad and for timber cut on the reservation for construction purposes, involving the sum of $21,458. The payment was entirely satisfactory to the Indians, as I took especial pains to see that no person entitled to payment was left off the list. The task was a great one, as the Indians are scattered all over the reservation, living in their farm-houses, hamlets, and lodges, and in such an inclement season, and considering the vast extent of the reservation, I feel especially elated that no complaint has yet reached me of a man, woman, or child having been forgotten or overlooked in the payment.

Sanitary.

The health of the Indians was very good during the past year, with exception of the Kootenais. A malignant disease broke out among them early in spring, which carried many of them to the grave. The sickness first visits the patient by severe pains in the body and stomach, followed by an eruption resembling chicken-pox. Where advice of the agency physician was followed the disease as a general thing yielded to his remedies; but the Indians of this unfortunate tribe are isolated by a distance of 70 miles from the agency, and in reaching them the Flathead Lake must be crossed by an Indian ferry-boat. It will thus be seen that medical attention from the agency physician could not have been of the most desirable character. Owing to the long distance from the agency to the settlement of the Kootenais Indians the agent cannot give the desired attention to their relief and advancement, but it is to be hoped that in the near future the agency may be removed to a more central portion of the reservation, as has been so repeatedly advocated from this office.

Irrigating Ditch.

The irrigation ditch authorized in letters dated, respectively, October 11 and December 8, 1884, and which was made the subject of a special report in a communication from this office dated November 21, 1884, has been excavated and nearly completed for a distance of over 5 miles, including a large amount of blasting and an estimated expenditure of 60,000 feet of lumber for fluming. With the additional amount asked for in my estimate, forwarded on the 7th instant, I am confident I can thoroughly complete the ditch, which would prove a credit anywhere, and it would be hard to estimate the advantages that can be derived from it.

Education.

Special attention is given to the subject of education, and among these people will be found separate industrial schools for boys and girls and a church that would be a credit to any community. The[s]e schools have 171 scholars, of both sexes — an increase of 71 over last year — and the Government pays $150 annually for the board, tuition, and clothing of each scholar to the number of 150.

On the 2d day of August, of this year, the annual exhibition of these schools was given, and attended largely by citizens of Montana, who take interest in the advancement of such institutions. From the report of the editor of the Missoulian, published in that paper, I extract the appendix marked A, which will convey the news of a non-interested party concerning the schools of this reservation.

[The enclosed newspaper clipping was not published with Ronan's report.]

I have the honor to inclose herewith the statistics called for, and remain,

Very respectfully, your obedient servant,

Peter Ronan,
United States Indian Agent.

The Commissioner of Indian Affairs.

August 17, 1885

William S. Holman and S. W. Peel, "To Provide for the Appointment of a Commission to Inspect and Report on the Condition of Indians, Indian Affairs, and for Other Purposes," House of Representatives Report No. 1076, 49th Congress, 1st Session (1886), serial 2438, pages 71-74.

> William S. Holman was a United States Congressman from Indiana for almost forty years in the late nineteenth century. He worked to minimize government expenditures and was especially interested in Indian affairs. Samuel W. Peel was a congressman from Arkansas for ten years between 1883 and 1893.[11]
>
> Much of Ronan's testimony in this excerpt was general, but he did include some valuable information about stock herds on the Flathead Reservation in 1885. The table of stock owners complimented Ronan's table giving farm acreage and grain production in his August 1885 annual report.

Flathead Agency, Montana Territory.
Peter Ronan.

St. Ignatius Mission,
Montana, August 17, 1885.

Peter Ronan, being duly sworn, made the following statement, in reply to questions by the committee:

Question (by the Chairman). Please state what official position you hold, how long you have held the same, and how long you have been acquainted with Indian affairs in the Jocko Reservation.

Answer. I am United States Indian agent for the confederated tribes of Flathead, Pend d'Oreilles, and Kootenay Indians, on the Flathead or Jocko Reservation, in Montana, and have held the same since June 1, 1877, which includes the period of my acquaintance with Indian affairs on the reservation.

Schools.

Question. Please state what schools have existence in your agency among the Indians named since your agency commenced, governmental or denominational, and the condition of the educational facilities of the Indian children on the reservation at the present time.

Answer. The Government has never built a school-house on the reservation. All the educational facilities established in the agency have been under the auspices of the Catholic Church. I have understood that the first steps of that church to establish schools within the agency occurred in 1859 or 1860, but in earnest in the year 1864. Since 1879 there have been two boarding schools at this place, St. Ignatius Mission — one for boys and the other for girls. During the last fiscal year the boys' school averaged in attendance 74, including certain Blackfeet pupils, and the girls' school averaged 82. The contract with the Government for that year was $100 for each pupil up to the number of 50 for each school of the children of this agency and 25 of the Blackfeet tribe for each school. For the present year the contract is $150 for each of 75 children in each school. At this time, being a partial vacation, there are in attendance at the boys' school 75 pupils, and at the girls' school 83. These children are to remain in the school the year round. There is a partial vacation in the month of August, but it extends only to a suspension of certain studies. Some of the girls now in attendance at the girls' school have been there ever since I became the agent.

In addition to the usual branches taught in school — reading, writing, arithmetic, grammar, music, and geography — the pupils are taught house-keeping, such as washing, ironing, sewing, dairy work, cooking, and general household duties in the girls' school, and in the boys' school the pupils are taught blacksmithing, carpentering, working in saw and grist mills, running shingle machines, farming work, gardening, teaming, and all general farm work, tailoring, painting, and all work incident to the institution. Some years ago two of the boys were employed in a mission printing office. The pupils are employed under persons competent to teach the several branches of industry named, the pupils being employed only in the industries connected with the respective schools.

Farmers.

Question. How many farmers are employed in your agency, and in what manner and at what salary?

Answer. One farmer is employed at a salary of $800 per annum. He is the overseer generally of the Indian farms, and gives instruction and aid to the In-dians in their farming operations. He is a practical farmer, but does not speak the language of the Indians.

Buildings.

Question. What buildings have been erected at your agency by the Govern-ment?

Answer. A house, occupied by the agent, one for the doctor, one for the clerk, one for the blacksmith, one for the interpreter and assistant miller, a storehouse, a large barn and storehouse attached, a shed for storage, a root-house, a blacksmith shop, a carpenter shop, a granary, and a grist and saw mill combined. Most of these buildings were erected prior to my appointment as agent.

Carlos Band.

Question. How many of the Carlos band of Flatheads still remain in the Bitter Root Valley, and how many families of that band have removed to the Flathead Reservation during the past twelve months?

Answer. Including men, women, and children, about 300 still remain in the Bitter Root Valley. About 15 families have removed to the reservation within the past twelve months.

Question. In what manner was the appropriation made for the benefit of the Flatheads remaining in the Bitter Root Valley and for those of them who removed to the reservation expended during the last fiscal year?

Answer. I erected and aided in the erection of 10 comfortable buildings, and the fencing in of 10 acres of land each for 10 families who removed to the reservation. I purchased 26 cows for the Indians who removed to the res-ervation, and furnished them with rations ever since their removal, and for agricultural implements and seeds[,] plows, wagons, and agricultural imple-ments generally were purchased.

Question. According to your best information, how many of the Carlos band still remaining in the Bitter Root Valley live in houses and are actually cultivating land, either held under patent or otherwise?

Answer. I should think between 30 and 40 families are living in houses and actually cultivating lands. Some are cultivating lands in that valley who do not live in houses. Some of these hold their lands by patent, and some of those removed to the Flathead Reservation still hold lands by patent in the Bitter Root Valley.

Indian Labor.

Question. To what extent are you employing Indians in the duties of your agency?

Answer. The interpreter and assistant miller are Indians, also 10 policemen, and 3 judges without salaries. When I have freighting to do or cutting logs and hauling the same to the saw mill, and also all the work on the ditching I have mentioned, except the skilled labor, I employ Indians.

Employés.

Question. Please furnish a list of the employés of your agency and the salary paid to each.

Answer. The following is a complete list of all such employés, and the salary paid to each:

	Per annum.
Doctor	$1,200
Clerk	1,200
Farmer	800
Carpenter	800
Blacksmith	800
Miller	900
Assistant Miller	600
Interpreter	300

Live-Stock.

Question. How much Government live-stock do you hold in connection with your agency?

Answer. I have 7 horses only.

Farming and Character of Lands.

Question. Please state what progress the Indians of your agency are making in agriculture; the character and extent of their farming and gardening; the kind of houses occupied by them; the character of the lands of the reservation; the extent to which they are adapted to agriculture; whether irrigation is necessary and the extent to which you are providing for irrigation, and to what extent are the Indians of your agency engaged in raising live-stock, especially as to cattle distributed to them by the Government.

Answer. At the present date (not including Indians who are making a beginning, and those engaged in making rails for a preliminary), we have 139 heads of families engaged to a considerable extent in agricultural pursuits occupying an acreage of 13,490 acres, and raising in about equal proportions 38,170 bushels of wheat and oats; they also raise more than a sufficiency for family use of the usual garden truck, such as potatoes, turnips, onions, peas, beans, carrots, parsnips, rutabagas, cucumbers, melons — musk and water — and in some favored localities corn is also raised in moderate quantities; fruit, such a plums, apples, and cherries, are showing evidence of culture, and the attention given to the care of tame berries is perceptible. Sixteen families purchased a quantity and variety of fruit trees this spring, which shows the spirit that animates them to compare with, if not rival, their white neighbors in the ownership of an orchard. All the leading farmers, in addition to the crops they look after, cut and stack sufficient hay for winter provender for their stock, and some of the more thrifty Indians have large inclosures, from 200 to 400 acres, fenced in to pasturage. The houses erected by the Government, under my supervision, for the Indians removed from the Bitter Root Valley, are substantial log dwellings, 16 by 24 by 10, shingled (cedar) roof, with good flooring and ceiling, panel doors, and full windows, with a convenient flue in center of house; those erected by the Indians by their own labor (except the manufacture of lumber from logs hauled by them to agency mill and there handled and sawed by the regular agency employés, and locks, nails, screws, glass, &c., issued to them from agency supplies) are of substantial build, generally of hewn log, but some of frame, weather-boarded, and in not a few instances ornamented with an L addition. The majority of the Indians who have erected homes have also added ample stables and outhouses for domestic fowls, milk, butter, &c.

The greater portion of the land lying along the valley of the Jocko, Mission Valley, Pend d'Oreille, Camas Prairie, Little Bitter Root, and about Dayton Creek is well adapted to the growing of wheat and oats, and the general garden vegetation. Irrigation is necessary all over the reservation, although not absolutely so in the bottom lands adjoining the river and larger creeks, but on the north side of the Jocko irrigation is more especially required. Already an irrigating ditch over 5 miles long is nearly completed at a cost of $5,000, and an estimate has been forwarded covering the amount needed to bring it to a successful completion ($1,250), which will render fertile a vast extent of land; and should the vast plateau on the south side of the Jocko, directly on the the road from Arlee to the agency, be supplied with a system of ditches, the possibilities of the soil cannot be estimated. Four hundred thousand acres of the reserve is tillable, and the balance, about 900,000 acres, grazing land and timber. I would in this connection invite your attention to the claims of the Kootenay Indians. This poverty-stricken tribe are isolated from the agency by a distance of 70 miles, have but one farm in common, and are situated at such a remote place from the agency that it is almost impossible to render the assistance needed or to supply the services of an employé to aid and instruct them, and I would earnestly recommend that an additional farmer be authorized for this poor tribe and authority granted me to hire and select the person to fill the office, as it is essential he be capable and willing to assist this tribe in the art of agriculture and aid them in making separate homes and farms. Provision was made in the appropriations for the present fiscal year for this very purpose.

As to the extent in which the Indians of the agency are engaged in stock-raising, I submit herewith a list of the principal owners, with number of cattle and horses, although nearly every Indian on the reservation is a possessor in his own right of at least one horse, and many females are owners of one or more cows, which are not taken into consideration in this statement:

Name	Horses	Cattle	Name	Horses	Cattle
Alex. Matte	45	50	Partee	30	
Joe Coture	20	50	Felix	100	60
Arlee, Chief	100	150	Samwell	40	200
Louison	200	160	Salowani	30	40
Michelle Rivais	25	5	Michel Colville	60	30
Charles Allard	30	700	Oryste	30	30
Joseph	250	200	Abraham Finlay	25	30
Octave Rivais	15	30	Red Mountain		30
Alex. Morrijeau	60	120	Little Nicholas	150	100
Isadore Laderoute	70	25	Deaf Louis	40	30
Big Sam	20	10	Vetal	80	40
Alex. Poirrier	10	30	Espanol	25	25
Michelle, Chief	20	15	Spokan Jim	25	40
Eneas	20	10	Gregoire	25	30
Peter Finlay	20	60	Paul Andre	10	25
Antoine Rivais	40	200	Marceal	20	50
Lorrette Pablo	60	100	Benwa Nenema	60	40
Baptiste Eneas	20	25	Joseph Finlay	15	20
Michelle Yoe-them-mee	160	300	Joseph Ashley	50	15
Joseph, Sil-elp-que	100	150	Charles Moolman	15	25
Nicholas, Chill-loo	40	80	Louie Moolman	10	25
Louie Pierre	30	100	Pierre Moolman	10	15
Roman Nose	300	10	Isaac	15	30
Grand Joe	15	10	Francois	40	30
Joseph, Who-lem-too	50	30	Lowmain	30	40
Maxime	40	30	Aleck the Snake	40	30
Big Leo	40	15	Pierrish	15	20

As far as cattle issued by the Government is concerned, I can state that during my incumbency of this office but 200 head have been received at this agency, although through a clerical or other error it appears upon record in the office of Indian Affairs as 400; the 200 head alluded to were received from Kleinschmidt Brothers, of Helena, Mont., 4 per cent. of which were bulls; the cattle was delivered as per contract, but owing to arrangements then in progress for the approval by the Indians for right of way for the Northern Pacific Railroad, they declined at the time to receive them, entertaining the idea it was a bribe from that company. I was then necessarily compelled to winter and care for them; this, however, without a dollar of expense to the United States excepting pay for the herder, engaged specially to look after the band of cattle; but in the following year, after having the matter thoroughly explained to and understood by the Indians, they accepted the gift, and accordingly I issued to the poorer Indians the stock cited. During the severe winter in which they were held by me and under my bond, for the care and responsibility of the same, several head died, but the increase more than made up for said loss. No gift the Government ever made to Indians could have proven more beneficial than the cattle referred to, and the increase thereof is a portion of the cattle enumerated in the foregoing list.

October 14, 1885
LR 24,767/1885, RG 75, National Archives, Washington, D.C.

White complaints about off-reservation hunting escalated during the 1880s. Montanans wanted to protect wild game from extermination but also wanted to reserve the game that was left for white sport hunters. Tribal members wanted to protect their right to hunt under the 1855 Hellgate Treaty.[12] According to an account in *The Weekly Missoulian*, at the same time white conservationists were complaining about Indian hunting off the reservation, white sportsmen from Helena were visiting the Flathead Reservation to help themselves to reservation fish and game.[13] See also Ronan's October 22 and 27, 1885, letters, and October 1, 1886, letter.

On November 11, 1885, the Commissioner of Indian Affairs replied to Ronan's letter about off-reservation hunting. He acknowledged the treaty right to off-reservation hunting, but claimed that tribal members still needed permits to leave the reservation. The Commissioner argued that tribal members should be encouraged to stay on the reservation in order to avoid any "pretense for conflict with white settlers."[14]

Major Robert C. Walker, originally from Pennsylvania, was an army paymaster in the 1860s and 1870s. He moved to Helena, Montana, in 1871 and retired in 1878. Thomas H. Smith ran a saloon in Noxon.[15]

United States Indian Service,
Flathead Agency,
October 14th, 1885.

Hon. Commissioner of Indian Affairs
Washington, D.C.

Sir,

In my regular report for the month of September I stated that a large number of Indians of this Reservation after harvesting their crops, went forth to the hunting grounds to secure wild meat to cure for winter use; I also stated that the bounty laws of Montana giving to the slayer of each bear the sum of eight dollars for every skin produced and properly vouched for as having been Killed within the boundaries of the territory and not on any Indian Reservation is a great incentive to the Indians to go hunting, as the bounty is promptly paid to the Indian hunter as well as to the white. I held also that while such a temptation is held out to the Indians, to hunt off the reservation, the press and citizens should not be so loud in their denunciation of Indians leaving the reservation for the chase while such a bribe is offered by law to disobey the regulations of the Indian Office.

I herewith enclose two letters from citizens on this subject, and would respectfully inform you that I have sent out "runners" to the different Indian camps ordering them back to the Reservation, and that I feel assured my order will be obeyed.

It has been the custom of the Confederated tribes of this Reservation, to go out to the hunting grounds every fall to secure meat and robes; in later years, however, since the disappearance of the buffalo, the largely increased cultivation of the soil by the Indians, and their attention turned to stock raising and civilized pursuits, hunting parties began to disappear, with exception of small parties who scatter out in different directions from the reservation to hunt deer, elk, mountain sheep, etc, both for amusement and profit. This year however a greater number have gone hunting after harvesting their crops, owing, I think, to the enactment of the bounty laws already alluded to, I have never offered any serious objection to the Indians leaving their reservation to hunt, after work was completed about their fields and farms, especially where each party, was accompanied by a trusty Indian, either a policeman, chief or head man, whose business it was to see that the Indians conducted themselves properly, and committed no improper acts among the settlers; in fact, I never had any department orders or instructions upon this point, but was guided by the Indian's claim of having such rights guaranteed to them by the treaty proclaimed April 25th 1856 (See Page 7. Revision of Indian Treaties) also April 18th 1859 (See Art. 3. Pages 385-386).

The Hon. Commissioner will perceive that in the letter of Mr. R. C. Walker no complaint is made except that the Indians are Killing game. The letter from the other party it seems to me to be a complaint from a white hunter whose occupation is gone, when brought into competition with the Indian hunter. His story of depredations I do not believe.

My object in forwarding this report is to obtain your views and instructions in regard to holding peaceable Indians upon their reservations who claim the right to hunt and fish "according to treaty" off the same, and against whom there is no authenticated complaint of committing any crime save to cross the boundary of their reserve line to hunt and fish for a few weeks after the harvesting of their crops.

I trust you will give this matter your early attention and your suggestions and instructions will be obeyed to the best of my ability.

I have the honor to be

Very Respectfully
Your obt svt
Peter Ronan
U.S. Ind. Agent.

First enclosure:

Helena M T, Oct. 10, 1885

Dear Major

Complaints are numerous from citizens that the Flatheads are out in great numbers from the Big Black Foot through to the Musselshell occupying every game pass in the mountains. It is thought a great imposition that these Indians who are supposed to be supplied by the Government with what meat they need on their reservation, are off of it, interfering with the rights of citizens in hunting deer at this season. Can't you hearken to the prayers of our people and call these Indians back & Keep them on their reservation. Or if there is any thing you will advise as to calling upon the military to escort these people back to their reservation we will readily follow your directions and act at once.

Respectfully your friend &c.
Robt. C. Walker

Second enclosure:

Noxon Mont oct 10th 1885

to Magor Ronen Esq

Dear Sir,

i beg leafe to ask you to be Kind anuf to keep your indians at home and on the Reservasion as they are a bothering some here at present there is a gang of them Camped Now at bull river 2 miles West of here and they are a Stealing game out of our traps and a takeing the traps also and if there Cant be a Stop put to it Rite away i wil for my part put 2 Winchester Rifels and 2, 45 army Revolvor to work at them and i will make Short Work of uncle Sams pets i have plenty of firearms and plenty amannishion and i wil Shote an indian as Soon as i would a Wolf or Ciotey if they Dont keep out of here and let the traps and game alone that is in them and i wont be alone in the mater as there is 5 more trapers that are fighting mad by ther acshions here but i told them that i would Write to you to Day and Se What Could be Dun about it before we Commenced, on them but if we Do have to Drive them out with fire arms take my Word for it it wil Cost the government something for lumber to box them up With after We get through With them or the Wolvs wil have a feast for a Couple of months to Come.

Hopeing to hear from you Soon on the Subject, i Remain yours

Thomas H. Smith
Noxon Montaina, T.y.

October 22, 1885
Montana Live Stock Journal *(Helena, Mont.), vol. 2, no. 7 (November 1885), page 5, col. 3.*

Indians Recalled.

Some time since Major R. C. Walker, of Helena, complained to Agent Ronan that the Flatheads were off their reservation slaughtering great numbers of deer, elk, etc., on the Big Blackfoot, and in the ranges on to the Missouri. The following is Maj. Ronan's reply:

Flathead Agency, October 22, 1885. — R. C. Walker, Esq., Helena, M. T. — Dear Sir: Yours of the 10th inst. to hand and contents noted. I have this day dispatched a "runner," ordering all Indians of this reservation to return here at once, and am confident they will obey the same. If not I will take the necessary steps to compel them to do so.

Very respectfully,
Peter Ronan,
U.S. Indian Agent.

October 27, 1885
The New North-West *(Deer Lodge, Mont.), October 30, 1885, page 3, col. 6.*

With this letter Ronan was responding to an earlier article in *The New North-West* newspaper about tribal hunting rights off the reservation.[16]

James H. Mills was the editor of the *Montana Post* newspaper in Virginia City and Helena during the late 1860s and *The New North-West* in Deer Lodge between 1869 and 1891. In 1878 and 1879, Mills published Duncan McDonald's history of the Nez Perce War from the Nez Perce perspective. In 1884, he was elected as the first president of the Press Association of Montana.[17]

About Flathead Indians.
How They Came to be Off the Reservation —
Inducement in the Bounty Laws.
Small Per Capita Appropriation.

To the Editor New North-West:

I feel grateful to you for publication in your paper of October 23d of an article headed, "Recalling Indians," as it does justice to my efforts in restraining the Indians under my charge from having any trouble with citizens, and also gives information to residents of the Territory that they seem to lack, viz:

"That an Agent cannot, as a matter of legal fact, compel an Indian not accused or convicted of crime, to remain on the Reservation, as that would practically deprive him of personal liberty, to which he is entitled under the Constitution. The Ponca Indian case, tried in Omaha, decided that, and it has not been reversed that we have noticed."

In your article you kindly add that Major Ronan understands the case and "will do all he can, when advised, to right or redress a wrong; and it should also be borne in mind that unless accused and arrested for violation of law, it is altogether a moral pressure that compels and Indian to remain on his reservation. Agent Ronan is therefore entitled to more credit than seems to be conceded to him."

In a special report to the Indian Office, under date of October 14, I stated that a large number of Indians of this Reservation, after harvesting their crops, went forth to the hunting grounds to secure wild meat for family use. I also stated that

The Bounty Laws of Montana,

giving to the slayer of each bear the sum of eight dollars for every skin produced and properly vouched for as having been killed within the boundaries of the Territory, and not on any Indian Reservation, is a great incentive to the Indians to go out hunting, as the bounty on bear and numerous other animals is promptly paid to the Indian hunter, as well as to the white. I held, also, that while such a temptation is held out to the Indians to hunt off the Reservation, the press and citizens should not be so loud in their denunciation of Indians leaving the Reservation for the chase while such a bribe is offered by law to disobey the regulations of the Indian office and the efforts of the Agent to keep them at home.

In said report to the Commissioner of Indian Affairs, I stated that it has been the custom of the confederated tribes of this Reservation go out to the hunting grounds every fall to secure meat and robes. In later years, however, since the disappearance of the buffalo, the largely increased cultivation of the soil by the Indians, and their attention being turned to stock raising and other civilized pursuits, hunting parties from this Agency began to disappear, with the exception of small bands, who scatter out in different directions from the Reservation to hunt deer, elk, mountain sheep, etc., both for amusement and profit. This year, however, a greater number have gone hunting after harvesting their crops, owing, I think, to the enactment of the bounty laws already alluded to. I have never offered any serious objections to the Indians leaving their Reservation to hunt, after work was completed about their fields and farms, especially when each party was accompanied by a trusty Indian, either a policeman, chief or headman, whose business it was to see that the Indians conducted themselves properly and committed no overt acts among the settlers; in fact I never had any Department orders or instructions upon this point, but was guided by common sense and the Indian claim of having such

Rights Guaranteed by the Treaty,

proclaimed April 25, 1856, (See page 7, Revision of Indian Treaties), and also the treaty of April 18, 1859, concluded at Hell Gate, in the Bitter Root Valley, Art. 3, page 385-386, from which I quote:

"The exclusive right of taking fish in all the streams running through or bordering said Reservation is further reserved to said Indians; as also the right of taking fish at all the usual and accustomed places, in common with citizens of the Territory, and of erecting temporary buildings for curing; together with the privilege of hunting, gathering roots and berries, and pasturing their horses and cattle upon open and unclaimed land."

No complaint has been made except that the Indians are killing game. But I

Ordered Them to Their Reservation,

and as thirty lodges returned to-day from the vicinity of the Big Blackfoot, it will be seen that the Indians accepted my advice and counsel, and obeyed the order without a question, except a mild protest that they had a treaty right to hunt off the Reservation, but would obey the orders of their Agent.

The Matter of Rations.

It has been stated in the press of Helena that the Indians of this Reservation receive ample annuities, and a supply of beef from the government sufficient for their support. How far this statement is from the truth will appear from a paragraph I copy from my annual report to the Commissioner of Indian Affairs, for 1884, page 112:

* * * * "In the list of appropriations for Indians for the fiscal year 1883-1884, those who run may read: For the subsistence and civilization of the Flatheads and other confederated tribes, including pay of employees, $13,000. That this munificent sum was not exceeded can be verified at your office. Therefore it will be evident that had the amount expended in their behalf been equally distributed among the 1,700 Indians of this Reservation, each would have been benefitted to the extent of nearly eight dollars. It is unnecessary to explain that a wagon, for instance, valued, let us say, at $80, could not well be distributed in ten equal parts, and that when one Indian, of necessity, became the recipient of the vehicle, the portions of the appropriations assigned others were correspondingly reduced, nor will it be requisite to prove that even had each received the full sum of $8, the amount would scarcely suffice during a twelve-month for "subsistence and civilization." I shall therefore allow the fact itself to work its own way toward a proof that the Indians of the Flathead Reservation are rapidly learning to work according to the methods of the white man, which, indeed, is about the only manner they now have of supporting themselves."

They All Like to Do It.

I leave it to the generous public to draw their own conclusions as to the right of those Indians to cross the boundaries of their reserve, after the toils of their harvest is over, to secure wild meat, robes and furs, as an assistance toward their support, as well as to gratify their natural taste for the chase, which is not altogether eradicated from the most refined of our own race.

Peter Ronan,
U.S. Indiant [sic] Agent.

Flathead Agency, Oct. 27, 1885.

———————

To James H. Mills:

Dear Sir:

Yesterday I sent you a communication in regard to the return of Indians etc., upon notification from me — that is, the camps that were found by the runners I sent out. To-day I was informed by an Indian that, upon their return toward the Agency through the Big Blackfoot valley, an Indian set fire to the grass, which communicated to a hay stack belonging to a settler. Now, whether it was done through malignity or thoughtlessness, I cannot say; but I wish to have a stop put to all malicious mischief or crime committed by an Indian off the Reservation, and this is the sentiment of all the law-abiding Indians of the Reserve. Should my information prove true, I trust a complaint will be made out, and that an officer will come here with authority to arrest the Indian. I will do all in my power to place him in the hands of the officer, and, if guilty, will be doing a great favor to the Indians of this Reservation to make an example of him.

I am yours truly,
Peter Ronan,
U.S. Indian Agent.

November 5, 1885

LR 26,599/1885, RG 75, National Archives, Washington, D.C.

See also Ronan's letter of June 20, 1885, on the same subject. The Commissioner finally replied on November 23, 1885, that no mental health facilities were available for tribal members and Ronan would have to improvise. Lorette Pablo's story adds a personal dimension to the problem. His wife's side of the story is not available. In the earliest surviving Flathead Reservation census, Lorette Pablo was 40 years old and his wife, Mary, 30 years old in 1886. They had three children ranging in age from 8 to 2 years old in 1886. Lorette had worked as Flathead Agency interpreter during the 1870s and during the Nez Perce War in 1877. In 1879, he was accused of furnishing whiskey to Indians off the reservation. In Ronan's August 1885 annual report, he had 160 acres under fence and raised 800 bushels of wheat and oats in the Mission Valley. In Ronan's August 17, 1885, testimony, Lorette was listed as owning 60 horses and 100 cattle. He died in a horse accident in 1887.[18]

United States Indian Service,
Flathead Agency,
November 5th, 1885.

Hon. Commissioner of Indian Affairs
Washington, D.C.

Sir,

While inviting your attention to my communication of June 20th in relation to demented Indians, to which no reply has ever been received by me, I also have the honor to enclose herewith a letter from an Indian of this reservation in relation to his wife, another unfortunate person, and a new case which has lately developed.

I respectfully and earnestly ask that some measures be adopted and the necessary authority and instructions be issued to place this and the other poor demented Indians in some safe retreat, where they can harm no one and receive the care and attention which they are so much in need of.

Very Respectfully
Your obt. svt.
Peter Ronan
U.S. Indian Agent.

Enclosure:

Foot of Flathead Lake,
November 1st, 1885

Major P. Ronan,
U.S. Indian Agent,
Flathead Agency, M.T.
Dear Sir:
I wish to ask your advice about my wife. On Friday I returned from hunting horses and my wife had gone and taken the baby with her. I thought she had gone to some of the neighbors' houses and did [not] go to hunt her but as she did not return that night I went next day to Bisson's on the road to Mud creek and he told me she had spent the night There but had gone that morning saying she was going to the Jocko to get her brother to come back with her and take my children away; also that she was going to sell my ranch to some one on the Jocko; that she would yet Kill me etc. etc. She is undoubtedly crazy and is unfit to [be] left alone but I have no means to send her to Deer Lodge and do not Know what to do. Will you please tell me what I am to do with her, if I find her; and can you get the Sisters to take care of my little ones as They are too young to be without a woman's Care. I am in a very bad way and am having much Trouble on account of my wife's misfortune.
Please send me a reply to this so soon as you can.

Very Respectfully
Lorette Pablo.

November 6, 1885
LR 26,702/1885, RG 75, National Archives, Washington, D.C.

This letter by Ronan and its enclosures give some of the most detailed accounting of the status of Salish land in the Bitterroot Valley during the middle 1880s. Many Salish did not receive patents under the 1872 law, some of those who were issued patents had removed to Jocko, and others had died without heirs. Ronan's list does indicate that about 14 Salish were farming on their patented land and others who had patents were farming elsewhere in the valley. See especially Father D'Aste's second point about whites filing on and claiming Salish farms that were not on land covered by the 51 patents from 1872. Unfortunately the available documents do not allow us to calculate exactly how much Bitterroot land Salish farmers controlled in 1885. See Ronan's February 12, 1885, letter about Charlo's hopes for more patents for Bitterroot Salish farmers.

Jasper A. Viall (or Vial) was Montana Superintendent of Indian Affairs between 1870 and 1872. Viall accompanied then Congressman James A. Garfield to the Bitterroot Valley in August 1872 to negotiate with the Bitterroot Salish. He fought with Montana Territorial Governor Benjamin Potts over patronage in the Indian Service.[19] John W. Winslett was a storekeeper and sheep rancher in Stevensville. He came to Montana in 1865 after fighting

Indians in California as a volunteer. In Stevensville much of his trade was with the Bitterroot Salish. He was judged insane in 1889 after a series of business reverses.[20]

United States Indian Service,
Flathead Agency,
November 6th, 1885.

Hon. Commissioner of Indian Affairs
Washington, D.C.

Sir,

Referring to your letter of May 8th (Land 3554-85) which instructed me to ascertain, in relation to Carlos Band of Bitter Root Indians "how many have died leaving no heirs and how many of those to whom patents have issued for lands in the Bitter Root Valley, have removed to and reside permanently on the Flathead Reservation." Your instructions add: "This information may be of assistance in case it shall be decided to ask Congress to authorize the transfer of the lands patented to Indians who have died leaving no heirs, and the sale of lands patented to those who have removed to the Flathead Reservation.["]

I enclose herewith "List of Patents" issued to Charlos Band of Bitter Root Flatheads, with description and remarks on face of same which will give a carefully collected and brief statement of the whereabouts, etc. of the holders of the patents.

Believing it to be the desire of the Indian Office to ascertain the full facts in regard to the status of Carlos Band of Flatheads, I requested the venerable and Revd. Father J. D'Aste, of the Jesuit Mission of St. Mary, founded by Father De Smet, nearly fifty years ago, in the Bitter Root Valley among the Flatheads, to give me his views in regard to the sale of the Indian lands, etc.

Father D'Aste has been a Missionary with this tribe for over twenty years, the trusted friend and adviser of the tribe, and I respectfully submit his views to the Hon. Commissioner for consideration.

Major Peter Ronan,
U.S. Indian Agent,
Flathead Agency

Dear Sir,

I herewith return the papers you furnished to me in regard to the land of the Flathead Indians in Bitter Root Valley.

To the few remarks I wrote opposite to the several names on the list of patents I would respectfully add the following:

Though in general I approve as a wise one the law passed by Congress that the Indians who received patents of land as homesteads, be forbidden to sell them for a number of years; however, in the case of these Flatheads, in order to encourage them to leave the Bitter Root Valley and go to their Reservation, where the Government wants them to go, I think that an exception to the general law might be the quicker and easier way to Solve this too-long unsettled question. I am confident that a good many, if not all, will Sell out and then they will be obliged to go to the reserve; but in order that no injustice be done to any of these Indians I would submit the following remarks:

The surveying of these Indian lands has been pretty near an arbitrary doing of Some party or parties to make money out of it, disregarding the rights of Some of the Indians concerned in the matter.

1st. In the first place, when Some time after the making of General Garfield's agreement or treaty, J. A. Vial, then Superintendent of Indian Affairs for Montana, came to the Bitter Root to urge the removal of the Flatheads to the Jocko Reservation, the conclusion came to was: that the Indians who would like to abandon their tribal relations and become citizens, Should give their names to one [John] Winslett, who was then Keeping store in Stevensville, near St. Mary's Mission. At that time a good many Indians were absent on their buffalo hunt and consequently could not give their names, and yet, only upon the grounds of this list Sent to the Government, the surveying was ordered of as many ranches as there were names on the list.

2nd. The surveying was done without even consulting the Indians interested in the matter, and almost only according to the caprice of the Surveyor, locating a good many of the Indians w[h]ere he pleased; and Some on worthless lands, and the Indians concerned have never been notified where the land surveyed for them was located, consequently the Indians went on as before, picking up here and there parcels of land, and some making on them substantial improvements, whilst their surveyed farms were idle, and now, naturally the whites, finding these lands occupied by Indians, not filed on, file on these lands, leaving for the moment the Indian settler alone until they can get the title, and they then will oblige the Indian to quit the land he has been farming on for several years, and this will be the cause of discontent for the Indians and increase the bitter feelings some of them entertain already for the whites.

3rd. According to General Garfield's agreement fifty thousand dollars were to be paid to the Indians in compensation of the abandonment of their claims in Bitter Root Valley; therefore those Indians who then moved to the Reservation, having got a large share (because of the small number who went) of the fifty thousand dollars, no lands should have been surveyed for them nor patents issued for these lands.

Therefore, in justice, either these patents issued for them should be withdrawn or sold to the profit of those among the Flatheads who having no patent be willing to move to the Reservation, but I think it would be unjust to give these lands to those who by going from the beginning to the Reservation renounced their claims and for which they were well paid by the Government.

I would suggest that as a compensation to those who could get no patents and to the numerous new families that were formed Since Garfield's agreement, a small appropriation be made to distribute in equal Share to each individual of these families, if they be willing to move to the Reservation. This in my opinion would facilitate their removal from Bitter Root, they are so poor, those who have no land, that the paltry sum of say from twenty five to fifty dollars that would come to every member might be quite an inducement to move.

From the remarks appended opposite to the names of the list, it appears that eight of the patents, i.e. Nos. 14, 22, 26, 37, 39, 40, 46, 48, should not have been issued, the Indians to whom they were issued, having renounced their claims to Bitter Root land, and got the money. That six of those that had patents issued, i.e. Nos. 7, 21, 30, 34, 43, 51, moved lately to the Reservation, so that the Indians in Bitter Root have only thirty seven patents, less than half the number of families among them, moreover there are two couples which have each two patents, i.e. 3, 25–21, 30.

Finally there are four families that have been farming several years on good farms, but have no patents and their claims are Sure to be taken, and probably they are already filed on by whites, these Indians cannot avail themselves of the privilege of filing on these lands free of charge, because these lands not lying in square parcels, they cannot get without the help of a Surveyor, a full description of the land they occupy.

I also have the honor of inviting your attention to my communication of February 12th, 1885, which entirely bears upon the subject of Carlos Band of Bitter Root Flathead Indians, and in submitting these views, remain.

Very Respectfully
Your obt. svt.
Peter Ronan
U.S. Indian Agent.

Enclosure, original tabular format is reproduced here in text. Some of the legal descriptions have handwritten corrections, which were added later, but are not included here, so there are probably mistakes in the legal descriptions given here:

List of Patents issued to Carlos Band of Bitter Root Flathead Indians

No. 1. Widow Therese Brooks; S. $\frac{1}{2}$, N.W. $\frac{1}{4}$, N. $\frac{1}{2}$, S.W. $\frac{1}{4}$, Sec. 15, Town. 9, N. range 20 W.; 160 acres. Remarks: Dead, four children living, one brother married, living in Bitter Root Valley and has no patent. No improvements on land.

No. 2. Joseph Collyer, E. $\frac{1}{2}$, S.W. $\frac{1}{4}$, N. $\frac{1}{2}$, S.E. $\frac{1}{4}$, Sec. 10, Town. 9, N. range 20 W.; 160 acres. Remarks: Dead.

No. 3. Mary Mouchelle, N. $\frac{1}{2}$, N.W. $\frac{1}{4}$, N. $\frac{1}{2}$, N.E. $\frac{1}{4}$, Sec. 16, Town. 9, N. range 20 W.; 160 acres. Remarks: Married to James De La Ware, has a boy from 1st husband. No improvements on patent.

No. 4. Medicine Pere, N. $\frac{1}{2}$, N.W. $\frac{1}{4}$, Sec. 10, S. $\frac{1}{2}$, S.W. $\frac{1}{4}$, Sec. 3, Town. 9, N. range 20 W.; 160 acres. Remarks: Dead, the widow is living and three children. No improvements on patent.

No. 5. Narcise Trochee, N. $\frac{1}{2}$, N.W. $\frac{1}{4}$, Sec. 8, S. $\frac{1}{2}$, S.W. $\frac{1}{4}$, Sec. 5, Town. 8, N. range 20 W.; 160 acres. Remarks: Dead, Widow married to Joseph Lumphrey the daughter married an Indian, a very good workman who has no patent, although living several years on a farm.

No. 6. Joseph La Moose, N.E. 1/4, Sec. 12, Town. 8, N. range 21 W.; 160 acres. Remarks: Living on his patent.

No. 7. Battice Mouchelle, N.W. 1/4, Sec. 7, Town. 8, N. range 20 W.; 147⁶⁴/₁₀₀ acres. Remarks: Move to the Reservation last year, part of the patent fenced.

No. 8. Peter Brown, S. 1/2, N.W. 1/4, N. 1/2, S.W. 1/4, Sec. 8, Town. 8, N. range 20 W.; 160 acres. Remarks: Living on his patent.

No. 9. Charles Qualchinee, S. 1/2, N.E. 1/4, S. 1/2, N.W. 1/4, Sec. 6, Town. 8, N. range 20 W.; 151¹⁰/₁₀₀ acres. Remarks: A small parcel of patent fenced.

No. 10, Charles La Moose, S.E. 1/4, Sec. 6, Town. 8, N. range 20 W.; 160 acres. remarks: Living on his patent.

No. 11. John Kiser, S.W. 1/4, Sec. 6, Town. 8, N. range 20 W.; 145⁸/₁₀₀ acres. Remarks: Dead, Widow married to Dutch Lumphrey who has no patent.

No. 12. Stephen James, S.E. 1/4, Sec. 24, Town. 7, N. range 21 W.; 160 acres. Remarks: John Hill living on the patent.

No. 13. Sapelle James, S.W. 1/4, Sec. 19, Town. 7, N. range 20 W.; 155²⁰/₁₀₀ acres. Remarks: Not living on the patent.

No. 14. Big Samuel, N.E. 1/4, Sec. 18, Town. 10, N. range 19 W.; 160 acres. Remarks: Moved to the Reservation under the "Garfield agreement" before the patents had been issued.

No. 15. Antoine Numchee, S.E. 1/4, Sec. 7, Town. 10, N. range 19 W.; 160 acres. Remarks: Living on his patent.

No. 16. Francois Kiser, S.W. 1/4, Sec. 8, Town. 10, N. range 19 W.; 160 acres. Remarks: Has 160 acres fenced and in an improved condition but on worthless ground he holds a patent, about 12 miles farther north than his location now.

No. 17. Eneas Kiser, S.E. 1/4, Sec. 8, Town. 10, N. range 19 W.; 160 acres. Remarks: His patent is almost worthless, he has fenced in and cultivated a large tract of land on Three Mile creek, but I believe it is on School land.

No. 18. Esuck Red Wolf, S.E. 1/4, Sec. 1, Town. 9, N. range 20 W.; 160 acres. Remarks: Dead, daughter married to Lame Michel. Two grandchildren are married in Bitter Root Valley.

No. 19. Widow Susteen, S.W. 1/4, Sec. 1, Town. 9, N. range 20 W.; 160 acres. Remarks: Dead, left a married son in Bitter Root Valley who has no patent.

No. 20. Indian Quinley, S.W. 1/4, Sec. 6, Town. 9, N. range 19 W.; 157⁷⁴/₁₀₀ acres. Remarks: Not living on his patent, probably on school land.

No. 21. Widow Pallacino, S.E. 1/4, Sec. 6, Town. 9, N. range 19 W.; 160 acres. Remarks: Married one Thomas Coosah, moved to the Reservation, one married son also moved to the reservation, the other married son in Bitter Root Valley, but has no land.

No. 22. Westiminee James, S.W. 1/4, Sec. 29, Town. 9, N. range 19 W.; 160 acres. Remarks: Dead. Moved to the Reservation. I believe he left no heirs.

No. 23. Joseph Pehotcee, S.E. 1/4, S.E. 1/4, N. 1/2, S.E. 1/4, Sec. 30, Town. 9, N. range 19 W.; 120 acres. Remarks: Living on his patent.

No. 24. Sapelle Chinlough, S. 1/2, N.W. 1/4, Sec. 31, Town. 9, N. range 19 W.; 79⁷⁵/₁₀₀ acres. Remarks: Living on his patent.

No. 25. Deleware Jim, N. 1/2, N.E. 1/4, Sec. 36, S. 1/2, S.E. 1/4, Sec. 25, Town. 9, N. range 20 W.; 160 acres. Remarks: Living on his patent.

No. 26. Henry Aurley (Chief), N. $\frac{1}{2}$, S.W. $\frac{1}{4}$, Sec. 30, Town. 9, N. range 19 W.; N. $\frac{1}{2}$, S.E. $\frac{1}{4}$, Sec. 25, Town. 9, N. range 20 W.; 159$^{62}/_{100}$ acres. Remarks: Moved to the Reservation before the patents were issued.

No. 27. Widow Nine Pipes, S.W. $\frac{1}{4}$, Sec. 25, Town. 9, N. range 20 W.; 160 acres. Remarks: Living together [with Antoine Nine Pipes].

No. 28. Antoine Nine Pipes, N.W. $\frac{1}{4}$, Sec. 36, Town. 9, N. range 20 W.; 160 acres. Remarks: Living together [with Widow Nine Pipes].

No. 29. Gabrielle Lamphrey, N. $\frac{1}{2}$, N.W. $\frac{1}{4}$, Sec. 35, S. $\frac{1}{2}$, S.W. $\frac{1}{4}$, Sec. 26, Town. 9, N. range 20 W.; 160 acres. Remarks: Living on patent. Most of the patent is worthless land.

No. 30. Thomas Coosah, N.E. $\frac{1}{4}$, S.W. $\frac{1}{4}$, Sec. 26, Town. 9, N. range 20 W.; 40 acres. Remarks: Moved to the Reservation, married to the Widow Pallacino (No. 21). No improvements on patent.

No. 31. Eneas Fronsway, N. $\frac{1}{2}$, S.E. $\frac{1}{4}$, Sec. 15, Town. 9, N. range 20 W.; 80 acres. Remarks: Most unjustly this well doing Indian and old settler was given only 80 acres. Living on patent.

No. 32. Peter Fronsway, N. $\frac{1}{2}$, S.W. $\frac{1}{4}$, Sec. 14, Town. 9, N. range 20 W.; 80 acres. Remarks: This patent is worthless, he is living with his father.

No. 33. Eneas Victor, N. $\frac{1}{2}$, S.W. $\frac{1}{4}$, Sec. 27, Town. 9, N. range 20 W.; 160 acres. Remarks: Dead, Peter Fronsway (No. 32) is the nearest relative. Charles Victor's son (No. 41) I believe claims the patent.

No. 34. Antowine Palloo, S. $\frac{1}{2}$, S.E. $\frac{1}{4}$, Sec. 27; S. $\frac{1}{2}$, S.E. $\frac{1}{4}$, Sec. 28, Town. 9, N. range 20 W.; 160 acres. Remarks: Moved to the Reservation, the land now belongs to his wife, Mary Prudhomme, but the son claims to own it.

No. 35. Josephine Slocum, N.W. $\frac{1}{4}$, S.E. $\frac{1}{4}$, Sec. 27, Town. 9, N. range 20 W.; 40 acres. Remarks: Dead, three sisters all married are the nearest relatives, the land adjoins the Stevensville townsite.

No. 36. Josephine Enumsco, E. $\frac{1}{2}$, N.E. $\frac{1}{4}$, Sec. 34, Town. 9, N. range 20 W.; 80 acres. Remarks: Very old and blind women, has a son Alexander married, with a family, but no land or patent, no fence on patent.

No. 37. Alex Bear Tracks, W. $\frac{1}{2}$, N.E. $\frac{1}{4}$, E. $\frac{1}{2}$, N.W. $\frac{1}{4}$, Sec. 34, Town. 9, N. range 20 W.; 160 acres. Remarks: Dead, Moved to the Reservation before patents were issued.

No. 38. Louise Vanderburgh, S.W. $\frac{1}{4}$, Sec. 33, Town. 9, N. range 20 W.; 160 acres. Remarks: Not living on patent, cultivating and farming on other land for many years, has a large number of married children, who hold no patents.

No. 39. Battise Matte, E. $\frac{1}{2}$, N.W. $\frac{1}{4}$, W. $\frac{1}{2}$, N.E. $\frac{1}{4}$, Sec. 26, Town. 9, N. range 20 W.; 160 acres. Remarks: Moved to Reservation before patents were issued.

No. 40. Joseph Matte, W. $\frac{1}{2}$, N.E. $\frac{1}{4}$, Sec. 31, S.W. $\frac{1}{4}$, S.E. $\frac{1}{4}$, Sec. 30, Town. 9, N. range 20 W.; 120 acres. Remarks: Moved to Reservation before patents were issued.

No. 41. Hereditary Chief, Charlo Victor, S. $\frac{1}{2}$, S.E. $\frac{1}{4}$, Sec. 32, Town. 9, N. range 20 W.; N. $\frac{1}{2}$, N.E. $\frac{1}{4}$, Sec. 5, Town. 8, N. range 20 W.; 160$^{80}/_{100}$ acres. Remarks: Living on his patent but the best part of his farm has been given to a White man by the Surveyor.

No. 42. Cecellia Parker, N.W. $\frac{1}{4}$, Sec. 33, Town. 9, N. range 20 W.; 160 acres. Remarks: Dead, the two married daughters and the grandchildren of Esuck, Red Wolf (No. 18).

No. 43. Chief Adolph, S.E.. $\frac{1}{4}$, Sec. 29, Town. 9, N. range 20 W.; 160 acres. Remarks: Moved to reservation. No improvements on patent.

No. 44. Cierelle, N. $\frac{1}{2}$, N.W. $\frac{1}{4}$, Sec. 34, Town. 10, N. range 20 W.; 80 acres. Remarks: Dead, widow very old, one daughter married to a crippled Indian, who has no patent.

No. 45. P. Fronsice Cirelle, S. $\frac{1}{2}$, S.W. $\frac{1}{4}$, Sec. 27, Town. 10, N. range 20 W.; 80 acres. Remarks: Living on his father's patent.

No. 46. Widow Suseen, N. $\frac{1}{2}$, S.W. $\frac{1}{4}$, Sec. 27, Town. 10, N. range 20 W.; 80 acres. Remarks: It is uncertain who this party is, probably a Blackfoot living on the Reservation now, has a married daughter in Bitter Root Valley.

No. 47. Gabereille Cecellin, S. $\frac{1}{2}$, N.W. $\frac{1}{4}$, N. $\frac{1}{2}$, S.W. $\frac{1}{4}$, Sec. 34, Town. 10, N. range 20 W.; 160 acres. Remarks: Living on his patent.

No. 48. Battise Marengo, S. $\frac{1}{2}$, N.E. $\frac{1}{4}$, Sec. 34, Town. 10, N. range 20 W.; 80 acres. Remarks: Dead, moved to the Reservation before the patents were issued.

No. 49. Shawnee Jake, N.E. $\frac{1}{4}$, Sec. 4, Town. 6, N. range 20 W.; 159^{68}/$_{100}$ acres. Remarks: Dead, Widow old and almost blind, one son, dumb, who has land, two married daughters in Bitter Root.

No. 50. Louise Dominick, E. $\frac{1}{2}$, N.W. $\frac{1}{4}$, S.W. $\frac{1}{4}$, N.W. $\frac{1}{4}$, N.W. $\frac{1}{4}$, S.W. $\frac{1}{4}$, Sec. 4, Town. 6, N. range 20 W.; 159^{72}/$_{100}$ acres. Remarks: Dead, the widow is living, they sold the improvements some years ago to a white man who is living on the patent.

No. 51. Frank Marengo, N.E. $\frac{1}{4}$, N.E. $\frac{1}{4}$, N.W. $\frac{1}{4}$, N.E. $\frac{1}{4}$, Sec. 15, Town. 9, N. range 20 W.; 80 acres. Remarks: Dead, widow living. Moved to Reservation.

December 4, 1885a

LR 30,991/1885, SC 55, RG 75, National Archives, Washington, D.C. The cover for this letter includes a note: "Presented by Hon. J. K. Toole." It was received by the Office of Indian Affairs on December 29, 1885.

Ronan apparently wrote this letter in response to accusations in a report filed in the fall of 1885 by M. J. Haley, Special Timber Agent for the U.S. General Land Office. Haley mentioned writing a series of reports in a letter published in "Montana Improvement Company," *The Helena Weekly Independent,* October 15, 1885, page 1, col. 5, but he did not mention the Flathead Indian Reservation specifically. Ronan pointed out that tribal members were employed to cut the timber used in the railroad construction through the reservation.

Haley also investigated a timber trespass on Bitterroot Salish land in 1889.[21]

United States Indian Service,
Flathead Agency,
December 4th, 1885.

Hon. J. K. Toole, M. C.
Washington, D.C.
    Sir:
    For time past I have been occasionally amused but oftener annoyed by reading an extract from a report said to have been made *by one Haley, a Government timber inspector,* in relation to the cutting of timber on the Flathead Reservation, and being entirely cognizant of the whole transaction, and being desirous of placing the matter in a right light to counteract his statement if made as reported in the public press. I respectfully submit the official correspondence quoted below and after perusal it will become apparent that he not only made wild and extravagant assertions but even failed to consult the

records of the bureau which employs him to ascertain if authority had ever been granted for the right to cut timber on the Flathead Reservation.

In the first place it appears from official letters and telegrams that the Northern Pacific Railroad Company made application to the Department of the Interior to cut timber on the Reservation, and on the 26th day of October, 1882, I was notified by telegram as follows:

> "Office of Indian Affairs
> Washington D.C.
> Oct. 26th, 1882.
>
> Ronan, Agent
> Flathead Agency,
> Missoula, Montana
>
> Authority has been granted by this Department to Northern Pacific Railroad Company to cut timber on Flathead reserve for use in constructing railroad thereon, subject to consent of Indians and payment of two dollars per thousand feet, board measure, to Secretary of Interior for use of Indians. Letter by this mail. Consult your Indians and advise result.
>
> H. Price
> Commissioner.
>
> L. 19314 — 82."

On November 12th I received a communication on the same subject enclosing copy of Mr. H. Villard's acceptance of the condition imposed by the Indian Department, official extracts as follows:

> "Department of Interior
> Office of Indian Affairs
> Washington, Oct. 26, 1882.
>
> Peter Ronan, Esq.,
> U.S. Indian Agent,
> Flathead Agency,
> via Missoula, Mont.
>
> Sir:
>
> Upon application of the Northern Pacific R. R. Co., to this Department representing that the work of Construction of the road upon the Flathead Reserve is liable to be greatly impeded by the inability of the Company to cut timber thereon; that the Indians are willing to grant the privilege and the Company ready to pay stumpage, and employ Indian labor in the cutting; authority was yesterday granted by the Department to the said Company to take such timber from the Flathead reserve as may be necessary for the purpose of constructing its road through the same (but not further or otherwise) subject to the consent of the Indian occupants being obtained and signified through you, and upon making proper compensation for the same.
>
> The terms of compensation and manner of payment approved by the Department and submitted to the Company for acceptance are as follows: — two (2) dollars per thousand feet board measure for all timber cut by the R. R. Co., upon the reserve — payment to be made to the Secretary of the Inte-

rior for the benefit of the Confederated tribes occupying the reserve — the quantity of timber cut to be accurately measured by competent persons, and a correct account thereof, verified by the affidavit of the Chief Engineer, or other other [sic] duly authorized officer of the Company to be filed with the Secretary of the Interior, and to be subject ot such further verification as he may direct. Upon the Company signifying to this Department its acceptance of these conditions, and the consent of the Indians, through the Indian Agent, obtained, the work to proceed.

Telegram, substantially to this effect, with instructions to consult your Indians and advise result was dispatched you this morning (see copy enclosed).

As soon as the R. R. Co., is heard from you will be further notified.

Very respectfully
(signed) H. Price
Commissioner."

[Line of text unreadable in original document.]

"Northern Pacific Railroad Company
Presidents Office,
New York, 28th Oct. 1882

Hon. H. L. Joslyn,
Acting Secretary of the Interior
 Sir:
  I have the honor to acknowledge receipt of your communication of the 25th of October, granting permission to this Company to cut timber on the Flathead Reservation on condition that the Company pay the usual stumpage and employ Indian labor in the cutting. I respectfully beg to state that this Company willingly agrees to the conditions imposed.

  I am sir, very respectfully yours

(signed) H. Villard, President."

Under this authority the N. P. R. Co., did cut and use in the construction of their roadway 2,729,006 feet of lumber, the stumpage amounting to $5,458.00, which amount was paid to the Hon. Commissioner of Indian Affairs (H. Price) and by him transferred to me in letter dated October 8th, 1884, as follows:

"Department of the Interior
Office of Indian Affairs
Washington, Oct. 8, 1884.

Peter Ronan,
Ind. Agent
Flathead Agency, Montana
 Sir,
  I enclose you herewith my check No. 116.711, on the Treasurer of the United States for five thousand four hundred fifty and eight dollars ($5,458.00) being amount paid by the Northern Pacific R. R. for lumber cut on the Flathead Reservation and which the Hon. Secretary of the Interior has directed to

be paid per capita to your Indians. You will take this amount up in your account current as "Received from Commissioner of Indian Affairs, being amount paid by Northern Pacific R. R. for 2,729,006 feet of B. M. lumber cut on Flathead Reservation at two dollars ($2.00) per M." and pay it to your Indians per capita.

x x x

Very Respectfully
H. Price
Commissioner."

After taking a careful census of the Indians entitled to share in the amount placed to my credit and paid by the Northern Pacific Railroad Company as stumpage on the amount of timber cut and used by them in the construction of their road through the Reservation i.e. 2,729,006, I found that 1,510 (persons irrespective of age sex or condition) were entitled to shares therein and between the 5th and 9th days of January, 1885, I paid to each of the persons so found entitled, the sum of $3.61 696/1510 and accounted for the said sum to the proper officers on the 31st day of March 1885.

The report of the Inspector as read and understood by me, is false, erroneous and malicious — false in that the timber cut on Reserve was authorized by the Interior Department; erroneous in that *but* 2,729,006 feet were cut instead of the enormous amount he stated; and malicious in that he charges it to a corporation and firm that had nothing whatever to do in the premises as the correspondence will show, and the Records of the Dept. will attest.

Again in the same report as appeared in the Newspapers that a large number of men (thousands) were employed by the Montana Improvement Company or Eddy, Hammond & Co., in cutting timber on the Reservation and that two saw mills were running day and night manufacturing the same into lumber. This I emphatically deny. No one outside of those employed by Mr. J. I. P. Weeks, Division Engineer and in charge of the work and operations of the Railroad Company were at work, or cutting timber, or employed in any other way on this Reservation save and except the regular employes of the Agency, and those employed at the Mission of St. Ignatius, constructing school houses and other buildings for the benefit and use of Indian Children; and further, I distinctly assert that with the exception of the Agency Mill and the one at the Mission for the use and advantage of the Indian schools, no mill or mills have been or are in operation within the confines of the Flathead Reservation; nor has any attempt been made to operate one, and as far as I am aware no one has ever even contemplated such a scheme.

I am very truly Yours
Peter Ronan
U.S. Indian Agent.

December 4, 1885b

Records of the Board of Indian Commissioners, Letters Received, entry 1384, RG 75, National Archives, Washington, D.C.

In this 1885 letter Ronan appeared confident that he could convince the tribes of the Flathead Reservation to accept allotment. See his June 3, 1887, and November 16, 1892, letters below for his second thoughts about selling the policy to the tribes after years of friction over the survey of the reservation boundaries. Ronan does make it obvious in this letter that he agreed with the allotment policy, even though he later despaired of selling it to the tribal members.

United States Indian Service,
Flathead Agency,
December 4th, 1885.

E. Whittlesey Esq.
Sect'y Bd. of Indian Commissioners
Washington, D.C.

Sir,

In reply to your favor of 26th ulto, it gives me pleasure to state in answer to your several inquiries;

1st. Fifty one (51) Indians have received allotments of land in Bitter Root Valley, but that country is not embraced in the limits of the Reservation and the recipients are those Indians known as "Carlos Band" of Bitter Root Flatheads.

2nd. Fifty-one (51) Indians, the same alluded to in reply to question 1st, have been forwarded, but have not accepted, patents.

3rd. Many Indians would be glad to receive patents for their homes. Allotments I could easily arrange here if authorized so to do and make the necessary survey.

4th. All, or nearly all the Indians over whom I exercise jurisdiction are well fitted to receive and occupy any land either alloted to, or patented to them.

Many of the Indians residing on the Reservation are living upon occupying and cultivating land which has never been surveyed, they have all of them, more or less improved the same, but owing to absence of an accurate map of an actual and authorized survey no definite boundaries are established and should an allotment be determined upon, a careful, thorough and complete survey would be necessitated in order to make a fair, equal and impartial distribution of the land.

Very Respectfully
Peter Ronan
U.S. Indian Agent.

December 17, 1885

LR 30,739/1885, RG 75, National Archives, Washington, D.C.

This December 1885 incident at Arlee was a good example of Ronan relying on the chiefs to maintain law and order. During the course of events, the Missoula County Sheriff and his deputies were disarmed by tribal leaders to avoid trouble. Ronan feared the U.S. Army would come on the reservation and aggravate the tension. He made his arguments to the tribal members that the injured Indian, Big Jim, should be turned over to Missoula County authorities.

After much debate, a tribal council finally agreed to surrender Big Jim to the Missoula County Sheriff. The dead man was Baptist Kakashee's son. The incident was widely covered in the newspapers.[22] The conflict was even reported in *The New-York Times*.[23]

Big Jim was quickly released for lack of evidence. The two white men involved — V. H. Coombs and P. Bader — were freed on grounds they acted in self-defense.[24] Father

Lawrence Palladino, S.J., of St. Ignatius Mission, wrote a report on the incident which agreed with Ronan's version. A copy of Palladino's letter was sent to the Secretary of the Interior.[25] Big Jim died of exposure near Ravalli, in January 1890.[26]

In the context of Ronan's efforts to undermine the authority of the chiefs, his dependence on their influence seems ironic.

Valentine H. Coombs, the storekeeper at Arlee in 1885, had been a partner with Andrew Hammond in the cattle business in the Upper Flathead Valley in the 1870s. In the 1880 census he was living in Missoula and listed his occupation as farmer.[27] No further information was located about P. Bader, the Arlee Postmaster involved in the incident. Robert L. Lane was elected Sheriff in Missoula County on the Republican ticket in 1884. Originally from New York State, he came to Cedar Creek, near Superior, Montana, to work as a miner and merchandiser in 1870. After one term as sheriff, Lane homesteaded in the Upper Flathead Valley.[28] No information was found about F. W. Gilbert, the Missoula Superintendent for the Northern Pacific Railroad in 1885.

United States Indian Service,
Flathead Agency,
December 17, 1885.

Hon. Commissioner of Indian Affairs
Washington, D.C.

Sir,

Owing largely to the abandonment by the Railroad employes of the station at Arlee, as also telegrams for troops, a rumor was spread of Indian troubles at this Agency; as no trouble or even an apprehension of such, has agitated the Agency or its people, I have the honor to address you and report all the circumstances which caused the said employes to leave their posts, and the unnecessary calls upon the military authorities.

A couple of drunken Indians arrived at Arlee, from without the confines of the Reservation, on the east bound train and made some demand for goods upon the clerk at the traders store, to these demands the clerk (Mr Coombes) would not accede, and they then forcibly attempted to obtain the same, which attempt was resisted; the clerk seeing danger called upon Mr Bader, the Postmaster, who came armed with a shotgun loaded with bird shot and the clerk likewise armed himself with a revolver, then suddenly one of the Indians drew a bull-dog revolver, aimed at the clerk, when the Postmaster seized him by the wrist of the armed hand; then the Indian with his left drew a large Knife, and while attempting to make a desperate plunge, the Clerk shot him dead, the confederate raised his gun and fired at the Postmaster, but missed his aim, when he in return emptied his shot gun wounding him in the thigh; (the Indian escaped to the brush was subsequently found and arrested) the Postmaster and clerk fearing for their lives telegraphed to Missoula for an armed posse and sent a messenger to me.

Upon arriving upon the scene, the Sheriff and posse having also arrived from Missoula; the clerk was immediately placed in arrest and taken to Missoula leaving a deputy and assistant to arrest the wounded Indian and the Postmaster, in order to bring them to Missoula for preliminary examination; in the meantime I notified Chief Arlee and several of the headmen to come at once to the scene of the tragedy, and after their arrival it was then and there agreed upon to take the wounded Indian as well as the white man to Missoula; everything being so arranged and agreed upon befor the arrival of the east bound train, and having full faith in the agreement, I returned to Agency as everything was quiet at the depot and no signs nor apprehension of either danger or trouble; soon after my departure a party of mounted Indians, accompanied by the father and relatives of the dead man arrived at the depot, and informed the Sheriff "that he could take the white man who did the shooting to Missoula, but they would hold the Indian, and try him according to Indian laws and usages," to this the Sheriff objected when himself and deputies were immediately disarmed by the Indians, the wounded Indian was then placed upon a horse behind another Indian who galloped off with him, the Indians then returned their arms to the Sheriff and deputies and directed them to return to Missoula upon the train; the railroad employes including the Agent, I presume fearing danger, leaped upon the train and the Postmaster who was then under arrest also departed, leaving the depot tenantless and the Agency without mail or telegraphic facilities.

Knowing that intense excitement would be created at the next station, I immediately despatched a messenger to that point (Evaro) conveying the following telegrams to the Commanding Officer, Fort Missoula, Robert Lane, Sheriff Missoula County, and F. W. Gilbert, Supt. N.P.R.R. Missoula M.T. viz:

Commanding Officer
Fort Missoula, M.T.

The Indians prevented the Sheriff from Arresting an Indian prisoner, there is no excitement here among the Indians, neither do I fear any trouble from any Indian source in fact, I apprehend neither trouble or danger. The fact of the R.R. employes leaving the station will no doubt create excitement. I hope to be able to turn the prisoner over to the civil authorities myself. Answer.

(Sgd) Peter Ronan
U.S. Ind. Agent.

* * * * * *

Robert Lane
Sheriff Missoula M.T.

I think there will be no trouble, Indians excited on account of Coombes leaving before having a talk, let the matter rest until you hear from me. I am of opinion that I can turn the prisoner over to you myself when the excitement is over. Answer.

Peter Ronan
U.S. Ind. Agent.

* * * * *

F. W. Gilbert
Supt. N.P.R.R.
Missoula, M.T.

The excitement occasioned by the death of the Indian at Arlee has subsided. I apprehend no trouble, am convinced there is no cause for alarm.

Peter Ronan
U.S. Ind. Agent

The Indians conveyed the wounded man to a house near the Agency, his wounds were attended and there he is at present. I immediately called a Council of all Indians and explained to them clearly and intelligently the trouble that was liable to arise from their hasty action in rescuing the prisoner from the officers of the law; that unless they agreed to turn the prisoner over to the civil authorities for an examination, trouble would surely follow and probably a large posse of armed men, if not the military, would soon appear, demand and force the surrender of the prisoner and all connected with his rescue. The Indians deliberated for over ten hours, and after heated discussions, finally acquiesced in all my suggestions.

Having heard that the military authorities had been called upon by some party or parties the dispatch quoted before reached Missoula in time not to introduce them upon this reservation, as they were armed and equipped and had already boarded the train at Missoula.

Intense excitement, I have no doubt, prevailed in Missoula and the surrounding country owing to my inability to hold communication, but as soon as the dispatches heretofore cited were received the excitement was allayed.

The dead Indian has been buried, the wounded Indian is here subject to any order from the civil authorities; everything in and about the Agency and reservation is quiet, peaceable and orderly, and even during the excitement at the depot nor [sic] an echo, could be heard at any other point, except when the Council met here for deliberation over the delivery of the Indians to the civil authorities, wherein stormy speeches were delivered, but by the calm, cool and deliberate reasonings and arguments of older and more experienced and enlightened headsmen, the latter eventually prevailed.

Very Respectfully
Your obt svt.
Peter Ronan
U.S. Indian Agent.

1886

January 1, 1886
St. Ignatius Mission file, Bureau of Catholic Indian Missions Papers, Marquette University Archives, Milwaukee, Wisconsin.

See also Ronan's letter of December 17, 1885.

> United States Indian Service,
> Flathead Agency,
> January 1st, 1886.

Captain John Mullan,
President Bureau Catholic
Indian Missions,
Washington, D.C.

Dear Sir:

In reply to your favor of the 22d of December inquiring into the reported trouble among the Indians at Arlee Station in this Reservation, I respectfully forward the following report to the Bureau of Catholic Indian Missions, which I copy from my report of the affair to the Hon. Commissioner of Indians Affairs which give full details:

[Here Ronan quoted his December 17, 1885, letter to the Commissioner of Indian Affairs which has been reproduced above. The text below is from Ronan's monthly report of January 1, 1886, which was not preserved in the National Archives.]

From my regular monthly report of Jan. 1st, 1886 to the Hon. Commissioner of Indian Affairs I quote:

"The Commanding officer at Fort Missoula, (when I got communication with him) refrained from forwarding the soldiers at my request. I am pleased to add now that I was enabled to carry my part of the agreement into effect and delivered the Indian prisoner over to the civil authorities. He was promptly tried before a committing magistrate and as promptly discharged for lack of evidence to hold him for the next session of the grand jury. Upon legal examination of the Traders Clerk Coombes and the Postmaster Bader, it was adjudged that the shooting was done in self defense and the Territorial court exonerated them from blame. I deemed it not prudent for either of these parties to resume their positions again at the Railroad station and both men have resigned their positions and their places are filled by others. I was favored with the following from Col. Gibson Commanding Fort Missoula.

> "Fort Missoula, Montana
> Dec. 18th 1885.

Peter Ronan
U.S. Ind. Agt.
Arlee Station,
North Pacific Railroad.

"Your prompt action in quieting the Flathead Indians has been duly reported by me to Military Headquarters. The excitement attendant upon the Railroad people leaving the station, as well as the repeated calls of the Sheriff for Military assistance, together with existing ignorance of the extent of the disaffection among the Indians on account of the shoot-ing affair, induced me to direct Major Jordan to proceed to Arlee yesterday evening with three companies to confer with you in regard to the prevention of further trouble should his services be needed. Happily your Well timed explanitory tele-gram from Evero, enabled me to recall him.

Gibson,
Commanding."
Respectfully submitted
Peter Ronan
U.S. Indian Agent.

March 2, 1886
LR 7,019/1886, RG 75, National Archives, Washington, D.C.

> Ronan tried to open employment opportunities on the reservation. Advertising the work and letting it for government contract would have disadvantaged tribal workers. Ronan mentioned that he had been swamped by requests for employment from tribal members. On March 23, 1886, the Commissioner granted Ronan authority to spend up to $210 to hire tribal members to break 70 acres of land.[1]

United States Indian Service,
Flathead Agency,
March 2d, 1886.

Hon. Commissioner of Indian Affairs
Washington, D.C.

Sir,

Referring to your communication of 11th ult marked F. Letter 31026/85 Authy. 12057, in relation to purchase of fence rails, and employment of labor and purchase of material for building houses for Carlos' Band of Bitter Root Indians, as also to advertise by poster inviting proposals for furnishing 14 cows and breaking seventy (70) acres of land, I have the honor to State that the same reason as set forth in my communication of December 24th last for a modifica-tion as to the building of houses and purchase of rails under contract, apply equally to the breaking of land, and as I stated in my monthly report for Febru-ary I was overtaxed with applications for work. I would earnestly request that the authority conveyed in the Department letter referred to be so far amended as to authorize me to hire Indian labor to break the seventy (70) acres of land alluded to at a rate not exceeding three dollars ($3.00) per acre, (the figure paid last year) or at a less rate if it can be obtained and submit the following additional reasons for my application which I earnestly hope will meet with the favorable consideration of the Department and the consideration also to which I believe it entitled.

1st. Under contract it is almost impossible to have an acre of ground bro-ken by white men, (who will be the only bidders) at a less rate than three dollars ($3.00) per acre.

2d. The Indians here are willing anxious and desirous to labor, hence in my opinion should have the preference all things being equal.

3d. By giving this employment to the Indians it will re-assure them of the desires of the Department to assist them, and

4th. It will be a means to avoid the introduction of white men upon this Reservation, to which I have always and ever strenuously object.

I have the honor to be

Very Respectfully,
Your obt. svt.
Peter Ronan
U.S. Ind. Agent.

March 5, 1886

LR 7,213/1886, SC 55, RG 75, National Archives, Washington, D.C.

The original complaint by the Western Union Telegraph Company was made in January 1886. Ronan argued that the vandalism had been committed by Indians from the west who rode the railroad to Flathead.[2] The railroad and the telegraph companies seemed to believe the agent's main responsibility was protecting their property on the reservation.

United States Indian Service,
Flathead Agency,
March 5th, 1886.

Hon. Commissioner of Indian Affairs
Washington, D.C.

Sir,

I have the honor to acknowledge receipt of your communication marked L. 5072. 1886, with enclosure in relation to the interference with the telegraph lines by Indians, and in reply respectfully state that I have carefully examined into every complaint which has reached this office and find that nearly all the mischief could be traced to Indians from the lower country around Spokane Falls and vicinity, whose only object in visiting this Reservation was to gamble and carouse, by some means they would obtain transportation on the R. R. and in self protection and for the welfare of the Indians under my care, I have in every instance when their presence was made Known to me, instructed my police to bring the Indians to the Agency and I have furnished them a pass to return to their homes and rid this Reservation of their undesirable presence, as a class they are worthless gamblers and drunkards and while attempting to return when ordered off by my police and not securing the requisite pass, the conductors or others in authority compell [sic] them to leave the train and then in retaliation are ready for any mischief. I have no doubt in some cases insulators have been broken by young boys, but am convinced no grown Indian of this reserve has been guilty of the act and I adhere to the statement already made that the breaking of the insulators was done by wandering Spokans but in order to be doubly convinced I will instruct one or two of my most reliable policeman [sic] to watch the particular points where most of the trouble complained of has taken place, and as soon as I receive their report and personally make further investigation into the matter, I will again lay the matter before you.

Very Respectfully
Your obt. svt.
Peter Ronan
U.S. Indian Agent.

March 25, 1886
LR 11,303/1886, RG 75, National Archives, Washington, D.C. Left at Office of In-dian Affairs by Hon. G. G. Vest.

There is no way now to determine how realistic Ronan was in his expectation that Charlo would agree to remove to Jocko. An article in the Missoula newspaper presented a similar argument, but it was probably based on information from Ronan.[3]

Department of the Interior,
Office of Indian Affairs.

See Mr [Wong ?] and inquire of the [****] to money to spare to bring Ronan & Carlos & an interpreter from Flat Head Agency to Washington to Consult about Carlos & his band's removal to Flat Head Reservation.

Atkins.

Above note attached to the following letter:

United States Indian Service,
Flathead Agency,
March 25th, 1886.

Hon. G. G. Vest
Washington, D.C.

Sir,

As you perfectly understand the question of Carlos, (or Charlot) and his Bitter Root band of Flathead Indians, and the refusal of that Chief to consent to the removal of his tribe from that valley to this Reservation, on his visit to Washington in 1884, and as you are also perfectly conversant with the whole history of this Chief and his greivances [sic], as also the great advantages ob-tainable both to the Indians and to the white settlers of Western Montana should Carlos be induced to remove his whole band to this reservation where he properly belongs, I have in view of this induced the Chief to visit the Reser-vation this month, it being the first time he came here since he accompanied Garfield, when he took such a bitter aversion against removing to the reserve on account of his name having been signed to the agreement to remove without his Knowledge, and other misunderstandings with Genl. Garfield and his com-mission, which has ever since embittered him and prevented his abandonment of the lands at Bitter Root. The trip of Carlos here has altogether changed his views and he intimated that if he removed now after his former refusal, that he would have to come and take the common advantages which are held out to each member of his tribe who removes here and besides he claims the special advantages offered him before, as Arlee would be Chief under the Garfield agreement, and the heriditary [sic] claims of Carlos would be ignored, in short I believe if you take an interest in placing the matter before the government in the light which your Knowledge of the facts would warrant, and give the old Chief one more chance to visit Washington, I feel assured he would consent to remove here with all of his people.

He claims now that he was improperly advised and expresses a wish to have one more opportunity; of course I would like to accompany him with an interpreter, and I feel almost confident that this vexed question could be fi-nally settled to the advantage of the Indians, the Government and the citizens of Montana should you Kindly interest Yourself in the matter.

I was by your Kind interest in my affairs re-appointed here in November, and have watched with considerable solicitude for my confirmation by the

Senate. Can I tresspass [sic] once more upon your Kindness to see that my confirmation will be reached by the Senate before adjournment?

I remain with sincere friendship

Yours very truly
Peter Ronan.

March 29, 1886
LR 9,212/1886, RG 75, National Archives, Washington, D.C.

> Ronan pointed out that the agency did not support the Flathead Reservation tribes economically. Rations were very limited and issued to the sick and indigent and in exchange for labor performed for the agency. According to Ronan, the shortage of agricultural equipment such as plows, harness, and grain cradles restricted agricultural development on the reservation.
>
> As mentioned in his August 1885 annual report, the Kootenais at Dayton Creek had a large communal farm. Ronan wanted to help expand Kootenai farming but also wanted to make sure they farmed the white man's way — on individual family plots.

United States Indian Service,
Flathead Agency,
March 29th, 1886.

Hon. Commissioner of Indian Affairs
Washington, D.C.

Sir,

In reply to that portion of your communication of March 20th "A" 6793-86, that "nothing less than a very great improvement over former years will be Satisfactory, as the law requiring all able bodied male Indians to perform Service on their reservations for themselves or their tribe, to entitle them to subsistence (Sec. 18. Stat. 176 and Sec. 346. Regulations 1884) has not been strictly enforced at Some Agencies hitherto, but it will now be applied to the fullest extent possible, that an increase in production, and a decrease in estimates for the purchase of subsistence may at once result." I would respectfully submit, (before alluding to the extent in which agriculture has been carried on at this Agency,) to the following table of subsistence stores estimated for for the fiscal year 1886-7, and the prorata of each article that would in a common distribution be the allowance of each Indian under my charge.

The last census shows the Confederated tribes of Flatheads, Pen D'Oreilles and Kootenais, including the Bitter Root Indians of Carlos Band who have removed here to be 1662, and of Carlos Band of Flathead Indians remaining in the Bitter Root Valley 341, a total of over 2000 Indians, dividing the subsistence supplies estimated for among them, should the quantities be received, the following handsome result would appear.

Articles, lbs of	Total estimated for	Allowance for 1 Year for each Indian
Bacon	12,500	$6\frac{1}{4}$ lbs
Beans	1600	$\frac{4}{5}$ lb
Coffee	3500	$1\frac{3}{4}$ lbs
Flour	25000	$12\frac{1}{2}$ lbs
Rice	1300	$\frac{13}{20}$ lb
Oatmeal	700	$\frac{7}{20}$ lb

Sugar	9500	4³/₄ lbs
Tea	700	⁷/₂₀ lb
Salt	1400	⁷/₁₀ lb

of course there are many Indians on the Reserve who are self supporting, and never apply for subsistence, and the stores are issued only to the sick, indigent, crippled and those who work for their own benefit or the benefit of their respective tribes, to this latter class the majority of the stores are distributed, and the section both of the Statute and the Regulations to which you refer have at all times been rigidly enforced under my administration.

The very practical and excellent views set forth by you, I am proud to say, have been my guide since I took charge of this Reservation and the good results which have followed are to be seen from the fact that last season one hundred and thirty nine heads of families were engaged to a considerable extent in agricultural pursuits, occupying an acreage of over thirteen thousand acres, and raising in about equal proportions over thirty thousand bushels of wheat and oats; they also raised a sufficiency for family use of the usual garden truck, such as potatoes, turnips, onions, peas, beans, carrots, parsnips, rutabagas, melons, cucumbers and in some favored localities corn is also raised in moderate quantities.

Among other improvements last year, I induced sixteen heads of families to purchase from the Geneva New York Nursery at their expense and transportation to this Agency, young fruit trees, such as plum, apple and cherry, which were planted out into orchards, and which shows the spirit that animates them to compare with, if not rival the white farmers of the County of Missoula.

Most of the Indians live in houses and the well fenced farms and the fields of grain which were being harvested at the time of the visit of Mr. [William S.] Holman of Indiana with the Congressional Committee of which he was Chairman, elicited from that gentleman and his companions, the warmest terms of praise for the evidences of civilization, thrift and advancement which manifested itself as I drove them over different localities of the Reservation; unlike the average Inspector, those gentleman [sic] had words of encouragement and expressed appreciation for the patient and painstaking efforts which were being put forth at this Reservation to educate the Indians up to civilizing pursuits, and the good results which were manifest to them on every side.

A greatly increased number of farms have been fenced in during the past winter, and as the weather was very mild a good deal of plowing was done in the month of February. March has however been cold and boisterous and as the ground froze up, plowing ceased but will be resumed this week; a largely increased acreage will be cultivated this season, as the Indians now feel that their future depends upon their own efforts and to this end I shall bend my energies.

As you state you would be pleased to have me give my views and make such suggestions as I think would further the work, I would say that the great object at present is to furnish implements of labor to the Indians, large as my issues of plows has been heretofore, I have not nearly enough to satisfy the demand this Spring; wagons and harness are also necessary to the new beginner, as without these articles rails for fencing cannot be hauled nor can plowing be done. I made requisition for harness last year but received none. Grain cradles on this years requisition should be forwarded so as to reach here no later than the 20th of July.

In order to increase the yield per acre, a system of irrigation should be inaugurated in most of the agricultural valleys of this Reservation, employing Indians to dig the ditches at fair wages. A large granary for storage of Indian grain should be built at the Agency, no root houses would be required as the Indian farmers generally have small root houses upon their farms. The granary would be required to store grain either to be ground into flour at the Agency Mill, or in case of a surplus, to be shipped to market from the depot at Arlee, which is only about four miles from the Agency, by the Indian owners of the Same.

Another threshing machine will be required this fall, (it has been estimated for in the fiscal year 1886-7) as the Indian farms are So widely Separated it is impossible to accommodate all with one machine, a large number were compelled to tramp out their grain last fall with horses, which occasioned great loss. A good market for all Kinds of farm products can be found in the various towns of the Territory, and shipments can be made to several points from the Northern Pacific Rail Road Stations, along the line of the route, which runs for fifty miles through the Reservation. I expect Some Indians cultivating the largest farms will take advantage of those facilities to dispose of Surplus produce.

The unfortunate band of Kootenai Indians, who are included with the tribes of the Reservation, and to whose peculiar condition your attention was invited in my communication of Aug. 20th 1885, need more attention than any others, isolated as they are from the Agency, being Settled some seventy miles away and in reaching them the Flathead Lake must be crossed by an Indian ferry boat. It will be readily seen under such circumstances that the Agent cannot give them or their wants as much personal attention as their necessities demand, I would therefore suggest that if authority can be granted for an additional farmer and I be allowed to select a person, either a well informed half breed who understands their language or a whiteman, capable and willing to assist this tribe in the art of agriculture and civilizing pursuits, I feel assured that success will crown the effort. This matter if possible should be acted upon at once, and arrangements could be made this spring for largely increased agricultural pursuits, among that poverty stricken band of Indians.

I have the honor to be

Very Respectfully
Your Obt. Svt.
Peter Ronan
U.S. Indian Agent.

April 13, 1886
LR 10,775/1886, RG 75, National Archives, Washington, D.C.

Tribal rights for persons in mixed marriages was already a problem in 1886. Ronan proposed having a general council of tribal members decide which white people married to Indians could live on the reservation. The Commissioner replied that white people who married into the tribes should only be allowed on the reservation if they were "men of good character" and "their presence is not objectionable to the Indians." Ronan was instructed to call upon the military, if needed, to expel from the reservation any white men who were living in adultery.[4]

United States Indian Service,
Flathead Agency,
April 13th, 1886.

Hon. Commissioner of Indian Affairs
Washington, D.C.

Sir,

Whitemen who married women of Indian blood, related to the tribes of this Reservation, and who lived and raised families outside of the reserve, are now giving trouble by quietly removing here with their families, on one pretext or another, one will say he is hired to cut rails for his Indian relative; another that he is cultivating the land on shares etc. On desiring these people to remove from the Reservation, I am sometimes confronted by a Chief or head man, who will say: "these people are blood relatives of mine and I desire they not be disturbed." I can see that if a peremtory [sic] stop is not put to this that the choicest locations on the reserve will be located on by such people under the pretext of being related to the tribes and having permission of some chief or head man to occupy the land.

As a great majority of the Indians are opposed to those people removing here, I have advised them to call a general Council to enquire into the matter, and to give me the name and location of any white person or head of half breed family, who is living on the Reservation without proper right, and if in the opinion of the Agent and a majority of said Council that such persons have not said right or permission of the Indians to live on the reserve, I will take the necessary steps to cause their removal.

I would respectfully enquire if an Indian woman who marries a white man, loses her tribal right by that action and if it is proper for the Agent to oppose the man in taking up a farm or living on the Reservation.

Indians generally are opposed to their young women marrying white men, and claim with a good deal of truth that their women are only sought after by worthless fellows merely to obtain a foothold on the reserve, and when a young woman marries one of them she must sever her reservation rights and remove with her husband from the reserve. As a rule this may be proper, but under it some cases of hardship might arise.

I respectfully submit the matter for advice and instructions, and will try to deal with it justly and in a manner satisfactory to the Indians and the Department.

I also respectfully request information as to what course, if any, I should pursue in the case of a white man, who is supposed (with very strong circumstantial evidence of the fact) to be living in adultery with an Indian woman of this reservation, who has a husband here, and who with his friends resisted my police in the discharge of their duty, endeavoring to recover the woman from a life of shame and returning her to her husband.

Very Respectfully
Your obt. svt.
Peter Ronan
U.S. Ind. Agent.

April 30, 1886
LR 12,154/1886, RG 75, National Archives, Washington, D.C.

Work was being completed on a Jocko Valley irrigation ditch to water the farms of the Bitterroot Salish families who had recently removed to the Flathead Reservation. Most of the labor digging the ditch was performed by tribal members.

The question of locating the Lower Pend d'Oreille Indians on the Flathead Reservation would occupy much of Ronan's time in later years. At this point, however, the Commissioner requested that Ronan not pursue the removal until a formal agreement was negotiated and Congress appropriated money to pay the costs involved.[5]

United States Indian Service,
Flathead Agency,
April 30, 1886.

Hon. Commissioner Indian Affairs
Washington, D.C.

Sir:

I am in receipt of Letter 9212 – '86 – F. in relation to the condition and wants of the Indians under my charge, in which you state that I am authorized to submit an estimate in detail of the amount of labor and material required in irrigating, with a plan of the proposed ditch and any and all information which may enable your office to act understandingly in the consideration and determination of this question. In reply I beg to submit the following report:

I am now drawing to completion and will have in full readiness for the irrigation of the crops of this spring's planting by the Indians, a ditch which is intended to divert the waters of the Jocko river from its main channel to a vast plateau of rich agricultural land which when properly irrigated and cultivated will furnish homes for hundreds of families, and upon which plateau I am constructing houses, fencing in fields, breaking up and seeding lands for the families of Charlos' band who have removed from the Bitter Root valley to this Reservation. This ditch is of the following dimensions, viz: Two feet deep; three feet wide in the bottom and four feet wide on top. The ditch was necessarily constructed until it reached the head of said plateau through a rough and rocky cañon for a distance of about two miles, and required a great deal of fluming and blasting. The flume like the ditch is three feet in the bottom of two inch plank; two feet high of inch and a half plank; bottom sills 4 x 6; side pieces 4 x 4; cap pieces 2 x 6, all morticed and tenanted and like the ditch has a fall of one quarter of an inch to the rod. About eighty thousand feet of lumber is required for the full completion of the ditch which is continued along the foothills of the plateau for some four miles, making about six miles and covering the fields and farms of the present Indian settlers in that locality, and will furnish abundance of irrigation for others who may come. The principal work of this undertaking was done by Indians, with exception of one or two whitemen who worked on the flume. The Indians were willing and anxious to earn wages, and the construction of the ditch furnished them profitable employment and was a means of encouragement to labor and also to keep them on the Reservation and away from the whisky drinking towns and the hunting grounds. After a careful examination I have concluded that the building of another irrigation ditch will not be required this season, as I have turned another water course, in a small way, with Indian labor, which also furnishes irrigation for a number of farms. I conclude therefore that it will not be necessary to construct another ditch at present unless the entire band of Chief Charlos conclude to remove here from the Bitter Root valley.

In this connection I wish to inform the Hon. Commissioner that last week I was in receipt of a letter from Victor, Chief of Calispels or Lower Pen d'Oreilles, whos[e] band is under the charge of the Colville Indian Agency, and who lives outside of any Indian Reservation, in a valley near Lake Calispel in Eastern Washington Territory. That Chief sent a messenger and asked me to send passes over the Northern Pacific Railroad, from a station called Sand Point on the Pend d'Oreille Lake to this Agency for himself and seven of his Indians, as they wished to come here and visit the Reservation with a view of removing here should they get my consent and that of the Indians — after making proper arrangements in the Indian Department for such removal. As I am fully aware of the disturbed condition of Victor and his band, who live in a beautiful valley containing fine hay meadows very much coveted by the whites of that region. As the land has been surveyed it is now doubtless open for settlement, and could this Chief be induced to move here with his band and the Indians of this Reserve give their consent for him to do so, I think it would be an easy and most satisfactory way to settle the question. I sent the passes to Victor and expect he will arrive here within a few days. Should you have any instructions to give me in regard either to the encouragement or the discouragement of this movement I would be glad to serve your views. This is another reason that I do not deem it advisable to make any preliminary survey or other arrangement looking to the bringing of another ditch, for should any move be made towards removing the Calispels here, it would be time enough to decide upon a waterway to be brought upon the land they might select for a home on the Reservation, which could be utilized both for the new settlers and the general good of the other Indians of the Reservation. The views as expressed in your letter in relation to my sug[g]estion that the Government furnish these Indians with another threshing machine and build them a granary are very practical and I will make the effort, as sug[g]ested by you, to induce the Indians to do this from their own exertions and funds, and feel confident that I will succeed as some of the more thrifty ones from year to year evince more of a disposition of independence and self reliance. All other advice and sug[g]estions conveyed in our letter will be carefully followed.

Very Respectfully
Your ob't. servt.
Peter Ronan,
U. S. Indian Agent.

May 4, 1886
LR 12,560/1889, now an enclosure in 15,507/1886, RG 75, National Archives, Washington, D.C.

> The Bitterroot Valley Indian farmer whose land was being filed on by Thomas H. Gibbons, a white man, was Baptiste Pierrish. Gibbons and his family had moved to Stevensville in 1879. He originally filed on Pierrish's farm in April 1885.[6] Pierrish was three quarters Nez Perce but his parents had lived in the Bitterroot Valley for many years. He was born on the plains while on a buffalo hunt with the Bitterroot Salish and was about twenty years old in 1886. For many years he was a prominent stockman in the Bitterroot before removing to the

Jocko Reservation.[7] In response to Ronan's report, the Commissioner of Indian Affairs moved aggressively to protect Pierrish's rights. On May 21, 1886, the Commissioner of Indian Affairs wrote the General Land Office, and a day later he wrote Ronan, to insist that Pierrish be protected. He stated to Ronan that: "If the facts are as stated by Father [Jerome] D'Aste, I am satisfied that the Indian will be protected in his rights, and kept in possession."[8] The General Land Office replied on June 8, 1886, that the local land office in Missoula had been ordered to consider Pierrish's claim.[9] On June 15, 1886, Ronan was instructed: "You will cooperate with the local land officers looking to the protection of the Indian in his lawful rights."[10] Despite the protestations of protecting Pierrish's rights, on August 30, 1889, Gibbons received his final patent to the land both claimed.[11]

S. W. Langhorne, the register of the United States Land Office in Helena in 1886, moved to Montana in 1865. Over the years he held various public offices and also worked as a journalist.[12]

United States Indian Service,
Flathead Agency,
May 4th, 1886.

Hon. Commissioner of Indian Affairs
Washington, D.C.
Sir:

I have the honor to to enclose herewith a series of correspondence relative to the filing on land occupied by an Indian, named Baptist Pierrist, in the Bitter Root Valley. The filing it appears was made by a white man named Thos. H. Gibbons, the notice of his intention to make final proof is also forwarded. From the letter of Rev. Father D'Aste S.J. in charge of St. Marys Mission, at Stevensville M.T. it would appear that the Indian has lived upon, occupied and improved the land in question, during a period of over five years: as will also appear I referred the matter to the Register of the U.S. Land office at Helena, M.T., but his reply does not afford me any tangible means for protecting the Indian in what I consider his just and equitable rights, hence I refer the whole matter to you for instructions.

Very Respectfully
Your obt. Svt.
Peter Ronan
U.S. Indian Agent.

First enclosure:

Stevensville, Apr. 30th, 86.

Maj. P. Ronan
U.S. Indian Agent.
Dear Major,

The bearer of this comes to you asking of your Kindness to help him. I enclose the notice of Final Entry of Th Gibbons who filed, some time last year, on the land upon which the bearer and his family, mother and two married sisters are living these last five or six years, and on which they built a large building that cost them over 1200 dollars. Last winter the bearer cut 4000 rails, or rather bought them of a white man, intending to fence in most of the land; but now this new comer steps-in and wants to take away from him his land.

I hope that you will be so Kind as to help these people, who by the poor management of the bearer are fast becoming poor.

Please to give my best respects to your lady, and Mr. Livingston and family.

Yours Respectfully
J. D'Aste S.J.

Enclosed was a clipping from an unidentified newspaper of "Notice of Final Entry," dated April 22, 1886, for Thomas H. Gibbons, claiming a homestead in the Bitterroot Valley. Four white men from Corvallis swore that Gibbons had resided on and was cultivating the land claimed.

Second enclosure:

United States Indian Service,
Flathead Agency,
May 1st, 1886.

S.W. Langhorne Esq.
Register U.S. Land Office
Helena, M.T.

Dr Sir,

I enclose herewith a letter from Rev. Father D'Aste S.J. enclosing a copy of notice of final entry of one Thomas H. Gibbins, from the letter you will perceive that he has filed on land which an Indian (Baptiste Pierrist) and his family have resided for over five years.

The enclosed circular No. 133, from the Dept. of the Interior, being an extract from an Act of Congress, gives the Indian the same right as a white man to homestead land, and they (the Indians) having lawful possession, have the first right. I would thank you to look into this matter and advise me what steps I may take to protect the Indian's right, if you can offer no advice, I will refer the matter to the Hon. Secretary of the Interior, through the Commissioner of Indian Affairs for instructions.

Very Respectfully Yours
Peter Ronan
U S Indian Agent.

Please return the enclosed papers with your reply and oblige.

Enclosed was a copy of Circular No. 133, July 28, 1884, from the Commissioner of Indian Affairs quoting an Indian appropriations act approved July 4, 1884, which allows for Indians to secure homesteads on public lands. Deeds were to be held in trust for twenty-five years, and no fees were to be charged the Indian homesteaders.

Third enclosure:

United States Land Office,
Helena Mont.
May 3rd, 1886.

Hon. Peter Ronan
Indian Agent

Sir,

I have the noted the contents herewith enclosed. Am of the opinion that this settler from this showing should be defeated in his rights and my advice would be for Baptiste Pierrist to appear on the day set for making proof and contest the entry and offer his own and any additional evidence, or submit the

JUNE 3, 1886   359

case upon a statement of the facts to the Hon Com Genl Land office. In the meantime I think the Indian had better file [Hmstd?] on the land, if you are sure they the entries are identical. I must confess that my experience does not cover such a case, and it is one which perhaps the Comr ought to pass on.

Yours Truly
S. W. Langhorne
Register.

May 27, 1886
LR 14,592/1886, RG 75, National Archives, Washington, D.C. Action notation: File.

Flathead Agency
May 27, 1886

Respectfully forwarded to Hon Com Indian Affairs for information.

Peter Ronan
U.S. Ind. Agt.

Enclosure:

St. Ignatius Mission
Flathead Reservation
May 25/86

Major P. Ronan, U.S. Ind. Agent.

Dear Sir

There is considerable sickness prevalent amongst the Indians of this Reservation at large as well as amongst the pupils of the St. Ignatius Mission School under my charge. I regret to have to state that these poor people have had for a good while little, and for nearly the last two months, no medical attendance of any kind; and that several of them have lately died who, in all likelihood, with proper medical care and treatment could have been saved. I call your attention to this and to the urgent necessity there is of securing at once the services of a competant [sic] physician for the suffering wards in your keeping. In hopes that this my appeal may meet with a favorable response and secure a timely succor in our needs, I remain

Yours truly & respectfully
L. B. Palladino, S.J.

June 3, 1886
LR 15,349/1886, RG 75, National Archives, Washington, D.C.

> Operating the new irrigation ditch required additional labor to protect the ditch and allocate the water to the different farms.

United States Indian Service,
Flathead Agency,
June 3rd, 1886.

Hon. Commissioner of Indian Affairs
Washington, D.C.

Sir:

In as much as the irrigation Season is now opened, and the presence of a ditch is a novelty to the Indians and as more than ordinary care must be exercised to protect the Same from injury through the pranks of Indian children and the ignorance of the Indians themselves, who are unacquainted with the methods of operation and the quantity of water required for the harvesting of a successful crop and as allowed in my monthly report for the month of May, I have the honor to request that authority be granted me for the employment of an irregular employee for the period of 30 days, Sundays included, from June 1st to June 30th at the rate of ($50) fifty dollars per month, to protect the ditch, guard the flood gates and distribute the water as required.

Very Respectfully
Your obt. Svt.
Peter Ronan
U.S. Indian Agent.

August 15, 1886
U.S. Commissioner of Indian Affairs, Annual Report of the Commissioner of Indian Affairs*(Washington, D.C.: U.S. Government Printing Office, 1886), pages 396-399.*

> Ronan repeated his argument from his March 29, 1886, letter that the Indian people on the Flathead Reservation were primarily self-supporting. Most of the rations distributed by the agency were used to pay for labor benefitting the agency or the tribes as a whole.
>
> Considerable progress was being made expanding farming and ranching on the reservation. Many tribal members worked for wages in the construction of the Jocko Valley irrigation ditch and developing farms for the Bitterroot Salish families recently removed to the Jocko Valley.
>
> The Kootenai at Dayton Creek had developed a communal farm which offended Ronan's nineteenth century white sensibilities. Chief Eneas was mentioned frequently in Ronan's later letters. Eneas was able to fight to protect his tribe and its interests despite repeated harassment and provocation by Upper Flathead Valley white settlers.
>
> Like all of Ronan's annual reports, this one expressed his prejudices and biases in favor of nineteenth century white American culture and values and against traditional tribal ways of life.

Flathead Agency, Montana
August 15, 1886.

Sir: In accordance with instructions, I herewith submit my tenth annual report from the Flathead Indian Agency, Montana Territory.

The confederated tribes of this reservation, consisting of the Flatheads, the Pen d'Oreilles, and the Kootenais, including the Bitter Root Indians of Charlos' band, who have removed here, the last census shows to be 1,662, and of Charlos' band or Flathead Indians remaining in the Bitter Root Valley 341, a total of over 2,000 Indians. Dividing the subsistence supplies estimated for among them for this fiscal year, the following result would appear:

Articles.	Estimated. Pounds.	Allowance for one year for each Indian. *Pounds.*
Bacon	12,500	$6\frac{1}{4}$
Beans	1,600	$\frac{4}{5}$
Coffee	3,500	$1\frac{3}{4}$
Flour	25,000	$12\frac{1}{2}$
Rice	1,300	$\frac{13}{20}$

Oatmeal	700	$7/20$
Sugar	9,500	$4^{3}/_{4}$
Tea	700	$7/20$
Salt	1,400	$7/10$

Of course there are many Indians on the ressrve [reserve] who are self-supporting, and never apply for subsistence, and the stores are used only for the sick, indigent, crippled, and those who work for their own benefit or the benefit of their respective tribes. To this latter class the majority of the stores are distributed, and the law requiring all able-bodied male Indians to perform service on their reservations for themselves or their tribe to entitle them to subsistence (sec. l8, Stat. 176, and sec. 356, Regulations 1884) has been enforced at this agency. I quote above table for the careful study of those who claim that the Indians of this reservation are furnished with a large percentage of substence by the Government. The figures will show but slight assistance from the Government in subsistence, and next year's estimates will be greatly reduced.

In reply to a portion of a communication from the honorable Commissioner of Indian Affairs, under date of March 20, 1886, I made the following statement, which will do to repeat in my annual report: The very practical and excellent views set forth by, I am proud to say, have been my guide since I took charge of this reservation, and the good results which followed are to be seen from the fact that last year 139 heads of families were engaged to a considerable extent in agricultural pursuits, occupying an acreage of over 13,000 acres of wheat and oats; they also raised a sufficiency for family use of the usual garden truck, such as potatoes, turnips, onions, peas, beans, carrots, parsnips, rutabagas, melons, cucumbers, and in some favored localities corn is also raised in moderate quantities.

Among other improvements, last year I induced 16 heads of families to purchase from the Geneva (New York) Nursery, at their expense and transportation to this agency, young fruit-trees, such as plum, apple, and cherry, which were planted out into orchards, and which shows the spirit that animates them to compare with, if not rival, the white farmers of the county of Missoula.

Dwelling-Houses.

Most of the Indians live in houses, and the well-fenced farms and the fields of grain which were being harvested at the time of the visit of Mr. [William] Holman, of Indiana, with the Congressional committee of which he was chairman, elicited from that gentleman and his committee warm terms of praise for the evidence of civilization, thrift, and advancement which manifested itself as they were driven over the different farming localities of the reservation. Unlike the average inspector, those gentlemen had words of encouragement, and expressed appreciation for the patient and painstaking efforts which were being put forth at this reservation to educate the Indians up to civilizing pursuits and the good results which were manifested to them on every side.

Fencing.

A greatly increased number of farms have been fenced in during the past winter and spring, and as the weather was mild considerable plowing was done in the month of February. In March the ground froze hard, but plowing was resumed early in April. A largely increased acreage has been cultivated this season. The Indians are beginning to realize the fact that their future depends upon their own efforts, and to this end every aid and encouragement shall be exerted at this agency. Farming implements are in great demand, and large as my issue of plows has been heretofore I had not enough last year to satisfy the demand.

The greater portion of the land lying along the valley of the Jocko, Mission Valley, Pen d'Oreille, Canvas [sic] Prairie, Little Bitter Root, and about Dayton Creek is well adapted to the growing of wheat and oats, and the general garden vegetation. Irrigation at this reservation is necessary, although not absolutely so in the bottom lands adjoining the rivers and larger creeks. About 400,000 acres of the reserve is tillable, and the balance, 900,000 acres, grazing land and timber.

Irrigation.

This season I completed and had in full operation an irrigation ditch which diverts the waters of the Jocko River from its main channel to a vast plateau of rich agricultural land which, when properly irrigated and cultivated, will furnish homes for hundreds of families. The irrigation ditches are about 6 miles in length and of the following dimensions: Two feet deep, 3 feet wide in the bottom, and 4 feet wide on top. The water, in order to be converted from the bed of the Jocko River, to reach the plateau intended to be irrigated, was raised some 200 feet, and the ditch had necessarily to be constructed, in order to raise it upon said plateau, through a rough and rocky cañon for a distance of about 2 miles, and required a great deal of fluming; some blasting was also necessary to its completion. The flume, like the ditch, is 3 feet in the bottom, of 2-inch planks; bottom sills 4 by 6; side pieces 4 by 4; cap pieces 2 by 6, all mortised and tenoned, and like the full continuation of the ditch, has a fall of one-quarter of an inch to the rod. About 80,000 feet of lumber were required for the completion of the ditch, all which was manufactured at the agency saw-mill. The ditch is continued down the plateau along the foot-hills, and is spread out among the Indian fields by the use of a furrow run by a plow, which conveys the water over the small gardens and grain fields, which certainly would not mature but for this system of irrigation. By proper cultivation and irrigation grain can be and is made to yield from 30 to 50 bushels to the acre.

Employment of Indians.

The Indians generally are willing and anxious to earn wages, and the excavating of the ditch furnished them employment, and during its construction was a means of encouragement to labor, and also to keep them on the reservation and away from the white settlements and hunting grounds. Such expenditures result in general good to all, as it furnishes paid employment to those who seek labor, encourages and teaches habits of industry to all who would rise above the level of savagery and indolence, and who try by industry to imitate the modes and living of the white race. Along the plateau watered by the ditch I have been and am now engaged in settling the families of

Charlos' Band

of Bitter Root Indians, who choose to abandon their lands in that valley and remove to this reservation. Seventeen houses have been constructed for the families so removed, 10 acres of land broken up for each family, and rails furnished for the fencing in of the same, and with exception of two fields, all are under fence and cultivation.

The members of Charlos' band who removed from the Bitter Root to this agency cannot be classed among them most industrious and civilized members of the tribe. In fact the colony is composed mostly of Indians who, with their families; followed the buffalo until this game became almost extinct, and continued to make a precarious living by hunting, fishing, and wandering among the settlements. It will therefore readily be perceived that no easy task is imposed upon the administration of affairs at this agency to bring these Indians suddenly into the ways of strict attention to the cultivation and harvesting of their fields, proper irrigation of the same, and to restrain them from wandering and the chase. But having made a beginning in a small way encouragement and assistance will induce them to enlarge their operations. I confidently believe that another year of proper management and encouragement will place those families on a basis of self-support and beyond the necessity of any subsistence from the Government.

Kootenais.

The band of Kootenai Indians who are included with the confederated tribes of this reservation are in great want, and need the fostering hand of assistance more than any others on the reservation, and yet are the most neglected, owing to the fact of their being isolated from the agency by a distance of about 70 miles, and the impracticability of sparing the service from the small force of agency employés to assist their efforts.

This tribe or band have one large enclosure which they cultivate in common, a practice which should at once be broken up, and each head of a family be placed in possession of an inclosure for himself, and taught self-reliance, by the cultivation of the soil for the exclusive benefit of himself and family. Authority should be given to employ an additional farmer to reside at their settlement, a capable man, competent and willing to assist and teach this poor tribe in the cultivation of the soil, and to aid them in building houses and making separate and individual farms and houses. Until this is done the unfortunate Kootenai will continue to be a wretched, dirty, wandering vagrant. Eneas, the chief of this band, is a sensible, generous man, fully devoted to the welfare of his tribe, but without encouragement and the assistance of a resident farmer, devoted to his duties, the chief is almost helpless, and his efforts unaided will result in hopelessness and failure.

Education.

There are two industrial schools on this reservation at Saint Ignatius Mission, one for boys and the other for girls. The, Government has never built a school-house on the reservation. All the educational facilities established in the agency have been under the auspices of the Catholic Church. I have understood that the first steps of the church to establish schools within the agency occurred in 1859 or 1860, but in earnest in the year 1864. Since 1879 there have been two boarding schools at Saint Ignatius Mission, one for boys and the other for girls. During the fiscal year 1884 the boys' school averaged in attendance 74, including certain Blackfeet pupils, and the girls' school averaged 82. The contract with the Government for that year was $100 for each pupil up to the number 50 for each school of the children of this agency, and 25 of the Blackfeet tribe for each school. At the present time and for the past year the contract is $150 for each of 75 children in each school. These children remain in the school the year round. There is a partial vacation in the month of August, but it extends only to a suspension of certain studies.

In addition to the usual branches taught in school — reading, writing, arithmetic, grammar, music, and geography — the pupils are taught housekeeping, such as washing, ironing, sewing, dairy work, cooking, and general household duties in the girls' school, and in the boys' school the pupils are taught blacksmithing, carpentering, working in saw and grist mills, running shingle-machines, farming work, gardening, teaming, and all general farming work, tailoring, shoe-making, saddlery and harness painting, and all work incident to the institution. The art of printing is also taught in a neat little printing-office where dictionaries of the Kalispel language, the Gospels, and innumerable pamphlets and circulars have been neatly printed.

The Indian schools of Saint Ignatius Mission, on the Flathead Reservation, are pointed to with pride by citizens of all denominations in Montana, and they should be encouraged and sustained by the Government as the best and only means that can be employed with any hope of success to educate the young Indian generation. In those conclusions my own observations are borne out by such men as the Rev. L. B. Palladino, S.J., who has spent almost a lifetime among the Indians, and who well says, The Indian is a savage, and to civilize him means to make him cease to be what he is by elevating him from his savage condition to a state more in harmony with reason and man's nature. There is no doing a thing without a way, means, and process of doing it, and here way, means, and process are what I understand by education. On the other hand, grown-up people, be they red, black, or white, cannot be trained easily into new ways and new habits. Theirs is the case of the aged, knotty tree. No ordinary force can give it or make it retain a shape contrary to its natural bend. It is unyielding, and will sooner snap under the strain. Hence, as the young Indian of to-day will be the grown-up Indian of to-morrow, if he be not trained when he can, when plastic and capable of being formed, most likely he will remain when old what he ceased to be when he was young, and thus the savage condition of the race must need be perpetuated.

Rules Governing the Code of Indian Offenses.

On the 12th of February, 1885, I had the honor of submitting to the Indian Office a code of laws drawn up and submitted by me to the Indians in general council, which were adopted by them and approved by the honorable Secretary of the Interior, and are now the rules or laws which govern the Indians of this reservation. On that date a police force was organized, and three judges were selected to administer the laws, who were chosen from the best men of the tribe. Culprits are sentenced to imprisonment, hard labor, and fines, and the administration of the rules governing Indian offenses are enforced with good judgment and dignity. Two new jails are necessary to the enforcement of discipline, one of which should be constructed at Saint Ignatius Mission and the other at the agency. The judges of the court should also be paid for their services as well as the police, as upon their strict attention to duty rests all the good that the police can perform in keeping order on the reservation. As this is a non-ration agency no provision has as yet been made to furnish the police with subsistence, nor have they received clothing or equipments to present date. This state of affairs is very discouraging to the police force, but I am hopeful that provision has been made in accordance with requisitions to relieve those wants during the present fiscal year.

Very respectfully, your obedient servant,

Peter Ronan,
United States Indian Agent.

The Commissioner of Indian Affairs.

September 1, 1886
LR 23,856/1886, RG 75, National Archives, Washington, D.C.

United States Indian Service,
Flathead Agency,
September 1st, 1886.

The Hon. Commissioner of Indian Affairs
Washington, D.C.

Sir:

The month of May was so very warm for this latitude that the melting snow of the mountains raised the currents of the brooks and rivers of this reservation to an unprecedented height, which threatened at one time to sweep away the bridges. As a precautionary measure to save the flume in the irrigation ditch, and also, the inundation of the Same, I caused the dam at the head of the ditch to be cut away and give the water full flow through the channel of the Jocko river. This precaution, I believe, saved the ditch and flume from great damages. The freshet in the rivers continued through almost the entire month of June, during which month a considerable amount of rain fell; and the appearance of the growing crops gave hope of an abundant harvest. During the months of July and August, no rain fell; the forests surrounding the reservation were on fire, and forest fires are still raging in every direction. Where irrigation was available the Indian grain crops averaged well, but where dependence was placed upon natural moisture, the grain is shriveled up and the yield will fall far below the estimates in my annual report.

The grain cradles so much needed for the harvest fields have not yet arrived, but old ones were repaired, and by the use of the combined mower and reaper which I was authorized to purchase, and also the one I had on hand at the Agency and some other machines owned and purchased by individual Indians, the harvest will be successfully gathered.

The thresher was put in repair and the machine set in motion last week, but owing to the breaking of a cog-wheel on the horse-power, the machine will be idle until the necessary repair can be made at the foundry at Helena.

I started the machine early in order to try to get the Indians' grain threshed before winter sets in. The fields and farms are so far distant from each other, that three machines are actually required to successfully thresh the Indians' crops. As I am only supplied with one machine, it requires energetic movements to get around to all.

The grist mill will be in thorough repair for the grinding of grain, as fast as delivered, this month.

The hay crop was short this year, but the Indians who own considerable stock, have been energetically engaged in cutting and stacking wild hay in anticipation of a severe winter, which the Indians hold, follows a warm, dry summer. I have succeeded during the month in putting up about twenty tons of hay for Agency use.

The doctor appointed for this Agency reported for duty during the month and was hailed with delight by the Indians and the Missionaries and school contractors, as considerable sickness prevailed among the children.

Inclosed please find monthly statements of funds and indebtedness and also the sanitary report.

I have the honor to be

Very respectfully,
Your obd't. svt.
Peter Ronan
U.S. Indian Agent.

September 2, 1886
LR 23,858/1886, RG 75, National Archives, Washington, D.C.

Surveying the boundaries of the Flathead Reservation proved to be loaded with problems. Mistakes in the surveys cost the tribes valuable land north of Elmo and along the southwest corner of the reservation. The northern boundary near Elmo was especially troublesome. White settlers made homestead claims in the hills north of the reservation and then grazed their cattle on reservation grass. See the introduction to Ronan's August 20, 1883, annual report for more information about the boundary problems on the reservation.

United States Indian Service,
Flathead Agency,
September 2nd, 1886.

The Hon. Commissioner of Indian Affairs
Washington, D.C.
Sir:
In reply to your communication "L" of 21st August '86, I have the honor to state that I do not think it will be necessary to make any surveys for allotments to Indians on this reservation this year but I would respectfully ask that the boundaries of the reserve be surveyed as soon as possible for the reason that the country to the north of the reserve in the vicinity of Flathead Lake is fast settling up with farmers and stock-raisers and the question of that boundary will soon be mooted and until satisfactorily established, will be a source of trouble and annoyance to the Indians and whites. There are settlements, also, along the west line, at Horse Plains, and, in time, the same trouble is likely to arise there.

The Cost of a survey, according to the Estimate herewith enclosed, made by the U.S. Surveyor General of the Territory, will be about 7000$ for the entire boundary, but I do not think it necessary to have more than the north and west lines run, which are through a much more accessible country than are the East and South boundaries. If it is not deemed practicable to have even all the North and West lines surveyed I would earnestly urge that a line from the west shore of Flathead Lake "one half way in latitude between the Northern and Southern Extremities of the Lake" to the west boundary line be established so as to set at rest the vexed question of the Northern line of this reserve.

Your obdt. servt.
Peter Ronan
U.S. Indian Agent.

Enclosure:

Office of the United States Surveyor General, Montana.
Helena, August 31st, 1886

Peter Ronan, Esq.
U.S. Indian Agent
Flathead Agency

Sir:

In answer to yours of 28th inst. I would beg leave to say,

That it is very difficult to make an estimate of the cost of surveying the boundaries of the Flathead Reserve, because the Country is so little Known, and the map so incorrect.

The line run in 1870-71 was a correction line or Standard Parallel, such as are run at every 4 Townships. It may nearly coincide with the Northern Boundary of the Reserve, but is not the boundary itself. That would have to be fixed as the Law defining the Reservation directs viz. ½ way in Latitude between the Northern and Southern extremities of the Lake.

Taking such maps as are at hand, which are doubtless very incorrect, and protracting thereon the Reservation as defined by law, the length of the whole boundary would be about 225 miles. As the country is very rough it would require much exploration, many Corners to be established also the taking of astronomical observations which would require a higher grade of Knowledge than is generally possessed by the ordinary Surveyor.

To secure a proper survey of the boundary would probably cost about $30 per mile, making an approximate total cost of $7000.

If the Survey was advertised and given to the lowest competent bidder; as is now done with the public land surveys, it might be done cheaper, but probably not as well.

> Very respectfully
> B. H. Greene
> Surveyor General.

September 28, 1886
LR 26,395/1886, RG 75, National Archives, Washington, D.C.

There is a note on the letter: "Not approved JBR."

> United States Indian Service,
> Flathead Agency Agency [sic],
> Sept. 28th, 1886.

Hon. Commissioner of Indian Affairs,
Washington, D.C.

Sir:

Referring to your letter (Education) dated at Washington, Sept. 6th 1886, in which I am advised that congress made an appropriation for purchase of horses, cattle, Sheep, goats and Swine for Indian Schools; and asking for a Statement Showing the number, Kind and value of all animals now belonging to the Schools under my charge and also requesting certain other information.

I have the honor to state that all the educational facilities established in the Agency had been, and are under the auspices of the Catholic church, and that the two Industrial Schools in operation one for boys and one for girls are contract Schools and are already provided with different Kinds of Stock, which belong to the missionaries, who have charge of the Schools, and in consequence the pupils have all the desired facilities for being taught herding, and are also provided with meat, milk etc. from the place itself the end arrived at by your letters Seems to be attained without additional Stock from the Government. However if the Stock mentioned are intended to give the pupils a Start in life after they leave the school, the Same would be very desirable; and the Agency would be the proper place for their consignment and care.

Two hundred (200) head of two year old hiefers [sic] including two bulls would be ample for the necessities, and in my judgment would be the most advisable to provide for the Schools, if it be intended to give the pupils a Start in stock upon marriage or graduation. Such cattle would cost, delivered at the Agency, in the neighborhood of ($35.00) thirty five dollars per head.

Having no stock on hand except the Agency horses, I have no facilities for taking care of any Stock that may be purchased: however, a branding corrall and winter Sheds, which would cost about ($500.) five hundred dollars; a mowing machine and a rake; at a cost of about one hundred ($100); and the Services of one herder at fifty ($50.) per month, with rations; and also the Services of one laborer, Say for two months in the haying Season, at a cost of ($50.) fifty dollars per month and rations; two horses for herding the cattle would also be required, each to cost one hundred ($100) dollars and the necessary amount of feed for Same, at a cost of one hundred ($100.) dollars. This outlay I believe would be ample for the proper care of two hundred head of cattle on this reservation and their increase for a reasonable time.

I am very respectfully
Your obt. Svt.
Peter Ronan
U.S. Indian Agent.

October 1, 1886
LR 27,066/1886, RG 75, National Archives, Washington, D.C.

> Tribal hunting and fishing off the reservation came up in Ronan's October 14, 1885, letter, but then the Commissioner only advised Ronan to do what he could to keep tribal members on the reservation and avoid conflict with white sportsmen. Relative to white people hunting and fishing on the reservation, on October 27, 1886, the Commissioner instructed Ronan to "notify all [white] parties found hunting on the Reservation, that they must desist therefrom, and that if they fail to do so, proceedings under the statute will be instituted."[13] Conflict over hunting rights would occupy the tribes well into the twentieth century.

United States Indian Service,
Flathead Agency,
October 1st, 1886.

The Hon. Commissioner of Indian Affairs,
Washington, D.C.
Sir:

The past month at this Agency ended in its usual quiet manner. A large number of the Indians having harvested their crops took advantage of the pleasant fall and are now out hunting — some beyond the limits of their reservation. It has always been the custom of some of the Indians of this reservation after harvesting their crops to go in pursuit of game for winter use, which I consider a healthy and useful recreation, especially for Indians, who have been brought up to such habits. A further inducement is found in the fact that a reward of eight dollars if offered by the territory for every bear Killed outside the limits of Indian reservations, which reward is as promptly paid to Indians as to whitemen. As before reported to your office, I have never offered any serious objection to their leaving the reservation in quest of game for food supply, after they had finished harvesting, especially as it has been my custom to send a trusty Indian — either a policeman or Chief — with each hunting party to maintain order and see that they were guilty of no misconduct; and for the further reason that the Indians have claimed the right to do so under treaty stipulations, I am of the opinion that it will be found, upon examination, that the privilege of hunting upon open and unclaimed land was guaranteed to the Indians by treaty, and I do not see how they can be denied the privilege which they still claim, especially as they are not Complained of for misconduct, but their offence [sic] is that being successful hunters they interfere to more or less extent with the sport of whites, either professional hunters, or amateurs of the Rod and Gun Clubs of the various Territorial towns. I offer every discouragement to the Indians for going beyond their borders, and try to teach them to avoid every pretense for conflict with white settlers. Every day the Indians encounter sportsmen upon their own reservation, with whom they do not interefere [sic] so long as they confine themselves to fishing and hunting and it can hardly be expected that the Indians of this reservation should feel that they should not have the Same rights so long as they behave themselves in a proper and becoming manner.

The Agency threshing machine is Kept moving from one Indian ranche to another threshing out the grain. The Grist mill is in active operation, and about one thousand bushels of the new Indian crop has already been made into flour for the Indians. Each day brings its loads of wheat to the mill, and I have some five hundred bushels now ahead of the grinding. Scarcely one third of the grain crop is threshed, but the weather is fine and I trust the threshing machine will be able to reach the remotest Indian farm before winter sets in.

Every industry pertaining to the service is receiving attention at this Agency, and I have no further especial report to make.

Inclosed please find monthly statements of funds and indebtedness and also the sanitary report.

I have the honor to be,

Very respectfully,
Your obdt. svt.
Peter Ronan
U.S. Indian Agent.

October 23, 1886
LR 28,914/1886, RG 75, National Archives, Washington, D.C.

> This report has a valuable survey of traders and commerce on the reservation in 1886. The "Scotch half-breed" trading at Ravalli was Duncan McDonald. See the annotation to Ronan's February 4, 1878a, for basic information and references on Duncan, whose father Angus had been adopted into the tribe. For Andrew B. Hammond, see the annotation to Ronan's September 25, 1882, letter.
>
> Alexander L. Demers, a Canadian by birth, was a brother to T. J. Demers of Frenchtown, who was also a trader on the Flathead Reservation. Alexander traded at St. Ignatius Mission for many years but between 1885 and 1901 owned the store at Arlee after the previous storekeeper, V. H. Coombs, had to leave because he shot an Indian customer in a fight. In 1907, he returned to Arlee and opened a store that was later operated by his son, Louis.[14]

For Henry A. Lambert, see the annotation and Ronan's letter of September 7, 1889. T. G. Demers' mother was Pend d'Oreille. See Ronan's letters of August 20, 1881a, and August 13, 1883b, for biographical information on T. G. Demers and his family.

United States Indian Service,
Flathead Agency,
October 23d, 1886.

The Hon. Commissioner of Indian Affairs
Washington, D.C.

Sir:

In compliance with instructions contained in letter A. C. dated at your office October 9th, 1886, in which you ask for a complete and accurate investigation of the gross amount of trade done annually at the different trading posts on this reservation and other information, I beg leave to submit my report as follows:

At Arlee, A. B. Hammond has conducted under license from the Indian office a trading post which is built on the right-of-way of the Northern Pacific Railroad Company, about four miles from the Agency proper, and which, to the best of my knowledge and belief has always been conducted in a lawful and proper manner. The gross annual trade at this post, is given at $14,335. It is an accomodation not only to the Indians, but to the Railroad employés, and to this Agency to continue this post, as necessary supplies are here purchased, and the clerk in charge is Postmaster for the Arlee Post Office.

The next trading post is also built on the line of the Northern Pacific Railroad, at a Station called Ravalli, and some ten miles west of Arlee and fifteen miles from the Agency. The trader is a Scotch half-breed, born on the Reservation, an educated, sober and industrious man. The gross amount of receipts at this post is reported to me at $13,000. At Ravalli station all passengers and emigrants for the Head of the Flathead Lake leave the Railroad and travel by team to their destination which is now rapidly filling up with settlers North of the line of the Reservation. The mail coach also meets the train at this post where the mail is transfered for the various post offices of the North. The accomodation of the traveling public as well as that of the Indians require a station and trading post at this point.

A. L. Demers is the regular licensed trader at the St. Ignatius Mission, and is the Postmaster at that place. The post is situated about six miles north of the Northern Pacific Railroad and in the largest Indian village of the Reservation. Here the Indian schools are carried on, and here St. Ignatius Mission is located. The trader is a respectable man and carries on a lawful and legitimate business. The gross annual receipts of the trade is reported to me to be eight thousand dollars. This trading post is situated about twenty miles Northwest of the Agency proper.

Thirty-miles further on, at the foot of the Flathead Lake, was situated the trading post of H. A. Lambert. At this point a ferry crosses a narrow portion of the Lake, and teams, freight and passengers are crossed on the ferry boat, on the public road leading to the settlements at the head of the Flathead Lake. This post is also a station for accomodation of the U.S. Mail, coach and passengers, where meals and lodging are obtained. A small steamer also plies between this point and the white settlements at the head of the lake, and carries freight and passengers up the lake to the new settlements already mentioned. It will be readily seen that for accomodation of the traveling public as well as for the Indians settled around the foot of the lake, a discontinuation of the post would cause great hardship. This trading post is situated about fifty miles Northwest of the Agency proper. The gross annual trade last year was only three thousand five hundred dollars, but hopes were entertained from the increased travel of next year for an increase of business, or it would not pay to keep the station.

Across the lake and twenty miles further on towards the Northern boundary of the Reservation, is another trading post kept by T. G. Demers. This post is located near the Kootenaii Indian settlement — is also a stopping station for travelers and for the mail coach and passengers going up into the Northern settlements. The licensed trader, T. G. Demers, reports his gross trade per annum at seven thousand dollars. This post is a great convenience to travelers and is also the only place the Kootenai Indians can trade without crossing the lake or going North some fifty miles to stores kept in the white settlements at the head of the Lake. The trader here is of Indian blood — belonging to the tribes of this Reservation — is a man of good character, and industrious.

Each of the above named traders made application for a renewal of license, accompanied by proper bonds, but I have not been yet officially notified as to whether their licenses were granted or not; the only license of which I have any official knowledge as being renewed is that of A. L. Demers, which was received under date of August 5th, 1886.

Very respectfully,
Your obdt. serv't.
Peter Ronan
U.S. Indian Agent.

November 1, 1886
LR 29,835/1886, RG 75, National Archives, Washington, D.C.

United States Indian Service,
Flathead Agency,
November 1st, 1886.

The Hon. Commissioner of Indian Affairs
Washington, D.C.

Sir:

I have the honor to submit my report for the month of October, and in doing so, it affords me pleasure to state that the usual good behavior, industrious habits and steady advancement in all civilizing pursuits, prevail among the Indians of this reservation.

During the past two months the Agency threshing machine has been in general employment and is doing very good work. The crops, this year, are light, owing to the unusually dry season — wheat, oats, potatoes, etc., yielding poorly. Where irrigation was provided by ditches, and proper care taken to flood the fields in season, good crops resulted.

The saw and grist mills have been in almost constant employment during the month. The Indians have been hauling a large quantity of logs to the mill, which I cut for them to suit their convenience for building. The running of the mills has kept the Agency employes in constant employment. I have commenced work on the picket fence which is to enclose the Agency buildings, and if, during the month of November, the weather will continue pleasant, I hope to have the work completed and the Agency nicely enclosed with a handsome and substantial fence.

I have nothing to add to my report for the past month save to state that everything pertaining to the service here is in good condition and the Indians under my charge are contented, peaceful and advancing in all the pursuits of Industry, which, at no distant day, will place them self-supporting and a self-r[e]liant people.

Enclosed please find monthly statement of funds and indebtedness, and, also, the sanitary report.

I have the honor to be,

Very respectfully,
Your ob'd't serv't
Peter Ronan
U.S. Indian Agent.

December 1, 1886
LR 32,315/1886, RG 75, National Archives, Washington, D.C.

> Undermining the traditional authority of the chiefs resulted in problems that required an elaborate and expensive structure to enforce law and order on the reservation. The new Indian police and Indian courts were under the nominal control of the agent, but they required salaries, weapons, and jails. See Ronan's letters of December 17 and 28, 1886, for his detailed requests for funds.

United States Indian Service,
Flathead Agency,
Dec. 1st, 1886.

Hon. Commissioner of Indian Affairs
Washington, D.C.

Sir:

I have the honor to submit my report for November. The month has been attended by unusual Storms, and Snow covered the country from the 15th untill [sic] the 28th of the month, when a warm Chinook, or Southern wind Set in Sweeping the Snow before it and leaving the landscape bare, releaving [sic] the Indians from the dreary prospect of an early and Severe winter, with attendant loss of stock. During the past month Several Indians delivered a large number of logs to the Agency Saw mill, to be cut into lumber for their use in building houses, barns and outbuildings; and, the present month will be devoted to cutting the Same into the desired dimensions. The grist mill is also well filled with wheat, which will be ground into flour for the different Indian owners. The threshing machine has been Kept in constant employment Since harvest time, and has been transported from one farm to another, from the thickly Settled Indian ranches to the far off fields and farms of Scattered tillers of the soil. The yield of grain this year will fall far Short of estimates in my annual report, owing to the fact that when that document was written, the Season Seemed propitious, and all Signs bid fair for an abundant harvest. An unusual drouth [sic] Set in later and where irrigation was not amply provided for and especially attended to, a return of the Seed Sown was barely realized in a great many instances. During the Severe and unlooked for cold snap the pump barrel on our new steam engine froze up and burst. I immediately ordered another one from the Atlas works in Indianapolis, Indiana, Where the engine and boiler was built, and the Same arrived at the Agency by express in a very short time, and has been placed in position and the mill is running at this date as usual. The uniforms for the Indian police have been received and will greatly tend to proclaim their authority: However the police should be armed, and untill that is done and at least two Jails are built, one at the Agency and one at St. Ignatius Mission, the police authority will be little respected: This is a matter which Should meet with due consideration, as it is obvious that authority cannot well be enforced among evil doers, unless backed up by resolution and force; but resolution and force can hardly be exspected [sic] from unarmed men provided with a Jail which cannot retain a prisoner unless Surrounded by guards. In reference to your letter A.C. 28914 – 1886, in regard to my report upon the traders and condition of trade upon this reservation, and in accordance with your orders, the traders who were doing business upon an expired license were directed to file a new bond in the Indian office and have their license renewed. The bond of Duncan McDonald and that of T. J. Demers, will be forwarded Soon as approved by the Judge of the District Court. The store of Mr Lambert has been closed, and that gentleman will ask for a renewal of his license, Soon as spring opens and travel commences to the head of the Flathead lake. During the month Inspector [Geo. B.] Pearsons visited this Agency. A heavy snow Storm prevailed at the time of his arrival, but I believe his inspection was thorough.

Enclosed please find monthly statement of funds and indebtedness and also the Sanitary report.

I have the honor to be

Very respectfully
Your obt. svt.
Peter Ronan
U.S. Indian Agent.

December 2, 1886
LR 32,554/1886, RG 75, National Archives, Washington, D.C.

A full copy of Inspector Geo. B. Pearsons' November 11, 1886, report to the Secretary of the Interior can be found in the National Archives Microfilm Publication of inspection reports. [15]

Flathead Indian Agency,
Montana Territory
December 2d, 1886.

Hon. Commissioner of Indian Affairs
Washington, D.C.

Sir:

Under reference 31022 – 86 I am in receipt of the following from your office:

"Inspector [Geo. B.] Pearsons recommends that your farmer Mr Lambert, whom he says does but little farming, be discharged and his place filled by an Indian."

I desire to fully report to you in reference to this matter:

Inspector Pearsons arrived at this Agency about noon on the 8th day of November, and the next day in a cold and gloomy storm of snow left the Agency. During the time he was here he made an inspection of the books and accounts of the Agency, the buildings and the Government property. In looking over the manner in which property of all description was carefully stored, he was pleased to make complimentary remarks. Now in regards to his report that "the farmer does but little farming," he is perfectly correct, as no farming is done in this latitude at this season. But I claim the farmer is as necessary at this time of the year as in planting season as he is the general overseer of all government property in tools, agricultural implements, etc., the use of which articles by the Indians he requires to attend to, in addition to the care of stock, etc.

2d. I am just now receiving the goods estimated for the confederated tribes of this reservation and also for the Indians of Charlos band of Bitter Root Flatheads. On the morning of the arrival of Inspector Pearsons at Arlee, the railroad station where goods for the Indians of this reservation are shipped, a carload of wagons and other agricultural implements were lying in the snow as unloaded from the car. The farmer's duty, as detailed by me, was to receive, check off, weigh, make out weigher's returns, and that the goods were freighted to the Agency and properly stored, this duty he was performing at that time.

3d. The Honorable Commissioner is well aware of the efforts which are being put forth by the Indian Department to remove Charlos band from the Bitter Root Valley without force, and to settle them upon this reservation. This is being slowly but successfully accomplished; and I have assurances that the whole business will be successfully carried out soon as the chief can have an interview either with the expected commission which I was notified would arrive here this year, or an arrangement directly with the Indian Office which he much prefers, and has so requested. In all those arrangements I am ably seconded by the energy and intelligence of this employee whom the Inspector desires to be replaced by an Indian. By reference to my annual report of this year you will find that I stated that ["]the members of Charlos band who have already removed from the Bitter Root valley to this Agency cannot be classed among the most industrious or civilized members of the tribe. In fact the colony is composed mostly of Indians who with their families followed the chase and the Buffalo until the game became almost extinct, and continued to make a precarious living by hunting, fishing and wandering among the settlements. It will therefore readily be perceived that no easy task is imposed upon the administration of affairs at this Agency to bring these Indians suddenly into the ways of strict attention to the cultivation and harvesting of their fields, proper irrigation of the same and to restrain them from wandering and the chase. But having made a beginning in a small way encouragement and assistance will induce them to enlarge their operations." In such work, again I submit, am I asking too much to retain an intelligent, energetic, moral and educated white-man to second my efforts, or will an order issue to discharge him and employ an Indian?

I have now seventeen families of Charlos band from Bitter Root settled in comfortable houses and surrounded by well fenced fields, and who raised crops the past season. Five more new families removed here last month and five other families reported here earlier in the fall, leaving ten families to care for and provide temporary shelter until the department furnishes means to provide homes as in case of the first seventeen, in accordance with promises made by the the Indian Department. In those matters the farmer is called upon by the Agent to second him in his efforts to see that no suffering prevails, until means are provided to house and open farms for the recent removals. It will also be seen in my report of this year that the band of Kootenai Indians, who are included with Confederated tribes of this reservation "are in great want and need the fostering hand of the government more than any others on the reservation, and yet are the most neglected, owing to the fact of their being isolated from the Agency by a distance of about 70 miles and the impracticability of sparing the services from the small force of Agency employes to assist their efforts. This tribe or band have one large enclosure which they cultivate in common, a practice which at once should be broken up, and each head of a family be placed in possession of an enclosure for himself, and taught self-reliance by the cultivation of the soil for the exclusive benefit of himself and family. Authority should be given to employ an additional farmer to reside at their settlement — a capable man, competent and willing to assist and teach this poor tribe in the cultivation of the soil and to aid them in building houses and making seperate [sic] and individual farms and homes. Until this is done the unfortunate Kootenai will continue to be a wretched, dirty, wandering vagarant [sic]."

Entertaining such views I intended before spring to request an additional farmer to assist those Indians, but if other views outweigh the settled convictions of an Agent who has resided on the reservation and been their director for almost ten years, and striven conscientiously for their well being and advancement, I would rather be without a farmer to direct them unless I can select a man in whom I can have confidence. I wish to say that I do not desire an Indian as an overseer over Indians, and I sincerely hope the Honorable Commissioner will not insist upon such an order, and recognize the benefit of employing whitemen as farmers at this Agency for the present.

I am very respectfully

Your ob'dt servt.
Peter Ronan,
U.S. Indian Agent.

December 17, 1886

LR 33,952/1886, RG 75, National Archives, Washington, D.C.

According to a note filed with this letter, on January 14, 1887, Ronan was authorized to employ five additional privates on the Flathead Indian Agency police force.

United States Indian Service,
Flathead Agency,
Montana, Dec. 17th, 1886.

Hon. Commissioner Indian Affairs
Washington, D.C.
Sir:

According to instructions contained in "F" — Letter 31022 '86, I have the honor herewith to submit estimates for revolvers, holsters and belts for the Indian police of this reservation. At present the force consists of nine privates and one officer, which is entirely too small for the proper enforcement of discipline on this reservation for the following reasons:

1st. The Indian settlements and farms are scattered at wide distances — some settlements being about seventy miles from the Agency. The force should be composed of representative Indians from different localities.

2d. The Northern Pacific Railroad runs for fifty miles through a settled portion of the reserve and a great deal of complaint has been made at times by the Company against Indians for malicious mischief — the shooting off of insulators from telegraph poles, throwing stones through the car windows &c. I am called upon with the Indian police to stop such doings along the line.

3d. A great portion of the occupants of the reserve are half breeds, and the young men are more vicious and harder to control than the Indians of full blood. They are addicted to drinking, gambling and bringing whisky on the reserve; and often resist arrest by the Indian police, owing to lack of arms and sufficient force to overawe them. The young half breeds consider themselves superior to the Indians and above the law governing offences [sic] on the reservation, and it therefore requires nerve and force to maintain order among them.

4th. Some of the Indians of Charlos' band of Bitter Root Flathead Indians who have and are moving from that valley to this reservation are vicious and hard to control especially when furnished with whisky by the half breeds. A number of this class are also half breeds.

5th. The band of lower Kalispels now living in the Kalispel valley on the Columbia river in Idaho Territory, through their Chief, informed me that they have concluded to remove to this reservation, and are only awaiting a conference with the commission which they are advised will visit and negotiate their removal within the year. This is considered one of the most lawless bands of Indians in this section of the country. I trust therefore that the Hon. Commissioner will recognize the fact that in place of ten I should have at least fifteen policemen, well armed, to strengthen my hands, to maintain order over the wide and scattered settlements and different bands of Indians which comprise the confederated tribes of the Flathead Reservation. I have estimated for an increas[e] of five policemen and trust that my request will be granted. The estimate for arms is based upon prices asked by dealers in the town of Missoula, and are as cheap, I presume, as such class of articles can be purchased in Montana.

I am now preparing and will have in readiness for transmission to your office in a few days, detailed estimate for materials and labor required for a suitable building for a jail on the reserve.

In am very respectfully,

Your obd't serv't.
Peter Ronan
U.S. Indian Agent.

Enclosed is an "Estimate of Indians Supplies, &c." for $325.00 for 15 Colt 44 caliber revolvers, 15 cartridge belts, 15 pistol holsters, and 1000 rounds of ammunition.

December 28, 1886

LR 518/1887, RG 75, National Archives, Washington, D.C.

> The Commissioner did not approve this construction request for a new jail and council room at the Jocko Agency. A note written on the letter said "No funds."

United States Indian Service,
Flathead Agency,
Montana, Dec. 28th, 1886.

Hon. Commissioner Indian Affairs:
Washington, D.C.

Sir:

Under date of December 17th 1886, I had the honor of addressing a letter to you, in compliance with instructions in "F" — Letter 31022 – '86, submitting estimates for revolvers, holsters and belts for the Indian police of this Reservation. In said letter I stated that I was preparing and would submit to you soon as practicable estimates for materials and labor required for a suitable building for a jail on the Reservation. Having submitted my plans to a competent and reliable contractor the enclosed specifications and estimates were returned. I will only refer the Honorable Commissioner of Indian Affairs to the letter above cited for information and reasons given of the urgent necessity for the erection of a good and substantial Indian jail on this Reservation.

By constructing the jail with Indian labor, paid for by the issue of wagons, harness, plows and other useful articles, besides supplies, I can get out 41,880 feet of hewed timber, which will save according to estimates $502.56.

As a fence will not be required this season to enclose the jail it will make a saving of 5,400 feet of lumber ($18.00 per M.) at a cost of $97.20.

I can also leave out 1,500 feet of matched flooring (at $30.00 per M.), saving $45.00 (use other material).

From the estimated items of "work in addition to above," I propose to employ two carpenters for thirty days each at $3 per day for each which will make a savings of two hundred and six dollars from the item of "Work in addition $476.["]

I can also save the item "contractor's profit 10 per cent $170."

From item "12 cell and lobby doors, locks, bolts, etc." by the employment of an extra blacksmith, I can save sixty-two dollars, by constructing the doors from iron purchased.

It will therefore be seen that for less than half of the contractor's estimates I can construct a jail which will be as substantial, and completed in workmanlike manner, and will scarcely vary from plans herewith submitted.

Owing to the fact that St. Ignatius Mission is in the center of the Indian population, and also of the Reservation; and also that the Industrial Schools are located at that place I recommend that the jail be built there.

In anticipation that my views and recommendations will receive favorable consideration at your hands, I have already put on a force of Indians cutting, hewing and hawling [sic] logs in recompense for the issue to them of the wagons and other articles before mentioned. The snow which now covers the country to a heavy depth furnishes a good opportunity to do the hawling of the hewed logs from the timber to cite [sic] of the jail; and the Indians being so eager to work I deemed it to be for the best interests of the service to get the logs on the ground pending your decission [sic] and instructions in the matter.

I am very respectfully,

Your obd't Serv't.,
Peter Ronan
United States Indian Agent.

Estimate for $837.54 for construction of a 67 by 23 foot building with 10 cells, a lobby, and a council room.

St. Ignatius Mission in the late 1880s. Left to right: School for girls conducted by Sisters of Providence, the Church, the shops, boys school, and Father's house. Oregon Province Archives, Gonzaga University, Spokane, Washington, negative 114.1.02b

View of Indian camp along road during Easter celebration at St. Ignatius Mission, undated. Oregon Province Archives, Gonzaga University, Spokane, Washington, negtive 114.3.03a.

Judge Baptiste Kakashe, Pend d'Oreille
Montana Historical Society Photograph Archives, Helena, Montana
detail from negative 954-528.

1887

The friction between the judges of the government sponsored Court of Indian Offences and the traditional chiefs was to continue through the rest of the nineteenth century. When the court was establish in 1885 Ronan claimed it has been approved by a general council of tribal members.[1] Ronan chose judges and police from "among the most influential" Indians on the reservation which must have strengthened the influence of the government law and order structure.[2] In 1888 Ronan described how he used the judges to reduce the authority of the chiefs.[3] A side effect of the government policy to undermine the influence of the traditional authority structure was to increase law and order problems on the reservation.

Ronan's relations with Chief Arlee were rocky over the years, but nothing compared to the open warfare that broke out in the middle 1870s between Arlee and Ronan's predecessor, Agent Charles Medary.[4] Arlee complained to Indian inspectors about the operation of the St. Ignatius Mission and the Jocko Agency, but he also assisted Ronan in keeping the peace and trying to arrest white whiskey sellers.[5]

The Commissioner of Indian Affairs replied on January 24, 1887, to Ronan's letter. Ronan was told to lecture Arlee and explain that "if they [the Indians] are refractory and refuse to obey the orders of the Agent and the decisions of the Court, prompt measures will be taken to compel their obedience."[6]

United States Indian Service,
Flathead Agency,
Montana, January 1st, 1887.

Hon. Commissioner of Indian Affairs
Washington, D.C.
Sir:

As reported to you upon several occasions, it requires strenious efforts upon my part to suppress lawlessness and crime upon this reservation, growing out of gambling, the introduction of whisky upon the reservation by Indians and half-breeds, the breach of marital relationship, horse thieving and murder. In 1885 I was in receipt of the following letter:

Office of Indian Affairs,
Washington, D.C.
March 5, 1885.

Peter Ronan, U.S. Indian Agent,

Sir: In reply to your letter of the 12th Ult., enclosing a code of Rules for the Government of the Court of Indian Offences for your Agency, I have to say that the Honorable Secretary of the Interior, under date of the 2d instant, approved of the same, and hereafter your court will be governed by said rules.

In your letter of the 14th of February, you nominated Baptist, Joseph and Louison, Judges, and on the 25th of the same month their commissions were forwarded duly approved.

                                                    Very respectfully,
                                          (Signed) H. Price, Commissioner.

The three Indians mentioned in above letter, are at present date Judges of the Court of Indian offences. They are three of the most intelligent, honest and industrious Indians on the reserve and administer the laws with firmness, respect and dignity, and more than all, they appreciate largely the new order of things and the necessity for self support by honest industry. They also fully appreciate the fact that this latter cannot be attained unless strong measures are taken to suppress the introduction of whisky upon the reservation by Indians and half-breeds; the suppression of gambling, horse stealing, adultry, murder etc.

Until recently my management of the police force and the Rules governing Indian offences, worked well. But a jealousy has arisen on the part of Arlee the Sub Chief of Flatheads, who removed to this reservation, under the Garfield Agreement, from the Bitter Root Valley, some fourteen years ago, and who is thus mentioned on page 231, in the Report of the Sub-Committee of the Special Committee of the United States Senate, appointed to visit the Indian tribes in Northern Montana, Composed of Senator [G. G.] Vest and Major M. Maginnis:

> "Charlot (the Chief) told us that he would never go to the Jocko reservation alive; that he had no confidence in our promises," for "said he your Great Father Garfield put my name to a paper which I never signed, and the *renegade Nez Percé Arlee*, is now drawing money to which he has no right. How can I believe you, or any whiteman after the way I have been treated?"

This same Arlee, having grown rich upon the distribution of the fifty thousand dollars in cash, among his few followers and himself, allowed by the Garfield Agreement, upon their removal to this reservation, has also grown arogant, and claims that he is the "Chief and the law."

This occurred yesterday when the police went to arrest, at his house, a lawfully married squaw who was living in adultry (as reported to me) with an Indian under Arlee's roof.

In a council with his followers Arlee advised to resist arrest, stating that the laws were made by the Agent, and that he had no right to promulgate or enforce any arrest and that the Judges were set up by the Agent to break his power and set him aside. This old man is seventy-three years of age. I have time and again explained to him, although he is not regarded as head Chief, that the Rules governing Indian Offences, and that the establishment of Indian Court, Judges and Policemen was done by order of the Indian Department and for the good of the Indians, for suppression of crime on the reservation.

Unless this insubordination is suppressed it may ripen into trouble among the Indians.

I summoned Arlee to come to the Agency and explain his conduct but he refused to come while the Judges and policemen were present. I sent him word not to come again to the Agency to consult me in the capacity of a Chief — that I no longer regarded him as head man or Chief among his people unless he came with an apology for advising his people to resist the rules governing the reserve. It may be necessary to use harsh measures for suppression of this uncalled for proceeding in Arlee, especially as he is urged on and supported by the lawless young men — those who desire to be free from arrest for crime and debauchery upon the reservation.

I stated that Arlee had grown rich, but the rest of his followers who accompanied him here from the Bitter Root valley, with exception of one family, under the Garfield agreement, are wretchedly poor, having spent $50,000, paid to them in ten annual instalments, mostly in gambling. Arlee and his followers are jealous that the present administration is assisting the rightful Chief Charlot and his unfortunate band of Bitter Root Flatheads, and as a number of the latter are moving here from said valley and are being helped to establish themselves in their new homes, and in a sustained prosperity, he cannot conceal his vexation that the payment of five hundred dollars a year to him by the Government as Chief of Flatheads, and also the large payment to himself and family from the annual cash payments, which were made quarterly, under the Garfield Agreement, has entirely ceased. Hence, as a pretext, his denunciation of the Missionaries, the Schools and the Agent, and his advice to his followers to go back to the old laws of the Chiefs and to renew their dances and feasts, which are prohibited in IV clause of the Rules Governing Indian Offences, as follows: "The Sun dance, war dance and scalp dance, and all other so called feasts, under penalty for the first offense, witholding all annuities and for any subsequent offense, incaseration [sic] in the reservation jail for thirty days."

It is unnecessary for me to remind the Honorable Commissioner of Indian Affairs that if the advice of Arlee is allowed to be followed it means, to a great extent, an abandonment of religion, schools, industry and self support from the cultivation of the soil, and a return to savagry and the chase.

If I may be allowed to suggest, I am of the opinion that a strong letter upon this subject from the Honorable Commissioner of Indian Affairs, sustaining the Agent, the Indian Judges and the police in enforcing the Rules Governing Indian Offences in a proper manner; and also warning the old chiefs that they are not above the reservation laws and any infraction of the same on their part will subject them to arrest and punishment the same as the meanest lawbreaker on the reserve. The said letter to be read in general Indian Council Called for that purpose. By such proceeding and a firm stand assumed by the Judges and Indian police, with the Agent to assist and direct them will overcome the evil advice of this selfish and malicious old man.

I am respectfully
Your obedient Servant,
Peter Ronan,
United States Indian Agt.

February 2, 1887
LR 3,847/1887, RG 75, National Archives, Washington, D.C.

William and Ralph Ramsdell established a trading post on Tobacco Plains in 1886. Apparently both could speak Kootenai, and Ralph even worked on a Kootenai dictionary that was never published. Ralph was part of the 1888 mob that "arrested" two Kootenai Indians accused of murdering white men. The whites lynched the Kootenais without a legal trial.[7]

In 1889 Ronan and one of the Ramsdells traded charges in the columns of *The Helena Journal*. Ramsdell listed a series of alleged murders of white people by Indians in western Montana and accused Ronan of indifference. Ronan replied that he had turned evidence of the crimes over to the United States Marshall in Helena and charged the Ramsdells sold liquor to Indians.[8]

In March 1890, however, William Ramsdell wrote to a local newspaper to defend Chief Eneas and the Dayton Creek Kootenai against charges that they were preparing to attack the white settlers in the Flathead Valley.[9] In 1889 William Ramsdell was elected to the Montana Constitutional Convention as a Democrat and in 1894 and in 1896 he was elected to the Montana State Senate from Flathead County as a Populist.[10]

In August 1890 Ralph was deputy sheriff in the hunt for several Kootenai accused of killing white men. In the conflict surrounding the arrests of Pascale and Antee he interpreted for Sheriff William Houston. The white lawmen held Kootenai Chief Eneas hostage for the surrender of the accused Kootenais. Ramsdell was also a leader in the posse that arrested Pierre Paul, a Pend d'Oreille. The three men were tried by a white jury, convicted along with Lalasee, and the four were hung in Missoula in December 1890.[11] Ralph Ramsdell's version of the Kootenai-white hostilities can be found in a manuscript at the Montana Historical Society Archives.[12]

Israel Wood Powell, a medical doctor, was Superintendent of Indian Affairs in British Columbia from 1872 through 1889. He supported limiting Indian reserves to twenty acres per family. Local British Columbia officials wanted to allow even less land.[13]

United States Indian Service,
Flathead Agency,
February 2d, 1887.

Hon. Commissioner Indian Affairs,
Washington, D.C.
Sir:
I have the honor herewith of enclosing certain correspondence between myself and the Indian Commissioner at Victoria, British Columbia, and am
Very respectfully,

Your obedient Servant,
Peter Ronan,
U.S. Indian Agent.

First Enclosure:

British Columbia

Indian Office
Victoria Jany 14th, 1887

Sir,
I am informed on credible authority that Messrs. Ramsdell Bros. traders on Tobacco Plains, about six miles south of the Boundary Line, are in the habit of selling Indians from Kootenay spirituous liquors, in quantities, and that many of the Natives of that place have lately been intoxicated.

I should be glad if you would take immediate steps to put a stop to the traffic referred to, or, if out of your power, that you may Kindly acquaint me accordingly.

I have the honor to be

Sir,
Your Obdt. Servant.,
I. W. Powell
Indian Commissioner.

P. Ronan Esqr.
U.S. Indian Agent.
Second enclosure:

Copy

United States Indian Service,
Flathead Agency,
Montana Territory, Feb 2d, 1887.

J. W. Powell [i.e., I. W. Powell],
Indian Commissioner,
Victoria, British Columbia

Sir:

I am in receipt of your letter of January 14th, 1887, and in reply thereto would state that the store or trading post of Ramsdell Brothers, on Tobacco Plains is in the neighborhood of one hundred miles North of the Boundary Line of this Indian Reservation, and embraced in the County of Missoula, Territory of Montana. You complain that the above named firm are in the habit of selling spirituous liquors, in quantities, and that many of the natives of that place have lately been intoxicated. I should be glad to put a stop to the trafic [sic] referred to if it were in my power; but I can only refer the matter to the authorities of Missoula County and to the United States Marshal of Montana Territory. As the store of Ramsdell Bros. is in the neighborhood of only about six miles from the British border, if your information is correct in regard to the sale of intoxicating liquors to the natives, no doubt it affords an opportunity for the Indians of either side of the line to indulge in their habits of intoxication and should be looked after the the proper authorities, the trafic broken up and offenders punished.

I am respectfully
Your obedient servant
Peter Ronan
United States Indian Agent.

March 11, 1887
The Weekly Missoulian, *May 13, 1887, page 1, col. 3.*

> In 1887 the federal government treated the Bitterroot Salish Indians as non-tribal citizen Indians as a result of the 1872 negotiations with Congressman James Garfield. The conflict over Salish hunting rights in the Bitterroot Valley grew out of the failure of the federal government to fulfill the provision of the 1855 Hellgate treaty providing for a Bitterroot Valley reservation. See also Ronan's letter May 28, 1887.

Deer-Killing by Indians.

Some months since a citizen of the valley wrote to a Missoula member of the Rod and Gun club that certain Indians had gone up the Lou Lou valley for the purpose of killing deer, and thought it his duty to report it to the game club. The Missoula man sent the letter over to Major Ronan, agent of the Flatheads, Pen d'Oreilles, etc., and requested information about the right of the Indians to kill deer at that early season of the year, receiving the following reply, which expresses the ideas of many others:

Flathead Agency, March 11, 1887.

Sir — Your favor has been received by me through the hands of Dr. Lombard, of Missoula, and in reply I would regretfully state that I have been informed that the Indians alluded to by you as having gone up the Lou Lou for the purpose of hunting deer, belong to Charlot's band of Bitter Root Flatheads who claim their homes in that valley, and as they do not live on this reservation it is altogether a moral pressure which compels such Indians to remain at their homes.

The regulations of the Indian department prohibit Indians from leaving their reservations without written permission from the agent, and it is the instruction to discourage them as far as possible from going beyond their borders. Every pretense for conflicts with white settlers should be carefully avoided, and it has been my endeavor to encourage friendly feelings on both sides. In conclusion I can only say that as in the past, as well as in the future, I shall continue to do all in my power to prevent the winter slaughter of game by Indians as well as whites. Indians committing crime off of their reservation, I presume, are amenable to the laws of the county and territory, but I am not prepared to say if it is a crime for any Indian to kill game for food at any season of the year.

I am, very respectfully yours,

Peter Ronan,
U.S. Indian Agent.

May 18, 1887
LR 13,478/1887, RG 75, National Archives, Washington, D.C.

This report was written in response to a May 2, 1887, inquiry by the Commissioner of Indian Affairs asking about the conflicting land claims of Newton Tillman and two Salish Indians, Joseph and Paul.[14] The claims of Joseph and Paul were rejected by the local land office on technicalities. Tillman's attorney argued in one of the letters Ronan enclosed, that the Indian improvements "were of little value." The case illustrated how white settlers were able to circumvent provisions in the land laws that were supposed to secure the rights of Indian farmers. Ronan's efforts to protect the claims of Joseph and Paul proved unsuccessful.[15] The federal government never did approve the money to survey Salish farms on unpatented Bitterroot land so Indian homestead claims could be filed in the United States Land Office.

The Tillman family came to the Bitterroot Valley in 1880 and later moved to Florence. In 1886, Newton J. Tillman married Julia Whaley, the daughter of a former Flathead Indian agent. In 1886 an unnamed Salish Indian shot Newton Tillman's horse after it had destroyed the Indian's crop. The Indian was acquitted by a white jury in Stevensville. Tillman offered to pay for the Indian improvements on the contested land claim Ronan referred to, and, according to one account, he allowed the Indian farmers to remain on the land even after he won his claim.[16] Gust Moser had a real estate office in Stevensville. In later years he worked for the Missoula Mercantile Company and practiced as a lawyer.[17]

United States Indian Service,
Flathead Agency,
May 18th, 1887.

The Hon. Commissioner of Indian Affairs
Washington, D.C.
    Sir:

Referring to "L" dated at Washington, May 2d, 1887, in reference to Newton J. Tillman, who filed preemption declaratory statement for lots 2-3 and 4 and N.E. ¼ S.W. ¼ Section 18. Township 10. N of Range 19 West, Bitter Root Valley, and on May 28th, 1886, submitted his final proof, against which two Indians named Joseph and Paul, one of whom claims a house and the other a cultivated field on the land in question.

I would respectfully state that my attention was first called to the above filing, by a notice Published in the "Missoulian," a local paper of Missoula County, Montana, and that I notified the Indian claimants to appear at the town of Missoula and there contest the Case, which was done by them with counsel.

Under date of February 14th, 1887, I received from the United States Land Office, at Helena, Montana, the enclosed letter marked "A" a copy of which I forwarded to Stevensville, Montana, in the Bitter Root Valley, to be read to the Indian contestants, and with instructions to contest the same before the Register and Receiver, if they wished to protect their rights, as there was ample time to do so.

I also forwarded a copy of the same letter to Revd. J. D'Astè, who has been a missionary for twenty years among the Bitter Root Indians, and herewith Enclose reply, marked "B."

A letter from the Bitter Root Land Agency, directed to me, will also be found attached, marked "C."

A letter from Stevens and Bickford is also herewith submitted. I trust enclosures will show, that, under the circumstances, I did all in my power to protect the rights of the Indians.

Very Respectfully,
Your obdt. servt.
Peter Ronan
U.S. Indian Agent.

First enclosure:

United States Land Office,
Helena, Montana,
February 14th, 1887.

Hon. Peter Ronan
Flathead Agency
Sir:
In the matter of the final proof of Newton J. Tillman on his Pre-Filing No 0736 for Lots 2-3 & 4 & NE 4 SW 4 sec 18 T 10 N R 19 W, Bitterroot in which a protest seems to have been filed by Indian claimant or claimants. I have the honor to inform you that the Register & Receiver have this day united in an opinion holding that the Indian claimants have failed to make out a case, in that they have not identified the land claimed as being within the boundaries of the land claimed by Tillman and have recommended that the proofs of Tillman be accepted and that he be allowed to make entry of the land. You are advised that your wards have 30 days in which to appeal from said decision.

Very Respectfully
S. W. Langhorne
Register.

Second enclosure:

Stevensville, Feb. 22d, 87.

Maj. P. Ronan
U.S. Indian Agent
    Dear Major
    I return to you the inclosed, as directed. I do not Know what to say in the case, not being well posted about the claims interfering. You wrote me last year that you had stopped the entry of Newton Tillman on behalf of the Indian, who claimed the land, but I do not Know what arrangements you made in Missoula. Foreseeing the troubles which were liable to come from several Indians occupying lands which were not patented to them, though for many years were living upon them, I suggested several times the last two years, that these claims should be surveyed at Government's expense, which would have amounted about 100 dollars, and filed, in the Land Office, on behalf of the Indians occupying them, but the amount of money required could not be appropriated for this purpose, and thus all the Indians occupying such lands are bound to lose them, for want of [not] having been filed, in the Land Office. Among other claims there is Louis Vandebourgh claim, whose sons having been living on it over ten years. The result is bound to badly impress the minds of the Indians, seeing that an Indian has to give up a piece of land to the white man, because the latter could prove priority of occupation, but the Indian, because he is not able to file on his claim which he has occupied for many years, cannot get hold of it, and has to give it up to the white man who came several years after him. If you come up, as you promised, you may get better information from Gust. Moser.
    The Indians continue to lose their horses, and if the snow Keeps on much longer, only a few will have teams able to put in any crop with, next spring. If you want to issue some provisions, the sooner you do, the better. The road from Missoula to Stevensville is very good for sleighs, impossible for wagons.

Yours Respectfully
J. D'Aste, SJ

Third enclosure:

Woody, Marshall & Moser,
Bitter Root Land Agency,
Stevensville, Montana, 3/17 1887.

Peter Ronan,
Arlee, M.T.
    Dear Sir —
    In the matter of the Contest against N. J. Tillman by the Indian—
    Tillman and the Indian agreed on arbitrators to settle on what sum Tillman should pay the Indian, and the Indian agreed to this arrangement, but previous to this time (that is the time for the arbitrators to meet) the Indian saw Charlos and he (Charlos), told the Indian not to compromise under any circumstance. The Indian now refuses to let this matter go to the arbitrators. Tillman is still willing to pay whatever they say is right.

Your &c
Gust. Moser.

Fourth enclosure:

Office of
Stephens & Bickford,
Attorneys-at-Law,
Missoula, M.T., May 14th 188 [sic]

Maj. P. Ronan U.S. Indian Agt.
Arlee Mont.

Dear Sir:

In answer to your inquiry of today, relative to the contest filed by an Indian against the preemption entry of N. J. Tillman we would say: The Indians appeared, as you state, and a hearing was had. Neither the records of the Land Office nor any evidence introduced by the parties, showed that the Indians had any valid claim or right to the land. It was shown that the Indians occupied the land at times, and had some fencing on it, but that the improvements were of little value. Tillman has offered to pay the Indians what the improvements are worth, since the Register & Receiver decided the case in his favor[.] There can be no uniform manner of deciding cases of this kind, nuless [sic] the Register and Receiver continue to hold as they have done in this case. The law plainly requires the Indian to file on the land claimed by him, and if this law was not enforced it would enable a few wandering Indians to claim and hold all the land in the Bitter Root Valley, by simply occupying a tract for a short time, and placing a few improvements on it, as was done in this case.

There has never been any disposition manifested on the part of the settlers in the valley to in any way molest the Indians, where they have filed on the land occupied by them, which fact may not perhaps, be so much an evidence of "goodness" on the part of the people of the valley, as of your watchfulness over the welfare of your wards.

In the present case the Indians had a full and impartial hearing of their claims to the land and it was decided that they had no claim.

The officers of the land office do not receive filings on any land which is already filed upon by an Indian, and this rule is so well understood by all persons doing business with the land office that no effort is ever made by any person to infringe upon it.

To answer your questions more particularly, all the action was taken in the case that could be taken, to protect the rights, or supposed rights, of the Indians. They had no claim on the land. The fact that the Indians lived on the land, without filing, or any asserted right there to would give them no claim to the land under the Act of June 25th 1872, or any other law or treaty.

Very truly,
Stephens & Bickford

May 28, 1887

The New North-West *(Deer Lodge, Mont.), June 3, 1887, page 2, col. 6.*

> Protecting Salish and Kootenai hunting rights off the reservation was a battle that continued well into the twentieth century. Montana laws regulating hunting tried to protect wild game from extermination but were written to favor sports hunters at the expense of subsistence hunters. In 1887 the Office of Indians Affairs and many white Montanans argued that state game laws applied to off-reservation hunting by tribal members. See also Ronan letter, March 11, 1887.

The Flathead Treaty.

Articles Conveying Certain Privileges and Regulations Concerning Absence from the Reservation.

Flathead Agency, May 28, 1887.

Editor New North-West:

Dear Sir: While absent from this reservation, on duty with the Northwest Indian Commission in the Territory of Idaho, the following paragraph was published in your paper and escaped my notice until the present date:

"A passenger train on the Northern Pacific, between Bearmouth and Missoula, last Friday ran into a band of deer and killed four of them. This is a clear infraction, not only of the game laws, but of the Indians' assumed exclusive right to slaughter any game the laws try to protect at any season. We base this on the claim made for the Flathead and other confederated tribes, that their treaty reserves to them the right to hunt anywhere in this country, irrespective of any laws made by Montana. We would be glad to have Major Ronan, agent of the confederated tribes, state if such a provision exists in the treaty."

I am not aware that the claim has been made for the Flatheads and other confederated tribes that their treaty reserves to them the right to hunt "anywhere in this country, *irrespective of any laws made by Montana.*" Whatever right is claimed for the Indians to hunt outside the boundaries of their reservation, I presume, is taken from the following paragraph in the third artitle [sic] of their treaty, made and concluded at Hell Gate, in the Bitter Root Valley, on the 16th day of July, 1855, which reads as follows:

"The exclusive right of taking fish in all the streams running through or bordering said reservation is further secured to said Indians; as also the right of taking fish at all usual and accustomed places in common with citizens of the Territory, and of erecting temporary buildings for curing, together with the privilege of hunting, gathering roots and berries, and pasturing their horses and cattle upon open and unclaimed ground."

Under date of November 11, 1885, a letter was directed to me from the Indian Office in Washington, in answes [sic] to inquiries and instructions asked for by me, under date of October 14th of the same year, in regard to the hunting privileges of these Indians, and I herewith quote a paragraph from it for your further consideration:

★ ★ ★ "In reply I have to say that the privilege of hunting upon open and unclaimed land was guaranteed to the Indians by the treaty of July 16, 1855, Art. III, Stat. 12, p. 976, and unless the conditions existing at that time have so changed as to render the guarantees inoperative, I do not see how they can be denied the privilege which they still claim. ★ ★ ★ ★

"The regulations of the Department prohibit Indians from leaving their reservation without written permission from their agent. Even with such permission they incur risk by wandering from their reservations, and they should be discouraged as far as possible from going beyond their own borders. Every pretense for conflict with white settlers should be carefully avoided, and you will endeavor to encourage friendly feelings on both sides."

(Signed) A. B. Upshaw,
Acting Commissioner.

To Peter Ronan, U.S. Indian Agent.

* * * * *

The above, silence concerning which by the courteous agent of the confederated tribes had been the occasion of some surprise to us, gives a fair understanding of the right of the Indians to hunt and fish on and off their reservation, and the policy of the Department concerning their absence from their reserve. They have "exclusive" rights of fishing on the reservation, which not being under our Territorial control, is not covered by the game laws of Montana. *Off* the reservation they have rights "in common with citizens of the Territory." These rights are now defined and limited by law, and apply to Indians just the same as citizens. If they violate our game laws they are just as amenable as other citizens. That they have violated them by killing game out of season is a fact — and they counteract wholly the purpose of the law in western Montana by destroying it in the breeding season, hanging around our valleys, foothills and mountains, and destroying it until, despite the observance of the laws by the whites, our larger game is diminishing in numbers year after year. As these Indians have the best fishing in Montana on their reservation, they have no excuse for coming off it to fish. They can no longer "go to buffalo," because the buffalo are exterminated. The policy of the Government is to break up their nomadic habits and inculcate industrial ideas, and as they "cannot leave the reservation without written permission from their agent," and it is recommended their wanderings be "discouraged," we think it would be best for all if Agent Ronan could see his way clear to stop these migrations around the Territory. The people have grown tired of seeing their game laws persistently violated by the red men, and will certainly prosecute them if it is continued. It is better they should stay on their reservation. We are satisfied Agent Ronan wishes to do the best he can for all concerned, and if any Agent in the West has the influence to lead the way in breaking up this nomadic habit, which is fraught with many other evils than those mentioned, he is the man. His efforts in that direction will be appreciated by all of us who have deemed him the right man in the right place through several administrations.

June 3, 1887
LR 14,895/1887, RG 75, National Archives, Washington, D.C.

On May 12, 1887, the Commissioner of Indian Affairs wrote Ronan asking about the feasibility of applying the new Dawes Act to the allotment of the Flathead Reservation. The allotment policy was based on coerced cultural change and theft of tribal assets. The Commissioner seemed anxious to use the Flathead Reservation to demonstrate the new policy. The stated goal was to give tribal members allotments on "the choicest parts of the reservation," but it also involved bargain sales of the remaining "surplus" lands to white farmers.[18] In Ronan's December 4, 1885b, letter he indicated that he agreed with the philosophy behind the allotment policy and thought he could sell the policy to the Flathead Reservation tribes, but in this letter he wrote that he did not want to fight to apply the policy on Flathead. During the nineteenth century allotment officially required the consent of the affected tribes. In 1904 Congressman Joseph Dixon was able to use the recent U.S. Supreme Court decision in the Lone Wolf case to open the reservation without tribal consent. The action notation on this June 3, 1887, letter from Ronan was "File," and the Office of Indian Affairs went on to subject other reservations to the policy. Ronan also recommended against allotment on November 16, 1892.

If allotment had been forced on the Flathead Reservation in 1890, the twenty-five year restrictions on selling the allotments would have expired in 1915 rather than during the 1930s as was the case under Dixon's allotment bill. The fifteen year difference would have resulted in even greater land loss for the tribes.

For more information on the survey problems with the northern boundary of the reservation see the introduction to Ronan's August 20, 1883, letter.

> United States Indian Service,
> Flathead Agency,
> June 3d, 1887.

The Hon. Commissioner of Indian Affairs
Washington, D.C.

Sir:

Replying to your letter of May 12th, 1887 — "L" respecting the Act of Congress approved February 8th, 1887, wherein "the President is authorized, when in his opinion any Indian reservation or any part thereof is advantageous for agricultural and grazing purposes, to cause said reservation or any part thereof, to be surveyed or re-surveyed if necessary and to allot the lands in said reservation to any Indian located thereon, in quantity as specified in said act," I would respectfully report, that in my opinion, the enforcement of this act upon this reservation at present would cause a great deal of trouble as the Indians are averse to allotments of land in sev[e]ralty, owing partly to their deep prejudice against the word "Survey." The Indians of the Flathead reservation claim that they have been robbed already by a survey, and it is a great task to eradicate that idea. It is claimed by Them that the boundary designated by the Stevens treaty, and pointed out to them as the line of their reservation is not at all the line described in the printed treaty, and therefor all surveys of their reservation at present, is looked upon by Them as a pretext to encroach upon their lands.

I quote from the report of the sub-committee of the special committee of the United States Senate, appointed to visit the Indian tribes in Northern Montana, at a council held at the Flathead Agency, September 5th, 1883, page 238.

Agent Ronan: — In the course of my official duties I was directed to locate the Northern boundary of this reservation, and in proceeding to make an examination in connection therewith, found certain monuments and posts placed and marked in order to designate such boundary, by Surveyor Thomas, sent for that purpose from the Surveyor General's office in Helena in this Territory. Now the Territory claims the line as surveyed by Thomas to be the correct boundary, while the Indians claim a line some four or five miles farther North running through Medicine Lodge. The strip of land in dispute is generally unfit for settlement there being only a small portion of it, sufficient perhaps for one or two occupants, suitable for pasture. This quantity, however, may not be inadequate to cause trouble, as the Indians have already removed one settler therefrom and I desire Eneas, (the Chief of the Kootenais) whose home is in that vicinity, to express his views on the subject to the Commission.

Eneas, (Chief of the Kootenais) — We don't know anything about the surveyor's line, or the authority under which he acted; but we do know the line as to which we made the treaty, and it is a well-defined natural boundary, marked by a ridge of hills.

Senator Vest: — No one has a right to run any line unless sent from Washington, and until such is done the boundary described by Governor Stevens must be regarded as the proper one."

I have been informed that a contract for the survey of the Northern boundary line running West from shore of Flathead Lake and connecting with west boundary line, has been let by the Surveyor General of Montana, by instruction from the Hon. Commissioner of Indian Affairs. The surveyors will be in the field next month, and the disputed line will again come up for reference and settlement. Therefor I trust that the Hon. Commissioner will realize the difficulties which will arise this summer in regard to surveys upon this reservation and that he will give ample time to the Agent and his employes to induce the Indians to take allotments in sev[e]ralty, and to pursuade [sic] them to forget their prejudices against the word "Survey."

Your obdt servant,
Peter Ronan
U.S. Indian Agent

June 10, 1887
LR 15,493/1887, RG 75, National Archives, Washington, D.C.

> In 1887 British Columbia Indian policy allowed each Indian family only ten acres of land while white settlers could pre-empt 160 acres. The British Columbia government even sold the traditional Kootenai village site on Joseph's Prairie to a white politician and demanded the Kootenai move. The final straw for Kootenai Chief Isadore was the arrest of Kapula, a Kootenai Indian, on flimsy evidence for murdering two white miners, when whites who murdered Indians were not prosecuted. Isadore and a group of armed Kootenai forced the local officials to free Kapula from jail. Kapula was later tried and released because of insufficient evidence. The land issues were never settled, but the Kootenai were able to keep an uneasy peace with the white settlers after 1887. Unfortunately Isadore's side of the story was not recorded.[19]
>
> The Commissioner of Indian Affairs authorized Ronan to travel to the Kootenai settlement on Dayton Creek but declined to cover the travel expenses to Tobacco Plains.[20] In June 1887 the United States Army sent twenty five men from Fort Missoula to Tobacco Plains to assess the risk of conflict in the area.[21]
>
> See also Ronan letter, September 13, 1887.

United States Indian Service,
Flathead Agency,
June 10th, 1887.

The Hon. Commissioner of Indian Affairs
Washington, D.C.

Sir:

I have the honor to call your attention to annexed enclosures "A" "B" and "C" and in connection therewith would respectfull[y] state that I am of the opinion that no fears may be entertained that the band of Kootenai Indians residing on this reservation under Chief Eneas, have any sympathy with any war movement of the Kootenais, across the British line. However, there is a large country extending from the Northern boundary of the Flathead reservation to the boundary line of the British possessions, which affords low classes of whites and half-breeds, as well as wandering bands of outlaw Indians an isolated locality for hatching disturbances and passing to and fro across the frontier, "ignoring national lines and frequently the laws and regulations of of [sic] both countries." Complaints have reached this office of certain whitemen who have established a trading post on Tobacco Plains on the American side, about six miles from the British border where in this isolated locality they carry on unrestricted traffic, both illicit and otherwise with the bands at and adjacent to the border on both sides. I deem it my duty to lay the correspondence before you for instructions and authority to make the journey if it is thought proper by the Indian Office. As the question seems to be of an International character, I desire to report fully and intelligently, and without visiting the localities it would be impossible for me to do so. The necessary transportation which might be obtained by authoritive [sic] requisition upon Fort Missoula — one interpreter and two employees and the expenses of the trip, is all I would require.

Very respectfully,
Your obdt servt.
Peter Ronan
U.S. Indian Agent.

First enclosure:

Copy
Headquarters Department of Dakota,
St. Paul, Minn. June 3, 1887

Peter Ronan, Esq.
U.S. Indian Agent,
Flathead Agency, M.T.

Sir:

Referring to the copies, herewith enclosed, relative to the condition of Indian matters in the vicinity of a portion of the boundary line between British Columbia and Montana &c., &c.: I have the honor of requesting, for the Commanding General, — information, — so far as you may be able to furnish it, — particularly as indicated by the following:

What number of our Indians, and of what tribes, have of late, — for a year or so past, — frequented the region to the north of Flathead Lake, — particularly the Tobacco Plains or any part of the valley of the Kootenay therein, near the boundary line?; What was the object of the "War Council" referred to in the paper?; Whether the straggler Indians from the West, with others, who were near the Flathead Lake some time ago, are still in that vicinity; whether there is much visiting back and forth, between the Kootenais, north of the boundary and those belonging to your agency; and, generally, any facts pertinent to the subject. In addition your opinion, as to the probability of Indians or half-breeds, belonging on our side of the boundary, going to join, or giving assistance to, Indians or half-breeds who may be inclined to give trouble to the Canadian authorities, will be deemed valuable.

Further, please state the number of settlers in the Country referred to, — the number in the Tobacco Plains region to be given separately.

I have the honor to be
Your obedeint [sic] servant,
Thomas M. Vincent
Assistant Adjutant General.

Enclosure in Vincent letter to Ronan:
(Copy — extract)
2833, D.D., 1887.

Certified copy of a report of a Committee of the Honorable the Privy Council for Canada, approved by H. E. the Governor General in Council on the 5th of May, 1887.

* * * * * *

On a report dated 2d May, 1887, from the Superintendent General of Indian Affairs submitting the annexed communication from D. J. W. Powell [i.e., I. W. Powell], the visiting Superintendent of Indian Affairs in British Columbia.

The Minister states that it is feared that disturbances of a serious character may arise at any time along the frontier from the lawlessness of the people, white as well as Indians, infesting the border. A body of Mounted Police is held in radiness [sic] to proceed to the locality on requisition from the Provincial Government, but their attempts at Keeping the peace can not be very successful so long as there are unchecked means of escaping across the boundary open to marauders, white and red. The Minister therefore concurs with Dr Powell in the opinion that it is expedient to apply to the Government of the United States to place a military force as close to the frontier as circumstances will permit, so that by joint action of the military bodies peace and order may be restored in that part of the country.

John J. McGee
Clerk Privy Council, Canada
Ottawa, April 27, 1887.

* * * * *

Sir:

I have the honor to report to you upon the present condition of Indian matters in the District of Kootenay in the vicinity of the boundary line separating that portion of the Province of British Columbia from Montana in the United States.

The small tribe of Kootenay Indians residing in the locality referred to, has for some time been a source of anxiety to settlers and to the peace authorities of the Province on account of their attitude and apparent hostility to the further settlement of the District by whites, — not that there exists apprehension of any successful outbreak, if confined to the band alluded to, but a combination between them and quite a large number of renegade Indians who belong to the United States, and, who are in the habit of passing to and fro across the frontier, ignoring national lines and frequently the laws and regulations of both countries, would, unchecked, create serious and fatal troubles.

Disturbances are also, more or less fermented by the low class of whites who often seek such isolated localities for trading purposes and the immunity they enjoy from unrestricted traffic, both illicit and otherwise with the bands at and adjacent to the border on both sides. Last Autumn I have the honor of requesting the attention of the U.S. Authorities to the report of the local officer at Kootenay that some white traders on the Tobacco Plains in Montana were demoralizing our Indians by supplying them with liquor, and unless they were stopped, we should be certain ere long to experience troubles of a more serious character.

During my late visit to that part of the country I was informed that a War Council had been held at the boundary line which was attended by the Kootenay Indians and those from various bands belonging to the U.S. Agency in Montana. I have also had the honor of reporting to you, a few days since the circumstances connected with the forcible rescue from the local authorities of a Kootenay Indian alleged to be guilty of having robbed and murdered a well-known white miner two years ago. This Indian had been arrested by the local constable and some armed specials in the camp of the Kootenays at St. Mary's, and had not been long imprisoned in the goal at Wild Horse Creek, ere Isadore, the Chief, and twenty five armed braves liberated him and compelled the Constable to leave the District. The local Government feel themselves powerless to enforce obedience to the law under such circumstances and have therefore requested the federal authorities to send into Kootenai from the N. W. Territories a force of Mounted Police, so that the law may be maintained, and the protection and safety of settlers, who have become greatly alarmed and very urgent in their appeals for assistance assured. From my knowledge of the circumstances, however, it has occured [sic] to me to suggest, for your consideration, that the pressure of mounted police may to a certain extent be neutralized if not indeed ineffectual, owing to the facility with which the Indians can cross the frontier, not only obtaining in their way, a base for their operations, but the assistance of their friends in U.S. Territory, which would strengthen and foster a feeling of active hostility, *not otherwise probable or possible*. In support of this view I need only point out the fact that kindred bands in Kootenay, such as the Shuswaps and others on the Upper Columbia River, do not sympathize with Chief Isadore in his present movement, and as his own band is small, he only relies in case of trouble on the assistance of those who he has met in Council from the other side of the line. I am informed that a U.S. Military force is stationed in Montana but too far from the boundary (about 150 miles) to be of practical service in co-operation with our mounted police. I venture therefore to suggest for your approval that the subject herein adverted to might be brought to the notice of the proper authorities at Washington, and, in the event of mounted police being, as proposed, sent from this side to be stationed near the frontier that the presence of a small military force of the U.S. in the adjacent locality on that side of the line would ensure obedience to the laws of both countries, and Certainly put a stop at once to any hope that the Indians may at present entertain of successful raids or open revolt.

I have &c.

J. W. Powell [i.e., I. W. Powell],

Supt. Indian Affairs, B.C.

★ ★ ★ ★ ★

Official Copy:

Thomas M. Vincent,

Assistant Adjutant General.

Second enclosure:

United States Indian Service,
Flathead Agency,
June 10th, 1887.

Thomas M. Vincent, U.S.A.
Asst. Adjt. Gen'l. Department Dakota,
St. Paul, Minnesota.
    Sir:
    In reply to your letter, with inclosures, dated June 3d, 1887, I would re-
spectfully state that in order to furnish a full and concise report, which the
nature of the correspondence calls for, it will involve a journey, first to Dayton
Creek, some seventy miles from the Agency on this reservation, where the Kootenai Indians reside belonging to the Confederation of Flatheads, Kootenais,
and Pen d'Oreilles, and perhaps, a journey to the boundary line at Tobacco
Plains, in order to make a proper investigation and report. I shall be happy to
accord you all the information on the subject possible to obtain, and shall immediately communicate with the Indian Department, and ask for authority to
make the journey and investigation.

Very respectfully,
Your obdt servt.
Peter Ronan
U.S. Indian Agent.

August 6, 1887
LR 21,347/1887, RG 75, National Archives, Washington, D.C.

Note on back of letter by Land Division of Office of Indian Affairs: "Tel. to Ronan Oct 15, 87, asking result of Busha's visit & whether Flatheads will allow Cree Refugees to come on Resn."[22]

Several unidentified newspaper clippings were enclosed with this letter, including one which charged the Crees with arming and organizing to invade Canada and a racist editorial railing against allowing the Crees to remain in the United States. Filed with the letter was a three page "Memorandum" from Charles F. Larrabee, longtime Office of Indian Affairs clerk, sympathetically spelling out the sufferings and travails of the Crees in Montana, including: "They are wanderers on the face of the earth homeless and helpless, driven here and then there. The women and children at least are innocent. We cannot allow them to starve to death on our territory! Would it not be well to allow them to go to Flathead Reservation, the Indians there consenting, and get the President to feed them out of the starving fund, till otherwise provided for?" Larrabee mentioned that even the Montana Legislature had appropriated $500 to help alleviate their destitution.

On October 16, 1887, Ronan informed the Commissioner that the Flathead Reserva-
tion Indians would not agree to let the Crees settle on Flathead. The reservation leaders argued that with the Bitterroot Salish, Lower Kalispel, and Spokane Indians being removed to Flathead there would not be enough agricultural land left on the reservation to provide for the Cree. On October 29, 1887, Ronan relayed a request from Pierre Busha for the Cree to settle on the Blackfeet Reservation. The Commissioner responded on October 31, 1887: "Tell Pierre Busha Indian Department can make no promises in regard to lands for British

Cree refugees."²³ In December 1888, Busha returned to the Flathead and was again denied refuge.²⁴ In 1888 Ronan was considerably more negative about the Cree than he had been in 1887. For a broader discussion of the travails of the Crees in Montana see Verne Dusenberry, *The Montana Cree: A Study in Religious Persistence.*²⁵

Very little biographical information was located about Pierre Busha (or Boucher). A short biographical sketch written by Lawrence Barkwell of the Louis Riel Institute, Winnipeg, Manitoba, says he was born in Canada in 1824 and died at St. Ignatius, Montana. No death date was given.²⁶

United States Indian Service,
Flathead Agency,
August 6th, 1887.

Hon. Commissioner of Indian Affairs
Washington, D.C.

Sir:

On the 3d day of this month, Pierre Busha, the Cree halfbreed associated with Louis Riel in the halfbreed rebellion in the British Northwest Territory, who was executed by the British Authorities, at Regina, arrived at this Agency and held an interview with me. The executed chief had as his second in command, Gabriel Dumont, and Pierre Busha, it is stated ranked as third officer. Busha stated to me that he had come to the Flathead Agency from Dupouia [Dupuyer] Creek, near Sun River, and close to the Blackfoot Agency, Montana, where are now living sixty families of exiled Cree halfbreeds — in all two hundred — Who took part in the conflict against the Canadian Authorities; which ended in the execution of their leader and the flight of Dumont and Pierre Busha, with sixty families, across the border, where they have lived ever since upon American soil. "Busha" stated that he was here to look at the country and, if possible, find a place upon which to locate these people, where they can make a home and a living. And if successful in negotiating with the Indians will appeal to the Government to give them an asylum. In reply to the statement that a report is now going the rounds of the press, that "Dumont" and "Busha" were gathering the disaffected Indians and halfbreeds of the British Territory, and those in sympathy with their course [sic] on the American Side, to invade the Northwest Territory and seek revenge. "Busha" said that such was not the case, — and his only object in coming here was to see if homes could be provide[d] for these families, who are in poverty and starvation. He further states that Gabriel Dumont is now on his way to France to ask aid, advice, and influence from that country with the government of Great Britain, to be allowed to return and occupy the lands from which they Claim to have been wrongfully driven, and which caused their rebellion, and their flight to American Territory. Failing in that, Busha said it was their hope to secure homes on the American Side, and to see this reservation — talk with the Indians and learn from them if they could make a home with them, provided he got the consent of the "Government" is the only object of his visit.

As this band of Cree refugees has attracted the attention of nearly all classes of people on both sides of the bound[a]ry line, I deemed it my duty to report the presence of Busha upon this reservation, and also to give his statement of the object of his visit. He has agreed to report to me after he interviews the Indians upon the subject of negotiating for homes for the Cree families, on this reservation.

I desire, if you think the matter of importance enough to give it any attention, to Know your views upon the subject of such removal, should I again be consulted.

I herewith enclose some newspaper Clippings, on the subject, published in Some of the Territorial papers today.

I am very respectfully
Your obt. Svt.
Peter Ronan
US. Indian Agent.

First Enclosure. Ronan enclosed three newspaper clippings with this letter. Only the two clippings that refer to the Cree request to settle on the Flathead Reservation are reproduced here. The sources for the clippings have not been identified:

The British Crees.

It is stated that the band of British Cree Indians who have been for two years a constant source of annoyance trouble and expense to Montana want to settle on the Flathead reservation and have made a request to that effect of Major Ronan. These Crees are not an admirable lot. They were in rebellion in the Canadian northwest and, instead of accepting the amnesty extended when the rebellion was over, came across the line as refugees. Their chief is said to have boasted around Fort Assinaboine of the number of white women he had outraged and exhibited trinkets that he had taken from them as trophies of his abomination. Since then they have been in a chronic state of poverty, beside their natural state of laziness. The territorial legislature has paid them $500, and private bounty doubtless as much more, beside what they have stolen, or taken from natural resources. There is not the slightest obstacle, except their own inclinations, to their return to their own country. They will not be molested upon their return. Montana has enough Indians and more than enough. The folly of allowing non-resident pauper Indians to come in here and camp down is illustrated in the case of the Cheyennes who settled in Custer county and have been more trouble since they have been there than all Montana Indians put together. Send these Crees back to their own country. Give them no asylum here. The whole Cree nation will be down here in a few years if this detachment is allowed to settle and is supported by the United States government, as they must be — or else by the territory and its people as they have been in the past.

Second enclosure. No title:

While Riel's rebellion has ended, its leader paid the penalty of his treason with his life, and the tribe with which he identified himself was compelled to wander in exile. They seem, however, to have tired of their nomadic existence and have sent out representatives to find a permanent abiding place. As stated in our special yesterday the emissaries have been to the Flathead country and may locate there. The question naturally arises, in case the wanderers prove incapable of self-support, will the United States be compelled to issue annuities to these wards of the Canadian Government? There would seem just cause for complaint in such event.

August 21, 1887

LR 22,552/1887, RG 75, National Archives, Washington, D.C.

On September 8, 1887, the Commissioner of Indian Affairs instructed Ronan to have Lawrence Finley tried for rape in the Missoula County courts.[27] On September 26, 1887, however, Ronan reported that he had to have Finley released from the Fort Missoula stockade because the rape victim had died and there was not enough evidence to try Finley for the crime. According to prison records and various newspaper accounts Finley was one quarter Indian and was born in Minnesota. Flathead Reservation enrollment records have him as 5/8 Kootenai.[28]

In 1885 Finley was reported to be bootlegging alcohol to the Indian workers digging an irrigation ditch in Jocko.[29] In 1888 reports placed Finley in Washington State where he allegedly ran off with another man's wife and horses.[30]

In 1889 Finley was arrested for killing a Kootenai Indian named Jocko north of Flathead Lake. While being questioned by the state authorities about the killing, Finley accused two other Indians, Pierre Paul and Lalasee, of having murdered two white men. Finley was frequently mentioned in Ronan's 1889 letters. Finley was convicted of manslaughter and sent to Montana State Prison from 1890 to 1896.[31]

After his release in 1896, Finley was accused of kidnapping his half sister and convicted of assault.[32] He was sent to the Montana Prison for a one year sentence and was released in 1897.

A few years later, in January 1904, Finley was accused of assaulting his brother's wife. He was held over for trial but the case was dismissed that fall. According to a newspaper report, Finley was transferred to the Missoula jail because authorities feared he would be lynched if held on the reservation.[33]

Despite his criminal record, in 1906 Finley was added to the Flathead Reservation rolls over the objections of then agent Samuel Bellew.[34] According to his enrollment record he was married on August 18, 1906.

Thomas E. Adams was appointed Flathead Agency clerk in 1886. Originally from Mississippi, in the 1890s he went on to become special agent for the U.S. Treasury Department for the Alaska seal fisheries.[35] Col. Horace Jewett, in command of Fort Missoula in 1887, was a Civil War veteran. Ranked lieutenant-colonel in 1886, he became a full colonel in 1891 and died in 1897.[36]

United States Indian Service,
Flathead Agency,
August 21st, 1887.

Hon. Commissioner of Indian Affairs
Washington, D.C.

Sir:

I have the honor to report that a certain half-breed Indian Known by the name of Laurence Finley, Who has the reputation of being a horse thief and outlaw, and who was confined in the Indian Jail, from which he escaped, charged with the commission of rape upon an Indian woman, from the brutal effects of which, it was reported to me, she died, was arrested by me yesterday and turned over to the Military authorities at Fort Missoula, under the following circumstances: Finley was under the influence of liquor, and followed me into the railroad station at Arlee; and demanded, in language which could not be misunderstood, if I was looking for him, being unarmed, I made evasive answers, untill I procured a gun from the railroad agent, when the Indian ran up the track. I finally halted him and had him securely tied with a rope. The prisoner informed Mr. [Thomas] Adams the agency Clerk, that he would kill me upon his release from the Reservation Jail. Knowing that the Indian Jail was not a safe place for such a Character, and also Knowing from former experience, that the county officials would not take action against the Indian, which would involve expense, in a protracted confinement I conveyed the Indian to Fort Missoula and addressed the following note to the Commanding officer:

Copy

Col. H[orace] Jewett.
Commanding Post
Fort Missoula, M.T.
    Sir:
    I would respectfully report that I placed under arrest today an Indian belonging to the Flathead Reservation, and would respectfully request, that I be permitted to turn him over to your charge, untill I report my action to the Indian Office.

I am
Your obt. svt.
(sgd) Peter Ronan
U.S. Indian Agent

Flathead Agency
Aug. 20th, 1887

The Indian is now confined at Fort Missoula, and as he is not a safe character to be allowed his liberty at present upon this reservation I respectfully request instructions in regard to the disposition of the prisoner.

Very respectfully
Your obt svt.
Peter Ronan
U.S. Indian Agent.

August 27, 1887

U.S. Commissioner of Indian Affairs, Annual Report of the Commissioner of Indian Affairs (Washington, D.C.: U.S. Government Printing Office, 1887), pages 137-141.

Much of Ronan's 1887 annual report involved a review of topics covered in many of his earlier letters reproduced above. The continued progress in developing agriculture on the reserve — highlighted this time by the expansion of orchards — was presented as a moral imperative rather than an economic necessity. The problems with the survey of the northern boundary of the reservation would give the tribes problems well into the twentieth century. Indian police and judges were part of Ronan's efforts to control police powers on the reservation. Finally Ronan returned to tribal opposition to allotment; the operation of the St. Ignatius Mission schools; and the need to fulfill promises of assistance for Bitterroot Salish who removed to the Jocko.

The most important new topic Ronan introduced in this report was the agreement between the Northwest Indian Commission and the Lower Kalispel and the tribes of the Flathead Reservation. In April 1887, the Northwest Indian Commission met the Lower Pend d'Oreille Indians at Sand Point, Idaho, and offered various types of economic assistance if they would remove to the Jocko Reservation and give up their claim to lands in the Pend Oreille River Valley. Most of the tribe under Chief Victor and his son Masseslow refused to remove, but one band under Chief Michel signed the agreement on April 21, 1887. The Commission then moved to the Jocko Reservation where they toured the St. Ignatius Mission, were entertained by student programs, and met the Flathead Reservation leaders in a general council. On April 27, 1887, the reservation leaders agreed to accept the Lower Kalispel, Spokane, and "any other non-reservation tribes or bands of Indians who desire and agree to said removal." At the request of the Indians, the St. Ignatius Mission was granted two sections of land "for educational and religious purposes, as long as they are used for said purposes and no longer." The United States was to erect a saw and grist mill and blacksmith shop for the tribes. Ronan expected the new saw and grist mill and blacksmith shop to be centrally located on the reservation.[37] Apparently the United States Congress never ratified the agreement with the Lower Kalispel and so the promised aid was never delivered. The unratified agreement caused considerable complaint and ill feelings over the years.[38] See also Ronan letters of September 25, October 19, and December 30, 1887.

No biographical information was located on Commission members Dr. Jared W. Daniels and Henry W. Andrews, but John V. Wright was a lawyer from Tennessee. During the Civil War he served in the Confederate Army and the Confederate Congress. In addition to chairing the Northwest Indian Commission, he also was a member of the Sioux commission in 1899.[39]

Flathead Agency, Montana,
August 27, 1887.

Sir: In accordance with instructions I herewith submit my eleventh annual report from the Flathead Indian agency, Montana Territory.

The confederate tribes of this reservation, consisting of the Pend d'Oreilles, the Flatheads, and the Kootenais, including the Bitter Root Indians of Charlos' band, who have removed here, the latest census shows to be 1,738, and of Charlos' band of Flathead Indians remaining in the Bitter Root valley, 278, showing a decrease of 63 from last year's census, the remainder having removed to this reservation during the year.

Charlos' Band Living in Bitter Root Valley.

Whole number of Indians	278
Males over eighteen years of age	80
Females over fourteen years of age	87
Children between six and sixteen years of age	51

Total Number of Confederate Indians on the Reservation.

Whole number of Indians	1,738
Males over eighteen years of age	518
Females over fourteen years of age	585
Children between six and sixteen years of age	405

Agricultural Pursuits.

It is a notable fact that the Indians of this reservation each year increase their acreage of planting, and that new families break up and fence in land, until now, in all directions from the agency, the eye is gladdened by the sight of Indian fields of grain, vegetables, and meadows, and also the numerous

Planting of Orchards.

In my last annual report I stated that sixteen heads of families had been induced to purchase from the Geneva, N.Y., nursery, at their own expense and cost of transportation to this agency, young fruit trees, such as plum, apple, and cherry, which were planted out into orchards. Such was the thrift and growth of the trees that other families followed the example this year, and an agent from the house of L. L. Mann & Co., nurserymen of Saint Paul, Minn., arrived here this spring with a shipment of trees for delivery to the following-named Indian residents of this reservation:

Name	Amount of order	Location
Joe Gardipe	$44.50	3 miles north of Saint Ignatius mission.
C. Matt	25.00	6 miles north of Saint Ignatius mission.
C. B. Vitell	15.00	At mission.
Peter Pain	50.00	At mission.
Louis Finley`	5.00	16 miles north of Saint Ignatius mission.
Parish Ashlin	25.00	2 miles northeast.
Frank Elmic	10.00	At mission.
Alex Sarel	25.00	4 miles east mission.
Gideon Gangras	35.00	16 miles north mission.
Isaac Bonapart	27.50	16 miles north mission.
Isaac Koodnai	5.00	16 miles north mission.
Kiccdlie Moses	25.00	30 miles Horseshoe Bend.
Salowan Malta	50.00	3 miles northwest mission.
Andre Spokane	17.00	10 miles west of mission.
Alex Pairier	32.00	8 miles south of mission.
Bob Irvin	115.00	16 miles north of mission.
Michel, chief of Pend-d'Oreilles	31.00	16 miles north of mission.
Louis Sac Sac	50.00	Mission.
J. Larose	25.00	3 miles north of mission.
Louis Camille	15.00	4 miles north of mission.
Joe Finley	10.00	10 miles east of mission.
Baptiste Michell	25.00	16 miles east of mission.
Antoin Marse	35.00	17 miles east of mission.
John Lumphrey	35.00	16 miles east of mission.
Joe Barnaby	30.00	16 miles east of mission.
Wm. King	15.00	15 miles east of mission.
Frank Secund	30.00	18 miles east of mission.
Adolph Finley	25.00	9 miles east of mission.
Isadore Ladaroot	50.00	9 miles east of mission.
Alex Finley	50.00	6 miles east of mission.

These large orders were sold to the Indians with the understanding that they were to be cash on delivery, and as the trees were delivered this spring by an agent of the nursery and planted into orchards by the Indians, it is presumable that both parties were satisfied. As fruit trees already planted have yielded abundantly on this reservation and at maturity, it will be readily seen that in a few years the raising and selling of fruit will be a marked industry on the Flathead Indian reservation.

Survey of Reserve.

The Indians claim that the boundary line designated by the Stevens treaty, and pointed out to them as the line of their reserve, is not the line described in the printed treaty, and therefore all survey of their reservation is looked upon by them as a pretext to encroach on their lands. I quote from the report of the subcommittee of the special committee of the United States Senate appointed to visit the Indian tribes in northern Montana, at a council held at the Flathead agency September 5, 1883, page 238:

> Agent Ronan. In the course of my official duties I was directed to locate the northern boundary of this reservation, and on proceeding to make an examination in connection therewith found certain monuments and posts placed and marked in order to designate such boundary by Surveyor Thomas, sent for that purpose from the surveyor-general's office at Helena, in this Territory. Now, the Territory claims the line as surveyed by Thomas to be the correct boundary, while the Indians claim a line some 4 or 5 miles farther north, running through medicine lodge. The strip of land in dispute is generally unfit for settlement, there being only a small portion of it, sufficient perhaps for one or two occupants, suitable for pasture. This quantity, however, may not be inadequate to cause trouble, as the Indians have already removed one settler therefrom, and I desire Eneas (the Chief of the Kootinais,) whose home is in that vicinity, to express his views on that subject to the commission.

> Eneas (chief of Kootinais). We don't know anything about the surveyor's line, or the authority under which he acted, but we do know the line to which we made the treaty, and it is a well defined natural boundary, marked by a ridge of hills.

> Senator Vest. No one had a right to run any line unless sent from Washington, and until such is done the boundary as described by Governor Stevens must be regarded as the proper one.

This summer a contract for the survey of the northern boundary line, running west from shore of Flathead lake and connecting with west boundary line, was let by the surveyor-general of Montana, by instructions from the honorable Commissioner of Indian Affairs. The survey was completed before I was notified that it was being done. I am not aware where the initial point was established, but infer that the surveyor had his proper instructions and that this vexed question will not come up again, and trust that the Indians will be satisfied with the boundary as recently surveyed. But few Indians are aware as yet that the line has been run out by order of the Government.

Indian Police.

Living close to and bordering upon commercial towns, it can not be expected otherwise than that the Indians and half-breeds of this reservation can purchase all the whisky they want despite the laws governing such traffic. The Indian police are inadequate at times and loath to meet emergencies, and the agent is called upon to act and make arrests when the police hesitate. No matter how much an Indian may annoy or even injure his brethren, my experience is that as soon as the culprit is in the custody of white men his people shrink from assisting in his prosecution and exhibit a vast amount of sympathy in his misfortune. In case a crime is committed by an Indian, no matter how revolting, and the culprit seeks the reservation, he generally has the sympathy of the Indians, and they will assist him in every way to evade arrest by white men. However, the Indian police and the laws governing Indian offenses have a good effect in preserving peace and quiet on the reservation. The judges of the Indian court should be paid a salary as well as the police, as to their vigilance and efficiency all the good arises from the efforts of the police. A good jail should also be provided for the confinement of prisoners. It is a great farce to provide for the payment of Indian police and establish a code of rules governing Indian offenses when there is no proper jail for the confinement of prisoners.

The Northwest Indian Commission.

The agreement which was made and concluded at Saint Ignatius mission on the Flathead Reservation, on the 27th day of April, 1887, by and between John V. Wright, Dr. Jared W. Daniels, and Henry W. Andrews, the gentlemen composing the commission, on the part of the United States, and the chiefs, headmen, and other adult Indians of the confederated bands of Flatheads, Pend d'Oreilles, and Kootenais Indians —

> That whereas it is the policy of the United States Government to remove to and settle upon Indian Reservations scattered bands of non-reservation Indians, so as to bring them under the care and protection of the Government of the United States; and whereas a part of the Upper and Middle bands of Spokane Indians have expressed their desire and consent to remove and settle in permanent homes upon this reservation; and whereas the Lower Pend d'Oreilles or Kalespel Indians also express their desire and consent to remove and settle in permanent homes upon this reservation; and whereas it is the policy of the United States Government first to obtain the consent of the reservation Indians before removing the Indians on said reservation:
>
> Article 1. In consideration of the desire and consent of said Spokane and Pend d'Oreilles Indians as set forth in their respective agreements made with the above-named commissioners of the United States and our desire that this reservation shall be occupied by Indians only, the undersigned chiefs and headmen and other adult Indians belonging to the confederated bands of Flatheads, Pend d'Oreilles and Kootenai Indians now residing on the Jocko Indian reservation in the Territory of Montana, do hereby agree and consent that the said Spokane and Pend d'Oreilles Indians may come and settle upon the lands of said Jocko reservation in permanent

homes on terms and conditions contained respectively with
the agreement made with said Spokanes, at Spokane Falls, in
the Territory of Washington, and with the said Pend d'Oreilles
at Sand Point, in the Territory of Idaho. And we do further
agree and consent that the United States may remove to and
settle upon the said Jocko reservation any other non-reservation tribes or bands of Indians who desire and agree to said
removal, on such terms and conditions as may be hereafter
agreed on between the United States and any of the said Indians.

Article 2. In consideration of the large amount of money
expended by the Saint Ignatius Mission in the erection of a
church, school-houses, mills, barns, shops, and other useful
buildings, and in the opening and fencing of farms and gardens, and in consideration of the religious and educational
facilities afforded thereby to our children, and our anxious
desire that our posterity in all times to come shall continue to
have such advantages and facilities, the undersigned Indians
agree that the United States may have a parcel of land not
exceeding one section for the boys' school under the charge
of the Society of Jesus, and one section for the girls' school
under the charge of the Sisters of Providence, on which is
situated said buildings and improvements; which land and
improvements may be occupied and held by said Saint Ignatius Mission for educational and religious purposes as long as
they are used for said purpose and no longer: Provided, That
nothing herein contained shall interfere with the rights of Indians living on said tracts of land.

Article 3. In consideration of the above agreements on
the part of the Indians, and the necessity therefor, the United States agree to erect on said reservation a saw and grist
mill, and furnish a miller for the same, at such place on said
reservation as may be selected by the United States Indian
agent in charge of said reservation, under the direction of the
Commissioner of Indian Affairs. And the United States further agree to furnish a competent blacksmith, and pay for the
service of the same, to be located at or near the said saw and
grist mill, and to furnish suitable tools for his use.

This agreement not to be binding upon the parties hereto
until the same shall be ratified by Congress.

The above agreement was signed on the 27th day of April, 1887, by the
Northwest Indian Commission, and a majority of the chiefs, headmen, and
adults of the confederated tribes living on the Jocko or Flathead reservation
in presence of United States Indian Agent Peter Ronan, and the agency clerk,
Thomas E. Adams, and the interpreter, Michael Revais.

Should Be Ratified.

The agency is situated at the extreme end of the southern habitable portion of the reservation, a fact which will be readily admitted when it is known
that not a single farm of even Indian lodge is in existence between it and the
southern boundary. It is also placed at the immediate foot of the mountains

forming the eastern line, thereby precluding any settlement in that direction. On the other hand, to the north and west there are farms extending in the one case to a distance of 40 miles, and in the other at least 60 miles. Owing to this state of affairs it will be evident that the use of the mills and the services of the mechanics connected with the agency can not be utilized by a great majority of the Indians except at considerable cost and inconvenience, consequently they have not the encouragement which it is the intention of the Government to afford them to follow civilized pursuits. This is especially apparent in connection with building and grain raising, two matters to which attention is most strongly urged by your Department, showing that the transportation by wagon of lumber or wheat for any considerable distance exceeds the value of the article itself. As the Bitter Root Flatheads of Chief Charlos' band are steadily removing from that valley and settling in close proximity to the agency, the mills and shops of the agency are of necessity where they are now located. If the agreement cited between the Indians and the Northwest Commission should be ratified it will place mills and mechanics in the very center of Indian settlements, where are now being opened new farms and new homes by thrifty and progressive Indians, who should be encouraged in their efforts to scatter out from Indian villages and settle upon land which they will soon ask to be set aside for them.

In Severalty.

At present the Indians of this reservation look with suspicion upon this bill, which no doubt arose from a common inspiration to secure legislation having for its object the making out of the Indian a self-supporting citizen of the United States, and it is hoped and advocated by a large number of the real friends of the Indians that by a wise administration of the severalty act in a few years the Indian as an Indian will cease to exist on the reservations and will give place to the self-supporting, law-abiding citizen. A large majority of the Indians of the Flathead reservation are averse to taking land in severalty, as they labor under the impression that the residue will be sold by the Government to white settlers, thus breaking up their reservations and mixing the Indians up promiscuously with the white settlers. It is apparent, and I seek to impress upon the Indians, that the severalty provisions of this act has only the legal effect whereby one or more of several owners of land in common can secure the separate and exclusive enjoyment of his share apart from the rest, and that in law not an acre of land can be taken from an Indian without his consent and in conformity with his title. It will take some time and patience to bring the Indians here to this understanding of the act, but I trust it can be accomplished.

The Schools

On this reservation consist of two industrial establishments, one for boys and one for girls, and are situated at St. Ignatius Mission, about 20 miles north of the agency, and within the boundaries of the reservation. Those schools are conducted under contract with the Government by the Jesuit missionaries of St. Ignatius Mission and the Sisters of Providence. The contract is $150 for each of 75 children in each school. These children remain in the school the year round. There is a partial vacation in the month of August, but it extends only to a suspension of certain studies. It is hardly necessary to report that the Indian schools of this reservation, under the careful teaching of the missionaries, Jesuits of St Ignatius and the Sisters of Providence, are excellent institutions of education for Indian children, and are fast attaining a national reputation. They should be encouraged and sustained, not only by the Government, but by the good people of all denominations, as education and religion are the best and only means that can be employed with and hope of success in elevating the Indian to citizenship and usefulness.

Charlos' Band of Bitter Root Flatheads.

The original families of Bitter Root Flatheads of this band who removed to this reservation, and who were furnished with fenced fields, seed, houses, cows, and agricultural implements, provisions, etc., may now be said to be self-supporting. Could they be induced or forced to give up their drinking or gambling habits they would soon be in comfortable circumstances. As the census shows, several other families of this band removed from the Bitter Root Valley and are living here but have not been provided with houses, fenced fields, etc., as were the other families who previously removed. It is certain that nearly every family of Bitter Root Flatheads would remove to the reservation if they were offered the encouragement of the first families who preceded them to the reservation, and the privilege of selling their land there. Those who choose to remain should be made to understand that they need look no further for Government aid; that they are amenable to the laws of the country, and to taxation, in common with their white neighbors who are struggling around them to acquire homes and independence.

I am, very respectfully, your obedient servant,

Peter Ronan,
U.S. Indian Agent.

The Commissioner of Indian Affairs.

September 5, 1887
LR 24,118/1887, SC 143, RG 75, National Archives, Washington, D.C.

United States Indian Service,
Flathead Agency,
September 5th, 1887.

Hon. Commissioner of Indian Affairs
Washington, D.C.

Sir:

In accordance with your directions, as contained in circular, dated at Washington, D.C. August 19th, 1887, but just received at this office. I respectfully report: that the Missionaries of the Catholic Church are located on the Flathead Reservation employed in Christianizing the Indians and teaching the Children.

The boys school is tought [sic] by the Fathers; and the girls school by the Sisters.

The land used by the Fathers for Church, school buildings, work shops, residences, mills, stables with Corrals agregates about Sixty acres. The land used by the Same fathers for farm and pastures agregate about 470 acres. It was set apart by the Indians for the above purposes.

The Fathers have been located at St. I[g]natius Mission on this reservation Since 1853 or 1854.

The Sisters located at the Same place in 1864. Their buildings for School purposes etc., occupy from twelve to Sixteen acres: Their farm amounts to about 160 acres.

The buildings of the fathers are valued at about $55,000. — Those of the sisters at about $20,000.

During the summer of 1887 the Confederated Tribes of this Reservation petitioned the Government to Set aside one Mile square of land embracing the above for the Fathers and as much also for the Sisters.

Very respectfully
Your obt. svt.
Peter Ronan
U.S. Indian Agent.

September 13, 1887
LR 25,010/1887, RG 75, National Archives, Washington, D.C.

See editor's annotation to Ronan's letter, June 10, 1887.

Very little biographical information was found for Michael Philips (or Phillips). He was born in England and married a Kootenai Indian woman. He was acting Indian Agent for the Kootenay Agency in 1887 and 1888 and agent between 1890 and 1893. He died in 1916. His annual reports as Kootenay agent dealt mostly with the agricultural adjustment of the Kootenays and problems with land claims.[40]

United States Indian Service,
Flathead Agency,
September 13th, 1887.

The Hon. Commissioner of Indian Affairs
Washington, D.C.

Sir:

In conformity with telegraphic authority, dated at Washington, D.C. June 10th, 1887, I have the honor to present my report in regard to Indian matters at Tobacco Plains, on the border of British Columbia:

On the 13th of June 1887, in accordance with instructions from Headquarters Department of Dakota, to the commanding officer at Fort Missoula, a detachment consisting of two Commissioned officers, six noncommissioned officers, one hospital steward and eighteen privates, left Fort Missoula for Tobacco Plains, through which runs the dividing line between the American territory in Montana, and the British Possessions. At the head of Flathead Lake, which is not included in the Flathead reservation, there lives around the country from ten to fifteen families of Indians, who move their lodges to different parts of the country to suit their notions. They are a detached band of British and American Kootenais, who claim the head of the Lake as their homes, and who are sometimes joined or visited by gambling Indians from the Flathead reservation or by wandering Nez Percés of the same class. Their number is constantly varying as some of them often go up into the Tobacco Plains country, to Sand Point, in Idaho, or down to the Flathead reservation to visit other bands of Indians. They belong to no reservation and have no chief resident with them; They are entirely vagabond in their habits; hunt just Enough to procure a meagre sustenance and spend their time principally in gambling. The settlers complain of their depredations, such as stealing vegetables from gardens, letting down fences, and compelling women to give them food when the men are absent; but no great charges are made against them except an occasional row with whitemen which generally Emenates [sic] from whiskey. Taking them all together they are a harmless set though very annoying to settlers. When it is considered that there is nearly seven hundred white people settled in the valley of the Flathead river, and as their [sic] are peace officers there, it seems the people should be able to control these wandering vagrants, without aid from military authorities or without making complaint to the Agent of the Flathead reservation who has no control or authority over their movements. The country known as

Tobacco Plains

extends from Elk river in British Columbia, to about eleven miles south of the boundary line. That portion in the United States is about eight miles wide. It is watered by a few small streams — by Grave Creek, sometimes called Tobacco river, and by the Kootenai river which forms the western boundary. The western portion has considerable open timber, the remainder is principally treeless rolling hills. The whole is covered with bunch grass. It is an excellent stock range but there is comparatively little agricultural land, probably not more than enough for Twenty or Thirty fair farms. There are now ten white settlers in the Plains, with a few prospectors who live there a part of the year but cannot be regarded as permanent settlers. There are no law officers resident here and the nearest Post office is at Ashley, at the head of Flathead Lake. There are at present in the Plains on this side of the boundary line only twelve lodges of Indians, but the remainder who make the Plains their home is greater, being about twenty-five lodges. There is a trader, or storekeeper, on Tobacco Plains, who talks their language and who is well acquainted with their habits. He states there are about fifty Indian men between the ages of sixteen and sixty, who consider this portion of Tobacco Plains (the American side of the line) their home. These all belong to the Kootenai tribe, which is divided geographically, into five different bands: those in British Columbia; those in Tobacco Plains, south of the boundary line; those at the head of Flathead Lake; those near Bonner's Ferry, on the Kootenai river, and those on the Flathead reservation. They are practically the same tribe, though the Kootenais on the reservation and on the Kootenai river, at Bonner's Ferry, in the vicinity of Sand Point, seem to be somewhat separated in feelings and interests from the remainder. There are

Four Chiefs

the limits of whose jurisdiction seems to be somewhat indefinite. The Chief Isador, who resides in British Columbia, and is probably the most influential, has some authority over the Kootenais in the United States, more particularly those in Tobacco Plains and some of the other Chiefs, says he will be obeyed by them. The Chiefs David and Edwald residing in Tobacco Plains claim obedience not only from those living with them but also those living in British Columbia and at the head of Flathead Lake. None of the chiefs claim much power over the Kootenais under Chief Eneas, on the Flathead reservation. The Indians in Tobacco Plains, on the United States side do not recognize the boundary line as dividing them from their relatives on the British side. They say they lived and occupied this country as one tribe.

Before the Boundary line was Established; that They were not consulted in making the line; that They are still as closely related as before the line was made, their feelings and interests remaining the Same, and that they do not, therefor, regard the boundary line as separating them.

A New Reservation

was surveyed on the British side of the line for those Indians, but They refused to confer with the Commissioner on the subject of going over there. In July a British commissioner was at Kootenai about sixty miles North of the line to treat with the Kootenai Indians there, with a view of locating them on a reservation. The Tobacco Plains Kootenais have never been subject to control, as they never lived on a reservation. They are impoverished and demoralized by their drinking and gambling habits. They claim all the land on Tobacco Plains on both sides of the International boundary and the whitemen who have settled there have been compelled, to avoid trouble, to pay the Indians something for the right of occupancy.

Michael Philips

a son of one of the old high officials of the Hudson Bay Company who married into the Kootenai tribe and who has lived among them from a boy, and is the father of a large family of half-breeds, was recently appointed Agent for the Kootenai of British Columbia, and also designated as a Crown Commissioner for the purpose of settling these Indians on a reservation. He recently held a consultation with the Indians on Tobacco Plains, on the American side of the Boundary line, with a view of getting them to decide which of them in future will remain on the American side of the line and which go North on the British reservation. In other words he wishes them to state definitely whether they desire to be considered as British or United States Indians. They refused to give a decision at present but promised to do so when he returns, in a few weeks, after settling matters with the Upper Kootenais.

About eighty

Mounted Police

have arrived from Canada and are now camped near Galbraith's Ferry, on the Kootenai river, with orders to remain during the winter. They are now engaged in building barracks.

The Anticipation of Indian Trouble

in the district, which led to the ordering of troops from Fort Missoula to the British border, and also to the ordering of Canadian Mounted police to the border, arose from two causes, 1st, the forcible rescue last March of two Indians who were confined in jail at Wild Horse creek, charged with the murder of two whitemen, two years ago. 2d, the fear that the Indians would not submit peaceably to being placed on a reservation which had been set apart for them.

The first difficulty has been settled by the Chief giving bond to deliver up the Indian prisoners. One of them has already been given up and the other will be when found.

It is the expressed opinion of Mr. Philips, the British Indian Agent, that the Indians will go on the reservation set aside for them without trouble and that all danger of an outbreak has been averted.

Two Reservations

have been laid out, one in the vicinity of Kootenai for the Kootenai Indians in British Columbia, and the other adjoining the boundary line for such of the Kootenai Indians on Tobacco Plains, on the American side as may desire to go to the British side of the boundary. A consultation has been held with the Tobacco Plains Indians in regard to going on the reservation and a report of the result sent to Ottawa.

Very few Indians of the Kootenai band living on the Flathead reservation have visited Tobacco Plains this summer and those were composed of wandering vagrants, with no particular end in view save to gamble and carouse.

I reiterate the statement made in my report to your office under date of June 10th, 1887, that the Kootenai Indians of this reservation under Chief Eneas, will take no part whatever, if trouble arises across the British border, with the Indians of the Kootenai tribe belonging and residing in the British Possessions.

I am, Very respectfully,
Your obdt. servant,
Peter Ronan
U.S. Indian Agent.

September 25, 1887
LR 26,035/1887, RG 75, National Archives, Washington, D.C.

> On October 31, 1887, the Commissioner of Indian affairs authorized Ronan to pay transportation expenses for fifteen Lower Kalispel families and spend $1500 for subsistence and removal aid.[41] See editor's annotation to Ronan's annual report, August 27, 1887, for more information about the Northwest Indian Commission agreement with Michel's band of Lower Kalispel Indians. Ronan's letters of October 19 and December 30, 1887, have more about the removal of Michel and his band to Flathead.
>
> In 1893, the Lower Kalispel Indians hired John Mullan, a Washington lawyer who had spent considerable time with the Rocky Mountain tribes as a member of the railroad survey in the 1850s, to lobby in Washington, D.C., to get the Northwest Indian Commission agreement ratified by Congress. In 1900 Father Augustine Dimier, S.J., reported that the priests visited the Camas Prairie Kalispel three time a year and Chief Michel kept a special room reserved to accommodate the missionaries. In 1902 Frank C. Armstrong, a government agent, commented that the Camas Prairie Kalispel were prosperous and "very good workers." The Kalispel "have a colony to themselves and do not allow the mixed bloods to settle among them." Later in 1902, the Kalispel refused to cooperate with the tribal enrollment: "they are a peculiar isolated lot and they claim that Government men have lied to them so often that they want nothing to do with any representative of the Government."[42]

United States Indian Service,
Flathead Agency,
Sept. 25th, 1887.

Hon. Commissioner of Indian Affairs
Washington, D.C.

Sir:

I have the honor to report that "Michel," one of the Chiefs of the wandering band of the Lower Kalispel Indians, Who Met the Northwest Indian Commission, at Sand Point, Idaho Territory, and who signed the agreement to remove to this reservation, with the families of the band who acknowledge him as chief, is now at this agency. He came here to request rail road transportation from a station, in Idaho, called Hope, on the line of the Northern Pacific Railroad to this Agency, for fifteen families, consisting of about seventy five men, woman [sic] and Children. Ten other families of this band are also camped at

Hope; but are provided with horses and are prepared to move on their own account. "Michel" fully understands that the agreement with the Commission, which he signed must be ratified by Congress, before it can go into effect, or that any means are at the disposal of the Indian Office to transport or take care of those families, until such provisions are made by Congress. But he now appeals to the Hon. Secretary of the Interior and the Commissioner of Indian Affairs to grant them the aid and facilities, he desires to remove his wandering band at once while they are anxious and willing to go to this agency where they can cultivate the soil; and abandon their wandering and vagabond lives. I can only add that if it is the policy of the Government to gather those roving bands upon reservations, that the opportunity should not be lost, to take those people up at once and at least feed them untill it is Known whether the Agreement with the Commission will be ratified. Chief Michel will expect a reply to his petition to the Hon. Secretary of the Interior, as soon as possible; as he states the band will have no other resource, but to scatter out into the mountains to prevent starvation by hunting.

> Very respectfully
> Your obt. svt.
> Peter Ronan
> U.S. Indian Agent.

September 26, 1887
LR 26,036/1887, RG 75, National Archives, Washington, D.C.

For information about Lawrence Finley see editor's annotation to Ronan's August 21, 1887, letter.

> United States Indian Service,
> Flathead Agency,
> Sept. 26th, 1887.

Hon. Commissioner of Indian Affairs
Washington, D.C.

Sir:

Referring to your letter L 22552–1887 under date of Sept. 8th, 1887, I would respectfully report, that I ordered the release of the halfbreed Lawrence Finley from confinement at Fort Missoula. The Woman upon which the rape was committed has Since died, and as I cannot obtain evidence upon which he would probably be convicted, I had the prisoner released. I arrested and conveyed the outlaw for safe Keeping to Fort Missoula because after he escaped from the Indian Jail, he made a personal attack upon me, and threatened to take my life for having insisted upon his arrest by the Indian Police for rape. His arrest and incarceration at the Military post has had a good effect upon the conduct of some other young ruffians, who attempt to terrorize the reservation and who laugh at confinement in the reservation Jail, out of Which they can make their escape when they choose to go. Enclosed I forward statement of expenses connected with confinement of Finley at the Military post, Fort Missoula.

> Very respectfully
> Your obt. svt.
> Peter Ronan
> U.S. Indian Agent.

October 16, 1887

LR 27,548/1887, telegram, RG 75, National Archives, Washington, D.C.

See editor's annotation to Ronan's letter, August 6, 1887, and see Ronan telegram of October 29, 1887, and letter, December 18, 1888.

Oct. 16, 1887
Arlee Mont

Comr Indian Affairs
Washn, DC

Indians held council and refused pierre busha permission to remove Cree refugees to this agency. Principal opposition stated at council was that permission had been granted to Kalispels and Spokanes to remove here and also that all of Charlos band of bitter root indians expected to remove here which if accomplished would be enough indians to occupy agricultural lands of reservation.

Ronan Agent.

October 19, 1887

LR 28,329/1887, RG 75, National Archives, Washington, D.C.

United States Indian Service,
Flathead Agency,
October 19th, 1887.

The Hon. Commissioner of Indian Affairs,
Washington, D.C.

Sir:

Referring to your telegram of 12th inst and my replies thereto on 18th and 19th insts, relative to cost of feeding and care of Twenty-five families of Kalispels and transportation for fifteen families of the same tribe to this reservation from their Camp at Hope, Idaho, I have the honor to report that the chief, Michel, is gathering his people preparatory to moving to this reserve and that a portion of his tribe (some of those who have means of transportation) have already reached Camas Prairie, the spot which they expressed a desire to occupy. The Chief is anxiously awaiting your decision in the matter of transportation for the fifteen families referred to in my letter of September 25th, 1887.

Very respectfully
Your obdt servt.
Peter Ronan
U.S. Indian Agent.

October 29, 1887

LR 28,899/1887, telegram, RG 75, National Archives, Washington, D.C.

Oct. 29, 1887
Arlee Mont

Commr Indian Affairs
Washn.

Pie[r]re Busha of Cree refugees is now at this agency & will leave for Cree encampment in three days from date. Is desirous to learn if encouragement will be given to the Crees by the govt. to either settle upon public lands or give them homes on some reservation. Blackfoot reservation would suit if they cant remove here await answer if he can encourage his people to this effect.

Ronan Agent.

December 30, 1887

LR 438/1888, RG 75, National Archives, Washington, D.C.

United States Indian Service,
Flathead Agency,
Montana, Dec. 30th, 1887.

Hon. Commissioner Indian Affairs
Washington, D.C.

Sir:

Referring to the removal of fifteen families of Michel's band of Lower Kalispel Indians from Hope Station Idaho, to the Flathead reservation, Montana, as authorized in telegram from your office, dated October 31st, last, I would respectfully report that when said authority was received, the families had scattered to hunt in the mountains. Learning of the locality in which Chief Michel was hunting, I sent a runner to notify him to come to the Agency. He arrived about the middle of December, but was sick and unable to accompany me to gather up the families. I took my interpreter and two Indians and proceeded to Sand Point and to Hope, in Idaho where we found but few Indians. However I succeeded in the removal of fifteen families of Michel's band, and now have them camped on this reservation on the Pend d'Orille river, in close proximity to Camas Prairie, where they propose to locate farms and commence to cultivate the soil. I shall keep them in their encampment until Spring, as fishing and hunting are good on that portion of the reserve; and besides the camp is near a railroad station where I can visit them at any time. The Indians also preferred to camp there as some of the men can go to Camas Prairie and split rails during the winter months, and visit their main camp once a week. The cost of transportation was very small as you will perceive when the accounts are rendered, as most of the families had horses and preferred to travel in that way. Herewith I attach list of families, giving the name of the head of each, and number in family, now encamped on the reservation, and to whom I issue provisions under authority 16565 from your office dated Nov. 9th, 1887. I submitted an estimate of their requirements for support, but as yet have not received a reply. I learned of an encampment of Lower Kalispels, on Priest river, Idaho, but as the camp was twenty-five miles from any railroad station and deep snow covered the country, I found no way to communicate with them. Chief Michel informs me the camps are of his people, and when he can get word to them they will likely try to get to a railroad station and communicate with me. The rest of the Lower Kalispels are in the valley of that name, with the head chief of the tribe Victor, and communication cannot be obtained with them until the river is open fore [sic] canoe travel:

1 Michel Chief of Lower Calispels	7 in family
2 Felix Kie Too	8 in family
3 Felix Took Koss Smel	4 in family
4 Gregoire Kalteel Sqhaw	5 in family
5 Widow Eliza	4 in family
6 Antoine Halpa Sam Hay	5 in family
7 Chel-Chess-tel	4 in family
8 Luke Nau Talakan	2 in family
9 Baptiste Cateel Ensee	2 in family
10 Louie Qui-Qui You	4 in family
11 Piere Hei Coo	3 in family

12 Louie Chee-me-Whaken   3 in family
13 Michel Que Que-La   4 in family
14 Widow Sophie   3 in family
15 Charles Smoo   2 in family
In all sixty-one people.

Footnotes

Abbreviations Used in Footnotes

AS — *The Anaconda Standard*

Bigart, *Getting Crops* — Robert J. Bigart, *Getting Good Crops: Economic and Diplomatic Survival Strategies of the Montana Bitterroot Salish Indians, 1870-1891* (Norman: University of Oklahoma Press, 2010)

Bigart, *St. Mary's Mission* — Robert J. Bigart, ed., *Life and Death at St. Mary's Mission, Montana: Births, Marriages, Deaths, and Survival among the Bitterroot Salish Indians, 1866-1891* (Pablo, Mont.: Salish Kootenai College Press, 2005)

CIA — Commissioner of Indian Affairs

DAB — *Dictionary of American Biography*

Heitman — Francis B. Heitman, *Historical Register and Dictionary of the United States Army* (Washington, D.C.: U.S. Government Printing Office, 1903)

Leeson, *History of Montana* — [Michael A. Leeson], *History of Montana, 1739-1885* (Chicago: Warner, Beers & Company, 1885)

Miller, *Illustrated History* — Joaquin Miller, *An Illustrated History of the State of Montana* (Chicago: The Lewis Publishing Co., 1894)

MCT — *Missoula County Times* (Missoula, Mont.)

NA — National Archives, Washington, D.C.

NA CIA LR — Letters Received, Records of the Commissioner of Indian Affairs, RG 75, National Archives, Washington, D.C.

NA CIA LS — Letters Sent, Records of the Commissioner of Indian Affairs, RG 75, National Archives, Washington, D.C.

NAmf — National Archives Microfilm Publication

NAmf M1070 — U.S. Department of the Interior, "Reports of Inspection of the Field Jurisdictions of the Office of Indian Affairs, 1873-1900," National Archives Microfilm Publication M1070, reel 11, Flathead Agency

NNW — *The New North-West* (Deer Lodge, Mont.)

PNTMC — Robert C. Carriker and Eleanor R. Carriker, eds., "The Pacific Northwest Tribes Missions Collection of the Oregon Province Archives of the Society of Jesus" (Wilmington, Del.: Scholarly Resources, Inc., 1987)

Sanders, *History of Montana* — Helen Fitzgerald Sanders, *A History of Montana* (Chicago: The Lewis Publishing Company, 1913)

Whealdon, *Meat for My Salish* — Bon I. Whealdon, et. al., *"I Will Be Meat for My Salish": The Buffalo and the Montana Writers Project Interviews on the Flathead Indian Reservation* (Pablo and Helena, Mont.: Salish Kootenai College Press and Montana Historical Society Press, 2001)

WM — *The Weekly Missoulian*

Introduction

1. S. S. Benedict to Secretary of Interior, July 10, 1883, NAmf M1070, 3093/1883.

2. *The Northwest Illustrated Monthly Magazine* (St. Paul, Minn.), vol. 8, no. 7 (July 1890), p. 46, col. 3.

3. P. McCormick to Secretary of Interior, Feb. 17, 1895, NAmf M1070, 1628/1895.

4. Ronan's Aug. 14, 1890, annual report.

5. Ronan's Aug. 14,1890, annual report.

6. Ronan's Aug. 14, 1890; Aug. 26, 1892; and Aug. 1885 annual reports.

7. Robert J. Bigart, ed., *Zealous in All Virtues: Documents of Worship and Culture Change, St. Ignatius Mission, Montana, 1890-1894* (Pablo, Mont.: Salish Kootenai College Press, 2007), p. 77; "Items from St. Ignatius," *Missoula Gazette* (daily), Jan. 9, 1891, p. 5, col. 2; Ronan's Jan. 2, 1891, and Jan. 31, 1891, letters.

8. Ronan's Oct. 31, 1890a, and Dec. 1, 1890, letters.

9. "Flathead Fears," *The Helena Journal* (daily), Apr. 27, 1889, p. 1, col. 8.

10. Ronan's Dec. 17, 1885, letter.

11. Ronan's Aug. 1, 1890, and Nov. 1, 1890, letters.

12. Ronan's Dec. 4, 1885b, letter.

13. Ronan's June 3, 1887, letter.

14. Ronan's Nov. 16, 1892, letter.

15. There is some disagreement in the sources about the exact year of Ronan's birth. This biographical sketch was compiled from: Peter Ronan, "Discovery of Alder Gulch," *Contributions to the Historical Society of Montana*, vol. 3 (1900), pp. 143-52; "Biographical," MCT, Aug. 31, 1887, p. 3, col. 3; "A Montana Pioneer," *The Spokane Review*, Nov. 7, 1891, p. 3, col. 1-2; "Passed Peacefully Away," *The Evening Missoulian*, Aug. 21, 1893, p. 1, col. 5-6.

16. "New Indian Policy," *Rocky Mountain Gazette* (weekly) (Helena, Mont.), Oct. 28, 1872, p. 2, col. 2; "Transferring the Charge of the Indians," *Weekly Rocky Mountain Gazette*, Dec. 31, 1872, p. 2, col. 2; "New Indian Reservation," *Weekly Rocky Mountain Gazette*, Aug. 13, 1873, p. 2, col. 2.

17. *The Northwest Illustrated Monthly Magazine* (St. Paul, Minn.), vol. 8, no 7 (July 1890), p. 46, col. 3.

18. Estate of Peter Ronan, Probate file 339 (1893), Clerk of District Court, Missoula County Courthouse, Missoula, Mont.

19. W. Turrentine Jackson, "The Irish Fox and the British Lion," *Montana: The Magazine of Western History*, vol. 9, no. 2 (Apr. 1959), pp. 28-42; "Henry Bratnober," *The Engineering and Mining Journal*, vol. 98, no. 13 (Sept. 26, 1914), p. 579; "A Bear Story," *The New-York Times*, July 21, 1890, p. 4, col. 7.

20. DAB, vol. 4 (1930), pp. 144-46; William D. Mangam, *The Clarks: An American Phenomenon* (New York: Silver Bow Press, 1941), pp. 32-33; Ida Smith Patterson, *Montana Memories: The Life of Emma Magee in the Rocky Mountain West, 1866-1950*. Second edition. (Pablo, Mont.: Salish Kootenai College Press, 2011), p. 22.

1877

1. A slightly modified version of Peter Ronan's description of Bishop James O'Connor's sermon has been published in Margaret Ronan, *Frontier Woman: The Story of Mary Ronan*, edited by H. G. Merriam (Missoula: University of Montana Publications in History, 1973), pp. 138-39. Also published in "Bishop O'Connor," *The Helena Independent* (daily), July 4, 1877, p. 3, col. 3, with June 23 date for the speech. Bishop O'Connor's account of his visit to the Flathead Reservation was published in Rev. James O'Connor, "The Flathead Indians," *Records of the American Catholic Historical Society of Philadelphia*, vol. 3 (1888-1891), pp. 85-110.

2. See Philip Rappagliosi, *Letters from the Rocky Mountain Indian Missions*, edited by Robert Bigart (Lincoln: University of Nebraska Press, 2003), pp. 55-58.

3. DAB, vol. 13, p. 618.

4. William N. Bischoff, S.J., *The Jesuits in Old Oregon, 1840-1940* (Caxton Printers, Ltd., Caldwell, Id., 1945), pp. 228-29.

5. Ibid, p. 234.

6. Philip Rappagliosi, S.J., *Letters from the Rocky Mountain Indian Missions*, ed. Robert Bigart (University of Nebraska Press, Lincoln, 2003), p. 108, 140.

7. "Making Medicine," WM, July 13, 1877, p. 2, col. 4.

8. Andrew Garcia, *Tough Trip Through Paradise, 1878-1879* (New York: Houghton Mifflin Co., 1967), pp. 273-77.

9. Clark C. Spence, *Territorial Politics and Government in Montana, 1864-89* (Urbana: University of Illinois Press, 1975), pp. 74-149.

10. Alvin M. Josephy, Jr., *The Nez Perce Indians and the Opening of the Northwest* (New Haven, Conn.: Yale University Press, 1965), pp. 566-87; Heitman, vol. 1, p. 817.

11. CIA to Ronan, July 18, 1877, U.S. Office of Indian Affairs, "Letters Sent by the Office of Indian Affairs, 1824-1881," NAmf M21, reel 134, accounts, p. 434.

12. James A. Teit, "The Salishan Tribes of the Western Plateaus," ed. by Franz Boas, *Annual Report of the Bureau of American Ethnology*, 45th (1927-1928), p. 377; Daniel Shanahan to CIA, Oct. 11, 1877, U.S. Office of Indian Affairs, "Letters Received by the Office of Indian Affairs, 1824-1880," NAmf M234, reel 496, fr. 117-19; C. S. Medary to CIA, Sept. 12, 1874, *Annual Report of the Commissioner of Indian Affairs* (1874), p. 263; C. S. Medary to CIA, Sept. 13, 1875, *Annual Report of the Commissioner of Indian Affairs* (1875), p. 304.

13. WM, Jan. 17, 1877, p. 3, col. 1; WM, May 4, 1877, p. 3, col. 2.

14. Philip Rappagliosi, S.J., *Letters from the Rocky Mountain Indian Missions*, ed. Robert Bigart (Lincoln: University of Nebraska Press, 2003), pp. 109, 140; William L. Davis, S.J., *A History of St. Ignatius Mission* (Spokane, Wash.: C. W. Hill Printing Co., 1954), pp. 122-23.

15. Alvin M. Josephy, Jr., *The Nez Perce Indians and the Opening of the Northwest* (New Haven, Conn.: Yale University Press, 1965), pp. 374, 537, 616.

16. Mary Ronan, *Girl from the Gulches: The Story of Mary Ronan*, ed. Ellen Baumler (Helena, Mont.: Montana Historical Society Press, 2003), pp. 155-56, 161-62, 170; Peter Ronan, "Eagle-of-the-Light," AS, May 14, 1893, p. 9, col. 1-3.

17. Allan Peskin, *Garfield* (Kent, Ohio: Kent State University Press, 1978), pp. 351-53.

18. *The Helena Daily Herald*, Oct. 20, 1877, p. 2, col. 1.

19. DAB, vol. 12, p. 199; *The National Cyclopædia of American Biography*, vol. 24, pp. 198-99.

20. Peter Ronan, "Discovery of Alder Gulch," *Contributions to the Historical Society of Montana*, vol. 3 (1900), pp. 143-47.

21. Bigart, *St. Mary's Mission*, pp. 295-96.

22. Peter Ronan, "Eagle-of-the-Light," AS, May 14, 1893, p. 9, col. 1-3.

23. See enclosure to Ronan letter of Mar. 3, 1879a.

24. William Tecumseh Sherman and Philip Henry Sheridan, *Travel Accounts of General William T. Sherman to Spokan Falls, Washington Territory, in the Summers of 1877 and 1883* (Fairfield, Wash.: Ye Galleon Press, 1984), pp. 59-64.

25. John Fahey, *The Kalispel Indians* (Norman: University of Oklahoma Press, 1986), pp. 10, 12-14, 25, 61-63, 70-71, 80.

26. Ibid, pp. 18, 61, 63.

27. WM, Nov. 7, 1879, p. 3, col. 2; WM, Nov. 11, 1881, p. 3, col. 1; U.S. Census Bureau, "Population Schedules of the Ninth Census of the United States, 1870," NAmf M593, reel 827, Montana, p. 329b, nos. 9-15; U.S. Census Bureau, "10th Census, 1880," NAmf T9, reel 742, Montana, Missoula County, 26th District, p. 460, nos. 8-9.

28. The viewpoint of some of the white settlers was recorded in Bud Ainsworth, "Neptune Lynch Family Were First Settlers in Plains...," *Rocky Mountain Husbandman* (Great Falls, Mont.), Aug. 4, 1932, p. 1, col. 1-3; Ellen Nye, "Old Days in Montana as Seen by Pioneer Woman," *The Daily Missoulian*, July 1, 1934, Pony Express Section, p. 4, col. 1-7.

1878

1. WM, Oct. 18, 1876, p. 3, col. 2; U.S. Census Bureau, "10th Census, 1880," NAmf T9, reel 742, Montana, Missoula County, 26th District, p. 460, nos. 20-21.

2. For a detailed report on the summer 1877 meeting at Spokane Falls referred to by Simon see O. O. Howard, "Supplemental Report: Non-Treaty Nez Percé Campaign," *Annual Report of the Secretary of War* (1877), vol. 1, pp. 642-51.

3. See Indian Depredation Claim files 1783 (RG 75), 8422 (RG 205), and 8422 (RG 123), NA.

4. John C. Ewers, *Gustavus Sohon's Portraits of Flathead and Pend d'Oreille Indians, 1854*, Smithsonian Miscellaneous Collections, vol. 110, no. 7 (1948), pp. 37-38; Bigart, *St. Mary's Mission*, pp. 232-33; "Making Medicine," WM, July 13, 1877, p. 2, col. 4; WM, July 13, 1877, p. 3, col. 2.

5. John Gibbon, *Adventures on the Western Frontier* (Bloomington: Indiana University Press, 1994), pp. ix-xvi.

6. Whealdon, *Meat for My Salish*, pp. 255-56; Leeson, *History of Montana*, p. 1313.

7. See Carle F. O'Neil, *Two Men of Demersville* (privately printed, 1990), pp. 3-57.

8. Leeson, *History of Montana*, p. 1319; "Dissolution of Copartnership," WM, Aug. 30, 1878, p. 4, col. 5; "Death's Decree," WM, Mar. 22, 1893, p. 7, col. 4.

9. Mary Ronan, *Girl from the Gulches: The Story of Mary Ronan*, ed. Ellen Baumler (Helena: Montana Historical Society Press, 2003), pp. 188-89; Bigart, *St. Mary's Mission*, pp. 320-21; "Michel Revais' Life Ends After Many Useful Years in Service of Government," *The Daily Missoulian*, Jan. 15, 1911, p. 1, col. 3-5.

10. Robert Bigart and Clarence Woodcock, eds., *In the Name of the Salish & Kootenai Nation: The 1855 Hell Gate Treaty and the Origin of the Flathead Indian Reservation* (Pablo, Mont.: Salish Kootenai College Press, 1996), pp. 31-38; John C. Ewers, *Gustavus Sohon's Portraits of Flathead and Pend d'Oreille Indians, 1854*, Smithsonian Miscellaneous Collections, vol. 110, no. 7 (1948), pp. 52-53; Charley Shafft, "Big Canoe," *The Council Fire* (Washington, D.C.), vol. 3, no. 11 (Nov. 1880) pp. 174-75; WM, May 14, 1880, p. 3, col. 3.

11. Jerome A. Greene, *Beyond Bear's Paw: The Nez Perce Indians in Canada* (Norman: University of Oklahoma Press, 2010).

12. Bigart, *St. Mary's Mission*, pp. 275-76.

13. See "The Murder of Joy, Elliott and Hayes," NNW, July 19, 1878, p. 2, col. 2-3.

14. Duncan McDonald, "An Appeal to Reason," NNW, Aug. 16, 1878, p. 3, col. 4.

15. Robert H. Ruby and John A. Brown, *Half-Sun on the Columbia: A Biography of Chief Moses* (Norman: University of Oklahoma Press, 1965).

16. WM, Oct. 25, 1878, p. 3, col. 2.

17. Miller, *Illustrated History*, pp. 729-30; "Married," WM, Sept. 5, 1879, p. 3, col. 5.

18. Roster of Agency Employees, 1889-1890, vol. 19, p. 22, entry 978, RG 75, NA.

19. "Baptiste Aeneas," William F. Wheeler papers, MC 65, box 1, folder 13, Montana Historical Society Archives, Helena.

20. Territory vs. Baptiste Matte, July 2, 1878, case 375, criminal, Missoula District Court Records, Missoula County Courthouse, Missoula, Mont., Territorial, microfilm reel 6, fr. 719-55.

21. Bigart, *St. Mary's Mission*, pp. 296-302; "Court House Cullings, WM, July 17, 1889, p. 4, col. 5; Rosters of Indian Police, vol. 11 (1895-1896), p. 10, and vol. 12 (1897-1899), p. 12, entry 982, RG 75, NA.

22. Miller, *Illustrated History*, p. 69.

23. "List of Pioneers Who Have Died During the Years 1907-8-9," *Contributions to the Historical Society of Montana*, vol. 7 (1910), p. 326; U.S. Census Bureau, "Population Schedules of the Ninth Census of the United States, 1870," NAmf M593, reel 827, Montana, Cedar Junction, p. 314a, nos. 19-23; "Horse Plains," WM, July 26, 1876, p. 3, col. 4; WM, July 11, 1884, p. 3, col. 2.

1879

1. Robert S. Gardner to Secretary of Interior, Jan. 30, 1885, NAmf M1070, 585/85.

2. U.S. Bureau of Indian Affairs, "Indian Census Rolls, 1885-1940," NAmf M595, roll 107, fr. 221.

3. Whealdon, *Meat for My Salish*, p. 251; Charles E. Simpson, "The Snake Country Freeman, British Free Trappers in Idaho," masters thesis, University of Idaho, 1990, DAI 1341382, p. 248; "Terrific Hail-Storm," *The Missoula Pioneer,* Aug. 10, 1871, p. 3, col. 3; Robert J. Bigart, ed., *Crossroad of Cultures: Sacramental Records at St. John the Baptist Catholic Church, Frenchtown, Montana, 1866-1899* (Pablo, Mont.: Salish Kootenai College Press, 2009), p. 60, no. B10.

4. CIA to Ronan, May 22, 1879, vol. 25, p. 177, civilization, NA CIA LS.

5. WM, Apr. 25, 1879, p. 3, col. 2; and May 2, 1879, p. 3, col. 2.

6. Felix S. Cohen, *Handbook of Federal Indian Law* (Washington, D.C.: U.S. Government Printing Office, 1942), pp. 176-77.

7. Whealdon, *Meat for My Salish*, pp. 265-66.

8. See "Savages on the Big Blackfoot," *The Helena Daily Herald*, July 10, 1879, p. 3, col. 2; "Further Particulars of the Indian Outrage on the Big Blackfoot," *The Helena Daily Herald*, July 11, 1879, p. 3, col. 2.

9. "Indian Difficulty," *The Helena Independent* (daily), July 13, 1879, p. 3, col. 3.

10. Summarized in "The Murders Near Lincoln," NNW, July 18, 1879, p. 3, col. 2.

11. "The Lincoln Indian Affair," NNW, Aug. 8, 1879, p. 3, col. 2.

12. Margaret Ronan, "Memoirs of a Frontiers Woman: Mary C. Ronan," unpublished masters thesis, State University of Montana, Missoula, 1932, pp. 319-21.

13. Gerard G. Steckler, S.J., *Charles John Seghers: Priest and Bishop in the Pacific Northwest, 1839-1886: A Biography* (Fairfield, Wash.: Ye Galleon Press, 1986), pp. 125-26, 130-31; "Arch-Bishop Seghers on Montana," WM, Oct. 17, 1879, p. 1, col. 3-5; DAB, vol. 16, pp. 558-59.

14. Paul C. Phillips, *Medicine in the Making of Montana* (Missoula, Mont.: Montana Medical Association and Montana State University Press, 1962), p. 276; Leeson, *History of Montana*, p. 1302.

15. William N. Bischoff, S.J., *The Jesuits in Old Oregon, 1840-1940* (Caldwell, Id.: The Caxton Printers, Ltd., 1945), p. 222.

16. Wilfred P. Schoenberg, S.J., *Jesuit Mission Presses in the Pacific Northwest: A History and Bibliography of Imprints, 1876-1899* (Portland, Or.: The Champoeg Press, 1957), pp. 18-20.

17. Joseph Seltice, *Saga of the Coeur d'Alene Indians*, ed. Edward J. Kowrach and Thomas E. Connolly (Fairfield, Wash.: Ye Galleon Press, 1990), pp. 305-336.

18. William N. Bischoff, S.J., *The Jesuits in Old Oregon, 1840-1940* (Caldwell, Id.: The Caxton Printers, Ltd., 1945), pp. 218-19; Robert Ignatius Burns, S.J., *The Jesuits and the Indian Wars of the Northwest* (New Haven, Conn.: Yale University Press, 1966), pp. 371-72.

19. Mary Ronan, *Girl from the Gulches: The Story of Mary Ronan*, ed. Ellen Baumler (Helena: Montana Historical Society Press, 2003), pp. 161-62.

20. Jerome A. Greene, *Beyond Bear's Paw: The Nez Perce Indians in Canada* (Norman: University of Oklahoma Press, 2010), pp. 118, 135-50.

21. George Conford, Depredation Claim 1863, RG 75, NA.

22. Sanders, *History of Montana*, pp. 870-72; Miller, *Illustrated History*, pp. 709-710; Leeson, *History of Montana*, pp. 1319-20.

23. Bigart, *St. Mary's Mission*, pp. 320-21; Ernest Ingersoll, "The Last Remnant of Frontier," *The American Magazine*, vol. 6, no. 2 (June 1887), pp. 136-39; Robert S. Gardner to Secretary of Interior, Jan. 30, 1885, NAmf M1070, 585/85.

24. *Bozeman Avant Courier*, Sept. 18, 1879, p. 3, col. 5; "St. Ignatius Mission," WM, Nov. 13, 1885, p. 2, col. 2.

1880

1. Heitman, vol. 1, p. 453.

2. Jerome A. Greene, *Beyond Bear's Paw: The Nez Perce Indians in Canada* (Norman: University of Oklahoma Press, 2010), pp. 162-70.

3. CIA to Secretary of Interior, Aug. 23, 1880, U.S. Office of Indian Affairs, "Report Books of the Office of Indian Affairs, 1838-1885," NAmf M348, reel 37, pp. 245-46.

1881

1. CIA to Ronan, Feb. 8, 1881, letterpress vol. 30, pt. 2, pp. 38-39, civilization, NA CIA LS.

2. "An Exhibit," WM, Mar. 31, 1882, p. 4, col. 1-2.

3. Territory vs. Morris and Preece, case 488, criminal, Oct. 20, 1881, District Court Records, Missoula County Courthouse, Missoula, microfilm reel 7, fr. 1892-95.

4. "Died," WM, Jan. 27, 1882, p. 3, col. 4.

5. Leeson, *History of Montana*, p. 1313; Sanders, *History of Montana*, vol. 2, pp. 910-11.

6. "In Memoriam," WM, Oct. 13, 1882, p. 3, col. 3.

7. U.S. Census Bureau, "10th Census, 1880," NAmf T9, reel 742, Montana, Missoula County, 26th District, p. 460b, lines 19-27; WM, Apr. 15, 1887, p. 3, col. 3.

8. U.S. President, "Message from the President of the United States, Transmitting a Letter from the Secretary of the Interior Respecting the Ratification of an Agreement with the Confederated Tribes of Flathead, Kootenay, and Upper Pend d'Oreilles Indians, for the Sale of a Portion of Their Reservation in Montana Territory," Senate Executive Document, No. 44, 47th Congress, 2d Session (1883), serial 2076.

9. CIA to Ronan, May 20, 1881, land, letterbook 81, pp. 13-20, NA CIA LS.

10. See Ronan letter of Mar. 10, 1882.

11. CIA to Ronan, Feb. 17, 1881, letterpress vol. 26, part 2, pp. 158-59, accounts, NA CIA LS.

12. WM, July 8, 1881, p. 3, c. 2; Territory vs McKenney and Farraher, case 486, criminal, Nov. 12, 1881, District Court Records, Missoula County Courthouse, Missoula, territorial microfilm reel 7, fr. 1823-29.

13. WM, July 29, 1881, p. 3, col. 2; Indictment Record Book, 1879-83, District Court Records, Missoula County Courthouse, Missoula, pp. 17-18, June 30, 1881; Montana State Prison Records, 1879-1981, State Microfilm 36, Montana Historical Society Archives, Helena, reel 4, p. 73.

14. DAB, vol. 13, p. 602.

15. *The National Cyclopædia of American Biography*, vol. 33, pp. 47-48.

16. *New Catholic Encyclopedia* (1967), vol. 2, p. 823.

17. Whealdon, *Meat for My Salish*, p. 247.

18. CIA to Ronan, Sept. 5, 1881, letterpress, vol. 33, part 2, pp. 73-75, accounts, NA CIA LS.

19. CIA to Ronan, Sept. 7, 1881, letterpress vol. 32, part 2, pp. 385-87, civilization, NA CIA LS.

20. CIA to Ronan, Sept. 30, 1881, letterpress, vol. 73, part 2, pp. 84-85, finance, NA CIA LS.

21. Bigart, *Getting Crops*, pp. 161-64.

22. The enclosed clipping was "Sublime Ignorance," WM, Nov. 4, 1881, p. 2, col. 1.

23. Sanders, *History of Montana*, vol. 2, pp. 930-31; Miller, *Illustrated History*, pp. 211-12.

24. Heitman, vol. 1, p. 584.

25. Heitman, vol. 1, p. 718.

1882

1. "Indian Interference," *The Helena Daily Herald*, Jan. 10, 1882, p. 3, col. 3; WM, Jan. 13, 1882, p. 3, col. 2.

2. "Railroad Obstruction," NNW, Mar. 17, 1882, p. 3, col. 1.

3. WM, Feb. 24, 1882, p. 3, col. 1.

4. "The Flathead Reservation," *The Helena Independent* (daily), July 12, 1882, p. 3, col. 2.

5. See Ronan's Jan. 22, 1881b, letter.

6. CIA to Ronan, Mar. 31, 1882, telegram, letterpress, vol. 31, part 1, p. 101, accounts, NA CIA LS; CIA to Ronan, Apr. 1, 1882, letterpress, vol. 39, part 1, pp. 102-104, accounts, NA CIA LS.

7. Ronan to Rev. J. B. A. Brouillet, Mar. 20, 1882, and Chas. Lusk to Ronan, May 9, 1882, St. Ignatius Mission file, Bureau of Catholic Indian Missions Papers, Special Collections, University Library, Marquette University, Milwaukee, Wis.

8. CIA to Ronan, July 13, 1882, telegram, land, letterbook 99, p. 1, NA CIA LS.

9. CIA to Ronan, July 19, 1882, telegram, land, letterbook 99, p. 83, NA CIA LS.

10. *The National Cyclopædia of American Biography*, vol. 19, p. 288; Sanders, *History of Montana*, vol. 2, pp. 998-99; Miller, *Illustrated History*, pp. 803-804.

11. CIA to Ronan, Sept. 18, 1882, letterpress vol. 37, part 1, pp. 171-74, civilization, NA CIA LS.

12. U.S. President, "Message from the President of the United States, Transmitting a Letter from the Secretary of the Interior Respecting the Ratification of an Agreement with the Confederated Tribes of Flathead, Kootenay, and Upper Pend d'Oreilles Indians, for the Sale of a Portion of Their Reservation in Montana Territory," Senate Executive Document, No. 44, 47th Congress, 2d Session (1883), serial 2076, p. 11.

13. Ibid, p. 14.

14. See Ronan's Oct. 1, 1883, letter.

15. U.S. President, "Message from the President of the United States, Transmitting a Letter from the Secretary of the Interior Respecting the Ratification of an Agreement with the Confederated Tribes of Flathead, Kootenay, and Upper Pend d'Oreilles Indians, for the Sale of a Portion of Their Reservation in Montana Territory," Senate Executive Document, No. 44, 47th Congress, 2d Session (1883), serial 2076, pp. 16, 19.

16. "They Have Bad Records," AS, Dec. 3, 1899, p. 14, col. 2.

17. *Who Was Who in America* (1897-1942), p. 798; Ronan's Feb. 3, 1884, letter.

18. Dale L. Johnson, "Andrew B. Hammond: Education of a Capitalist on the Montana Frontier," unpublished PhD dissertation, University of Montana, Missoula, 1976.

19. WM, Oct. 20, 1882, p. 3, col. 2.

20. Jerome D'Aste, S.J., diaries, PNTMC, reel 29, entries for Sept. 19 – Nov. 5, 1882; "Bitter Root Items," WM, Nov. 17, 1882, p. 3, col. 4.

21. "Small-Pox in Missoula," *The Helena Daily Herald*, Sept. 25, 1882, p. 3, col. 4.

22. CIA to Ronan, Nov. 17, 1882, letterpress, vol. 37, part 2, pp. 355-57, civilization, NA CIA LS.

23. "The Western Invasion," NNW, Dec. 8, 1882, p. 3, col. 4.

24. Paul C. Phillips, *Medicine in the Making of Montana* (Missoula, Mont.: Montana Medical Association and Montana State University Press, 1962), pp. 76-77.

25. Whealdon, *Meat for My Salish*, pp. 249-50.

26. "Murder on the Jocko," WM, June 23, 1882, p. 3, col. 3.

27. WM, June 30, 1882, p. 3, col. 3; WM, June 30, 1882, p. 2, col. 1; "The Kuntza-Marengo Murder Trial," NNW, Jan. 12, 1883, p. 3, col. 4.

28. "District Court," NNW, Dec. 22, 1882, p. 3, col. 4.

29. WM, Jan. 26, 1883, p. 1, c. 4-5.

30. E. D. Banister to Secretary of Interior, Oct. 20, 1888, NAmf M1070, pp. 4-5, 5261/88.

1883

1. Clark C. Spence, *Territorial Politics and Government in Montana, 1864-89* (Urbana: University of Illinois Press, 1875), pp. 96-97; Miller, *Illustrated History*, pp. 66-67; *Progressive Men of the State of Montana* (Chicago: A. W. Bowen & Co., ca. 1900), pp. 1640-41.

2. WM, Jan. 26, 1883, p. 3, col. 2.

3. Leeson, *History of Montana*, pp. 1067-68.

4. Heitman, vol. 1, p. 1037.

5. Ronan's Dec. 14, 1891b, letter; T. C. Carter to CIA, Mar. 9, 1896, 9381/1896, NA CIA LR; "Their Hearts Are Bad," AS, Mar. 8, 1895, p. 6, col. 3; "All At Liberty Again," AS, Mar. 14, 1895, p. 6, col. 3.

6. Thomas R. Wessel, "Historical Report on the Blackfeet Reservation in Northern Montana," U.S. Indian Claims Commission, docket 279-D (1975), pp. 42-53; Howard L. Harrod, *Mission Among the Blackfeet* (Norman: University of Oklahoma Press, 1971), pp. 67-81; Helen B. West, "Starvation Winter of the Blackfeet," *Montana: the Magazine of Western History*, vol. 9, no. 1 (Winter 1959), pp. 2-19.

7. Bigart, *Getting Crops*, pp. 115-36.

8. Col. Thomas H. Ruger, "Report of Col. Thomas H. Ruger," *Annual Report of the Secretary of War* (1883), pp. 122-23.

9. CIA to Ronan, Oct. 13, 1883, letterpress, vol. 41, part 2, pp. 441-43, civilization, NA CIA LS.

10. Confederated Salish and Kootenai Tribes vs. United States, docket 50233, decision Nov. 12, 1965, U.S. Court of Claims, vol. 173, p. 398.

11. S. S. Benedict to Secretary of Interior, July 10, 1883, NAmf M1070, 3093/83; "The Flatheads Object," *The Helena Independent* (daily), Aug. 25, 1883, p. 5, col. 3; Confederated Salish and Kootenai Tribes vs. United States, docket 50233, Nov. 12, 1965, decision, U.S. Court of Claims, vol. 173, p. 398.

12. "Judge Eugene McCarthy of Kalispell...," *Rocky Mountain Husbandman* (Great Falls, Mont.), July 21, 1938, p. 7, col. 2-5.

13. "Heavy Taxpayers," WM, Dec. 10, 1886, p. 2, col. 1.

14. "Another Quartz Discovery," WM, Jan. 6, 1875, p. 3, col. 3.

15. "For Sale," WM, June 5, 1885, p. 2, col. 5; "Jottings by the 'Husbandman' Traveling Man," WM, Jan. 27, 1888, p. 1, col. 3-4.

16. DAB, vol. 8, pp. 402-403; Sanders, *History of Montana*, vol. 2, pp. 880-81; John W. Hakola, "Samuel T. Hauser and the Economic Development of Montana: A Case Study in Nineteenth-Century Frontier Capitalism," unpublished PhD dissertation, Indiana University, Bloomington, 1961, DA 61-4441.

17. G. G. Vest and Martin Maginnis, "Report of the Subcommittee of the Special Committee of the United States Senate Appointed to Visit the Indian Tribes of Northern Montana," in Senator H. L. Dawes, et. al., "Report of the Special Committee of the United States Senate....," Senate Report No. 283, 48th Congress, 1st Session (1884), serial 2174.

18. See Ronan's Oct. 31, 1890a, letter for more information.

19. "Villard's Guests," *The Helena Independent* (daily), Sept. 25, 1883, p. 5, col. 2; WM, Sept. 28, 1883, p. 3, col. 3; Arthur L. Stone, *Following Old Trails* (Missoula, Mont.: Morton J. Elrod, 1913), pp. 165-72; Nicolaus Mohr, *Excursion Through America*, ed. Ray Allen Billington. (Chicago: R. R. Donnelley & Sons Company, 1973), pp. 240-49.

20. DAB, vol. 19, p. 260; Marian Elaine Dawes, "The Senatorial Career of George Graham Vest," unpublished masters thesis, University of Missouri, Columbia, 1932.

21. Clark C. Spence, *Territorial Politics and Government in Montana, 1864-89* (Urbana: University of Illinois Press, 1975), pp. 150-57; DAB, vol. 4, pp. 568-69.

22. DAB, vol. 19, pp. 273-75.

23. See also Ronan's letters of Sept. 5, 1883, and Aug. 18, 1884, to Hauser, and Oct. 5, 1883, to Senator G. G. Vest.

24. Fort Missoula Post Orders, Oct. 3, 1883, RG 98, NA. Also U.S. War Department, Book Records of Fort Missoula, reel 11, pp. 168-69, University of Montana Library microfilm 978.6 U586.

25. S. S. Benedict to Secretary of Interior, July 10, 1883, NAmf M1070, 3093/83.

1884

1. WM, Oct. 26, 1883, p. 3, col. 3-4. See the introduction to Ronan's Dec. 1, 1882, letter for more information about Koonsa Finley's life and legal problems.

2. *U.S. Statutes at Large*, vol. 23 (1883-1885), pp. 362, 385.

3. WM, Jan. 18, 1884, p. 3, col. 3.

4. C. H. Howard to Secretary of Interior, Dec. 4, 1883, NAmf M1070, 5061/83.

5. WM, June 19, 1885, p. 3, col. 1.

6. Robert J. Bigart, editor, *Crossroad of Cultures: Sacramental Records at St. John the Baptist Catholic Church, Frenchtown, Montana, 1866-1899* (Pablo, Mont.: Salish Kootenai College Press, 2009), p. 30; "Married," WM, Apr. 27, 1877, p. 3, col. 3; U.S. Census Bureau, "10th Census: 1880," NAmf T9, reel 742, Montana, Missoula County, Missoula, p. 447a, numbers 1-4; MCT, Nov. 18, 1885, p. 3, col. 4.

7. See also Ronan letter, Feb. 18, 1884.

8. "Killed at a Dance," *Butte Semi-Weekly Miner*, Jan. 28, 1888, p. 3, col. 6.

9. U.S. Bureau of Indian Affairs, "Selected Records of the Bureau of Indian Affairs Relating to the Enrollment of Indians on the Flathead Reservation, 1903-08," NAmf M1350, reel 1, fr. 16, numbers 570-576; WM, Apr. 11, 1894, p. 8 col. 2; "A Painful Accident," AS, Dec. 16, 1899, p. 12, col. 3.

10. "School," *The Pioneer* (Missoula, Mont.), June 15, 1872, p. 3, col. 3; WM, Oct. 18, 1876, p. 3, col. 1; "Trip to the Lower End of the County," WM, Sept. 14, 1877, p. 3, col. 3; U.S. Census Bureau, "10th Census: 1880," NAmf T9, reel 742, Montana, Missoula County, Flathead Agency, p. 458a, number 29; "Murder and Robbery," NNW, Dec. 12, 1884, p. 3, col. 7; "Robbery and Murder," MCT, Dec. 3, 1884, p. 2, col. 2; "The Baird Murder Trial," MCT, Mar. 3, 1886, p. 2, col. 3.

11. Paul C. Phillips, *Medicine in the Making of Montana* (Missoula, Mont.: The Montana Medical Association and Montana State University Press, 1962), p. 277.

12. G. G. Vest, "Charlot: Chief of the Flathead Indians: A True Story," *The Washington Post,* July 26, 1903, p. A11.

13. "Indians and Ice Cream," MCT, Feb. 6, 1884, p. 2, col. 2; *The Washington Post*, Feb. 5, 1884, p. 4, col. 4.

14. Bigart, *Getting Crops*, pp. 131-35.

15. "Returned from Washington," WM, Mar. 14, 1884, p. 2, col. 1-2; "Montanians in the East," *Independent* (Helena, Mont.), Apr. 13, 1884, p. 5, col. 2; "Chief Charlos," *The Helena Independent* (daily), Feb. 9, 1884, p. 7, col. 2.

16. Bigart, *Getting Crops*, p. 164; Rosters of Agency Employees, volumes 21-29, entry 978, RG 75, NA; Robert Bigart and Clarence Woodcock, "The Rinehart Photographs: A Portfolio," *Montana: The Magazine of Western History*, vol. 29, no. 4 (Oct. 1979), pp. 30-31.

17. Jerome D'Aste, S.J., diaries, PNTMC, reel 29, entry for Aug. 12, 1883; J. Verne Dusenberry, "Samples of Pend d'Oreille Oral Literature and Salish Narratives," in Leslie B. Davis, ed., *Lifeways of Intermontane and Plains Montana Indians* (Bozeman, Mont.: Museum of the Rockies, Montana State University, 1979), p. 119; U.S. Secretary of the Interior, *Annual Report of the Secretary of the Interior* (1891), p. xlvi; Bigart, *St. Mary's Mission*, pp. 327-29.

18. Bigart, *St. Mary's Mission*, p. 275; "Colonel Williams Gives History of the Birth of Fort Missoula," *The Daily Missoulian*, Dec. 25, 1927, p. 7, col. 1-3; "Land of Their Fathers," AS, June 4, 1894, p. 6, col. 2.

19. Bigart, *St. Mary's Mission*, pp. 231-32; *Daily Missoulian*, Mar. 8, 1895, p. 4, col. 2.

20. DAB, vol. 18, pp. 362-63.

21. DAB, vol. 13, pp. 319-20; Robert J. Bigart, editor, *A Pretty Village: Documents of Worship and Culture Change, St. Ignatius Mission, Montana, 1880-1889* (Pablo, Mont.: Salish Kootenai College Press, 2007).

22. T. A. and M. C. Bland, "Our Latest Reception to Indians," *The Council Fire and Arbitrator* (Washington, D.C.) vol. 7, no. 2 (Feb. 1884), pp. 1-2.

23. "The President's Public Levee," *The New York Times*, Feb. 6, 1884, p. 1, col. 4.

24. "Obituary," *The New York Freeman's Journal and Catholic Register* (New York, N.Y.), Feb. 16, 1884, p. 8, col. 3.

25. "Charlo's Eyesight Restored," *The Washington Post*, Feb. 9, 1884, p. 4, col. 2.

26. *The Evening Star* (Washington, D.C.), Mar. 1, 1884, p. 5, col. 3.

27. Robert Harris, Northern Pacific Railroad, to CIA, Mar. 17, 1884, telegram, 5,378/1884, NA CIA LR.

28. CIA to Ronan, May 8, 1884, finance, letterpress vol. 100, part 1, pp. 425-27, NA CIA LS.

29. *U.S. Statutes at Large*, vol. 23, (1883-1885), pp. 76, 90.

30. *The Bozeman Weekly Chronicle*, Apr. 16, 1884, p. 2, col. 4; "Murder of Two Indians," *The Bozeman Weekly Chronicle*, Apr. 16, 1884, p. 3, col. 3; "Foully Murdered," *Weekly Avant Courier* (Bozeman, Mont.), Apr. 17, 1884, p. 3, col. 1; NNW, May 9, 1884, p. 2, col. 5.

31. Belgrade Centennial Committee, *Belgrade, Montana: The First One Hundred Years* (Dallas, Tex.: Taylor Publishing Company, 1986), pp. 53-54.

32. Bigart, *St. Mary's Mission*, p. 159 (entry 408), 294.

33. St. Ignatius Mission, "Liber Baptismorum, " 1855-1873, PNTMC, reel 5, fr. 114a, p. 110.

34. CIA to Ronan, July 2, 1884, land, letterbook 127, pp. 171-73, NA CIA LS.

35. Leeson, *History of Montana*, p. 1331; *Progressive Men of the State of Montana* (Chicago: A. W. Bowen & Co., ca. 1900), p. 1656.

36. "Indian Reservation Jollification," *The Livingston Enterprise*, Nov. 22, 1884, p. 1, col. 3-4.

37. "The Flatheads," WM, Jan. 2, 1885, p. 1, col. 6-7.

38. See introduction to Ronan's Sept. 4, 1882, annual report.

39. Acting Secretary of Interior to CIA, July 15, 1884, 13,427/1884, NA CIA LR.

40. S. S. Benedict to Secretary of Interior, July 10, 1883, NAmf M1070, 3093/1883.

41. WM, Oct. 24, 1884, p. 3, col. 2; "Great Joy on the Reservation," MCT, Jan. 14, 1885, p. 3, col. 2.

42. "A Denial," MCT, Jan. 21, 1885, p. 3, col. 2.

43. See Ronan's June 11, 1884, letter.

44. "Railroad Racket," WM, Sept. 5, 1884, p. 2, col. 2.

45. WM, Sept. 5, 1884, p. 3, col. 2; Lt. Col. Geo. Gibson to Adjutant General, Sept. 11, 1884, Fort Missoula Letters Sent, RG 98, NA, pp. 36-37.

46. CIA to Ronan, Dec. 5, 1884, accounts, letterpress vol. 63, part 1, pp. 295-96, NA CIA LS.

47. See also Ronan's Feb. 12, 1885, letter.

1885
1. CIA to Ronan, May 8, 1885, land, letterbook 135, pp. 371-77, NA CIA LS.

2. "Land Entries," WM, Nov. 6, 1885, p. 2, col. 4-5; "Another Change," WM, Sept. 2, 1874, p. 3, col. 1; "Bitter Root Valley," MCT, Oct. 3, 1883, p. 2, col. 4-5; U.S. Census Bureau, "10th Census: 1880," NAmf T9, reel 742, Montana, Missoula County, Bitter Root Valley, p. 438a, number 31.

3. WM, Feb. 6, 1885, p. 3, col. 1-2.

4. Rosters of Agency Employees, volumes 18, 20-21, 23-26, 29-38, entry 978, RG 75, NA; War Department to Secretary of Interior, Jan. 15, 1886, 1,789/1886, NA CIA LR; T. C. McKeogh, "The New Scholasticate Amid the Rockies," *Woodstock Letters*, vol. 26, no. 1 (1897), pp. 73, 78; Jerome D'Aste, S.J., diaries, PNTMC, reels 29 and 30, entries for June 11, 1891; Feb. 5, Mar. 9, Mar. 11, June 26, and July 17, 1902; July 9, 1904; Mar. 21 and 23, 1905; and July 4, 1906; Ky-Ky-Shee to CIA, Apr. 3, 1907, 33,669/1907, NA CIA LR; "Rites for Flathead Chieftain Big Event, *The Daily Missoulian*, Dec. 24, 1922, p. 4, col. 2.

5. See Ronan's Jan. 15, 1889, letter and annotation.

6. Ronan's July 6, 1891, letter and annotation; *Evening Missoulian*, Aug. 13, 1894, p. 4, col. 2.

7. A. V. Swanberg, "A. V. Swanberg Came To This Area in 1890," *Kalispell News-Farm Journal*, Feb. 2, 1950, p. 2, col. 4-7; WM, July 13, 1892, p. 4, col. 2.

8. CIA to Ronan, Feb. 25, 1885, finance, vol. 110, pt. 2, pp. 489-90, NA CIA LS.

9. WM, Mar. 13, 1885, p. 3, col. 2; "How It Is Done Nowadays," NNW, Mar. 20, 1885, p. 3, col. 4; J. H. Mitchell to Secretary of Interior, Mar. 12, 1885, 5,369/1885, NA CIA LR.

10. CIA to Ronan, Nov. 23, 1885, land, letterbook 142, p. 109, NA CIA LS.

11. DAB, vol. 9, pp. 158-59; *Biographical Directory of the American Congress, 1774-1927* (Washington, D.C.: U.S. Government Printing Office, 1928), p. 1396.

12. See also "The Indian Nuisance," NNW, Oct. 16, 1885, p. 3, col. 1.

13. WM, Oct. 23, 1885, p. 3, col. 2.

14. CIA to Ronan, Nov. 11, 1885, land, letterbook 141, pp. 476-78, NA CIA LS.

15. Leeson, *History of Montana*, p. 1258; *Missoula Gazette*, Aug. 28, 1891, p. 4, col. 1; R. L. Polk & Co., *Minnesota, North and South Dakota and Montana Gazetteer and Business Directory, 1892-93* (St. Paul, Minn.: R. L. Polk & Co., 1892), p. 1726.

16. "Recalling Indians," NNW, Oct. 23, 1885, p. 2, col. 2.

17. Leeson, *History of Montana*, pp. 1082-83; Miller, *Illustrated History*, pp. 139-41; Duncan McDonald, "The Nez Perces: The History of Their Troubles and the Campaign of 1877," NNW, Apr. 26, 1878, through Mar. 28, 1879.

18. U.S. Bureau of Indian Affairs, "Indian Census Rolls, 1885-1940," NAmf M595, reel 107, fr. 14; Daniel Shanahan to CIA, Jan. 21, 1874, U.S. Office of Indian Affairs, "Letters Received by the Office of of Indian Affairs, 1824-1880," NAmf M234, reel 500, fr. 262; Peter Whaley to CIA, Nov. 20, 1874, U.S. Office of Indian Affairs, "Letters Received by the Office of of Indian Affairs, 1824-1880," NAmf M234, reel 500, fr. 1287; Capt. A. E. Rothermich, "Early Days at Fort Missoula," in John W. Hakola, editor, *Frontier Omnibus* (Missoula and Helena: Montana State University Press and Historical Society of Montana, 1962), p. 387; NNW, Mar. 28, 1879, p. 3, col. 2; "Court Proceedings," NNW, Dec. 12, 1879, p. 3, col. 4; Ronan's Aug. 1885 annual report; Ronan's Aug. 17, 1885, testimony; "Killed," MCT, Nov. 23, 1887, p. 3, col. 5.

19. Oliver W. Holmes, editor, "Perigrinations of a Politician," *Montana: The Magazine of Western History*, vol. 6, no. 4 (Autumn 1956), pp. 34-45; Clark C. Spence, *Territorial Politics and Government in Montana, 1864-89* (Urbana: University of Illinois Press, 1975), pp. 82-83, 139; Richard D. Seifried, "Early Administration of the Flathead Indian Reservation, 1855 to 1893," unpublished master's thesis, University of Montana, Missoula, 1968, pp. 74-91.

20. Leeson, *History of Montana*, p. 1319; Miller, *Illustrated History*, pp. 362-64; "Adjudged Insane," *Missoula Gazette*, Jan. 30, 1889, p. 3, col. 3.

21. General Land Office to CIA, Jan. 2, 1889, 192/1889, NA CIA LR.

22. See "Bad Indians," WM, Dec. 18, 1885, p. 3, col. 4; "Murderous Indians," *Semi-Weekly Miner* (Butte, Mont.), Dec. 19, 1885, p. 1, cols. 5-6; "Trouble on the Reservation," MCT, Dec. 23, 1885, p. 3, col. 5; "The Indian Troubles," WM, Dec. 25, 1885, p. 2, col. 1.

23. "An Indian Uprising Feared," *The New-York Times*, Dec. 19, 1885, p. 1, col. 7.

24. WM, Jan. 1, 1886, p. 2, col. 1.

25. L. B. Palladino, S.J., to Capt. John Mullan, Jan. 2, 1886, St. Ignatius Mission file, Bureau of Catholic Indian Missions Papers, Marquette University, Milwaukee, Wis.; CIA to Secretary of Interior, Jan. 25, 1886, land, letterbook 144, pp. 110-11, NA CIA LS.

26. "Big Jim, a Notorious Outlaw....," *The Inter-Lake* (Demersville, Mont.), Jan. 17, 1890, p. 4, col. 2.

27. "Matters at Flathead Lake," WM, Apr. 7, 1875, p. 3, col. 3; WM, May 25, 1877, p. 3, col. 2; U.S. Census Bureau, "10th Census: 1880," NAmf T9, reel 742, Montana, Missoula County, Missoula, p. 448b, no. 29.

28. Leeson, *History of Montana*, p. 1312; "The Republican Candidates," WM, Sept. 12, 1884, p. 2, col. 1-2; Bob Raffety and John C. Moe, *Sheriffs of Missoula County, Montana, and Their Times, 1860 to 1978* (n.p., n.d.), pp. 102-104.

1886

1. CIA to Ronan, Mar. 23, 1886, letterpress, vol. 121, part 1, p. 289, finance, NA CIA LS.

2. CIA to Ronan, Jan. 14, 1886, telegram, letterbook 143, p. 359, land; CIA to Western Union Telegraph Co., Jan. 16, 1886, letterbook 143, p. 432, land, NA CIA LS; Leonard Whiting, Western Union Special Agent, to CIA, Feb. 15, 1886, 5,072/1886, NA CIA LR.

3. "The Indians," WM, Mar. 19, 1886, p. 2, col. 3.

4. CIA to Ronan, July 9, 1886, letterbook 150, pp. 131-32, land, NA CIA LS.

5. CIA to Ronan, May 26, 1886, letterbook 148, pp. 406-407, land, NA CIA LS.

6. "Ed Gibbons, 91, Dies in Hamilton Hospital," *The Missoulian*, Oct. 31, 1967, p. 7; "Land Entries," WM, May 22, 1885, p. 2, col. 3.

7. Bigart, *St. Mary's Mission*, pp. 313-14; CIA to Secretary of Interior, Sept. 25, 1905, letterbook 795, p. 6, land, NA CIA LS; "Indians Draw Crowds to Stevensville," *The Western News* (Hamilton, Mont.), Sept. 15, 1911, p. 1, col. 2 and p. 4, col. 3-4.

8. CIA to General Land Office, May 21, 1886, letterbook 148, pp. 292-96, land; CIA to Ronan, May 22, 1886, letterbook 148, pp. 318-21, land, NA CIA LS.

9. General Land Office to CIA, June 8, 1886, 15,507/1886, NA CIA LR.

10. CIA to Ronan, June 15, 1886, letterbook 149, p. 190, land, NA CIA LS.

11. U.S. Department of the Interior, Bureau of Land Management, General Land Office Records, Land Patents, www.glorecords.blm.gov/ accessed Mar. 30, 2011.

12. Leeson, *History of Montana*, p. 1138.

13. CIA to Ronan, Oct. 27, 1886, letterbook 153, pp. 166-67, land, NA CIA LS.

14. Sanders, *History of Monana*, vol. 2, pp. 1138-39; WM, Jan. 11, 1884, p. 3, col. 1; "Trouble on the Reservation," MCT, Dec. 23, 1885, p. 3, col. 5; MCT, Dec. 30, 1885, p. 3, col. 3; S. O. S. Writers' Club, *Montana's Little Legends* (Hamilton, Mont.: Daily Ravalli Republican, 1963), pp. 38-40; Missoula Publishing Company, *Flathead Facts: Descriptive of the Resources of Missoula County* (Missoula, Mont.: Missoula Publishing Company, 1890), p. 18.

15. Geo. R. Pearsons to Secretary of Interior, Nov. 11, 1886, NAmf M1070, 6543/1886.

1887

1. See Ronan's Dec. 30, 1884, and Feb. 12, 1885b, letters.

2. Ronan's Feb. 14, 1885, letter.

3. Ronan's July 26, 1888, letter.

4. Robert Bigart, "The Travails of Flathead Indian Agent Charles S. Medary, 1875-1877," *Montana: The Magazine of Western History*, vol. 62, no. 3 (Autumn 2012), pp. 27-41.

5. Ronan 's Feb. 1 and Nov. 24, 1883; Jan. 15, 1884b; and Dec. 17, 1885, letters.

6. CIA to Ronan, Jan. 24, 1887, letterbook 155, pp. 304-305, land, NA CIA LS.

7. Ogla Johnson, ed., *The Story of the Tobacco Plains Country* (Caldwell, Idaho: Pioneers of the Tobacco Plains Country, 1950), pp. 63-65, 71-73; Ronan's Apr. 17, 1888, letter.

8. Ronan's June 3, 1889, letter.

9. "Unnecessary Alarm," *The Inter-Lake* (Demersville, Mont.), Mar. 7, 1890, p. 4, col. 2.

10. Ellis L. Waldron, *Montana Politics Since 1864: An Atlas of Elections* (Missoula: Montana State University Press, 1958), pp. 50, 78, 82.

11. "Cleverly Caught," *Missoula Gazette* (daily), Aug. 5, 1890, p. 1, col. 3-4; "One of Them Caught," *Missoula Gazette* (daily), Aug. 7, 1890, p. 1, col. 5; "Death's Decree," *Missoula Weekly Gazette*, Dec. 24, 1890, pp. 1-3, 5.

12. Ralph Henry Ramsdell, "Cleaning Up Northwest Montana," Ralph Henry Ramsdell reminiscences, SC 394, Montana Historical Society Archives, Helena.

13. *Dictionary of Canadian Biography*, vol. 14, pp. 845-46; Robin Fisher, *Contact and Conflict: Indian-European Relations in British Columbia, 1774-1890*. Second edition. (Vancouver, B.C.: UBC Press, 1992), pp. 180-87.

14. CIA to Ronan, May 2, 1887, letterbook 159, pp. 261-62, land, NA CIA LS.

15. CIA to Ronan, Jan. 22, 1889, letterbook 180, p. 409, land, NA CIA LS.

16. Anonymous, *Some Bitterroot Memories, 1860-1930: A Homey Account of the Florence Community* (Missoula, Mont.: Gateway Printing and Litho, n.d.), pp. 17, 55; Bigart, *Getting Crops*, pp. 153, 166, 170; "Married," WM, Nov. 12, 1886, p. 3, col. 5; "R. L. Tillman," *Missoulian*, Nov. 24, 1993, p. B3.

17. Tom Stout, *Montana: Its Story and Biography* (Chicago: The American Historical Society, 1921), vol. 2, p. 570; "Republican Nominees," WM, Oct. 1, 1886, p. 2, col. 1-4; "County Correspondence," WM, Mar. 18, 1887, p. 2, col. 3.

18. CIA to Ronan, May 12, 1887, letterbook 159, pp. 487-89, land, NA CIA LS.

19. Robin Fisher, *Contact and Conflict: Indian-European Relations in British Columbia, 1774-1890.* Second edition. (Vancouver, B.C.: UBC Press, 1992), pp. 164-66, 198-204; Col. S. B. Steele, *Forty Years in Canada* (London: Herbert Jenkins, Ltd., 1915), pp. 244-56; *Dictionary of Canadian Biography*, vol. 12, pp. 465-66.

20. CIA to Ronan, June 24, 1889, telegram, letterbook 161, p. 309, land; CIA to Ronan, July 7, 1887, letterbook 162, pp. 76-77, land, NA CIA LS.

21. Thomas H. Ruger, "Report of Brigadier-General Ruger," *Annual Report of the Secretary of War* (1887), p. 146.

22. See CIA to Ronan, Oct. 15, 1887, telegram, letterbook 166, p. 52, land, NA CIA LS.

23. CIA to Ronan, Oct. 31, 1887, telegram, letterbook 166, p. 350, land, NA CIA LS.

24. Ronan's Dec. 18, 1888, letter.

25. Verne Dusenberry, *The Montana Cree: A Study in Religious Persistence* (Stockholm: Alquist & Wiksell, 1962), pp. 28-46.

26. See http://scribd.com/doc/94454775/Pierre-Boosah-Sr-Boucher-Busha-Bouchie, accessed July 2, 2012.

27. CIA to Ronan, Sept. 8, 1887, letterbook 164, pp. 159-60, land, NA CIA LS.

28. U.S. Bureau of Indian Affairs, "Selected Records of the Bureau of Indian Affairs Relating to Enrollment of Indians on the Flathead Reservation, 1903-08," NAmf M1350, reel 1, fr. 73, number 2323.

29. Flathead Reservation," WM, May 8, 1885, p. 2, col. 4.

30. "Flathead Items," *Missoula Gazette* (weekly), June 16, 1888, p. 2, col. 5.

31. "Larry Finley," *Missoula Daily Gazette*, Mar. 1, 1890, p. 1, col. 3 "Finley the Murderer," *Missoula Daily Gazette*, Mar. 14, 1890, p. 4, col. 2; "State Prison Convict Register," Montana State Prison Records, State Microfilm 36, Montana Historical Society Archives, Helena, reel 1, pp. 3 and 36 and reel 10, vol. 6, p. 41.

32. *The Inter Lake* (Kalispell, Mont.), June 12, 1896, p. 4, col. 2; *The Call* (Kalispell, Mont.), Sept. 17, 1896, p. 4, col. 2.

33. "Criminal Assault Charged," AS, Feb. 3, 1904, p. 12, col. 5; "Assaults His Brother's Wife," *The Missoulian* (daily), Feb. 3, 1904, p. 3, col. 4; "Larry Finley a Bad Breed," *The Missoulian* (daily), Feb. 4, 1904, p. 3, col. 1; "Is Accused of Assault," *Missoula Daily Times*, Feb. 25, 1904, p. 1, col. 3; "Lawrence Finley Is Tried," AS, Feb. 26, 1904, p. 12, col. 6; "Indians Before Grand Jury," *The Missoulian* (daily), Sept. 29, 1904, p. 6, col. 2.

34. CIA to Samuel Bellew, July 30, 1906, land, letterbook 882, p. 248, NA CIA LS.

35. Missoula Publishing Company, *Flathead Facts: Descriptive of the Resources of Missoula County* (Missoula, Mont.: Missoula Publishing Company, 1890), p. 18; "From Far and Near," AS, Oct. 12, 1894, p. 1, col. 3; "In Behring Sea," WM, Oct. 10, 1894, p. 2, col. 3-4.

36. Heitman, vol. 1, p. 573.

37. "Reduction of Indian Reservations," House of Representatives Executive Document No. 63, 50th Congress, 1st Session (1888), serial 2557, pp. 40-46, 56-60; John Fahey, *The Kalispel Indians* (Norman: University of Oklahoma Press, 1986), pp. 68-72.

38. CIA to Secretary of Interior, Jan. 4, 1898, letterbook 370, pp. 41-47, land, NA CIA LS; W. H. Smead to CIA, Sept. 23, 1902, 57,496/1902, NA CIA LR.

39. *Who Was Who in America*, vol. 1, p. 1385; *The National Cyclopædia of American Biography*, vol. 21, p. 189.

40. Frederike Verspoor, British Columbia Archives, to Bigart, June 28, 2012, email; *Canadian Sessional Papers*, 1888, vol. 13, pp. 122-23; 1889, vol. 13, pp. 110-11; 1890, vol. 10, pp. 111-12; 1891, vol. 15, pp. 87-88; 1892, vol. 10, pp. 127-28; 1893, vol. 9, pp. 245-47; 1894, vol. 10, pp. 126-27; Naomi Miller, "Michael Phillipps: Prominent Kootenay Citizen," in Wayne Norton and Naomi Miller, eds., *The Forgotten Side of the Border* (Kamloops, B.C.: Plateau Press, 1998), pp. 29-39.

41. CIA to Ronan, Oct. 31, 1887, letterbook 166, p. 352, land, NA CIA LS.

42. "Will Push an Agreement," *The Inter Lake* (Kalispell, Mont.), Jan. 20, 1893, p. 1, col. 6; Dimier to Friedl, Mar. 1900, Robert Bigart and Clarence Woodcock, editors, "St. Ignatius Mission, Montana: Reports from Two Jesuit Missionaries, 1885 & 1900-1901: (Part II)," *Arizona and the West*, vol. 23, no. 3 (Autumn 1981), p. 270; Frank C. Armstrong, "Condition of Reservation Indians," House of Representatives Document No. 406, 57th Congress, 1st Session (1902), serial 4361, p. 37; Chas. S. McNichols to CIA, Dec. 31, 1902, 822/1903, NA CIA LR.

Index

Since there was no standard spelling for Indian names in the nineteenth century, most of the full blood Indian people in this index were entered under their Christian names, except in cases where the Indian name later became a family name. As a consequence some individuals appear under both their family and their Christian names. Since more than one person had the same Christian name, it was not possible to tell who was referred to in some of the letters. Mixed bloods usually used family names and they are entered in the index in the traditional way. Despite these shortcoming, the editor hopes this index will help the reader locate information about individuals and topics of interest.